THE LATIN AMERICA READERS
Series edited by Robin Kirk and Orin Starn

THE WORLD READERS
Series edited by Robin Kirk and Orin Starn

THE

CHILE

READER

HISTORY, CULTURE, POLITICS

Elizabeth Quay Hutchison, Thomas Miller Klubock,
Nara B. Milanich, and Peter Winn, editors

DUKE UNIVERSITY PRESS   *Durham and London*   2014

Library of Congress Cataloging-in-Publication Data
The Chile reader : history, culture, politics /
Elizabeth Quay Hutchison, Thomas Miller Klubock, Nara B. Milanich,
and Peter Winn, eds.
pages cm — (Latin America readers)
Includes bibliographical references and index.
ISBN 978-0-8223-5346-1 (cloth : alk. paper)
ISBN 978-0-8223-5360-7 (pbk. : alk. paper)
1. Chile—History. 2. Chile—Civilization.
3. Chile—Politics and government.
I. Hutchison, Elizabeth Q. (Elizabeth Quay)
II. Klubock, Thomas Miller.
III. Milanich, Nara B., 1972–
IV. Winn, Peter.
V. Series: Latin America readers.
F3081.C485 2013
983—dc23
2013020980

For our boys—Dante, Pasqual, Giacomo, Luca, Ishan, Kiran, Ethan and Sasha.

Contents

III   *The Honorable Exception: The New Chilean Nation*
in the Nineteenth Century   121

IV   *Building a Modern Nation: Politics and the Social Question*
in the Nitrate Era   193

Acknowledgments

A work of this size and complexity requires that a great many people share the editors' pain—as well as their success—in bringing the project to fruition. The editors would like to start by expressing our gratitude to each other for persevering in this project over the last decade. Although finishing this book has been a shared enterprise, many of our most important debts are individual. Liz Hutchison would therefore like to thank Regina, Dante, Pasqual, Tita, Beth, Justin, Miguel, Kymm, Jason, Sam, Heidi, Ericka, Sole, and Nara for their unwavering support. Tom Klubock would like to thank Ishan, Kiran, and Sandhya. Nara Milanich thanks Nicola, Giacomo, and Luca. Peter Winn would like to thank Ethan, Sasha, and Sue for their patience and support.

   This book would not have been possible without the support and generosity of our many colleagues and friends, on whose specialized advice we have relied to identify and obtain many of the texts and images that make up this book. This long list includes many of those named elsewhere in these acknowledgments, as well as Marjorie Agosín, Margarita Alvarado, Lisa Baldez, Merike Blofield, Brenda Elsey, Mario Garcés, Alfredo Jocelyn-Holt, Katherine Hite, Mala Htun, María Angélica Illanes, Jadwiga Pieper, Julio Pinto, Ericka Verba, Angela Vergara, and Soledad Zárate. Although the Selected Readings indicate some of the vast bibliography we have relied on for the book's scholarly apparatus, we are particularly indebted to Brian Loveman for his enduring work, *Chile: The Legacy of Hispanic Capitalism*, without which many more errors of fact and interpretation would have surely crept into our manuscript. We extend special thanks to colleagues who gave us access to their archival materials, Ericka Beckman and Leonardo Leon, and to those who shared their original interview transcripts, namely Lisa Baldez, Ricardo Balladares and Alison Bruey, Florencia Mallon, and Margaret Power. For permission to reprint excerpts of their published interviews, we thank Luis Cifuentes and Pilar Molina. We are deeply indebted to colleagues who have authored major published collections of historical documents, including Peter Kornbluh, author of *The Pinochet File*; Sofía Correa, Consuelo Figueroa, Alfredo Jocelyn-Holt, Claudio Rolle, and Manuel Vicuña, editors of *Documentos del siglo XX chileno*; Sergio Grez, editor of *La cuestión social en Chile: Ideas y debates precursores, 1804–1902*; and to the curators and scholarly contributors to the Chilean National Library's remarkable digital archive, *Memoria chilena* (www .memoriachilena.cl).

Almost all of the selections in *The Chile Reader* are from primary sources, but Elicura Chihuailaf, Jacques Chonchol and Julio Silva Solar, Alejandro Foxley, Sergio Grez and Gabriel Salazar, Joaquín Lavín, and Tomás Moulián did grant us permission to publish translated excerpts of their longer works. Most of the remaining texts selected for the book required permissions granted by authors' agents and publishers, including the Sociedad Chilena de Derechos de Autor, LOM Ediciones, and Editorial Universitaria. Other permissions were granted directly by the authors' families or estates, such as the Orden Franciscana de Chile, the family of Radomiro Tomic, and the Victor Jara, Pablo Neruda, Salvador Allende, and Jaime Guzmán foundations. We particularly wish to thank Angel Parra for the rights to publish his mother's work, as well as assistance with the English-language lyrics, and Juan Flores for his generosity in granting rights to republish the translation by his father, Angel Flores, of Benjamin Subercaseaux's *Crazy Geography*.

The guts of this book—its historical documents—were made possible by a crew of translators who worked tirelessly to render them in English: we thank Justin Delacour, Enrique Garguín, Ryan Judge, Timothy Lorek, Jane Losaw, Melissa Mann, Trevor Martenson, Carson Morris, David Schreiner, Carolyn Watson, and John H. White for their translations of this material. We are particularly grateful to Rachel Stein for her masterful work with challenging colonial texts, to Bea Rodríguez-Balanta for expert translations of literary materials, and to Ericka Verba and Gloria Alvarez for rendering poetry and song in beautiful English. Kristina Cordero, Karin Rosemblatt, Eliot Weinberger, and Enrique Zapata also generously granted us the rights to their excellent published translations of Chilean texts. These translations, as well as the reproduction and permissions costs, were funded by generous financial support from UNM's Latin American and Iberian Institute and the Department of History, Duke University Press, and Columbia University's Institute of Latin American Studies. The editors particularly wish to thank Esteban Andrade at Columbia University's ILAS, for processing permission payments, and Karen Poniachik and Paula Pacheco at Columbia's Global Center in Santiago, for their assistance in bringing *The Chile Reader* to a broader audience.

Turning *The Chile Reader* into a book that would provide readers with visual as well as textual sources required tremendous cooperation from dozens of artists, photographers, and activists, as well as the agents, archivists, and family members who often manage their work. Alejandro Barruel, Juan Carlos Cáceres, Tom Dillehay, Marcos González Valdéz, Alvaro Hoppe, Hugo Infante, Fernando Maldonado Roi, Marcelo Montecino, Victor Hugo Robles, John Spooner, David Tryse, Spencer Tunick, and Guido Vargas gave us permission to publish their original photographs, while José Balmes, Guillo Bastias, and Ricardo Morales allowed us to reproduce their graphic art. Many others gave permission to publish images belonging to their families and/or organizations, including Lidia Casas and Adriana Gómez Muñoz of the Corporación Foro Red de Salud y Derechos Sexuales y Reproductivos; the widow of Nemesio Antuñez for her late husband's work; Horacio Salinas (and Augusto and Malena Samaniego, who put us in touch with him) for photos of Inti-Illimani; Mario Aguirre Maldonado for his father's historic photos of Sewell (www.imagenesdesewell.cl); Fernanda Rubio for her father's photos of Plaza Yungay and Minister Allende; Elizabeth Lira and Viviana Diaz for assistance with *arpilleras*; and Sebastián Ríos O., for use of his grandfather's Klein-Saks poster. We received extraordinary help in securing reproductions and rights from Carolina Suaznabar of the Museo Histórico Nacional, Jimena Rosenkranz of the Biblioteca Nacional, Alena Zamora of CreaImagen, Marlena Penna of the Archivo del Arzobizpado de Santiago, and Father Samuel Fernández of the Centro de Estudios y Documentación Padre Hurtado. Suzanne Schadl graciously provided access to the Sam Slick Collection of Latin American Political Posters at the University of New Mexico, while Ivan Boserup of the Danish National Library, Katie Mishler of the Artists' Rights Society, and Gerben van der Meulen of the International Institute of Social History provided other reproductions. The editors particularly want to thank Marjorie Agosín for generously allowing us to place Irma Muller's remarkable *arpillera* on the book's cover, as well as photographer Addison Doty and curator Tey Mariana Nunn of the National Hispanic Cultural Center for providing the reproduction for our use.

During the long gestation of *The Chile Reader*, busy colleagues have invested their time in reading our proposals, drafts, chapters, and manuscript. We deeply appreciate the support and feedback we have received from John Dinges, Paul Drake, Brian Loveman, Caterina Pizzigoni, and Fernando Purcell; Heidi Tinsman has spent so much time with this book that she knows it better than some of the editors! We thank Bill Nelson for creating his fine maps of the "long narrow country," and at the University of New Mexico, Liz Hutchison wishes to thank Kellie Baker, Patricia Kent, and Alicia Romero for their tireless work to obtain authors' permissions; Dana Ellison,

Yolanda Martínez, and Barbara Wafer for a variety of rescue operations; and Shawn Austin for his arduous labor on the index. For their help in obtaining and processing copyright permissions at Duke we thank Vanessa Doriott Anderson, Elena Feinstein, Mitch Fraas, China Medel, Tom Robinson, Isabel Rios-Torres, Megan Williams, and particularly Lorien Olive, who gave so much time and heart to make this book turn out well. Miriam Angress has patiently shepherded this project through multiple editorial stages over many years, and Liz Smith and Chris Crochetière have supported our work at the production stage. Martha Ramsey was a dedicated and sympathetic copy editor. Above all, we warmly thank Valerie Millholland, senior editor and creator of the Readers' series, for her patience and heartfelt devotion to *The Chile Reader*. We hope that our whole community of colleagues, friends, family, translators, contributors, and publishers finds satisfaction and recompense in what we have created together.

Introduction

In September 2010, after making world headlines with a major earthquake, the inauguration of a new conservative president, and the ongoing drama of thirty-three miners trapped underground, Chile marked its bicentenary with an outpouring of public celebrations. For weeks before and after the September 18 national holiday, Chilean media brimmed with reflections on the country's 200 years of national life. In concerts and performances, lectures, and parades, and in the pages of the press, Chileans examined, celebrated, and critiqued every aspect of their history and identity as a nation. Major public events, such as the inauguration in Santiago's Santa Lucía Park—site of the first Spanish settlement—of a commemorative statue dedicated to Chile's indigenous peoples and symbolically "returning" to them the park's main plaza, also foregrounded significant events and themes in the national memory. Especially noteworthy was the diversity of perspectives represented; alongside the rosters of "official" festivities a plethora of "alternative" events proliferated whose organizers promised a less conventional, more critical vision of the nation.

The bicentennial reflections on—and competing arguments about—the past were by no means a unique occurrence. After the arrest of the ex-dictator Augusto Pinochet in 1998 and again during a wave of 2011 student protests, Chileans engaged in passionate debates about their society that were simultaneously debates about the country's past. *The Chile Reader* takes its cue from this impulse to think about the meanings of national history and the relationship of Chile's past and present.

For much of its history, Chile has embraced the mantle of exceptionalism—the notion that Chile is somehow different from its Latin American neighbors. In recent years both inside and outside Chile, in Latin America and beyond, this sliver of a country has been touted for its economic performance, political stability, and modernity. In fact, this aura of historical exceptionalism itself has a long history. During the colonial period, Chile's distinct character derived from its status as a remote backwater of the Spanish Empire, a colony plagued by a perpetual war with an unusually resistant indigenous population. In the early nineteenth century, observers inside and outside the newly independent republic observed that Chile had avoided the violence and political chaos that characterized most of the hemisphere's new nations, adopting a stable and centralized, if authoritarian, political system.

In the mid-twentieth century Chilean exceptionalism reached its peak. Chile enjoyed a reputation as a "model country," a participatory democracy that boasted peaceful electoral politics in a hemisphere plagued by military interventions in political life. During the Cold War, Chile became one of the world's key ideological battlegrounds, bringing Salvador Allende to power as the first democratically elected Marxist president in the world. This backdrop also helps explain the global impact of the coup of 1973, when that storied democratic tradition met a brutal end at the hands of the dictatorship of Augusto Pinochet. Then again during seventeen years of military rule, Chile was touted as a model by both critics and defenders of the dictatorship: a disturbing emblem of the violent political repression that swept the region at the height of the Cold War, Chile was also seen as a success story of neoliberal market reform in Latin America. The transition to civilian democracy in the 1990s—which presented the remarkable case of a brutal, long-running dictatorship terminated through a nonviolent plebiscite—has further strengthened notions of Chilean exceptionalism, as has the "Chilean economic miracle," more than a decade of high growth with low inflation and a dramatic drop in poverty. Today, for many in Chile and beyond, the country enjoys an enviable status as a stable, modern, capitalist democracy without peer in the region.

The Chile Reader probes this distinctive character, seeking to explain how and why, in the present as at key moments in the past, Chile has followed a path that appears so different from that of its Latin American neighbors. But it also probes exceptionalism as myth, that is, how particular ideas about Chile's exceptional character have been central to national identity and have both emerged from and helped shape Chile's historical development. One goal of this volume is to help readers recognize these "myths," the history on which they are built, and how they have served nationalist, class, and ideological agendas. Travelers and students of contemporary Chile who are fluent in the stories Chileans tell about themselves—and that others tell about them—will be better able to navigate the political and cultural terrain of "the model country" in the twenty-first century.

The Chile Reader is composed of primary documents, including both written texts and illustrations, spanning more than 500 years of Chilean history. Most of these works are by Chilean authors, and many of these are published here in English for the first time. Brief introductions accompany each document, providing historical context and explaining its significance. While this significance is in some cases obvious—as in an 1812 proclamation calling for independence from Spain or President Salvador Allende's final radio address to the nation—we also present materials that reflect unofficial expressions and points of view. The *Reader* makes available interviews, literature, artwork, cartoons, correspondence, manifestos, ethnographies, and photographs that reflect the perspectives of a wide variety of people, dissenting views, and contested memories of the past. Thus we hear from Mapuche Indians and Spanish colonists, peasants and aristocrats, feminists and military strongmen, entrepreneurs and workers, priests and poets. These documentary selections also provide points of departure for readers to examine themes of gender, class, and ethnic relations in Chile across time. In the end, this selection is neither comprehensive nor exhaustive: rather, the editors have chosen emblematic texts and images that speak to themes such as democracy, social inequality, economic development, the environment, and ethnicity that are particularly relevant in today's Chile.

The *Reader* is organized around a series of recurring tensions linked to the persistent narrative of Chilean exceptionalism. One of the most enduring of these narratives has been the discussion of economic modernization —and its recurring nemesis, socioeconomic inequality—throughout Chile's national period. Chileans have been debating what it means to be modern and how to achieve economic development since the birth of the nation. This debate runs through early nineteenth-century struggles over the legacy of Spanish rule, over foreign economic influence, and over the shape that the state should take. By the end of the nineteenth century, Chile had embraced a surface modernization through an economy based on exports of primary commodities to world markets (notably copper and nitrates). Yet even as the early twentieth century brought such apparent signs of modernity as the growth of cities, the founding of factories, and a broadening political sphere, it also spurred critical voices who condemned unregulated capitalist development's other face, including social inequality, deepening poverty for many Chileans, and sharpening class divisions. Conflicts over these very different visions of how to produce economic modernization escalated throughout the 1960s and 1970s, as Chile passed through reformist and revolutionary socialist attempts to generate development while also increasing social equality and political participation, experiments that ended abruptly with the U.S.-supported military intervention of 1973. A defining event of Chile's national history, the coup brought to power a military dictatorship that pursued a neoliberal free market model for economic growth, which was largely maintained by the democratically elected coalition governments that ruled Chile for two decades after the end of military rule in 1990. In 2010, Chile became the first South American member of the Organization for Economic Cooperation and Development, the elite club of thirty-four developed nations. But recent studies show it has the worst income inequality and most socioeconomically segregated educational system of any nation in that club. The *Reader* gives readers access to texts and images that document the enduring tensions between economic modernization and social inequality that have plagued Chilean development and marked its political discourse.

A second and related tension evident in even a cursory reading of Chile's national history is the competing pressure between authoritarian and democratic forms of governance. From the conservative constitution of the early republic to the geographically and administratively centralized force of twentieth-century statehood, Chilean political elites and historians alike have lauded the relative success of their increasingly stable, democratic, and centralized state. The powerful myth of Chilean democratic rule is seemingly confirmed by its two periods of dictatorship (1927–1931 and 1973–1990), which are viewed as "exceptional"; the myth also elides the delay of universal suffrage to all its citizens (universal male suffrage 1887, female suffrage 1949). On closer examination of the state and party formation that undergirds Chilean democracy, moreover, historians have noted the systematic exclusion of particular groups—such as the peasantry—even in periods of civilian rule. Chilean politics in the twentieth century also evidenced the concentration of power in the hands of a small political and economic elite, even as popular political participation expanded under populist and revolutionary governments. Finally, although Pinochet's regime institutionalized authoritarian practices, this "state of exception" was in some ways unexceptional, as Chile was ruled through states of exception or siege for much of its history. In addition, the military exercised subtle forms of influence on the political and economic life of the nation both before and after the dictatorship. Tellingly, the rendition of Chile's national history produced for the bicentennial celebrations by the new conservative government ended before Allende's socialist government, the military coup, and the seventeen-year dictatorship, ignoring one of the most symbolically powerful moments in Chilean history: the bombing of the presidential palace, La Moneda, a symbol of Chilean democracy, by the military on September 11, 1973.

One of the least examined of the overarching tensions informing national history is the assertion that Chile—in contradistinction to some of its closest neighbors—is composed of an ethnically homogeneous population. In fact, this national attribute has long been invoked to explain its political, economic, and military achievements. Relegating indigenous populations and their histories either to the past as conquered peoples or marginalizing their significance in the present, Chilean nation-building has typically homogenized ethnic difference and left Mapuches and other native and African-descended groups out of the national narrative. This tendency was most clearly expressed by some turn-of-the-twentieth-century intellectuals, who advocated Europeanization and viewed Chile's indigenous population as an impediment to "progress," while others celebrated Chile's Indian warrior roots and vaunted the mestizo population as the basis of the nation's military triumphs and potential economic success. Even in the latter view, however, the glories of the Mapuche were relegated to a distant past and nationalist writers looked forward to the biological and cultural absorption of Mapuches into a national, ethnically mestizo citizenry. The exclusion of the Mapuche, who compose 10 percent of the Chilean population, from both the country's democracy and from the fruits of economic modernization was again evident in the country's bicentennial celebrations. Even as the Chilean state "returned" the Santa Lucía hill to the Mapuche, almost every major leader of the government, including the president himself, were enjoying a more conventional bicentennial celebration in the city of Valparaíso where the Congress is located, demonstrating the minimal importance they attributed both to Mapuche history and Mapuches' current condition as a marginalized ethnic minority.

By contrast, Chile's immigrant populations, though smaller than those of some of its neighbors, have received greater recognition. A place has been made in the national imaginary for immigrant communities (from German farmers in the south to Palestinian manufacturers in Santiago and British mining entrepreneurs in the north). The cultural and racial contributions of North Americans and Europeans to national progress have been celebrated. *The Chile Reader* addresses the historical roots, as well as demographic and cultural effects, of this ethnic diversity, a part of Chile's history that reveals a variety of distinct cultural and regional identities and informs episodes of territorial, economic, and religious conflict. By examining the varied history of ethnic communities in the Chilean nation and illustrating how racial hierarchies and ethnic differences have structured Chilean notions of class and nation, the *Reader* prepares readers to engage thoughtfully with the ways Chileans have—and have not—confronted the politics of ethnic difference in the past and the present.

In apparent contrast to current scholarly trends that emphasize global and transnational frames of analysis, *The Chile Reader*, like all the readers in the Duke series, is organized around a nation. This contrast, which we

PERU

ARICA

Arica

BOLIVIA

BRAZIL

TARAPACÁ

Iquique

Tocopilla   Calama

PARAGUAY

ANTOFAGASTA

Antofagasta

Copiapó

ATACAMA

La Serena

Coquimbo

Ovalle

COQUIMBO

ARGENTINA

URUGUAY

PACIFIC
OCEAN

VALPARAÍSO

Viña del Mar   Quilpué

Valparaíso

METROPOLITAN
REGION
(Santiago)

Santiago   San Bernardo

O'HIGGINS   Rancagua

Linares   Talca   Curicó

Talcahuano   MAULE

Concepción   Chillán

Los Angeles

BÍOBÍO

LA ARAUCANÍA   Temuco

Valdivia   *LOS RÍOS*

Osorno   LOS LAGOS

Puerto Montt

Chiloé

ANTÁRTICA
CHILENA

Coihaique

AISÉN

ATLANTIC
OCEAN

ANTARCTICA

Punta Arenas

MAGALLANES

N

0   200 mi

0   300 km

Political Map of Contemporary Chile.

suggest is also apparent, points to yet another tension that has marked Chile throughout its history, that between isolation and global insertion. Since colonial times Chile's geographic isolation has been frequently highlighted; the territory has often been described as a long, thin sliver enveloped between the formidable peaks of the Andes and the vast expanse of the Pacific, cut off to the north by the hostile Atacama Desert, the world's driest, and to the south by the remote and forbidding lands and waters of Patagonia, Tierra del Fuego, and Antarctica. This peculiar geography served as the basis for the region's administrative isolation under Iberian rule and later as the template for territorial claims made by the Chilean nation-state against neighboring Argentina, Bolivia, and Peru. But such isolation masks a historical reality of vital global connections between Chile and the rest of the world, connections that long predate late twentieth-century "globalization," although they have multiplied greatly in recent decades. Claims to isolation (and by implication, exceptionalism) are belied by evidence of regional trade networks, trans-Andean indigenous communities in the south, migration and territorial expansion in the north, and oceanic shipping networks that connected Valparaíso to ports in North and South America, Europe, Australia, and East Asia. In the nineteenth and twentieth centuries, Chile's economy relied on substantial foreign investment and trade, linkages that have shaped everything from the nation's ethnic communities to its social and political movements. During the nineteenth century, British merchants, who would come to compose some of Chile's leading families, played a central role in the economy and society, dominating trade and exercising considerable influence in banking, railroads, and even nitrate production, while during the twentieth century U.S.-owned copper mines in the Andes and Atacama desert produced the country's major source of foreign revenue. The tension between national isolationism and global integration was particularly evident during the military regime, whose violent excesses drove a diplomatic wedge between Chile and the international community and whose rigid censorship isolated Chile culturally, even as the regime embraced a model of neoliberal economic integration. Since the return to democracy in 1990, this integration with regional and global markets has only increased. A *Reader* dedicated to a "national" history remains relevant in an increasingly global and transnational world: the story of Chile's emergence as a nation illustrates how deeply the story of nations is predicated on international flows of people, ideas, and capital. This national history also illuminates important comparative and regional dimensions in the country's national development, revealing dynamics and relations that demonstrate

Chile's similarity with, as much as exception from, broader regional and world historical developments.

Although *The Chile Reader* is a substantial tome, we hope that it will serve students and travelers new to Chile as a faithful and useful companion in their journeys, both actual and imagined. The *Reader* is therefore both a tool and a point of entry that can be approached in multiple ways: read from cover to cover, digested in documentary selections on a particular theme, or explored through a single chronological chapter about an era of particular interest. Whatever one's approach, chapter and document introductions will orient one to the key events, actors, and moments in Chilean history and society. All notes, other than those indicated as written by a text's author or translator, are by the editors of this volume. We also hope this *Reader* will be of interest to experienced teachers and specialists—even if they take issue with certain selections and interpretations. Finally, The *Reader* benefits enormously from the extensive corpus of scholarly work on which it draws. Readers are encouraged to consult the selected readings to access the rich and informative scholarship on Chile that will enable them to delve deeper into its history and explore new themes and other perspectives.

By adopting a historical perspective and employing primary sources, *The Chile Reader* presents Chile's many voices and allows readers to make decisions for themselves about the complex realities behind Chile's career as a model for Latin America and to judge for themselves the debates over its past and present. The authors, historians from the United States with long experience in research, scholarship, and teaching about Chile and Latin America, have learned from and contributed to Chileans' ongoing efforts to understand and interpret that country's past. They have sought through their writing and teaching to deepen U.S. understandings of the region and the U.S. role in its history. Those efforts—like this book—have contributed to the critical remembering of Chile's past, both within Chile and for U.S. audiences accustomed to narratives of U.S. exceptionalism and Latin American inferiority, violence, and victimization. The history of Chile, like many other national histories south of the Rio Grande, provides an important vantage point from which U.S. readers may not only learn about this long, thin country, but also think critically about their own country—and its own claims to exceptionalism. As our Chilean colleagues have expressed so well, "history is projection. It is the social construction of future reality."[1]

Note

1. Sergio Grez and Gabriel Salazar, *Mannifiesto de historiadores* (Santiago: LOM, 1999), 19.

I

Environment and History

Chile does indeed appear at first glance to be a country with "a crazy geography," in the famous words of the essayist Benjamín Subercaseaux. Straddled by two mountain cordilleras, the Andes and the coastal range, the country extends 2,600 miles in length along the Pacific Ocean coast and averages only just over 100 miles in width. The Pacific on the west, the Andes cordillera to the east, the Atacama Desert to the north, and Cape Horn in the far south are ecological barriers that make Chile an island, isolated, both in political and environmental terms, from its neighbors. Yet in spite of its apparent isolation, Chile has also been something of a thoroughfare: until the opening of the Panama Canal in 1914, the straits of Magellan were the only waterway connecting the Atlantic and Pacific oceans, giving Chilean ports tremendous maritime and commercial importance. Chile's crazy geography includes the world's driest desert, in the north, one of the world's largest remaining temperate rain forests, in the south, the frozen wastes of Antarctica, and a Mediterranean climate in the center. Chile also has two distant Pacific island possessions, Easter Island (Rapa Nui) and the Juan Fernández Islands (the setting for *Robinson Crusoe,* the fictionalized account of a shipwrecked sailor), both hundreds of miles off the coast.

This unusual geography has played an outsized role in Chile's national imaginary from the days of the Spanish conquest to the present. It is not by chance that when Chilean schoolchildren study their nation's past, the subject is called history and geography. Ever since its conception as a colonial possession, Chile's boosters have publicized the products of nature's bounty there, from the wheat cultivated on central Chile's large estates and the livestock pastured on its meadows during the colonial period and the nineteenth century to the nitrates and copper extracted from the Atacama desert and Andes cordillera during the late nineteenth and twentieth centuries. The earliest conquistadors, beginning with Pedro de Valdivia, the founder of the Spanish colony, extolled the natural beauty and bounty of Spain's new possession. Similarly, the builders of the modern nation-state during the

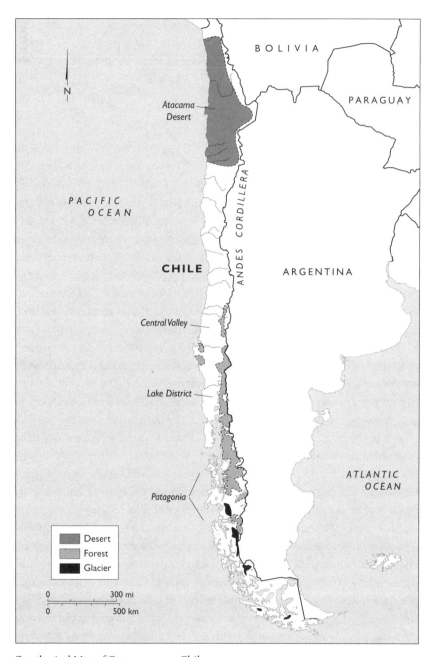

Geophysical Map of Contemporary Chile.

nineteenth century linked the singularity of Chile's identity as a nation, and the apparently exceptional trajectory of its history, to its geography. Today, as Chile mines it forests, oceans, and soil to produce timber, fruit, fish and shellfish, and copper for markets abroad, triumphalist accounts of nature's bounty continue to celebrate the country's model free-market economy and democratic government. In a similar vein, modern writers like Benjamín Subercaseaux and the poet Gabriela Mistral have often looked to Chile's geographic isolation and remote location "at the extreme end" of the world, in the words of conquistador Pedro de Valdivia, to explain its purportedly unique position within Latin America. Both Subercaseaux and Mistral celebrate the country's isolation as the foundation of an exceptional political and economic history, as well as a robust national identity.

Narratives of Chilean historical and geographic exceptionalism have been tempered by three crosscutting discourses about Chile's nature or the nature of Chile. The first is an acute awareness of the changing configuration of the nation. Frontiers, like nature more generally, have played a major role in Chile's national formation. Until the late nineteenth century, Chile's northern border lay in its "near north," or *norte chico*, south of the port of Antofogasta. What is today considered northern Chile, consisting of the provinces of Tarapacá and Antofogasta, belonged to Bolivia and Peru and was acquired by conquest during the War of the Pacific (1879–1883). To the south, the territory sandwiched between the Toltén and Bío Bío rivers, known as "the frontier" or "Araucanía" (for Chile's native araucaria pine tree), was independent of the nation, ruled by indigenous Mapuche groups until the late nineteenth-century military campaigns known as "the pacification of the Araucanía." In Patagonia to the far south, disputes with neighboring Argentina have made defining Chile's southernmost borders a conflictive process since colonial days. The question of where the lines between the two nations would be drawn in Patagonia was only resolved in the early twentieth century and has left bitter feelings on both sides. So too has Chile's conflict with Peru and Bolivia (which continues to demand access to the Pacific Ocean) and forcible incorporation of Mapuches into the nation at the close of the nineteenth century. By some accounts, Chile's unstable borders and the history of violent national integration of frontier territories, from the Atacama to the Araucanía and Patagonia, have underwritten an exceptionally stable national identity and robust nationalism. As in the United States, Chile's exceptional place in the Americas has often been attributed to its frontier experiences and its aggressive expansionism since the mid-nineteenth century.

Second, while nature has often appeared to endow Chile with exceptional beauty and limitless wealth, natural disasters—from earthquakes, volcanic eruptions, and tidal waves to floods, droughts, and epidemics—have been an ever-present reminder, like the shifting national borders, of the nation's fragility. For some writers, such as the historians Cristián Gazmuri and Rolando Mellafe and essayists like Subercaseaux, constant natural disasters, like the chronic frontier wars with Mapuche groups and the country's geographic isolation, have created a specifically Chilean "mentality," one defined by stoicism, sobriety, and modesty, as well as the capacity to overcome adversity and "begin again."[1] These national characteristics were acclaimed in responses to the 2010 earthquake in southern Chile and have been a staple of writing about Chilean national identity for generations. In celebrating the *roto chileno* (a once derogatory term for poor Chileans, literally "broken one") as the pillar of the nation, writers since the late nineteenth century have distinguished the roto's capacity to overcome natural adversity, whether the rugged topography of the mountain cordilleras or the inhospitable environment of the Atacama. The miner who suffers nature's wrath in explosions, landslides, falls, and silicosis, or black lung disease, has been a representative figure of Chilean nationhood, just as mining itself has fueled the economy since the nineteenth century. But the (always male) miner conquering (female) nature, overcoming danger and disaster to extract ore, the bounty granted to Chile by nature, has also been a source of national pride. Chileans' perseverance in the face of natural adversity has been a defining feature of nationalist sentiment. For many Chileans the miraculous rescue of miners trapped underground for sixty-nine days after a terrible accident in 2010 symbolized both Chilean success in overcoming natural disasters and the strength of Chilean nationalism. The workers came out of their confinement hundreds of feet beneath the ground shouting "Viva Chile mierda!"[2] The use of the expletive reflected how fraught, even uncertain, nationalist celebration of triumph over nature could be. For many Chileans, it was difficult not to recall the 355 miners killed in a tragic accident in the North American–owned El Teniente copper mine in 1945, one of the most terrible tragedies in the history of mining across the globe.

Third, Chilean nationalism has historically been fractured by conflicts over the distribution of the wealth generated by the commodities extracted from nature. Pablo Neruda's poem "Catastrophe in Sewell" denouncing North American capital's control of the mining industry and lamenting the 1945 El Teniente catastrophe reflects tensions over the ownership and distribution of Chile's natural resources. Chile's mines, the motor of the national economy, generated profits for foreign companies until their nationalization in 1971. Today, while Chile has enjoyed the fruits of export-oriented production, the benefits of this prosperity have rarely been evenly distributed. In 2010, Chile was one of the fifteen most unequal countries in the world in terms of income distribution. Social inequality has often been exacerbated by ecological degradation. In fact, accounts of economic modernization in Chile frequently emphasize the twin processes of environmental crisis and social dislocation throughout Chilean history. During the nineteenth century, for example, the expansion of wheat exports led to the expulsion of thousands of rural workers from the large estates that dominated central Chile's countryside, generating a mushrooming landless labor force. At the same time, wheat monocultures provoked drought, flooding, and soil erosion within decades of a midcentury export boom, leading to Chile's first environmental regulation on deforestation in 1873. Similarly, a midcentury boom in copper exports led to devastating conditions for mine laborers and an environmental crisis provoked by the destruction of the short north's native forests, a development described vividly by naturalists like Claudio Gay and Charles Darwin.

Indeed, throughout Chilean history, human-manufactured natural disasters have drawn as much attention as the "tragic events" described by Mellafe. Nineteenth-century concerns with climate change, soil erosion, and flooding caused by deforestation and cereal monocropping laid the foundation for the growth of an "environmental consciousness" during the twentieth century. During the 1940s, Pablo Neruda evoked the desolation caused by the destruction of unique temperate forests in southern Chile in his famous poem "Ode to Erosion in Malleco." In the late 1950s the writer Rafael Elizalde described ecological catastrophes as threatening the foundation of the nation in *The Survival of Chile*. This nationalist vein in conservationist writing drew on earlier *criollista* (creolist) genres and can be found in Neruda's poetry as well. Neruda often evoked the magnificence of the Chilean landscape in his poetry, writing in his memoirs, "anyone who has never been in the Chilean forest doesn't know this planet. I have come out of that landscape, that mud, that silence, to roam, to go singing through the world."[3] His "Ode to Erosion" reflected a growing environmentalist concern in Chile that was ignited by massive forest fires, set to clear land for crops and livestock and to clear underbrush and abet logging, which destroyed thousands of acres of southern temperate forest. By the 1980s, a burgeoning environmentalist movement organized in groups like Defensores del Bosque Chileno (Defenders of the Chilean Forest) and Comité Nacional Pro Defensa de la Flora y Fauna (National Committee in Defense of Flora and Fauna) called increasing attention to the environmental costs of high growth rates during Chile's neoliberal economic miracle. Environmentalist groups pointed out that free-market growth, beginning during the dictatorship of Pinochet and maintained by transition demo- cratic center-left governments during the 1990s, had created a new moment of profound ecological degradation. A boom in forestry exports led to the rapid destruction of southern temperate rain forests and their replacement by plantations of eucalyptus and North American Monterey pine. Industrial fishing along Chile's lengthy Pacific coast and the spread of fish farms led to the collapse of marine ecosystems and the depletion of a number of spe- cies of Chilean fish and shellfish, including the "Chilean sea bass," which is not a bass at all but the species formerly and less appetizingly known as the Patagonian toothfish. In the fruit industry, workers were exposed to high doses of pesticides, some banned in the developed world, and suffered a number of work-related illnesses. In the forestry industry, logging compa- nies sprayed cleared land with chemical defoliants, including a component of Agent Orange, poisoning regional ecosystems that included remnant old- growth temperate forests and were inhabited by large populations of Mapu- che peasants. These ecological disasters were accompanied by some of the worst working conditions in Chile. Forestry and fruit workers composed a chronically underemployed, migrant labor force, laboring seasonally for subcontractors, without the protection of unions or basic benefits. In the fishing industry, large "factory" fishing boats competed with a once thriv- ing population of small, independent "artisanal" fishermen along the coast, producing high unemployment in coastal towns.

While exploiting natural resources has driven export-led growth over the last decades, today ecotourism plays a significant role in the Chilean economy. As foreign tourists travel to Chile in increasing numbers to ex- perience the natural wonders of the country's temperate rain forests, the glacial formations of the Torres de Paine in the south, the Andes cordil- lera and its mountain lakes, and the stunning Pacific coast, the environ- mentalist movement's critique of the unregulated exploitation of natural resources has taken on more weight. Admiration for Chile's natural envi- ronment, which constituted a wellspring of creole nationalist sentiment from Pedro de Valdivia to Mistral and Subercaseaux, today motors the country's profitable tourist economy, placing conservationist pressure on resource-extractive industries like forestry, mining, and fishing. During the 1940s, the Chilean state promoted domestic tourism as a means to foment nationalism and national strength. Travel throughout the country on the state-owned railroad would, like the writings of Mistral and Subercaseaux, acquaint Chileans with the extraordinary natural and geographic gifts bestowed on the country and instill in them a profound identification with the nation. In addition, travel in nature outside the city was believed to be a healthful exercise that would increase the strength of "the Chilean race." Today, however, tourism initiatives have been reoriented toward attracting foreign travelers and currency with the still "pristine" natural wonders in Chile's numerous national parks and nature preserves. The hidden underbelly of these natural attractions, threatening to unravel Chile's continued self-representation through nature, is a series of "tragic events" human in origin. These include tree plantations that have replaced temperate forests, collapsed marine ecosystems, and environmental pollution caused by mining and the usual urban contaminants—diesel-powered buses, dust, and industrial output—that make the nation's capital, trapped in a valley between the two cordilleras, one of the most polluted cities in Latin America.

Notes

1. Cristián Gazmuri, "Lejanía, aislamiento, pobreza y guerra. La mentalidad histórica del chileno," *El Mercurio*, 22 April 2006.
2. This expression literally translates as "Long live Chile, shit!" "Shit" is employed here to express a determined pride. A better, though less literal, translation, might be "Long live Chile, damn it!" This articulates well the idea of the nation overcoming an obstacle, be it a natural or humanmade one. For example, the nation will prevail despite mine cave-ins and earthquakes.
3. Pablo Neruda, *Memoirs* (New York: Farrar, Straus and Giroux, 2001), 6.

"No Better Land"

Pedro de Valdivia

Five years after embarking on the conquest of Chili, Pedro de Valdivia penned this famous missive to Emperor Charles V. Like many petitions of conquistadors seeking royal favor for their enterprises, the letter extols the wealth and latent potential of the new territory. In Chile, this consisted primarily of (allegedly) abundant gold as well as fertile land. Valdivia's eloquent descriptions of Chile's natural beauty, fertility, and riches would be echoed by numerous colonial naturalists and missionaries, whose annals abound with descriptions of the "luxuriance" of Chile's native forests, its "proud mountains . . . so tall they make the Alps and Pyrenees seem like pygmies," the abundance of its harvests, and its seas "populated by an infinity of fish." Valdivia's descriptions also resonated well beyond the colonial period: his letters laid the foundation for a strain of criollismo—*creolism or literature of national pride—that would flourish in modern Chile. Today a quotation from Valdivia's letter is engraved in a stone at the base of Santa Lucía Hill in Santiago, reputed to be the site where he founded that city in 1541.*

Your Majesty should know that one hundred leagues and seven valleys lie between here and the Valley of Copiapó, measuring twenty-five leagues across at the widest parts and fifteen or less at others. Anyone needing to come to these provinces from those of Peru will find difficulty only in that stretch from Copiapó to here, for up to the Valley of Atacama there is food everywhere, since the Indians of Peru are at peace with the Spaniards thanks to the good order that Governor Vaca de Castro has established. At Atacama they can restock their provisions to cross the large, sparsely populated, 120-league tract from there to Copiapó; the Indians of this and all other parts gather and hide food where it cannot be found whenever they receive word that people are coming, and not only do they refuse to give any to those passing through, but they wage war against them. Here in this land, however, everyone already present and anyone who should come can count on having enough food, for three months from now, around December, which is the middle of summer, ten or twelve thousand *fanegas*[1] of wheat and a countless amount of corn will be harvested in this city, and from the two hogs and suckling pig that we salvaged when the Indians burned the city, there are already eight to ten thousand more, and from the male and female chickens, as many hens as grass, which breed abundantly in the winter and summer. . . .

And I have sent word . . . to Governor Vaca de Castro . . . to inform and encourage merchants as well as anyone else desiring to settle here to come, for there is no better land in the whole wide world to live and thrive, as it is very flat and healthy and one can be very happy here. Winter lasts for no more than four months with a lovely sun shining all the while, so there is no need to build fires; it only rains for one or two days when there is a quarter moon. The summer is so mild and there are such delightful breezes that you can walk under the sun all day without being bothered by the heat. This land is more abundant than any other in pastures, sown fields and the conditions for raising every class of livestock and plant imaginable.

There is plentiful and very beautiful wood to build houses and infinite firewood to serve them. Moreover, the mines are extremely rich in gold— the whole land is full of it—and in any place where anyone should desire to extract it, they will find land to sow and on which to build, together with water, firewood and grass for their livestock. Indeed, it seems that God developed this land with the express intent that man should have everything within his reach. . . .

Therefore, Your Majesty, this city, Santiago del Nuevo Estremo, is the first step upon which we should build and go about settling all this land for Your Majesty, until reaching the Strait of Magellan and the North Sea. And the land I kindly ask Your Majesty to grant me by way of a royal privilege should start here, as I have only suffered the trials of maintaining and sustaining it in order to be able to continue to push ahead. If I had not established this foothold and instead kept moving forward without settling this land first, few would have come, understandably—unless men and horses had fallen from the sky—due to the state of the land, and even less due to the lack of provisions. Furthermore, horses cannot be transported by sea, for sailing is not cut out for that, so by settling here and with Coquimbo already precariously supplied, anyone who would like to may now come and go as they please. And if people come now to attend to the city's safety— even if not many—and bring some horses to give to the footmen I already have, I will move onward with my men to find a place for them to eat and settle and patrol up to the Strait, if necessary. In short, the aforesaid account conveys what I have already managed and what I plan to do in the future, along with the reasons thereof. . . .

Chile's native palm and araucaria pine. Colonial writers often dwelled on exotic aspects of Chile's natural landscape. From the treatise by Giovanni Ignazio Molina, *Compendio della storia geografica, naturale, e civile del regno del Cile* (Bologna: Stamperia di S. Tommaso D'Aquino, 1776). Courtesy of Colección Archivo Fotográfico, Biblioteca Nacional de Chile.

Thus, oh Victorious Cesar, in order to safeguard this land and those ahead, as well as their sustenance, maintenance and discovery, it is essential that no captain be equipped by Your Majesty to come here from Spain or through the Strait of Magellan to disrupt me. I am writing the same to Governor Vaca de Castro in Peru, with the wholehearted aim of serving Your Majesty's best interests. I advise and beg this of Your Majesty herein because, if people were to come through the Strait, they would not be able to bring horses, which are absolutely necessary, since the land is as flat as the palm of one's hand. Moreover, if people unaccustomed to the food of these parts were to partake of it before their stomachs had built up a thick enough skin, half of them would die, and the rest would be killed off promptly by the Indians. And our hold over this land is so delicate that if the Indians saw us dispute over it, it would crumble; we would never be able to start the game over and put the pieces back into place. I am telling Your Majesty the truth down to the letter, so that it and Your Majesty may always be on my side. I do not want anyone to come and deprive me of serving Your Majesty or disrupt the current state of things, because I hope to apply the life and property I have now, and any property I should acquire in the future, to discovering settling, conquering and pacifying all this land up to the Strait of Magellan and the North Sea, and to seeking suitable land to repay those of Your Majesty's vassals who are here with me for all the hard work they have done, thereby relieving Your royal conscience and mine. And once I have done this, which is my principal desire, and once Your Majesty has received news of me and my services as is fitting, my only wish is to hear and see—in charters from Your Majesty—that you are pleased by the services I have and am performing for Your Imperial person, and that you kindly consider me among the number of your royal house's loyal subjects and vassals and servants. . . . These are the privileges which I set out to request at the beginning of my letter, in return for the small service I have performed for You until today and the much greater ones I hope to carry out over the rest of my life, with the continual aim of increasing Your Majesty's wealth and royal income.

Translated by Rachel Stein

Note

1. *Fanega:* obsolete unit traditionally used to measure agricultural areas; equivalent to 0.66 hectares.

The Poetry of Place: "My Country"

Gabriela Mistral

Gabriela Mistral, winner of Latin America's first Nobel Prize in literature, wrote poetry rooted in the landscape of her native country, although she lived much of her life abroad. Her poems spoke to a new criollista *movement in Chilean letters and art, with an emphasis on local and national social and cultural realities. This movement produced art that especially reflected the natural and social worlds of the Chilean countryside. In the following excerpt from "My Country," Mistral provides a twentieth-century rendition of Pedro de Valdivia's paeans to Chile's geography. She ascribes basic features of Chilean identity to the country's natural peculiarities, with lyrical descriptions of the country's natural wonders that could just as well be found in a travel guide. Like many writers she locates Chile's exceptional place in Latin America in its geography. For Mistral, Chile's small size and isolated location led it to organize a stable political system before other Latin American countries and gave Chileans a determination born of geographical adversity. This Chilean will to overcome the strange historical fate of geography also led Chileans, she argues, to work tenaciously for the development of the nation. This nationalist sentiment is reflected too in Mistral's claim that the exposure to sea air because of the country's narrow waist and lengthy coast "strengthened" its children's lungs. The forbidding Atacama Desert, which some might view as an extraordinarily difficult landscape, she celebrates for its position as a barrier to Inca conquest, thus summoning an early nationalist bellicosity that would flourish with the Chilean military conflicts with Peru during the nineteenth century. Summing up this criollista celebration of a nation singularly blessed by nature, she declares: "the whole land is like one favored spot for human life," and certain regions constitute "the blessing of the planet," "the marvel of geographers and naturalists."*

In the partition of the continent of giants, in the geographic Pantagruelism of the conquest, much was left to the Captaincy General of Chile—570,000 square kilometers which were hung like a superfluous tassel onto rich Peru.

Precisely because the country was small, she organized herself before the larger ones, and with a determination born of a will that comes to the

Andean border between Chile and Argentina. Photograph by Carlos Tapia. Courtesy of Colección Museo Histórico Nacional de Chile.

fore in trying times, she carried out her own development more intensely than the others.

If the continent has given us a foot-stool instead of a chair, the sea has offered us every opportunity along a coast 2,600 miles long. It is within six hours reach even from a city or village walled in by the mountains. We have such access to the sea that though we live in mountain ravines it can be said that the sea air has strengthened the lungs of all our children. Sea of the north with radiant warmth and the drowsy life of tropics, white blue sea, the luxurious surf of the gay *Constitucion* beach, livid grey sea toward the south, the father of great tempests which challenged the classic mariners.

After the omnipotent sea, the mountains give us their tonic and as a theologian said, leave their imprint on our character. One cannot think of any segment of Chile without them looming up as any dramatic backdrops to city or country. The whole land is like one favored spot for human life.

Where there is a broad sky there will be found *Tupungato, Tres Cruces* or *Osorno*, peaks authoritatively ruling the valley with their presence.

The great Pedro de Valdivia wished the capital of the country be ruled by this geological hierarchy to remind the people not to forget their maternity in rock.

The desert, which halted the Incas with its stony reverberations, stretches through three provinces so great in relation to Chile's territory that it might have been a curse had it not soon yielded us riches. We might have faced the decided calamity of a Sahara eating away a third of our country.

As a panorama, the *Atacama* desert appears forbidding to those who have eyes only for delightful landscapes. If seen in fragments, the Chilean desert is plebeian with its savage, implacable rockiness and a nakedness which neither the sparse, colorless herbiage nor a seven-month spring could ever clothe. The drought tears at the tear ducts and makes them bleed; the air, free of any particle of humidity, seems made for the vulture.

But the nitrate pampa is beautiful in breadth. There is a nobility about it when at the siesta hour it merges into a single reflection to the point of brilliance, and at night beneath the full moon, it merges again, now in a whitish grey plain, broken at intervals by fantastic hills. Only on these pampa nights does the earth forget herself to savor the joy of an astronomer—enemy of fog—a heaven of burnished enamel, without the banality of clouds, which to the tired eye seems almost an artificial horizon of pure perfection with sharply defined constellations.

After the stark desert there is a transitional region which resembles a battlefield between the arid and the fertile, such as is found in Palestine and in Morocco.

This region produces a fig as beautiful as that of Sicily; a long sun-drenched raisin better than the Greek; a papaya smaller than the oilier tropical kind, fragrant and sharp-flavored; and a brandy that ranks among those least detrimental to the human system. Perfect summers, are these, yielding an aristocracy of fruits worthy of an Asiatic table. Pomona, of the fruit trees, rather than Ceres, mother of grains and abundant pastures, has journeyed with Oriental feet through this tiny bowl of earth.

The robust body of San Cristobal is formed by the so-called Central Valley that unfolds between the Andean range and the quasi range of the coast. It forms the agricultural arm of a nation wealthy in strong hands.

A pleasantly mild valley, it undulates with wheat-sown hills and is interrupted by one or two volcanoes tending its vast green mercifulness—the *Descaezado*, the *Chillan*, the *Llaima*, the *Osorno*. Without geological exaggeration it can be called, like the Valley of the Rodano, "the blessing of the planet," a generous gift from its provinces, a loyal offering for agricultural pursuits so man need neither break his back with overwork nor undertake some ill-starred project.

Where the verdant vineyard is brusquely broken by the "Bio-Bio," another extraordinary region of our territory begins. This is the cold tropics, the marvel of geographers and naturalists.

The real tropics dazzle the eye with their Dionysian hues which excite, lacerate and end by exhausting the senses. These tropics are as vast as the other, but disciplined and almost austere. A narrow sky presses which, when seen in July, seems never to have loosened its dark cloud cover and jungle masses appear to have grabbed the mountains by the feet and to carry them on their shoulders. Or, if one sails when the evil fog lifts, there comes to view an island not of rocky volcanic spewings but an enormous sylvan platter, without a sandy border, with ivies, cypresses and nüptines seemingly diving into the very sea.

In this region of sombre vigor may be found countless aristocratic species of conifers and ferns.

Seek, from Valdivia island, the larch which Lafont called "the first tree of the world" and which it might well be if we were to establish a plant hierarchy under a joint standard of economics and aesthetics. The larch has the magnificent stature of the captains of vegetation; living two months mired in humidity, it remains incorruptible when summer comes and with it the breeding of insects on its trunk which leave no marks or holes. Thus it defends itself like a Homeric hero, and far from being obstinate its bark lends to carding and to yielding a very fine wool.

And, finally, as though as this were not enough, it is generous and prolific, unlike the so-called precious woods and the scarce sandalwood.

Something like a synthesis of the planet is fulfilled in the geography of Chile. It starts in the desert, which is like beginning with sterility that loves no man. It is humanized in the valleys. It creates a home for living beings in the ample fertile agricultural zone; takes on a grandiose sylvan beauty at the end of the continent as if to finish with dignity, and finally crumbles, offering half life, half death, in the sea which wavers between its blessings of water and its Buddhic blessings of eternal ice.

Crazy Geography

Benjamín Subercaseaux

When Benjamín Subercaseaux's book appeared in 1941, Gabriela Mistral heralded it as an exhaustive guide to Chile in the tradition of travel writing, bringing together the art of poets and the science of naturalists. The work quickly became a bestseller in Chile and required reading in school curricula.[1] Like Mistral, Subercaseaux's paean to Chile's natural "extravagance" or, in a different translation, "crazy geography," extols the variety and abundance of natural environments. Yet Subercaseaux also bemoans the fact that most Chilean writers and observers ignored the expanse and diversity of Chile's geography to focus narrowly on the central agricultural valleys and the capital city of Santiago. Meanwhile, in addition to celebrating Chile's "crazy geography," Subercaseaux underlines a characteristic of this geography that had been similarly part of the creole imagination since Pedro de Valdivia: Chile's isolation. Subercaseaux, like Valdivia, who emphasized Chile's location "at the extreme end of the world," views this geographic remoteness as a defining element of Chilean national character and an explanation for Chilean exceptionalism in Latin America.

The word *Chile* has a juvenile flavor, irresponsible, like the first ray of sun which, caressing our land, in one leap reached the sea.

For the land of Chile is narrow. There are regions in which it suffices to climb a mountain to be able to encompass it all with the naked eye, from cordillera to ocean.

If the sea were to dry up, we could descend from a height of 4,000 meters on the mountain range to a depth of 3,000 meters below the sea without having to walk more than 120 kilometers in a straight line from the Argentine frontier to the bottom of the Pacific (near Illapel).

But besides being narrow this land is long: it prolongs itself endlessly toward the south; it curves a trifle, now to the west, now to the east; it breaks, in an incredible way, farther down; it bends somewhat to the west; and, after a mad race across thirty-eight parallels, it sharpens and ends in

"Laguna del Inca in Portillo, Chile." Photographer unknown. Courtesy of Colección Museo Histórico Nacional de Chile.

a point—in Horn, a bleak, rocky little island lashed by the storms of the southernmost reaches of the world.

In the map of South America, Chile looks like a long yellow fringe bordering Argentina on the west. One might say that it was simply a cartographical coquetry to prevent the chilly water of the Pacific from wetting the Argentine frontiers.

When seen on a regional map, Chile appears a little wider and divided into provinces of different colors. This is called a political map. Its aspect is then deplorable, confusing. Its study, too. From the very first glance one wishes to avoid so much complication and to limit oneself to that "long narrow fringe" which we have been studying since childhood. We are accustomed to look at the darker line of the range and tell ourselves that that point of reference suffices: what extends from there to the sea must be Chile. Is it worth while to burn our eyes out studying such a tiny country?

This is the geography of many decent persons. They seem to ignore that Chile is bigger than any European country except Russia (I am thinking in terms of the "legitimate" map of Europe). They do not know that its mountains are, next to the Himalayas, the loftiest in the world; that its coastline is among the longest and most complicated in existence; and finally that along its 4,200 kilometers of length there is a little world of its own with the most varied climates and types.

If, instead of this indolent, apathetic character which is ours, we had been born with the enthusiastic and imaginative spirit of North Americans, we would have had geography books, moving pictures, and adventure stories wherein against a torrid desert background the dark men from the pampas rub shoulders with the hieratic Indians of the Atacameñan nitrate works, while in the Pacific we would see the Polynesian "caucus" of Easter Island alternating with the fishermen of Lord Anson Valley, offspring of some shipwreck survivors on the beach of Robinson Island. We would see combative Araucanians and hefty women rowing in the Calbuco Seas; the Chilotes of Japanese features, small and garrulous; the Alacalufs of the somber canals, navigating their primitive canoes; the cowboys of the Magellan pampas, with their high boots, their blue jackets, and the caps with the visors turned backward, struggling against the pampas wind. We would follow the steps of the gold diggers across Tierra del Fuego; and at Beagle Canal we would hear yarns about sea wolves, mixture of fishermen, smugglers, and pirates who in their cutters ply the canals of the Far South, imposing their wills, unbridled by anything save their own laws.

But we Chileans spend our lives gazing at the agricultural and administrative belly button of the country. When the films try to be nationalistic they show only fields and threshings, as if threshings were not the same the world over. Perhaps the merchants and geographers are right in assuming this attitude. (Current geographies are *economic*, as if written for merchants.) And there is no sense in artists imitating the merchants. But every man should have something of the artist in him in order to understand the world, in order to understand something about each thing. Perhaps even the merchants may also need art in order to conceive other realities more attractive and worth while than their everyday prosaic reality.

Chile is more than a simple capital in process of construction. It is more than a small agricultural center, or group of communes mentioned only in some electoral count. It is a vast, imposing country, pride of geographers, naturalists, and travelers. A country, in short, which is man's joy and, more so, an artist's joy, who, after all, is the man possessing the greatest vision and sensibility.

Chilli, "where the land ends," as the Aymarás were wont to say.

And they were right, unless Chilli be where the land begins.

In an area of 750,000 square kilometers, Chile extends its territory before the sea like a silent offering. With its back to America, removed from all commercial routes which would make it turn its glance toward Europe, it has remained there contemplating the infinite ocean, as if it had lost something in it in times gone by and still longed for it. Marooned on a desolate coast, it follows with its eyes the ships that sail in the distance unnoticing, and lets them disappear beyond the horizon without any desire to change its position.

For the truth is that it would be necessary to tour half the globe before encountering any habitable land beyond the sea.

If we sailed westward in a straight line from Valparaíso, in two days we would pass the Juan Fernández Islands, about 350 miles away. We would cross them northward, without seeing them.

After three weeks we would brush past Easter Island, some 400 miles to the south, without even suspecting its presence. After more weeks of sea and sky we would reach one of the Kermadec Islands, in Oceania, or perhaps the extreme north of New Zealand. If the current should change our course, slightly, in two weeks more we would reach the Australian coast, a little to the north of Sydney.

If we sailed westward from Magellan Strait, we would make a world tour in a straight line, returning to the Strait this time a little to the south. In this long voyage we might possibly see—although we cannot be sure of this—some British colony in the southern Pacific, or in the Indian Ocean or the Atlantic. An ideal tour, no doubt, for someone seeking total spiritual isolation.

In Chile we live immersed in this isolation, and not because we have looked for it with the spleen of a romantic lady. In addition to this inexorable sea, we have on the east a tremendous granite wall with only a few gaps through which, in the center, the Trans-Andean train creeps laboriously, and, farther south, the smugglers of cattle, and finally, on the other end, the rats which every so often infest the fields of Puerto Montt.

By means of the southern fjords the sea perforates the last remnants of the Andes and advances till it almost washes the Argentine frontier. This leads to a strange rendezvous of races. In Puerto Natales, deep in Ultima Esperanza, I have sat in the dining room of the Hotel Cruz del Sur, next to a gaucho from Río Gallegos, a Chilean landlord, and an Alacaluf Indian (rara avis). The Indian was dressed in European style and did not smell of fish. He told me that in summer he devoted himself to the fur trade in Argentina. In winter he discarded his comfortable clothes, put on his seal furs, and went out with his men in canoes after the otters and seal. I asked him if he felt cold on ridding himself of his clothes in the coldest weather. He answered that it was only now in his Sunday best that he felt cold. "When one is naked, the whole body becomes a face," he explained.

At the extreme north Chile is separated from the world by a wide deserted expanse. In the south it faces the polar ice; to the west, the ocean; and to the east, the immense mountain range.

Such a country should be called an island even though this does not fit in with the geographical definition of an island.

Of course islands are havens for sailors and fishermen, but our country is the haven only of farmers and politicians.

In Chile there are few maps, and not all of them are good.

Translated by Ángel Flores

Note

1. Gabriela Mistral, "Contadores de patria: Benjamín Subercaseaux y su 'Chile o una loca geografía,'" *La Nación* (Buenos Aires), 27 April 1941.

Catastrophe and National Character

Rolando Mellafe

In this essay the historian Rolando Mellafe describes a very different relationship between national identity and geography. Rather than celebrate Chile's exceptional natural beauty, he chronicles a lengthy history of natural disasters from earthquakes, tsunamis, and volcanic eruptions to droughts, floods, and epidemics. For Mellafe, these "tragic events" have played a fundamental role in shaping the "Chilean mentality." In this passage, a major earthquake in 1647 that razed the city of Santiago, destroying every last structure, stands as a foundational event, forging a particular Chilean mentality.

Mellafe calculates an average of one major earthquake every eight years in Chile. Frequent earthquakes, he writes, produce a sense of national community, shaping society and distilling its basic psychological characteristics during periodic moments of crisis. Just as Mistral and Subercaseaux underline Chile's geographical peculiarities and isolation to make Chilean national identity intelligible, Mellafe contends that constant confrontation with natural disasters has played a formative role in the psychology of Chilean society.

You can understand [why Chilean historians have traditionally told a history that focused primarily on describing events that were ultimately positive and contributed to progress]: one would have to be morbid to accumulate and describe only the facts of disasters, the calamities and catastrophes that our ancestors suffered. Morbid or not, a history of mentalities requires, among other things, a list of tragic events, in order to explain the formation and maintenance of some of the characteristics of a people. The continual recuperation from and survival of tragic events, reiterated over the long centuries, reinforces many of the most valiant elements of the collective and individual egos of the people.

Every historian who has been preoccupied with economic facts, social facts, or those related to the population knows, for example, how difficult it is to describe normal situations. It is often nearly impossible to say if that which we are analyzing is or is not a normal situation. Generally, we dis-

Houses destroyed by the 1960 earthquake in Valdivia. The earthquake that struck southern Chile in May 1960 was the strongest quake ever recorded, touching off tsunamis as far away as Hawaii and huge waves in Japan and the Philippines. Photographer unknown. Courtesy of Colección Archivo Fotográfico, Biblioteca Nacional de Chile.

cover normality when it experiences crisis, when it begins to transform or fall apart. Thus, the importance of examining connected moments, the crises, that are generally also chapters of historical misfortune.

At a first stage, the history of tragic events should be carried out in the form of a quantitative history. This is to say, we aren't interested in one singular calamity or catastrophe, which happened in a given moment of the nation's past, but rather in all of the catastrophes that occurred in our history. In this way we can reduce a part of our unfortunate history into a system, with a frequency, regularities and irregularities, and which, finally, could pass for a model. This isn't to say, of course, that each of the individual facts lacked value or importance as a singular occurrence.

Droughts, and especially earthquakes are very important in economic history. Earthquakes, in the history of credit, for example, because mortgage loans known as double-taxes, almost the only ones that existed during the colonial period, were granted over urban personal property, [and] once that was destroyed by an earthquake, the system was also ruined. Perhaps the most important economic crisis of the colony was the result of the 1647 earthquake that totally destroyed Santiago.

A simple mathematical account of the disasters that occurred in Chile leaves us feeling terrorized. First, put to the side wars, revolutions, the devastation and destruction of cities that resulted from the actions of man, as well as the burning of entire cities, incursions by pirates and corsairs (which often paralyzed commerce for several years), plagues that attacked crops and livestock, etc. We are concentrating only on: earthquakes, flood years, large droughts, epidemics that attacked humankind, and plagues of locusts and rats. Even when considering only the truly significant phenomena, those which devastated at least one-third of the inhabited territory, we come to an incredible statistic.

Our calculation begins before the arrival of Almagro in 1520, with accounts of a terrible earthquake that the Indians gave to the first conquistadores. There was probably also an early viral epidemic at this point, but we ignore its possibility because of the uncertainty of the data. Our calculation ends in 1906, with the earthquake in Valparaíso. In these 386 years there were 282 disasters; 73 percent of the years in our history have been harmful: 100 earthquakes, 46 years during which everything was flooded, 50 years of absolute drought, 82 years of different generalized epidemics and 4 years during which insects or rodents ate everything including the trees. I believe that this account is not exact, but if it contains errors, they are due to omissions, because there were almost certainly more tragic years than this. In any event, our ancestors suffered an earthquake every 3.8 years, a season with flooding every 7 years, a dry year every 7, and an epidemic every 4.

These calamities are organized in short cycles, the most common being that an earthquake follows a year of storms and flooding, and then an epidemic, in an interval of three or four years. On a side note, a curiosity, the worst year in Chile's history for natural disasters was 1851, during which there were two earthquakes, a disastrous winter, and a viral epidemic; on top of this, there was a bloody revolution. This is only curiosity, but, for motives which will become clearer later, it is possible that this 1851 revolution was so passionate and inflamed precisely because the four previously noted phenomena—two earthquakes, a flood, and an epidemic—broke apart ethnocentric national ties and oriented the peoples' collective anguish in the direction of violence, which ultimately would have had the object of creating greater security to the collective and individual ego.

Throughout the years of an average Chilean's life during past centuries there were, without doubt, certain years of grief that resulted from these disasters. On average, every family in the country, before falling apart, had three deaths from epidemics or earthquakes, as well as various years of economic hardship resulting from years of drought and flood.

When we speak of tragic events, in the sense that we are doing so here, we refer to them in the past. This is because in our time, man doesn't feel the effects of earthly disasters with the same force that he did a few decades ago. Geologic and climatic processes haven't changed very much, but contemporary man, who had learned how to surround himself with defenses against the effects of the elements, has. Dams, canals, and dykes relieve us of the effects of floods and droughts, epidemics are practically under control; even special earthquake-resistant construction has diminished our fear of earthquakes. At the same time and as a result of this, a much shorter and less preoccupied dialogue with things of the earth is producing in us another profound change with unforeseeable effects. At least for now, this is neither good nor bad, but it is something that is simply happening that merits our reflection.

The purpose of my words at this point, however, isn't to describe with direct causality the social and economic character that natural disasters produce. We would like to go a little deeper into the maturation process of the national individual and collective ego and, precisely, tragic events lend themselves well to this task.

In this day and age, if there is an epidemic outbreak, the Ministry of Health, for good or ill, takes charge of the problem. It seems that, in general, this has worked well in the past few decades, because smallpox, polio, yellow fever, etc. have nearly been eradicated. In any case, we understand any problem as coming from a bacteria, virus, or germs, as a biological question that is clearly defined and delimited. But little more than a century ago, the question was not so clear, or better stated, not so simple. Tragic events had a supernatural origin, they were sent by God or by a powerful deity; the appearance, development, and final consequences of such a phenomenon were related intimately with the individual and collective behavior of the society that suffered. It was related to sin and grace, with evil and its redress. Death that resulted from such occurrences was not natural and because of this it was wrapped up in the mystical-cultural symbolic trappings of the period.

At this point, Spanish, Indians, blacks, those of mixed race (*mestizo*) reacted in quite a similar fashion. Smallpox, for example, had a supernatural origin for all of them, "preternatural" as it was called at the time. For the Spanish it was a punishment from God for their unchaste, impious, licentious life, and its cure was likely found in the Church. In response to the same sickness, Indians supposed that it was induced by occult enemy forces. Father Rosales tells us "The Indians say that the Spanish carry the smallpox in sealed jars from one place to another and wherever they want to they

open the jars to destroy the Indians," and this idea doesn't seem strange
to them, because according to what Father Rosales adds, "that which kills
some gives life to others."

For the blacks and the mestizos, the soul wandered in the night, while
the body slept (at night there are no shadows, the shadow is the soul), committed misdeeds and got in trouble with other souls. When the soul argued
with that of a god or a wizard it got something bad in return as vengeance—
such as smallpox—with which the soul later infected the body. You couldn't
find a better example of the unity of the natural and supernatural worlds,
which was just mentioned above.

Perhaps you are wondering "what does all this have to do with Chilean
character?"

You will have noted that we are at a more obvious position than that
which has generally been called "telluric." The American and the Chilean
have been defined as essentially of the earth. But telluric is not simply a love
of the earth, nor a simple affinity for the natural; it is a constant and unconscious dialogue between the psyche and Nature. Tragic events oppress this
dialogue and press an entire society to confront, through its ego, the deepest layer of its spiritual existence, the dawn of its own psyche. The tensions
that this repeated meeting produces, the terror that often inspires us, pro-
vokes collective phenomena that express themselves in modes of being and
acting: love of and indifference toward the earth, for example. One loves
the place where he was born, but he also escapes from there. He loves his
wife, his mother, and his family, but he abandons them. A woman carries
on, due to another type of connection, but for that same reason must play
a more practical role of greater integrity, which explains a lot of women's
historical behaviors.

If smallpox can bring us to these reflections, earthquakes tell us much
more. The psychic effect of an earthquake is that the physical world that is
perfectly stable and balanced becomes undone, becomes unstable, it produces a chaos that is the most unnatural that can be conceived of. Evangelical priests from the sixteenth century told the Indians that God, on creating
the world, had put "each thing in its place." For the Indians this wasn't very
novel; their gods had done the same. But earthquakes, eclipses, and less so
the darkness of night, unmade that which God had made. For a man with
a mystically oriented mentality this signified a return to the first night of
chaos. Earthquakes have the effect of hypnosis or a self-guided, collective,
and almost automatic dream. A mystic connection is charged with ordering
this disintegrated, natural world, and it does so using archetypal symbols.
This means, until the Earth stops moving, each ego lives as if for the first

time the most primary chapters of the formation of its self. The phenomenon of an earthquake goes beyond just that which concerns earth, just as do effects of various epidemics of smallpox, though suffered in minutes. It produces the collective, social effect of reaffirming one's own personality, of characterizing—that is to say putting in characters—that which already exists; and this is another of the traits of the Chilean way of being.

Translated by David Schreiner

Deforestation in Chile: An Early Report

Claudio Gay

In this 1838 report to the Chilean government, "On the causes of the diminishing woodlands of the province of Coquimbo," the French-born botanist Claudio Gay describes the deforestation wrought by the copper mining industry in Chile's northern province of Coquimbo. As a counterpart to celebrations of Chile's natural beauty, in the nineteenth century politicians and scientists became increasingly alarmed by ecological degradation and the loss of valuable natural resources. For decades during the mid-nineteenth century, Chile was the world's largest producer of copper and acquired the mining riches that had eluded it during the colonial period, when it remained one of the poorest provinces of the Spanish Empire. Copper generated growth underwrote the country's unusual political stability as a young republic. It also produced modern Chile's first great ecological catastrophe, the almost complete elimination of Coquimbo's native forests. As Charles Darwin also observed during his voyages down the Pacific coast on the Beagle, *the loss of forests meant that the mines had little wood for smelting and thus had to export their ore abroad, primarily to Great Britain, where it was converted to metal, depriving Chile of the value added during processing. Deforestation in Chile's* norte chico *(near north) and the loss of revenue due to dependence on smelters abroad sparked some of the first efforts to regulate deforestation in Chilean history. Gay wrote this brief report as part of a broader program, spearheaded by the landowners' trade association, the Sociedad de Agricultura (later the more famous Sociedad Nacional de Agricultura), to promote legislation regulating the mining industry and the destruction of forests. During the same period prominent writers and politicians like Benjamín Vicuña Mackenna joined the fight for environmental regulations, penning important studies of the effects of deforestation on soil erosion, river flooding, and the advance of dunes from the coast. Gay embarked on this campaign during the 1830s; the first major legislation regulating the destruction of forests was not passed until 1873.*

Mr. Minister.

Although the great drought of the year 1837 prevented my visiting the province of Coquimbo in its totality, I nevertheless cannot let more time pass without declaring to you, sir, how much the declining state of its vegetation surprised me, and the disastrous consequences which may result.

To the less attentive observer, this province presents a completely unfavorable appearance. Nearly all of its woodlands have disappeared; the bushes are weak, small, and stunted, and the rocks, already revealing their flanks in the most dreadful nudity, seem to portend to this beautiful province an unfortunate future.

However, the ambience is not completely contrary to grand and robust vegetation; in various isolated places, and above all distant from population centers, one still encounters trees of great size; there you still see carob trees, hawthorns, *talhuenes*, *litres*, etc., of notable beauty and height, and if moving forward the vegetation changes and these species disappear, they are replaced by the willows, *lormatas*, *chañales*, *carbon*, and many other trees and shrubs marvelously suited to the nature of that terrain and the force of that climate. The locality ought not then be accused of worthlessness, with respect to the aridity of this province. Rather man, and only in man, is where one has to search for the root (of these charges); this exists in the shortcomings of our laws governing the arrangement of forests and fields, and in the defects of the Mining Ordinances, which authorize miners to tear out and destroy everything.

At the beginning of the conquest, or when the population was still weak and sparse, the government could watch the devastation of our forests with indifference. And before, on the contrary, these forests were the property of the State, which cleared the land from which agriculture would later take great advantages. But today the scene has completely changed; the population has increased and the forests have diminished in equal proportion! What will our homes and refineries be reduced to if, moving forward, this ruinous vice is not contained? How has the great rigidity of the laws governing the forests of old Europe not caught the attention of our government? It is time to consider them, and to modify the Mining Ordinances that have hitherto governed the tasks and labor of miners.

Originally created for use in Mexico and Peru, in many cases they [the Mining Ordinances] cannot be applied to this Republic: the miners are convinced of their insufficiency at the local level, and for a long time there has been demand for other laws better suited to the country's nature and wealth. The government, without a doubt, cannot delay a remedy of such urgent necessity, and in such cases as the articles relative to the cutting of wood, should not lose sight of the fact that both the landowner and the miner should be consulted, and after discussing the interests of both parties, a completely impartial third party should adopt the measures most convenient to the general interest; the opposite would result in a depravity that, favoring mining production, would occasion true harm to the most valuable and useful of industries: agriculture.

I do not base this assertion solely on the diminishing of wood, as a sufficient quantity remains to feed the ovens, and the miner can, at present, with fewer extra expenses, meet his needs; but it is not from this point of view that the government should consider things: what jealous village father would attend as much to the present as to the future, and stubbornly insist on bequeathing to his children a province in which poorly understood resources have been wiped clean of everything needed for agriculture, reducing the land to extreme aridity? We must not deceive ourselves; in the dry and burnt countries the trees are very slow to grow, and today's numerous devastated places will for a long time remain without the cover of their native vegetation. On the other hand, and this is the principal purpose of the question, the disappearance of the forests influences atmospheric phenomena in a mysterious manner; the seasons become more intense, the air drier, the rains more scarce, and the combination of all of these results in the decrease of the rivers' water level, declining more each day since a geometrically growing civilization places greater and greater demands on them. As one attentively views the banks and beds of the rivers, it is not necessary to be a physicist or geologist in order to know that in another time they had carried very considerable quantities of water: the evidence is all too clear, and if we believe some of the older people, there is not much time before the desperate farmer will see, for the first time in certain places, the Coquimbo and Limari rivers entirely cut off throughout their width.

It is true that the means to prevent such terrible misfortunes are scarce and difficult to find: they cannot propose plantings of indigenous trees in the hills because the bovine and wool-bearing livestock would very quickly destroy them; nor is it possible to impede the cutting of the trees; the work of the mines would suffer too much, and they constitute one of the principal branches of commerce in this province!!! It is still probable that mining operations will expand, and then the climate and vegetation will find new enemies that contribute powerfully to the devastation of this beautiful region. In these conflicting circumstances, it is the duty of every individual to search for a remedy, and although the inhabitants of the north can in this case, through deep-seated experience, propose perhaps more adequate means, I will take the liberty upon myself to present to you, sir, some ideas that my travels have brought to mind.

Of course it is true, of which you sir should be convinced, that the trees attract electricity, and thus the rain: theory and experience prove that the cause of this phenomenon lies in their tall form and in the pointed branches of which they consist. Now then, in order to achieve this result, one needs to find some trees that may fulfill these conditions; the botanical gardens of Europe would supply many of this sort; but as Chile still lacks such establishments, it is necessary to search for those that are situated in this country. None better for the desired objective, following my opinion, than those known under the name of poplars and willows: they have the additional advantage of growing rapidly, and offer the farmer all of their benefits very quickly. In all of my travels and excursions I have never failed to see the usefulness of such plantings: the landowners agree on it, but whether out of indifference or some other motive, they have not made an effort to put such a beneficial project into execution. In which case it falls to you, sir, to consider the situation from the point of view of public utility, and order intelligent persons to examine this project, and once approved oblige the large landowners and small farmers to plant one or more rows of these trees on the banks of the rivers, canals, and even around their fields; these forced plantings, far from harming their interests, beautify their properties, providing them within very little time not only excellent wood for construction but also an abundant quantity of firewood. When one reflects that said trees suffice for the demands of Mendoza and its environs, one cannot be less than surprised that in the towns of Huasco and Copiapó, where firewood and lumber are as expensive as they are scarce, the proprietors have entirely neglected this division of industry.

If, due to the scarcity of rivers and canals, one does not achieve the desired end through the decreed proposal, that is, to alter the atmospheric conditions in favor of agriculture, it would be necessary then that the government foster a new venture directed to transport and smelt copper minerals in another province, thereby conserving the woodlands of Coquimbo, and favoring its vegetation. This project, though considerable, does not seem risky or difficult to me. The woodlands are becoming so scarce at various points that the miners see the sad necessity of selling their minerals to foreigners at a loss, who, with rising costs, transport them unrefined to Europe or the United States.

Now it remains to be seen if this new branch of commerce is advantageous to the country! A very simple calculation will prove the contrary.

According to Customs records, 179,200 quintales of unrefined minerals have been extracted in 1836, which, sold at 120 pesos per container of 64 quintales, have made a quantity of 336,000 pesos. Supposing, as shown by repeated assays, that the average purity of exported copper minerals is 25 percent, these metals smelted in the country would have yielded 44,750 quintales of copper bars, which, sold at the average price of sixteen pesos per quintal, amounts to a sum of 716,000 pesos! Here is an effective loss of 381,000 pesos for the Republic: the loss to the National Treasury is no less considerable, for in place of the 43,000 pesos that it should receive, it does not earn more than 20,000.

These losses will increase with time due to the growing scarcity of firewood to fuel the kilns. The same Customs records confirm this truth: the export of minerals doubles from one year to the next, and you, sir, should not ignore that a copper mine is not a resource in and of itself, if not combined with the benefit that results from smelting and manufacturing; because in that case the owner of the mine sells no more than the work of the miner; and in a country such as ours which lacks labor, rather than take advantage of this genuine resource, a mere paltry yield is taken out, which is almost void, especially if one were to compare it with the damages done to future agriculture and industry. If the country's statistics were more developed, it would be very easy for me to prove that the expenditures of labor and transport absorb the majority of the product of sale, and thus these mines cannot be considered a resource in this sense; they only sustain their profits more or less individually. On the other hand, mines do not grow like plants; that which is taken from them does not reproduce, and given the limited duration of a mineral's extraction, its product cannot be placed on the same level with that offered by agriculture. In good economic policy, it [agriculture] has to be preferred in many cases to the mining of certain minerals. And in the province of Coquimbo, the notion that it has always considered itself the exclusive realm of mining, in reality, has harmed its agriculture, destroying more and more the elements it counts on to impede the diminishing of its water. When one visits the lovely and fertile valleys of Limari, Guanti, Hurtado, and Elqui, one cannot help but admire the richness of their vegetation, and then one laments that the rivers do not supply enough water to make good use of the vast plains that border these valleys, and that a non-renewable resource every day advances closer to being used up; because, I cannot close without repeating, climate will be favorable to agriculture when the [tree] plantings multiply and one knows how to appreciate the influence of the forests over this important branch of our industry.

In order to achieve this objective and partly remedy these inconveniences, which the government should not regard with indifference, I do not expect obstacles to be placed before the operation of the mines: on the contrary, the mines require of you, sir, the greatest and most resolute protection; but they [the mines] ought also to search for means of getting all of the advantages of which they are capable. These advantages may be achievable in part if the government could initiate the appropriate undertaking, that is, a company that takes on the responsibility of transporting and smelting the minerals in a province, such as Concepción, which offers raw materials in abundance. It is not necessary here to analyze the immense advantages that the company would attain as a result of such an undertaking; the calculations are very simple and the facts so very clear that they could easily stand up to a rigorous evaluation. And you, sir, will agree with me that if foreigners, in spite of the rising costs of transport (which equal the cost of purchase exactly), obtain a profit in this kind of commerce, the Chilean association, saving these expenses, ought necessarily to find the greatest advantage.

If we now consider this enterprise in relation to public advisability, we will see that it would give a new impulse to coastal trade, being able to employ 25 vessels monthly of no less than 250 tons, which would maintain permanent communication between these two rich provinces. The Chilean nation would not lose the true value of the metals which the foreigner exports in such quantity, and the country would provide itself an income of 400,000 pesos annually and the National Treasury more than 20,000.

Translated by Timothy Lorek

"Catastrophe in Sewell"

Pablo Neruda

In 1945, Chile experienced its worst mining accident. Three hundred and fifty-five workers in the North American–owned El Teniente copper mine, located in the Andes cordillera near Rancagua, perished during a mine fire. Like deforestation and soil erosion, the mining disaster reflected the often catastrophic consequences of extracting nature's wealth from the soil. If geography had blessed Chile with extraordinary natural resources, disasters or "tragic events" were also part of the bargain. The El Teniente accident was, of course, both humanly produced and natural. For many Chileans "the Tragedy of 'the Smoke,'" as the accident was known, reflected the unequal distribution of both mining's riches and its costs. The hundreds of dead miners were victims of the foreign mining company, which held a monopolistic control of Chile's most valuable natural resource. (Copper produced in North American mines accounted for well over 50 percent of the country's foreign earnings.) Press accounts of the accident noted the lax security in the mine, the failure of the Braden Copper Company (a subsidiary of the better-known Kennecott) to take prompt measures to rescue the miners, and the generally difficult and perilous working conditions in the mine tunnels. The miners' funeral was attended by President Juan Antonio Rios as well as dignitaries like Pablo Neruda, and three days of national mourning were declared. For many, the workers' exploitation at the hands of Kennecott reflected the more general exploitation of Chile's natural resources by foreign capital. The El Teniente tragedy helped fuel a national movement to wrest control of the copper industry (still today the motor of the Chilean economy) from its North American owners, the Kennecott and Anaconda copper companies, and in 1971, Chile's copper mines were nationalized by a unanimous vote in Congress. Neruda, who wrote the poem "Catastrophe in Sewell" as part of his epic Canto General, *was at the time of the accident a senator for the Communist Party representing the northern mining districts. The poem highlights both the exploitation of Chile's natural resources by foreign companies and the exploitation of workers' labor and bodies; in the poem, the (always male) workers stand in for Chile and Chileans more generally.*

Sánchez, Reyes, Ramírez, Núñez, Álvarez.
These names are like Chile's foundations.
The people are the country's foundation.
If you let them die, the country keeps collapsing,
keeps bleeding until it is drained.
Ocampo has told us: every minute
there's a wound, and every hour a corpse.
Every minute and every hour
Our blood falls, Chile dies.
Today it's smoke from the fire, yesterday
    firedamp,
the day before the cave-in, tomorrow the sea or
    the cold,
machinery and hunger, the unforeseen or acid.
But there where the seaman dies,
but there where people from the pampa die,
but there in Sewell where they disappeared,
everything is maintained—machinery, glass,
iron, papers—
except man, woman, and child.
It's not the gas: it's greed that kills in Sewell.
That tap turned off in Sewell so that not even a
    drop
of water for the miners' poor coffee would fall,
there's the crime, the fire's not to blame.
Everywhere they turn off the people's tap
so that the water of life won't be distributed.
But the hunger and cold and fire that consume
our race (the flower of Chile's foundations),
the tatters, the miserable house,
they're not rationed, there's always enough
so that every minute there's a casualty
and every hour a corpse.
We have no gods to turn to.
Poor mothers dressed in black
already wept all their tears while they prayed.
. . . .

This human cave-in cannot be,
this bleeding of the beloved country,

this blood that falls from the people's heart
every minute, this death
of every hour.
My name's the same as theirs, as the ones who
    died.
I, too, am Ramírez, Muñoz, Pérez, Fernández.
My name's Álvarez, Núñez, Tapia, López,
    Contreras.
I'm related to all those who die, I'm people,
and I mourn for all the blood that falls.
Compatriots, dead brothers, from Sewell, Chile's
dead, workers, brothers and sisters, comrades,
as you're silent today, we're going to speak.
And may your martyrdom help us
to build a severe nation
that will know how to flower and punish.

Translated by Jack Schmitt

A Call to Conservation

Rafael Elizalde Mac-Clure

After a wave of fires had devastated southern forests during the 1940s Rafael Elizalde Mac-Clure wrote this foundational text in Chilean conservationist and environmentalist writing during the 1950s. He makes an impassioned plea for the conservation of Chile's natural resources, with individual chapters charting the ecological degradation of soil, water, forests, flora and fauna, and "scenic beauty." His book, Chile's Survival, *also proposed a series of measures to ensure the nation's sustainable management of renewable natural resources, including an extensive educational program to advocate environmental awareness. Elizalde frequently wrote for the state railroad publication* En Viaje *(Traveling), which promoted domestic tourism with lengthy articles on national parks and natural attractions throughout the country. Elizalde's* En Viaje *articles, like others in the publication, were directed at a growing urban blue-collar working class and white-collar middle class who had little knowledge of their country's vast and diverse geography. The goal was to build the domestic tourist economy, stimulate conservation, and construct a stronger national identity founded on a consciousness of the national territory. In addition, Elizalde, like many other writers, advocated conservationist measures and travel in nature as essential to the health of the "Chilean race," increasingly threatened by ecological crises and the ambient ills of modern, urban living.*

Four hundred years of civilization have completely transformed Chile's countenance. The little vegetation there was in the northern oases has been reduced to narrow strips along the squalid rivers and streams. The hills near the towns are stripped of chaparral and cracked with erosion, which is exacerbated by the herds of goats that devour every last blade of grass. The reservoirs that were built at great expense to store the meager rainfall are gradually being choked with the sand washed from the neighboring mountainsides.

In central Chile, the wide river beds are covered in the summer with stony ground and pebbles of all sizes, punctuated here and there by the zigzagging course of two or three river branches that seem more like streams.

In the winter, the floods sometimes make them overflow; since the basins and riverbanks have been denuded of vegetation, they are eaten away by the force of the swift current.

The mountain range of the north-central coast, although it partly conserves its scrublands of hawthorns, *boldos* and *litres*, has not been reforested.

The Maule range to the south has lost all its oaks, and though efforts have been made to reforest it with pines, it looks withered and desolate. On the mountainsides wheat is still being cultivated on exhausted land that yields less each year, while in the dry brown meadows, sheep and cattle waste away from the rickets.

This region's coast is invaded by gray dunes that advance, undaunted and uncontainable, into the interior, sterilizing the fertile lowlands and burying trees and even villages.

All the rivers sweep along millions of tons of sand that obstruct their beds and mouths, making navigation impossible and killing fish and shellfish.

The only encouraging note is the green ribbon of the Longitudinal Valley with its well-irrigated lands stretching to Puerto Montt, intersecting to the east and west with other fertile valleys. These lands, irrigated with water from nearby rivers, are the best in the country.

The remaining lands are dry; almost all are overgrazed fields of wild grasses. Every year many animals are lost due to drought and lack of fodder.

Similarly, the overabundance of flocks grazing on the steep deforested land of the Andean foothills and in the overgrazed summer pastures has caused erosion on the mountainsides that has gradually extended to the lower lands.

Moving briefly from the center to the far south, the Patagonian jungle has been insulted as its most vulnerable and sacred sites, its numerous river basins, were barbarously burned to the ground. And Magallanes, the cold and desolate steppe, still feeds immense flocks of sheep that miraculously survive thanks to the heat of their wool and the plants of the *coironales*, in spite of their own voraciousness and the violence of the winds.

But it is the romantic Araucanía, where renewable resources have been most cruelly abused, that has most inspired the poet.

If our forefathers Ovalle, Olivares, Rosales or Molina[1] were brought back to life and saw with their own eyes the region they had so highly praised, they would surely weep.

While fire has been used to clear the flat land for sowing, it has not been controlled and the damp forests have gone up in flames, even those located on the steepest slopes.

The view seen from the window of a train is distressing, particularly in some stretches of that region: Cemetery after cemetery of charred trees parade before the passenger, some atrociously twisted, mummified in a final rictus of pain. Their black branches stab the air like amputated arms; others, reduced to squat stumps, lift their severed limbs only a few meters from the ground. They gradually disintegrate into dust and are scattered by the wind and the rain, like the funeral rite of scattering the ashes of the dead.

The national writer Luis Durand describes the tragic landscape thus: "Dry sticks jutting up before the eyes, engulfed in poetic sadness. Dry sticks, jutting up in anguish to the black, hollow wind. Others like lepers, full of holes; twisted into bizarre contortions, like an unsteady drunk on the sidewalk; imploring like an inscrutable plea."

It would seem as though the white man, with a crass sense of vengeance for the fierce resistance of the Indian who defended his soil, had wanted to take revenge on the Araucanian land, stripping it of its jewels, its trees, flowers and ferns, silencing its songbirds, exterminating its graceful South Andean deer, leaving it naked and defenseless, at the mercy of the elements. And then subjecting it to thousands of tortures and violations, force feeding it with seeds until it sickened, stabbing it with the plow up and down its slopes, opening up furrows until the interminable rains ate away at its insides, until it sunk in impressive craters, red and bloody, that stretched, deepened and widened infinitely, aborting all its fertility, thus creating an earthly desolation that will lead to the destruction of mankind.

Faced with the horrifying work of the white man in the four hundred years that he has dominated the country, we should ask ourselves if so-called material progress is compatible with the conservation of renewable resources. It is a dilemma that must be resolved as soon as possible, for the increasing exhaustion of our vital resources is indisputable. The survival of the nation is at risk.

Translated by Jane Losaw

Note

1. Colonial-era Jesuit missionaries who wrote foundational works on Chile's natural and political history.

In Defense of the Forests

Ricardo Carrere

In this selection, published by one of Chile's earliest environmentalist organizations, Defenders of the Forest, Ricardo Carrere analyzes the ecological costs of Chile's much-heralded forestry boom during the 1980s and 1990s. In this celebrated essay, Carrere observes that accelerating forestry exports during this period of free-market reform relied on the unsustainable logging of Chile's unique temperate rain forests and the substitution of native forests with plantations of eucalyptus and the North American pino radiata *or Monterey pine, which grows rapidly in Chilean soil and supplies the raw material for Chile's booming paper pulp and cellulose industry. Indeed, Carrere argues that while proponents of industrial forestry contend that tree plantations relieve pressure on native forests, during the 1990s, a number of Chilean environmentalist organizations and forestry experts demonstrated that beginning with the military regime of Augusto Pinochet, which provided large forestry companies subsidies for foresting with pine, tree plantations replaced native forests as frequently as they reclaimed already cleared land. In effect, environmentalist groups such as Carrere's have demonstrated that during the military dictatorship the state effectively encouraged the substitution of Chile's temperate forests, which contain a high degree of biodiversity and numerous species endemic to Chile, with monocultural plantations of exotic species. From Maule and Concepción provinces to Cautín, Valdivia, and Llanquihue further south, the landscape defined by one of the world's largest and most ecologically diverse temperate forests, a forest celebrated by writers from Pedro de Valdivia and Rosales to Mistral and Neruda, has been increasingly replaced by Monterey pine, which composes about 90 percent of Chile's tree plantations. The publication of Carrere's essay also reflects the growth of the environmentalist movement during the 1990s, when environmentalist organizations like Defenders of the Forests have provided an important counterbalance to the proponents of export-led, free-market growth based on the extraction of Chile's natural resources.*

The main effect of the forestry industry originates in the conversion of vast expanses of native forests into industrial pine and eucalyptus plantations

Pine plantations near Concepción. Photographer unknown. © Pool fotográfico Zig-Zag. Used by permission of Empresa Editora Zig-Zag S.A. Courtesy of Colección Museo Histórico Nacional de Chile.

through clear-cutting or burning. Some fifty thousand hectares of native forest disappeared in two of the main forest regions between 1978 and 1987 (Regions VII and VIII). Almost one third of the forests along the coast of the VIII Region have disappeared as well, to be replaced with pine plantations.

This conversion has had a significant impact on the survival of some plant and animal species. Among them are three tree species (Nothofagus alessandri, Gomortega keule and Pitavia punctata) and a shrub (Berberidopsis coralina), native to Regions VII and VIII that are on the list of ten woody species in danger of extinction. The plantations, whose density inhibits the development of accompanying vegetation, also crowd out native plant communities containing between 20 and 158 species of vascular plants.

Animal species have also been devastated. Schlater and Murúa offer the following description of the unmanaged pine plantations of the central zone:

. . . *on the ground is a lawn of fallen needles, a reddish brown color. Once in a while fungus could be seen—especially after a rainfall—and one or more small plant. The fauna was very scarce, the forests silent, without the singing of birds or amphibian life. There was a complete absence of reptiles and mammals. Only along the edges, along the fire breaks and clearings is there some evidence of life.*

According to the National Forest Corporation, the vast monoculture forests constitute a threat to the survival of several wild species, such as the pudú (deer), the güiña (leopard), the Chilote fox, the long-nosed mouse (comadreja trompuda), the huemul (deer), the little mountain monkey, and Darwin's frog, to mention only a few.

Of course, the plantations also favor the development of some species. The homogenous nature of monoculture allows such species to easily find food, quickly transforming them into a plague capable of wiping out entire plantations. For example, two species of field mouse accustomed to eating roots adapted to eating pine as a result of the change in their environment. In some zones this translated into the destruction of up to 30 percent of the pine trees. Similarly, in the last few years the European pine-shoot moth (Rhyacionia buoliana) has also appeared in Chile. It consumes the pine shoots from the inside and forces the pine to produce new shoots, resulting in loss of growth and directionality. Weakened, the tree is susceptible to fungus infections that kill it. The Diplodia pinea fungus (that kills mainly the top of the tree) and the Dithistroma pinea (which causes a loss of needles) are serious infections in the plantations, while the stick insect (Bacunculus phyllopus) consumes the trees' needles, crippling the process of photosynthesis. These types of plagues pose serious problems for the local populations that have become economically dependent on the forestry industry.

Other species can also become a problem. As Schlater and Murúa note, *the introduction of pine plantations altered the vegetation structure in such a way that it prevented birds from building nests and hindered the fox's roaming inside the forest. Rodents and rabbits, competitive species, have increased in numbers, damaging the young pine plantations and causing economic losses for the forestry companies.*

In response to this infestation, the companies resorted to the use of chemicals that not only poisoned the rabbits, but also other mammals and birds. The number of carnivores capable of regulating the herbivores declined, thereby altering the natural equilibrium and facilitating the increase of rabbits, creating a vicious circle. The herbicides (including one that contains a component of Agent Orange) are also used in young plantations to control weeds, and undoubtedly constitute another important factor in reducing the diversity of native plants and animals.

Another harmful element for biodiversity is the use of fire as a management method. Cavieres and Lara note that fire . . . *kills almost all the existing*

fauna in the area in its different stages of development: eggs, young, adults, etc. . . .
but not only do they kill entire populations of various species, this type of action
also destroys the habitat and micro-habitat (burrows, nests, etc.), a situation that
persists for a long time and sometimes indefinitely.

In the Bio-Bio Province an important—and symbolic—example of the loss of biodiversity due to burning can be noticed with the copihue [Chile's national flower]. Its presence has decreased so much because of burning brush that only some scarce, weak plants exist.

Substituting plantations for native vegetation also impoverishes the landscape: the natural diversity is replaced by homogenization. The diversity of life, the result of which is a landscape of unique characteristics, becomes a monotonous landscape, composed of ordered rows of only one species of pine. A recent study has shown that pine is less attractive to tourists than the native forests.

Translated by Carolyn Watson

Pollution and Politics in Greater Santiago

Saar Van Hauwermeiren

This 1994 analysis of the ecological impact of the neoliberal economic reforms imposed by the Pinochet dictatorship and maintained by the center-left democratic governments that succeeded it offers a grim picture of Santiago's process of urbanization during a period of radical deregulation. The piece highlights the major sources of air pollution in the city, including industries, unpaved roads, and an enormous fleet of cars and diesel-fueled buses, as well as the meteorological and geographic conditions that contribute to it: the city's location in a basin trapped between the Andes and coastal cordilleras. The considerable pollution, toxic gases like carbon monoxide, as well as particulate matter generated by the rapidly expanding metropolitan area, which grew from six to nine million inhabitants during the 1970s and 1980s, is a cause of major public health problems. During winter when the "thermal inversion" is at its worst and pollution is trapped in the city, unable to rise out of Santiago's valley and escape over the mountains, pedestrians often wore masks to filter the air, and bronchial ailments become chronic. As one doctor notes in the piece below, during the winter there are days when the amount of air pollution breathed in by children is the equivalent of smoking ten cigarettes.

After 1990, the democratic governments began to tackle some of the principal problems associated with the Pinochet dictatorship, such as the lack of urban planning and centralized public transportation. Among other policies, they sought to rationalize the system of buses and expanded the city's metro, while restricting private automobiles' access to downtown Santiago during days when air pollution reaches "emergency" levels. However, the capital's geography and rapid demographic expansion have proven an intractable problem, leading to often fantastic and unrealizable schemes to improve air quality, perhaps the most notable of which was a proposal to blast a gigantic hole in the side of the coastal cordillera to provide a valve through which polluted air might escape.

Air pollution in greater Santiago clearly shows the negative effects that the Chilean economic boom and environmental deregulation have caused to the environment and human health. The increased pace of production (and

Buses ("micros") in the streets of Santiago, 1969. The city's bus fleet was a major source of pollution in the city prior to the implementation of pollution controls in the 1990s. Photograph by Josep Alsina. Courtesy of Colección Museo Histórico Nacional de Chile.

its associated services) that has tended to take place around the "pole" of the country's modernization, "Greater Santiago," have caused serious environmental damage to the Metropolitan Region. We will only understand the final implications of this damage in the long run.

It is important to note that these environmental and health effects act as subsidies that the community, nature, and future generations are forced to pay to the commercial activities that the military regime has been supporting since 1974.

Chile, Your Pure Skies Were Blue

The adult population, and even adolescents, almost certainly remembers a time when the skies over Santiago were a clean blue, and we could see the mountains, in all of their imposing beauty, from almost anywhere in the city. Today, however, we have a dirty environment which is full of toxins that not only affect our physical health, but also our state of mind. One only has to climb San Cristóbal Hill to see the desolate panorama of our city, as well as those who live there, who are covered by a permanent layer of brown-lead colored smog.

Air pollution has turned Santiago into one of the most polluted populated places on earth. It now represents one of the greatest public health problems in the country. The effects of air pollution are most severe during the winter months, when they reach their yearly highs. At this time of year, besides the cold weather, it is common that children go to the health clinics because they have problems of bronchitis, asthma, and other respiratory complications.

But how did Santiago become this "monstropolis"?

A Brief History of Air Pollution in Santiago

. . . More than five million people currently live in Santiago. It is estimated that there will be more than six million by the year 2000, and nine million by 2020.

From the latter half of the 1970s through the end of the 1980s, the process of deregulation affected the zoning of urban space, the public transportation sector, and inadequate location of industries. We summarize these main processes within this framework.

Regarding the zoning of urban space, the pressure to develop new urban spaces around the periphery of Santiago (due to the lower land costs vis-à-vis the more centralized areas), the pressure from economic groups that are interested in new housing developments and the free market ideology led the Ministry of Housing and Urbanization (MINVU) to modify the urban development policies in a radical way in 1979. Decree 420 increased the developable urban area from thirty-eight thousand hectares in 1979 to almost one hundred thousand. Santiago currently occupies fifty-four thousand. . . .

The revisions to the location of "fixed sources" of air pollution and the high traffic areas where the number of "mobile sources" are increasing show environmental inconsistencies and imbalances.

Because industries and housing are located in the periphery, while services and commerce are in the downtown area, the daily commute in Santiago is long. This commute exacerbates the problem of air pollution. The intensity and velocity of the urban concentration problem has become one of the highest in the world over the past forty years.

Reports from the Ministry of Transportation show that the number of 12,000 public transportation vehicles is overestimated by about 30 percent. The number of public transportation vehicles doubled between 1980 and 1988, while the number of private cars increased by 30 percent. It is estimated that there will be one million vehicles in Santiago by the year 2000. This increase in the number of vehicles makes traffic even worse. . . .

Eseudero discusses the background of the problems facing public transportation:

> Fifteen years ago, the Ministry of Transportation decreed a policy known as "Freedom of Routes." This policy eliminated any entry requirements and regulations. Whoever wanted to provide public transportation could do so without any authorization. When the democratic government took office in 1990, the Ministry of Transportation did not even have a list of the transportation routes at the time, or a registry of the vehicles that were offering their services.

Public transportation cannot function without a centralized management system. That is why the companies managed themselves for the ten years that the "Freedom of Routes" policy was in effect. The nearly seven thousand bus owners organized themselves into a union whose economic actions resembled those of a cartel. The ensuing increase in prices made it profitable for more vehicles to enter the system and justified the expansion in the fleet, which led to an excess in capacity.

A Few Technical Details

We classify the factors that explain the phenomenon of pollution into two large groups: (a) the growing number of sources of pollution; and (b) the interplay of the weather and geographical conditions in the basin in which the capital is located. These conditions trap pollution over Santiago. Air pollution in Santiago began to be a major environmental and public health problem as a consequence of the increase in the first group of factors and as a consequence of the economic "progress" associated with the neoliberal model.

In the city of Santiago, pollutants come from fixed sources (industrial processes, incineration of garbage, and the incorporation of particles into the air from mainly unpaved roads) as well as mobile sources (private vehicles and public transportation).

"Thermal inversions" are one of the reasons why these pollutants do not disperse sufficiently. These inversions produce a thermal screen which impedes the mixing of polluted air at the city level and the clean air above this screen. The thermal screen is like a lid over a container (the Santiago basin) that does not allow the gasses and polluted particulates to disperse into the atmosphere. Conditions are better in the spring and summer, when the inversion layer occurs at a higher altitude. Sometimes this layer breaks down completely.

A second problem is the absence of winds that are strong enough to diffuse or remove the air pollution from the city in a horizontal manner. There are also mountains that surround the city and impede atmospheric flows and natural ventilation. Finally, there is a lot of solar radiation.

The two most abundant pollutants, as measured by tons of emissions, are total suspended particulates and carbon monoxide.

Total suspended particulates (TSP) mainly arise from people driving in the streets, which causes 69.8 percent of the total. Of this amount, 46.4 percent stems from unpaved roads, while 23.4 percent stems from paved roads. Industries create 17 percent of the total of total suspended particulates.

The most important part of the suspended particulates is what is called the breathable fraction (BF, which are particles that are smaller than 10 microns), because they cause the most harm to the respiratory system. Twenty percent of total suspended particulates belong to the breathable fraction, within which 49 percent is made up of floating dust, and 24 percent stems from transportation. Among this last percentage, diesel motors produce 71 percent.

Carbon monoxide (CO) is the main pollutant gas in the atmosphere in Santiago. Mobile sources create 80.6 percent of it. Cars are the primary source of CO, creating 78.2 percent of the total CO emissions.

Other important pollutants are nitrous oxide (NOX), sulfur oxide (SOX) and volatile organic compounds (VOC).

Public transportation creates two-thirds of nitrous oxide. When it comes into contact with volatile organic compounds (VOCS), this pollutant turns into ozone (O_3) through photochemical processes.

The main source of sulfur oxide (SOX) is factories. Industry produces 74.6 percent of total sulfur oxide emissions. Mobile sources are responsible for 13.4 percent, two-thirds of which stem from public transportation.

Volatile organic compounds (VOCS) are released about evenly from fixed and mobile sources. Ninety percent of the emissions of VOC stem from cars and the other 10 percent is from public transportation.

From these figures, we can see that the amount of pollution in Santiago has frequently surpassed the limits permitted by the Chilean Air Quality Regulations for several years. Every measuring station detects levels of particulate matter that exceed the (75 micrograms per cubic meter of air) limit. The CO and O3 concentrations also exceed the permissible limits. The data also show that breathable size particles pollute the city of Santiago nearly all year. The highest levels recorded at each of the MACAM [air quality monitoring] network stations in 1990 were considerably larger than an INCAP [index of particulate matter] of 400 (which is considered dangerous), with a recorded measurement of up to 858.

However, in spite of these alarming numbers, the official monitoring system of the air that we breathe appears to produce incorrect measurements. In June 1994 the Chilean Medical Association presented a serious charge when it publicly announced that the official data did not correspond to reality because the officials were using inadequate instruments. In reality, the air quality in Santiago is worse than what the government says it is. According to the Association, air pollution is sometimes so severe that its health effects on a nine-year-old child are similar to smoking ten cigarettes a day.

The danger of air pollution for people living in Santiago is so severe that it has forced the government to adopt a series of policies aimed at stopping the worsening of air pollution. These policies have nevertheless been incapable of solving the problem.

Translated by Ryan Judge

II

Chile before Chile: Indigenous Peoples, Conquest, and Colonial Society

If ever there were an unpromising imperial enterprise, it was the Spanish colony known as Chili. In 1541, after almost a year trekking from Cuzco, Peru, through arid deserts, skirmishing with hostile Indians, and facing dissension in his own ranks, Pedro de Valdivia arrived at the fertile Mapocho Valley. There his fractious, bedraggled band of would-be conquerors established a precarious foothold and baptized it Santiago del Nuevo Extremo. Seven months later, the settlement was attacked by local Amerindians and burned to the ground. Thereafter, hunger haunted them as they struggled to maintain a constant vigil against further attacks. The "bad times that in these parts have been abundant up to the present," as Valdivia described them in a letter to the king, would eventually catch up with the intrepid conquistador. Twelve years into his Chilean venture, he was killed in battle, still attempting to secure new territories for the Spanish Crown.

These inauspicious events presaged the travails the Spanish colony would endure over the next century and more. Remote, precarious, poor, and repeatedly ravaged by disasters both human and natural, Chile remained for much of the colonial period a political and economic backwater on the southernmost periphery of Spain's vast American empire. The dreams of the Spaniards who set out from Peru in search of new empires to conquer and new riches to capture would remain largely unfulfilled. Modest discoveries of gold and silver in Chile paled in comparison to the great mines of the Andes and northern Mexico.

The wealth of Chile would instead be found in Indian labor, but as Pedro de Valdivia discovered, subjugating the native inhabitants of Chile presented unique challenges. The remarkable resistance of the peoples whom the Spanish called Araucanians (a variety of groups including the Mapuche) would become legendary. Indeed, they would wage what was arguably the longest running and most successful indigenous resistance to European rule anywhere in the hemisphere. The colony was in a perpetual state of war for its first century and a half and experienced periodic violence thereafter. The conflict, which was concentrated on the colony's southern frontier, sapped resources and lives, yet the Crown was committed to Chile's survival due to its strategic location on the far periphery of its empire, where the threat of encroachment by other European powers was ever present.

Over the course of several centuries, colonial society gradually evolved. As elsewhere, colonialism proved devastating to native populations; more than 200 years later, the population of Chile was still smaller than it had been prior to the arrival of the Spanish. But stable Hispanic settlements eventually emerged, the colony achieved modest wealth through mining, herding, and agriculture, and with increasing administrative autonomy it ceased to be a marginal appendage of the Viceroyalty of Peru. Meanwhile, Hispanic and Mapuche society developed ever closer ties of commercial interdependence that were solidified in peace treaties and trade relations, even as conflict periodically convulsed the frontier. Chile's history as a poor, peripheral, and violent frontier of the Spanish Empire gave rise to social and ethnic relations, labor structures, and landholding and settlement patterns that cast the colony in a different mold from more central Spanish territories. This history would shape Chile's development long after the end of Spanish colonial rule.

Of course, the history of Chile begins long before Pedro de Valdivia claimed those lands for the Spanish crown. By the time of the Spaniards' arrival, the territory that would become first the kingdom and later the republic of Chile had been inhabited for at least 12,500 years, according to recent archaeological research. In fact, the earliest site of human habitation yet located in the western hemisphere is in southern Chile. The discovery in the 1970s of this site, Monte Verde, would incite scholarly controversy and challenge accepted truths about the peopling of the Americas. One of the most arresting finds from the site is a single human footprint, preserved in mud.

The population of the Americas at the time of European contact is a topic of long-standing controversy, but an estimated one million people lived in the territory now recognized as the nation of Chile. Dispersed across a vast territory ranging from the arid northern desert to the frigid southernmost reaches of the continent, this population was composed of a patchwork of indigenous societies with cultural beliefs, social and political systems, and languages as varied as the geoclimatic environments they inhabited. While the indigenous peoples of Chile would be dismissed by the Spanish, and often in traditional historical scholarship, as "poor," their poverty was relative. As semisedentary hunter-gatherers, herders, and fishermen, none boasted the imperial political organization of the Inca or Aztec empires. They were "poor" in the sense that they had little in the way of material wealth—other than their labor—that could enrich their European overlords. Moreover, their dispersed political and social systems made them much more difficult to dominate than the densely populated, centralized empires of the Aztecs in central Mexico and Inca in the Andes. Nevertheless, their complex cultural and religious systems and material cultures belie the characterization of poverty.

Because none of these peoples practiced writing, the "documents" reproduced here so as to describe Chile's native populations are visual images that showcase aspects of indigenous material cultures. These include a mummy of the northern Chinchorro culture, whose mummification practices are the oldest known in the world, and pottery of the Diaguita people of the center-north, whose ceramic traditions were prized first by the Inca and then by the Spanish. Finally, a photograph illustrates the Mapuche culture's rich textile tradition—a tradition still much in evidence in modern-day Chile's handicraft markets. Collectively, these material objects offer a window onto the spiritual beliefs, social organization, and historical development of just a handful of the many diverse cultures that inhabited the region over the course of millennia.

In the period immediately prior to the arrival of the Spanish, many of the indigenous groups in northern and central Chile had been incorporated into the Inca Empire. That empire had its heartland in present-day Peru but extended outward to encompass a large swathe of western South America. To the south, it reached an abrupt halt 50–200 kilometers south of present-day Santiago, somewhere between the Maipo and Maule rivers. There the Inca encountered the staunch resistance of the Mapuche, who prevented their advance in a pitched battle estimated to have occurred around the 1480s. This event was recorded more than a century later in Spanish chronicles, one of which is Garcilaso de la Vega's lively *Comentarios Reales de los Incas*, excerpted here.

The Incas' unsuccessful attempts to subjugate the Mapuche anticipated the challenges experienced by two other would-be overlords—first the Spanish Empire and later the Chilean nation-state. The Spanish attempted to establish a string of fort towns southward, only to see their settlements repeatedly annihilated by the Mapuche, events that at times threatened the very existence of the colony. The southward expansion of the Spanish Empire thus came to a grinding halt at approximately the same latitude as the Inca one before it, more or less thirty-six degrees south. After a century of struggle, Spanish officials were forced into a treaty that recognized Mapuche political and territorial autonomy to a degree unique in the Americas. Thus, when Chile gained its independence from Spain in the early nineteenth century, the Spanish conquest was in a sense still incomplete: fully one-third of present-day Chile (and much more of its territorial extension at the time) remained under Indian rule.

Feared and reviled by the Spanish, the Mapuche were also romanticized by them. The defiance of the "Araucanians" contributed to their image as a proud and noble people, an image immortalized in Alonso de Ercilla's sixteenth-century epic poem *The Araucaniad*. Often called the first work of Chilean literature, Ercilla's poem introduced the "Arauco War" and its indomitable native protagonists to a European audience. The poem marks the origin of the romantic vision of Chile's indigenous peoples as a noble but bellicose race who, in intermixing with the Spanish, would give rise to Chile's "mestizo" (mixed Indian-Spanish) identity. Centuries later, the poem would serve as a key referent for nationalist writers.

Meanwhile, the violent conflict between Hispanic and Amerindian society belied the degree of cultural, economic, and technological exchange between them. At strategic moments, the Mapuche entered into alliance with or accepted subordination to the Spanish, and they also gained valuable knowledge from the Hispanic deserters in their midst. The Spanish divided indigenous peoples into two neat categories, "indios de paz" (peaceful Indians), who were willing to cooperate with them, and "indios de guerra" (rebellious Indians), who would not, but in the shifting vicissitudes of the conflict, alliances proved tenuous and, for the Spanish, the categories frustratingly, sometimes dangerously, porous. Pedro de Valdivia lost his life at the hands of Lautaro, a famed Mapuche cacique (chieftain) who had once served as Valdivia's groomsman. We will describe some of the reasons for the remarkable tactical and political successes of the indigenous "rebels."

If the Arauco War proved lethal, it was also potentially lucrative. For Hispanic society, the frontier was a social escape valve and war an economic engine. The arrival of soldiers to fight in the conflict increased demand for agricultural products, especially after 1600, when the Crown was forced to dedicate a standing army to a conflict previously staffed by mercenaries and funded by private individuals. And while war was a drain on Spanish coffers, it was also a source of enrichment. Unfree labor was the fuel for all economic enterprises throughout the New World, and in chronically labor-scarce Chile, Indians captured in war were a major source of labor for Spanish mines and fields.

Despite the tremendous challenges it presented, the colony of Chile was of strategic importance to Spain as the outer defense of silver-rich Peru against European rivals. Periodic incursions by Dutch and English pirates and corsairs would remind the Crown of this importance. Given this reality, Madrid was willing to make special concessions to attract settlers there, and certain institutions and practices thus developed in Chile that looked very different from central areas of the empire.

One such institution was the *encomienda*, a grant of Indian workers or tribute bestowed by the Crown on deserving conquistadores, known as *encomenderos*. In central areas of the empire, the Crown kept tight control over encomiendas, taxing and regulating them in order to prevent the harsh exploitation that might benefit encomenderos but would jeopardize the long-term productivity of Indian labor and, moreover, give rise to a class of feudal lords who threatened the Crown's authority. In these areas, taxation, regulation, and the decline of Indian populations spelled the end of the encomienda within a few generations. But in poor and peripheral regions the institution survived. In Chile it persisted until the very end of the colonial period in the 1790s, and Chilean encomenderos tended to exercise much greater autonomy from Crown authority than in the empire's central areas.

Another colonial institution that assumed a peculiar form in Chile was slavery. African slavery was of course a widespread feature of Spanish (and European) colonialism in the New World. Indians were subject to many coercive work arrangements, but after the first years of the colonial enterprise, Spanish imperial policy protected them from legal enslavement. In Chile, however, the desperate situation of the war and the need to placate colonists prompted the Crown to legalize the enslavement of Indian war captives, a policy that endured for most of the seventeenth century. The issue of Indian slavery gave rise to animated ethical, doctrinal, and practical debates within Chilean society. These polemics are highlighted in two treatises excerpted here, one by the Santiago resident Melchor Calderón in favor of slavery, the other by the Jesuit scholar Diego de Rosales against it. In another selection, we catch a glimpse of the everyday practice of slavery. While the perspectives of those subject to bondage—as opposed to those who observed, discussed, or benefited from it—are notoriously difficult to find in the historical record, a certificate of enslavement provides subtle clues about the experiences of enslaved Indians themselves. It also hints at the wide gap between law and practice, which was a hallmark of many institutions in colonial Chile.

Meanwhile, and again in contrast to many other New World societies, African slavery was not widely practiced in Chile. This reflected the expense of importing Africans all the way to Chile, the lack of lucrative cash crops (such as sugar) that would justify the expense, and the ready availability of Indian labor. But while Africans have not figured prominently in Chilean historical scholarship, recent research suggests that they were more of a presence, especially in urban areas, where they primarily served as household servants, than national myths of a Chilean mestizo identity have allowed. As the population of encomienda Indians dwindled, devastated by disease and overwork, the population of mixed-race peoples, known as *castas*, gradually increased. Scholars have begun to document the African presence in colonial Chile and to ponder its disappearance from historical memory.

Chile's peculiar colonial development would shape two additional social structures, with far-reaching consequences for future historical development. The first was its system of landholding. In other colonial settings, the Crown made efforts to check the concentration of property in a few hands, but the balance of power on the margins of the empire was, once again, different. Local officials in Chile handed out generous grants of land because of the weakness of royal authority and the need to appease private colonists whose cooperation was indispensable to the colony's survival. *Latifundismo*, or the concentration of land in the hands of a few, would have economic, political, and social consequences down to the present. For example, because of the free-for-all land grab that ensued in central Chile, the Crown made no attempt to protect Indian communities or their lands. Consequently, no autonomous Indian communities survived in the central areas of Hispanic settlement, a pattern that contrasts markedly with places like Mexico and Peru.

The early development of large landholdings and the encomienda system gave rise to a rural social order in which elites wielded inordinate power over dispossessed laborers who worked their land. In some places, such as the *norte chico* ("near north": the arid terrain between the central valley and the Atacama Desert), descendants of the early sixteenth-century beneficiaries of land grants managed to hold onto their properties into the twentieth century. Elsewhere, the original landowners did not necessarily retain their holdings, but patterns of rural social relations were established nonetheless. The concentration of land in great estates, or haciendas, resulted in a landless, rootless underclass of sharecroppers, tenants, migrant peons, and squatters, who eked out a living on the margins of the estates. These groups would prove a perennial headache for colonial and later republican authorities, who accused them of vagabondage and banditry. Meanwhile, landownership became strongly associated with aristocratic status, fostering a seigniorial rural culture that would characterize the Chilean countryside until the 1960s.

A second feature of colonial Chilean society with long-standing historical consequences was its distinct pattern of urban settlement. Travelers will
note that contemporary Chile boasts none of the old colonial cities that
grace other parts of the former Spanish Empire—cities like Antigua, Guatemala; Quito, Ecuador; or Cartagena, Colombia. This absence reflects the
multiple challenges of urbanization in the colony. Key towns were repeatedly destroyed when the Spanish suffered military defeats at the hands of
the Mapuche in 1553, 1598–1604, 1655, and 1723. Pirates attacked coastal cities
in 1578, 1680, and 1686. Meanwhile, natural forces proved equally detrimental to Spanish designs, with earthquakes, tidal waves, and flooding wreak-
ing major destruction in 1570, 1647, 1657, 1730, 1751, and 1783. Concepción, the
largest urban settlement after Santiago, was destroyed and resettled multiple times, coming to occupy its current location only in 1765, more than
two centuries after its initial founding. Finally, the hacienda's monopolization of rural land and people inhibited the formation of urban nuclei. Even
in an era when most of the world's population was rural, Chile's settlement
patterns struck observers as peculiar. As a new governor who toured the
colony wrote in 1717, "the way the people live in Chile seems to me greatly
disordered, and neither in Europe nor in Peru and Mexico . . . do I know of
a similar way of life . . . [with] so many people distant from each other such
that . . . [even in] the most populated parts of the Kingdom, there is not to
be found a single village with a number of houses together."[1]

The governor's comment heralded a new imperial policy of reorganizing
the widely dispersed rural population into discrete urban settlements. Over
the course of the eighteenth century, at least twenty-four new villages and
towns were founded, although the policy was only partially successful, as
it was resisted by poor rural denizens and landowners alike. The landowners in particular opposed the creation of towns that required expropriating
their lands and removed dependents who worked for them or paid rent to
them.

By far the colony's largest urban settlement and its commercial capital
was Santiago, although at 24,000 souls in 1778, it was hardly a booming metropolis. By way of comparison, Mexico City had a population of more than
118,000 around this time; Lima two decades before had 54,000 inhabitants.
Below, a traveler's lively portrait of Santiago in the 1790s captures the tex-
ture of a city that had become a microcosm of colonial social and ethnic
stratification.

Incipient urbanization was part of broader social, political, and economic
changes. By the eighteenth century, Chile had become a more stable, modestly prosperous outpost of the empire. The frontier south had also changed

significantly. The open warfare of the colony's first century and more had gradually waned, superseded by a steady, if still often mutually hostile, rela tionship of commercial interdependence and cultural exchange. Faced with their utter failure to subjugate the Mapuche, creole authorities adopted a policy of diplomatic and commercial engagement that recognized the po- litical and territorial autonomy of the Mapuche. This posture is reflected in the *parlamentos*: periodic summits between representatives of the Span- ish Crown and indigenous leaders whose purpose was to renew the peren- nially fragile peace. We reproduce here the proceedings of a parlamento held in 1774, which show the quite remarkable political relationship that had evolved between the two societies as they sought to manage diplomatic, economic, and social exchange along their shared frontier.

Meanwhile, at the other end of the colony, the north was home to a growing mining economy. In a letter reproduced here, mine owners in Copiapó enjoin colonial authorities to help control their "disorderly" and "insolent" peons. While the relationship between workers, owners, and the state would change over time, such dynamics are of enduring political and economic importance to Chilean history and are a central theme of this book.

But first, we begin with a Paleolithic footprint.

Note

1. Quoted in Santiago Lorenzo Schiaffino and Rodolfo Burgos, *La política de poblaciones en Chile durante el siglo XVIII* (Quillota: Editorial el Observador, 1978).

A Paleolithic Footprint

For decades scholars believed that the Western Hemisphere's first inhabitants arrived via the Bering Strait some 12,000 years ago. In the 1970s and early 1980s, an archaeological site in southern Chile challenged that orthodoxy when a research team led by Tom Dillehay made a remarkable discovery: evidence of the oldest human settlement yet found in the Americas. Their findings included dwellings, tools, animal hides—and this footprint of a small adult or child who stepped in clay next to a hearth some 12,500 years ago.

The site, known as Monte Verde, raised an intriguing question. If human settlements already existed 12,500 years ago in southern Chile, almost 10,000 miles away from the Bering Strait, when did people first arrive in the hemisphere? On this score, the site continues to yield intriguing clues. Near the artifacts of incontrovertibly human origin are even older materials—dating back more than 30,000 years—whose provenance is less clear. Should they ultimately prove to be associated with human habitation, Monte Verde will again upend established orthodoxies about the peopling of the Americas.

Photograph by Tom Dillehay. Used by permission of the photographer.

Chinchorro: The World's Oldest Mummies

Two to three thousand years before the Egyptians, the Chinchorro peoples of present-day northern Chile and southern Peru practiced elaborate mortuary rituals on their dead. The Chinchorro were fishermen and hunter-gatherers who adapted to the arid climate of the Atacama Desert. Theirs are the oldest known mummies in the world.

Chinchorro mummification was a complex procedure, in which all organs were removed from the cadaver and replaced by clay, mud, sticks, llama fur, and plants. Sometimes the skin was replaced with mud. The mummies were then colored with shiny black manganese or rich red ochre. Sometimes they wore elaborate facial masks as well as helmets or wigs of long human hair. As such, the mummies were simultaneously religious objects but also artistic ones, in which the body became a vehicle of aesthetic expression, a statue that "artisan-morticians," as researchers have called them, elaborately fashioned and painted. Later mummies were less complex, involving simple desiccation.

The mummies also yield clues about Chinchorro social organization. In contrast to the Egyptians, as well as most other cultures that practiced mummification, the Chinchorro peoples apparently practiced these mortuary rituals on the dead regardless of their social rank. As a result, hundreds of mummies have been recovered, including those of children and fetuses, who are rarely mummified in other cultures. While the unique mortuary practices of the Chinchorro apparently ceased around the first century BCE, their techniques would be echoed by other cultures of the region in succeeding centuries. These included the Inca, who are also known for the preservation and display of their dead. While the Atacama Desert challenged the cultural resources of ancient peoples who inhabited its harsh environment, it also made possible certain cultural and aesthetic practices whose material products have survived down to the present.

Photograph by Fernando Maldonado Roi. Used by permission of CREAIMAGEN, Santiago, 2012.

Diaguita Ceramics

From approximately 1000 until the 1500s CE, *the Diaguita culture thrived in the region of Chile known as the* norte chico *(near north), between the Copiapó and Choapa Valleys. The area is one of geoclimatic transition between the arid Atacama Desert to the north and the temperate central valley further south. Part of a broad Andean culture area whose peoples had been in contact for thousands of years, the Diaguita were hunters, fishermen, and agropastoralists best remembered for their unique ceramic tradition. Diaguita pottery is distinguished by distinctive white, red, and black geometric motifs and zoomorphic and anthropomorphic vessels in which birds, cats, and humans predominate. They display a great diversity of motifs, and the fact that the vessels tend to vary subtly suggests that each piece's uniqueness was valued by those who made and used them. The ceramics are believed to have served utilitarian, decorative, and ceremonial functions, particularly in funerary rituals.*

In the late fifteenth century, the Diaguita came under the political dominion of the Inca empire, triggering important social and political changes that are reflected in ceramics. Local craftsmen incorporated Incan techniques into their pottery and began to copy pieces introduced by their Inca rulers. By the end of the sixteenth century, the Diaguita culture, its language or languages, and its ceramic traditions were dying out. In the succeeding centuries of Spanish colonialism, this cultural and patrimonial complex largely disappeared as the native inhabitants of the region became laborers and their lands were swallowed up by Spanish haciendas. In the early twentieth century, Chilean archaeologists rediscovered—or one might even say, "invented"—the Diaguita. The peoples who inhabited the valleys of the norte chico *exhibited important differences, such as distinct languages, and were not politically unified. But modern archaeologists identified them as part of a distinct Diaguita cultural complex, of which their shared ceramic tradition is a key commonality. Recently some local communities have reclaimed a Diaguita identity, and the Chilean state has recognized legal claims of individuals based on their status as descendants of the indigenous inhabitants of the region. Meanwhile, there is an ongoing effort to recover the ceramic traditions of the Diaguita in present-day Chile.*

Photograph by David Tryse. Used by permission of the photographer. Courtesy of El Museo Archaeológico de La Serena.

Mapuche Textiles: Culture and Commerce

The sophisticated textile tradition of the Mapuche of southern Chile and Argentina dates from well before the pre-Hispanic period, though few early examples have survived the humid climate of the south. What we know about early textile practices comes from sparse archaeological remains as well as European accounts beginning in the sixteenth century. Textiles were originally produced using the fibers of llamas and guanacos (another Andean camelid), but with the arrival of the Spanish, sheep wool became the fiber of choice. Serving as ponchos, for domestic use, and to outfit horses, they were utilitarian but also conveyed meanings—related to myth and cosmology, status and lineage—through color, design, and symbols. Meanwhile, the social identities expressed in the textiles were hardly static: they emerged in part out of the long struggles of Mapuche communities to resist the Spanish Crown and later the Chilean state.

Textiles also had great commercial value, belying the notion that recent commodification has corrupted once "pure" forms of cultural expression. Bartered, bought, and sold among different indigenous groups as well as between the Mapuche and the Spanish, woven products served as a currency with which the Mapuche obtained goods such as horses. Far-reaching trans-Andean textile trade networks eventually reached from Chilean Araucania across the Argentine pampas to the Atlantic coast, and south into Patagonia. In 1753, a traveler in the southernmost reaches of Argentina came upon a local chieftain wearing an "Araucanian" poncho that would have originated more than 1,200 miles away. Around this time, an observer estimated that the Mapuche produced some 60,000 ponchos annually for colonial markets. Meanwhile, textiles conferred social and economic status on the women who made them: according to nineteenth-century accounts, brides recognized as good weavers commanded higher dowries.

This image of women weaving dates from the nineteenth century, when photographers travelled to the south seeking to capture an "essential" indigenous culture thought to be dying out. Today textiles remain perhaps the best-known material emblem of Mapuche culture, yet they are not timeless artifacts of some distant and unchanging past but have a long social and economic history.

Photograph by Odber Heffer Bissett. Used by permission of the Heffer family. Courtesy of Colección Museo Histórico Nacional de Chile.

The Inca Meet the Mapuche

Garcilaso de la Vega

The Incas' vast empire, which they called Tawantinsuyu, incorporated disparate peoples within its domain. From its capital in Cuzco, Peru, the empire stretched across large parts of present-day Bolivia, Ecuador, Peru, southern Colombia, and northwest Argentina, as well as Chile. After achieving dominion over the peoples of the northern desert and central valley of Chile, the Inca moved southward, but around the Maule River their geopolitical domination halted abruptly. In events estimated to have occurred between 1470 and 1490, the empire's southward advance was checked by the Mapuche.

The Incas' unsuccessful attempt to conquer the Mapuche is narrated here by the chronicler Garcilaso de la Vega. Also known as "El Inca," de la Vega was a mestizo born in Cuzco, the illegitimate son of a Spaniard and an Andean noblewoman. Penned in the early 1600s, his Comentarios reales de los Incas *is a trove of information on Andean customs, beliefs, practices, and history, much of it culled from stories and experiences from the author's childhood. The conflict between the Mapuche and the Inca was presumably preserved in oral history, as neither group had alphabetic script. Garcilaso de la Vega was among the first (though not the very first) chronicler to narrate these events in writing, more than a hundred years after they had occurred.*

The Mapuche-Inca encounter is important because it reminds us that the Mapuches' storied resistance to imperial domination predated Spanish colonialism. But Mapuche-Inca relations, like Mapuche-Spanish ones, did not just involve unmitigated conflict. Archaeological and linguistic evidence suggests that relations between these indigenous groups also included economic and cultural reciprocity and that these influences extended beyond the formal military or geopolitical boundary separating the two. Ceramic artifacts and the presence of certain Quechua words (the language of the Inca) in Mapudungun (the language of the Mapuche) suggest as much. Thus, the southern frontier was a site of hostility, as de la Vega's chronicle tells us, but also of political, cultural, and commercial exchange, a dual role it would maintain in succeeding centuries.

Inca and Mapuche in battle. This image from Huamán Poma de Ayala's *Nueva Corónica y Buen Gobierno* portrays a military confrontation between the Mapuche and Inca that occurred some time in the late fifteenth century. Illustration by Huamán Poma de Ayala. Courtesy of Royal Danish Library, Department of Manuscript and Rare Books.

Given that the Incas' main goal and source of honor was to bring new people under their empire, customs and laws, and that they were so powerful at the time, they did not consider idleness an option. Rather, they had to conquer new lands, both to keep their vassals busy in the service of the Crown's growth and to put to use the income—supplies, arms, clothing and footwear—that each province and kingdom contributed every year. . . . In light of all this and seeing as the Inca King Yupanqui[1] was loved and obeyed and so powerful, both in subjects and in possessions, he decided to embark upon a great endeavor: the conquest of the Kingdom of Chili. After consulting with his council, he gave the order to commence preparations. Leaving his usual ministers at court to govern and oversee the administration of justice, he went to Atacama, which was the province nearest to Chili that had been settled by him and was subject to his rule. He did this to rouse his men at a closer distance from the conquest, as there was a large unpopulated tract of land to cross before arriving in Chili from there.

The Inca sent runners and spies from Atacama throughout that uninhabited land to find a route to Chili and take note of the difficulties along the road in order to prepare for them. These scouts were Incas because the Inca kings of those days did not entrust tasks of such great importance to anyone outside their lineage. Equipped with Indian guides from Atacama and Tucma (from whom . . . the Incas received news about the Kingdom of Chili), they would go out and return at two-league intervals to bring word of what they had discovered; in this way, they could also remain adequately provisioned. The scouts carried on in accordance with these measures, suffering great trials and difficulties throughout those deserts and leaving markers as they went not only to find their way back, but also so that those who were following would know where they were. They came and went in this way like ants, bringing news with them about what they had discovered and, most important, heading back out with supplies. Through these procedures and work they covered the eighty leagues of uninhabited land that lay between Atacama and Copiapó, which is a small but highly populated province surrounded by large, long deserts. Since there were another eighty leagues of desolate land to cross from there to Coquimbo, the scouts stopped at Copiapó. Once they had gathered all the information they could from that province by sight, they returned as quickly as possible to inform the Inca about what they had seen. . . .

When the first [10,000 warriors dispatched] got close to Copiapó they sent messengers, as was the ancient custom of the Incas. They told [the people of Copiapó] to surrender and bow to the son of the Sun, who would give them a new religion, new laws and customs under which they would live like men and not brutes. [The messengers also said] that if they refused to do so, they should prepare their weapons, because whether by force or voluntarily they were going to obey the Inca, lord of the four parts of the world. This message riled up the people of Copiapó and they took up arms to keep the Inca out of their lands. There were some skirmishes and light fighting as both sides tested the other's strength and willingness to fight. For their part the Incas, in accordance with what their king had ordered, did not want to unleash an all-out war, but rather show tolerance toward their enemies to convince them to surrender for their own good. The people of Copiapó were conflicted as to how to defend themselves: on the one hand, the son of the Sun deity terrified them and they thought they would suffer a great curse if they did not receive the Sun's son as their lord. On the other hand, their desire to maintain their age-old freedom and love for their own gods inspired them: they did not want change, but wished instead to live as their ancestors had. . . .

When the second army dispatched to assist the first arrived, they came upon this scene of confusion. The people of Copiapó surrendered as soon as they saw the second army, believing themselves unable to resist so many people, and thus they negotiated with the Incas as best they knew how as to what they would receive and what idolatries they would have to abandon. The Inca received notice of all of this and was very relieved to have a clear path ahead and such an auspicious beginning to his conquest of Chili, a kingdom he feared he would not be able to overcome because it was so large and far removed from his empire. . . . He decided to pursue this good fortune and ordered another 10,000 warriors be prepared. When they were equipped with everything they needed, he sent them to assist the earlier armies. . . . The Incas went on conquering all the other nations that lay between there and the Valley of Chili, which gets its name from the kingdom called Chili. Throughout the entire length of the conquest, which they say lasted more than six years, the Inca always took particular care to help out his men with reinforcements, arms and supplies, clothes and footwear so that they would not want for anything, because he was well aware that his honor and majesty rested on his men not retreating an inch. Thus, he eventually had more than 50,000 fighters in Chili who were as well supplied as if they were in Cuzco.

Once the Incas had brought the Valley of Chili under their empire, they sent word to the Inca to tell him what they had done and kept informing him of their activities each day on an hourly basis. As they imposed order and set up seats [of authority] in every place they conquered, they continued advancing toward the south, moving constantly in that direction and conquering all the valleys and nations up to the Maule River, which is almost fifty leagues from the Valley of Chili. We do not know what battles or smaller confrontations took place, but one would assume that the Incas won their new subjects peacefully and on friendly terms, as in their conquests they always tried to appeal first to the Indians by acting benevolently rather than violently. The Incas were not satisfied with having extended their empire more than two hundred and sixty leagues from Atacama to the Maule River over both populated and uninhabited territories—that is, eighty leagues from Atacama to Copiapó, another eighty leagues from Copiapó to Coquimbo, fifty-five from Coquimbo to Chili and almost fifty from Chili to the Maule. Instead, they decided to proceed with the same ambition and greed for new states. To this end, they incorporated the lands won to that point into their empire in the usual orderly and skillful fashion, always leaving behind the necessary garrisons as a shield against any misfortunes which war might bring upon them. Setting out with this degree of determination, the Incas crossed the Maule River with 20,000 warriors, and in accordance with their ancient customs sent demands to the people of the Purumauca province, whom the Spanish call Promaucaes,[2] to receive the Inca as their Lord or gather up their weapons. The Purumaucas had already heard about the Incas, were prepared to fight and were allied with some of their neighbors, such as the Antallis, Pincus and Cauquis, who all together were determined to die rather than lose their ancient freedom. They replied to the Incas that the victors would rule over the vanquished and the Incas would soon find out what it was like to bow before Purumauca rule.

Three or four days after this answer the Purumaucas and their allied neighbors emerged in full, totaling about 18,000 to 20,000 armed men, and that day they concentrated their efforts on setting up camp right where the Incas could see them. The Incas sent new requests for peace and friendship, putting on a grand show in which they swore to the Sun and the Moon that they were not going to take their lands and property, but instead were affording them the opportunity to live like men on the condition that they recognized the Sun as their god and his son the Inca as their king and lord. The Purumaucas responded by saying that they were determined not to waste their time on meaningless words and reasoning, but rather to fight until victory or death, so the Incas should prepare for battle on the next day and stop sending messages that the Purumaucas did not want to hear. . . .

After the Inca captains discussed it among themselves, and in spite of the fact that some of them insisted on fighting until victory, in the end the Incas decided to return to the lands they had conquered and leave the Maule River as the end of their empire, holding off on any further conquests until receiving new orders from their Inca King, Yupanqui. They informed him of everything that had happened and the Inca ordered them not to conquer any more lands, but rather to take great care in cultivating and bettering those which they had already won, always pleasing and benefiting the vassals so that the surrounding populations would see how much better off those communities were under the Incas' domain and choose to enter their empire as other nations had already done; if they did not, they would lose more than the Incas anyway. With these orders, the Incas ceased their conquests of Chili and strengthened their borders, setting limits and placing boundary markers. At the southernmost part of their empire, that limit was the Maule River. They made sure that their justice system got up and running, as well as the royal treasury and the treasury of the sun, and that all of these particularly benefited the vassals, who lovingly embraced the Incas' rule and their privileges, laws, and customs, under which they lived until the Spaniards arrived in those lands.

Translated by Rachel Stein

Notes

1. Túpac Yupanqui (whose reign lasted from 1471 to 1493) was known as the "traveling Inca" for his many campaigns to conquer neighboring peoples and expand the empire.

2. *Purumauca,* derived from the Quechua word for "wild people" and corrupted in Spanish as Promaucaes, was the term the Inca used to refer to peoples who had not been incorporated into their empire. In this case it refers to subgroups of the people later known collectively as the Mapuche.

A Conquistador Pleads His Case to the King

Pedro de Valdivia

The Spanish conquest of the Americas occurred relay style, with the conquerors establishing footholds in subjugated territories and spreading from there. First, they established themselves in the Caribbean islands before moving on to mainland Mexico. A second thrust moved from Panama down to Peru, which in turn served as a launchpad for expeditions into present-day Chile. The Spanish in Peru during the period of the Inca conquest were a fractious group. As part of an ongoing effort to divvy up the spoils of war, one prominent conquistador, Diego de Almagro, was awarded rights to the conquest of Chile. It would prove a decidedly ambiguous prize. Thanks to the rigors of the Andes and the Atacama Desert, hostile Indians, and the elusiveness of hoped-for gold, the expedition Almagro launched in 1536 ended in failure. When Pedro de Valdivia, another veteran of the conquest of Peru, embarked on a second attempt four years later, many observers thought it folly. Valdivia had already secured considerable wealth in Peru, and the conquest of Chile involved physical risks and great personal expense.

Valdivia's expedition encountered many of the same challenges as Almagro's, but it survived, and a precarious Spanish settlement took root. Here is a famous letter that Pedro de Valdivia wrote to Emperor Charles V several years into the Chilean enterprise. Conquistadors routinely sent petitions to apprise the Crown of their progress and to secure royal support for their endeavors (as well as favor for the writer). True to the genre, Valdivia dwells on the personal costs and many hardships he and his entourage have suffered in their attempts to subdue rebellious natives and secure the territory. The letter conveys the author's strong voice and suggests he desired a place in the glorious annals of empire as the individual responsible for extending Spanish dominion literally to the ends of the earth.

While Valdivia's self-serving motives must certainly be kept in mind, his letter is nevertheless an invaluable account of the founding of Santiago and the earliest years of the colony. Between the lines, we can read, for example, for a sense of how the Indians reacted to the invaders: biding their time, they observed carefully and waited for strategic moments to attack. Valdivia's vivid portrayal of the many chal-

lenges facing the Spanish reminds us of the utter precariousness of this outpost on the fringes of empire.

La Serena, September 4, 1545
Your Sacred, Catholic, Imperial Majesty,

Five years have passed since I first set out from the provinces of Peru equipped by Governor and Marquis Francisco Pizarro to conquer and populate Nueva Extremadura, formerly known as Chili . . . and in all this time I have not been able to inform Your Majesty of what I have done in these lands, wholly caught up as I have been in serving your empire. . . .

Your Majesty should know that when Marquis Francisco Pizarro charged me with this task, it was impossible to find any man willing to come to this land. The men whom Diego de Almagro had brought here were the most evasive of all; they avoided it like the plague, stigmatized as it was by his desertion. Even many of those who were very loyal to me and who, moreover, were known for their good sense, judged me to lack that same quality when they saw me spending all my possessions on an enterprise so far from Peru, in the same place where [Almagro] had decided to give up once he realized that the 500,000 gold pesos spent by him and his company's men served only to redouble the Indians' verve. Nonetheless, I recognized what a service it would be to Your Majesty to officially acquire it for You, as well as to populate and hold onto it so that thereby I might discover the lands up to the Strait of Magellan and through there to the North Sea. Thus I decided to find a shrewd way to do this, seeking out merchants willing to lend me money. And endowed with those funds, together with my own possessions and help from friends, I gathered as many as 150 infantry and cavalrymen to come with me to this land, suffering along our journey hunger, wars with Indians, and other misfortunes—the great hardships that have always abounded in these parts and still do to this day.

Sometime around April of 1539 the Marquis delivered supplies to me, and I arrived at the Mapocho Valley, where I am today, toward the end of 1540. Next I managed to speak with the caciques of the land, and thanks to the diligence I invested in making our presence felt all over, the Indians believed us to be a great many Christians and most of them agreed to peace, serving us well for five or six months because they knew that they would lose the food they had in their fields if they did not.[1] At this time, they built us houses of wood and straw in an area of the aforementioned valley according to the designs I gave them. There I founded this city, calling it "Santiago del Nuevo Estremo" in Your Majesty's name, since I arrived on [the day of your birth,] February 24 in the year 1541.

Once this settlement was established and some order was brought to the land, I was wary that the Indians would do what they always do when they harvest their food: rebel. Moreover, I knew very well that they were counting our numbers, as it is a customary precaution of theirs. Given that they watched us settle and judged us to be few, and since they had witnessed so many men return with [Almagro] out of what they thought was fear, the Indians waited in those early days to see if we would do the same. But when they realized we were not leaving, they decided to make us retreat by force or kill us. The first thing I did, in order to adequately defend ourselves . . . , was to safeguard as much food as possible, because I knew they were determined to do us ill and I did not want to lack provisions. Thus I ordered my men to gather a supply that would last us two years or more, as there was plenty available to last us that long. . . .

Later, I received word that all the Indians of the land were joining together in two groups to wage war on us. I went to confront the larger group with ninety men, leaving my lieutenant to guard the city with fifty, thirty of them on horseback. While I was off against the one contingent, the other entered the city and fought the Christians for an entire day, killing twenty-three horses and four Christians. They burned the whole city and with it all the food, clothing, and property we had, leaving us with nothing but our tattered war clothes, the arms slung over our backs, two hogs, one suckling pig, two chickens, one female and one male, and two handfuls of wheat at most. Thus all-out war began. Since the Indians were on the offensive, they decided not to sow their fields, subsisting instead on a few scallions, some small seeds like the oats of an herb and other legumes that this land naturally produces in abundance without the need for farming; they were able to survive as they did with this sustenance and some corn sown in the mountains. . . .

Men are able to endure the tribulations of war, oh Victorious Cesar, because praise goes to the soldier who dies fighting. But to endure hunger in addition to battle, a soldier must be more than a man. Such have your vassals proved themselves under my protection, with me under the protection of God and Your Majesty, to keep this land for You. For it was not until the last of these three years past that we established a good position for ourselves and had plenty of food; the first two years we suffered a need so dire I can barely put it into words. On any given day, many Christians were forced to dig up scallions to sustain not just one person, but three; once eaten, they would go back for more. All our slaves, servants, and children had to live off these scallions, for there was no meat at all. If any Christian acquired fifty grains of corn a day, he considered himself fortunate, and any who had a handful of wheat would not grind it so as not to lose the bran. Thus have we lived, and the soldiers would have been happy if this basic income had allowed them to stay at home. However, I needed thirty or forty men continually patrolling the country on horseback throughout the winter and summer. As soon as those men's backpacks were empty, they would return and others would go out. Thus we toiled like spirits of the night, and the Indians called us *zupais,* which is what they call their devils, because anytime they came looking for us—as they know to come fight at night—they would find us awake and armed and, if necessary, on horseback. I was so careful to be prepared in this way at all times that, although we were few and they were many, I put them in a real predicament. This brief account should suffice to show Your Majesty that, as the saying goes, he who would eat the kernel must first crack the nut. . . .

Once I had entered this land and the Indians had risen up against me, in order to fulfill my intention of keeping it perpetually for Your Majesty, I occupied myself with the task of being Governor, in your royal name, with the authority to govern your vassals and the land, as well as their captain, inspiring them in battle and going out to confront danger before any other. For they needed a father to aid them in every way possible and suffer their trials with them, helping them endure their hardships as if they were his sons; a friend with whom to converse; an architect to plan and settle; an engineer to dig irrigation channels and distribute water; a laborer and farmhand to sow the fields; a steward and pastor to lead them in the raising of livestock; and, finally, a settler, raiser, sustainer, conqueror and discoverer. In light of all this, I leave it to Your imperial will to deem whether I deserve to have the authority of Your Majesty that Your religious men and vassals granted me in Your royal name, and whether I deserve to have that authority newly confirmed with the aim of doing you even greater service with it. And I believe I deserve this confirmation most of all because, aided first and foremost by God, I have known how to get by with 200 Spaniards so far from Christian settlements. Moreover, even though, due to the events of the past, the settlements in Peru abound in everything a soldier could desire to possess, my men have remained here with me, subjected to, suffering through, and dying of hunger and cold, plowing and planting with their own hands to sustain themselves and their children with weapons on their backs; and despite all this, they do not abhor me, but love me, because they are beginning to see that all this has been necessary in order to live by and receive from Your Majesty that which we came seeking. With this motivation, they are eager to penetrate the land beyond here so that You may compensate them for their services, in Your royal name. And out of my desire to look after Your Majesty's best interests, I am advancing bit by bit rather than acting under the same intention as other governors—to not stop until they find gold to fatten themselves—for despite the small number of men with which I came, I myself could have sought gold and left it at that. However, since it is more of a service to your Majesty and more favorable to the perpetuation of this land, I have gone about settling and maintaining it slowly. And if God deigns to allow me to carry out this service for Your Majesty, I will still have time to do more, and if not, whoever may succeed me will at least find the land in good order. For I have no interest in buying even a few inches of land in Spain, and would not desire it even if I had a million ducats; my interest is to serve Your Majesty and that you may grant me land here so that my heirs may enjoy it and my memory and theirs may be preserved in the years to come.

Translated by Rachel Stein

Note

1. That is, the Indians were aware that as long as their crops were in the fields, their food supply was vulnerable to destruction by the enemy.

Exalting the Noble Savage

Alonso de Ercilla

The sixteenth-century epic poem La Araucana *(The Araucaniad) has been baptized with the qualifier "first" on multiple counts: it has been called the first work of Chilean literature, the first American epic, the first Chilean poem, and Chile's first history. Its author, the young Spanish nobleman Alonso de Ercilla, arrived in Chile in 1557 and served as a soldier in the war with the Mapuche. His epic consists of three parts: the first recounts events prior to his arrival in Chile, which he reconstructed from conversations with older soldiers, and the other two narrate events he himself witnessed during the military campaigns. Each night the "soldier poet" took notes on the day's events, and he later composed the epic. Written in a complex stanza structure, the poem hewed to the epic genre but in contrast to traditional epics, which take an individual hero as their subject, Ercilla's poem exalts the collective heroism of the "Araucanians." The work was written at a time when Spanish writers and statesmen were hotly debating the nature of Indian peoples and the policy the Crown should pursue toward them. Ercilla's epic is shot through with contradictions in this regard: he shows the Spaniards committing despicable acts of gratuitous cruelty but also argues that victory justifies even questionable means. The poem glorifies the Indians' noble struggle to preserve their honor, dignity, and autonomy but also condemns them as barbarians who resist the Crown's rightful struggle to subjugate them—a struggle in which the author was, of course, a participant.*

It was Ercilla who first called the indigenous peoples in southern Chile "Araucanians" (Araucanos) and who helped introduce the Chilean conflict to a broad public in the Spanish-speaking world (his poem is even mentioned in Don Quijote*). In Chile, the epic's legacies were even more profound and long lasting. Ercilla's descriptions of the Mapuches' indomitable courage and skill mark the origin of the romantic national myth, nurtured by Chilean intellectuals and statesmen in the early twentieth century, of Chile's "mestizo" identity as a marriage of two warrior races. The Nobel Prize–winning poet Pablo Neruda dedicated two works to the soldier-poet Ercilla, declaring that he "not only saw stars, mountains, and waters, he discovered, separated, and named men. And in naming them he gave them existence. The silence of the races had ended." This was perhaps a more ambiguous project than*

85

Neruda acknowledged. If Ercilla's epic ended the "silence of races," it did so by giv-
ing indigenous peoples an existence for European audiences that was firmly rooted
in the conquerors' worldview and language. In this regard, it is interesting to note
the appearance in 2007 of a new edition of La Araucana—*this one published in*
Mapudungun, the language of the Mapuche.

> Chile, fertile province, famous
> In the vast Antarctic region,
> Known to far-flung mighty nations
> For her queenly grace and courage,
> Has produced a race so noble,
> Dauntless, bellicose, and haughty,
> That by kind it ne'er was humbled
> Nor to foreign sway submitted.
> . . . .

> Land runs North to south, a ribbon,
> And the sea bathes western shoreline.
> On the East in one direction
> Stretch a thousand leagues of mountains.
> In their midst war's point is sharpened
> By fierce exercise and custom.
> Love and Venus have no part here;
> Only wrathful Mars is master.

> At this district's demarcation,
> Where 'tis broadest, lies the nation
> Thirty-six degrees projected.
> Costly to itself and aliens,
> Toll it takes of strange usurpers,
> Fetters Chile in strait shackles,
> And with warfare undiluted,
> With sheer grit outrocks the earthquake.

> 'Tis Arauco self-sufficient
> That with stratagem and splendor
> Holds the soil in far dominion
> From the one Pole to the other,
> Trapping Spaniards in crass meshes,
> As my writing soon will picture.
> Twenty leagues contain its landmarks.
> Sixteen Toqui chiefs[1] possess it.

Praeeunte Deipara Hispanorum exercitum, Indi qui Ciuitatem obsidebant, eam Videntes in ipsorum oculos puluerem conspergentem perteriti fugerunt in Chile.

A divine power intervenes on behalf of the Spanish. What explains the remarkable success of Mapuche resistance to Spanish domination, perhaps unique among indigenous peoples in the New World? At the outset the Mapuche did not have guns or horses, but they proved able to adopt new military tactics and technologies with great ingenuity. They devised their own gunpowder of volcanic sulphur, nitrate, and charcoal to use with captured firearms, and after capturing horses, they became skilled equestrians and developed sixteen-foot pikes for use against Spanish cavalry. Beyond their military resourcefulness, they adopted wheat cultivation, less vulnerable to the Spaniards' scorched-earth attacks than the traditional maize because of its rapid time to maturity. Finally, the Mapuches' decentralized social organization proved highly resistant to domination, but later, as ongoing warfare necessitated greater political organization, they successfully developed coordination among once loosely organized clans. Illustration by Alonso de Ovalle, from *Histórica relación del Reyno de Chile* by Alonso de Ovalle (Rome: Francisco Cavallo, 1646). Courtesy of Colección Biblioteca Nacional de Chile.

. . . .

Beardless men, robust of gesture,
Theirs are full-grown, shapely bodies,
Lofty chests and massive shoulders,
Stalwart limbs and steely sinews;
They are confident, emboldened,
Dauntless, gallant, and audacious,
Firm inured to toil, and suffering
Mortal cold and heat and hunger.

Never has a king subjected
Such fierce people proud of freedom,
Nor has alien nation boasted
E'er of having trod their borders;
Ne'er has dared a neighboring country
Raise the sword and move against them;
Always were they feared, unshackled,
Free of laws, with necks unbending.
. . . .

Victory was with rightful reason
Only to Valdivia granted;
And 'tis well to praise his memory,
Since his sword has hewn such progress.
In Arauco was encompassed
Glory hitherto unequalled.
Proud, the race he yoked in bondage,
Shrouding freedom with oppression!
. . . .

Waxed self-interest, greed, and malice
At the cost of others' sweating.
Ravenous Avarice in tatters
Skulked, uncurbed, and grazed, licentious.
Statutory law and justice
Pleased the heart of kind Valdivia.
Lenient in grave wrongs, forgiving,
He was harsh in trivial cases.

Thus ungrateful, mad Castilians
Swelled in self-esteem and mischief,
And pursued vain, proud intentions,
Chasing after prosperous fortune;

But the sovereign Heaven's Father
Barred them on this way, permitting
That the one they yoked to hardship
Be the knife of execution.

    Araucanian states accustomed
To enforce dread laws and mandates,
Viewing how their throne had toppled,
Tasting mortal men's oppression,
Swore to win again their freedom,
And condemning levies suffered,
They resumed the use of falchions²
Which in idle peace had rusted.
. . . .

    This is worthy of attention,
Nor should lightly pass neglected,
That a folk obscure, sequestered
From the haunts of man's society,
By unnavigable gulfs surrounded,
Should attain what global heroes
Have achieved with difficulty
Through the course of war and travail.

    Let all writers cease extolling
Military art's discoverers,
Celebrating not the inventors
First to forge hard steel and metal,
For primeval, backward dwellers
Of the Araucan state so managed
Discipline and war's maneuvers
That they furnish us a lesson.
. . . .

    Ages have engendered heroes
Who by length of years were sullied.
Ah, the world would love them better,
Had an early death enshrined them!
Hannibal is our exemplar,
Pompey also, in Pharsalia
Routed, who for life o'erlengthy
Lost this planet's foremost dais.

Well Caupolicán[3] confirms this,
Famous captain and great warrior,
In American Indian boundaries
First in arms, through storm-racked decades;
But his fist by fate was freighted,
And his boon supreme retarded.
His collapse so swift, so wretched
Far outshone the ascent laborious.

Understanding that his tribesmen
Staggered in their faith, and tottered,
Seeing Fortune's prosperous crescent
To its nadir swiftly sinking,
He would fain address Reinoso.[4]
Keen to learn his resolution,
Avid listeners congregated,
Whilst the grave barbarian ranted:
. . . .

"I am Chief Caupolicano,
Dashed to earth, by Fate o'ertoppled.
I have absolute dominion
Over Araucanian heroes.
Peace is in my hand and choosing,
And each compact's confirmation,
Since my providential office
Curbs the earth in bestial bondage.

"In Tucapel I slew Valdivia,
And I left Purén[5] dismantled.
I am he who throttled Penco,
He who won so many battles;
But the opposing bowl inverted
Of the sky, beringed with triumphs,
Bows me at thy feet to beg thee
For my life a short span longer.

"If my cause be wrong, remember
He who most forgives is kindest,
And if passion prompts thy vengeance,
'Tis enough that I beseech thee.

Cool thy wrathful breast, for anger
Is impertinent in victors.
If thou'lt give me death, 'tis pity
Of a sort to give it quickly.

  "Think not, though I die at thy hands,
That my state will lack a leader.
More Caupolicáns by thousands
Will there be, yet none so wretched.
Since though know'st the Araucanians,
Gaze on me, their least of warriors!
Tempting luck anew were folly,
Though mine own slides down the hillside.
. . . .
  More the Indian said not, waiting
For his answer, calmly gazing
On his eyes, and stolid-featured,
Craved swift death of life full precious.
No adversity could crush him.
Though a prisoner, bound and vanquished,
He preserved in deed and discourse
Freedom's dignified demeanor.

Translated by Charles Maxwell Lancaster and Paul Thomas Manchester

Notes

1. Literally "axe" or "axe-bearer," a title conferred by the Mapuche on those selected as military chieftains.
2. A kind of sword.
3. Famous military leader (*toqui*) who helped coordinate a major uprising against the Spanish in the 1550s, during the course of which Pedro de Valdivia was killed. Caupolicán died at the hands of the Spanish five years later.
4. Alonso de Reinoso, a military official who oversaw the execution of Caupolicán by impalement.
5. Purén and Penco were Spanish forts and settlements destroyed by the Mapuche.

Debating Indian Slavery

Melchor Calderón and Diego de Rosales

In 1598, almost six decades after the founding of Santiago, a huge Mapuche rebellion came very close to destroying the entire Spanish colony in Chile. The most dramatic in a series of indigenous uprisings, the revolt resulted in the death of the Spanish governor, the destruction of all mainland Spanish settlements south of the Bío Bío River except Concepción, and the loss of key agricultural lands on which the colony depended. It would take almost two centuries for the Spanish to reestablish control over the territories lost in the rebellion.

The uprising also helped prompt the legalization of Indian slavery in Chile. It was a policy virtually unique in the Spanish Indies, where African bondage was of course widespread but Indian slavery had been rejected during the early years of colonization (significantly, the only other place it was legal, northern Mexico, was also a conflict-ridden frontier). Yet Indian enslavement was controversial. The two well-known treatises presented here lay out competing positions for and against it.

Produced in the climate of fear and desperation engendered by the 1598 rebellion, Melchor Calderón's treatise captured the reasoning of an increasingly broad swathe of Spanish society in Chile, including that of most high officials, who embraced slavery as a just and effective policy. A respected resident of Santiago and holder of various prestigious titles, Calderón may have collaborated with other learned individuals in writing the treatise, which was presented to the public at a meeting in Santiago's cathedral. According to accounts, the city's authorities unanimously endorsed his disquisition, notarized it, and sent it to the king. In this excerpt Calderón makes a series of pragmatic arguments in favor of Indian slavery, declaring that the prospect of obtaining war captives would be a powerful incentive for Spanish conscripts to fight, that slaves would free up "peaceful" Indians to fill skilled jobs in Spanish society, and even that slavery would improve the colony's moral conditions.

Ten years later, in 1608, the Crown legalized the enslavement of the rebellious Mapuche, but key voices spoke out in opposition to the policy for reasons both practical and moral. The Jesuit missionary and historian Diego de Rosales, who served for years on the war front, where he became involved in successive peace negotiations with the Mapuche, was one prominent critic. In this treatise, Rosales accuses the

Spanish of fomenting warfare to profit from the capture and sale of Indians, includ-
ing "friendly" Indians who were supposed to be exempt from bondage. Rather than
pacifying the rebellious natives, Rosales charges, slavery perpetuates the cycle of
war. In 1674, the Crown reversed course and outlawed the policy. Thereafter, the
enslavement of Indians ceased to enjoy the legal imprimatur of the king, but it nev-
ertheless continued as de facto practice.

Treatise on the Importance and Utility of Enslaving the Rebellious
Indians of Chile, by Melchor Calderón

This past Christmas of 1598, our good Governor Martín García de Loyola
and another forty Spaniards died an unspeakable death. In view of these
events, Melchor Calderón, a licensed university graduate, Treasurer of the
Cathedral, priest serving on the tribunal of the Holy Inquisition and Cru-
sade, and general vicar of this bishopric . . . deemed it necessary to . . . examine this question: is it lawful to enslave these rebellious Indians? . . . He
gathered and recorded all of the noteworthy arguments offered by a group
of learned men of this city of Santiago, as it seemed right that the learned
people who reside here in Chile and are witnesses to the current affairs
should be the ones to determine the answer to this vital question and present the arguments for and against the lawfulness of enslavement. . . . With
all [the learned men, ecclesiastics, laymen, and war veterans] gathered in
the choir of the central church of Santiago, Melchor Calderón read aloud
that paper in which he had gathered . . . the aforementioned arguments
as to the lawfulness of enslaving Indians. Once recited, everyone present
agreed that it was necessary to appeal to the Viceroy and the Royal Court
and ask them to rule on this matter as quickly as possible, and that in their
appeal they should include all the reasons read at the meeting, which were
the following. . . .

First, forty-six years of experience have shown that no form of aid—
neither defense in the form of manpower nor money from the Royal Treasury, nor the expenses and extraordinary taxes continually levied on the
local residents of the kingdom to the point of impoverishment—has sufficed
to stop this war. . . . The majority of those who go to war are not rewarded
or paid for their service, and though so many new soldiers come to fight,
they quickly flee the kingdom once they find themselves stuck in their forts,
unclothed and starved and uninterested in their jobs. And we can be certain
that if these Indians were awarded as slaves, people from outside the kingdom would willingly come to acquire them; we would no longer need to
force them to fight as if they were sentenced to jail. Furthermore, the king-

dom's residents would willingly fight in return for slaves to work on their small farms and haciendas and homes. And the Royal Treasury, moreover, could save a wealth of funds since the slaves taken in His Majesty's name or the portion corresponding to Him could be put to work in the mines and thus extract more gold for the war effort. Or at the very least, the soldiers' interest in acquiring slaves would inspire them to fight with such determination that the war would end in two or three year's time. The rebellious Indians would see that their children and women were being taken from them; that the desire to possess slaves was attracting a great deal of outside aid; and that their very own persons were paying for the war. As a result, they would more promptly accept a truce under whatever conditions His Majesty should mandate.

Second, the enslavement of rebellious Indians would be of great benefit to those peaceful Indians who have free status, since they would in large part be relieved of their jobs as personal servants. If there were slaves, the reasons for making free Indians serve as they do, with so much work, would cease to exist. Moreover, more than one-third of girls are taken from their villages in order to be placed in servitude and thus they remain unmarried for a long time. Once personal servitude is put to an end, the population of peaceful Indians will increase because it would mean the end of the great impediment that this kingdom's female servants face when it comes to marriage: since their masters never wish to lose their service, they do not allow them to marry, either through threats or persuasions, and therefore these Indian girls stay unmarried for many years and out of natural weakness or lack of reason become involved in illicit unions. Also, since personal service deprives the Indian villages of inhabitants, they are also deprived of religious indoctrination and education; in the cities, moreover, Indian servant girls are not sent to get a Christian education out of fear that they should marry. Along the same lines, the peaceful Indians, in large part, would no longer need to go to work in the mines as they do every year—some of them for eight months without a substitute—because the captured slaves would supplant that need, in the same way that His Majesty has decreed that labor be supplied with black slaves [elsewhere in the empire].

There is a third reason why slavery would be advantageous for the Spanish colonies. Given that so many Indians are destined for servitude, there are currently no workers who are not tied to their masters, and as such these Indians cannot dedicate themselves to trades. If Indians were free to work as they wished, only having to pay a tax, the cities would abound with tradesmen such as carpenters, blacksmiths, tailors, cart makers, etc., which are in very high demand. Furthermore, there would be more frequent open markets where one could buy vegetables, potatoes, beans, chickpeas, and other necessary legumes. These are currently nonexistent because there is nobody to organize them—it is even impossible to find food many Fridays because there are no Indian fishermen. If the Indians were free to do so, they would apply themselves to these things out of interest and gain. . . .

Fourth, enslaving rebellious Indians would incidentally secure their spiritual well-being, because if enslavement were deemed lawful, they could be educated in our faith. And they would all accept our religion, as experience has shown in other places where we have sovereignty over them.   ✗

Translated by Rachel Stein and Dave Schreiner

Treatise Acknowledging the Damage Caused by Slavery in the Kingdom of Chile, by Diego de Rosales

Some kinds of war are geared toward harm and destruction, such as those waged against the Moors and the Turks, who are enemies of the Faith and Christianity. Others are aimed at doing good and bringing peace . . . such as that carried out against the Indians. If the Catholic kings make war against them, it is for their own good, . . . with the object of introducing them to the Christian religion, pacifying them, and compelling them to obey Christian principles. . . .

It follows from this that if slavery, which was considered a means of pacifying and converting the Indians of Chile, actually leads to their ruin, brings them greater harm, and perpetuates the war . . . the medicine has become poison and the solution has turned into despair. What was ordered for their well-being and pacification has ultimately been to their detriment. Slavery was prudently thought at first to tame the ferocity and arrogance of these Indians, but experience has shown that, on the contrary, it has made them more fierce and obstinate.

The reason that the war is never-ending is not so much the Indians' stubbornness as it is the greed of the Spaniards who, gaining good profits from slavery, do not want peace with the Indians because of the interest they have in selling them as slaves. Hence, it is certain that as long as there is slavery, there will be war. When the decree allowing slavery was sanctioned, the well-experienced prophesized the length of war, saying: "Slavery in Chile? Well then, our great-grandchildren and great-great-grandchildren will see war as well." And their predictions have come true, for in all the lands controlled by the Spanish monarchy, as of this day in 1670 his Majesty has no war older than that against the Indians in Chile. While the Crown has made peace with every other hostile nation, the war in Chile has endured since the beginnings of the conquest and will persist unless his Majesty puts an end to the enslavement of Indians.

The Indians have desired peace many times, but peace has always been rejected in order to have people to raid, from whom slaves could be sold for a profit. Though peace treaties have been established at different times, some provinces were always left open to warring so as to maintain a source for slaves. This has been justified by the claim that it is necessary for war to persist somewhere so that soldiers may benefit and remain occupied—thus preventing them from becoming depraved by idleness—and so that friendly Indians may be kept busy fighting the Indians of the interior—thus preventing them from developing negative feelings toward us [the Spaniards]. Verily, these are political justifications and reasons of state that do not accord either with good conscience or with his Majesty's orders, established in different decrees, that any truce offered by the Indians must be accepted. But since these reasons serve [the colonists'] interests, they are intoxicated and pleased by them rather than heeding the call of their consciences. And wherever there is a disinterested governor willing to serve God and the King, there are many officials whispering in his ear, asking him what it is he seeks if not money, telling him that they gave fifty thousand pesos earned from slaves to one governor and sixty thousand to another and they will give him money as well, and that he should continue the war and not miss the opportunity for making a profit. And so with this cajolery they not only maintain the war, but embalm it so that it may last forever. . . . No one comes here to govern without promising, with righteous zeal and noble intentions, to bring peace to Chile. But as soon as they are wooed by the charming and cunning Circe, goddess of slave profit and greed, they set off on a different course and endeavor to earn and spend. Thus they leave Chile as they found it. . . .

The wrongs have reached such an extent that, having no enemies to raid, or because they are too far away, some officials have organized raids on peaceful and friendly Indians. . . . This, in turn, shocks neighboring provinces, inciting them to take up arms out of the justifiable fear that today's strike against their neighbors will be visited upon them tomorrow. Since the Indians are familiar with the Spaniards' insatiable greed, knowing that no number of slaves will ever satisfy their desire, they rightly mistrust them and prudently take up arms to justly defend themselves. On the other hand, those who have not done so, whether due to simplicity or fear, have paid for inaction with their own destruction. And because the war officials require no more to brand Indians rebels than the mere sight of weapons in their hands—without distinguishing between those who take up arms in fair defense and those who rebel—they wage war on them indiscriminately. . . .

The overall, large-scale picture painted above should be more than enough to convince pious minds that such an evil slavery, the cause of so much harm, should be put to an end. These arguments gain even greater weight, however, if we consider particular cases as a manner of proof. . . .

The case of Cacique Mencuante is woeful and appalling. Peace had been granted to him under the royal word that he and his family would not be harmed. To further assure him of the validity of this agreement, the Spaniards showed him a paper that they said contained that royal oath. (This was an order by the Governor . . . stipulating that . . . any offering of peace made by the Indians should be accepted, punishing only the rebels.) Yet once this cacique and his thirty-six-person family approached our men in peace, these good officials fulfilled that royal oath and governor's order by distributing the Indian women as slaves among themselves and bringing the cacique with them bound to a horse. And because some enemies attacked the officials on the road to free prisoners enslaved in other raids, they killed the cacique with the blast of a harquebus. . . . This was the reward the cacique received for accepting peace. What an appalling and woeful death! Worst of all, the cacique had sent word to two of his sons who were not with him, telling them how he was going to live in peace with the Spaniards and asking them to join him with their families. Obeying their father, the sons arrived peacefully with their wives and children. But just when they thought they were about to enjoy their father's company and peace with the Spaniards, they came across his naked body splayed across the road, shot to death by the Spaniards—the very same ones to whom their father had offered peace—and discovered that all their people have been taken captive. This sight and tragic event had them weeping bitterly for a long time, saying: "Is this what happens when you offer peace to the Spaniards? Is this the royal oath, their greed for slaves? Is this what they call Christianity?" Such are the damages wrought by slavery! These injustices, these atrocities and these scandals brought upon a new people! How do we expect them to accept the divine faith, which is all about that which we cannot see, if they are given such bad examples of human faith before them? . . .

With such injustices and atrocities, how will this war not go on forever!

Translated by Rachel Stein and Enrique Garguin

"To Sell, Give, Donate, Trade, or Exchange":
Certification of Indian Enslavement

In addition to being the subject of heated political debates among theologians and statesmen, the enslavement of Indians was an everyday practice. A routine judicial inquiry provides a glimpse of how that practice was conducted, the experiences of those enslaved, and the often large gap between the prescriptions of the law and the actual realities of slavery in colonial Chile. The inquiry began when the protector de indios, an official charged with Indians' legal representation, asked the court to investigate the circumstances surrounding the bondage of Luisa Colmey, a woman who had been enslaved as a child some thirty years before. Women and children were often the targets of slave raiding, and narrations of battle scenes suggest that whereas adult men were often killed, women and children were captured and sold. Coupled with the fact that Spanish society coveted them as personal servants, the young and the female—people like Colmey—may have accounted for a dispropor-tionate number of those subjected to enslavement.

Because only Indians captured in warfare could be legally enslaved, Spaniards were required to certify captives' origins before they gained the right to "sell, give, donate, trade, or exchange" them. It seems that the protector de indios in this case had doubts as to whether Colmey had actually been captured in war. For her part, due to the passage of so many years, Colmey could not remember "the name she had, nor her nationality [which Mapuche group she belonged to], nor who captured her, nor her age." Her testimony hints at the process of forced acculturation experienced by captives removed from their natal kin group, community, culture, and language.

Meanwhile, the inquiry also reflects how, royal mandates and bureaucratic forms notwithstanding, illegal practices thrived. According to law, girls over age nine and a half could be subjected to perpetual slavery (whereas younger children could only be placed in temporary bondage); conveniently, Luisa Colmey's captors placed her age at capture at ten. And while we do not know the precise circum-stances of her seizure, Spaniards routinely misrepresented such events and reduced "peaceful Indians" to bondage. The archives even hold records of the purchase and sale of Indians in periods when slavery was supposedly illegal. In other words, legal slavery cast a long shadow in which illegal practices of bondage thrived. In Colmey's case, the court was apparently satisfied by its investigation and, over the objections of the protector, deemed her bondage lawful.[1]

[*Introduction.*] I, Admiral Pedro Porter Casanate . . . Governor and Captain General of this kingdom of Chile . . . hereby declare:

That Captain Juan de la Barra, an inactive military officer working in my close and personal service, appeared before me and stated that an *auca*[2] Indian named Luisa Colmey, captured in war and in enemy rebel territories, belongs to Ana Pajuelo, a resident of the city of Santiago. He asked me to grant the said Ana Pajuelo a deed of enslavement for the said Indian, and for this purpose presented me with the certificate and other documents required of him, attaching a power of attorney as well. The originals have been registered in the government office, to remain on permanent record, and their contents are included hereunder.

Request. I, Captain Juan de la Barra . . . declare, on behalf of Ana Pajuelo, widow of General Juan Sánchez Abarca, by virtue of the power of attorney duly presented herein, that: having appeared before your Lordship to request enslavement certification for an Indian named Luisa Colmey, an *auca* and slave who was captured in war and in enemy territories, your Lordship graciously ordered by decree that the fathers of the Society of Jesus examine the said Indian according to the usual procedures, for the purpose of obtaining the ordinary documents. In accordance with the foregoing, the said Indian appeared before the said fathers of the Society of Jesus and was examined for the purposes of issuing the corresponding certificate, as is recorded in the examination. . . . Therefore, I respectfully request that, in light of all these documents, as well as the proof I have provided for my part, your Lordship order that the deed of enslavement for the said Indian be granted to me as is customary in cases like this. . . . *Juan de la Barra.*

Decree. In Concepción on July 7, 1657. By order of his Lordship. The fathers of the Society of Jesus have examined the Indian in question and have recorded that she was captured in war and in enemy territories. . . . Moreover, payment of the royal fee corresponding to one-fifth the value of the slave has been guaranteed. . . .

Certificate. I, Captain Juan Fernández Rebolledo . . . hereby certify: that in a *maloca*[3] which I carried out during September 1627 in the Pellahuen territories by order of the . . . Governor and Captain General of this kingdom, one of the young men under Second Lieutenant Luis Verdugo de Zarria captured a girl named Colmey, aged 10, daughter of Minchaqueupu, subject of Cacique Anganamón, born in Pancaco, who is a slave. In accordance with the applicable royal privilege and by request of the aforementioned Second

Lieutenant, to whom this slave belongs, I am issuing this certificate [so that the enslavement may be decreed]. *Juan Fernández de Rebolledo.*

Examination: I have examined an Indian girl named Luisa belonging to . . . Ana Pajuelo, the woman referred to in the certificate of her capture. . . . Despite the fact that, in response to my questions, she said that she does not remember the circumstances described in the aforementioned certificate, she did say it is true that she was captured in war at that time, more than thirty-two years ago. Given this passage of time, it is no wonder that she does not remember her old name, homeland, or who captured her. In light of the foregoing, as well as the trustworthiness and legality of the man who issued the aforementioned certificate, I judge its contents regarding this captured Indian to be true. . . . *Juan Junel.* . . .

[*Reply by the Public Defender.*] Your Eminence: I, Doctor Antonio Ramírez de Laguna, your Public Defender and Protector General, hereby declare that for the purpose of defending Luisa, an Indian in the service of Ana Pajuelo . . . in the case which I have been following regarding her freedom, I requested that the aforementioned Ana Pajuelo present the requisite documents certifying that the said Indian belonged to her and was her slave, and in response she presented a simple certificate with a signature that says Juan Fernández Rebolledo, holding no other authority, dated at the Fort of San Felipe on 20 October 1627. . . . A hearing was held by your President and Ministers of the Tribunal on 5 March 1653 . . . and the said Indian was handed over to the said Ana Pajuelo, and I was not informed or notified about the aforementioned hearing until now. Now that this news has reached me, I beseech, with all due respect, that it be revoked, on the following grounds and for the following reasons.

First: because all Indians are entitled to freedom according to his Majesty; the many and repeated privileges he has granted in their favor state that he wishes them to be free. Moreover, anyone claiming to legally own a slave must do so through the sufficient amount of legitimate documents required to revoke the general privilege that declares all Indians to be free.

Second: the certificate presented by the said Ana Pajuelo, signed by the said Juan Fernández Rebolledo, is not sufficient. On the contrary, I counter that it is false under civil law, and as such should not be trusted or believed in or out of court, since, according to the ordinance laid down by your Viceroy . . . certificates issued by *maestros de campo,* sergeant majors, captains and other ministers of war are not to be trusted or believed in or out of court unless the certificate is proven valid by witnesses or a deed of enslavement issued by the Government. This ordinance also states that the governor and bishop or the oldest minister of the tribunal must participate in this process with regard to declarations of age, and . . . the formalities for declaring age are not contained in the said certificate, and this in itself is enough to expressly render it null. . . .

Third: even if the certificate in question were legitimate, thirty years have passed since its execution. As such, any right therein has expired and therefore the said document has no power to take away freedom from the said Indian or her children.[4] In light of the foregoing . . . I ask and beseech your Lordship to . . . declare the said Indian and her children free, allowing them to enjoy their liberty. . . .

[*Conclusion.*] In accordance with all of the above and in light of the records stating that the said Luisa Colmey is an *auca* who was captured in war and in enemy rebel territories, and thus is included under the royal privilege regarding enslavement, and that the payment of the royal fees corresponding to one-fifth the value of the Indian has been guaranteed, I hereby declare in the name of his Majesty, as his Governor and Captain General, that the aforementioned Indian . . . is a slave subject to servitude and perpetual enslavement. [Concepción, 7 July 1657]. *Pedro Porter Casanate.* By order of his Lordship.

Translated by Rachel Stein

Notes

1. This document and others like it appear in Alvaro Jara and Sonia Pinto's two-volume compilation *Fuentes para la historia del trabajo* (Santiago: Editorial Andrés Bello, 1982–83).
2. A word derived from *promaucae,* the term the Inca used to refer to unsubordinated groups and that came to refer to the peoples of southern Chile who refused to submit to their authority. The Spanish subsequently adopted the term in altered form.
3. A raid, usually with the object of enslavement.
4. It is unclear what the protector is referring to here, but he may be invoking a temporary form of bondage that applied to indigenous children up to age twenty.

Portrait of Late Colonial Santiago

Vicente Carvallo y Goyeneche

Several decades before independence, Santiago was a modest urban center, but one in rapid expansion and far removed from the precarity of its first century of existence, when Indian attacks, floods, and earthquakes repeatedly reduced it to ruins. The city was the political center of Chile and a commercial hub for a wider swathe of South America, home to wealthy merchants, holders of noble titles, and various religious orders, as well as a multiethnic plebe; according to census figures, half of the population was comprised of Indians, mulattos, and blacks. Informal street vendors jostled with established merchants, and the periphery was populated with humble ranchos, or dwellings of the poor, which according to one estimate accounted for a quarter of the city's buildings. These urban peripheries would become the city's slums in succeeding decades.

The author of this account, Vicente Carvallo y Goyeneche, grew up in southern Chile and served as a soldier in the Arauco War before becoming a historian and chronicler. In the 1780s and 1790s, he wrote a multivolume work that narrated the colony's history and described Chile's contemporary cities and towns in the manner of a traveler's account. In this selection, he paints a lively portrait of Santiago shortly before independence: its social and occupational groups, its customs, and the cultural and economic life of its elite and plebeian inhabitants. His comparisons to life in Madrid suggest that his intended audience was Spanish, and as someone originally from the south, Carvallo y Goyeneche may well have experienced Santiago as a "foreign" city. He had a keen eye for the symbolic trappings of power and status—clothing, carriages—and offered a moral condemnation of the poor as vagrant and vice-ridden that was characteristic of contemporary elite accounts. The social stratification he describes became increasingly acute in the nineteenth century.

This city has driven war away from its limits and surrounding areas for almost as long as it has existed, and since the middle of the last century, no one has dared to bring the fatal ravages of war across the great currents of the Maule River. Thanks to the tranquility of this perpetual peace, the city has been able to grow, becoming the commercial center of the entire king-

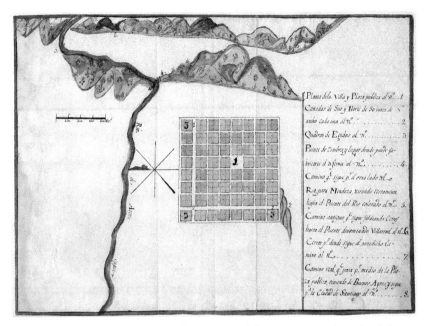

Plan of the town of San Felipe, founded in 1740. While Santiago was the only Chilean city of any size, in the eighteenth century officials attempted to concentrate the colony's widely dispersed rural population within newly founded towns. They associated urban existence with proper political and spiritual order and worried that dispersed populations could not be taxed and supervised. Some two dozen towns were founded over the course of the century, among them San Felipe, whose projected expanse, according to this map, was just eight square blocks. Courtesy of Colección Archivo Fotográfico, Biblioteca Nacional de Chile.

dom for business among its own provinces, as well as between these realms and those of Peru and Buenos Aires.

Santiago, constructed as a traffic hub and adorned with such qualities as a benign climate and an abundance of everything its inhabitants need to live, and in comfort, has prospered significantly, to the point that its population now totals 40,000,[1] a number composed of Spaniards, Indians, blacks and the castes that result from these three classes.

The Spanish represent half the population, and in that half there are some 200 noble families, many of whose origins can be traced to this country's conquistadors. Some are descendants of . . . its governors who, enamored with the country's beauty, became wedded to it as if in the close bonds of matrimony. The rest have immediate ties with distinguished European families. . . .

The noble families in this city stand out brightly, as most of them live

Map of Santiago, capital of the Reino de Chile, 1776. Occupying a tiny fraction of its present-day expanse, late eighteenth-century Santiago is nevertheless recognizable to modern viewers thanks to such features as the Mapocho River, the Alameda, and Santa Lucía Hill. From the treatise *Compendio della storia geografica, naturale, e civile del regno del Cile*, by Giovanni Ignazio Molina (Bologna: Stamperia di S. Tommaso D'Aquino, 1776). Courtesy of Colección Archivo Fotográfico, Biblioteca Nacional de Chile.

off of more-than-moderate fortunes. They are very decorated and opulent both inside and outside their homes, ride expensive coaches, and dress their help in fine liveries. They can be seen in public strolling down promenades, and in the event of visits and balls they wear beautiful clothing and very expensive jewelry. The families of moderate means use calash carriages, which are only different from coaches in that they do not have four wheels and are drawn by only one horse. The household services, exterior pomp, and personal decorum of these nobles, moreover, abound in proportion to their means. The Spanish commoners also have a certain luster because, since they are white, they are not made to work as servants for nobles, as they are in Europe.

The female commoners do all the sewing-related work needed for the undergarments that noble families wear: they wash, mend and beautify them and knit lace adornments, which they call *trencillas* or braids, for stockings, high socks, embroideries and other garments. The earnings they make from this and other honest occupations such as kneading bread and making sweets and pastries allow them to live with some measure of leisure. The lower-class Spanish men do not keep as busy. They live off the lesser commercial activities of shops and taverns, which in the Americas are called *mesón* and *pulpería*, and the majority of those who do not dedicate themselves to such jobs live an idle and lazy life, given over to gambling and other delinquent diversions. Meanwhile, government officials make no attempt to deliberate how this kind of conduct, which stems from a lack of employment in the kingdom, might be remedied. Instead, they manage to discipline these men and keep them in line with the rigor of punishment, which if it does not make them useful to the state, at least serves to teach them a lesson.

The other half of the population is made up of some Indians and mestizos and many blacks, mulattos, free zambos,[2] and slaves. The slaves work as house servants, coachmen and footmen. The Indians and mestizos work as farmers on small farms; sell fruits, vegetables and all types of foodstuffs; and transport provisions. For their part, the free blacks and mulattos bear the brunt of the mechanical arts, in which a few Europeans are also employed. . . .

The city's men, in keeping with their natural gallantry, are inclined above all else to the art of weapons. At the same time, however, docility comes very naturally to them, and this quality has a tempering effect, ridding them of the vices of pride and provocation so that they strive to defend themselves without causing insult. They begin to ride horses when they can barely walk, and thus many become famous riders and skilled cavalrymen. The nobility of this city has always produced a great number of excellent captains, as proven over the course of the country's lengthy war against the Indians, and they have demonstrated their military talents not only in this conflict, but also in a handful of clashes against the European enemies who used to pirate in the seas of these parts. In truth, I do not think there is any difference between dying pierced by a bullet fired by an Englishman or stabbed by a spear couched under an Indian's arm. But today, despite their natural propensity for this profession, the lack of opportunities to exercise it has distanced them from it, and so they are afforded little chance to increase their profit or honor—those powerful incentives that move a man and determine his worth—by arms. A military career here destines one to poverty: after forty or fifty years of service, the men meet their eternal end, leaving their families mired in misery and begging. With these examples before them, even the military men themselves direct their sons away from this path, and if they lack the means to steer them to a career as a laborer or merchant, they encourage them to join the clergy, which is the most common way to keep them from falling into the web of poverty.

The sons of this city are well aware of the maxims of commerce, but few of them advance in business. Seeing as though they are raised in lavish conditions and are naturally generous and giving, they have difficulty becoming accustomed to economic frugality, which is indispensable for increasing one's income. Some apply themselves to mining, but in order do well in this field, it is likewise essential to think economically and avoid squandering money; these concerns, however, are far from the minds of miners, who find vanity in their profession, so few increase their earnings there either. Others think reflectively and pragmatically, and managing their affairs with a judicious hand, they dedicate themselves to agriculture and raising livestock. They establish opulent ranches that bring in more than middling fortunes, enjoying the advantageous conditions afforded by an unfailing enterprise free from bankruptcy and irreparable contingencies.

They generally are clear of mind and intelligent and have a particular ability in the sciences, so their colleges and universities produce outstanding theologians and lawyers, and they would be excellent in other fields if they had time to dedicate to their study. However, they only apply themselves to the sciences because there they can obtain some reward, albeit a modest one. . . .

There are no comedies, operas, or bullfights to divert the public in this city, but this defect might be owed to the fact that the population does not want a visible arena for poor manners, as one finds in other American cities that do have such diversions. Nonetheless, Santiago's inhabitants are very good at making up for this deficit. In the spring, they frequently take excursions to country estates and homes where they put on fine banquets, dance a great deal, and enjoy themselves all day long. Both the masses and the nobility frequently go picnicking in the area around San Cristóbal Hill as well. In the summer, they spend time at the baths of Colina, Angostura, and Cauquénes, where along with restoring their health, they are able to unburden their minds thanks to the simple dealings of the countryside, where there is no place for the fastidious ceremonies and requirements of the city. In the fall, the estates and ranches make up for their expenses with the slaughter of livestock and abundance of seasonal fruits. And in the winter, when there are fewer people about, most of the city's residents go to some place where they can enjoy music or dance, for rare is the house that lacks a lady who can sing and play some musical instrument. Other homes host *tertulias,* or evening get-togethers where they consider educational topics and listen to a variety of discussions on different matters, and at a certain hour, set according to the fact that they all have to retire at eleven, a light refreshment of chocolate, biscuits, excellent sweets, and drinks from lemons, oranges, or seasonal fruit is served. And this is so common here that one need not be rich to provide it. After that, the modest entertainment continues with card games such as mediator or manille, using quarters as chips with the sole aim of having fun. Moreover, every family, according to its social condition, celebrates its saint days with large banquets followed by complimentary drinks and dancing. This is how they compensate for the absence of theater.

Basic provisions are very cheap. No European good is lacking here, but in contrast to Europe, the essential goods and comfort and luxury items can be purchased at low prices. Three ten-ounce loaves of bread as fine as the best eaten in Madrid cost no more than half a real; four loaves of bread of a bit lesser quality cost the same, as do five or six of the common kind. No groceries are expensive, with the exception of fresh seafood. About three or four pounds of beef can be bought for half a real, and the same goes for other kinds of meat. Three half-liters of mediocre wine cost one *real,* and the same amount of the class served in Madrid's taverns costs two. Legumes and vegetables cost so little that the highest quality is also accessible to the poor. . . . At the risk of appearing to exaggerate, I will say no more about the abundance, fine quality, and low cost of foodstuffs and fruits; many people in Madrid and all over Spain have been to this privileged country and experienced it for themselves, so they know full well that there are times when everything I have mentioned sells for even less. And I do not want anyone to think that this is owed to poverty or a lack of consumers, for there is nothing of the kind here—there are no less than 40,000 inhabitants, many of whom have more-than-middling fortunes and a great many of whom boast no small wealth totaling 50,000 to 100,000 pesos.

The city does not, however, have factories to exploit the good materials it has, and its inhabitants could produce even more if they applied themselves. For if they did have factories, they would prosper infinitely in every branch of business thanks to the abundance and low prices of every operational necessity, together with the low wages that would correspond. The foregoing is already evident in the industries they do have: bricklayers and carpenters earn six reales a day plus a mid-morning ration, without lunch, afternoon rations or dinner; peons, moreover, earn forty reales over 30 days of work, and though this includes a mid-morning ration, lunch and dinner, the cost of the meals comes to no more than one real per day.

Translated by Rachel Stein and David Schreiner

Notes

1. If taken as the population of the urban nucleus, this figure would seem to be inflated.
2. A person of mixed African and indigenous descent.

From War to Diplomacy:
The Summit of Tapihue

After the first hundred years, unremitting warfare between Hispanic and Mapuche societies gave way to a more complex mix of dependency and exchange, albeit with recurring spasms of violence. Hispanic authorities had learned through hard experience that territorial subjugation of the Mapuche was futile, and their goal shifted to maintaining a mutually acceptable peace with indigenous vassals who pledged obedience to the king even as they retained their essential autonomy. A centerpiece of these efforts was the parlamentos *or* paces, *periodic peace summits between colonial and indigenous authorities that the historian Leonardo León has called a "colorful political assembly peculiar to the Reino de Chile." Initiated in the mid-seventeenth century, the highly ritualized parlamentos gave both sides the opportunity to elaborate the "rules of the frontier game."*

Involving several thousand attendees, the gatherings occasioned significant expenses for the Spanish hosts, thanks to the large quantities of food and wine consumed (an average of more than 10,000 liters, according to one estimate) and the exchange of gifts. Indeed, "gifts for the Indians" was a permanent item in Spanish budgets, an institutionalized aspect of colonial politics in Chile. The Spanish would present Mapuche authorities with a list of capitulaciones, *or conditions for establishing peace, which resembled a European-style peace treaty. But while the parlamentos have traditionally been interpreted as reflections of Spanish power and European cultural forms, recently historians have drawn attention to the extent to which Mapuche symbols and rituals pervaded the assemblies. These included the sacrifice of animals (especially alpacas); the burial of arms; the offering of branches of the winter's bark tree (Drymis chilensis), a Mapuche symbol of peace; as well as the use of staffs tipped with silver, a Mapuche symbol of power. The assemblies included days of speeches by Mapuche leaders, in what was clearly an indigenous rhetorical form. While the capitulaciones were formulated in Spanish and records of the summits written in that language, thanks to the longwinded caciques, the great bulk of the oral proceedings were actually in Mapudungun, with interpreters on hand to provide translation. Meanwhile, if the capitulaciones resembled European*

peace treaties, the procedure by which these documents were subjected to public dis-
cussion to reach collective consensus echoed indigenous political forms.

The proceedings reproduced here are from the Parlamento of Tapihue, which
brought together more than 3,000 attendees near Yumbel (southeast of present-day
Concepción) in 1774. By equal turns conciliatory and threatening, the conditions the
Spanish presented reflect their preoccupations of the moment. These included recent
English territorial incursions (hence the exhortation that the Mapuche be "friends
of our friends, and enemies of our enemies"); the recrudescence of intertribal conflict
within Mapuche society, which imperiled peace with the Spanish; malocas, or raids
of livestock and captives; as well as banditry and illicit commerce across the frontier.
As Leonardo León has noted, interethnic relations no longer involved a simple equa-
tion of Mapuche versus Spaniard but rather delicate alliances between the Crown
and certain caciques against other uncooperative chieftains, Spanish bandits and
rebels, and would-be English invaders.

Finally, if the Spanish set the summit's agenda, this document was a reflection
as much of their concessions as of their demands. They insisted on Mapuche subor-
dination to their monarch but promised that faithful indigenous vassals would not
forfeit their political or territorial autonomy or pay taxes or tribute. A particularly
innovative proposal was the creation of a corps of cacique ambassadors who would
reside in Santiago as representatives of their "nations." The creation of indigenous
ambassadors implied a tacit recognition of Mapuche political autonomy and the
acknowledgment (and reinforcement) of the chieftains' social and political status.
Finally, the offer to educate the sons of Mapuche leaders raises the possibility that
the king intended to create a Mapuche ruling corps who would bypass local Chilean
officials and deal directly with the Crown.[1]

On December 21, 1774 in the fields outside Tapihue . . . an arbor [had been]
prepared to hold a General Peace Summit with caciques, distinguished Indians, and *mocetones*[2] from the four *butalmapus*[3] . . . for the purpose of ratifying peace agreements to enhance the strength, tranquility and safety of the
Kingdom. . . . [With] the said Caciques and Indians sitting by order of their
reducciones[4] and the four ambassadors or spokesmen of the aforementioned
butalmapus sitting separately on the right-hand side of those in attendance
with the President,[5] his Lordship ordered that the General Interpreter, Juan
Antonio Martínez, and the Capitán de Amigos,[6] Blas Yañes, swear . . . by
the Lord our God and under the true sign of the cross, to tell the truth and
faithfully and literally translate everything proposed by the President to
the Indians as well as their responses. . . . [And] his Lordship exhorted . . .
other ecclesiastical figures versed in the Indian language to inform him as
to whether the General Interpreter was proposing to the Indians everything
he was ordered to and faithfully translating their responses.

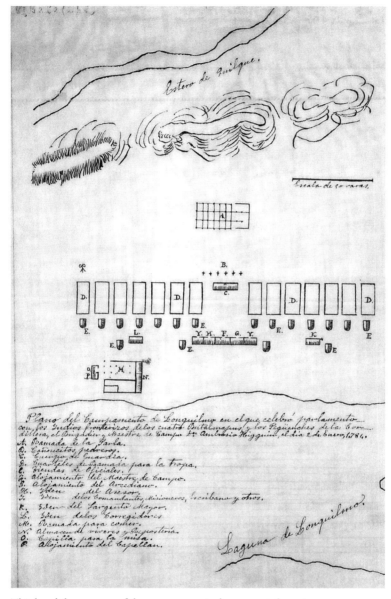

Plano del Campamento de Longuilmo en el que celebró parlamento
con los Indios fronterizos delos cuatro Butalmapus, y los Peguenches de la Cor-
dillera, el Brigadier y Maestre de Campo Dn Ambrosio Higgins, el día 2 de enero, 1784.
A. Ramada de la Parla.
B. Cañoncitos pedreros.
C. Cuerpo de Guardia.
D. Cuarteles de ramada para la Tropa.
E. Tiendas de Oficiales.
F. Alojamiento del Maestro de Campo.
G. Idem del Arcediano.
H. Idem del Asesor.
I. Idem delos Comandantes, Misioneros, escribano y otros.
K. Idem del Sargento Mayor.
L. Idem delos Corregidores.
M. Ramada para comer.
N. Almacen de viveres y Repostería.
O. Capilla para la Misa.
P. Alojamiento del Capellan.

This hand-drawn map of the encampment where one *parlamento*, or peace summit, was held at Lonquilmo in 1783 suggests the careful planning that went into
these assemblies. The map indicates the arbor from which speakers addressed
the assembly, lodgings for Spanish officials, the dining arbor, and provisions
storage. Everything about the summits, from the seating arrangement to the
order of speakers, was orchestrated with assiduous regard for political symbolism. Courtesy of Colección Sala Medina, Biblioteca Nacional de Chile.

With these formalities concluded, the Governing Cacique of the Reducción of Santa Fe, Ignacio Levihueque, elected and named by the Indians . . . asked for permission to finalize his appointment as spokesman. This request was granted by the Captain General, and the said Cacique went about his rituals and ceremonies, collecting the staffs of all of the conference participants . . . and with all these staffs he formed a bundle of sorts, placing the Captain General's staff at the very top. . . .

[The Governor begins his presentation:] I have traveled to this border and summoned you to this Peace Conference now purely for your own good and benefit, to admonish and demand of you, in the name of the King, to pledge the most firm and proper loyalty to his sovereignty. Moreover, I warn you that if you do not keep this peace . . . you will see my demeanor so changed that I will not sheathe my sword until I have laid down a punishment so horrific that it will forever serve as a lesson. . . . And I will inform the King of my actions, explaining how you have abused his royal benignity and the great benefits his powerful hand affords you all. However, as long as you assure me that you . . . will be very faithful vassals of his Majesty, and that the ratification of peace agreements, which is the main objective of this Peace Conference, will be so strong and constant in all of your hearts that none of you would even think to break it, I will now set forth the terms of peace . . . so that you may plainly say if you accept them. Once this has been carried out, I will continue in my duties as your benevolent Father, treating all of you as humble and obedient sons. Therefore, I advise you to pay close attention to these terms, as you will be held responsible for perfectly fulfilling all those you accept, just as the Spaniards will have to fulfill, for their part, all those applicable to them.

- You shall ratify all the terms which you voluntarily agreed upon . . . with respect to appointing and conferring powers to your nations' ambassadors or spokesmen, in order for them to reside in the city of Santiago. . . . They will be supported by the Royal Exchequer and will discuss and accept, just as they would in a general peace conference, any agreements geared at bringing about a stronger peace. . . . Moreover, you must fully understand and take seriously that the main objective of these conferences and peace treaties is that, once established, they may not be broken or altered for any reason . . . however serious it may be . . . and now that you have sworn and promised to live in peace and friendship with the Spaniards, and to never consider taking up arms or causing any damage or prejudice to their persons, haciendas, or livestock, you are hereby informed that you are required to comply with your word and promises forever. . . .

- You shall remain loyal . . . to the King forever. Otherwise—and we do not presume or hope it will come to this—you will experience the . . . ravages of war in all their force. Remember how much his Majesty has tolerated you until now, out of pure benevolence, and how he has honored you by sending me here to keep the kingdom in tranquility and peace. . . . We are only accepting you as our friends because we wish for you to reap the same benefits that we, the rest of his Majesty's vassals, enjoy. . . .

- May it hereby be known that if any Spaniard causes you any humiliation, grievance, or damage, you may arrest him, but you may not do him harm or punish him by your own hand. Rather, you must immediately deliver him to the *corregidor*[7] or another judge so that they may punish him accordingly, if the cause is justified. . . . Likewise, the caciques must promptly punish any Indians who rob or harm the Spaniards in any other way.

- Moreover, with the same objective of executing punishment when due, you may not allow into your lands any Spaniard, Black, Mulatto or Yanacona[8] who has fled from ours to escape the sentences they must suffer for their crimes. . . . As has been stated in other peace summits, men of this sort are capable of leading your lands to ruin, inciting many damages and robbing as they are accustomed to do. . . .

- Knowing that I am only concerned with what is beneficial and convenient for you, you may, equipped as you are with this assurance, sell your fruits and services, going through the ordinary and sanctioned entries to the towns of Santa Barbara, Purén, Nacimiento, Santa Juana and San Pedro. . . . Likewise, you may send your mocetones to work in the service of hacienda owners, and if they fail to pay the mocetones' daily wages in a timely fashion or in full, you may report them to the corregidores, so that they may carry out justice.

- If any mocetón commits a robbery, the cacique of the corresponding reducción shall investigate the matter and identify the robbers; confiscate the stolen goods so that they may be returned to their proper owners; and turn the delinquents over to the authorities so that they may be punished. . . .

- Your ambassadors or spokesmen . . . in Santiago . . . will live at his Majesty's expense, enjoying every comfort and amenity. . . .

- Our friends shall be your friends, and our enemies, your enemies, and whenever you see any foreign ships along the Coast, you must report this to the commanding officer of the closest towns, in order for them to be warned. . . .

- Given that all nations are equal, and as such it is not right . . . for any one to insult or offend another with impunity, ferociously spilling blood among yourselves by way of those barbarous attacks called *malocas*,[9] in which you destroy each other, losing lives and lamenting the deaths of your women, children, and relatives and the loss of your houses, livestock, animals, and sown fields . . . , from now on may it be . . . established, forever and with the strongest conviction possible, that . . . there shall be no more malocas on your part, and may we even forget that evil word, *maloca*. . . .

- In order to punish your reducciones' delinquents and other malicious people and to serve justice to those who seek it . . . I suggest, if you deem it suitable, that you follow the example of the Spaniards and, like them, appoint mayors or judges at proportionate distances, selecting the most well regarded, capable and sound Indian Nobles. . . .

- Whenever a President or the Maestre de Campo General[10] dispatches mail, supplies, or other provisions to Valdivia, you shall not harm or extort these dispatches in any way.[11] On the contrary, you shall clear the roads, and each cacique shall provide one or two guides until the next closest cacique is reached, expressly recommending that the following do the same . . . so that the dispatches may travel safely and with assistance to that town. . . .

- You may not allow any Yanaconas born, baptized, and married among us to abandon their women or children or Christian duties to go and live among you to disturb your possessions and tranquility and . . . lead you into ruin with bad advice. On the contrary, as has been stated, you must detain them and return them to their place of origin. . . .

- Shortly before leaving Santiago, I received a royal privilege from his Majesty who . . . has ordered me to spend . . . all the funds necessary to . . . instruct in schools the children of caciques, Indian nobles, and even those of lesser rank or status. . . . Therefore, anyone who wishes to do so may deliver their sons to me so that they may be educated and indoctrinated in the true principles of our religion and so that, if they apply themselves, they may learn to read, write, and perform any other skills to which they are so inclined. They will be cared for, attended to, and respected, and will not be employed in the service of the King. . . . Moreover, I hereby promise in the name of the King that they will enjoy the utmost liberty and decent treatment, not only under the care of the teachers and directors assigned to them, but, above all, under mine and that of any President and Captain General who should succeed me. . . . In this manner, your children, with time, will be able to earn privileges and distinctions even among Spaniards. . . . In other words, they will be treated as nobles and be able to receive the honors corresponding to their diligent work and good customs, thus allowing their fathers and relatives to boast capable and educated family members who can honor, protect, and defend them and make requests without having to turn to an interpreter or anyone else to represent them.

- You must fully understand that you are free, and the sale of any captive Indians . . . shall be void. Any buyer will lose such a purchase . . . and any judge made aware of such a case must take the captive from the buyer and put him in the custody of a person of good habits who can instruct him in the mysteries of our religion and treat him kindly.[12] . . . Moreover, the buyer shall be subject to whatever punishment the Superior Government should determine. . . .

- If you ask for and are granted missionaries to instruct you in the truths of our religion, you must treat them with all due respect, just as you would treat a minister of God, without harming, humiliating, or damaging their persons.

And once the General Interpreter . . . had conveyed the aforementioned articles to all of the Indians, one by one, without moving on to the next until the former had declared to have perfectly understood everything said to him, they unanimously agreed that all the terms were to their benefit, replying that they intended to be good vassals to his Majesty and keep the peace, enjoying their lands and the calm of their homes. The [Cacique of Angol] spoke of all this at length, expressing how pleased they were with all the conditions proposed and stating that they would firmly observe and fulfill them. Thus concluded that day's negotiations.

Translated by Rachel Stein

Notes

1. Leonardo León provides a full analysis of the capitulaciones of Tapihue in "El Parlamento de Tapihue," *Nütram* 32:9 (1993).

2. *Mocetones* occupy a rank below the caciques in Mapuche society and are dependent on and obedient to them.

3. A territorial division; the area south of the Bío Bío River in this period was commonly said to be divided into four butalmapus.

4. Another territorial division, smaller than the butalmapu.

5. Agustín de Jáuregui y Aldecoa, the governor of Chile at the time. He is referred to alternately throughout as president, captain general, and "his Lordship."

6. Literally, "Captain of Friends": a Spanish or mestizo official who acted as an intermediary between the Spanish authorities and the Mapuche.

7. Judge or mayor appointed by the king to carry out justice and other governing duties in a given territory.

8. An Indian who works as a personal servant to a Spaniard.

9. Raids, usually with the object of enslavement.

10. Military rank that is a step down from captain general.

11. Valdivia was separated from the rest of the colony by the Mapuches' autonomous territory.

12. An apparent reference to the illegal enslavement of Indian children, who were captured or purchased in Mapuche territory and then sold in Hispanic towns, where they worked as servants.

"The Insolence of Peons"

Mine Owners of Copiapó

Far from the conflict in the south, the arid norte chico *(near north) witnessed the emergence of a very different colonial society. By the eighteenth century, this region was home to silver, gold, and copper mines that exported these metals to international markets. While dwarfed by the great mining centers of the Andes and Mexico, Chile's mines were nevertheless an important source of wealth to the growing colony. With the decline of the encomienda, the system in which individual Spaniards exercised control over Indian laborers granted to them by the Crown, the mines were worked by a growing, mobile, multiethnic plebe. Conflict between mine owners and this nascent mining proletariat is reflected in this 1780 petition from a group of owners near Copiapó. (Interestingly, this is the same region where thirty-three trapped miners made world headlines in 2010 when they were rescued from a collapsed shaft.) The mine owners sought to control a workforce of peons and day laborers whom they considered undisciplined and dishonest, and they enjoined state authorities to help them by promulgating ordinances restricting workers' movements and tying them to their employers. State authorities were apparently sympathetic, if somewhat slow to respond: a proclamation issued fifteen years later largely fulfilled the mine owners' requests. This appeal for state support and regulation portended patterns in later years, especially as workers organized to demand better working conditions and higher wages. The mines would eventually serve as the cradle of the Chilean labor movement.*

We, the undersigned miners, present the following request to your Worship with every due respect, thanking you first and foremost for the distinguished and tireless efforts you have invested in spreading and promoting the mining industry to help boost both our community and the Royal Exchequer of Spain. We find ourselves obliged to report to your Worship, however, that the disturbances caused by our peons are preventing us from continuing to carry out these activities as we all so desire, as they are insolent and fail to fulfill their obligations more and more every day. Furthermore, since they are in such short supply, they make many demands:

as is common knowledge, they refuse to take on work without being paid two, four, or sometimes eight months' salary up front to pay off their debts and attend to their needs, and this advance is almost never repaid in labor; rather, they frequently desert their worksites. . . . At times, mining activities must be suspended; at others, we miners must take over their duties, persevering through days of hard work that reap no benefit because of the shortage of laborers. This lack is aggravated by the fact that we must search for the peons far from their worksites, removing them from the custody of others who aid them either in friendship or in the interest of using their services.

With the aim of remedying such serious damages, the laws of this kingdom contain provisions regarding the steps to be implemented when a laborer flees, and when he abandons one mining area for another, and it would be fitting to order that [local] officials . . . be responsible for enforcing these provisions. Moreover, since we know that mining work is usually delayed because the peons are protected by this valley's other miners and residents who bring them under new labor agreements, it would be fitting to [emit an edict] that provides that nobody may rent a peon . . . without the peon first presenting a document from his last employer stating that he has carried out each and every one of the obligations provided under their agreement, and that, if some debt remains, it shall be delivered in straightforward terms, with payment of any damages incurred to the first employer because of that laborer's absence. . . .

Those who hide the said peons in their ranches and mining areas deserve harsher punishment. Therefore, it would also be fitting to emit an order that prohibits housing them for more than one hour, even for the purpose of providing lodging, and that all persons, including the caretakers of haciendas and farms, must take special care to send these peons on their way. And if the peons refuse to leave, the said persons must immediately inform the authorities, who in turn must send the peons to the Copiapó jail to receive fifty public lashes in the pillory, with the same punishment applicable to those who fail to send the peons away or inform the authorities, unless they are Spaniards, in which case the corresponding fine shall be imposed.

We are fully aware of the practical difficulties this order entails: since your Worship is the only judge residing in Copiapó, it would be incredibly burdensome for those who wish to report deserters hiding on ranches to travel great distances to notify you, and likewise, it would be very burdensome for you to have to go chase after them, leaving the many other matters required of you unattended. All of these problems could be solved by appointing a magistrate specifically dedicated to these matters in [various localities in the area]. To this end, an edict could be posted in their respective jurisdictions to announce their appointment, stating their responsibility for seeing to this matter. . . . Through this edict, . . . we should be able to eradicate the kinds of disturbances described above. . . .

Translated by Rachel Stein

III

The Honorable Exception: The New Chilean
Nation in the Nineteenth Century

If the Kingdom of Chile was in many ways an exceptional colony within the Spanish Empire, the newly independent Republic of Chile would gain a reputation for a very different, and much more enviable, kind of exceptionalism. The collapse of the Spanish Empire in the first two decades of the nineteenth century gave rise to more than a dozen independent nations in Latin America. But their initial prospects as republics were discouraging: militarism, political violence, and civil strife plagued the new nations, and weak states and economic contraction were the rule of the day. Against this backdrop, Chile appeared to be, as one newspaper put it, "the honorable exception of peace and stability, order and liberty."[1] The Chilean nation-state was the first in South America to achieve relative territorial control and political stability. This early consolidation would undergird the nation's trajectory of relative political continuity as well as economic expansion for much of the rest of the century. As a result the origins of Chile's twentieth-century political exceptionalism are often traced to this period.

Yet the same observers attribute less salubrious patterns to this period as well. The stability that emerged in postcolonial Chile was rooted in a distinctly authoritarian political order. Moreover, amid the emergence of a robust economy based on the export of commodities such as wheat, copper, and silver to global markets, the country witnessed acute poverty and worsening social inequality. The constitution enacted in 1833 and in effect until 1925 declared all Chileans to be equal under the law. Yet this legal equality was rendered largely moot by the prevailing social structure, which was characterized by a small politically and economically powerful elite who dominated a large, overwhelmingly rural, landless mestizo underclass. By the end of the nineteenth century, the distance between social groups had widened considerably as elites benefited from the wealth generated by expanded agricultural and mining production that caused severe dislocations for the poor. Given that marked social inequalities continue to afflict contemporary Chile, it is worth thinking about the historical antecedents of this problem.

The selections that follow trace the birth of Chilean nationhood, the competing visions of what that new nation should look like, and struggles over the sometimes contradictory promises of order, liberty, and equality. The selections also explore the origins and effects of an export-led, liberal economic model that would last until the Great Depression. Thereafter it would fall out of favor, but economic liberalism would be resurrected during the Pinochet regime in the 1970s.

The story of independence in Spanish America begins in 1808, when Napoleon invaded Spain and dethroned the king, leaving his empire without its legitimate head. Spanish-American creoles responded by organizing local juntas, or governing bodies, to rule in his absence. While the juntas initially pledged loyalty to their deposed monarch, the invasion also gave a fortuitous opening to creoles with economic or political grievances against the Crown. Events in Europe provided an unexpected opportunity to those in the colonies who had imbibed ideals of liberty and republicanism from the French and American revolutions a few decades before and desired the end of Spain's absolutist monarchy.

In Chile, there had been few early signs of discontent with Spanish dominion. Yet here, too, on the western flank of South America, the sentiment of revolution gradually swelled and spread. It was aided by the arrival of the printing press, which the fiery revolutionary Father Camilo Henríquez called "the great and precious instrument of universal enlightenment." A priest turned revolutionary writer, Henríquez founded Chile's first newspaper, the aptly titled *Aurora de Chile* (Dawn of Chile) in 1812. His treatise on independence in the paper's inaugural issue is excerpted here.

An attempt by royalist troops sent by Peru's viceroy to quell revolutionary activity in Chile sparked all-out war between patriots and royalists. The royalists initially won the day, restoring Spanish authority in the wayward colony, but an army of Argentine patriots and Chilean exiles crossed the Andes and, after celebrated battles, took back Santiago. At this point Bernardo O'Higgins, who had been appointed supreme director and is today considered Chile's "founding father," declared Chile's independence, in 1818. One of the liveliest portraits of O'Higgins and of everyday life in the new nation comes from the pen of the British travel writer Maria Graham, who lived in Chile a few years later.

The first decades of the new nation witnessed debates, which at times erupted in violence, between competing visions of this new nation. The basic conflict was between liberals, who advocated a more radical republican break with colonial political and social structures, and conservatives, who valued order above liberty. The two sides fought over the relative distribution of power between the branches of government and between federal and regional powers, over the extent of suffrage, and over the role of the Catholic Church and religion in the new republic.

By 1830, conservatives had gained the upper hand, and they proceeded to maintain it for several decades. The conservative order of this period was and is strongly associated with the figure of Diego Portales, a businessman in Valparaíso whose influence over the new nation's political structures far transcended both his office as chief minister and his life span, which was cut short by assassination in 1837. Known as the "Portalian state," early republican Chile was characterized by a strong centralized executive authority that frequently reverted to emergency powers, states of siege, and the suspension of civil rights. Another common feature of politics was widespread vote buying, or *cohecho*, a practice that persisted well into the twentieth century.

We may trace the origins of Chile's vaunted political stability to this period. The unbroken string of regular, five-year presidential elections from 1831 to 1891 stands in sharp contrast to Mexico, for example, where the presidency changed hands almost forty times in the three decades from 1822 to 1855, yielding an average term of less than eight months in office. It contrasts too with Argentina, where a caudillo ruled through force and patronage for more than two decades during this period. The relative consolidation and stability of the Chilean nation-state has been attributed to various factors, including the small expanse of the country (700 miles from north to south), Santiago's ability to triumph over regional tensions, the cohesiveness of elites, and the imagined ethnic homogeneity of the Chilean nation.

Chile's electoral stability certainly set it apart from other countries, yet the authoritarian elements of its political structure meant that it was not a political democracy. Autocracy did not go unchallenged, however. A vigorous culture of liberal dissent emerged in Chile, challenging the republic to achieve a more democratic, egalitarian order. Among this "Generation of '42" were some of nineteenth-century Latin America's most important intellectuals, including Francisco Bilbao, whose writings are excerpted here. Bilbao is remembered for his blistering critiques of imperialism, despotism, and the Catholic Church. Charged with blasphemy and sedition, he spent much of his life in exile.

Over time, conservative hegemony gradually gave way to a more liberal vision of state and society. While the democratic vision of more radical dissidents like Bilbao remained unrealized, outright repression was relaxed and executive power reined in. A key trend later in the century was the progressive loss of power of the Catholic Church and the secularization of various domains, from marriage to education, that the Church had previously overseen. What did not change was the practice of electoral manipulation, enthusiastically indulged in by all members of the political class regardless of ideology or party.

Of course, the formation of a nation-state involves not just a political entity known as a state but also a social or cultural identity—a feeling of collective identity, of nationhood or nationalism. Even prior to independence, Chile had begun to develop a sense of its own political and cultural distinctiveness, a process encouraged by the colony's geographical isolation. By the end of the eighteenth century, for example, Chileans already spoke Spanish with a recognizably distinct accent. In the context of the new republic, the development of a Chilean national culture became a pressing political priority.

One arena where ideas about nationhood were explored was literature. In 1861, the writer Alberto Blest Gana, said to be Chile's first novelist, declared the importance of developing a Chilean literature that promoted the progress of the nation. In *Martín Rivas*, his best-known work, he paints a vivid portrait of politics and society in midcentury Santiago. Another realm for the consolidation of the nation was education. The University of Chile, founded in 1843, played a central role in the modernization of the nation-state by promoting the generation of knowledge, professionalization, and the education of a political class. We present here the vision for the new university promoted by its first rector, Andrés Bello. Almost from its founding, it was a center not only of learning and knowledge but also of political activism and dissidence, a role it continues to play today.

On the southern frontier, home of the Mapuche Indians, the formation of the Chilean nation looked very different. As discussed in part II, by the end of the colonial period a fragile peace existed between imperial officials and the Mapuche, whose territories south of the Bío Bío River remained politically and territorially autonomous. During the independence wars, the Mapuche, in deference to their peace treaties with the Spanish king, tended to side with royalist forces. During the first half century of Chilean nationhood, the Mapuche continued to inhabit Araucanía, a territory the size of the state of Connecticut. How to incorporate these peoples and the increasingly commercially lucrative lands they occupied into the nation was a looming political question when Polish scientist Ignacio Domeyko conducted an expedition to the region in the 1840s at the behest of the Chilean government. The account he wrote of his encounters with the Mapuche, excerpted here, spurred great controversy because of his sympathetic posture toward them and his call to pursue a nonmilitary strategy of assimilation.

The southern territories are treated from a very different perspective in an account by Vicente Pérez Rosales, a diplomat, politician, and adventurer who worked as a colonization agent promoting German immigration to southern Chile. Critics charged that such policies gave away Mapuches' historic lands to foreigners even as many poor Chileans remained landless. Here Pérez Rosales defends the policy as a way to civilize the barbarous south and describes the conflicts over land that the policy generated.

The political consolidation of the Chilean nation in turn stimulated, and was reinforced by, economic development. Adopting a policy of commodity export, the new nation was decisively inserted into an expanding global economy. The total value of foreign trade increased fivefold from the 1840s to the 1870s, and while cyclical downturns were frequent and sometimes acute, Chile experienced economic expansion for much of the century. These processes established a pattern of dependence on a handful of export commodities that would last, in Chile as elsewhere in Latin America, until the Great Depression. Meanwhile, as the economy expanded, so did the foreign, especially British, presence within it, presaging a pattern that would become a major political issue in later decades. The frequency of English surnames such as Edwards and Ross among the Chilean oligarchy reflects the economic and commercial importance of this immigrant community.

One consequence of economic expansion was the development of the port at Valparaíso, which enjoyed a strategic location as a way station for ships passing around the tip of South America, the only seafaring route between the Atlantic and the Pacific oceans prior to the construction of the Panama Canal. A sleepy town of 5,500 in 1810, the "Jewel of the Pacific" became a bustling center of commerce and finance of more than 60,000 by the 1860s. Among that population was a significant contingent of foreign merchants, many of them British. Meanwhile, Chile's first banks, railroads, mining and industrial concerns, insurance companies, and mercantile houses were located there.

While nitrates would later become the star commodity, Chile's export economy initially rested on gold, silver, and copper, extracted from the mines of the arid north. In 1832, a herder discovered a vein near Copiapó that became the richest silver mine in the history of Chile. In succeeding decades, silver production rose vertiginously. Copper followed a similar pattern: by the 1870s, one-third to one-half of the world's copper originated in Chile. As exports grew, extractive technologies remained rudimentary and production increases relied on the grueling labor of the growing numbers of workers who migrated to the mines from elsewhere in Chile. In the 1830s, as part of his storied world travels on the *Beagle*, the naturalist Charles Darwin surveyed various parts of Chile and vividly described the miners who excavated ore and carried it, with brute physical strength, to the surface.

The other source of export wealth was agriculture. Prior to the mid-nineteenth century, landownership was a wellspring of social status for Chilean elites, but it was not necessarily a way to get rich. Local markets were limited, external markets were few, and poor transportation hampered the ability to move products to potential consumers. Beginning in the late 1840s, this situation changed dramatically. The California gold rush provided the century's first major international market for Chilean grain. The frontier society could not feed itself and relied on imports from places like Chile, which enjoyed a geographic advantage as the only grain producer on the Pacific. Wheat and flour exports soared. Shortly thereafter, a gold rush in Australia provided another boom. The development of railroads linking once remote haciendas to urban centers and the port of Valparaíso gave further impulse to the export economy.

California's gold rush involved another sort of Chilean export as well: people. Tales of spectacular wealth touched off an exodus of several thousand Chilean fortune seekers, who ranged from the sons of distinguished families to poor peons. Several skilled writers among them recorded their experiences for eager Chilean audiences. Reproduced here are the perceptive, sardonic observations of Pedro Combet, a native Frenchman resident in Chile who like so many others sought, but did not necessarily find, his fortune in California. The gold rush episode reflects Chile's growing integration into a global economy and the dislocations and opportunities it engendered.

If the promise of gold proved evanescent, so did the wheat boom that the gold rush triggered in Chile. Within a few years, both California and Australia became self-sufficient grain producers, and these markets evaporated as quickly as they had materialized. While Chile continued to export to other markets (such as England and Peru), the boom times were over. Worse still, Chilean grain was soon eclipsed by the more efficient breadbaskets of North America, Australia, Russia, and later Argentina.

Such boom-and-bust cycles notwithstanding, agriculture remained central to Chilean society in the nineteenth century, not least because 80 percent of the population at midcentury lived and worked in the countryside.

Rural Chile was dominated by the institution of the hacienda, the large landed estate that constituted one of the central features of Chilean social, economic, and political life up until the 1960s. In the nineteenth century, haciendas controlled perhaps 75 percent of agricultural lands, and most rural dwellers were landless and dependent on them. Bound to the estates by paternalistic custom rather than law, *inquilinos*, or tenant farmers, provided labor to the hacienda in exchange for access to land to cultivate their own crops. To the hacienda's critics, these workers looked suspiciously like feudal serfs. Yet inquilinos were in many ways better off than another class of workers, the itinerant *peones* or *gañanes* (peons, day laborers) who traversed the national territory seeking seasonal work for a miserly wage. In a manual excerpted here, a wealthy landowner gives readers instructions on how to run an hacienda. His manual attests to the finely tuned hierarchy of these estates, the often hidden role of women's work, and the forms of labor discipline at the disposal of the *hacendado*, or landowner.

Overall, the growing agricultural economy did not increase efficiency or stimulate the adoption of new production methods: for example, ox-driven carts remained the technology of choice until the 1930s. Nor did this economic expansion challenge the distribution of land or the organization of labor. Rather than undermining the hacienda, commercial expansion in the nineteenth century consolidated the central role of the large landed estate in Chilean agriculture. But if the burgeoning agrarian economy did not alter production methods, it did affect people. Haciendas turned out superfluous workers so as to dedicate more land to cultivation, and the number of rootless male peons swelled. Around 1865 this "errant mass," as observers called it, accounted for a third of all workers. Unskilled, unmarried, with no fixed residence or job, these workers migrated in search of work between the countryside, the mines, and the cities and across the border to Argentina and Peru.

Women too left haciendas to seek work in urban areas, mostly as poorly paid servants and seamstresses. Households headed by women were common in urban and semiurban areas. Some of the most dramatic evidence of the conditions of the poor is found in the records of Santiago's orphanage, which received tens of thousands of children in the latter half of the nineteenth century. Notes and letters left with these youngsters attest to the growing impoverishment of the lower classes and the feminization of poverty in a city where women outnumbered men and experienced higher unemployment and lower wages.

The specter of widespread poverty, the transient population of rootless male laborers, and the apparent disintegration of family structures among the poor provoked an outpouring of concern over "the social question," the phrase elites invoked to refer to the material and moral poverty of the majority of their compatriots. Were the causes of poverty and inequality to be found in the degenerate character of the poor themselves or in features of the society they inhabited? In a famous essay, the doctor and congressman Augusto Orrego Luco makes the latter argument. First published in 1881, the essay foreshadows the social and class conflicts that would animate Chilean politics into the twentieth century.

Note

1. *El Araucano*, 1841.

A Revolutionary Journalist:

"Fundamental Notions of

the Rights of Peoples"

Camilo Henríquez

The arrival of the first printing press in Chile in 1811 coincided with the explosion of revolutionary independence movements there and elsewhere in Spanish America. Chile's first newspaper, Aurora de Chile, *became a mouthpiece for the patriots. No one did more to advance the revolutionary press than Fray Camilo Henríquez, a friar with a gift for writing who is widely considered the founder of Chilean journalism. A native of Valdivia, Henríquez completed much of his education and entered a religious order in Lima, where he imbibed antimonarchical, republican ideas and had run-ins with the Inquisition for possessing banned texts (such as work by Rousseau). In 1810, with the Spanish Empire convulsed by revolt, he returned to Chile, eager to work for "the great effort of public enlightenment."[1] Excerpted from one of Henríquez's best-known essays, the passage here explores the origins of the social compact and the relationship between monarchs and their people. The essay appeared as the opening editorial of* Aurora de Chile's *first edition. The weekly lasted a bit more than a year before wary authorities shut it down, but by then the political press was well established, and newspapers would continue to serve as a key forum for expounding revolutionary principles.*

Every man is born with an underlying social character that inevitably unfolds, sooner or later. His weakness during childhood and the long length of that stage; the perfectible nature of his spirit; the maternal love he receives and the gratitude and tenderness born from it; the faculty of speech; and the natural events that bring wandering and free men together and join them in a thousand ways: all this proves that man is destined by nature for society.

Man would be unhappy in this new state of being if he lived without rules, without subjection, and without laws designed to maintain order. But who could establish . . . these laws when all were equal? No doubt a body of partners, forming a mutual pact to subject themselves to certain rules determined precisely by them in order to ensure the tranquility and permanency of the new body they comprised. Therefore, the instinct and necessity that led them into this social state could not but gear all moral and political laws toward achieving order, safety, and a longer and happier existence for each and every individual, along with the social body as a whole. . . . Such was the origin of society.

Order and liberty cannot survive without a government, and so the same hope of living peacefully, happily, and safe from internal violence and hostile affronts compelled men, once assembled, to rely on a freely agreed upon public authority. By virtue of this consent, the institution of *Suprema Potestas* was established and its exercise entrusted to one or many individuals from the same social body.

In this great body, there is always a central force constituted by the will of the nation in order to guarantee the safety, happiness, and preservation of all and guard against any serious troubles that should arise from the passions. There is also a centrifugal force born from the aspirations and unjust and violent actions of neighboring peoples, whereby each labors against the rest to expand and grow at the expense of the weakest; unless, that is, each party makes itself respected by force. On the basis of this principle, history shows us slavery, ravages, atrocities, misery, and the extermination of the human species at every turn. Thus it is impossible to find any people who have not suffered the tyranny and violence of another, stronger group.

This state of peoples is the origin of monarchy, because in war the people needed a general to lead them to victory. In ancient times, according to Aristotle, when captains displayed valor and skill and felicitous outcomes in battle they were raised to royal power out of public recognition and in the public's interest.

The origin of the Spanish monarchy was none other than this. What else were the Visigoth kings in their beginnings but captains of a conquering people? . . .

Let us establish as a principle, then, that supreme authority finds its origin in the free consent of the people, which we may call a social pact or alliance.

Every pact has its conditions, and those of the social pact are none other than the objectives of the group.

The parties to the contract are the people and the executive authority. In a monarchy, these are the people and the king.

The king agrees to guarantee and preserve safety, property, liberty, and order. This guarantee comprises all the monarch's duties.

The people agree to be obedient and provide the king with all the means necessary to defend them and to preserve internal order. It is on this principle that the people's duties are based.

The nature of the social pact requires that the manner in which the public authority is to exercise power be determined: under which circumstances and at what times must it listen to the people? When does it have to report the Government's operations to the people? What measures should be taken to avoid arbitrariness? In sum, what is the scope of the powers of the Prince?

Therefore, a foundational set of rules is needed, and this set of rules is the constitution of the state. In essence, these are no more than the manner and order whereby the political body is to achieve the aims of its group. . . .

By virtue of what has been shown above, the executive authority lies with the prince; he is the first judge and the protector of the law and the people.

The kingdom, then, is not a patrimony of the prince; the prince is not an owner of the kingdom free to sell, bequeath, and divide it as he sees fit.

Despite all this, base courtiers easily managed to persuade arrogant monarchs that the nations had been made for them, and not them for the nations: from then on, the monarchs considered the people as they would herds of beasts: from then on, authority had no limits. How unhappy the fate of humanity was from then on! . . .

For about eighteen centuries throughout a large part of the world, philosophy was forced to keep quiet. [But] in the end it won out. Truth is fearlessly rearing its luminous head in the current century. . . .

We said that one of the rights of the people was to reform the constitution of the state. In fact, the constitution should be adjusted to the people's current circumstances and needs at any given time; whenever circumstances vary, the constitution should vary. There is no law or custom that should endure if it can bring any detriment, inconvenience, or preoccupation to the political body. The health of the people is the supreme law. With the passage of time, states come to find themselves in circumstances very different from those in which the laws developed. Colonies multiply and grow and their well-being then ceases to be compatible with the primitive system; it must be changed.

In this case, the well-being of the colonies is what determines the permanence of the constitution. The prince and the system were made with the well-being of the whole nation in mind. . . .

I say here to the people: such are the principles from which your eternal rights emanate. They ennoble your being: you owe them to the sovereign

Author of nature: appreciate them; do not allow the injustice and evil nature of men to snatch and obscure them from you. The supreme hand that granted them to you gave you a heart and spirit to defend them. If you have been capacitated with heroic sentiments, lofty aims, and sublime virtues, it is so that you may preserve your dignity; none of these things are needed to be a slave.

I have laid out these principles as quickly as possible, so that they may be more easily stamped in your memories.

Have no doubt: ignorance of these rights keeps the chains of slavery intact. Countries have been moaning under the weight of despotism for as long as they have been under this reign of ignorance and barbarity. . . .

So, we have a lot of work to do to achieve happiness. The study of public law and politics should be the task of all good minds. Patriotism should make this study a kind of requirement: it should be the principal target toward which public institutions aim. Genius is no substitute for the kind of knowledge that should be priceless to the people—that which gives birth to liberty. Thus spoke the illustrious Condorcet in Paris in 1790: what would he have said in America? Oh! Would that the *Aurora de Chile* could contribute in some way to the enlightenment of my compatriots! Would that it were the dawn of more copious talents, eventually bringing to light writers with more natural ability than mine! At that point, my name will cease to live on. My meager work will undoubtedly fall into oblivion, its only merit being that it paved the way for other, greater feats; but my homeland will not forget that I did everything for it within my reach, and even, perhaps, laid the ground for a better fate from afar.

Translated by Rachel Stein and Melissa Mann

Note

1. Camilo Henríquez in a letter to his brother-in-law Diego Pérez de Arce, cited in Miguel Luis Amunátegui, *Camilo Henríquez*, vol. 1 (Imprenta Nacional, 1889), 23.

An Englishwoman Observes the New Nation

Maria Graham

In the early nineteenth century, the Englishwoman Maria Graham became well known for her professional travel writing on South America, South Asia, and Europe. Widowed during a sea voyage to South America, she buried her husband, a ship captain, in the port of Valparaíso and decided to stay on for a time. Published several years later, her Journal of a Residence in Chile during the Year 1822 *was among the first travel diaries penned by a woman and offered an astute portrait of the public and private life of the new nation, which had declared its independence just four years earlier. Graham had the opportunity to meet leading political figures of the day—not least the Chilean "founding father," Bernardo O'Higgins, himself— and she frequently commented on the vicissitudes of Chilean politics.*

Graham's travels presaged the growing British presence in Chile. During the independence struggle, British naval forces had collaborated with Chilean patriots against the Spanish. (Graham befriended the most famous British ally, the naval officer Lord Thomas Cochrane.) In succeeding decades, the expanding Chilean economy would attract an important contingent of British immigrants linked to the export trade.

In this excerpt, Graham demonstrates her ability to circulate among commoners and the well-heeled alike. She sketches scenes of street life and popular entertainment as well as elite households and manners, concluding with a rumination on the new republic's still precarious political structures. While Graham found Chile "far back with regard to the conveniences and improvements of civilized life," she developed an evident affection for the young nation, wishing it "well to the good cause of independence."

English tailors, shoemakers, saddlers, and innkeepers hang out their signs in every street; and the preponderance of the English language over every other spoken in the chief streets would make one fancy Valparaíso a coast town in Britain. The North Americans greatly assist in this, however. Their goods, consisting of common furniture, flour, biscuit, and naval stores, necessarily keep them busier out of doors than any other set of people. The more

Country house. In her travel diary, Maria Graham included her own sketches, as well as illustrations by others, to show scenes of everyday life in the new republic. Drawing "Costume of Chile" by Augustus Earle and engraved by Edward Finden, from *Journal of a Residence in Chile during the Year 1822* (London: Longman, Hurst, Rees, Orme, Brown, and Green, 1824). Courtesy of Colección Sala Medina, Biblioteca Nacional de Chile.

elegant Parisian or London furniture is generally dispatched unopened to Santiago, where the demand for articles of mere luxury is of course greater. The number of piano-fortes brought from England is astonishing. There is scarcely a house without one, as the fondness for music is excessive; and many of the young ladies play with skill and taste, though few take the trouble to learn the gamut, but trust entirely to the ear. . . .

Soon after dinner to-day, . . . I accompanied [some acquaintances] to the plain on the southwest side of the town, to see the Chinganas, or amusements of the common people. On every feast-day they assemble at this place, and seem to enjoy themselves very much in lounging, eating sweet puffs fried on the spot in oil, and drinking various liquors, but especially chicha,[1] while they listen to a not disagreeable music played on the harp, guitar, tambourine, and triangle, accompanied by women's voices, singing of love and patriotism. The musicians are placed in wagons covered with reeds, or regularly thatched, where they sit playing to draw custom[ers] to little

A *chingana* (celebration). Graham observed these outdoor celebrations for the popular classes where merrymakers ate, listened to music, and gambled. Here a couple dances the *cueca*, a dance associated with chinganas that was later declared the national dance of Chile. Illustration by Claudio Gay, from *Atlas de la historia física y política de Chile*, by Claudio Gay (Paris: Imprenta de E. Thunot, 1854). Courtesy of Colección Biblioteca Nacional de Chile.

tables, placed around with cakes, liquors, flowers, which those attracted by the songs buy for themselves or the lasses they wish to treat. . . . Men, women, and children are passionately fond of the Chinganas. The whole plain is covered with parties on foot, on horseback, in caleches,[2] and even in carts; and, although for the fashionables, the Almeida [Alameda] is most in vogue, yet there is no want of genteel company at the Chinganas. Everybody seemed equally happy and equally orderly. In so great a crowd in England, there would surely have been a ring or two for a fight; but nothing of the kind occurred here, although there was a good deal of gambling and some drinking. In the evening I joined the family tertulia,[3] where the usual music and dancing and gossip went on; and I found that even in Chile the beauty and dress of one young lady is criticized by another just as with us. And now I think of it, I am sure I never saw so many very pretty women in one day as I beheld to-day. . . . [However,] these pretty creatures have generally harsh rough voices, and about the throats of some there is that fullness that denotes that goiters are not uncommon. . . .

This morning, on looking out soon after day-break, I saw the provisions coming into town for the market. The beef cut in quarters, the mutton in halves, was mounted on horseback before a man or boy, who, in his poncho, sat as near the tail of the horse as possible. Fowls in large grated chests of hide came slung on mules. Eggs, butter, milk, cheese, and vegetables, all rode, no Chileno condescending to walk, especially with a burden, unless in case of dire necessity; and as the strings of beasts so laden came along one way, I saw women enveloped in their mantas, and carrying their alfombras . . . going to mass another.[4]

The cries in the streets are nearly as unintelligible as those in London, and, with the exception of *Sweep* and *Old Clothes*, concern the same articles. Judge Prevost came in soon after breakfast and settled my mode of paying my respects to Doña Rosa O'Higgins[5] in the evening. It appears that to walk even to a next-door neighbor on occasions of ceremony is so undignified, that I must not think of it, therefore I go in a chaise belonging to the family where I live, and two of the ladies will accompany me. . .

On arriving at the palace, we walked in with less bustle and attendance than I have seen in . . . most private houses: the rooms are handsomely but plainly furnished; English cast-iron grates; Scotch carpets; some French china, and time-pieces, little or nothing that looked Spanish, still less Chileno. The Director's mother Doña Isabella, and his sister Doña Rosa, received us not only politely but kindly. The Director's reception was exceedingly flattering. . . . His Excellency had passed several years in England, great part of which time he spent at an academy at Richmond in Surrey. He immediately asked me if I had ever been there, enquired after my uncle Mr., now Sir David Dundas, and several other persons of my acquaintance, by name, and asked very particularly about his old masters in music and other arts. I was very much pleased with the kindliness of nature shown in these recollections, and still more so when I saw several wild-looking little girls come into the room, and run up to him, cling about his knees, and found that they were little orphan Indians rescued from slaughter on the field of battle. It appears that the Indians, when they make their inroads on the reclaimed grounds, bring their wives and families with them; and should a battle take place and become desperate, the women usually take part in it. Should they lose, it is not uncommon for the men to put to death their wives and children to prevent them from falling into the hands of the enemy. . . . The Director now gives a reward for all persons, especially women and children, saved on these occasions. The children are to be educated and employed hereafter as mediators between their nations and Chile, and, to this end, care is taken that they should not forget their native tongue. The Director was kind enough to talk to them in the Araucanian tongue, that I might hear the language, which is soft and sweet; perhaps it owed something to the young voices of the children. One of them pleased me especially: she is a little Maria, the daughter of a Cacique, who, with his wife and all the elder part of his family, was killed in a late battle. Doña Rosa takes a particular charge of the little female prisoners, and acts the part of a kind mother to them. I was charmed with the human and generous manner in which she spoke of them. . . .

My mind, for a time after I arrived, was not sufficiently free to attend, with any degree of interest, to the political state of the country: yet a measure of vital importance is now pending.

On the first settlement of affairs after the battle of Chacabuco,[6] Don Bernardo O'Higgins had been chosen to preside over the nation. . . . A senate was chosen from among the respectable citizens to assist him, and a provisional constitution was adopted. The law of the land continued to be such as the old Spaniards had bequeathed it. The constitution gave equal rights to all; abolished slavery, limited the privileges of the mayorazgos,[7] diminished the power and revenue of the church, and adopted the English naval code for the regulation of its maritime affairs. But three years and a half of internal peace and success in all distant expeditions had given leisure to the northern provinces of Chile, and particularly to the capital, to see and feel the inconveniences of the actual form of government, which was in fact a despotic oligarchy. . . . By the absence or secession of the members of the senate, who were disgusted at the opposition they met with in a plan for declaring their office perpetual and hereditary, the whole power had been left in the single hands of the director: if he had had a spark of ordinary ambition, he might have made himself absolute. It is seldom that a successful soldier like O'Higgins has the sense to see, and the prudence to avoid, the danger of absolute power: he, however, has had both; and the senate being dissolved, he has convoked a deliberative assembly for the purpose of forming a permanent constitution. The members are to be named by him and his private council, from among the most respectable inhabitants of each township in Chile. . . .

If such an assembly should honestly do its duty, nothing could be wiser than this measure. But chosen by the executive, and therefore biased not unnaturally in its favor, it appears to me that every possible difficulty lies in the way of obtaining through that assembly an effective representative government; and it might have been wiser, and certainly, as the government is constituted, as legal, to have issued a decree for electing representatives for the towns at once.

These, as the people of the country increased and became enlightened, would naturally add to their numbers, and the government would grow along with the people. I am too old not to be afraid of readymade constitutions, and especially of one fitted to the habits of a highly civilized people applied too suddenly to an infant nation like this. . . .

I am interested in the character of the people, and wish well to the good cause of independence. Let the South American colonies once secure that, and civil liberty, and all its attendant blessings, will come in time.

Notes

1. An alcoholic beverage made from fermented grapes.
2. A kind of carriage.
3. Get-togethers in private homes for the purpose of socializing or for discussing politics, culture, and other "refined" topics. A common social custom among the upper classes, tertulias were often presided over by women.
4. Here Graham refers to the custom of women, especially wealthy ones, of covering their heads with shawls (*mantas*) and bringing small rugs (*alfombras*) with them to kneel on during mass.
5. In this section Graham pays a visit to supreme director of Chile, Bernardo O'Higgins, his half-sister Rosa, and his mother, Doña Isabella Riquelme.
6. A battle in 1817 in which patriots led by San Martín and O'Higgins defeated royalist forces, marking an important (albeit not definitive) military milestone in the process of Chilean independence.
7. Entailed estates, a legal mechanism used by wealthy families to keep their patrimony intact over time; eventually abolished in the new republic.

The Authoritarian Republic

Diego Portales

One of the most important as well as controversial figures in Chilean political life over the past two centuries is the conservative statesman Diego Portales, a businessman who headed a Valparaíso import-export company. His ill-fated ventures involving a monopoly concession from the government led him to enter politics. The 1820s was a decade of liberal ascendance, but by 1829 the tide had turned in favor of conservatives. As a cabinet minister and presidential advisor (due to a self-professed "aversion to politics," he refused to hold elected office), Portales became the intellectual and political architect of the "authoritarian republic" that prevailed for much of the nineteenth century and continued to shape politics into the twentieth. So closely is he associated with this structure that it became known as the Portalian state.

Institutionalized in the Constitution of 1833, the Portalian republic featured strong executive powers, a highly centralized state, the frequent use of extraordinary government powers, and the suspension of civil rights in the name of conserving public order. As Portales famously declared, "the stick and the cake"—punishment and reward—"justly and opportunely administered, are the remedies with which any group of people can be cured, no matter how deeply rooted their bad habits." The Constitution also imposed more restrictive property and literacy requirements on suffrage, reflecting the way the autocratic state tended to serve the interests of economic and political elites. In the following letter to a friend, recently appointed minister of the interior, who has asked for his advice, an irascible Portales expresses his suspicion of politics, politicians, constitutional rule, and popular representation. The letter contains another famous Portalian phrase: "the weight of the night," which refers to his belief that tradition and the passivity of the masses would guarantee political order in Chile.

Today the figure of Diego Portales continues to be ardently celebrated or reviled and remains powerful shorthand for conveying particular political ideas. It is not by chance, for example, that following the 1973 coup the military government rebaptized the hulking downtown high-rise it chose as its headquarters the Diego Portales Building. The name drew a symbolic link between the regime's own political ideals and the nineteenth-century authoritarian order identified with Portales. Just as pointedly, a center-left government that succeeded the dictatorship eventually removed his name from the building.

July 16, 1832
Valparaíso
Sir Joaquín Tocornal

Dear friend:

The same insufficiency that led you to hesitate in accepting the Ministry you now occupy is the same that should excuse me from answering your letter from the twelfth. What suggestions, what warnings could I provide that might contribute to your success? What could I possibly do when I lack the capacity, the time and perhaps even the will to do so? You have no idea how much I despise public affairs, or of the discomfort it causes me simply to hear them mentioned. Whether this is caused by the fatigue or selfishness common to all men, or by my own idiosyncratic fear of appearing ridiculous (resulting from the strange way I often see things); whatever the cause, the truth is that I have this aversion to politics, which I myself consider a virtue while others criticize me for it. This being the case, and since I am unfortunately not one of those people who knows how to control himself, what could you possibly stand to gain by hearing my warnings, even supposing that I had any to provide? Let us agree then that from now on, you should only count on me for personal matters.

Nonetheless, I cannot conclude this letter without giving my opinion with my customary frankness: by doing nothing in the Ministry, you do more than someone who tries to do a great deal!

We all trust that you will not do badly, nor permit that anyone else do likewise; this is the best that judicious, thinking men can do. On the other hand, no good comes from making decrees and creating innovations that, most of the time, produce either nonexistent or pernicious results. At every point you will use your position to do good things, of which you yourself are unaware, and together they will form a mass of good deeds that will become perceptible over time. With your every resolution, your every suggestion, etc., you will provide a good example of rationality, impartiality, order, respect for the law, etc. etc., that will imperceptibly advance the recognized progress of government. In this manner you will add the final touches to the defeat of the bullheadedness that in another time flaunted vice and sanctified crimes.

I believe that we now find ourselves fleeing from partial reforms that would only further complicate the labyrinth of our political machine, and that it is not a job for our times to contemplate the formal, systemic, and radical reorganization of that system. Even if such changes were not obstructed by the conciliatory character of our governor, this is a job that cannot be done by just one man, much less by someone who—as far as I can tell—does not have any support. In the first place, it would require continuous meetings of good councils for at least three years; the Congress will never do anything beneficial or substantial because of its excessively drawn-out sessions. One also needs some hard-working men who are nowhere to be found, brought together despite their differences because of their enthusiasm for the public good, and by an even greater impartiality than that shown in the present councils, which are the best councils we have had yet. The errors and nonsense going on in Bolivia demonstrate this well because even though the Bolivians are ridiculously organized, they have launched a plan, and the public officials have worked with a perseverance that stands in stark contrast to the laziness of Chileans and our inability to carry out even our own affairs.[1] It is for these reasons, and infinite others that I omit because they do not belong in a letter, that it is nearly impossible to successfully create the kind of organization that is needed in a nation where everything remains to be done, where the very laws that govern it are ignored, and where it is hard to know what the laws are, because it is difficult to have rule of law and pick out useful laws from the mountains of those that have been passed or are dark and unmanageable, etc. etc. One might say that at least the government could channel its efforts toward reforming one of its branches, but the truth is that since the different administrative branches are so tangled together, it is not possible to organize only one; one must address all of the administrative branches at the same time.

Social order is maintained in Chile by *the weight of the night* and because we do not have men subtle, capable and sensitive enough, the masses' general tendency toward passivity is the guaranty of public tranquility. If this were not so, we would find ourselves in darkness and powerless to contain disruption, aside from the methods dictated by reason or those which experience has proven useful. Meanwhile, however, we will not find officials of this sort who understand and can expedite this plan, because they do not know their own prerogatives. . . . If, for any of the reasons I have mentioned, it becomes difficult or perhaps inconvenient to make substantial innovations in the administration of justice, see to it that the laws are better than they would be, correcting the abuses that are caused more by judges than by the laws themselves. In this way you will fulfill your position better than all the others who have come before you.

But enough about common things and of disturbing you with a letter in which you find nothing that you wanted.

I am happy that you have nothing new to report, and feel free to call upon your friend and Your Honor

D. Portales

Translated by Trevor Martenson

Note

1. Here Portales appears to be referring to the ongoing conflict between Peru and Bolivia over the formation of a confederated state, an initiative Chile viewed with hostility. The confederation would emerge several years later, sparking a Chilean declaration of war. The mastermind behind the war, Portales would be assassinated in a conspiracy associated with the conflict's critics.

A Political Catechism

Francisco Bilbao

The Portalian order remained dominant for much of the nineteenth century, and its legacies would persist longer still. But this autocratic vision of the republic did not go unopposed. A generation of liberal writers and intellectuals challenged the prevailing political structure and called for a more thoroughgoing democracy. This so-called Generation of '42 included journalists and poets, lawyers, engineers, and educators, whose work was both literary and political. A number of its members were Argentine and Uruguayan exiles, reflecting Chile's role as a cultural and intellectual center for those fleeing political repression elsewhere on the continent. One member of this generation, the writer Francisco Bilbao, became an icon of radical liberalism. In the 1840s he caused widespread scandal with his mordant critiques not just of the political system but of Chilean society in general. Radically anticlerical in an era when the Catholic Church enjoyed great political power and moral authority, Bilbao was excommunicated and found guilty of blasphemy and immorality. He fled to Paris, where he witnessed the liberal revolutions that swept Europe in 1848. Back in Chile, Bilbao helped found the Society of Equality, a crossclass movement of Chilean artisans and intellectuals whose purpose was the political education and social empowerment of the proletariat. When the Society was repressed by the conservative government, he again went into exile.

This fiery liberal is also remembered for his strong anti-imperialism—he denounced the United States' war with Mexico (1846–1848), in which Mexico lost over half of its national territory, as well as the French invasion of Mexico in 1862. Indeed, Bilbao concerned himself with political developments not only in Chile but also elsewhere in Latin America, including Peru and Argentina, where he spent time in exile.

The following excerpt is taken from his final work, The American Gospel (El evangelio americano), *published the year before he died in Argentina. Among his most famous works, it has been called a "political catechism" that proclaims individual and collective sovereignty and self-government to be the highest of moral and metaphysical ideals.*

Man of America, your honor is to be a republican, your glory is having won the Republic, your right to govern yourself is the Republic, and your duty is to always be a Republican. Never permit another government, nor another authority over yourself other than one's own authority of conscience, one's personal rule of individual reason, for that is the Republic, that is democracy, that is autonomy, that is what is called *Self-Government*.

And there is no other true government.

Why? Because man is sovereign.

If man is sovereign, there can be no other legitimate form of government than the one that consecrates, institutes and accomplishes the sovereignty of man.

If man is not sovereign, then monarchy, empire, theocracy, aristocracy, feudalism, priestly, military and propertied castes, all forms of tyranny and despotism are not only possible, but just.

Metaphysics or theology, morals or religion, politics or management, the economic system over property, work, credit, production, the sharing and consumption of wealth, all of these issues must be resolved in the same way: by recognizing the sovereignty of man or negating it.

The metaphysics or theology that negates freedom is the root of slavery.

The morals or religion that negate liberty are the morals and religion of slaves. The politics or management that negates the rights of government and management of all is the politics and management of exploitation and privilege. The distribution of property, the organization of work, and the sharing of products that negate freedom and the right to credit for all are feudalism, proletarianization, despotism, and misery.

Sovereignty is, then, the main criterion of all the social sciences. . . .

He who does not think must be a slave. In order to be free and sovereign, it is necessary to think for one's self because, by thinking for ourselves, we judge according to the eternal principles of truth and justice that constitute man's ability to reason. By thinking you govern yourself, and you are free.

By not thinking, others govern you and you are a servant of someone else's interests or thoughts. It is for this reason that justice, freedom and law are self-government, the individual sovereignty of each person. . . .

Do you understand now why all religious and political despotisms condemn and persecute free thought?

Do you understand now that there can be neither liberty, nor rights, nor justice without the absolute liberty of individual thought and that the freedom of thought and conscience is the basis of all liberty?

You understand now that, by thinking for yourself and having the right to govern yourself through your own ability to reason, you will judge if there is justice in your being forced to be a soldier, in making you work by necessity or by force without the just payment of your salary; you will judge if it is right that your work enriches the wealthiest, caring for their livestock at the mercy of all the elements, cultivating the land, felling the trees, digging up rocks in the mines, without even accumulating what is necessary to provide for your family and to avoid being a slave among men.

Then you will understand that you, just like the rich, the powerful and the learned, have rights to sovereignty and should occupy yourself and interest yourself in all that is called the exercise of the rights of citizenship. You have the vote. With the vote you can elect the one whom you know to be an honest man, who will represent you in making the law. It is for this reason that you should vote with your own mind because, otherwise, it will be another who makes the law that will make you a soldier, that will impose taxes upon you, that will do you justice or injustice. Today you have the vote to elect men who represent you, but don't forget that . . . it is you who could one day become a legislator.

These examples will make you understand the importance of the right of free thought. . . . Detest, as the lie should be detested, that doctrine that they call *blind obedience. Blind obedience* is the decapitation of freedom. . . .

Your own thought is the revelation or vision of the truth that God incarnated in all men.

Abdicating your thought is abdicating your sovereignty.

Self-government is the government of the truth and the law.

And as this law shines in all, all are sovereign. This is what is called equality. Attacking the sovereignty of another is violating the law by which you are sovereign. Respecting the sovereignty of those like you is your duty.

And as you love yourself, so should you love all men, they are like you, sovereign and brothers. Sons of the same father, enlightened by the same law, men should love each other, just as the ideal goodness and beauty of one's existence is loved. . . .

You know the law. There is no happiness without it; there is only degradation. Wealth without the possession of the law is anguish. Life without the law of sovereignty in each person is contempt. Being a slave out of ignorance is pardonable, but it does not absolve you of your negligence to think, of your neglect of innate dignity. . . .

Being a slave and legitimizing one's own slavery with sophisms, cowardly excuses or lies is to make oneself worthy of being a beast.

So, my brother, don't forget your sovereignty, don't lose heart under the weight of the conspiracy of all the interests of the malevolent. Your cause is the cause of God that made you sovereign. Your sovereignty is the sacrosanct religion that makes you worthy of recompense or punishment, of glory or ignominy, of being an agent and ally of the Supreme Being for the happiness of the land, or an agent and ally of the malevolent for the degradation and slavery of the human species. And one day you will have to answer to Eternal Justice about the use of your sovereignty. And that Justice will judge you with the law of your own thought, calling out: "You the free, those who have suffered for freedom, go to my right! Be the blessed ones of the Father. You the slaves, instruments of all tyranny, go to my left! Receive the punishment of purification."

Translated by John White

A Literature of Its Own: *Martín Rivas*

Alberto Blest Gana

Written in 1863 and extolled as Chile's first novel, Martín Rivas *captures the role of literature in the forging of the new Chilean nation. Its author, Alberto Blest Gana, served as the first literature professor at the University of Chile. In a speech on the occasion of his university appointment, he declared the importance of Chile having "a literature of its own, which corresponds to the progress already under way and which would contribute powerfully to propel it down this path of happy advances."[1]*

Published a few years later, Martín Rivas *embodies this purpose. Originally subtitled "a novel of politico-social customs," the tale is a period piece that captures the manners, customs, and politics of a crucial moment in the nation's historical development. The story takes place in Santiago in 1850–1851, when disaffected liberal intellectuals in alliance with artisans formed the Society for Equality, an organization promoting the "sovereignty of the people" against the conservative government. Blest Gana's politically active family had direct ties to these events; his brother, a poet, would be exiled due to his involvement in the rebellion. The novel narrates the romantic and social development of Martín Rivas, a young and poor but virtuous and ambitious provincial, who arrives from the north seeking the patronage of the wealthy Don Dámaso Encina, his father's former business associate. It is an intimate portrait of class aspirations, both individual and collective: through the character of Martín, the book narrates the triumphant rise of the Chilean bourgeoisie and emphasizes the unity that prevails among Chile's ruling class in spite of the serious political conflicts of the period. In following the twists and turns of Martín's unrequited love for Don Dámaso's beautiful but haughty daughter Leonor, the novel echoes the penchant of nineteenth-century Latin American novels for portraying national politics through the trope of romantic dramas. Ultimately, Martín's story ends happily in marriage—just like, Blest Gana seems to say, the unified Chilean upper classes and the new nation they sought to forge.[2] In this passage, the young hero has just appeared on his patron's doorstep.*

The stately manor where we have just seen Martín Rivas introduce himself was the home of Don Dámaso Encina, his wife, their 19-year-old daughter,

Santiago's Plaza de Armas, 1830s or 1840s, line drawing by the German artist Mauricio Rugendas. In one celebrated scene from *Martín Rivas*, aggressive shoe peddlers accost the young provincial when he wanders into the Plaza de Armas, the city's stately central plaza. The Plaza served as a focal point for commerce, public ritual, and social interaction. Line drawing by Mauricio Rugendas. Courtesy of Colección Sala Medina, Biblioteca Nacional de Chile.

23-year-old son, and three small children who were away at a French boarding school.

At the age of 24, Don Dámaso had married Doña Engracia Nuñez, more for social advancement than for love. Back then, Doña Engracia's want of beauty was compensated by an inheritance of 30,000 pesos, which so incited the passion of the young Encina that he asked for her hand in marriage. Don Dámaso was employed by a commercial lending house in Valparaíso, and his meager salary was all that lined his purse. However, the day after his wedding he had at his disposal 30,000 pesos with which to paint the town, and since then his ambitions knew no limit. Sent away on business by his employer, Don Dámaso arrived at Copiapó a month into his marriage. Good fortune allowed Encina, who was sent to collect on a rather small note, to meet an honest man who told him the following.

"You could shut me down because I have nothing to pay you. But if you'd like to gamble, I'll double this note and make you my equal partner in a silver mine that I'm sure will strike rich within a month."

[The honest debtor is Don José Rivas, Martín's father. Taking advantage of his precarious position, Encina makes a deal with him that allows him to buy Rivas's shares; months after buying him out, a silver strike makes Encina instantly rich while Rivas remains in penury.]

Thanks to Don José Rivas, the Encina family was counted among the most aristocratic families of Santiago.

In Chile money dispels family disrepute more readily than in old European societies. Over there they have what is called *nouveau riche*, who, in spite of all their pomp and luxury, never manage to crawl completely out of the obscurity of their cribs. But in Chile nowadays, all that matters is all that glitters. This is hardly a step toward democracy, however, because those who base their vanity upon blind favors of fortune usually adopt an insufferable insolence. They try to deny their obscure past and disdain those who, unlike themselves, cannot afford to purchase respectability.

The Encina family was noble in Santiago by pecuniary right and as such enjoyed the social courtesy extended them for the reasons we have just noted. They were notorious for their luxurious tastes, and their prestige was enhanced by Don Dámaso's solid credit, due to his main line of business— namely: that of grand scale usury so common among Chilean capitalists.

Their luxury served as a magnificent frame around the beautiful Leonor. . . . Leonor was the apple of her parents' eyes because she was the best-looking child (the criteria used by most parents), and they spoiled her from the start. She had long grown accustomed to viewing her splendor as a weapon of absolute dominion over those around her, including her own mother.

Doña Engracia, also born willful and headstrong, took great pride in the 30,000 pesos she had brought into the marriage, the origin of the wealth the family now enjoyed. However, now that she was gradually being eclipsed by her daughter's ascent, she began to treat the rest of the family with indifference and spared no one from her "cool treatment" except her darling little lap dog.

At the time this story began, the Encina family had just hosted a grand ball to welcome home Agustín, who had brought back hoards of clothes and jewels from the Old World (instead of knowledge, which he had not bothered to acquire during his trip abroad). His curly hair, charming grace, and perfect elegance could almost make up for the emptiness of his brain and the 30,000 pesos that he spent roaming the cobblestones of the major European cities. . . .

Agustín's return and some good business deals had predisposed Don Dámaso toward the benevolence with which he had welcomed Martín Rivas into his home. These circumstances had also distracted him from his preoccupation with hygiene, which he swore maintained his good health. He surrendered himself wholly to Politics, which incited his capitalist patriotism and fueled his vehement desire to hold a seat in the . . . Senate. . . .

[In the days after the conservative government's crackdown on the Society of Equality, a group of relatives and friends, gathered in the Encina household, discusses the turn of events.]

After the attack against the Society of Equality on the 19th, there were fiery debates about Politics in tertulias [social gatherings] everywhere. Don Dámaso Encina's salon was no exception on the night of August 21st, for his guests were completely engrossed in the rumors that Santiago would be declared a state of siege.

"The Government must take this measure at once," declared Don Fidel Elías.

"That would be ludicrous," replied his wife. "Francisca," Don Fidel replied adamantly, "how often must I tell you that women should stay out of Politics?

"It seems to me that Chilean Politics is not so enigmatic that it is beyond comprehension," she said.

"Take heed of what my compadre says," said . . . Don Simón, "for it is true that you cannot fathom a state of siege without having studied the Constitution."

This gentleman, considered to be a man of some capacity (for the dogmatism of his phrases and the eloquence of his silence), generally ruled upon the frequent squabbles between Doña Francisca and her husband, who then clucked, "Precisely, and the Constitution is the foundation of our Government and without it we wouldn't have a Government."

Don Dámaso lacked the nerve to back his sister in this controversy because his friends had convinced him, through the threat of a revolution, to support the Government. Doña Francisca told him, "Thanks for defending me. Oh, George Sand said it aptly: Woman is a slave."[3]

"But, dear, given the threat of revolution, I believe that it would be prudent . . ."

"Señor George Sand can say whatever he damn well pleases," interrupted

Don Fidel, looking for the approval of his compadre, "but the truth of the matter is that, without a state of siege, the Liberals will take over. Correct me if I am mistaken, compadre."

"It sounds like you fear those poor Liberals," exclaimed Doña Francisca, "as if they were the northern barbarians in [the] Middle Ages."

"Worse than the seven plagues of Egypt," said Don Simón in a pedagogic tone.

"To tell you the truth, I don't know what I would fear more," exclaimed Don Fidel, "the Liberals or the barbaric Araucano Indians because Francisca is mistaken when she says they are from the north."

"I was referring to barbarians from the Middle Ages," said the lady, miffed by the stubborn ignorance of her husband, who insisted, "No, no! Age has nothing to do with it because Araucano Indians have wee folks and old folks, the same as Liberals, but they're all a bunch of thieves, and if I were in power I would declare a state of siege."

"The state of siege is the basis of domestic tranquility, Don Dámaso, my friend," said Don Simón, seeing that the host was still ambivalent.

"I agree, I believe in Governments which secure tranquility," said Don Dámaso.

"But, sir," exclaimed Clemente Valencia, biting the tip of his gold-crowned walking stick, "they want to beat us into tranquility."

"*A coups de báton,*" said Agustín.

"That's the way it should be," replied Emilio Mendoza, who . . . blindly pledged his allegiance to the authorities. "The Government must show itself to be forceful."

"Otherwise, the Constitution would topple tomorrow morning," said Don Fidel.

"I believe the Constitution makes no mention of clubs," observed Doña Francisca, who could not resist the temptation to rebut her mate, who shouted, "Woman, woman! How many times must I tell you . . ."

"But, compadre," interrupted Don Simón, "the Constitution has its amendments, and one of them is military ordinance, which would cover such measures."

"You see what I was saying!" answered Don Fidel. "Have you read the ordinance?"

"But that ordinance refers to the military," objected Doña Francisca.

"Every attempt of opposition against Authority," argued Don Simón dogmatically, "should be considered a military transgression because resisting Authority requires arms, and, therefore, those who resist must be viewed as militant."

"You see," said Don Fidel, impressed by his compadre's logic.

Doña Francisca returned to Doña Engracia, who was petting Diamela [the lap dog], and said, "To argue with those reactionaries can make one's blood boil."

"I know what you mean, my darling, it's stuffy in here and I can hardly breathe," answered Doña Engracia, who, as we said before, suffered from apnea. Doña Francisca, silently cursing the stupidity of her sister-in-law, replied, "I was referring to the heat of these disputes."

"I know what you mean, my darling," she added, "and it's plumb dreadful. All day long my head is burning and my feet are freezing." . . .

Don Dámaso, finding himself alone with his wife, began to recite the Conservative ideas to which his friends had converted him by the end of their debate. He said, "After all, they have a point. What good has ever come from the Liberal party? And their point is well taken, because all over the world the rich have always sided with the Government. Take England, for example, where all of the Lords are rich."

Having thus reflected, he went to bed thinking that this direction would be the quickest way to Congress.

Translated by Tess O'Dwyer

Notes

1. Alberto Blest Gana, "Literatura chilena: Algunas consideraciones sobre ella," Discurso de incorporación a la Facultad de Humanidades, Universidad de Chile, 3 de enero de 1861, in *Anales de la Universidad de Chile*, 1861, 84.
2. Doris Sommer, *Foundational Fictions: The National Romances of Latin America* (Berkeley: University of California Press, 1991).
3. The French writer Amantine Lucile Aurore Dupin, better known by her pseudonym, George Sand, known for her transgressive behavior and defense of the rights of women and the working classes.

The University and the Nation

Andrés Bello

The University of Chile was "one of the most massive institutional works of the nineteenth century," according to the historian Sol Serrano. Inaugurated in 1843, the university served as "the spine of public education, of intellectual life, and of the formation of a ruling elite."[1] Its founding was a milestone not just in the development of Chilean education but in the modernization of Chilean society. The university's task was twofold: to cultivate scientific, technical, and humanistic knowledge and to form a class of enlightened citizens. As such, it represented a massive public investment in the political and economic progress of the nation.

The university's first rector was the jurist, philologist, poet, and statesman Andrés Bello, one of nineteenth-century Latin America's most important men of letters. In his inaugural address, Bello spoke of "the special tasks to which, in my opinion, our university faculties are called in the present state of the Chilean nation." In this excerpt, he discusses the importance of the university in society and the broad spectrum of learning and knowledge that it should foster. Challenging both liberals who saw no place for theology in the pursuit of knowledge and conservative Catholics suspicious of secular humanism, Bello argued for the wide-ranging inclusion of both theological and secular fields of study: humanistic, scientific, and practical. Above all, he suggested that the university be devoted to producing knowledge and learning, whether about statistics or poetry, that served the needs of the new nation.

As his address makes clear, the new, state-sponsored university was envisioned as an essential element of the formation of a modern Chilean nation. This idea of the university's mission would prove enduring; in some sense, it was a version of this principle that motivated the student-led protests for educational reform more than a century and a half later at the dawn of the twenty-first century.

Are universities, are literary bodies, the proper instruments for the diffusion of learning? I can hardly imagine how this question can be asked in an age which is so peculiarly an age of association and representation; in an age where societies for agriculture, trade, industry, and charity abound everywhere, in the age of representative governments. . . .

If the diffusion of knowledge is one of the most important functions of letters (for without it they will merely offer a few points of light among dense clouds of darkness), then the bodies chiefly responsible for the rapidity of literary communication confer essential benefits both on learning and on mankind. No sooner has a new truth sprung up in the mind of an individual than the whole republic of letters appropriates it. The scholars of Germany, of France, of the United States, recognize its value, its consequences, and its applications. In this propagation of knowledge each of the academies, the universities, forms a reservoir where all scientific acquisitions tend to accumulate continually; and it is from these centers that they most easily spill over into the different classes of society. The University of Chile has been established with this special aim in mind. If it is true to the intent of the legislation that has reorganized it, if it responds to the desires of our government, the university will be an eminently expansive and disseminative body.

Others claim that the encouragement given to scientific instruction ought to be given instead to primary education. Certainly, I am one of those who consider general instruction—the education for the people—as one of the most important and privileged aims to which a government can turn its attention. This is a primary and urgent need, the basis of all solid progress, the indispensable foundation of republican institutions. But for this very reason, I believe that the development of literary and scientific education is both necessary and urgent. Nowhere has the elementary instruction demanded by the working classes, who constitute the larger part of mankind, become general except in places where science and letters have previously flourished. . . .

The diffusion of knowledge involves one or more hearths from which light is emitted and spread; and this light, expanding little by little through the intervening spaces, will at last seep into the furthest levels of society. Making education universal requires a large number of carefully trained teachers, and the skills of these, the ultimate distribution of knowledge, are in themselves more or less distant emanations of the great scientific and literary depositories. Good teachers, good books, good methods, and good guidance of education are necessarily the work of a very advanced intellectual culture. Literary and scientific instruction is the source from which elementary teaching is nourished and brought to life, just as, in a well-organized society, the wealth of the class most favored by fortune is the wellspring from which flows the sustenance of the working classes and the people's welfare. . . .

The legislation that has reestablished the old university on new foundations, adjusted to the present state of civilization and the needs of Chile, indicates the great aims to which this faculty must be dedicated. . . .

Encouragement of the ecclesiastical sciences [theological studies], whose aim is to educate worthy ministers of religion and ultimately to provide an adequate religious and moral education to the population of the republic, is the first and most important of these objectives. But there is another aspect under which we must regard the university's dedication to the cause of morality and religion. While cultivation of the ecclesiastical sciences is important for the functioning of the sacerdotal ministry, it is also important to disseminate an adequate knowledge of the dogma and annals of the Christian faith among all the youth who participate in literary and scientific education. I do not think it necessary to prove that this must be an integral part of general education, indispensable for any profession and even for any man who aspires to occupy more than the humblest place in society.

The broadest field, and the one most susceptible to useful applications, opens before the schools of law and political science. You have heard it said that practical usefulness, positive results, social improvements, are what the government chiefly expects from the university; they are what must chiefly justify its efforts to the country. Heirs to the legislation of Spain, we must purge it of the blots that it acquired under the evil influence of despotism. We must sweep away the inconsistencies that mar a work to which so many centuries, so many alternately dominating interests, so many contradictory inspirations, have contributed. We have to adjust it, restore it to republican institutions. And what purpose can be more important, or grander, than the formation and perfecting of our basic laws, the swift and impartial administration of justice, the protection of our rights, the integrity of our commercial transactions, the peace of the domestic hearth? . . .

The university will also study the special features of Chilean society from an economic viewpoint, which presents problems that are no less vast and no less difficult. The university will develop the field of statistics, will examine the results of Chilean statistical figures, and will read in their numbers the expression of our material interests. For in this as in other branches of study, the university is entirely Chilean: if it borrows from Europe the deduction of science, it does so to apply them to Chile. All the paths that the work of its faculty and students must follow converge on one center—our country.

Following the same procedure, medicine will investigate the peculiar modifications that confer upon Chilean man his climate, his customs, and his nutrition. It will dictate the rules of private and public hygiene. It will spare no effort to extract from epidemics the secret of their germination and devastating activity, and, insofar as possible, it will encourage widespread knowledge of simple means of preserving and restoring health. Shall I now enumerate the positive uses of the mathematical and physical sciences, their applications to a nascent industry which has only a few simple, rude arts in operation, an industry that does not have clear procedures, that has no machines and none of the commonest tools? Shall I enumerate the applications of those sciences to a land crisscrossed by veins of metal, a soil fertile in vegetable wealth and foodstuffs, soil on which science has scarcely bestowed a passing glance? . . .

In the course of this very rapid review, ladies and gentlemen, how could I fail to mention, albeit briefly, the most enchanting of literary vocations, the aroma of literature, the Corinthian capital, so to speak, of cultivated society? Above all, how could I fail to mention the sudden excitement that has caused to appear on our horizon that constellation of youthful minds who cultivate poetry with such ardor? I will speak candidly: there are errors in their verses, and things in them that a severe and censorious mind condemns. But correctness is the result of study and years. Who can expect it from those who, in a moment of exaltation that is at once poetic and patriotic, have burst into this new arena, determined to prove that a divine fire, of which they thought themselves deprived by unjust prejudice, also burns in Chilean hearts? . . . I find in these works undeniable sparks of real talent, and in a few of them even true poetic genius. . . . To encourage our young poets, perhaps the university will say, "If you do not want your name to be confined between the Andes and the Pacific Ocean, too narrow an area for the ample aspirations of talent; if you want coming generations to read you, then study well, beginning with the study of your native language. Do more than this: write about subjects that are worthy of your country and posterity. . . . Let moral feeling throb in your works. . . . And has not our young republic already presented you with magnificent themes? Celebrate its great days; weave garlands for its heroes, consecrate the shroud of the country's martyrs." . . .

As a counterweight—on the one hand, to the servile docility that receive[s] everything without examining it; and on the other to the unbounded license that rebels against the authority of reason and against the purest and noblest instincts of the human heart—freedom will undoubtedly be the university's theme in all its different departments.

Translated by Frances M. López-Morillas

Note

1. Sol Serrano, *Universidad y nacion: Chile en el Siglo XIX* (Santiago: Editorial Universitaria, 1993), 15.

A Polish Scientist among the Mapuche

Ignacio Domeyko

During the first decades of Chilean nationhood, the Mapuche communities south of the Bío Bío River enjoyed an ambiguous status. Bernardo O'Higgins had granted them citizenship, but most Chileans considered them barbarians. As in the colonial period, their territories were politically autonomous from the Chilean state, yet ever-expanding encroachments by illegal settlers on their lands, whose value was increasing in an era of commercial agricultural expansion, constantly threatened the fragile peace.

Ignacio Domeyko was a Polish chemist and mineralogist who arrived in Chile in the late 1830s, contracted by the government as a teacher. He undertook various geological expeditions, including one in the 1840s to Araucanía, whose safe passage required the agreement of several caciques. In Araucanía Domeyko met with Mapuche leaders and observed lifeways and cultural practices. In an era of unapologetic ethnocentrism, his approach to Mapuche culture is striking for its humility: "It is by no means easy to write about the morality of a people without having lived with it and taken part in its fate, good and bad," he wrote. "I would not want to go down the path of those wandering writers who, at the first encounter with a man, already have a long dissertation ready about his heart and spirit."

When Domeyko's account of his travels was published in a Chilean newspaper in 1845, it inspired considerable controversy. Chile's posture toward the semiautonomous territory and its "savage" inhabitants was an open question, with some favoring military conquest and others peaceful assimilation through religious conversion and education. Domeyko argued squarely for the latter. While still considering the Mapuche barbarians, he dwelled on the many commonalities they shared with "civilized" peoples: their monotheism and respect for the cross, intrinsic moral sense, demeanor, domestic relations, and practice of sedentary agriculture. Domeyko's insistence on the essential humanity of the Mapuche was an important intervention at a time when many Chileans rejected such a claim. At least initially, his account helped convince authorities to pursue a nonmilitary policy of assimilation, although later in the century it would give way to a policy based on force.

Mapuche heroic and savage. Among the favorite subjects of Mauricio Rugendas, a prolific German painter resident in Chile in the 1830s and 1840s, were the Mapuche. He never actually traveled to Araucanía, and his paintings, like this one of a *malón*, or raid for the purpose of capturing slaves, often portray scenes from the colonial past. Here the kidnapping of a white woman reflects the barbarism of the Indians, but the scene also contains a strong romantic element that communicates the nobility of the Mapuche as well as their savagery. This juxtaposition captures Chileans' ambivalent sentiments toward the Mapuche at this time. Painting by Mauricio Rugendas. Courtesy of Colección Sala Medina, Biblioteca Nacional de Chile.

[The Araucanians] believe and always have believed in God, creator of the whole world, and in the immortality of the soul. Because they are men they have always been certain of the existence of God. They have the same assurances as we do, but not the same knowledge.

Missionaries have never entirely abandoned that country since the Spanish invasion. They have introduced the holy word of God and other terms that express the attributes of the Supreme Being into the Araucanian language. In contemporary times one finds old Indians, some with Christian names, and others who had been baptized in infancy, or descendants of parents or grandparents who had been baptized. And although these very same Indians often do not remember anything about Christianity except its name, every one of them, without exception, respects the cross, and they solemnly respect it without knowing what it means. In their graveyards they place crosses at the tombs of their rulers, and they also demand that a cross be placed to mark what has happened in their peace summits. As long as they see it, they have great fidelity and respect for it.

The Indian in times of peace is sensible, welcoming, apt to keep his word, grateful, protective of his own honor. His disposition and his manners are softer, and I would almost say more refined, at least on the exterior, than those of plebeians in many parts of Europe. He is serious and very formal in his manner, somewhat thoughtful, severe; and he knows how to respect authority, dispensing to each individual the corresponding deference and affection. But in general, [the Indians also] seem lazy, indulgent, given to drink and gambling. They carry everything to the extreme, to the point that from the breast of that calm, that peacefulness that makes them seem so impassive, they suddenly cede to a kind of tumultuous hurricane that issues from their breast, becoming enraged and their movements rapid and extreme.

There is absolutely no doubt that the Indian distinguishes between what is just and unjust, between goodness and malice, between generosity and baseness, like any other man endowed with a heart and soul. As a result of a sentiment governed either by natural intuition or by some obscure tradition, he carries a moral code in his spirit as if it were engraved there, and he is inclined to respect it as much as his brutal passions and inclinations— unchecked by any divine commandment or precept—permit.

Their houses are little states that enjoy so much independence and respect vis-à-vis one another that they appear to be capitals of distinct nations. Everything in them obeys the laws and old ceremonies: the threshold of the door is as feared and sacred as the frontier of a powerful empire.

Any guest of the dwelling of an Araucanian, whether neighbor or relative, does not dare to enter and must wait on his horse in front of a heavy beam that sits upon two or three poles, and serves to mark the patio. Nobody can cross it without the permission and knowledge of the owner. After it is known where the traveler comes from and what brings him, the careful women come out to sweep the patio and arrange it to receive the guest. Under the hallway, or under an arbor close to the door of the house, they place little benches covered with furs for the people of high rank and place sheep skins on the ground for everyone else in the group. And as soon as that task is over, the owner approaches his guests, extends his hand to each one of them, invites them to dismount from their horses, and almost without saying a word, shows them to their seats and sits down in front of them in an always pensive, formal, and strangely serious manner. . . .

Order, severity, and discipline appear to rule within the family. Children obey their parents and the women are busy; some taking care of their children, and others in the kitchen, while others are constantly spinning yarn and weaving clothes.

The Chilean Indian is a farmer. He farms because of his character, the physical nature of the country, his nature and customs. In this regard he is different from the Pehuenches and other transandean tribes who are shepherds, nomads, true scavengers whose leather tents move like thick clouds of locusts. The peaceful Araucanian has a well-built, large, spacious house. It is about twenty or more yards long, eight to ten wide, and is well insulated against the wind and rain. It is tall and built from good wood, coligüe,[1] and hay, with only one door and a hole in the highest part of the roof to let the smoke out. Next to the house there are gardens and fields of wheat, barley, corn, garbanzos, potatoes, flax, and cabbage, all well cultivated and fenced off. And as the habitations are usually near some river or creek, around them one can see quite open lands and flowery meadows where the Indian keeps horses and his fat and beautiful cattle, though they are not as abundant here as on the Chilean haciendas. . . .

We will add to this that these Indians make their pots, pitchers, and large jugs from clay that is so abundant in the Araucanian territories. They usually make them of the same shape and size as the old pots and little pitchers that chance discovered among the tombs of the Indians in Northern Chile, Peru, and Bolivia. They also skillfully make wooden plates, spoons, and bowls, while their women weave very durable, soft, and cozy wool products that they dye with long-lasting colors. Finally, there are among them silversmiths who produce, albeit in a crude and rude manner, spurs and diverse ornaments for bits, gear, and breast collars for horses. . . .

As much as one ponders the energy, patriotism, and civic virtues of this nation, one can not ignore the sad signs in it that prove the degradation of the Araucanian state since the Conquest.

These signs are apparent first in the lack of political unity and in the extinction of the moral necessity that compels a nation to centralize its forces and power while the energy and will to work abound. There are no longer those meetings where chiefs from every tribe would discuss the well-being of the state and the election of its chiefs. The names of past authorities . . . have disappeared. The frontier lands have been sold or rented, changing the political divisions of the territory. Today the entire nation can be found divided up among the authority of the rulers, whose numbers have increased over the years to the point that now there are some who barely govern ten or twelve families in their district. The majority has inherited this title, but there are others who gained it from the Chilean government as reward for their services to the Republic against their brothers. Some of them are still rich and own a lot of land as well as many cattle and horses while others, to the contrary, are hardly distinguishable from the rest of the village. None has enough power or prestige to enforce his jurisdiction in times of peace and cannot always gather his vassals in times of war. Only an imminent danger, the invasion of territory or a mortal vengeance, could unite the citizens and awaken in them the ancient spirit.

But what better proof of the *political* decadence of that people who constitute a nation and of the disposition which must be found to unite them with the Chileans, than their conduct in the war for Chilean independence . . . ? There were some people here who fought for the king and others for the nation, while still others fought for the spoils of war and some who remained neutral throughout, but nobody thought to take advantage of the times to assure old Araucanía's independence. . . .

Another sign of this decline, or at least of the disappearance of the old moral idea that inspired in those people the fire and extreme zeal for liberty and for the independence of their territory, is the almost total extinction of ancient traditions surrounding the most eminent deeds and heroes of their history. . . . Nobody among them today knows who the diligent Lautaro, the wise Colocolo, the intrepid Caupolicán were, as they only live on in the memory and poetry of Christians.[2]

The pride of the old Arauco has been eclipsed. The prudent policies of the Spanish tamed it. Many of the rulers became used to receiving gifts that were more fatal weapons for the barbarian chest than the hard steel of the damask sword of Castille. Familiar with their contemporary state of decadence, some receive a miserable salary from their old enemies. Others are happy to accept overalls, shirts, or staffs as signs of the little authority they hold in exchange for their humiliation. Others uselessly desire the same favors, which they are denied because they are not as fearsome. . . .

Should the Chilean nation maintain [its] passive attitude regarding its brothers and limit itself to the show of force when its obligations call for it to take on a different task, more sacred and civilizing?

The main objective of the *pacification* of Indians must not, of course, be to make them good merchants, artisans, and manufacturers. Nor must it be to make them forget how to fire weapons, intimidate them, or feminize them with luxury and easy living. It must not be to make them poor so that they become submissive. The objective must be none other than to reform those ideas, customs, and inclinations of the Indian people that most stand in the way of their *true civilization*. And now, if we do not look for the main elements to do this in religion and divine light, how will we make the Indian freely and voluntarily give up his life of *revelries* and *drunken binges*, and his witches and fortunetellers? Why would he give up his laws of vengeance and his *natural* right to harm his enemy without submitting to adjudication? And with what arguments, promises, or reasoning would we make him emancipate his women, children, and slaves? And as long as these laws and customs exist, could an Indian call himself Chilean?

Translated by Ryan Judge

Notes

1. A native bamboo species.
2. Here Domeyko refers to a series of storied sixteenth-century Mapuche leaders who were immortalized perhaps most famously in Alonso de Ercilla's epic poem *The Araucaniad* (see part II).

German Immigrants in the South

Vicente Pérez Rosales

Discussions of Chilean nationhood in the 1850s raised many issues, among them the controversial topic of foreign immigration. While some saw European immigration as a means of civilizing and modernizing the young nation, others thought that immigrants, particularly Protestant ones, threatened Chilean cultural habits and religion.

The civil servant, statesman, and adventurer Vicente Pérez Rosales became one of the best known of the proimmigration advocates. Pérez Rosales worked as a colonization agent and consul in Germany and wrote treatises to persuade prospective immigrants to seek their fortunes in Chile. Believing that industrious Europeans would draw the south out of its barbaric languor, he was single-minded in his efforts to establish a German colony at Llanquihue and Valdivia, a remote area separated from the rest of the country by the autonomous Mapuche territories to their north. In his memoirs Pérez Rosales describes his tireless efforts to establish a community of new immigrants, to obtain land for them, and to defend them from fellow Chileans who opposed their presence or simply hoped to take advantage of them to make a buck. He describes the vexing situation of property rights in the south and how he readily engaged in legal sleights of hand to wrest lands from Chilean and Mapuche inhabitants in order to provide for "his" Germans. Finally, his zealous ministrations call attention to the extraordinary environmental changes wrought by colonization. Pérez Rosales pays an Indian guide to burn huge tracts of native forest to prepare the land for settlement. This was the first of a series of deliberate conflagrations that would destroy native forest stands and irreparably alter the temperate rain forests of the south.

Before I came to Valdivia, people in the north had such a low opinion of the agricultural production of this province that they believed that not even wheat could be grown there, when in the granaries . . . the weevils were eating the wheat, because what little was grown was more than enough for local consumption and there was no way to export the surplus. . . . Pretty much all of those fields, so productive now and so little prized then, were

The Plaza de Armas of Valdivia around 1865, shortly after the settlement of German colonists. Courtesy of Colección Museo Histórico Nacional de Chile.

held in common, whether by the descendants of the Spaniards or by those of the natives, who still considered themselves the legitimate owners of everything. . . . When a citizen wanted to become the sole proprietor of some communal land, all he had to do was look for the nearest Indian chief, get him drunk, or get his agent to get drunk along with the Indian, and supply the chief and his people cheap liquor and an occasional peso; that was enough to let him appear before a notary with a seller and witnesses, or declarations under oath, to certify that what was being sold lawfully belonged to that seller. . . .

This was the state of affairs when somnolent Valdivia was roused from its habitual lethargy by the news that the bark *Hermann,* proceeding from Hamburg, had reached Corral after a one hundred and twenty days' journey, with eighty-five German passengers on board: seventy men, ten women, and five children. . . .

The [German] immigrants . . . were not Japanese coolies drawn to leave their country by the wages we paid our day laborers; quite the contrary, they and their successors were all more or less well-off tradesmen [who desired] to buy lands that before their arrival had been considered totally worthless. . . .

In four short months . . . eight German houses were going up in the village of Valdivia on lots bought at inflated prices; and two rural properties, equally bought for cash, were receiving the baptism of European cultivation, the first to do so in the vicinity of town. . . . Among the immigrants came men of caliber . . . , tradesmen and manufacturers such as had never come to Chile, and many capitalists, who on their own account or in the name of European companies came to acquire lands on which to establish colonies. Immigration was, thus, for Valdivia a beneficent visit from learning, arts, and material wealth, coming to rouse it from its stagnation. . . .

[Pérez Rosales sets out in search of suitable land to make available to the immigrants.]
A methodological investigation convinced me that I should find what I wanted only in the very heart of the immense virgin forest that begins at Ranco and covers the extensive base of the Andes until its roots plunge into the salty waters of Reloncaví Bay.

Only the Indians could supply any significant information about this dark region, since it was impossible to enter it other than on foot, clearing a narrow path with a machete through dense foliage, only to have it soon wiped away by the vigor of the vegetation and the falling of dead branches. . . .

We spent the night in a place they called El Burro; and at dawn of the following day we penetrated on foot, and more by dint of determination than of physical strength, into a five-league-wide strip of forest so dense that in its shade we could not even read our maps. Tangled roots, thorny bushes, thickets of *quila* shrubs joined to the tree trunks with mighty lardizabala vines, and the muddy ground where we constantly sank into puddles camouflaged by decaying leaves, all offered determined resistance to our advance. . . .

All our discomfort and exhaustion, however, turned into joyful enthusiasm when we suddenly left the dark domain of the forest and without any transition saw the most splendid panorama stretch before us. . . . [I] found myself on the western shore of the great Lake Llanquihue. As with a sea, mists hid the northern and southern limits of the clear calm waters that seemed to be playing at my feet among the roots of the sturdy trees that bordered the beach where we had stopped. In the pure air to the east, the most delicate traces of the last snows that crowned the heights of Pullehue, Osorno, and Calbuco contrasted with the blue of the sky. . . . The thick muddy humus that covered all the land I had been traversing so clearly showed the benefit that agriculture could draw from this place that despite tiredness and lack of provisions, I determined not to return without first exploring this interesting country for at least another couple of days.

I was accompanied by one Juanillo or Pichi-Juan, a drunken native, celebrated for his knowledge of the most hidden forest paths and also as a genealogist ready to declare which of his ancestors had been the owners of the lands that the Valdivians used to purloin. . . . As I traveled I offered Pichi-Juan thirty days' wages, which at the time meant thirty pesos, to burn the forests between Chanchán and the mountains; and then I returned to Valdivia to soothe the discontent that was beginning to come over the immigrants, who did not know what to do with themselves in the provisional lodgings where, lacking lands, I had left them.

Immediately on my arrival I distributed the vacant lands of Osorno and La Unión, which cheered them all. I was also pleased to see that many of the wealthier immigrants had bought lots and farms in the neighborhood of Valdivia and that, encouraged by my reports, they were preparing to do the same farther inland, trusting that the roads I had promised them in the government's name would soon be built. . . .

The sun's disk, always unclouded when it appears [in Valdivia], had now been veiled for three months, which is how long Pichi-Juan had been burning the forests. As soon as the fire had died down I had to undertake another and more leisurely exploration of the area that it had laid open in the department of Osorno, and I therefore made a delightful expedition through all the land that lies to the north of Lake Llanquihue. The average width of the burned area was five leagues, and its depth, fifteen. All of it was level and of the best quality. The fire, which had so long devastated those impassable thickets, had whimsically drawn back from some stands of trees, as though the hand of Providence had deliberately spared them so that settlers, in addition to clear soil, might have wood for construction and the necessities of life. . . .

[*Stymied by local authorities, Pérez Rosales resorts to legal subterfuge to secure title over these lands for the immigrants.*]

My annoyance and surprise were . . . considerable when I found a letter from the governor . . . in which I was informed that if I wanted to found settlements in Cayenel I had to begin by buying that land, because all of it had lawful owners. Under the circumstances, if I hesitated I was lost; requesting funds from the government meant delay and no assurance of success, and bringing suit meant entering into a world without end. I thus resigned myself and began by buying the site of the future town and the immediate surroundings out of my own pocket; and taught by example and experience, I fought the squatters with their own arms by setting up simulated purchases from the Indians, the presumed owners of the vast territory of Chanchán. These purchases and another levy of six hundred duros [pesos] extracted from my puny purse allowed me to calm the storm.

Translated by John H. R. Polt

The Beagle Diary: "A Peculiar Race of Men"

Charles Darwin

In the 1830s, the naturalist Charles Darwin embarked on his storied multicontinent voyage on the Beagle. The observations collected during that expedition later gave rise to the theory of evolution. Toward the beginning of the trip, Darwin spent time in various parts of Chile, including Tierra del Fuego, the central valley, and the north, before continuing on to Peru, Ecuador, and of course the Galapagos Islands.

In this selection from Darwin's travel diary, he describes his visit to copper and gold mines. The Portalian political order taking shape at this time had as its economic basis the growing wealth generated by mining. Chile's mines were already well known to foreign entrepreneurs and of increasing interest to them. Darwin's own interest, however, lay in geology and in the methods used for extracting ore. Most Chilean mines at the time relied not on steam power but on brute human strength to lift ore up to the earth's surface. Darwin's diaries vividly portray the excruciating physical exertion required to perform these tasks.

The labouring men work very hard. They have little time allowed for their meals, and during summer and winter they begin when it is light, and leave off at dark. They are paid one pound sterling a month, and their food is given them: this for breakfast consists of sixteen figs and two small loaves of bread; for dinner boiled beans; for supper broken roasted wheat grain. They scarcely ever taste meat; as, with the twelve pounds per annum, they have to clothe themselves, and support their families. The miners who work in the mine itself, have twenty-five shillings per month, and are allowed a little charqui.[1] But these men come down from their bleak habitations only once in every fortnight or three weeks.

During my stay here I thoroughly enjoyed scrambling about these huge mountains. The geology, as might have been expected, was very interesting. The shattered and baked rocks, traversed by innumerable dykes of greenstone, showed what commotions had formerly taken place there. . . .

We slept at the gold-mines of Yaquil, which are worked by Mr. Nixon, an American gentleman. . . .

When we arrived at the mine, I was struck by the pale appearance of many of the men, and inquired from Mr. Nixon respecting their condition. The mine is 450 feet deep, and each man brings up about 200 pounds weight of stone. With this load they have to climb up the alternate notches cut in the trunks of trees, placed in a zigzag line up the shaft. Even beardless young men, eighteen and twenty years old, with little muscular development of their bodies (they are quite naked excepting drawers) ascend with this great load from nearly the same depth. A strong man, who is not accustomed to this labour, perspires most profusely, with merely carrying up his own body. With this very severe labour, they live entirely on boiled beans and bread. They would prefer having the latter alone; but their masters, finding they cannot work so hard upon this, treat them like horses, and make them eat the beans. Their pay is here rather more than at the mines of Jajuel, being from 24 to 28 shillings per month. They leave the mine only once in three weeks; when they stay with their families for two days. One of the rules in this mine sounds very harsh, but answers pretty well for the master. The only method of stealing gold, is to secrete pieces of the ore, and take them out as occasion may offer. Whenever the major-domo finds a lump thus hidden, its full value is stopped out of the wages of all the men; who thus, without they all combine, are obliged to keep watch over each other.

When the ore is brought to the mill, it is ground into an impalpable powder; the process of washing removes all the lighter particles, and amalgamation finally secures the gold dust. The washing, when described, sounds a very simple process; but it is beautiful to see how the exact adaption of the current of water to the specific gravity of the gold, so easily separates the powdered matrix from the metal. The mud which passes from the mills is collected into pools, where it subsides, and every now and then is cleared out, and thrown into a common heap. . . .

It is curious to find how the minute particles of gold, after being scattered about, and from not corroding, at last accumulate in some quantity. A short time since a few miners, being out of work, obtained permission to scrape the ground round the house and mill: they washed the earth thus got together, and so procured thirty dollars' worth of gold.

. . . .

We proceeded to Los Hornos, another mining district, where the principal hill was drilled with holes, like a great ants' nest. The Chilian miners are in their habits a peculiar race of men. Living for weeks together in the most desolate spots, when they descend to the villages on feast-days, there

Tres puntas.—Apires de la mina Buena Esper nza.

Workers at the Buena Esperanza mine, Atacama. This image of a mine in a different region from and several decades after Darwin's account nevertheless portrays *apires* (mining peons) in a similar light, with an emphasis on the physical exertions of workers weighed down by heavy loads. Behind them several upright figures, evidently of a higher occupational and social status, intently observe their work. From *Chile ilustrado*, by Recaredo S. Tornero (Valparaíso: Agencias del Mercurio, 1872). Courtesy of Colección Archivo Fotográfico, Biblioteca Nacional de Chile.

is no excess or extravagance into which they do not run. They sometimes gain a considerable sum, and then, like sailors with prize-money, they try how soon they can contrive to squander it. They drink excessively, buy quantities of clothes, and in a few days return penniless to their miserable abodes, there to work harder than beasts of burden. This thoughtlessness, as with sailors, is evidently the result of a similar manner of life. Their daily food is found them, and they acquire no habitual care as to the means of subsistence: moreover, at the same moment that temptation is offered, the means of enjoying it is placed in their power. On the other hand, in Cornwall, and some other parts of England, where the system of selling part of the vein is followed, the miners, from being obliged to act for themselves, and to judge with clearness, are a singularly intelligent and well-conducted set of men.

The dress of the Chilian miner is peculiar and rather picturesque. He wears a very long shirt, of some dark-coloured baize, with a leathern apron; the whole being fastened round his waist by a brightly-coloured sash. His trousers are very broad, and his small cap of scarlet cloth is made to fit the head closely. We met a party of these miners in full costume, carrying the body of one of their companions to be buried. They marched at a very quick trot, four men supporting the corpse. One set having run as hard as they could for about two hundred yards, were relieved by four others, who had previously dashed on ahead on horseback. Thus they proceeded, encouraging each other by wild cries: altogether the scene formed a most strange funeral.

. . . .

Captain Head has described the wonderful load which the "Apires,"[2] truly beasts of burden, carry up from deep mines. I confess I thought the account exaggerated; so that I was glad to take the opportunity of weighing one of the loads, which I picked out by hazard. It required considerable exertion on my part, when standing directly over it, to lift it from the ground. The load was considered under weight when found to be 197 pounds. The apire had carried this up eighty perpendicular yards,—part of the way by a steep passage, but the greater part up notched poles, placed in a zigzag line in the shaft. According to the general regulation, the apire is not allowed to halt for breath, except the mine is six hundred feet deep. The average load is considered as rather more than 200 pounds, and I have been assured that one of 300 pounds (twenty-two stone and a half) by way of a trial has been brought up from the deepest mine! At this time the apires were bringing up the usual load twelve times in the day; that is, 2400 pounds from eighty yards deep; and they were employed in the intervals in breaking and picking ore.

These men, excepting from accidents, are healthy, and appear cheerful. Their bodies are not very muscular. They rarely eat meat once a week, and never oftener, and then only the hard dry charqui. Although with a knowledge that the labour is voluntary, it was nevertheless quite revolting to see the state in which they reached the mouth of the mine; their bodies bent forward, leaning with their arms on the steps, their legs bowed, the muscles quivering, the perspiration streaming from their faces over their breasts, their nostrils distended, the corners of their mouth forcibly drawn back, and the expulsion of their breath most laborious. Each time, from habit, they utter an articulate cry of "ay-ay," which ends in a sound rising from deep in the chest, but shrill like the note of a fife. After staggering to the pile of ores, they emptied the "carpacho;"[3] in two or three seconds recovering their breath, they wiped the sweat from their brows, and apparently quite fresh descended the mine again at a quick pace. This appears to me a wonderful instance of the amount of labour which habit (for it can be nothing else), will enable a man to endure.

Notes

1. Beef jerky.
2. Mining peons who carry loads of ore to the surface.
3. *Carpacho* (or *capacho*)—a leather sling used to transport the ore.

How to Run an Hacienda

Manuel José Balmaceda

The hacienda, or great landed estate, was the backbone of Chilean rural society in the nineteenth century. The expansion of commercial agriculture encouraged Chilean landowners to rationalize administration and production on their properties. This guidebook, written by Manuel José Balmaceda, a very wealthy landowner and father of the future president José Manuel Balmaceda, reflects that impulse. Originally intended as informal instructions for his children when they took over the family properties, it was eventually published and appears to have circulated among other hacendados, having been found in the family papers of at least one. As the publisher noted in the manual's foreword, the Handbook *rendered "an important service" to the country's landowners because "the permanent conditions of our soil, our social way of being, and Chileans' customs and practices in the countryside" made European agricultural guides of limited value in Chile.*

The handbook provides meticulous instructions for running an estate, from advice on daily agricultural tasks to accounting techniques. In this section, the author discusses the management of the hacienda's workers, which included a panoply of ranch hands, cowherds, muleteers, shepherds, wheelwrights, service tenants, foremen, and overseers. But the most important distinction was between peons—hired day laborers—and inquilinos, *resident service tenants, who worked for the estate in exchange for access to land to cultivate their own crops. Balmaceda's instructions reveal the social and occupational hierarchies on haciendas, for example between those who worked on horseback (de a caballo) and those on foot (de a pie) and between different categories of inquilinos. He also dwells on how to discipline errant workers, hinting at tensions that must have been endemic to everyday life on the estates. Finally, he provides a glimpse into the importance of women's work to the functioning of the hacienda. If women's labor was often invisible from the outside, the manual suggests that landowners themselves were well aware of its value and eager to fold it into the many obligations that tenant households owed them.*

In the early 1970s, land reform policies sparked an interest in the history and sociology of the Chilean hacienda. In this context, Balmaceda's Handbook *gained a*

CARRETERO. CAPATAZ.

Portrait of rural workers, 1840s. The wheelwright and foreman are two of the many occupational categories discussed in Balmaceda's *Handbook*. The French naturalist Claudio Gay left many evocative scenes of rural life in Chile in the 1840s. Illustration by Claudio Gay, "Carretero y Capataz" from *Atlas de la historia física y política de Chile,* by Claudio Gay (Paris: Imprenta de E. Thunot, 1854). Courtesy of Colección Biblioteca Nacional de Chile.

second life he could not have foreseen. Republished by land reform advocates, it was
held up as evidence of the backwardness of rural social relations.

Every day before dawn, with the exception of holidays, the head caretaker
should ring the bell thirty times to wake up the peons and summon them
to work. Before the sun rises, he should distribute to the assistant caretakers the tools and implements needed for each job, along with the workers'
mid-morning and lunch rations. The peons should spend the time between
daybreak and sunrise feeding and giving water to the animals with which
they will be working. . . .

Before commencing any task, the head caretaker or, in his absence, one
of his assistants, should explain to the peons the work corresponding to
them and exhort them to work hard and well, with no need to scold them
repeatedly.

A peon's mid-morning ration is one-fifteenth an *almud*[1] of flour, or one
slice of bread out of the fifteen that would produce the same measurement.
The lunch ration is one-fifteenth an almud of beans or corn, since each almud consists of fifteen rations. If a dinner ration falls under the terms of the
peon's work agreement, it will be the same as either the mid-morning meal
or lunch—whichever the landowner deems most appropriate.

Work begins at sunrise. There is a half-hour break at nine in the morning
for the peons to have their mid-morning ration. There is another break at
noon for the same amount of time for lunch, with no further breaks until
the sun has fully set. . . .

Any peon who arrives at his worksite after sunrise should either not be
allowed to work that day or be punished by having his day's wages cut by
one-third or one-fourth, depending on how late he is.

Any peon who does not work as quickly as he should, fails to do his
job correctly, or acts in a disrespectful manner should be thrown off his
assignment.

Any peon who encourages others to be insubordinate so that they refuse to work unless paid a certain price or demand more food or a decrease
in work hours should be severely punished and even thrown off the hacienda. . . .

Any peon caught idle during work hours will lose one-fourth that day's
wages on first offense. If caught a second time he will lose half that day's
wages and on third offense, the whole day's pay.

If a peon, despite the caretaker's instructions, does his job incorrectly out
of negligence or ill will and thus causes some damage, that damage will be
taken out of his wages.

Any peon suspected of illicit behavior should be taken to the police immediately with an accompanying report detailing what is known of him and should not be allowed back on the hacienda until his return is duly justified. . . .

Peons should be forbidden from and severely punished for mistreating animals.

Peons must pay for any implements or tools lost or broken out of carelessness or misuse; the same applies to those that are lost or broken by assistant caretakers. . . .

The head caretaker should ensure that his assistants are present when food is distributed so that it is doled out equally and in due abundance; if any complaints are lodged regarding improper distribution, the cook should be punished.

If there are peons working far from the general group, their food should be brought to them in order to avoid wasting time. . . .

Peons not living on the hacienda should not be assigned to do house-related work; this work should correspond to the most trusted *inquilinos.* . . .

As a matter of habit up until this point, the term *inquilino* has only been used to refer to those persons living on the estate who do not receive daily wages, who provide their services without pay or, to give a better definition: all those who are not head caretakers, vice or assistant caretakers, foremen, cowhands, horse wranglers or any other kind of estate employee normally hired to work on a year-by-year basis and known as field hands.

Inquilinos are hands indebted to the hacienda owner to carry out all manner of work.

According to the current system, inquilinos can be divided into three types or sections. [The first are] inquilinos on horseback: these have some assets of wealth to their name, are more respectable and honorable, and carry out all the hacienda's services performed on horseback, among others of no lesser importance.

On estates of a certain size where it is useful to have inquilinos on horseback, these should not be given more than a pasture large enough for ten or twelve horses or cows and twenty-five sheep; enough land to sow four *fanegas*[2] of wheat; and about half a *cuadra*[3] to farm.

In order for the inquilino to pay back these benefits to the hacienda, he must provide: one peon on horseback for rodeos, grazing and other services; one peon on horseback for trips outside the estate, who will be paid twenty-five cents per ten leagues traveled; one peon for all fence repairs and canal cleaning, to whom the hacienda will provide food; one peon for sowing—but only up to 300 fanegas, beyond which the hacienda will pay him extra; one peon on horseback for threshing and grain-heaping to whom the hacienda will provide mid-morning meals and lunch, as well as dinner if he sleeps on the threshing floor; and one peon paid the same amount as the inquilinos, who work on foot, for any necessary work on the estate. . . .

He must also spend one day and night helping around the houses whenever it is his turn to fulfill that shift.

The second type or category is inquilinos who work on foot also known as "half-obligation" tenants. . . . These are given a pasture large enough for just two to four horses or cows and twelve sheep. In some cases, this allotment may also include enough land to sow one or two fanegas of wheat, as well as a small section to farm that should not exceed a quarter cuadra.

This type of inquilino can provide the following services: (1) Provide one peon on horseback, just like those mentioned for the first type, for round-ups, grazing, threshing, grain-heaping, and housework shifts. (2) Carry out short-distance errands on his own mounts if he has them, or on those belonging to the hacienda, without receiving any wages for that day's work. (3) Provide one peon daily for any manner of job on the hacienda; this peon should be paid the ordinary daily wages and the inquilino has no right whatsoever to raise them, though he may lower them by a maximum of two-thirds. (4) If there is a lot of work that needs to be done, the inquilino will be required to provide one more peon and put all those who live in his house to work; they will be paid the same amount as the peons from outside the hacienda.

The third type or category is peon-inquilinos. These have only housing and a small piece of land no greater than forty yards to raise chickens and grow vegetables when there is water to do so.

Their obligations are as follows: (1) Do housework shifts for free. (2) When needed, help with roundups once a week; in this case, the hacienda will provide mid-morning meals and lunch. (3) Provide one peon daily throughout the whole year who is paid the ordinary daily wages, just like those mentioned for the second type of inquilino. (4) Carry out any unforeseen services not considered a formal job. (5) Put all the peons who live with him to work when the hacienda needs them for the same day's wages that a peon from outside the hacienda would receive.

Women are also useful for many tasks and jobs; if not those in the first category of inquilinos, then at least those in the second and third categories should be required to knead bread; prepare food for the work crews; milk the animals; make butter and cheese; shear; sew and mend sacks; work in the grain shed to help winnow; sweep; sow and harvest, among many other things in which not only are they useful, but they perfectly substitute men and even do a better job. Each woman's salary and day's wages should be arranged in proportion to the amount the men are earning, unless some other form of compensation should become habitual.

It is not possible to excuse women from working because in periods when peons are scarce the landowner would have to delay work otherwise. Moreover, the benefits of having women earn a living are well known: their small incomes constitute a burden for inquilinos, so everyone's condition ultimately improves when they all join their efforts together.

Translated by Rachel Stein

Notes

1. An obsolete unit of measurement that varied according to the time period and region in use. In Chile, one *almud* would be equivalent to about 7.34 dry quarts.
2. An obsolete unit traditionally used to measure agricultural areas, equivalent to 0.66 hectares.
3. Another unit used by farmers to measure surface area, which varies by country but is equivalent to about 0.64 hectares.

A Franco-Chilean in the California Gold Rush

Pedro Isidoro Combet

The discovery of gold in central California at the end of the 1840s reverberated far beyond North America. News of the strikes arrived via ships docking at Valparaíso and was disseminated via sometimes sensational local press accounts. Almost immediately, Chileans began to embark on the two-month Pacific voyage to the gold fields, first in a trickle and then in a steady stream. As one paper noted, California is "the theme of the day, the conversation topic of all idle people, the goal of all who wish fortune, the thought of merchants and even the conversation topic for ladies."[1]

All told, at least 4,000–5,000 Chileans traveled to California. The well-heeled among them formed mining companies and contracted the plentiful peons who roamed Chile's central valley, paying their travel expenses. But in California Chileans encountered national, ethnic, and religious prejudice, which sometimes turned violent—most notoriously in an attack on the settlement of "Little Chile," near Telegraph Hill in San Francisco, in July 1849.

Pedro Isidoro Combet was a French printer and bookbinder resident in Santiago. Like others, he was caught up in gold fever and in 1851 traveled to California, where he stayed for a year. Upon his return a Santiago newspaper published his "Memories of California," an account that revealed the author's keen eye and dry wit. Combet renders with skill and humor the textures of California's rough-and-tumble frontier society of peoples of different nationalities, ethnicities, and religions. He portrays with perceptiveness how the social pretensions and class hierarchies that Chileans brought with them could be abruptly—and humorously—upended in this environment. In this selection the bookbinder, several months into his stay, contemplates his options for striking it rich—or perhaps just making a living.

I was due back in Chile with a fortune by this time (*El Mercurio* of Valparaíso had promised I'd have one). I put my intellectual faculties to work to see whether I could find an honorable way to make some money.

A man's industrial knowledge had the fullest scope [in California]. Everything was still to be done. This society was not like the sluggish and decrepit ones we had left behind in other countries, in which half the population lives on the sweat of the other half, where you have only to put a pair of glasses on your nose to have people point to you and say, "There is a wise man." In California they do not look at a young man with a pale bald forehead and say, "This is a poet." Instead they would say, "There is a poor fellow who ought to be in the hospital. Why didn't he stay at home in his own country?" A bad journalist or magazine writer who put the pompous words, "Literary Man," on his calling cards would die of hunger. Why?

The reason is that society does not recognize any kind of competence except the practical, industrial sort. If one went to them with a beautiful translation of Homer or Virgil in one's hand they would say, "Those were good men, no doubt, but they must have been stupid to waste all that time writing. We need some cabbage; have you got any to sell?" What can a man with an education say to that? What he had better do is plant cabbage and carrots. That is how I got to meet, on several occasions, some very distinguished writers for the French or Chilean press: buying lettuce or parsley.

The gentleman who brought peons from Mexico or Chile had to call them "my boys," and see to it that they got plenty of suet and chili in their food; otherwise they might have abandoned him—and he would have been helpless if he had to handle a pick and shovel himself. Merchants in California were not very different from miners; they wore the same wool shirts, were friendly and amiable with their customers, and offered a glass of brandy to workers and sailors when they came in to buy (and paid them very well in addition). . . .

Such was the society in which I found myself mingling in San José. I had to forget about writing books in a land where a mention of Homer brought the reply, "carrots." I had to ask myself, "What can you do?" After reflecting a while and making an exhaustive list of my various abilities, I ended by agreeing that I was capable of nothing. Meeting a Mr. Napoleon Charpin that night rescued me from this embarrassing plight. When I described to him the dilemma I found myself in, so far as choosing an art or profession in San José, he said to me, "If you want manual labor I am going to build an adobe house and the count of Narbonne will lay the adobes. You can help him to mix the mud, and I'll give you five dollars a day and board at my house."

Oh Napoleon, name twice great, I bless you!

I accepted.

The following morning at dawn I had my trousers rolled up above the knees and was treading the mud mixture, singing the cavatina from Romeo and Juliet: *"la tremenda ultrice spada . . ."*

At breakfast my boss complimented me and said he was satisfied with my work because I had reduced the mud to the consistency of butter. This showed there were great hopes that I could make my fortune in this line of work. "Many an adobe layer has begun by mixing mud," he told me confidentially. . . .

I couldn't sleep that night. I dreamed I was on a scaffold, a master adobe bricklayer, fitting adobes to the top of an edifice I had just finished. Oh, noble ambition! Open to all generous hearts! Source of such great hopes and misfortunes! . . .

Eight days later I . . . took a stroll down the streets of San José with a ruler in my hand. I dreamed the night before that I was an adobe builder making twelve dollars a day. Such builders were scarce then, and I had gone only a little way when a French gentleman came up to me and asked me if I were one. I did not even pale. "As you can see," I replied, "I am carrying a plane and ruler."

[The man hires him to build some rooms onto his store.]

Next day I tried to find a mud mixer to help me in the job. . . . All who applied, though, spoke with such elegance of diction and had such aristocratic manners I was afraid they would resent the kind of work I had for them. Then a Chilean youth showed up whom I had seen as an officer in the civic guard at Santiago. . . . He said to me with a humble air, "Oh Musiú Combet, I know you, I remember when you lived on Calle Ahumada.[2] You bound a book for me: *The Law of Nations*, by Bello.[3] If you want me to, I can mix mud for you; I know how to do it. I did that kind of work in San Francisco before going to the damned mines."

"You know how to do it?" I expostulated. "What do you mean by that? Do you think you can become a master craftsman by simply pouring water on a mix, and then treading on it for fifteen minutes without real interest? Are you then entitled to exclaim, with your face raised to the sky and all streaked with dirt and sweat, 'I know how to mix mud!' You have to put a lot of study and hard work into this craft to learn how to reduce mud to the consistency of butter. Believe me, Señor Bello is a man I venerate. . . . Nevertheless, even if you knew as much as our holy father, the pope, about his *Law of Nations*, his *Principles of International Law*, his *Castillian Grammar*, and his beautiful verses . . . —all of that would not make you a true craftsman in mixing mud. Abandon this vanity, which can only injure your case, and, instead, ask me to initiate you in the art of building."

He was hungry, so he submitted. Next morning he was dancing on Chilean cement, and showing a considerable interest and ability in the work. I was worn out trying to look calm when my employer looked at me, and to maintain an air of confidence worthy of a better job. The first row of adobes went down well enough; the second row was off level by an inch; the third row by two inches; and so it went from then on. At the fifth tier I found I'd formed a cornice. I told myself I could fill in the low spots with the mud my assistant was mixing and so cover up the defects. Four days later I demanded in a loud voice that a carpenter be brought to set the lintels of the doors and windows so I could finish the job.

The carpenter came. He knew his business, so he turned to me and said, "You must have been called in to redo this work. The man who put these walls up was certainly no builder. Nothing here is plumb. It will all fall in and bury the people who live here. I'm certainly not going to put any carpentry into these buildings if they are going to stay this way."

"How can it be, my friend, that you are not familiar with this method of building? Have you never been in Chile or other countries where they have earthquakes?"

"No."

"Well, in Chile they don't build any other way." (I humbly beg pardon from Juan, Pedro, and all Chilean builders—blame it on *El Mercurio de Valparaíso* for making those promises.) "This was all carefully planned. Now you seem to me an intelligent man, so I will explain to you the reason why we build this way. We used to build on the plumb, but found it a bad method. The least tremor knocked walls out of plumb—like these. But we found that if you build them out of plumb to begin with, the shaking straightens them up.". . .

When I had crawled into my tent, made of three blankets sewed together, and let myself fall on the one old pelt that served me as a bed, I started to reflect on the vicissitudes of human life: upon the ceaseless hunger for acquisition that is innate in man, so that neither home nor family nor friends are enough to keep him from the career of a vagabond when opposed to the dreams of his inexperienced mind! What a warning! "The son of a family," as they say in Santiago, a young man who is one of the most distinguished in the land, known for his elegance on the Alameda, and at Tajamar, reduced to selling cookies made by his partner, a peon. Other men whose articles had achieved great success in various periodicals of the capital were selling salad vegetables they had gathered in the countryside. A captain of the National Guard of Santiago, a man of martial bearing, was selling empanadas at the door of his tent in San José. A foreign baron whom we all knew in Chile for his eccentricities was shouting, "Oranges, four dollars a dozen!" in almost a scream. The count of Narbonne was an adobe mason, etc. These reflections forced me finally to admit that in this unique land each man had to do whatever his physical strength and capacity equipped him to do.

Translated by Edwin A. Beilharz and Carlos U. López

Notes

1. Fernando Purcell, "'Too Many Foreigners for My Taste': Mexicans, Chileans and Irish in California, 1848–1880" (Ph.D. diss., University of California, Davis, 2004), 9.
2. A street in downtown Santiago.
3. The writer, jurist, and statesman who became first rector of the University of Chile; see his inaugural address excerpted earlier.

"The Worst Misery":
Letters to the Santiago Orphanage

The expansion of the export economy in nineteenth-century Chile wrought major social dislocations that affected women as well as men, children as well as adults. Between 1865 and 1907, more than 100,000 women migrants arrived in Santiago, skewing the sex ratio of the urban population. The most common employment for poor women was domestic service, yet only 9,000 new service positions opened up during this time. Poor women thus experienced high rates of unemployment and miserable wages. Their plight was exacerbated by periodic downturns in the export economy, which caused food prices to spike.

Many poor urban women remained unmarried, and households headed by women were common. By the late nineteenth century, a third of children were born out of wedlock, and Chilean commentators claimed that the infant mortality rate in their country was the highest in the "civilized world." Santiago's public orphanage became the last resort of many desperate families, and between 1853 and 1924, more than 51,000 children were placed in the institution. Some children arrived there with notes attesting to their origins and the reasons for their abandonment. These ranged from formal letters by masters and mistresses who wrote on behalf of their servants to barely legible notes scratched on scraps of paper by mothers, midwives, and wet nurses. In these missives, we find poignant evidence of the conditions affecting the urban working classes in the late nineteenth century. They speak to the difficulties that migration and servitude imposed on parents, especially mothers; to endemic poverty; and to the specter of hunger and disease. The majority of the children left at the orphanage perished there, and those who survived were placed as servants in city households and as workers on haciendas nearby.

Today Huérfanos (Orphans) Street in downtown Santiago recalls the asylum's original location, and the Providencia neighborhood takes its name from the order of nuns who ran the orphanage when it was relocated to what was then the city's rural outskirts. The orphanage continues to operate (on a much smaller scale, and in a new building) on the same site. The letters reproduced here, which tell the stories of children left at the orphanage, were located in a closet there.

[On a paper left with a two-month-old, 1874:]

I certify that Salomé Pacheco is poor and has no way to raise her and she has done this out of necessity because her milk dried up, the baby causes no trouble at all when she's full . . . she eats everything and her name is Perpetua del Carmen Soto . . .

[On a semilegible note, sent with the baby José Hipólito, 1879:]

I am sending my little son there because I am a widow and very helpless I have no father or mother and my husband died and I was pregnant and now I am very sick and I have no one to leave him to and this is the reason that I send him because I may not live I am very sick, also he is being sent without oil or water [unbaptized] because I have no way to do it because I do not have enough even to eat myself. Rosa Hernández

[Scratched on a piece of paper, 1881:]

I am baptized and my name is Héctor Miranda my parents left me . . . because of poverty but later if fortune helps them they will come get me. . . . April 28 1881 [The "voice" then changes.] The baby . . . eats a lot and there is no way to satisfy him and the mother is sick and so it is out of poverty that I find myself in these circumstances.

[From a letter from a courthouse on the rural outskirts of Santiago, 1884:]

I certify that Mercedes Quezada has been left in charge of a nursling whose name is Manuel de la Cruz Mosqueira, and his father José Dolores Mosqueira (widower of Transito Zamorano) has left this place, going south to Talca and for four months now there has been no word of him; . . . lacking the necessary resources, Quezada requests [that you accept the baby] because she believes that, as a roving peon and an uncaring father, he will not return. Manuel S. Marchant.

[On a note remitted from another charity asylum, 1887:]

Dear Sister: the two children can be received without any worry. No one will reclaim them ever. They have no mother, and their father entrusted me with them, never to reclaim them. This unfortunate man, whose conduct is really bad, had *pawned* one of them. . . .

[From a letter sent from the small town of Los Andes, August 2, 1888:]

Reverend Mother. Yesterday, a few hours before the birth of the baby who today is going to seek shelter in your holy house, I gave lodging to its poor mother who is an entirely destitute unfortunate. The father is the son of a rich family who live in Valparaíso, in whose house she used to work as a servant, but they have refused to give her so much as an old rag; it could be that later when the father receives his inheritance, he will want to do something for his daughter.

The poor girl, who isn't a bad person, has had a hard time resigning herself to sending [the baby], but they won't accept her anywhere with a child, because while she is a good person she is inept . . . and I am a very poor widow who has to work from the night to the morning to maintain my children. The woman whose house she will go to [to work as a servant] as soon as she can get up has given us the necessary resources to send the baby [to the orphanage]. . . .

[On a scrap of paper left with a six-month-old, 1888:]

Your name is Julio Ernesto del Rosario Rodríguez born November 18, 1887 the person who is giving you this note is your sister Elena V. Guerra. . . . I am putting you there because I am in the worst misery and with two other siblings and you as the smallest one, I was obliged to leave you at the orphanage goodbye little brother until we see each other again if God wills it. Elena V. Guerra, Santiago 23 May 1888

[From the Santa Ana police station, 1896:]

I am remitting to the Casa de Huérfanos, a little baby of the masculine sex who was found alive in the southern bank of the Mapocho [River] in a ditch.

Translated by Nara Milanich

"A Race of Vagabonds"

Augusto Orrego Luco

By the mid-nineteenth century, commentators were increasingly concerned with the effects of modernization and urbanization on Chile's poor majority. Such concerns gave rise to a genre of critique known as the "social question," in which observers sought to identify the causes of rampant poverty.

The author of the essay excerpted here, Augusto Orrego Luco, was a medical doctor who had unusually intimate knowledge of the living conditions afflicting Santiago's poor. He served in the public hospital for mental patients and also treated the sick during a smallpox outbreak in 1872 that killed 5 percent of the city's population. During a stint as municipal physician for Santiago, he regularly performed autopsies on the infants abandoned daily on city streets. While police investigations sought to determine if there were criminal causes of death, usually their bodies bore the marks of a different kind of violence: premature and unattended births, disease, starvation. It was at this time that Orrego Luco wrote "The Social Question," a wide-ranging analysis of Chile's social ills, which was first published in 1884 in a Valparaíso newspaper.

Whereas many authors located blame for social problems with the poor themselves—their innate nomadism and laziness, their immorality and love for drink, their ignorance of proper childrearing techniques—Orrego Luco emphasized economic dislocation and dispossession. In this essay, he narrates the transformations of the preceding half century and describes the ways they have produced rural-urban migration, a mass of dispossessed peons, endemic infant mortality, and disrupted family structures. He then criticizes traditional "laissez-faire" approaches to the social question and calls for basic economic reforms, including wage hikes and protectionist policies to stimulate industrialization and create employment. Later a member of Congress, Orrego Luco was one of a number of distinguished medical doctors in Chile and in Latin America, among them Salvador Allende and Che Guevara, who became voices for social change as a result of their firsthand work with the poor. His essay anticipates many of the struggles and debates that would animate Chilean public life in the twentieth century.

An early twentieth-century *rancho*, or poor rural dwelling. Photograph by Einar Altschwager. Courtesy of Colección Museo Histórico Nacional de Chile.

As long as the lower classes are engulfed in misery and dwell in the horrible promiscuity of the shanties, there will prevail not only the physical conditions that make high levels of infant mortality inevitable, but also an even graver phenomenon: a dearth of the family sentiments on which our society is founded. Life in the shanties has turned family ties into an intractable problem. . . . This formidable issue has gone unnoticed up until now but is destined to make a dangerous appearance, perhaps in the near future.

And yet, this shanty life that is so disastrous in the cities, in rural areas is the most humane, most civilized form of life there is.

The system of *inquilinaje* [tenant farming] has been the target of bitter criticisms for many years, and its flaws and painful consequences have been exhibited. A system that does not concede any rights to the laborer over the land he works is obviously defective. The laborer is completely at the mercy of the owner, and the only thing that defends him against the capricious arbitrariness of the landlord is a vague and distant social protection. A system that has all the harshness of the feudal system without any of its picturesque side is obviously defective.

But in the shadow of this system the *inquilino* [tenant farmer] has a home, some land to cultivate, some animals to raise, and the possibility of savings. He even has those ties that unite him with the owner of the estate on which he was born and has spent his life working, ties which, though weak, none-theless establish a certain community of interest and affection.

So there one finds the guarantee of order, of sociability; there one finds the basis for family. That home, that plot of land, those animals, those chil-dren are all guarantees that the inquilino gives to society.

But in the shadow of this system, forty or fifty years ago the figure of the peon began to appear; that nomadic mass, without families, homes of their own, or social bonds, who traveled about searching for work at different haciendas. This floating mass plants roots nowhere, has no ties to constrain it, and constitutes the strength and weakness of Chile, her misery on the inside and her grandeur on the outside. . . .

This race of vagabonds is the atonement for the economic and social sys-tem . . . a system that could only be sustained as long as communication bar-riers separated the urban and rural populations. It was naturally bound to collapse the day that they established a link between city and countryside.

In the former days of isolation, the inquilino had no other terms for com-parison than the house and life of the landowner, whose house and life were not that different from his own. The comforts of civilized life had not yet reached his view; he could not feel the contrast between misery and opu-lence that has painfully appeared before his eyes over the past forty years.

Better forms of transportation and, above all, the banking establishment have made possible the construction of elegant and sumptuous dwellings and have carried all the refinements of urban life to the countryside. In do-ing so, they presented the inquilino with a new ideal, a new and dazzling aspiration.

This abrupt revelation of wealth logically and naturally produced a moral shock very similar to the shock experienced by the barbarians when they saw the magnificent monuments of the empire suddenly appear. . . . The arrival of the civilized world was a landmark in the lives of people who had only known misery. . . .

And at the same time the inquilino felt overwhelmed by that grandeur and was conscious of the enormous distance that stretched between his own dark condition and the other brilliant one, at the same time a road opened between his shanty and the city, his own artisanal activities began to collapse. The looms that foreign competition had stilled . . . began to crumble, as did the bridles, the carts, and plows, and all the products of his rough crafts. The railroads transformed rural life, obliterating the roadside stands and guesthouses that had been little entrepreneurial wellsprings for the inquilino and that provided employment to the women and children.

In all aspects it was a violent economic crisis, which diminished incomes, decreased employment, and directly increased poverty at the same time that it awoke new aspirations and opened a road to the city to escape this terrible situation.

It was natural that the son of the inquilino would abandon the farm to search for a job and would begin to constitute the proletariat, which here, as everywhere, "is comprised of the unfortunate leftovers of society; that remain outside the normal class system." . . .

Emigration has contained the effects of this social dissolution, removing from the country those elements that are set loose from the old system of inquilinaje and that would be enough to submerge us in an uncertain and disastrous situation were they to remain.

But aside from being a remedy that the statesman cannot accept in any event, mass emigration presents us with one of the most tremendous developments that a society can face; all over the feudal regions of Chile, the number of women exceeds the number of men. This monstrous fact—which is being addressed for the *first time* in these articles we are writing—cannot persist without inviting a moral and economic revolution. . . .

We have sketched the contours of this problem with sufficient clarity to be able to affirm that we are engulfed in a social situation that is threatening and dangerous . . . ; to affirm that we are experiencing a situation in which the outflow of emigration and the high infant mortality rate are two valves that prevent our society from falling into an even graver situation; to be able to assert that a proletariat is coming into being before our eyes, and that the organization of the family is crumbling in the shanties and the balance between the sexes is being destroyed. . . .

It follows that when faced with this grave and threatening situation, the doctrine of passive indifference—of *laissez-aller, laissez-faire*—is condemned as inexcusable. It is precisely in the context of this nearsighted doctrine that the very situation we deplore has developed, and it would naturally worsen if we continued to allow the doctrine to carry out its effects.

We need to intervene, then, with an active hand to establish new economic and moral conditions that remove us from this atmosphere in which the lower social classes feel asphyxiated.

We need to raise wages, and this can only be done by doggedly fostering the industrial development of this country; raising up industry and protecting that industry; renouncing openly and clearly the small advantages enjoyed by foreign competitors that destroy our small national industries and that we are paying for with the lives and well-being of our compatriots. . . .

This does not mean that we ask for some ill-advised protectionist policy for our industries, that we want to shut the door on all foreign products and convert our customs offices into a great Chinese wall that isolates us from the commercial world. Such an outlandish argument does not even merit the honor of a formal refutation. But we understand this view better than the opposite one that denies any protection for any national industry, and that in fact protects foreign industries in their competition with national ones insofar as the former are already organized and can obtain capital at lower prices.

The wage increase that stems from the development of industry would make possible [a series of material and moral improvements.]

A mass of people spurred on by the implacable demands of life cannot dedicate itself to intellectual betterment, nor can it think about savings or hygiene, but is condemned to vegetate in manual labor and in the material vices that devour it.

Now, if this same mass of people is a nomadic mass, wandering from shanty to shanty, from village to village, how can one seriously consider inspiring in them habits of hygiene and saving, developing their intelligence, and raising their moral condition?

The first step is to settle the mass, to gather them around organized work and encourage them to re-enter the class system. One needs to present them with a nucleus around which they can condense, and this nucleus is the fixed work of commerce and industry.

This process of settlement is, at the same time, indispensable for the organization of learning. Education needs to become obligatory if it is ever to make an impact, and this could never be possible when half of the population is scattered around the countryside or leads the life of vagabonds. Education is the basis of all reform and development; social disaggregation makes it impossible. . . .

If on top of this we add more serious efforts toward establishing the principles of hygiene, obligatory vaccination, medical services for children, and a more ample system of social charity, we would have the basic measures needed to confront this problem that, later on, may demand solutions of a violent and unpleasant nature. . . .

And the possibility of a situation like this is more than just fantasy for those who remember the social situation we experienced when war broke out five years ago.[1] We could see then that the social question began to make its dark and dreadful appearance. Destructive doctrines circulated in the atmosphere, people from the slums showed up in the very heart of Santiago to challenge public order, gangs of bandits roamed the countryside, and the police were on the lookout for arsonists. With the passing of each day, that rising black tide became more threatening and more daring, revealing one of those social upheavals governed not by ideas, but by the savage ferocity of instinct.

We were taken to that point thanks to a lack of foresight, low wages, a lack of national industries, and the misery and idleness of the slums. We will find ourselves there anew if we do not manage to eradicate the current economic calamities.

Translated by Trevor Martenson

Note

1. A reference to the War of the Pacific, a conflict between Chile and its Andean neighbors Peru and Bolivia, and the social dislocations it unleashed.

IV

Building a Modern Nation: Politics and the Social Question in the Nitrate Era

The late nineteenth century and the early twentieth century were a period of intense social, economic, and political change in Chile, and for many scholars represent the era when modern Chile was formed. As both the agricultural and copper-mining sectors declined, Chile gained a new engine for its export-based economy when it conquered the nitrate fields of the northern Atacama Desert from Peru and Bolivia during the War of the Pacific (1879–1883). This military conflict, followed by the conquest of southern territories from the Mapuche (1881–1883) and a civil war (1891) defined, in part, by the issue of national control of the northern nitrate industry and railroads, produced a strong sense of Chilean nationalism and made national identity and citizenship vital subjects of debate. In addition, the profound social inequalities produced by nitrate-driven economic modernization during this period gave birth to a militant labor movement in Chile's mining districts, ports, and cities, as well as national debate about how to deal with "the social question." Increasingly nationalist critiques of foreign domination of the Chilean economy were joined by attacks on the elite-dominated Parliamentary Republic established after the 1891 civil war and on laissez-faire approaches to both social problems and national development. By the 1920s, populist calls for nationalist policies that would protect Chilean control of basic infrastructure and industry were becoming more commonplace, as were demands for basic social legislation to improve the conditions of Chile's impoverished rural and urban working classes.

Documents in this section describe the development of nationalism and an expansionist Chilean foreign policy during the War of the Pacific. Chile's sustained economic growth, driven by exports of silver, copper, and wheat since the 1840s, began to enter into a prolonged crisis during the mid-1870s, when international prices for these commodities dropped and production in Chile's northern mines and central valley estates stagnated. Export-driven prosperity had underwritten the country's exceptional nineteenth-century political stability, but during the recession of the 1870s Chile experienced its first major crisis in the model of export-oriented development since independence. In the face of this crisis, a sector of the Chilean elite with financial interests in the nitrate fields of the Bolivian province of Antofogasta and the Peruvian province of Tarapacá pushed for confrontation with Bolivia and Peru over control of nitrate production. Proponents of war with Peru and Bolivia bolstered their case by emphasizing that not only had Chilean capital developed the nitrate industry but also that Chilean workers composed the bulk of the mining labor force and the populations of Antofogasta and Tarapacá.

The appropriation of the northern provinces from Bolivia and Peru was accompanied by expansion southward during the final military conquest of Chile's southern frontier or "Araucanía" territory in 1881–1883. With the defeat of independent Mapuche groups, Chile's national territory was expanded and consolidated from the north to the south. Mapuches were settled on small *reducciones* or reservations (also referred to as land grant communities), and their former territories, now defined as "empty" and "public," were auctioned off or granted as concessions. Mapuches were granted only land they could prove they had a history of cultivating and living on, a difficult task given their historically transhuman and pastoral economy, in which agriculture played only a minimal role. The Chilean government hoped to use the newly opened territory to settle European immigrants and granted hundreds of thousands of hectares of public land to colonization companies. However, relatively few Europeans settled in Chile. Instead, auctions of "public" frontier land held in Santiago allowed wealthy merchants and agriculturalists to build enormous estates, extending the regime of the hacienda from central Chile southward. Mapuche communities saw their already small allocations of land even further constricted by continual land usurpations, often accompanied by violence and fraud. By the first decade of the twentieth century, many communities had been reduced to extreme poverty without access to resources sufficient for subsistence. Conquest of the southern frontier produced debates about the racial basis of the nation, including the incorporation of the Mapuche population, while conquest of the northern deserts raised questions of whether and how to integrate Peruvian and Bolivian populations. A racial ideology of Chilean *mestizaje* (racial or ethnic mixture) fueled the nationalism and anti-immigrant xenophobia of writers like Nicolás Palacios, even as liberal positivists hoped that European immigration to southern Chile would pro-

PERU

Tacna

Arica

Returned to Peru in 1929

BOLIVIA

Conquered from Peru

Iquique

Territory Acquired
after War of the
Pacific, 1879-1883

Antofagasta

Conquered from Bolivia

N

PACIFIC
OCEAN

Copiapó

Present border of Chile

La Serena
Coquimbo

ARGENTINA

Valparaíso

Santiago

Talcahuano

Concepción

Bío Bío River

Territory Conquered
during the Pacification
of the Araucanía,
1861-1883

Valdivia

Toltén River

PARAGUAY

CHILE

Easter Island
annexed in 1888

0   100   200 mi
0 100 200 300 km

Modern Chile's Changing Borders.

duce economic and demographic growth. This era of Chilean expansion also included the 1888 annexation of Easter Island, 2,300 miles away from the Chilean coast, and the reduction of the small population of indigenous Rapa Nui to near slave-like conditions under the rule of the Chilean navy.

A decade after the War of the Pacific, during a period of tremendous prosperity due to bonanza nitrate revenues, Chile erupted in a violent civil war between military forces loyal to President José Manuel Balmaceda and forces loyal to Congress. At issue were Balmaceda's heavy-handed use of presidential powers, in line with the Portalian tradition, and the balance of power between Congress and the presidency. Balmaceda has been viewed as both a nationalist and a populist for his efforts to promote economic modernization by exerting greater Chilean control over nitrate production and revenues. Despite his use of military force to repress nitrate miners' strikes, after his death in 1891 he became a figure idolized by nitrate workers in the north. His defeat and suicide led to the fall of the autocratic republic and the establishment of what has been called Chile's Parliamentary Republic, a system of government dominated by the legislature and Chile's elite landowning class. Many of the documents here reflect nationalist critiques of the weaknesses of the liberal model of export-driven development, including foreign domination of the economy, and the limitations of the Parliamentary Republic, widely viewed as a vehicle for Chile's traditional aristocracy to exercise its political will through the widespread practice of buying votes to obtain congressional seats.

Debates over presidential and parliamentary powers and Chile's "economic inferiority," as the historian Francisco Encina put it, were accompanied by discussions about how to address the "social question." Widespread poverty and inequality and a large transient population of rootless male laborers, who traveled from rural and mining districts to the countryside and increasingly to cities and towns, as well as across the border to Argentina, provoked both new concern with social policy and critiques of traditional laissez-faire approaches to economic and social policy. The social question was made all the more urgent by a series of bloody massacres of working-class protests and strikes during the first two decades of the twentieth century, most notoriously an episode in the northern port city of Iquique in 1907 in which army units gunned down hundreds of nitrate workers and their family members, described here in the memoirs of Elías Lafertte, a nitrate worker and cofounder of the Chilean Communist Party. Increasingly, employers' reliance on military force to resolve the social conflicts engendered by vast inequalities during this period of rapid economic modernization was viewed as inadequate, and calls for social reform widened by the 1920s.

The selections here describe social conditions in the mines, cities, and countryside and the development of a radical labor and socialist movement. The nationalism developed during the late nineteenth century found radical expression first in popular Balmacedismo and support for Chile's first proworker party, the Democratic Party (founded in 1887), and then in the militant labor movement of the north, where the Chilean Communist Party was born after World War I. Chile's north became a cauldron of radical labor politics, with ideological tendencies ranging from support for the Democratic Party's basic reformism to anarcho-syndicalism and to revolutionary socialism. The selections here also consider women workers and their participation in labor politics. The nitrate-driven prosperity, accompanied by the spread of railroads that connected Chile's far-flung regions and newly acquired territories, drove a period of economic modernization and urbanization. Increasingly, migrant workers, both men and women, moved from the countryside or mining districts to urban areas in search of jobs. Male laborers found employment in an expanding urban manufacturing sector. Women participated in the stream of migration from the countryside to the cities. Often they settled with their families in one-room dwellings in *conventillos* (tenements) whose squalor contrasted starkly with the European architecture of aristocratic mansions and became the focus of debates about "the social question." Women workers found jobs as domestic servants and in factories producing textiles, clothing, and food, composing a large section of Chile's industrial labor force; women were the majority of workers in the textile and clothing industries. The selections here reflect women workers' role in labor politics and the growth of a working-class feminism that provided an alternative to the more middle-class feminism with which this period is associated.

In 1920, the election of Arturo Alessandri to the presidency ushered in a period of reform and mass politics. Alessandri sought to introduce basic social reforms but was confronted with a recalcitrant Congress who refused to approve his legislation or budgets, exacerbating the tensions between presidential and parliamentary powers. The standoff between Alessandri and Congress, which in many ways replayed the conflict that had led to the 1891 civil war, as the excerpt from Alessandri's memoir here makes clear, was resolved by two military coups, the first by high-level officers, and the second by mid- and junior-level officers, including Carlos Ibáñez, who supported some of Alessandri's reformist programs. When Alessandri returned from a six-month exile in 1925 to reassume the presidency, a new Constitution, which restored many presidential powers, was approved in a plebiscite. The military interventions in 1924 and 1925, and the 1925 Constitution, dealt a final blow to Chile's Parliamentary Republic.

Finally, this group of selections ends with excerpts from the works of two of Chile's greatest poets, Gabriela Mistral and Vicente Huidobro. The nitrate era was also a period of extraordinary cultural effervescence, both at the popular and elite levels. Mistral, who would go on to win Latin America's first Nobel Prize for Literature in 1945, emerged during the second decade of the twentieth century as the country's most important poet. Her poetry drew on some *criollista* themes, especially in its attention to local landscapes and folklore, and the concern with "chileanidad," but forged a set of new concerns that critics consistently described as "feminine," including an abiding interest in children, religion, and loss. Vicente Huidobro represented an alternative strand in Chilean literature. Unlike Mistral, he identified with modernist trends in poetry and became, while living in Paris and Madrid, an influential figure in literary circles in France and Spain. His own philosophy of poetry, "creationism," reflected themes developed by the European avant-garde during this period, including a fascination with new technologies and a vision of the artist as creator of experimental forms of language and expression.

"Audacious and Cruel Spoilations": The War of the Pacific

Alejandro Fierro

The origins of the War of the Pacific lay in the competition between Chile, Bolivia, and Peru to establish sovereignty over the nitrates-rich Atacama Desert. The war had two immediate causes. First, the decision of the Peruvian government in 1875 to nationalize Tarapacá's nitrate industry and organize a new nitrate monopoly damaged the financial interests of a number of leading Chilean figures, including the past and future presidents Manuel Montt and José Manuel Balmaceda. Second, in 1878 the Bolivian Congress imposed a new export tax on nitrates in violation of a 1874 treaty with Chile. The Bolivian government then appropriated the Antofagasta Nitrate and Railroad Company after it had refused to pay the new tax, which in turn threatened the financial interests of key sectors of Chile's elite, including the minister of foreign relations, Alejandro Fierro, and the Valparaíso merchant, banker, and newspaper magnate Agustín Edwards. The Chilean armed forces occupied Antofagasta and then, in response to the revelation of a secret 1873 Peru-Bolivia treaty and alliance, occupied Lima and other cities in Peru. Chile's victory in the war brought it the wealthy provinces of Antofagasta, depriving Bolivia of any access to the sea, and Peru's Tarapacá. The war wrested from Peru and Bolivia both territory and the engines of their national economies and remains today a source of tension between Chile and its two northern neighbors.

The "Manifest" selected here was written by the foreign relations minister Alejandro Fierro, who was a shareholder in the Antofagasta Nitrate and Railroad Company. It lays out Chile's arguments for going to war and emphasizes the Bolivian and Peruvian governments' actions against Chilean investors in the nitrate industry. In addition, Fierro alludes to the wave of patriotic mobilization that accompanied Chile's conflict with Bolivia and Peru. He emphasizes that the purported offenses of the neighboring governments were directed not just at the private nitrate companies but also at the thousands of Chilean workers who toiled in the industry. Indeed, the Chilean war effort was not just an elite affair; it enjoyed widespread popular support. The War of the Pacific was distinguished in Chilean history by the many patriotic demonstrations in support of the war and, following Chilean victory, an extraordinary proliferation of parades, exhibitions, poems, memoirs, and monuments extolling the glory of Chile's military success.

During and after the war, nationalist movements began to invest the figure of the once despised roto chileno with the virtues of the national soul. The roto (literally "broken one"), who had once been denounced as an uncivilized barbarian-vagabond and subjected to harsh disciplinary measures, was now extolled as the virile, hardworking, patriotic citizen-laborer and soldier who had helped turn the arid northern desert into a new source of wealth for the nation and who had helped make the nitrate fields Chilean. One of the major results of the war was, then, the dissemination of a powerful new nationalism that incorporated Chile's migrant working-class men, the peones and gañanes (itinerant laborers) who traveled throughout the country from estate to estate, to cities, and mines in search of work and livelihood. The conscription of thousands of laborers into the military abetted this process. That a monument honoring the "roto," shown here, could be built in a central plaza in Santiago alongside the statues of officers like Arturo Prat, who were the official military heroes of the war, indicates a significant shift in Chile's national imaginary during this period.

The especial characteristic of this country, the constant tendency of its foreign policy, and even its social and economic necessities, have withdrawn it from all spirit of adventure, and have stimulated it to maintain the most friendly relations with all nations. Chili lives by peace and industry; requires as a prime element of its prosperity, foreign immigration; and possessing a vast territory only partially fertilized by the rude labor of its sons, requires more than any people, foreign and internal tranquility. . . .

My government very recently complied with its duty in manifesting to those with whom it has the pleasure to maintain cordial relations, the circumstances, which obliged it to declare at an end the treaty existing with Bolivia, and to occupy the territory lying between parallels 23 and 24 S. lat.

Subsequently, and without previous declaration of war, the President of Bolivia issued a decree emanating from his single will, by which he expelled Chilian citizens from that state, confiscated their property, and sequestered the products of the industry and capital of this country. . . .

If Chili has been forced into war, it is not through its own act, but is the unavoidable consequence of the extraordinary conduct observed by the Government of La Paz. This . . . declined to fulfill the treaty of 1874, in virtue of which, and by whose sole title it occupied conditionally the territory whose possession was transferred by the treaty mentioned. . . .

If it be undeniable that before the treaty of 1866 the territory comprised

Monument to the "Roto Chileno." Photograph by Miguel Rubio, Chile. Used by permission of Fernanda Rubio. Courtesy of Colección Museo Histórico Nacional de Chile.

between parallels 23 and 24 belonged to Chili by right and by the constant exercise of veritable possession; if it be true that it was ceded to Bolivia by the treaty of 1874 on the emphatic condition that no new taxes should be levied on Chilian industry and capital; and if in fine, it is the melancholy truth proved by public documents of the Bolivian Government, that in, turning a deaf ear to all remonstrance, ceased in truth to impose taxation, but rendered illusory the right of property recognized by its own laws—it was necessary on the part of Chili to replace things in the state in which they stood before the extraordinary violation of the treaty mentioned. . . .

Official documents, and still more, the private history of Chilian indus-

Photo of the monument to Arturo Prat, c. 1906. From *Album Chile
en 1906*. Photographer unknown. Courtesy of Colección Archivo
Fotográfico Biblioteca Nacional de Chile.

try on the coast between 230 and 240 S lat. are witnesses that cannot be
refuted, to the fact that since 1866 to the date of the occupation of Antofogasta, the Bolivian government appears to have conceived, organized, and
put into practice an inflexible system of persecution against the development of Chilian enterprise, which have been the only origin and principal
element of the wealth of that locality, never suspected and never stimulated
by the private industry or national protection of Bolivia.

The capital of this republic, and that developed under the protection of
our laws without distinction of nationality, being embarked in costly specu-

lations, my government could not view with indifference the adoption by Bolivia of special measures tending to place Chilians in an exceptional situation. Soon after the treaty of 1866, and then after that of 1874, the painful certainty was realized that in Bolivia no idea existed of individual guarantees. Taxes were imposed under the pretext of municipal rates; disgraceful punishments were inflicted by the authorities on citizens of this republic, and finally, a Chilian enterprise for the working of nitrate beds, authorized by the Bolivian government afforded a pretext for a law irreconcilable with the most essential stipulation of the treaty of 1874.

My government could not and ought not abandon its citizens to caprice of that of Bolivia, and less to the discretion of its subalterns; and the official documents inserted in the reports of the Ministry of Foreign Affairs since 1866 render unnecessary any additional proof that since then till now it has been impossible to restrain the action of the Bolivian authorities.

These precedents showed sufficiently that the occupation of Antofogasta was urgently required, through the violation of the treaty; and my government found itself under the necessity of ordering it, for the protection of interests and persons threatened by measures which respected no rights at all. . . .

It was our duty then to confide in the loyalty of Peru; still more, we had the right to demand it, either on the ground of a sincere friendship, or as a slight return for the blood of our citizens and our treasure spent in giving that country a nationality and defending it at the price of our own ruin. . . .

There were, however, various antecedents, which contradicted in a great measure the declarations that now we might stigmatize as insidious, with full knowledge of the circumstances. The President of Peru did not hesitate to express his fears for the pressure that might be brought to bear in an opposite sense by a reckless popular opinion. He hinted at the not improbable event of the action of the authorities being interfered with, and recognized the influence of certain circles whose disaffection to Chili is only founded on the childish jealousy with which our prosperity is regarded. . . .

Respecting the belligerent attitude which Peru commenced to assume, its representative attributed it to the special condition of its territory, and to the necessity of preventing its violation by the operations of belligerents. . . .

These explanations were not tranquilizing because they were not conclusive, and confirmed my government in the conviction that it would be necessary to resolve so equivocal a situation before the cabinet of Lima itself, and even without knowing its antecedents, instructions were sent at the first moment to our minister at that capital to ask for a prompt declaration of neutrality. . . .

And, at the same time the government of Lima had to be reminded that it had confessed itself impotent to fulfill its duty, and that an explosion of hate as profound as unreasonable against this republic, had burst forth among the people of the pretended mediator. . . . On the said 24th of March peremptory instructions were sent to our minister at Lima. According to them he was to insist that the question of neutrality should not be discussed in Chili; that we demanded the immediate and guaranteed suspension of the armament, and the production of the secret treaty [between Bolivia and Peru] . . . and [that Peru] give us the requisite explanation for having negotiated in secret, while on terms of friendship with us, a treaty showing want of confidence in and even hostility toward Chili. . . .

The treaty of 1873 [the secret Bolivia-Peru treaty] wed its origin . . . in the measures adopted by Peru at that epoch, to justify one of the most audacious and cruel spoliations witnessed by countries submitted to a regime of common respect toward the industry of all nations.

It is evident that Peru sought in the treaty of 1873 to protect the financial measures it meditated against an industry that in any commonly scrupulous country would have had the right to develop itself freely. What it desired was to strengthen the nitrate monopoly, without considering the sums invested in that industry; for in vain are antecedents of any kind scraped up to justify the belief—not probable, but even possible—of any aggression against the independence or dominion of the contracting powers. . . .

The alliance [between Peru and Bolivia] is explainable by much less elevated motives and which decidedly were intended to embarrass the action of my government in exacting the due fulfillment of the treaty with Bolivia, and provide against the consequences of the indignant clamor of Chilian citizens, despoiled by the despotic hand of the monopoly established in Tarapacá.

It was Peru, which, if it did not declare war first, with the frankness of a noble resolution, commenced it first—and what is worse, a war hidden and sheltered under false p[r]otestations of friendship.

A Mapuche Chieftain Remembers "Pacification"

Pascual Coña

This selection from the memoirs of the Mapuche lonko (cacique or chief) Pascual Coña deals with the last massive Mapuche uprising or "malon" in opposition to colonization during the late nineteenth-century "pacification" of the Araucanía. In 1861, the Chilean government shifted its policy on the frontier region known as "la frontera" or "la Araucanía," sandwiched between the Bío Bío and Toltén rivers. This territory had remained under the control of independent Mapuche groups since the late sixteenth century, and the Spanish colonial government and then Chilean governments had recognized Mapuche governance in a series of treaties or "parlamentos" with Mapuche lonkos. Colonization of the territory was largely entrusted to religious missionaries. By the 1850s, however, Chilean merchants and landowners, having accumulated capital during the wheat and copper export booms, began to look southward for new investment opportunities and new territory to expand wheat production.

The drive to conquer the independent Mapuche groups through military force was sparked by Mapuche rebellions in the late 1850s in response to pressures from the increasing incursions of Chilean settlers across the Bío Bío. The Chilean military slowly pushed their line of garrison towns and forts on the frontier southward, until they succeeded in crushing the final Mapuche uprising in 1883, with an army staffed with many soldiers who had seen action against Peru and Bolivia during the War of the Pacific. The Chilean military offensive against Mapuches during the early 1880s coincided with a similar military offensive against independent indigenous groups, including Mapuche-Pehuenches, across the border in Argentina. Coña's testimonial, recorded by a Capuchin missionary during the 1920s, describes the crossborder alliance between Argentine and Chilean Pehuenche-Mapuche groups, as well as the general alliance of Mapuche lonkos in the south. He also describes the actions of Mapuches who allied themselves with the occupying Chilean military forces. Some Mapuche lonkos pursued a long-standing tradition, dating back to the colonial period, of negotiating treaties with the Chilean state as an alternative to military action.

The ancient Mapuche people mightily detested the foreigners. We have nothing in common with these foreigners; they belong to another race. Sometimes caciques who were neighbors of the *huincas* [non-Mapuches, Spaniards, or Chileans] launched raids against them; they fought and were defeated. Hatred against the foreigners grew with every battle.

Owing to the great aversion toward the huincas, every part of the indigenous world had been plotting to rise up against them. The first order by the Pehuenche caciques (Argentines) was given in a message to the Chilean chief Neculmán de Boroa. The message stated that they were ready for war in Chile, such as the Pehuenches had prepared in Argentina. In addition, a knotted cord was sent that indicated when the general malon would begin.

When the indigenous Argentine messenger arrived, he stated: "The chiefs Chaihuenque, Namuncura, Foyel, and Ancatrir have ordered me to visit the nobles of Chile. This is the reason for my arrival here. My chief orders me to say to you, the chiefs of Chile, the following: 'Alas, the huincas are there. The indigenous Argentines will rise up and finish the foreigners off; that you do the same with yours, that you also attack them; united we are going to make war against them.' In addition, take this knotted cord and adhere to the rebellion decidedly because the huincas are abominable." They gave me this order to tell the message to Neculmán. . . .

In this way news of the war was propagated everywhere; Colihuinca's messenger went with his knotted strings from cacique to cacique.

Pascual Painemilla de Rauquenhue and Pascal Paillalef de Alma were not advised [about the uprising]. They were in favor of the huincas; that is why the [cacique planning the uprising] wanted them dead.

All those who had received notice of the rebellion untied a knot each day. When the last day came, they called for general meetings of all the principal caciques.

When the meetings had already finished . . . the subject came to the attention of certain Chileans. So five men went to advise the Mapuches who were against the malon. . . . They went to address the cacique Colihuinca.

Upon hearing about their arrival the cacique Marimán, who was holding a meeting, sent some men to bring them to him. At night while they slept in Colihuinca's camp, they were captured. They were all taken prisoner and taken to where the Mapuches were meeting. Marimán and his followers were pleased, saying "we have already captured the victims, today we will celebrate a *nguillatún* [ceremonial assembly]." . . .

While in Toltén, Painemilla received a message from Calfupán relating the following: "You have been saved, I began the alarm when they [the Mapuches in rebellion] were still in view, but they have gone away. They demanded that I ally myself with them. Colihuinca, Painecur, Huichal, and Carmona, the leaders of the mob, stated: 'You must help us, we are going to assault the town of Toltén.' I refused them and they said: 'if you want to be defeated then walk alone if you believe you are strong enough to conquer the soldiers.' They had many weapons so I did not dare." Because of these words fear of the leaders of the rebellion took over and they retreated.

The messenger also told us: when the rebellion arrived at Boca-Budi, the chief Painecur of Pichihuenque killed the Chilean José Maria López. The same terrible fate befell his brother Martín López. Both men and several women were traveling down the river in a canoe when the warriors advanced from each riverbank, invaded the boat, and murdered the men. They did not kill the women, however; these fled to Toltén, as I found out afterward.

When the caciques who were in rebellion withdrew, the followers of Calfupán pursued them. . . . The rebels were intimidated and retreated running. Calfupán's people were amused by their fear and intensified the persecution; they took the horses of some; killed one Mapuche; and, took five others prisoner. They took these captives, natives of Mañiu, to Toltén. Much later, the captives were set free.

With this the insurrection ended. It never arrived in Toltén. The chiefs returned to their huts and remained peaceful.

We stayed in Toltén for five days before returning to the land of Rauguenhue. What the other insurgents did in other regions I do not know nor can I tell. I can only say that much later in Nehuentúe, on the other side of Cautín, the Chilean Severino Ibáñez was killed.

After remaining in the house for two days, a message arrived from Painemilla that said: "You should come, we are meeting in Toltén. Tomorrow, we have to leave again," said the messenger. We returned to Toltén on horseback and met with Chief Painemilla who pledged in the meeting to unite a great number of men, according to the orders of Governor Pascual López in Toltén. One hundred or so of us gathered there, the precise number I do not know. We were armed with spears. Ten of the Chileans carried firearms and I myself carried a shotgun.

Then we began to march to make war in turn against the mutinous Mapuche rebels. We went along the north bank of the river Toltén, passing by Peñehue, and arrived at Puculón. There, as we had hoped, we reunited with all the bands of warriors together in the great plain of Puculón. After massing together, we settled ourselves in the great mountains called Puqueno for a rest.

While in that place, we met an Indian who was asking for a pardon for his part in the raid. Later, the Chilean Juan Peña said: "This bad Indian sub-ject assaulted us in Peñehue." If memory serves me correctly, he told us that he had killed his mother and stolen her possessions. "Today you will die," Juan Peña said. He went alongside the Mapuche, took out his gun and fired it. The gun did not discharge. Then, he asked for the shotgun from Juan Aburto, one of the Chileans. Juan Peña fired the gun. The Indian fell to the ground and died instantly.

In addition, Chief Painequeu came to surrender. Juan Peña said again: "These people have invaded Peñehue and I will kill them too." But this time Painemilla did not permit it so Painequeu escaped. . . .

We stayed in the mountains for a long while. Unexpectedly, we encoun-tered fugitives, women, and a few other men. The women stayed with us but cried from fear believing that we were going to kill them. We did not. However, we asked that they give us their silver articles, including the spurs and stirrups that they had brought in great supply. We gave some of our warriors this task and the others gathered the cows and mares that we had.

We returned later to our old camp in Liuco. Half of the booty was handed over to Painemilla. The other half we buried. Painemilla gathered the lot of silver, filled a sack, and watched over it.

A few days ago we left for Quilaco. There we met with Pelquimán, son of Neculmán. In the time of his father, he led a great multitude of fighters armed with lances forming Mapuche raiders.

As Neculmán had never realized his goal of defeating the Chileans in Toltén, he sent a message to Imperial, protectorate of Pancho Jaramillo, in order to display his concern. The first half of the message told the Governor: "I did not take part in the rebellion of the caciques, that is why you cannot blame me, my Governor. If you wish, I am ready to help in the retaliation against the chief that started the insurrection."

The Governor agreed and answered Neculmán: "What is done is done. I presume that you are without fault. Punish all those caciques and their fighters and do not get involved in any new conspiracies."

In light of this response, Neculmán put his fighters under the command of his son Pelquimán who would lead the attack. Pelquimán and his armed fighters grouped along a low ridge. We marched the same way and prepared for the attack. But in the end Pelquimán succumbed to the threats, affably greeted Painemilla, and began negotiations. They conversed for a time and we separated. I do not know anything more about the events during the attack.

After the attack, the poor Mapuches no longer possessed houses as they had been reduced to ashes. They remained in a very lamentable state. Thus the insurrection ended. We returned to the land of Rauquenhue never to leave again. We lived there in complete tranquility. We heard that the Chileans of other regions did not tire of hunting down the unfortunate Mapuches.

The chiefs Huichal, Colihuinca, and Juanito Millahuinca addressed themselves to the Governor to ask for a treaty. They brought their saddle-bags full of silver objects as requested. But the Governor took the tokens of silver and made shackles for the chiefs. When they were released from prison, they were taken under guard to Boca-Budi. From most accounts it would have been just because these chiefs were the most to blame, especially Colihuinca who had surrendered five Chileans to those who ripped out their live hearts over there on the other side of Carahue.

Marimán, who had killed those men, did not surrender. He fled and remained hidden. Marimán was included in the pardon under the amnesty for the Mapuches that was declared later. . . . When he left his hiding place, he traveled for pleasure and reveled in his friendly relations with the authorities, more than before.

It's been heard said that in Nehuentúe, on the other side of the Cautín River, there was a Chilean by the name of Patricio Rojas. This monster took the Mapuches prisoner and locked them in a hut. Then he set fire to the hut and exterminated the Indians in the flames.

Such was the progress of the Indian uprising in the coastal region. The unfortunate Mapuches went from living in bad conditions to even worse. They had not taken much property from the Chileans, whereas a number of the Chileans enriched themselves thanks to the livestock they pillaged from the Mapuches.

Translated by Ryan Judge and John White

Chile and Its "Others"

One recurring national myth is that Chile—in contrast to its neighbors—is consti-
tuted of an ethnically homogeneous mestizo population. In this imaginary, ethnic
"others" have been located not within the nation, as in many other Latin American
countries, but outside it. This gallery showcases three of Chile's others as imagined
in the late nineteenth century: Peruvians and Bolivians north of its borders, Mapu-
che peoples in the south, and the inhabitants of the newly annexed Easter Island, or
Rapa Nui, far from Chile's Pacific coast. These images circulated at a time when ter-
ritorial expansion put the Chilean state into conflict with peoples, territories, and
nations that were viewed as ethnically distinct from, and inferior to, the mestizo
Chilean nation.

"Faces of the allied army," 1879. Published in a newspaper during the War of the
Pacific, this cartoon portrayed Chile's Andean enemies as racially inferior. According
to the accompanying article, the Peruvian army "is quite notable, most of all, for its
variety of races, which are almost a variety of species and which almost authorizes the
assumption that man comes from the ape or from . . . the elephant." Benjamín Vicuña
Mackenna, "Fisonomias del ejército aliado." *El Nuevo Ferrocarril,* 4 December 1879, 3.
Courtesy of Colección Biblioteca Nacional de Chile.

Mapuche con guagua

Mi querida Mimí

Mil gracias de recordarte de mi
yo no solamente pienso a mi Chilenita
pero me hace muchísima falta aquí
Adios y recibes los mejores besos de
este feo que se llama Pépé

Postcard of Mapuche women and child, c. 1902. As settlers, land speculators, survey-ors, and colonization officials moved into the "empty" lands once governed by Ma-puche groups, early anthropologists and photographers went with them. The images they produced, many of which circulated as postcards, represent an attempt to capture a "lost" culture, now transformed by military defeat, settlement, and colonization. Courtesy of Colección Biblioteca Nacional de Chile.

Moai on Rapa Nui (Easter Island), c. 1920. One of the most isolated places on earth, Easter Island was settled eight centuries ago by the Rapanui, Polynesian migrants who crossed the Pacific Ocean in double-hulled canoes. The Rapanui sculpted giant statues of their deified ancestors in an inland volcanic crater and somehow moved the enormous statues, known as Moai, to coastal altars. Evoking the amazement of European explorers who reached the island in the eighteenth century, the monoliths were displayed in museums in Europe as well as Chile, which annexed the island more than a century later, in 1888. Photographer unknown. Courtesy of Colección Museo Histórico Nacional de Chile.

Race, Nation, and the "Roto Chileno"

Nicolás Palacios

Nicolás Palacios's 1904 polemical book on the racial basis of Chilean national iden-
tity, The Chilean Race *(La Raza Chilena), acquired rapid popularity and noto-*
riety. Palacios's nationalist and anti-immigrant arguments, rooted in nineteenth-
century racial science and specious anthropological arguments about the racial
origins of Chilean mestizaje *(racial mixture), articulated an emergent conservative*
populist-nationalist ideology. Palacios romanticizes the Araucanian contribution
to Chilean racial stock and the figure of the "roto chileno" (literally "Chilean bro-
ken one," a derogatory term for poor and working-class Chileans), whose alleged
combination of German (or "Goth") and Araucanian blood was the source of Chile's
national character and strength. Palacios was an ardent critic of liberal economic
policy and programs to promote European immigration during the late nineteenth
century. The populism inherent in Palacios's xenophobic nationalism found expres-
sion later in his denunciations of the 1907 Escuela Santa Maria massacre of nitrate
workers, which he witnessed as a resident of the city of Iquique.

I love the *roto*; I know he is much better than it is currently supposed; I
admire in him the wittiness developed in his roughness and I believe the
country will be great if it manages to keep in the roto the valuable qualities
that distinguish him. It is just a matter of keeping him away from the vice
of liquor.

First of all, I think it necessary to express to you my opinion about who
is the Chilean roto as a human entity, what are the origins of his blood, and
what is the cause of the uniformity in his thought—which, in sociology, is
the most important condition that characterizes a human group as a race.

I have many conclusive documents, both anthropological and historical,
which allow me to assert that the Chilean roto is a clearly defined and characterized racial entity. This fact is of great importance for us, and all the
observers who have known us, from Darwin to Hancock, have stated it,
though it seems to be ignored by the ruling class of Chile.

The Chilean race, everybody knows, is a *raza mestiza* (mixed race) produced by the Spanish conqueror and the Araucano, and it was born massively since the first years of the Conquest owing to the frequent polygamy that the European conqueror practiced in our country. . . . The Father of the race. The discoverers and conquerors of the New World came from Spain, but their original fatherland was the Baltic sea coast, especially Southern Sweden, nowadays GOTIA. They were the direct descendants of those blond barbarians, warriors, and conquerors who destroyed the Western Roman Empire in their exodus to the south of the European continent. They were the Gothic, prototype of the Teutonic, German, or Northern race, who kept their caste almost entirely pure thanks to the pride of their lineage and the laws that prohibited intermarriage with the conquered races for several centuries. Based upon my knowledge of several portraits and depictions of the conquerors of Chile, I can affirm that fewer than 10 percent of them show marks of mixing with the autochthonous race of Spain, the Iberian race; the rest of them, such as Pedro de Valdivia, whose portrait is so well known, were of pure Teutonic blood.

The Chilean roto is, then, Gothic-Araucano.

Physical and Psychical uniformity of the race. Its cause and its importance. The Chilean race is not Latin.

The mixture of only two ethnic elements in our race gives to the Chilean physiognomy some features that are common to all of us, including to those with the most different faces. This is why foreign witnesses say that in Chile there is a unique race, which is different from every other race in the world. The same can be appreciated by a Chilean when he comes back to the fatherland after having visited other countries.

If the physical physiognomy of the Chilean has some common, characteristic features, his moral physiognomy has such a uniformity in its main lines, that it constitutes one of the most interesting phenomena of our race.

From the blond, blue eyes, and dolichocephalous roto, whose blood is 80 percent gothic, to the reddish Moreno, with scarce black and pig-like moustache, rough hair, and braquicephalous, whose blood is 80 percent *araucana*, we all feel and think in the same way about the key questions upon which all the other questions are organized. Around such key issues as the family and the fatherland, moral and civic duties, our moral and social criteria are one and the same.

This condition of our psychology, whose high importance our leaders seem not to know, can be explained by the peculiar similarity among our parents' souls. Precisely, Goths and Araucanos, though so different in their physical appearance, had both, with the same clarity and firmness, all the defining features of what experts call manly or patriarchal psychology—in which man's criteria absolutely reigns over the woman's in all the spheres of mental activity. It does not seem necessary to recall here the great importance sociologists give to patriarchal guidance in ethnic psychology. The perfect patriarchy of the Germanic race is well known, but the perfection of our native-ancestors' patriarchy seems to have been only appreciated by wise foreigners such as H. Spencer—who posits it as a [racial] type—, and Smith Hancock—who highly praises it.

The conquerors noticed the similarities between the Araucanos and themselves from the first moment. Valdivia himself compares them with the Tudescos for their art of war and the absolute nobility with which they fight. The chroniclers of those times frequently compare them with the Romans or with the Germans who destroyed the Empire. On several occasions Chile's Capitanes Generales did not reject personal duels, gentleman against gentleman, with Araucanian chiefs. Proud Sotomayor, Gothic, married into the royal family, did such a thing—something he would never have done with a plebeian or a villain.

Uriel Hancock, the wise North American writer just mentioned, compares the Araucanos with the Scottish highlanders, adding: "during three centuries and a half they have fought for their freedom against the dominating race, producing hero after hero, like the Scottish mountains; and Chile, like Scotland, is inflamed by the memory of its historical past. For that reason it is a bellicose, heroic and progressive country." "There was something in the Araucano spirit that inspired its enemies' admiration; rarely so little restraint has been seen when speaking of the cause of an adversary, as in the Spanish historians speaking of the Araucanos' campaigns."

The immortal Ercilla synthesized in his poetry the admiration born from the soul of those illustrious conquerors for this barbarian and copper race of the new world. They were, hence, two races with similar heart and mind, those who, during their two-centuries encounter, gave life . . . to the Chilean roto. This is the reason for the uniformity of the roto's mentality.

Disastrous results of the mixture between two different races. Settlers of the Latin race should not be brought to Chile.

[T]here is another way to degenerate and even destroy a race other than alcoholism, which some want to implant in Chile, and this has to be opposed with the same energy with which alcoholism is fought.

I am referring to the immigration on a large scale of families of the Latin race from the old continent, which is being fomented by sectors of the press from Santiago, by journal articles, and even by some Chilean public men. . . . The large scale, massive and forced immigration of Latin families has been tried in our country about ten or twelve years ago. More than 2.5 millions of pesos were spent in the attempt. Logically, the result was completely null. . . . No-one stayed here, except for some bartenders and toy sellers, who did not want to follow in their comrades' wake.

Very different will be the qualities of the immigrants if they are forced to come, whether this is achieved by paying their fare (either by our or their government, or the companies in charge of transferring the poor and unemployed people of those countries), or offering them a job here, a job which they would not have won by their own efforts. These people would come to work as day-laborers, competing with the roto—who would probably cross the Andes [to Argentina] as his ancestors did. East of the Andes there is lot of land and lack of workers, just the opposite from here, in Chile, which, aside from Uruguay, is the South-American country with least land for agriculture, having a surplus population who are forced to emigrate by thousands to neighboring and even remote nations.

If somebody thinks that attracting immigrants by creating for them a privileged situation, such as giving them our lands or priority in public jobs, or any other privilege, it is a mistake and an injustice. The Chilean roto, both the illiterate and those of us who have achieved some education, would unanimously object.

It would also be convenient to dissipate a very common illusion in relation to Latin immigration. Some people imagine that among the immigrants of that race can come, in person or in embryo, a Caton, or a Michelangelo, or a Cervantes, or a Gonzalo de Cordova. There is nothing more unfounded than that hope. The races which produced those geniuses were very different from those which populate Southern Europe today.

I developed this issue at length because, as I already said, especially in under-populated countries like Chile, the immigration problem has more importance than is usually recognized, for it is not always analyzed from the point of view of the races. . . .

Some courage is necessary nowadays to say "I love the roto." The poor of Chile, that roto who you are not ashamed to say you love, is today the Great Orphan, disinherited in his own fatherland which he loves so much, whose glories have been achieved with his own blood, and for which he is always ready to give his life.

Translated by Enrique Garguin

Nitrates, Nationalism, and the End

of the Autocratic Republic

José Manuel Balmaceda, Arturo Alessandri,

and a popular poet

José Manuel Balmaceda was a leading Chilean Liberal. Before becoming president in 1886, he had served in Congress as a deputy and in the Liberal administration of Domingo Santa María as minister of the interior. Balmaceda inherited conflicts with Congress that had been provoked by Santa María's heavy-handed method of wielding presidential power, a legacy of the Portalian autocratic republic. Santa María also bequeathed to Balmaceda tensions with Conservatives and the Catholic Church over a series of anticlerical measures. A proponent of national economic modernization, Balmaceda sought to invest nitrate revenues in an extensive public works system, expanding the country's railroad network, for example, and in public education. As his speech here reflects, he also advocated greater Chilean control over the production, marketing, and transportation of nitrates in the province of Tarapacá where British companies held a number of mining enterprises and a monopoly over railroads. Balmaceda's use of concentrated presidential powers to limit the role of Congress, including his intervention in congressional elections and efforts to name a successor, provoked a head-on collision with the legislature. Naval forces loyal to Congress initiated a civil war against Balmaceda that ultimately led to his defeat and suicide. The civil war put an end to presidential dominance of government and significantly increased the power of Congress, initiating the period known as the Parliamentary Republic.

In the speech here, Balmaceda asserts the need for Chilean control of Tarapacá's foreign-owned railroads and nitrate mines. He also suggests the importance of state ownership of railroads and the possibility of state intervention to guarantee conditions for Chilean investors in the nitrate industry. Balmaceda argues that state action, including ownership of some mines, is necessary to prevent monopolies from dominating an industry so vital to the health of the national economy. This kind of rhetoric won Balmaceda a posthumous reputation as a nationalist who fought to defend Chile's natural resources against foreign capital. Here also is a memoir by the later Chilean president Arturo Alessandri reflecting on the conflict between presidentialism and parliamentarianism in the 1891 civil war. Alessandri identifies his own presidency (1920–1924) with that of Balmaceda and sees his clashes with an obstructionist Congress, which precipitated a military coup, as analogous to the congressionalist insurrection that defeated Balmaceda. Alessandri notes accurately that both Congress and Balmaceda invoked the 1833 Constitution to defend their actions but followed courses of action that were unconstitutional. He laments the limits on electoral freedom imposed by the Constitution and Balmaceda's actions to sidestep congressional authority but views the congressional uprising as producing a political fiasco in which a corrupt aristocracy used its hold over Congress to build a "despotic dictatorship" that rendered the president impotent to pursue programs in the national interest.

These selections are accompanied by "La Balmacedista," a working-class poem dedicated to Balmaceda. Following the civil war of 1891 and Balmaceda's defeat and death, he became an idealized figure in the popular imagination, although his policies had rarely favored the working class or poor. Indeed, at the height of his conflict with Congress, he had sent troops to help suppress a general strike of railroad and port workers and nitrate miners in the north. As the historian Julio Pinto Vallejos has noted, despite his role in repressing the strike and the support of nitrate workers for the congressionalist cause, after his death Balmaceda came to be lionized in popular mythology as a populist and nationalist hero, representative of working-class interests in Chile's northern nitrate fields. "Popular Balmacedismo" expressed strains of working-class militancy and nationalism that would later come together in a powerful leftist labor movement.

President Balmaceda's Speech at Iquique

As head of the State and as a Chilean, I am extremely pleased to be with you, gentlemen. I find myself in the most active and populous heart of our land, which yesterday was the site of immortal exploits, and today is a center of culture, fruitful labor, a singular prosperity, and a manly cosmopolitanism. This spirit animates hundreds of industries and thousands of businesses, all of them created with complete liberty, and without any fear as to the rights of Chileans or foreigners, because here, as elsewhere, we are all equal under the rule of our national institutions. My fellow citizens are watching Tarapacá closely; and this is natural, because this region produces the substance needed around the world to restore exhausted soil, and because [our nitrates] are the restorers par excellence of the productive power of the land cultivated by man.

Everyone, especially legislators and men of State, must consider the extraction, manufacture, transportation, shipment, ocean freights, and application of nitrate (as well as mining and secondary industries), the business and use of credit, and the economic results of these various serious and interesting factors.

Nitrate extraction and manufacture are the domain of free competition in that industry: likewise, national ownership is now the object of serious reflection and study. Private ownership is almost all foreign and is actively concentrated in individuals of one nationality. It would be preferable that private ownership was also Chilean, but if national capital is lazy or jealous, we should not then be surprised that foreign capital has the foresight and intelligence to fill the void that, as the region progresses, is left by our compatriots' negligence.

The pending transfer of part of nitrate ownership to the state will open new horizons for Chilean investment, if the conditions in which it operates are modified and if the concerns that discourage it are corrected; the application of Chilean capital to that industry will allow us to benefit from the export of our own wealth and the normalization of production without the danger of creating a possible monopoly.

The moment has arrived to make a declaration in front of the entire Republic. The industrial monopoly of nitrate cannot be the business of the State, whose fundamental mission is only to guarantee property and liberty. Nor should the monopoly be the work of private individuals, whether national or foreign, because we will never again accept the economic tyranny of the few over the many. The State will always have to own a sufficient amount of the nitrate industry to protect, through its influence, the production and sale of nitrate, and to frustrate every possibility of industrial dictatorship in Tarapacá.

This is the right moment to set the course, and for that very reason I stress the advantages that greedy and selfish forces sought to obtain through monopolistic practices: improvements in manufacturing, reduced transport prices, easy and free shipments, reduction of freight costs and greater maritime safety, and principally the expansion of nitrate markets and consumption. This is a system condemned by morals and experience, since, in the economic regime of modern nations, it has been proven and demonstrated that only free labor enlightens and enlivens industry.

In relation to the above ideas, public transportation is here a serious local question. I am of the opinion that the railway question ought to be equitably resolved, without injuring lawful private interests or restricting the convenience and rights of the State. I hope that all the railways in Tarapacá will soon become national property. I am striving, gentlemen, to make Chile the owner of all the railways that cross her lands.

Private railways naturally respond to private interests, while State railways represent, above all, the people's interests: low fares to encourage industry, which increase the value of property itself. Finally, we ought to invest our surplus revenue in infrastructure, so that when the time comes that nitrate is exhausted, or its importance is diminished by the discovery of other nitrate fields or by the progress of science, we will have created a national industry and with it the State railways created the basis for new revenue sources and national greatness.

Let us invest in railways and public works the twenty million pesos of our yearly surplus, and in ten years we will create from our own resources two hundred million pesos' worth of useful public works.

With respect to railroad construction, our greatest priority is to build the line connecting this great emporium of wealth with the Chilean capital. I wish that all the most distant corners of our country were connected by rail, so that industry would spring up and flourish everywhere, and our people could travel on steel rails from north to south in all directions, so that wherever we need to defend the national territory, my fellow citizens would be there to defend it.

We have all the resources and credit we need to carry out this great enterprise, and foreign lands offer their advice, skills, labor to execute it.

Translated by Elizabeth Q. Hutchison

The Revolution of 1891: My Participation, by Arturo Alessandri

The days passed in this way until the 19th of September, when the tragic death of President Balmaceda took the city and country by surprise. Many celebrated; others, including myself, felt deeply sad. The heroic sacrifice of the President struck me as a clear demonstration of what that man had fought for, not for ambition or petty interests, but rather driven by honorable conviction, he had followed the only road that his duty indicated, defending the country's sacred interests, which, as he had said with such truth and sentiment, he loved above all else.

I insist that the revolution was a great historical calamity even though no one was directly responsible for it.

We have seen that, for many years, a general feeling had been born, later transformed into a true civic religion, which demanded that the immense presidential powers granted by the Constitution of 1833 be reduced in order to enjoy greater liberty.

Much was achieved with the 1874 and other reforms. Unfortunately, habits and customs, stronger than written law, were unable, through the years, to wrest from the hands of the President of the Republic the power derived from his ability to use elected offices at will, principally with respect to designating the successor to the presidential throne.

The people therefore felt it had been deprived of its most important right, and the great abuses under the Santa María administration intensified the desire and the need to return to the people, once and for all, the most sacred of rights: electoral freedom, the fundamental and true base of a democratic regime.

This was in essence the common feeling, which, mixed with passions, interests, ambitions, jealousies, etc. etc., converted that desire into a powerful psychic force that held too strongly in the subconscious of the politicians who emerged from the agitated political events that became the civil war of 1891.

The powerful sentiment of freedom and the inveterate repeated abuses over so many years fostered mistrust of the President, whose opponents sought guarantees and security by forming cabinets that represented the Congress, which would owe their existence to the Congress and have the Congress's trust. Their immense desire to achieve their goals and the passion of the fight prevented them from seeing that they revolted against the constitutional rights of the President. It did not matter: the hour of triumph had arrived, and it was necessary to achieve it. . . .

If he, in his fierce fight with Congress, was relying on the Constitution and had made himself the champion of this doctrine, he should not have abandoned that solid trench of stability. This resulted in the decline of his moral authority. . . .

It is undeniable that the Revolution of 1891 finally ended the President's absolute authority to select senators and deputies and, most important, choose his successor. Without exception, the presidents subsequent to 1891 have not been able to rely on the support or the affections of their predecessors.

All of these are actions that demonstrate how the President of the Republic's irresistible tool of absolute intervention was damaged and finally destroyed by the Revolution of 1891. . . .

Unfortunately this advantage, which undoubtedly could have been attained just through public opinion campaigns and with peaceful legal change over time, does not compensate for the considerable misfortunes that the tragedy cost the country.

The victors did not know how to lay down rules for the victory. The parliamentarianism that served as a banner declined into a true orgy that left all the public services in a state of absolute disorganization. The vote of censure, based in the Constitution, without any rule or restrictive measure; the failure to close the debates; the impotence of the executive to exact resolutions or pronouncements about its plans or laws that were necessary in order to know the will of the majority, the foundation of the democratic regime, enthroned the Congress at the head of a total and despotic dictatorship.

The legal responsibility of the President of the Republic existed; but, in fact, he became a simple slave of Congress, before whom he had to yield quickly in order to govern, since if he did not obey its orders he fell into the clutches of the censure and was left without ministers.

Translated by Elizabeth Q. Hutchison

"The Balmacedist," by a popular poet

Your eyes are two stars
That shine in the sky
And your smile is a crystal ball
In which I can see my happiness reflected
Balmaceda is not dead
I tell you,
Love of my life,
That he is very much alive
That he is very much alive, yes,
Who would believe it
That he will return triumphant
With his flag held high.

II
Those who today exploit the masses
Are tyrants and big shots
Who want to become rich by
Taking "contributions"
The poor and the worker
Through their work
Make the rich fat
And other rogues

And other rogues, yes
And this is the truth
Even if Montes
And Condorito don't like it.

III
The poor are dying of hunger
Because there is nothing to eat
And the rich don't care
If the poor man perishes
With laws and decrees
They want to drown him
Make him jump through hoops
And strangle him
And strangle him, yes
And this is the truth
Freedom is chafing
Against the chains that bind her

IV
Those who yesterday were free
Today are called saviors
And answer all protest
With a kick in the pants
They call Balmaceda a tyrant
Because he said to the poor
"You are my brothers"
You are my brothers, yes,
Without distinction
Even if your redemption
Costs me my life."

Translated by Ericka Verba

A Manifesto to the Chilean People

Democratic Party

This document from the inauguration of Chile's first proworker party protests the oligarchic politics of the Parliamentary Republic and demands a truly representative system of government. The Democratic Party's manifesto also articulated one of the earliest critiques of Chile's export-driven economic modernization, arguing that the country's focus on agricultural exports had led to the neglect of manufacturing. The party's support for protectionist policies reflected both its artisan and working-class base, as well as the realities of an increasingly urban economy and society. While organizing a vocal working-class press and building ties to workers' mutual aid societies, the Democratic Party advocated a strategy of winning social and political reforms at the ballot box. Indeed, over the following decades it would elect a number of its members to Congress. The party's demands for reforms to democratize the political system and its critique of the rural aristocratic order were indicative of a party whose base and leadership included intellectuals and members of the urban middle class, as well as artisans and workers, and the entrance of those social groups into the world of formal politics.

A new political party has just been constituted: the independent workers of the capital and of Valparaíso, in conjunction with the radical youth and all workingmen, have laid aside class differences to raise the banner for the social, political, and economic regeneration of the country. These forces have united to lay the foundation of the great Democratic Party.

The directorate believes that one of its most fundamental responsibilities is to make public the purpose, beliefs and goals of the new party; the means that it will employ and the causes that gave rise to its constitution.

To build ourselves into a great and sovereign nation by means of the efforts of the indomitable Chilean people, it has been established that the government of the republic should be *popular and representative*. This means that the people, free of coercion of any kind, should elect the officials of the State. In addition, these people's representatives in Congress should pass laws that work for the betterment of the nation. . . . All the parties adopt the great moral and religious interests of the nation as the pretext for their dissensions: they speak of civil and political liberties and freedom of conscience; they spill the blood of the people for the triumph of the Pope or civil power; they fight in the name of heaven or of hell.

All the while the material well-being of the people and the prosperity of the nation are considered of little importance. . . .

Because our nation's economy depends exclusively on agriculture, we live in a state bordering on barbarity. The poor man is condemned to the slave-like condition of tenant farming, to the laborious cycle of the ox and plow. Intelligent work and skilled labor have no place among us. The underprivileged are born into a dark cloud of misery and ignorance, of subservient and proletariat status. This fate that binds them is their only social inheritance and the only thing they can ever truly call their own. . . .

Such a lamentable and backward condition has not permitted our nation to contribute to the greater civilization, nor appreciate the merit of public institutions. Even more so, it blocks our people from having the voice that they deserve in the course of public policy and in the defense of their freedom and rights.

This is why we are inundated with attitudes of apathy, servitude, superstition and ignorance. This is why we are not a modern nation and have limited contact with other parts of the world. This is why we struggle with poverty and political impotence.

Where manufacturing industries flourish, however, the human spirit finds itself less hindered. The ideal of tolerance gains new ground, and moral truth replaces the restriction of conscious.

Factories and manufacturers are the mothers and daughters of civil liberty, electricity, arts, sciences, commerce, better navigation and modes of transport, civilization and political power.

But the existing parties want to keep us from realizing such a goal. In the midst of their great egoism, the deleterious practice of buying foreign merchandise has taken precedence over developing the productive forces of this country. The former practice leads to our economic demise. Employment of the latter would guide us toward an economy independent of outside forces and set us on a solid course to future prosperity and a better nation.

The current parties are so blind that they ignore the fact that factories have many times the value of arable land. They fail to see that the income generated by the increasing prices of consumer products will more than compensate for the current value and demand for agricultural products.

The other parties have not wanted, nor been able, to understand these realities. And an agenda based on these truths is exactly what the Democratic Party proposes to accomplish.

We want a general and comprehensive protection for national industries; a protection that precludes any privileges for the hateful monopolies.

We propose to suppress the system of taxes that weighs upon our jobs and our ability to feed ourselves.

We will promote training for industry.

We propose a government of the people, by the people and for the people; a government founded under the guidance of our most apt citizens.

We want a liberty founded on prosperity, because a miserable and impoverished nation cannot also be a free nation. There can be no social stability in a society where the majority of citizens lack general well-being. There can be neither progress nor civilization in a nation where men lead isolated lives and spend the greater part of the year looking to nature or to God for the success or failure of their crops.

We have united to accomplish this dream, and we implore others of good will to join us. We call out to men who love their country and are conscious of their rights and their interests. Our call makes no distinction between people of different classes or from diverse circumstances. We are confident that our ranks will quickly swell with those who long for the improvement of the fatherland.

This peaceful struggle can only occur through the ballot box. Dignified and honorable suffrage will be our only weapon. The ability to vote is our right and our power, and for this reason we will not let it be infringed upon or snatched away. Suffrage is sovereignty, and the sovereignty of man is inviolable. Every man is free and sovereign over himself.

As a result, man cannot renounce his right to sovereignty without abdicating his liberty, without renouncing his personality.

Until now the sovereignty of the people has existed in name only. The clergy and the government, the spiritual and earthly powers of theocracy and oligarchy, have all played a role in repressing the most sacred right of man: his moral and material liberty.

We shall demand, then, sovereignty of the people, a government based on reason, and the enjoyment of liberty and both material and moral well-being.

Translated by Trevor Martenson

"God Distributes His Gifts Unequally":
An Archbishop Defends Social Inequality

Mariano Casanova

Archbishop Mariano Casanova's 1893 pastoral letter articulated the Catholic Church's response to the growing militancy of workers' movements, calls for social reform, and the emergence of political parties like the Democratic Party. Casanova both denounced the spread of "irreligious and antisocial doctrines" and promoted Pope Leo XIII's 1891 Rerum Novarum *(Of New Things), which directed the Church to work for the improvement of conditions for the urban working class, while combating communism. The Church advocated on behalf of social reforms to ameliorate the poverty produced by modernization and urbanization, but also established the sanctity of private property as a natural and divine right, as well as the mutual interdependence of labor and capital, arguing strenuously against socialist programs of redistribution. Casanova argues here that socialism constitutes a danger because its espousal of social equality violates the natural order and thus God's order. Casanova's sermon reflects a period of social change accompanying economic modernization in Chile and the Church's weak support among the urban poor and working class as it faced stiff competition from radical labor organizations and anticlerical leftist parties.*

To the Clergy and Those Loyal to the Archdiocese,
Health and Peace in the Lord

A while ago, because of unrestricted freedoms, irreligious and antisocial doctrines were propagated in this country that imply grave danger for the faith of our people and threaten to undermine the foundation on which the social structure rests. A relentless work of discrimination has been undertaken against religion with the purpose of making it contemptible and hateful in the eyes of the people. It denies its dogmas, ridicules its holy practices, blasphemes God and his saints, and scorns his most noble mysteries.

As in the worst times of impiety, it tries to persuade the people that the entire body of doctrine taught by the Church, the sacraments, morals and the cult, are inventions of the clergy, made with worldly goals and temporary conventions. And above all, there is a decided determination to slander the Catholic priesthood and devise precautions of all kinds to bring about their loss of prestige and replace with hatred or ridicule the love and respect that it has professed to the Catholic people of Chile.

This propaganda against religion is bearing fruit. Never has been seen among us a greater number of sacrilegious thefts and profanation of things belonging to the saints. Never have manifestations of impiety been presented more explicitly nor significant disrespect shown against the priesthood. As well, we have never seen such a great number of anonymous publications intended almost exclusively to attack and denigrate religion, nor have such crudity and disorder ever been used in such attacks. Proof of the speed with which this impiety travels, the lack of effective correction and someone to apply it, and even the indifference of not a few Catholics is serving as stimulus to the enemies of the religion.

They have already stopped feeling the effects of irreligious propaganda in the invasion of the socialist plague, whose existence in the republic is manifested by unmistakable symptoms. No one ignores socialism, whose doctrines and consequences oppose the law of God; it is only propagated where religion has lost its authority.

In this way then, in view of these evils and in compliance with a vital duty of our pastoral ministry, we believe it appropriate to prevent the dangers that threaten the faith of the Catholic people, and to call attention to the injustice and the ingratitude with which the enemies of the religion, the Church and the social order advance.

IV

Another evil of the current time to which we want to call the attention of the Catholic people, is the socialist propaganda that is made in this country through the publications and meetings of the working class. We oppose the idea that our people thoughtlessly accept the doctrines that have brought other countries to the edge of the abyss and are producing social upheavals and offenses against property in some nations of Europe that have alarmed the most powerful governments.

Socialism establishes as a right the equal distribution of wealth among all citizens, and as a consequence the abolition of property. War on the rich! is the slogan of the communist; and the logical derivation of this slogan is the plundering or destruction of private property.

The simple enunciation of this doctrine is enough to persuade one that its acceptance would bring about the ruin of society such as God established it. In effect, the redistribution of wealth would destroy the unequal social conditions on which society is founded. In order for society to subsist it requires relationships of necessity among members, to the point that each member, to satisfy his own needs, relies on the competition and services of the rest. Therefore, the rich need the poor, and the poor the rich; the worker needs industry for his salary, and industry needs the worker to give impulse to production; the professional scientific man needs the client to obtain the benefits of his discipline, and the client needs the professional for the direction and protection of his interests. Man enters necessarily into society, because he needs the competition of other men to live; but socialist equality, making this competition unnecessary, would make the necessity of association disappear, which for us is imposed by the same nature.

"Man was born for society; everything that he has arranged in it is his testimony: society is a necessity for his body, a necessity for his heart, a necessity for his intelligence."

In contrast, the inequality of conditions is not the work of man but of nature, or rather, of God, who distributes his gifts unequally. As well as not having equal talent, equal strength, nor equal nobility, not all have the same fortune. And out of this inequality social harmony results, this variety in unity that is like the hallmark of divine works. Property, be it inherited or acquired, is a right as sacred as that which every man has to the fruits of his work, of his strengths or his talents. And the day that this right disappears, all stimulus to work will be lacking, and, consequently, progress in all laws of human activity will be stopped.

Socialist doctrine, then, is antisocial, because it tends to overturn the bases which God, author of society, has established. And it is not in the hands of man to correct what God has done. God, as sovereign lord of all that exists, has distributed wealth according to his approval, and prohibits committing an offense against it in his seventh commandment. But he has not left the poor without compensation. If he has not given them wealth, he has given them the means to acquire subsistence with a job that, if it overwhelms the body, makes the soul rejoice. If the poor have less wealth, in exchange they have fewer necessities: they are happy in their own poverty. If the rich have greater goods, they have in exchange more anxieties in their souls, more desires in their hearts, more grief in life. The poor live content-

Nitrate wealth and Santiago's architecture: the salon of Cousiño Palace. This Santiago mansion built by the wealthy Cousiño family reflects the extraordinary wealth amassed during Chile's explosive urban growth in the nitrate era, as the aristocracy moved its residences from the countryside and mining districts to Santiago. Santiago now had a modern urban infrastructure of paved streets, streetcars, electric lights, and automobiles. Nitrate revenues were poured into the construction of major public buildings in the center of the city, most built to imitate the architectural styles of Paris. Photographer unknown. Courtesy of Colección Sala Medina, Biblioteca Nacional de Chile.

edly with little; the rich are never satisfied. "Poverty as object of scandal for the ignorant and the man without faith is for the Christian a rich source of virtues and merits. The true fortune of man is his work, his activity, his intelligence. The poor know that their poverty is a treasure for future life, a fertile seed for the harvest of eternity."

According to the will of God, the surpluses of the rich should be inherited by the poor, in a way that if the rich comply with their duty, bread will never be absent on the table of the poor nor will misery take hold in his home. If God demands resignation to their privations from the poor, in exchange he demands generosity of the rich in favor of the poor. And, how they neglect this strict obligation! The evangelical parable of the miserly rich will not always be a fable for the poor but a severe lesson for the coldhearted rich.

To these temporary compensations are added still eternal compensations. Among those is the kingdom of heaven; the Savior of the world has said: *Beati pauperes, quoniam ipsorum est regnum coelorum.* The poor, says a Catholic writer, are like those settlers abroad who have nothing in one hemisphere, but have but millions in another. They have nothing in this world, but they can have all the treasures of heaven in the other if they tolerate with Christian resignation the privations of their poverty. If the world considers them unfortunate, in the eyes of God they are blessed. They are the object of special love by Jesus Christ, who, being lord of all, wanted to be the poorest of all the poor in the world. The wretched of this world will be the privileged of the immortal homeland. There they will be closer to the King of Glory, because they are similar to him through their poverty; and because of that those who want to live a perfect life on earth will embrace voluntary poverty.

This sublime doctrine, that explains the inequality of wealth in the plans of God, completely dispels the vain sophisms with which socialists try to justify their pretensions. They claim to disrupt society to make the poor happy: but what in reality they obtain, if they practice its doctrines, would make them all unfortunate, the rich and the poor, because all the goods of the earth, distributed in equal parts to all the inhabitants of the world, if this distribution were possible, would leave all deprived and in misery above and beyond the inappreciable benefits of society cemented in order and justice.

"If wealth were divided, says Dr. Beluino, would you like to know what each person would receive from all the revenue of France? Only something like seventy-five cents a day. Would that not be poverty?"

Do not then deceive yourselves, Catholic workers, as a result of the pernicious doctrines that they preach to you, being enemies of your faith, they are also enemies of your true happiness. God, who loves us infinitely more than those who call you friends, has not placed you in this social space you occupy save to make you happy. He wants you to sanctify yourselves in work in order to give you greater rewards in heaven. And in vain you try to look for well-being, violating his divine will and holy laws, because the only happiness possible on earth is to comply with the will of God. Those who violate it will sooner or later find their punishment coming to destroy their hopes and replace their happiness, that they hoped to attain through reprobate means, with misfortune.

Explain these principles to the faithful, beloved cooperators in the holy faith, sure that the truth will open a path in intelligence and make the lost see through their false doctrines to the edge of the abyss in which they want to take the nation, depriving it of the Catholic faith and its charitable influence. I trust in the common sense of our people who have seen where their true interest is and can clearly discern the truth of the error. The rich have resources to dominate their pains and give themselves pastimes; but upon depriving the poor of religious comforts they take away from them their greatest joys and their most satisfying hopes.

Trust in God, beloved brothers, in any case in his cause and ours, and all that we have to desire is the coming of his kingdom. Our duty is to work even when we believe that nothing will be enough, because then from the same God we will receive our reward.

Translated by Carolyn Watson

Workers' Movements and the Birth of the Chilean Left

Luis Emilio Recabarren

This 1902 letter from Luis Emilio Recabarren, secretary general of the Democratic Party and one of the major figures of the Chilean Left, expresses the radical ideas that would lead him to direct the Federation of Chilean Workers and organize the Socialist Workers Party in 1912 and the Chilean Communist Party in 1922. Recabarren, a typesetter by profession, founded and wrote for a number of labor publications in Chile's northern nitrate zone and was an important figure in the northern workers' mancomunales (brotherhoods, or associations of nitrate workers) and unions of the 1890s. Elected to Congress as a Democratic Party representative of these northern districts in 1906, Recabarren—an ardent anticlerical—was not seated both because he refused to swear the official oath on the Bible and because of his revolutionary writings in the press. He was elected once again to Congress in 1921, this time for the Socialist Workers Party, and was able to hold his seat until his suicide in 1924. His political career illustrates the diverse strategies that would characterize the Chilean Left for much of the twentieth century. In this letter written to the director of a mancomunal in Tarapacá, he describes the need for both elected working-class representation in Congress and a general strike in the northern nitrate port Iquique. He also voices one of the central demands of the northern labor movement: an end to the system of payment in scrip, tokens that were redeemable only at company stores and that over time left workers mired in debt to their employers.

Mr. Abdón Díaz

Distinguished friend,

With great pleasure I received a telegram bearing your signature, as president of the Mancomunal Workers Society of Iquique. I shall always remember your phrases because they are the first that a man of your stature directs toward a worker who struggles for the same principles.

Although great distances separate us, we share a community of ideas that unites hearts that beat with the same belief. And that belief, and those feelings are, my friend, those that every worker should feel: *The emancipation of workers, carried out by the very workers*, as the German sociologist Carlos Marx once said.

As a worker, as a working man, I am proud to contemplate, although from a distance, that omnipotent and powerful movement that is being carried out by my working brothers in those areas that are so far from the nation's heart yet so immensely rich. Their immense wealth reflects the immense poverty of the workers who extract that wealth from the common mother to give it to the lazy of the social hive called the rich.

As I write these lines, I ask myself with great distress how it is possible that the worker who extracts such wealth from the land is so poor and miserable he often does not have any food to give to his children.

Why does such a phenomenal anachronism exist?

In my mind the worker who extracts such wealth should own it and not give it to another just because he makes everyone call him the boss.

Such is the case, my friend, that when I learn that the workers rise up, awaken, walk off the job together to ask for more humanity from the boss because it is just to do so, I feel doubly enthused and wish that I could be in the middle of them to inspire them with my words, to help them with my efforts.

To me, the Iquique strike is the first cry of rebellion that the Chilean has given. It is the first cry of protest thrown in the face of the capitalists who, protected by the government and their armies, exploit us according to their inhumane whims, while all the while they claim that our protests of their savage acts are illegal.

There exists in that place a wealth that the poor paid for with rivers of their blood in 1879. This only made the rich happier. This is the place where one sees the most poverty and the most shameless exploitation; where, to defraud the hard worker even more, they force the worker to receive payment in a form of currency that is not legal tender.

The Old World has given us important examples with their massive strikes, fifty, one hundred, two hundred thousand men on strike, what a beautiful thing! The last strike in the United States involved *one million workers*.

All of the massive strikes always triumph because of the strikers' cohesion and because they also have lots of capital to cover their costs.

In addition, the foreign workers disable their workplaces when they go on strike so that other workers, those whom we shall call strike-breakers, can not work in their absence.

The workers at Iquique must do the same because that is the only way possible to win.

The striking worker must never be afraid of blood.

The scrip system must be abolished and you must not ever hope that a law written in Congress will get rid of it. That will never happen because many congressmen are interested in maintaining that very system.

Thus said, it is up to you and nobody else.

The general strike at Iquique, has been called as an extreme necessity and it must be carried out as quickly as possible.

The work shift must be reduced to eight hours and pay must be in the form of legal currency.

These words must be spoken in unison from the lips of every worker in the northern region. Its echo must lift every heart in one movement toward the great strike in order to obtain its laudable objective.

But before doing so it is necessary to be well prepared and have a few thousand pesos in savings to meet the needs of the strikers.

And above all, you must be united and decided.

We must divide society into two classes: rich and poor.

The rich, who are the minority, only think about making themselves richer at the expense of the poor, who are the majority. They affect the lives of countless workers without caring absolutely anything at all about the miserable lives that the rest of us lead. We will collapse one hundred times on the job and the rich will never come by to give us a glass of water to calm the fatigue that they make us suffer. They see us as worse than dogs. They abhor us.

So we, who already know this and are the majority, must extend our embrace broad enough to erase all borders. We must unite in solidar-ity and form one single family, that is, we must live for ourselves and help one another mutually. And once we are under the same roof, at the same time, we will let loose a powerful cry: *Down with the slavery of workers!* By destroying the chains in which the bourgeoisie currently have us together under the yoke of work, we will toss their remains into the face of those who up until now oppress us.

At that time we will impose our will, and together we will enjoy the wealth that Mother Nature provides humanity.

At the same time, my dear friend, up until now it has been the custom that workers, in election times, vote for the first gentleman who approaches them to ask to pay for their vote. Once in Congress they will work with those who exploit us, or they themselves are the exploiters.

Workers commit a true crime when they vote for gentlemen who never see us in a positive light. This equates to giving arms to the enemy so that he may attack us with greater fury.

If the worker wants to send representatives to Congress or the municipality, he must send his own workmates; he must send workers because they are the only ones who can represent his interests. He must never vote for those who are his oppressors.

You, my friend who is at the head of this movement, have the final word in this regard. You have the initiative to advise your friends and produce propaganda in the sense described above.

We wish to be free. We wish to improve our conditions of misery. Let us help one another mutually, relying only upon ourselves.

As it has been said, "The emancipation of workers must come from the very workers." This is the irrefutable truth which has been proven throughout the ages. For twenty years you have worked to fatten the villains, and up until now there has not been one man in Congress who has been able to change the current state of things. The experience of the years must show you a new path toward what is to come.

Never again at the service of the owners, of the bosses, of the rich.

Let us work only for ourselves.

The strike which has begun there is the first step; it is impossible to go back. The path has been taken, and must be followed until we reach our goals.

Hearts with resolve possess great energies; energies that cap their pursuits with success. Weakness must be put down and betrayal must be punished so that only justice and truth prevail.

My most fervent votes will be that you all continue in your great effort, that your children reap the rewards of what is to come, and that the clouds that darken the horizon of our most cherished hopes disappear.

Finally, be brave in this terrible war against the capitalists. They punish us and our enemies. We must hit them in the head.

The boss is a blood-thirsty hyena that jumps on us to devour us. It is our duty, if we wish to remain alive, to defend ourselves and kill this hyena to avoid the danger that it represents.

Go on brave legion of liberty!

Long live freedom and fraternity!

Death to oppression and the owner!

I extend the hands of all of the workers of Tarapacá unto you, my dear friend Díaz, and promise you that from time to time I will write articles for the newspapers that you support.

Union and fraternity.

Luis E. Recabarren S.
Secretary General of the Democratic Party

Translated by Ryan Judge

Nitrate Workers and State Violence: The Massacre at Escuela Santa María de Iquique

Elías Lafertte

This document from Elías Gaviño Lafertte's memoirs provides a vivid description of social conditions and cultural life in Chile's nitrate mines by a worker, union militant, and cofounder of the Chilean Communist Party. Lafertte describes his first jobs in the nitrate mines and ports as a child, reflecting the prevalence of child labor in the north. Lafertte and his family moved from nitrate camp to nitrate camp, and to the port city of Iquique, underlining the tremendous transience of Chilean workers, who had come to compose an unsettled, mobile labor force in both northern and central Chile, in the mines and cities as well as the countryside. Lafertte's memoirs also contain a powerful description of the infamous 1907 massacre of hundreds of workers and their families who congregated in a peaceful protest at the Escuela Santa María (Santa María School) in Iquique. Thousands of workers and their families came to Iquique from the nitrate camps to demand higher wages and occupied the Escuela Santa María. Army troops commanded by Colonel Roberto Silva Renard, who was ordered to dislodge the striking workers from the school by any means necessary, opened fire, leaving many hundreds of people dead and many hundreds more wounded. The massacre has come to symbolize the violent response of the Chilean state to any kind of popular protest or labor organization during this period.

The life of our poor is characterized by the disorganization that misery brings. Work causes families to separate, and children have to live far away from their parents, either because the parents cannot support them or because circumstances prevent the parents from staying. This happened to me at a very early age. First, my father disappeared from the house in search of a better life and never returned. Later, when I was ten years old, I had to leave my mother's side because her "great job" in the La Serena teachers' college didn't even allow her to see me. At that point, my mother decided to send me to Iquique, where my grandmother and uncles had moved. . . .

As soon as I arrived I learned that things were not going at all well: the nitrate camp had "halted" and everyone was leaving. . . . When the traditional horseshoe was nailed to the door of the "Providence" company store, we had to get going to the "Pearl" nitrate camp, where Uncle Juan had found work in the materials warehouse. The sun of the plains tickled my back, but soon I became accustomed to it. In the beginning, I just went around the encampment, observing the work, conversing with the *pampinos* [residents of the pampas], and in general making friends everywhere. When I became more familiar with the work, it began to seem less terrible, and one day it occurred to me that, in spite of my youth, I could work to help support the family.

And so it was that I took my first job in the nitrate fields, and this was the position of ore-crusher, or "toadkiller" as we were known. I worked with another boy of my same age, shoveling the fragments of ore that were too large to fit into the sacks or that were too heavy to carry. We worked twelve hours a day, in the full sun, reducing the large lumps of ore into smaller pieces. But because we were just a pair of kids, of little importance to the company, who only earned sixty cents a day each, nobody paid us any attention. . . .

Later, I took a job in the materials warehouse, where I worked with my uncle. . . . My work consisted of untangling the twine used to sew shut the sacks of nitrate so as not to lose a single ounce of the material. From what I earned in that first year in the nitrate fields, I was able to buy myself some clothing and even send 100 pesos back to my mother. . . .

Once again I had to depart for the north, where my family was now living, at the "Holy Water" camp, next to the nitrate railway. I left Coquimbo on the steamboat *Mapocho* and disembarked one Saturday afternoon in Caleta Buena, a port located between Iquique and Pisagua that had grown a great deal because of nitrate production. . . .

Finally, I arrived at "Holy Water," where I found work as a *herramentero* [tool-carrier], which was a job generally filled by boys my age [13 or 14]. This was one of the most cosmopolitan nitrate companies, given that alongside Chilean workers there were Argentine, Peruvian, and Bolivian workers as well. The boss of the tool-carriers was the "superior" Leonor Juárez, who supervised us each morning when we left, each one in charge of two mules that carried tools to the nitrate fields. There, right out in the fields, was a forge to fix the augers that belonged to each *barretero* [workers who dug or blasted preliminary holes in the desert floor] and the iron bars owned by the company.

The barreteros had to prepare the blasts that extracted the nitrate from the fields. I watched them intently as they worked, as they used the augers and iron bars to open up small shafts within the craters. These shafts were about one foot in circumference and their depth varied according to the terrain. Then, beneath the shaft the barreteros would open up a space, extracting the soil and sand from underneath, so that the [explosive] powder would fill more space and the explosion would be as large as possible, in order to extract as much nitrate as possible. Then they would set up the wick. The barreteros conducted their work with extreme caution. They were paid according to each foot dug out and the barreteros made it a matter of honor to avoid reckless charges—which threw the nitrates too far out—and "lazy" charges, which failed to explode altogether. . . .

At that point, following the custom of the residents of the pampas who got this custom from Bolivia, I learned to "arm myself," that is to chew coca leaves in a very organized and complex fashion. The company store sold coca leaves to the barreteros and miners at one peso per handful. Between lunchtime and the time the explosives were detonated, the workers sat upon the ground and "armed themselves," which consisted of placing in the mouth a large mass of jute and carbon ash, mixed with ground raw potato, that one mixed with the coca leaves in the mouth. The resulting pasty mass swelled up the cheeks of the *armadores* [coca-chewers], who smoked at the same time. No one spoke: they only watched the cars rise and descend during the half hour that the process lasted. The first time that I—imitating my elders—"armed myself," I got sick to my stomach and vomited violently.

The coca leaves, which were brought from Bolivia in large sacks or bundles on the backs of mules, represented one more source of profit—and not a small one—for the company stores. . . . After more than a year in the "Holy Water" camp, the family decided to move to "Puntachara," in the same district of Negreiros. At that time, the phenomenon that most characterized the plains was the mobility of workers from one nitrate camp to the other. No one took root in any one place. Rarely did anyone ever grow old in the same place. Indeed, the plains dwellers were nomadic and wandering in nature and did not stay in one place for long. . . .

Eventually, the family left for Puntachara because of the odd reason that my grandmother was having trouble maintaining her cow in Agua Santa. In Puntachara, I changed my job as toolman for the blue overalls of the workers of the dockyard. . . .

I became familiar with the tools of the mechanic, the distinct keys [or switches] with strange-sounding names. In the end, I learned about all of the instruments that were utilized in the dockyard. My salary was two pesos and ninety cents per day. They paid a small part of the salary in cash and the rest in tokens, exchangeable only in the general store. I liked the look of the tokens. They were silver-plated metal, polished, and shiny and very different from the bone and shell tokens used in the nitrate camps. The tokens came in denominations of one peso, and from ten to twenty cents.

The company's strategy was that the workers would spend their money at the company stores and not outside the camps. Buying provisions on a monthly basis in Negreiros was a convenient and less expensive option for the workers. But I had to buy everything in the general store with those infamous tokens, at high prices fixed by the company. It was often said that the companies did not profit as much from the sale of nitrates as they did from the business from their company stores.

At the end of 1904, I joined my family in Iquique. . . . I did not idle long in Iquique. Just when I was becoming familiar with the wharfs and streets, my grandmother took me by the arm to the railyard to see if there was work for me there.

They hired me and assigned me to the docks, in the lathe department, where train cars and locomotives were repaired. More than two thousand "stained ones" worked in this enormous workshop. In one area of the shop, locomotives with slight damage were repaired. The trains were fueled by burning large blocks of coal imported from Cardiff, England. The local coal from Lota did not have enough energy generating potential. The engineer worked on one side of the boiler and the coal stoker on the other. I began in the lathe room. . . .

I began working in the San Lorenzo *oficina* [mine] [in 1907]. . . . The night of December 10 the whistle sounded three times to wake the mechanic and his apprentice. Ernesto Araya got up and went to work. I remained sleeping and the next morning I was awakened with the news that a strike had broken out. Who had declared the strike? Everything had been done so silently, that for many, including me, the news came as a complete surprise.

What were the reasons for the strike? While I worked in the workshops of the Nitrate Railroad I had seen my salary rise and fall according to the fluctuations in the exchange rate. . . . But here in the pampa things were very different. Here one worked by the job, for a piece rate, or for a fixed wage. The exchange rate had fallen [by half] and as a consequence many basic goods, principally clothing and food, increased in price, in some cases by double.

There was misery and hunger in the pampa, above all for large families. . . . The strike movement had been underground because there were no union organizations that could legally represent the workers then. . . .

Twenty-four hours later a group of some thirty workers, carrying Chilean flags and banners, left for the nearest oficina, Santa Lucía, . . . and were able to halt production there. The column became larger as the pampinos joined it and the peregrination continued from oficina to oficina, until it arrived at La Perla. . . .

The columns of workers had to spend the night in the middle of the pampa at the edge of improvised campfires to combat the cold. . . .

The town was bubbling with energy, full of workers from different oficinas. Orators spoke spontaneously from the kiosk for musical performances or from the flatcars in the railway station. I listened to all the speeches—those leaders who had come out of the heat of the struggle said they were on strike; that we could not continue living with the miserable wages; here was oppression, repression and exploitation; a large loaf of bread cost a peso, that is to say a fourth of what a worker earned in a day. . . .

The word to go down to Iquique began to spread rapidly among the diverse group of pampinos since the province's intendant did not stoop to coming to Alto San Antonio. If the mountain didn't come to us, we would go to the mountain. . . .

The fifth day of the strike, that was a Sunday, there appeared in the morning in the hills, the first groups of workers. In Iquique there was a great deal of excitement. The maritime workers and other workers' organizations commented with enthusiasm on the heroism of the pampinos who had made this long and difficult march, driven forward by their desire for justice. The authorities, on the other hand, were prisoners of a tremendous alarm. They had the Huasares and Esmerelda regiments brought to the city, since the strike of the pampinos coincided with a strike of the port workers, who were also suffering economic problems. The great fear of the authorities was that the pampinos and the workers from Iquique would make contact and initiate an offensive together. To prevent this from happening, as the nitrate workers arrived in the city, they were pushed into closed precincts of the city in Iquique's suburbs. . . .

On Monday, the sixth day of the strike, the nitrate workers continued coming down from the pampa and filling the streets of Iquique. They came in large groups, with their women and children, on foot or on trains that they themselves operated. The railroad company had stopped service in support of the companies, but there were plenty of workers who knew how

Nitrate workers, c. 1906. Photographer unknown. Courtesy of Colección Archivo Fotográfico Biblioteca Nacional de Chile.

to drive locomotives and moved the convoys carrying cargoes of pampi-nos. . . .

The pampinos paraded through the streets and organized large assemblies in which the orators did not tire of recommending that the workers stay calm and maintain order; that nobody drink and that if any undisciplined pampino were to disobey these orders and get drunk, his own comrades would take him to the police station. In the days the pampinos were in Iquique there was not one act of disorder, not even the most minimal violation of private property, nothing that could provoke the intervention of the police. . . . In the assemblies, the orators, almost with tears in their eyes, condemned violence and called for respect for law and order. . . .

The streets filled with soldiers and marines and no groups of more than two were allowed to circulate. The strikers were cornered wherever they found themselves. . . . Around nine I went to the Escuela Santa María and I saw how the soldiers took the stoves away. How were my *compañeros* [comrades] going to eat? . . .

Upon returning in the afternoon I saw that they were setting up machine guns in front of the school. The police were pushing the people, telling them the intendant was going to respond to their petitions. But, in reality, the order that the army, marines, and police had received was to evacuate, by any means, the Escuela Santa María, an order the workers refused to follow. . . .

Around 3:30 to four in the afternoon a terrible expectation reigned in the Escuela Santa María. Army troops pointed their guns against the workers and against the roof where the movement's leaders were in a permanent meeting. The machine guns in the hands of the marines . . . were directed directly against the packed lines of the pampinos. . . . Then the voice of Silva Renard was heard ordering the pampinos to immediately evacuate the school. . . . But, nobody left and, on the contrary, they kept coming and increasing the numbers of those concentrated there, from the adjacent streets that had been carefully cleared previously by the army. . . .

"No . . . We will not move!"

"Nobody leaves . . ."

"We will not move as long as the strike is not resolved!"

"We want a settlement!"

Phrases like this were the response to Silva Renard's order. Then he ordered the coronet to sound and ordered the crime. He coldly gave the order to open fire. The noise of the gunshots was deafening. The fusils fired on the roof, while the machine guns discharged fatal charges three times against the huge crowd of pampinos, three volleys were enough to fill the school with cadavers.

After a silence provoked by shock and death, the cries of women, the screams of the wounded, the sobs of children, and the angry, indignant voices of the survivors of the crime that had just been committed.

Translated by John White

Women, Work, and Labor Politics

Esther Valdés de Díaz

In this short speech by the head of the Seamstresses' Association, we see the variety of concerns and rhetoric that motivated women workers' organization in the early twentieth century. During this period, male-led workers' associations, be they Democratic, anarchist, or socialist, often addressed the issue of women's inequality. While Democratic and socialist leaders like Luis Emilio Recabarren called for women's suffrage, they focused their energy instead on organizing working women in unions and promoting social legislation to protect women (and children) in the workplace.

For their part, upper-class women organized a number of feminist groups, including reading circles and women's clubs, influenced by the feminist movements in Europe and the United States. These women sought to shape movements for suffrage to fit local Chilean realities, in fact postponing any active campaign for the vote until the 1920s. Indeed many upper-class feminists criticized the more militant suffragette movements abroad and reaffirmed the importance of motherhood and the family, while promoting improvements in women's legal status, especially married women's rights to property, income, and custody of children, as essential to national progress and a precondition for female suffrage. Upper-class feminists also viewed extending the vote to poor and illiterate women as undesirable.

Women workers articulated a slightly different vision of the struggle for legal rights and social justice, building a movement that they themselves referred to as working-class feminism in the early decades of the twentieth century. They frequently went on strike, organized their own associations (as in the case of this seamstresses' union), and joined national unionization efforts such as Recabarren's Federation of Chilean Workers. The seamstresses' union, led by the seamstress and labor journalist Esther Valdés de Díaz, demanded the regulation of working hours, an end to night work, Sundays off, and just wages. Working-class women feminists during this period also began to advocate sexual egalitarianism and to critique the hypocrisy of male socialists' and anarchists' patriarchal practices within their own households.

Two years old! This is a cry that, in terms of the life and action of the Seamstresses' Association, sounds something like a victory song, one of joy, deep satisfaction and tenderness!

For those who follow every step in the development of modern workers' movements; for those who predicted that the organization of trade resistance societies would only last as long as the needs of the moment; for those who laugh sententiously, placing the success of women's organization in quarantine; for all of those people it will seem strange, incomprehensible and doubtful that the Seamstresses' Association, organized and founded by women workers, should have arrived quietly, with slow but sure steps, at the end of two years of existence.

Actually, this might be the first time in the life of female organizing in the capital that a women's trade organization—discussed and attacked so much since its foundation—presents the beautiful spectacle of completing two years of existence. Don't be surprised if they say that it's strange that a society such as the Seamstresses' Association should boast of entering a third year of life.

If we keep in mind the indifference and the almost complete lack of organizational spirit that characterizes women workers; if we remember that women resist everything that smells of violence and organized struggle; and then we note that in the actual case of the founding of the Seamstresses' Association, the statutes call for economic improvement through energetic trade organization activity and the practice of the redemptive doctrines of solidarity and union (until recently little known to our working *compañeros* [comrades]); we will see that, in reality, the triumph of the Seamstresses' Association's second anniversary is one of the greatest victories to be achieved in the recent years of trade organization. And we might add an important observation here: in these two years, working women have demonstrated their gifts of faith, action and perseverance. And what is even more valuable, we see what these two years of organized existence have meant for us: women have shown their deep and rigorous discipline, and demonstrated their new consciousness of their worth and of their important and crucial productive potential.

The love and kindness of my compañeras, as well as my love for the cause we defend, have obliged me to remain until today at the head of this wonderful organization, which a handful of modest *obreras* [women workers] started on June 24, 1906. Today, just as yesterday, I feel in my breast the beautiful and energetic longing for justice for the crushing and ill-paid work of the obreras, for these noble and bold collaborators of the increase of capital, who fuel employers' exploitation and luxury.

Washerwomen in a Valparaíso slum, c. 1900. Although many nineteenth-century observers dwelled on Chile's dramatic rural poverty, the cities increasingly attracted the attention of journalists, novelists, poets, and others. As land scarcity and early industrialization drew ever larger numbers of poor Chileans to urban centers in search of work, the shanties that ringed them gave rise to *conventillos:* poor dwellings organized around a central patio where washing and cooking took place; photographs of the era often show women at work there. Photographed by Harry Grant Olds. Courtesy of Colección Museo Histórico Nacional de Chile.

On the wings of memory I go back two years to examine the moral and physical state of my sisters of the workshop, comparing them with the women workers of today, who bear that noble and brave stamp that imprints on our acts the awareness that we know what we are and what we are worth. I see more self-assurance and energy in the formerly timid countenance of women workers, and as though to complement such a pretty picture, I find an atmosphere, a perfume of social solidarity that inspires all of their organized activities. These reflections are another valuable face of the victory that has been achieved with the spread of women's association and organization.

As for the rest, we all know about the change that has taken place in bourgeois practice and customs, in terms of the consideration and relative respect they now pay to women workers in the workshop and the factory. With a few brush-strokes, we can paint a water-color that shows the struggle and the victory that women workers have carried out during these past two years of female trade union organizing. The street actions achieved by women's organizations have been few—one could truthfully say that the strike itself has not existed. It would be more correct to say that a perfume—that powerful spirit of discipline, organization and solidarity—has pervaded the proletarian environment and has caused women's action and energy to take its place in the economic struggle, a place that modern progress had reserved for it. The relative gains in wages, work-hours and the personal consideration for the woman worker that have been achieved in some workshops and factories—in this category the Camisería Matas, the Fábrica de Tejidos and the Justiniano Military Workshop stand out—show that union spirit and pressure are slowly but surely taking deep root in women's trades. And the day is not far off in which the diverse and lost elements of women's organization will fuse together into one action and one force; and this will show working women the beginning of a dawn that will have no dusk, which will usher in an era of improvement and economic independence for working women.

The Seamstresses' Association, rightly enough, has not been far from this slow but sure female awakening. One can say that because of the initiative, energy and constant propaganda of the women workers who belong to those different workshops and factories (each of which contained members of the Seamstresses' Association), the timid women workers—the classic and slavish meat of exploitation—one day rebelled and refused to be automatic machines any more; they took hold of the book and opened their hearts to the committed voices of their sisters who want to save them from the opprobious and bestial yoke of capitalist exploitation.

Oh! How beautiful! What a touching event! How our spirits move at the memory of such an important victory, the noble victory of freeing the spirit of our sisters! Ah! The awaited hour has come: that hour glimpsed by the *visionaries*, by those noble [women] fighters who sowed the seed of economic redemption in the midst of jokes and indifference. They have accomplished what the skeptics called *impossible*. These classic and legendary sheep evolved into wounded lionesses—modest and quiet, conscious and lofty—and demanded of their boss, that usurper of their well-being and energy, the fair and legitimate payment for the work they do for 10 or 12 hours a day. The struggle did not last long. The furious and despotic boss laughed at the demands of the women workers and threw them out onto the street. Several days went by and the doors of the factory remained closed. However: the blindfold of pride and fatuousness that covered the avaricious eyes of the boss fell before the magnificent glimmer of iron-like female organization, and the boss of yore, who waited for the obrera to come begging for work, had to surrender before the evidence and recognize that the obrera of today had woken up and demanded what, as an agent of industry, corresponds to her.

Days went by and the Chilean obrera gave the most beautiful and noble example of union and social solidarity, perhaps for the first time. Union and force defeated the pride and gold of the despotic boss: he called his workers and made an agreement. "It is not possible," he said, "for me to give you all that you ask. This would ruin me. I will give you half and . . . afterward we'll see if I can give you more. But you must promise me that no other boss will find out what I am paying you."

Here I have sketched the outlines of my talk, the work and triumph of women workers' organization. With victory attained singly in different workshops and factories, the value of women's trade organization has been recognized, at the same time that the organization moves toward a future and colossal collective victory.

It would be a mistake to sleep on our laurels, or to give in to the biased propaganda of our enemies, who spread the idea that women's trade organization has no purpose. It would be a crime to betray the work we have begun and have already set in motion with bravery and foresight. It would be cowardly and reprehensible to get left behind on the way. We must continue energetically and confidently to the end, even if we do so at a slow pace.

Like other human actions—the great causes, the struggles, the innovations, the very progress of humanity—this movement also has its painful aspects: deep sorrows, profound discouragements, which wound, demoralize, and destroy the warmest spirit. This has happened in the very bosom of our dear institution. It is painful to say this, but our mission is like that of the surgeon, who rips open living flesh to extract the pus that suppurates inside, and heals the wound with fire if necessary.

Not just a few, but many compañeras have deserted our ranks—why not say it?—discouraged by the antipropaganda that some members have blindly and treacherously carried out, lending credence to the rumors and slander that vent their fury on even the most noble and honorable things. This has meant that we have had to carry out a mortal struggle within our own organization.

However, our enemies' propaganda against us have been countered in part by the constancy, bravery, and conviction of those courageous members, of those who have every day been like a sentinel, watching over the future of our beloved institution. And today, in spite of the vicissitudes and mishaps, in spite of the fact that the bone of contention has been sown in the very bosom of our association, in spite of mistrust and even demoralization, our Association has stayed virile and lofty, challenging the rigors of the division that some have tried to sow there. Like those armies, destroyers of universal peace, who after combat and victory call the roll of the brave ones who have remained at the foot of the cannon, we today—after the innumerable tests through which we have passed in our short organizational life of two years—call the roll of the courageous ones who remain, the fighters who make up the vanguard of the proletarian women's army. We are few, perhaps, but we know that we are foot-soldiers, seasoned and experienced in the field of battle, the anonymous proponents of the cause, who march unshaken to conquer the ideal that can be seen in the distance.

Translated by Elizabeth Q. Hutchison

The Lion of Tarapacá

Arturo Alessandri

Arturo Alessandri was leader of the Liberal Alliance, composed of the Liberal, Radical, and Democratic parties, and president from 1920 until his removal at the hands of a military coup in 1924. He was known as "the Lion of Tarapacá" for his famous populist senatorial campaign of 1915 in Chile's nitrate districts, in which he assailed the Chilean aristocracy and embraced the working class and poor as mi querida chusma *(my beloved rabble). Alessandri injected a personalistic populist style into Chilean politics, competing with the Left and organized labor for the loyalty of miners and urban workers. In the speech provided here, he makes the case for social welfare and labor legislation as vital for the resolution of the bitter labor conflicts and profound social changes produced by nitrate-generated economic modernization. In office, Alessandri sought to implement key social reforms, including a labor code, but met with an intransigent conservative Congress, who consistently refused to pass his legislation. The political stalemate was broken in 1924 when military officers placed pressure on Congress to pass a number of Alessandri's social and economic reforms and then took power after his resignation and departure into exile. A second coup, led by the army majors Carlos Ibáñez and Marmaduke Grove, who supported Alessandri's reformist program and opposed the more conservative upper-level officers who had taken power in 1924, led to Alessandri's return to the presidency in 1925. The Parliamentary Republic came to an end with a new Constitution in 1925 that restored a number of key presidential powers and imposed limits on congressional authority. Alessandri's government would last only months; he resigned once again in late 1925 under pressure from Ibáñez, who had become his minister of war.*

Despite his populist appeals to workers and efforts to build a state-directed system of labor relations, Alessandri, like his predecessors, responded to strikes with military force. In 1925, for example, he declared a state of siege and sent troops to Tarapacá to repress a general strike of railroad and port workers and nitrate miners who demanded a series of rights encoded in Alessandri's own social legislation, including the eight-hour day, as well as the nationalization of the nitrate industry. The crackdown on the strike resulted in the massacre of hundreds of workers who had occupied the La Coruña oficina *(mine). Nonetheless, Alessandri's government marked the ascension of middle-class and worker-based parties like the Radical and Democratic parties, as well as a new style of mass-based politics. In addition, the social and economic reforms finally passed in 1924–1925, with the backing of officers like Ibáñez and Grove, significantly modified the laissez-faire liberal model that had dominated since the nineteenth century.*

Throughout my recent travels across the country, I have felt the vibrations of the national soul. I have felt its pulse as well as its most noble yearnings, and though I am but a modest soldier of a great cause, I cannot resist the thrust of great popular aspirations. . . .

Men from the entire country are congregated here and it can be said that what pulsates in this Assembly is the synthesis of the Chilean soul, genuinely represented by all the tendencies, by all the aspirations and by all the yearnings that inspire citizens of the Republic's territory from one end to the other. . . .

The country is currently facing one of the most difficult moments in its history. For years, we have been living in the midst of anarchy and lawlessness. Fears and hardships of all sorts hinder the prosperous course of activities in this fatherland, so dear to us all. The country wants and demands a solid and strong government, with a defined agenda, oriented on the basis of a markedly national policy. . . .

I have spent all of my life serving the sacred cause of public freedoms. I have fought the most energetic struggles for them, with particular dedication to electoral freedom, for which I have made considerable sacrifices. I speak mainly here of electoral freedom. . . . It was won in our country by way of bloody sacrifices and is one of the achievements that all patriots who worship the religion of democracy must respect and serve with all their energy, with all the faith of their integrity. . . .

Our 1833 Constitution, the glorious monument upon which the Republic's greatness has been built, was drafted on the basis of an all-encompassing and absolute centralism, which was necessary given the period's social conditions. Taking into account the size of the territory and the population, and the limited circulation of culture and education in that period, this regime can be considered useful, appropriate and necessary for the formation of the Republic and for the orderly and peaceful consolidation of its institutions. But the years have gone by, the country has grown in every sphere of activity, the population has increased, culture has spread and powerful, energetic progress emerges everywhere. The exaggerated centralism of 1833 is no longer possible or appropriate, it is simply absurd. Our Fundamental Charter must be reformed in this respect, as provinces must be given legal personality so that they can see to all of their local services and so that they can directly intervene in electing the authorities who will govern them. Provinces should be entitled to: elect local authorities directly; tend to local needs by way of their own activities; and determine how they shall invest their own public monies. These three points constitute the indestructible and necessary basis of a methodical and reasoned decentralization. By raising the provinces' intellectual and material level, they will in turn contribute to the Republic's general progress.

When this takes place, we will have fine roadways, bridges and schools. Our prisons, hospitals and public buildings, now unfortunately an affront to civilization, will also have been improved. . . . The peoples' economic progress, which is the preferential preoccupation of all rationally organized governments, is precisely the result of the individual's personal effort and of the capital that uses this effort and remunerates it. Consequently, if the proletariat represents the muscle, the vigor, the intelligent effort in the immense economical laboratory that generates the country's wealth, then it constitutes an efficient and necessary factor for progress and it must be tended to, protected and supported. There are diverse reasons for this, some are moral and are related to justice and others are material and are related to convenience.

At this very moment, public opinion is assiduously following a movement of strikers that has suspended and paralyzed all coal production in the South.

This is not the appropriate time to analyze the causes or origins of that movement. Nor is it up to me to express my opinion regarding those who administer justice. My purposes only require that I recognize this movement's existence. A considerable strike carries on and brings with it hunger, misery and pain to many thousands of our fellow citizens. Hardships make themselves felt, and hours of distress touch not only men, but also women and children.

The capitalists, like all of society, see their interests affected. Railroad service is altered and the country's general economy is harmed.

This disastrous situation, furthermore, slowly deepens the abyss of resentment and enmity between capitalists and workers, both contributing factors of national progress. They are common associates in the economic life of peoples whose very growth and prosperity is based upon the harmony that must oversee all relations between these two weighty factors that are indispensable to any sort of prosperity and greatness.

The government's impotence in the face of this situation is deeply disastrous for the noble and sacred social interest. In such a situation, a government must have pre-established norms that allow it to deal with the danger. It cannot possibly be reduced to the status of impotent witness, inert and disarmed in the face of the disorder and the disorganization brought on by the prolongation of this state of things.

Precautionary legislation anticipating such emergency situations is necessary. Republican justice must create an obligatory arbitration tribunal so as to avoid these painful situations. Prevention is better than cure. The government must have at its disposal such a powerful instrument of order and progress.

These conflicts—that are unfortunately spreading to a great extent among us—always pit a weak side against a strong and powerful one. It is, accordingly, necessary, appropriate and indispensable that justice mediate between the weak and the strong and that this justice be sovereign and impartial, as cold as the law and as majestic as the moral force that it represents. This moral force should resolve conflicts, re-establish order and peace, producing harmony between capital and labor, the two hinges of the machine of progress.

The solution to this most pressing problem in our national existence no longer brooks delays. Whoever takes the luxury of discussing its appropriateness lacks due appreciation of the imperative demand for social order and for our country's firm and solid progress. It is impossible to deny that the proletariat's efficiency is an irreplaceable economic factor. This is why the State, represented by the government, must possess the necessary elements to physically, morally and intellectually defend the proletariat.

We must demand that the proletariat be given housing that is affordable, that is hygienic enough so as to protect workers' health and comfortable enough so as to keep them away from the taverns and so as to generate in their spirits the feelings of family and of belonging to a home. We must ensure that workers receive appropriate remuneration for their labor, allowing them to provide for their families and see to their lives' basic needs, in a physical sense and in relation to their moral improvement and their honest recreation. They must be protected in accidents, illness and in their old age. Society cannot and must not abandon to misery and hardship those who have dedicated their entire life's effort to serving it and furthering its progress. . . .

The machinery of our administrative organization lacks the appropriate body by which it would tend to, develop and supervise questions pertaining to socio-economical problems. This body is the Ministry of Labor and Social Planning that has yet to be created. Public opinion demands that it be created, and I've likewise been demanding that it be created with unshakeable determination. This pressing and unavoidable requirement that our social development has brought on allows no further delay.

The law of obligatory primary school education depends on the consideration of the Honorable Senate of the Republic. What was for so many years a great and deeply felt national aspiration only awaits the sanction of the Senate's final constitutional procedure to become a beautiful reality. All gathered here know how much I have fought for this law of public salvation. You also know that it is not sufficient for laws to be written and that they must be put into practice through their correct and appropriate application. This is why I declare to you that my soul would be most deeply satisfied if, as head of State, I had the honor of giving life, form and movement to a law that I have pursued with untiring persistence. . . .

Women's legal condition in Chile has not yet been freed from the narrow molds that humiliate and oppress them and that are not attuned to modern civilization's aspirations and demands. Women here are devoid of all initiative and freedom. Unjustly and inconveniently reduced to the whims of their husbands' capricious will, women vegetate.

All present-day legislation and all of this century's thinkers demand that woman be given the high position that her moral, legal and intellectual level entitles her to occupy, since she is such a noble and respectable part of society and so considerably contributes to the development of modern life. In this regard, our legislation cannot continue to be such a mediocre exception to the civilized world.

I want no uproar or violence. I abominate and condemn both with all of my spirit's honest energy. I want and demand that all the fundamental rights guaranteed by our institutions be respected. In the interest of order and of social stability, those who govern nevertheless have the unavoidable duty of addressing, fulfilling and meeting all of those public needs that have justice as their basis, all of those claims that seek to destroy any privilege that is not based upon high and noble considerations of a moral nature.

Translated by Beatriz E. Rodríguez-Balanta

Autocrats versus Aristocrats: The Decay
of Chile's Parliamentary Republic

Alberto Edwards

*Alberto Edwards was a deeply influential conservative politician and essayist,
elected several times to Congress and a cabinet member in the first government
of Carlos Ibáñez (1927–1931). Edwards's ideas about Chilean exceptionalism in
nineteenth-century Latin America, which he attributed to Chile's centralized state,
became common tenets of conventional wisdom about Chilean history. In his 1928
work* The Aristocratic Fronde, *he describes the consolidation of oligarchic rule in
Chile under the Parliamentary Republic, the historic struggle between executive and
parliamentary powers, and the distinctive characteristics of Chile's "fronda aristocrática." Writing against the predominant liberal vision of history as progress,
Edwards interpreted Chilean history in terms of the conflict between a centralized,
strong state and an aristocratic oligarchy, extolling the virtues of Portales and the
autocratic republic and denouncing Chile's decline during the Parliamentary Republic. His support for the Portalian system of presidentialist rule informs this critical portrait of Chile's aristocracy. The term* fronda aristocrática *refers to the dis-
contented French nobles who opposed the absolute authority of Luis XIV. Edwards's
essay hails the military interventions of 1924 and 1925 and the new presidentialist
Constitution of 1925, put in place by the government of Arturo Alessandri with the
backing of the military and the approval of a national plebiscite, as putting an end
to the feudal and corrupt aristocratic rule of the Parliamentary Republic.*

In 1891, for the first time in sixty years, a Government was overthrown
through violence in Chile; but the form in which the event produced itself,
gave it rather the traits of a legitimate restoration of the traditional political
status quo. With the old elite class had triumphed the old juridical order,
and also, it is necessary to recognize, the historical movement that since
the end of Bulnes's government (1841–1851) ended up accentuating the oligarchic predominance over absolute political power. The victors, for their

part, strengthened themselves by demonstrating that they had intended to combat an attempt at usurpation and that, with this attempt thwarted, all remained as before.

Effectively, the Republic continued "in this form." The legitimizing sentiment of hereditary aristocracy that constituted its spiritual foundation had been fortified and not weakened with the outcome of the crisis; of the social forces that served as the foundation of the political order, the one, that is, the monarchic power of the Presidents, weakened already for some time, was not, henceforth, but a shadow of itself; instead, the aristocratic and oligarchic element of old Chile reached the golden age of its predominance; for thirty years it was to dominate without limits. . . . The outcome of the long fight between presidentialism and the fronde brought as a consequence a period of political lethargy, such as the Republic had not before known. For more than a quarter of a century, all was about to stay immutable. . . .

This immobility also existed, apparently at least in the public spirit; but the old silence of opinion now took new forms. The great mass of the electorate, indifferent as always, put its votes up for auction; the leading members of the provinces, submissive before power, invested their loyalty in the different aristocratic circles of the capital; every one of these had its invariably submissive clientele. Elections followed elections, without changing, except in insignificant details, the relative power played by the old oligarchic associations in parliamentary politics in the drawing rooms of Santiago. . . . In Chile, by hereditary tradition, a public position, a seat in the Houses, was equivalent to a title of nobility; and the dignity of a patrician did not spare the money for attaining it. The electoral bribe reached monstrous proportions: there were "senatorships" that cost a million. And these sums were spent, most of the time, without ideological fanaticism or intentions of personal gain having intervened in them. . . .

They were buying seats in the House for the same reason that their fathers bought titles under the Colony. . . . The oligarchic domination, more and more tinged with plutocracy, was founded, then, spiritually, during the third phase of the formal Republic on a colonial hereditary sentiment that manifested itself through the dominating arrogance of the political vanity of patrician dignity and through the submission to the old hierarchies by the electorate. As for the popular element, incorporated into politics through legislative reforms and incapable of exercising the sovereignty that the theoreticians and the constitutions granted it, it only worked indirectly, through its venality, which by raising the price of the elections, strengthened the plutocratic forces of the oligarchy. . . . The parliamentarianism, already inert and mildly anarchic under the old oligarchy, began to enter into a period of open and quick decomposition, with the first triumphs of the "renovation of values."

Insubordination and disorder increased even more. We have seen the form in which the collapse took place, immediately thanks to the Army, but in essence, because of the incurable decrepitude of a regime that served to externalize juridically the Government of an oligarchy, but that was not able to continue functioning inside the new order of spiritual rebellion. . . . In this way, we understand that our current movement, constructive and not at all revolutionary in its essence, has constantly been hostile to every attempt at oligarchic and parliamentary restoration, which in the final analysis is a great benefit. Would it have been productive, or even, possible to restore through an act of force that whose soul was already dead? . . . Our parliamentary regime was not reformed through the deliberate work of a political majority, in an assembly of doctrinaires or ideologues. After long years of languid and respectable life, but a life of limited efficiency, it came to collapse almost spontaneously, and its death sentence was already signed by destiny when September 5, 1924 arrived.

Translated by Melissa Mann

Rescuing the Body Politic:
Manifesto of a Military Coup

On September 13, 1924, El Mercurio published this declaration by a junta composed of military officers who had attended a session of Congress to express their displeasure at its failure to pass Arturo Alessandri's social legislation and a budget for the military. Under pressure from the military junta, Alessandri appointed high-ranking members of the armed forces to cabinet positions and then departed for exile, leaving the military in charge, though he would return to the presidency six months later following the second coup led by Carlos Ibáñez and Marmaduke Grove. The declaration explains the junta's motivations for what was in essence a military coup, arguing that rampant political corruption and paralysis had compelled their "surgical" intervention to rescue the body politic. The junta's defense of its actions as necessary to protect the nation from a "gangrenous" political system would find echoes decades later in the pronouncements of the military junta that took power in 1973.

After 1925, the leading military officers in the junta went two ways. Marmaduke Grove would turn to the left, erect a short-lived socialist republic, and found the Chilean Socialist Party in 1933. Carlos Ibáñez, who had served in Alessandri's cabinet as minister of war, helped push Alessandri out once again in late 1925. In 1927, Ibáñez ran for president in a fraudulent election that won him over 90 percent of the vote and proceeded to build a dictatorship. As president, he cracked down on organized labor and its leftist leadership, banned the Communist Party, and sent hundreds of his political opponents into exile abroad or into internal exile to remote regions of the country, including a large number of anarchist and Communist union militants to the Más Afuera desert island (one of the Juan Fernández Islands). But he also implemented a number of reforms, such as a new labor code, massive public works programs, and state credit institutions to promote domestic industrialization and agricultural modernization. Ibáñez would remain in power until 1931, when a devastating economic crisis produced by the Great Depression and the decline of the nitrate industry precipitated his downfall. His combination of authoritarian rule and policies to promote economic modernization provided a template for the military dictatorship of Augusto Pinochet during the 1970s.

Manifesto from the Military Junta to the Country

So as to rectify slight errors that have made their way into the publication of this manifesto yesterday, we specify here its exact terms:

Before definitively exposing our purposes to the people, we have wanted facts to anticipate our words: the old and discredited system of making promises without guaranteeing that they'll be honored is repugnant to our integrity.

The corruption of the Republic's political life was leading our institutions into an abyss toward which the very Fundamental Charter, driven as it was by merely personal interests, was beginning to drift.

The healthy components had distanced themselves from public life for such a lengthy period of time that this abstinence took on for them the weight of guilt.

The people's misery, the speculation and bad faith of the powerful, the economic instability and the absence of any hope of regeneration within the existing regime, had produced a ferment that irritated the very entrails of those classes whose struggle for life is most arduous.

Out of all this came the imminence of civil strife. . . .

This movement is the spontaneous product of circumstances.

It aims to abolish gangrenous politics. Its energetic yet pacific method is a labor of surgery, not of vengeance or punishment.

It is a movement without sectarian or party allegiances, oriented equally toward all of the political factions that have corroded civic culture and are the cause of our organic corruption. None of these factions will be able to claim for itself the inspiration of our actions, nor can they expect to reap the fruits of our efforts.

We have not taken power to stay in power.

We have not and will not put a caudillo in power because our work must be done by all and for all. . . . We will maintain public liberties because creation is born of their rational exercise, and because we know very well that they are at the source of the most august of conquests: the recognition of the people's sovereignty.

This is a time of creation and not of reaction.

Our aim is to call a free Constituent Assembly from which should emerge a Fundamental Charter corresponding to national aspirations.

Following the creation of the new constitution, public powers will be elected by way of Registers established on the basis of free and wide-ranging criteria.

Once these powers will have been constituted, our mission will be completed. . . . In the meantime, we want our action to be viewed serenely and from a true conception of politics. We also ask that the robust cooperation of the live and uncontaminated forces of the Republic be added to the patriotic and tireless labor that will produce the new national consciousness.

Before adopting a hostile attitude toward this movement, keep in mind that the most respectable and logical attitude consists in attempting to understand—above all else—its meaning and scope.

Let us have faith in the cause that we are defending, let us thrust away the suspicions that divide, and, united by the healthy purpose of saving the nation, let us work to give back to our fatherland the free play of its fundamental institutions, as pure and honest as those upon which the Republic laid the foundations of its greatness.

Santiago, September 11th, 1924—The Military Junta.

Translated by Beatriz E. Rodríguez-Balanta

The Poet as Creator of Worlds: *Altazor*

Vicente Huidobro

Vicente Huidobro, who was a major figure in literary circles in Paris and Madrid as well as Santiago, embraced a cosmopolitan avant-garde style in opposition to the naturalist criollista or creolist literary movement of the time. Huidobro was born to an aristocratic Santiago family and educated in Jesuit schools. After 1916 he lived, wrote, and worked on literary journals in Paris and Madrid and participated in Europe's avant-garde artistic movements, forging his own "creationist" style, as in his epic poem Altazor, *whose preface appears here. Huidobro's "creacionismo" (creationism) articulated a philosophy of poetry that rejected the criollista focus on nature and the natural, as well as its interest in the rural and its search for the essence of "chilenidad." Huidobro argued, instead, that the poet and poetry created realities, instead of merely reflecting and describing them, and he sought a more international identity for his poetry. A work of art, he argued in 1916, is "a new cosmic reality that an artist adds to nature and must have, like the stars, its own atmosphere."[1] He expressed his understanding of the poet as a creator of worlds, and language, in his famous poem "Poetic Art," which concludes: "the poet is a little god."[2] Huidobro was consistent in his identification with the Chilean Left. In 1925 he published an attack on the military junta, and in the 1930s, he campaigned for Communist Party candidates and traveled to Spain to support the republic.*

Preface to Altazor

I was born at the age of 33 on the day Christ died; I was born at the Equinox, under the hydrangeas and the aeroplanes in the heat.

I had the soulful gaze of a pigeon, a tunnel, a sentimental motorcar. I heaved sighs like an acrobat.

My father was blind and his hands were more wonderful than the night.

I love the night, the hat of every day.

The night, the night of day, from one day to the next.

My mother spoke like the dawn, like blimps about to fall. Her hair was the color of a flag and her eyes were full of far-off ships.

One day, I gathered up my parachute and said: "Between two swallows and a star." Here death is coming closer like the earth to a falling balloon.

My mother embroidered abandoned tears on the first rainbows.

And now my parachute drops from dream to dream through the spaces of death.

On the first day I met an unknown bird who said: "If I were a camel I'd know no thirst. What time is it?" It drank the dewdrops in my hair, threw me 3 ½ glances and went off waving "Goodbye" with its pompous handkerchief.

At around two that afternoon, I met a charming aeroplane, full of fishscales and shells. It was searching for some corner of the sky to take shelter from the rain.

There, far off, all the boats were anchored in the ink of dawn. One by one they came lose from their moorings, dragging pennants of indisputable dawn like the national colors.

As the last ones drifted off, dawn disappeared behind some immoderately swollen waves.

Then I heard the voice of the Creator, who is nameless, who is a simple hollow in space, lovely as a navel.

"I created a great crashing sound and that sound formed the oceans and the ocean waves.

"That sound will be stuck forever to the waves of the sea and the waves of the sea will be stuck forever to that sound, like stamps to a postcard.

"Then I braided a great cord of luminous rays to stitch each day to the next; the days with their original or reconstructed, yet undeniable dawns.

"Then I etched the geography of the earth and the lines of the hand.

"Then I drank a little cognac (for hydrographic reasons).

"Then I created the mouth, and the lips of the mouth to confine ambiguous smiles, and the teeth of the mouth to guard against the improprieties that come to our mouths.

"I created the tongue of the mouth which man diverted from its role to make it learn to speak . . . to her, to her, the beautiful swimmer, forever diverted from her aquatic and purely sensual role."

My parachute began to dizzyingly drop. Such is the force of the attraction of death, of the open grave.

Better believe it, the tomb has more power than a lover's eyes. The open tomb with all its charms. And I say it even to you, you whose smile inspires thoughts of the origin of the world.

My parachute caught on a burnt-out star conscientiously continuing its orbit, as if it didn't know the uselessness of such efforts.

And taking advantage of this well-earned rest, I began to fill the little squares of my chessboard with deep thoughts:

"True poems are fires. Poetry is propagating everywhere, its conquests lit with shivers of pleasure or pain.

"One should write in a language that is not the mother tongue.

"The four cardinal points are three: South and North.

"A poem is something that will be.

"A poem is something that never is, but ought to be.

"A poem is something that never has been, that never can be.

"Flee from the external sublime, if you don't want to die flattened by the wind.

"If I didn't do something crazy at least once a year I'd go crazy."

Grabbing my parachute, I leap from the edge of my speeding star into the stratosphere of the last sigh.

I wheel endlessly over the cliffs of dreams, I wheel through clouds of death.

I meet the Virgin, seated on the rose, who says:

"Look at my hands, as transparent as light bulbs. Do you see the filaments where the blood of my pure light flows?

"Look at my halo. It has a few cracks in it, a proof of my antiquity.

"I am the Virgin, the Virgin without human stain, there's nothing halfway about me, and I am the captain of the other eleven thousand who were, in fact, excessively restored.

"I speak in a language that fills the heart according to the laws of the communicant clouds.

"I always say goodbye, and stay.

"Love me, my child, for I adore your poetry and I will teach you aerial prowess.

"I have a need for tenderness, kiss my hair, I washed it this morning in clouds of dawn, and now I want to sleep on the mattress of occasional drizzle.

"My glances are a wire on the horizon where swallows rest.

"Love me."

I got down on my knees in that circular space and the Virgin rose and sat on my parachute.

I slept, and then recited my most beautiful poems.

The flames of my poetry dried the Virgin's hair. She thanked me and went off, seated on her soft rose.

And here I am, alone, like the little orphan of anonymous shipwrecks.
O how beautiful . . . how beautiful.

I can see mountains, rivers, forest, the sea, boats, flowers, seashells.

I can see night and day and the axis where they meet.

Oh yes I am Altazor, the great poet, without a horse that eats birdseed
or warms its throat with moonbeams, with only my little parachute like a
parasol over the planets.

From each bead of sweat on my forehead I give birth to stars, which I
leave you the task of baptizing like a watered-down bottle of wine.

I can see it all, my mind is forged in the tongues of prophets.

The mountain is the sigh of God, rising in its swelling thermometer
till it touches the feet of the beloved.

He who has seen it all, who knows all the secrets without being Walt
Whitman, for I've never had a beard as white as beautiful nurses and
frozen streams.

He who hears in the night the hammers of the counterfeiters of coins,
who are only diligent astronomers.

He who drinks the warm glass of knowledge after the flood, obedient
to the doves, and who knows the way of weariness, the boiling wake the
ships leave behind.

He who knows the storehouses of memories, of beautiful forgotten
seasons.

He, shepherd of aeroplanes, guide to the unmatched poles for mislaid
night and experienced west winds.

His whimpering is a blinking net of unwitnessed aerolites.

The day rises in his heart and he lowers his eyelids to create the night
of agricultural rest.

He washes his hands in the glances of God, and combs his hair like the
light, like the harvest of those thin grains of satisfied rain.

Shouts wander off like a flock over the hills when the stars sleep after
a night of continual labor.

The beautiful hunter faces the cosmic waterhole for heartless birds.

Be sad, like gazelles before the infinite and the meteors, like deserts
without mirages.

Until the appearance of a mouth swollen with kisses for the vintage of
exile.

Be sad, for she awaits you in a corner of this passing year.

Perhaps she's at the end of your next song, and she'll be as beautiful as
a free-falling waterfall and rich as the equatorial line.

Be sad, sadder than the rose, that beautiful cage for glances and inexperienced bees.

Life is a parachute voyage and not what you'd like to think it is.

So let's fall, falling from our heights to our depths, let's leave the air stained with blood, so that those who breathe it tomorrow will be poisoned.

Inside yourself, outside yourself, you'll fall from high to low, for that is your fate, your miserable fate. And the greater the height from which you fall, the higher you'll rebound, the longer you'll remain in the memory of stone.

We have leapt from the belly of our mother, or from the edge of a star, and we're falling.

Oh my parachute, the only perfumed rose of the stratosphere, the rose of death, cascading through the stars of death.

Have you heard it? The sinister sound of closed chests.

Open the gate of your soul and get out and breathe. With a sigh you can open the gate it took a hurricane to close.

Here's your parachute, Man, wonderful as vertigo.

Here's your parachute, Poet, wonderful as the charms of the chasm.

Here's your parachute, Magician, which one word of yours can transform into a parashoot, wonderful as the lightning bolt that tries to blind the creator.

What are you waiting for?

But here is the secret of the Gloom that forgot how to smile.

The parachute waits tied to the gate like the endlessly runaway horse.

Translated by Eliot Weinberger

Notes

1. Vicente Huidobro, "La Creación Pura," in *Obra poética*, ed. Cedomil Goic (Nanterre, France: ALLCA, 2003), 1313.

2. Vicente Huidobro, "Arte Poética," in *The Selected Poetry of Vicente Huidobro*, ed. David M. Guss (New York: New Directions, 1981), 3.

"Mother of Chile"?
"Women's Suffrage" and "Valle de Elqui"

Gabriela Mistral

Gabriela Mistral was the first Latin American to win the Nobel Prize in Literature (1945). Mistral's life was one of unusual independence for a middle-class woman of the times. She started teaching public school at age fifteen out of economic necessity In 1914, at the age of twenty-five, she catapulted to national fame when she won a national poetry contest and then began publishing widely in literary magazines, while continuing to teach in schools throughout the country. In 1922, she was invited to help direct the public education and literacy programs of Mexico's postrevolutionary government.

Despite an extraordinarily unconventional life, most of which was spent outside Chile working in the consular service and for the League of Nations, and later teaching in the United States, Mistral has been viewed, in a traditional gendered stereotype, as "the mother of Chile" because of the "maternal" and religious themes in her poetry, as well as her verses for children, her work as a teacher, and her identification with the local landscapes of her youth. As the historian Nicola Miller argues, this apparently conservative image was later promoted by the dictatorship of Augusto Pinochet, which sought alternative national-cultural figures to leftist poets like Pablo Neruda.

The two pieces selected here demonstrate that reading Mistral solely through the lens of her image as a traditional "mother of the nation" is too simple. "Valle de Elqui" contains many of the themes that run through Mistral's poetry. The poem employs religious and mystical language to express nostalgia for the natural landscape of Mistral's birthplace and for childhood more generally. But it is also a meditation on loss and suffering, with unsettling religious imagery of aging and death. In her essay on female suffrage here, Mistral makes a fairly traditional argument for women's broader participation in politics, contending that women will bring the maternal virtues of the home to the public sphere of politics and provide an antidote to the sterile political and ideological debates of the halls of Congress. But in a twist on this conventional rhetoric, she not only argues that women's participation in

*politics, beyond simply voting, is necessary for defending the home but also foresees
a time when women's virtues would propel a woman to the presidency. As Miller
notes, Mistral translated her belief in women's maternal nature into a mandate for
social and political activism, supporting progressive causes throughout her life. She
was a staunch supporter of democracy, human rights, and pan-American solidarity, critiquing dictatorships and endorsing Latin American struggles for national
liberation.*

"Women's Suffrage" (1932)

Suffrage comes to us as a victory for the long demands, after campaigns that
came from Europe and the United States and that have finally convinced
the stolid masculine brain. Or maybe they have alerted the clever, who only
see us as votes for their campaigns. However it may be, Chilean women
can now vote. The important thing is not to vote as assistants, but rather as
women who long to contribute a little *feminization to democracy.*

   We all know that the masses of women, being inexperienced in political
skirmishes, could do little in their marginal state, somewhat like the He-
brews in the synagogue. Due to centuries of atavism, we were convinced—
or brainwashed to be more exact, that men have always produced ideas
easily, just like one who plays or pretends to try hard. No we do not give
them a servile amen to that proclaimed virile monopoly on intelligence: we
have shown just as many cases of women who are equal to, or above the recognized male "thinkers"; they can no longer treat us like helpless creatures
or sweet idiots with our brains only half developed. The fact that they have
given us the masculine right to vote proves this, which I always thought
that we had based on . . . zoology.

   But in the climate of today's political assemblies, where women will go
and put in their two cents—problems, needs, subterranean tragedies—they
run the risk of abandoning themselves, as well as their children there, to
quarrels and disputes, and remaining useless duplications of men.

   Why are they so excited to participate in those raucous halls if they can
not participate in the debates or if they have to follow along like affection-
ate sheep? They tell me that when dolphins swim, females and males lead
them. These animals have created a better team and parliamentary model
than we humans have.

   Whether we like it or not, Creole life is saturated with patriarchal ideas.
This is also an ancestral fabric and has been broken in very short stretches.
In the Chilean countryside, the matriarch, that jealous guardian of chil-
dren, was also alongside the patriarch. While the father values his growing

son only when he begins to look like him, the mother provides him with all of her love since the moment he is born and even before he is born, she begins a long back and forth conversation with him. Making the children visible, like when someone takes a fish out of the abyss, is one of the things that make our times more dignified by giving them spirituality. And that serious patriarch who used to say that little kids did not exist before they were ten, has just bumped into them and now treats them like people. This action gives him tenderness and ductility as he recuperates the infant that was once in him and still crawls around in his soul.

We must carry on the work of those tried and tested matriarchs and not burn our femininity in the crater of politics. Only by acting as women can we save life and the world.

Our earthly mission is to be men's muses, intercessors as well as redeemers, much like Dante's Beatrice. But now that we have the right to vote, that is a direct vote and not a whisper in men's ears (who sometimes smile, "supposedly respecting us") now is the time, side by side with the men who "represent" us, to represent ourselves in body and soul.

This will be the second part of our actual feminism. We must organize ourselves until we become completely acculturated—by studying history, law, sociology, and even math (which will be helpful with statistics, that swordfight with numbers in which men show off . . . without any swords). Perched on high, we will go to the elections, not merely as voters, but as *candidates*. If we vote, but only for men, we will continue to be relegated, without really taking control of the steering wheel.

Our Senate will *also* have women, doves among condors, contributing the nesty coo, the vocation of domestic stability, without which men have neither peace nor place to rest.

Some leaders will come forth from our multitude of women. Without being anti-home, may they take to the streets and belong to the Senate, precisely to defend the patrimony of their homes, that of their husbands, the Chile that they would otherwise be building only with men's decisions. Shoulder to shoulder, and on the prowl toward a nation seen as a great home for its children and their friends' children, women will complete the political undertaking in which more economy, much more economy is lacking; maybe just economy, because we left land and arrived at the table, from the tangible to the feasible, without inebriating ourselves on theories, or losing ourselves in the labyrinths of ideological discussions. That is why Chile will someday choose a woman to be the President of the Republic.

Translated by Ryan Judge

Valle de Elqui

I must come to the Valley
while the almond's still in flower
and the last figs are growing
blue on the fig-trees,
so I can walk in the evening
with my living and my dead.

The Valley burns: above it
hangs a dream lagoon
baptizing and sprinkling it
with everlasting coolness
when the Elqui River shrinks,
bleaching its thirsty banks.

The hills are going to look at me
like tremendous godfathers,
turning into animals,
with great drowsy flanks,
uttering the deep birthcry
I hear as I fall asleep:
for twelve of them hollowed
my cradle of stone and wood.

I want us all to be sitting
in the alfalfa or clover,
in the clan-ring, the circle of those
whose love for one another,
beyond time and words, speaks only
through the blood and breath.

We'll be there so and stay,
exchanging gaze and gesture,
contented, going over
the cord of memories,
the aged and the ageless,
the named and the unnamed,
people of the Andes,
tight in a burning knot,

sometimes singing,
sometimes keeping still.

They pass by, first to last,
the joys, the sorrows,
the ferment of the young folk,
the slow honey of the old;
they pass, in fire, in fervor,
the anguish and the agonies,
and more, and more: the Valley
passes in its serpent curves
from Peralillo to La Unión,
various and single and complete.

There's a peace and a passion,
fevers and cool airs,
in this human circle
held close by the thirty hills.
Eyes glance back and forth
as if keeping count,
and the missing ones arrive,
with or without a body,
struggling uphill, breathless,
with their defeats, their defiance.

Every time I find them
they're more defeated.
All I can bring them is the speech
and gestures they gave me,
and I open my heart to give them
the hope I do not have.

Here my childhood runs milk
from every branch I break,
and the sage, the rosemary
remember my face and turn
their mild eyes on me
as if they understood,
and I fall asleep in the lulling
of their knots and tangles.

I only wish they'd give me
the harvest of their hills,
and pass from hand to hand
a fragrant melon tender as a baby,
trading tall tales and true ones
for their humble food.

And if all at once my childhood
returns, leaps up, confronts me,
I yield wholly, melt,
then like a scattered grain-sheaf,
gather myself together and hold fast,
for how can I relive it
with hair as grey as ashes?

I'm going now, I'm hiding
my face so the hills won't know
and open their eyes on me
cloudy with resentment.

I'm going farther into the mountains,
on the track of my mule-drivers,
though thornbushes and carobs
hold me back with their reproaches,
sharpening their spines
to stab me in the heart.

Translated by Ursula K. Le Guin

As the writer Benjamín Subercaseaux observed, Chile exhibits "a cartographical coquetry" that is "the pride of geographers, naturalists, and travelers." The country extends 2,600 miles in length along the Pacific Coast but averages a mere 100 miles in width. Its "crazy geography," as Subercaseaux termed it, features the imposing Andes mountain chain as its eastern border, the majestic Pacific to the west, the Atacama Desert—the world's driest—to the north, and Cape Horn in the far south. Pictured here, the Torres del Paine in southern Patagonia is one of Chile's spectacular natural features, a national park of glaciers, lakes, and rugged mountains. Such features amaze visitors but also have historically cut Chile off from its neighbors, a geographic isolation that has nurtured the country's sense of separateness and uniqueness. Photograph by John Spooner. Used by permission of the photographer.

For most of its history, Chile was an overwhelmingly rural society. From the colonial period onward, land was concentrated in haciendas, large landed estates that conferred aristocratic status on their owners but were worked by impoverished tenant farmers who, critics charged, resembled feudal serfs. The hacienda's importance extended well beyond the countryside, shaping Chile's economic, social, and political structures up until the 1960s, when reforms altered land tenure and awarded belated rights to rural workers. Yet even today, when almost 90 percent of Chileans live in cities, the countryside continues to exercise a powerful hold on national identity. One enduring symbol of *chilenidad* or "Chilean-ness" is the *huaso*, or Chilean cowboy, portrayed in this nineteenth-century print. Illustration by Claudio Gay, from *Atlas de la historia física y política de Chile* by Claudio Gay (París: Imprenta de E. Thunot), 1854. Courtesy of Colección Biblioteca Nacional de Chile.

Since colonial times, Chile's economy has relied on exporting primary products to international markets. Wheat, silver, and leather first played this role, but in the nineteenth century a military victory over Peru and Bolivia gave Chile control over deserts rich in nitrates, a mineral valued for its use in fertilizer and explosives. Like other exports, nitrates experienced severe boom-bust cycles. This 1912 publicity poster, distributed in South Africa, reflects the international reach of Chilean nitrate exports but also portends their demise in the 1920s. Soon afterward, nitrates would be eclipsed by another lucrative export: copper. Courtesy of Colección Biblioteca Nacional de Chile.

EL PUEBLO UNIDO
JAMAS SERA VENCIDO

When Salvador Allende was elected president in 1970, he became the hemisphere's first elected Marxist head of state. In the heady climate of the time, art and music were deeply political. Emblematic is the slogan "The people, united, will never be defeated," which the artist José Balmes portrayed in this iconic poster and the musical ensemble Quilapayún transformed into a stirring march. In later years, social movements in Iran, the Philippines, and Ukraine would adopt this anthem of the Chilean—and international—Left. Courtesy of José Balmes and (Posters), International Institute of Social History (Amsterdam). © 2012 Artists Rights Society (ARS), New York / CREAIMAGEN, Santiago.

The military dictatorship that came to power in 1973 under the leadership of General Augusto Pinochet was characterized by massive human rights violations as well as by creative forms of resistance to repression. One of these were *arpilleras*, appliqué tapestries created by women who belonged to the Association of Families of the Detained-Disappeared, a group for those whose loved ones had been killed, detained, or "disappeared" by state security forces. Sold to raise funds for their activities but also to spread the word about human rights in Chile, *arpilleras* were purchased and exhibited by Chilean solidarity groups throughout the world. The sign held by the women gathered in front of a courthouse asks "Where are the Detained-Disappeared?" Tapestry by Agrupación de Familiares de Detenidos-Desaparecidos, from *Arpilleras: Otra forma de denuncia* (Santiago: Gráfica Andes Ltda, 1985).

In 1990, after seventeen years of dictatorship, a plebiscite forced General Pinochet from power. Redemocratization would prove a protracted process. At the 1992 World's Fair in Seville (which also marked the quincentenary of Europe's "discovery" of the Americas), Chileans eager to present a new face to the world devised an ambitious and unusual exhibit. A 140-ton iceberg from Antarctica was transported to Seville in ten refrigerated containers and put on display in a specially designed glass case. The exhibit was the subject of heated debate within Chile, where it was criticized as an attempt to mask the recent authoritarian past behind a sleek and celebratory but ultimately superficial modernity. As the sociologist Tomás Moulian observed, "the iceberg was the sculpture of our metamorphosis," symbolizing "the New Chile, clean, sanitized, purified by the long passage through the sea." Photograph by Alejando Barruel. Used by permission of the photographer.

On a frigid Sunday morning in June 2002, over 3,000 Chileans gathered in front of the Fine Arts Museum in downtown Santiago to pose nude for the renowned U.S. artist-photographer Spencer Tunick. Although the event competed with the simultaneous broadcast of the 2002 World Cup final match, Chileans were stunned by the turnout for the event, which also drew scores of onlookers and evangelical protestors. Media reports and talk shows analyzed the event for days, showcasing commentators' reactions to the Chilean "destape" (loosening, opening) as a rebellion against the social conservatism not only of the dictatorship but also of the civilian governments that had succeeded it. "Chile 2 (Museo de Arte Contemporáneo) 2002," c-print mounted between plexi, h: 71 x w: 89.25 in / h: 180.34 x w: 226.7 cm, edition of three. © Spencer Tunick, artist-photographer, used with permission.

Chile today enjoys an enviable reputation as a modern and increasingly affluent society. Over the past twenty years, it has experienced macroeconomic growth and a marked decline in poverty rates. Yet income inequality remains stubbornly high. By drawing attention to the gross socioeconomic segregation of the educational system, the student movement that erupted in 2011 placed the deep-seated inequities operating in society at the center of political debate. Indeed, inequality is perhaps the greatest economic, social, and ethical challenge facing Chile today. In this photograph, the shacks of Villa Ermita de San Antonio, a shantytown in Santiago, are framed by the high-rises of the affluent Las Condes neighborhood. Photograph by AP/Victor Ruiz Caballero, Image no. 671276206953. © 2012 The Associated Press. Used by permission.

V

Depression, Development, and the Politics of Compromise

The 1929–1930 world economic crisis dealt a death blow to Chile's nitrate-fueled export economy and initiated a new stage of economic and political development characterized by rural-urban migration, industrialization, and the growth of populist, nationalist, and leftist political movements. This section explores the rise of the Chilean Popular Front (1938–1941) and a shifting alliance, led by the Radical Party, of parties that governed Chile from 1938 to 1952, an experience that would later become a prototype for Salvador Allende's socialist Popular Unity coalition in 1970. Unlike Brazil and Argentina, where politics in this period were dominated by military men, in Chile the Popular Front and its successor coalitions combined ideologically diverse civilian leadership from the Radical, Socialist, and Communist parties with nationalist policies designed to promote industrialization, the modernization of the rural sector, and the political incorporation of hitherto excluded sectors of the population, including women. This powerful yet unstable ruling coalition ushered in the era of the "politics of compromise," defined by the tension between electoral alliance and the polarizing ideological frictions of the Cold War.

Like most of the world, in the years following the Great Depression Chile confronted a crisis of economic recession and unemployment, with thousands of unemployed nitrate miners flooding temporary hostels in Chile's major urban areas and accelerated migration of uprooted laborers from the countryside to the city. After 1930, Chilean governments turned away from a model of laissez-faire economic development based on the export of primary commodities to world markets, seeking instead to generate economic growth and diversify production through state policies that encouraged industrialization. The Chilean government stepped in to promote the development of Chile's manufacturing sector by providing tariff protection and other subsidies for the nation's industrial enterprises. The documents here describe how Palestinian immigrant families—most notably the Yarur family, who remain one of Chile's most powerful economic clans—launched Chile's textile industry with this kind of government support.

Chilean governments in this period also introduced a series of key social reforms in order to create demand for domestically produced goods in a country with a historically limited internal market, reforms that also addressed the growing social problems created by urbanization and economic recession. The 1931 labor code, passed during Ibáñez's last year in office, laid the foundation for expanding workers' rights during the 1930s and 1940s, including regulations for labor unions, social security, health care, worker safety, minimum wages, and benefits such as a "family allowance" for white- and blue-collar workers. While Chile's labor movement had been hit hard by the crisis in the nitrate mines, urban workers, often with the support of the Communist and Socialist parties, organized new unions and a new union federation, the Confederation of Chilean Workers, which played a key role in the Popular Front coalition. Another mass organization that joined the original Popular Front was the newly formed Movement for the Emancipation of Chilean Women (MEMCH), one of Chile's most important feminist organizations, which sought to organize both women of means and working-class women in support of women's social and political rights. The MEMCH became one of the leading organizations in the long struggle to allow women to vote in national elections. Because of the MEMCH's activism, women finally received the vote in 1949. The flavor of feminist politics is captured here in an interview with the lawyer and MEMCH founder Elena Caffarena.

The 1930s and 1940s also marked a significant change in Chile's cultural life. The Catholic Church, alarmed by its declining influence among Chileans both in the countryside and the rapidly expanding cities, sought to revitalize and broaden Chilean Catholicism through Catholic Action, a movement of lay Catholics seeking to reevangelize Chileans who had fallen away from the Church through a diverse array of new associations. Led by a new generation of priests who included Father Alberto Hurtado, this "social Catholicism" shifted the Church's focus away from wealthy neighborhoods and toward workers, women, and the urban poor. Addressing the problems of the large population of rural-urban migrants became particularly important, and the Church played a major role in organizing household workers, as reflected in an oral history interview with a woman active in the Catholic domestic service association during the 1950s. The Church's social activism was accompanied by the organization of the Catholic Falange Nacional in 1935, an offshoot of Chile's Conservative Party that shared many of the

Popular Front's social reformist goals but eschewed the secularism of the Radical, Socialist, and Communist parties. From this movement the Christian Democratic Party emerged in 1957, dedicated to a vision of Catholic political engagement that would define a "third way" in Chilean politics, an explicitly anti-Marxist agenda for social reform.

The ascent of the Left and of social reformist ideas during the 1930s and 1940s is also evident in the poetry of Pablo Neruda, who won Chile's national poetry prize in 1945 and the Nobel Prize in Literature in 1971. Arguably Chile's most important poet, Neruda entered Chile's Communist Party after serving in a diplomatic post in Spain during the Spanish Civil War. As the selections from his poems and memoirs here make clear, Neruda viewed his poetry as organically rooted in the ecological, social, and historical realities of Chile and Latin America. He wrote explicitly political poems about Spain and United States imperialism and poems that focused on the worlds of miners, peasants, and stevedores. In keeping with the politics of the times and his own political commitments, Neruda made a point of reading his poems in union halls and poor neighborhoods, visiting the southern coal mines, the northern nitrate fields, and the poor neighborhoods of Santiago. In a sense, Neruda's writing and activism reflected the new populist mass politics of the 1930s and 1940s and the growing mobilization and incorporation of Chilean workers into the nation-state.

The social and labor reforms that characterized the 1930s and 1940s notably excluded the countryside and its workers from the benefits of the populist state. Chile's profoundly unequal system of landownership remained intact, and rural laborers, both seasonal migrants (*peones*) and resident estate laborers (*inquilinos*), were denied the rights afforded to urban workers. Landowners employed their monopoly over land and access to cheap labor to make estates profitable, while flexing their political muscle to prevent any reform of rural labor relations or land reform. This represented what the historian Brian Loveman has referred to as the "compromise state," in which large landowners maintained often coercive control over the rural labor force while urban workers and industrialists benefited from state intervention in labor relations, price controls for basic goods, and protective tariffs. The populist state's pursuit of reform and industrialization was also limited by Chile's continued reliance on revenues from copper exports to generate economic growth. Despite the often militantly nationalist rhetoric of the Popular Front, Chile's large copper mines remained in the hands of the North American companies Kennecott and Anaconda. A famous 1950s book by the economist Aníbal Pinto, excerpted here, described Chile's development as "frustrated" by the country's failure to diversify its exports and its continued reliance on a single commodity, copper. In addition, lack of social reform in the countryside acted as a brake on Chile's industrialization and the modernization of the agricultural sector. With large, inefficient estates monopolizing land in the countryside, agricultural production stagnated; by the 1950s Chile had come to increasingly depend on imports of food, prejudicing its balance of trade.

Other limits to the Radical Party–led governments' populist policies became clear when in 1947 President Gabriel González Videla, under pressure from both the U.S. government and North American mining companies, sent in the armed forces to take control of the coal and copper mines and force workers to end their strikes. The following year González Videla went on to impose a law banning the Communist Party, which had until then participated in his own governing coalition. Hundreds of Communist Party members were sent to concentration camps or into exile, putting an end to the participation of the Chilean Left in the Radical Party coalition governments and definitively turning Chilean politics to the right, a shift that extended to the presidencies of the former military strongman Carlos Ibáñez (1952–1958) and of Jorge Alessandri (1958–1964). Ibáñez and Alessandri implemented austerity measures to combat inflation, a plan designed by a mission of U.S. economists in 1955, which represented Chile's first experiment with neoliberalism and a return to the orthodox economic policies of the pre-1930 period. These so-called Klein-Saks measures effectively put an end to Chile's experiment with populism and social reform, cutting real wages and restricting credit and public spending, which led to a significant deterioration of Chileans' standard of living and undermined the manufacturing sector that had developed with the help of government protections since 1930. But the measures helped reduce inflation and won Chile favor with development agencies, multi-lateral lending institutions, and the North American copper producers. The essay by the lawyer and feminist leader Elena Caffarena included here charts the chronic use of states of siege during the 1950s to quell social unrest as workers protested the effects of the turn rightward in politics and economic policy.

This set of excerpts ends with an account of the founding of the La Victoria squatter settlement (*población*) during the 1950s. The period following 1930 marked a significant increase in Chile's urban population as industrial development drew rural laborers and the landless poor from the countryside to urban centers, particularly Santiago. Stagnation in agricultural production, moreover, spurred the reduction of the resident labor force of inquilinos and pushed a large segment of the rural population to the city. By the end of the 1950s, Chile was an increasingly urban society with an economy focused on manufacturing. Production in the agricultural sector declined steadily during the post-1930 period so that by the 1960s Chile was a net importer of food, leading to significant trade deficits in a country that had once been a major supplier of Pacific wheat markets. Cities like Santiago were unprepared for the large influx of migrants, who often took matters into their own hands, invading empty land in marginal city neighborhoods and erecting shanties. *Pobladores* (residents of poblaciones) became an important presence in urban politics during this period, targets of organizing for both the Christian Democratic and leftist parties. While often depicted as marginal, uneducated, and immiserated, pobladores usually organized their own urban institutions and developed ties to reformist and revolutionary political parties, demanding basic urban services like pavement for roads, sewage systems, running water, and electricity. Organized with the support of Communist Party leaders, La Victoria established itself as a notorious bastion of Communist support, and the poblador movement would play a major role in Chile's increasingly radical politics during the 1960s.

"Their Work Has Laid the Foundation for Greatness": Chile's Arab Industrialists

Like many other Latin American governments facing the devastating economic effects of the 1929–1930 world economic crisis, the Chilean state implemented policies of import-substituting industrialization, giving rise to a number of new industries in Chile, including a vital textile industry that was founded by families of immigrants from the Middle East. Encouraged by Chilean subsidies and market protections, the Palestinian Yarur family moved to Chile after working as merchants and founding a textile enterprise in Bolivia. They quickly became one of the most financially powerful families in Chile, where they developed a dominant and nearly monopolistic role in the textile industry, as well as their own bank, insurance companies, and a number of other businesses. The Yarur factories employed hundreds of workers, many of whom were rural migrants; young women, who were viewed as more docile and productive than men as well as appropriate for work in textile production, were a particularly important part of this workforce. In addition, the Yarurs built housing for workers and cemented a deeply paternalist style of management practice, combined with a ruthless repression of strikes and union organizing drives in their plants. An interview with Juan Yarur in the nationally circulated Ultimas Noticias (Latest News) *and reprinted in* Mundo Arabe (Arab World) *and a Syria-Palestine Business Association pamphlet praising the Arab communities in Chile provide a window onto Chile's rapid post-1930 industrialization and the formation of a small but economically powerful and politically influential Arab immigrant community in Chile.*

Interview with Juan Yarur in Mundo Arabe *(1936)*

Editor's note: We are transcribing the complete text of the interview that the editors of *Ultimas Noticias* conducted with our distinguished compatriot and friend, Mr. Juan Yarur, in his offices, to explain to the country exactly what the great textile factories that Mr. Yarur's company is building in this capital city are.

This marvelous effort means the installation of this [textile] industry in Chile. The solemn grandeur of the factories being built is briefly summarized in the short declarations given to *Mundo Arabe* by *the powerful industrialist who,* as our readers know, *is the leading promoter of this industry. We are proud to publish this interview* since the companies belonging to our compatriots Said and Yarur have a prominent place in America. Because of this, we once again extend our congratulations to our distinguished friend, Mr. Juan Yarur.

The industrialist Juan Yarur, one of the most successful businessmen in the world cotton industry, arrived in Santiago on the latest flight from New York. Mr. Yarur controls the cotton industry from his factories in La Paz and other capital cities in the continent and has brought his activities to Santiago, which will become this industry's main headquarters. He is currently building a formidable technically advanced plant along "El Mirador" Avenue. The plans for this project come from the United States and according to the opinions of engineers and the New York press, it will have the features of the most modern cotton factories in the world.

AN INITIAL CAPITAL OF FIFTY MILLION

Even though Mr. Yarur has not made any declarations to the Santiago press in order to avoid speaking prematurely, thanks to Mr. Alberto Farrah, a prestigious member of the Arab neighborhood, we were able to ask him for an interview at his apartment.

Quick, nervous, and concise in his answers, the industrialist showed the temperament of dynamic strength that has allowed him to completely dominate the South American cotton textile industry. He showed us the blueprints for his factory. The most efficient engineers in Memphis, where the North American cotton industry is located, drew them up. Looking at the blueprints spread out across a desk, you see the outline of an urban neighborhood with its avenues, parks, and little houses for the workers. "It is a total of a thousand square blocks" the industrialist told us, "and the budget is a minimum of 50 million." After calculating the figures for the separate booths and machines, you arrive at the sum that is unrivaled in Chile's private sector.

THE LATEST WORD ON TECHNOLOGY

Taking out a series of correspondences and newspaper clippings, Mr. Yarur shows us concretely that he has incorporated the most modern techniques in his manufacturing fortress.

"Each machine is the most modern of its type. They all have individual motors and an ad-hoc apparatus that produces the artificial moisture needed for the perfect production. Each activity will be mechanical, even the clean-up process will involve a mechanical system of absorption, and the residues will automatically be deposited in an extensive underground tunnel."

"I have arranged for the shipping of the machines from the United States in 16 ships. The first ones will arrive this week. . . ."

THE COMPANY'S SOCIAL CONTRIBUTION

But everything pales in comparison with the social opportunities that the company offers. "I will need 700 workers" Mr. Yarur says, "and I have incorporated the greatest number of conveniences and accommodations for working conditions as well as living conditions. A community will live inside the compound, and have every type of resources. I will also install nurseries, clinics, conference rooms, training rooms, and other similar things on the grounds."

THE MAYOR, MR. ABSALON VALENCIA'S OPINION

"Because building the factory along 'El Mirador' Avenue," Mr. Yarur adds, "implies some modifications to the urban layout of the sector, as well as a contribution to the progress of this zone, I have spoken with the Mayor of Santiago. He offered me his valuable support while at the same time offering me his always favorable opinion."

"And this" Mr. Yarur declared as he was saying goodbye, "is just a little outline of what you will see if you attend the factory's official inauguration, which will be in August."

Translated by Ryan Judge

"The Industries of the Arab-Speaking Community in Chile"

The Arab speaking people who reside in this charming land and make up one racial family have played an essential role in the country's evolution toward progress. Their work has laid the foundation for greatness. . . .

Since arriving in Chile, the Arab Family has taken on an important role in developing business. And this land, which so needed vigorous stimulation, was able to count on the valuable contribution of these tenacious men who dedicated their efforts to conquering a position of honor where they could develop their great aspirations by being ingenious and progressive.

That is why, given the singular role that they play regarding the country's cultural, industrial, agricultural, mining, and commercial development, they make up one of the solid bases upon which the people's future rests.

THEIR BEGINNINGS

With a few exceptions, the first activities of the Arab Family were of an exclusively commercial nature. While some opened their businesses in the different sectors in the Capital, and in almost every city and town of the Interior, others offered their merchandise in neighborhoods as well as in the most isolated corners of the country where the train did not reach and there were no commercial markets.

And they brought something more than their varied merchandise. They brought a bit of civilization and the city's progress with them. They indirectly collaborated with this progress and practically improved the living standards of the inhabitants of those far off regions. They were the point of contact between progress and ignorance. . . .

As small business owners, they brought with them an almost unknown prosperity. They then went on to occupy a respectable position within the world of large-scale commerce, which they expanded as they increased trade relations with European markets. But members of the Arab Family dreamed of something bigger. They felt the attraction of industry.

Many of their men, who for business reasons constantly traveled to the most important industrial centers in Europe and the United States, saw the possibility of establishing industries in Chile. However, although they strongly felt this necessity, and as intelligent businessmen they understood the beneficial consequences that this step would have for the betterment of the country, they recognized the unfavorable conditions facing this type of project. Because of vitally important factors such as the public's desire for imported goods and the paltry protection that the Supreme Government gave to the majority of industries, it was only at the beginning of the year 1922 that they decided to take this important step that has turned out to be one of the country's most incredible sources of wealth.

THEIR INDUSTRIES

. . . As is only natural, the beginning involved great sacrifice. The public looked upon nationally manufactured products with distrust. People either out of custom, or if you will, out of tradition, were more familiar with imported goods. However, this was not an obstacle for those who would later follow the example of the forefathers of the Arab industrialists in Chile. Many others have given the textile sector a serious boost, as it has gone through a marvelous boom in a short time. And currently, only fifteen years after establishing their first factory, members of the Arab speaking community own more than 80 percent of the country's textile and thread making industries. With the recent opening of the Yarur brothers' magnificent thread factory, which constitutes the most outstanding and superb example of the Arab race's progressive spirit, this national industry has immediately taken a vanguard position among its South American counterparts.

The resulting benefits from the industries which these groups established have constituted the most transcendental step ever taken in Chile regarding the economic life of the nation in its many and varied aspects. Besides the enormous sums that they pay in taxes, insurance, customs fees, etc.; besides employing between 9,000 and 10,000 people, which lessened the unemployment that afflicted the country; besides replacing imported goods, which meant stopping capital flight, and benefited the consumer masses who can now afford the goods that are so necessary for human life and that were previously out of reach because they were too expensive; besides all of these factories that have contributed to the general well-being of the nation; there is another and maybe more important reason, and that is the boost that the creation of industries has given to our cities. In effect, throughout the different parts of this city, in the neighborhoods that were once completely abandoned, there are currently beautiful neighborhoods whose centers have more than one marvelous building whose chimneys send up thick clouds of smoke that signal the presence of one or more factories which give life to individuals who are conscious of the benefits to them and to the nation.

Translated by Ryan Judge

Is Chile a Catholic Country?

Alberto Hurtado

This selection from the book Is Chile a Catholic Country? *by the Jesuit priest Alberto Hurtado reflects the crisis of Chilean Catholicism during the post-1930 era. In both rural and urban areas, Hurtado points out, the Church had only a limited presence, and Chileans' commitment to Catholicism seemed superficial at best. Chileans' experience of a church identified with the wealthy elite and losing its sway among the poor was typical in Latin America, especially after 1930, when increased migration distanced many people from traditional religious practices and exposed them to competing religions and secular political ideologies in urban areas. Hurtado's treatise on the state of Catholicism reflects the rise of "social Catholicism" in Chile, a Church now oriented toward and engaged with the mass of urban working-class and poor rural Chileans. In addition to his central role in founding the Hogar de Cristo, a social welfare organization for the poor, Hurtado directed Catholic Action, a Church association that mobilized lay Catholics for religious and social activism. Hurtado urged the reorientation of the Church toward activism to organize workers and address problems of poverty, laying the foundation for the politics of Chile's Christian Democratic Party, the organization of Catholic unions during the 1940s and 1950s, and the powerful role played by liberation theology during the 1960s. In 2005, a half century after his death, he was canonized by the Catholic Church, becoming the second Chilean saint.*

The material and moral misery in which our people live, and of which they become more aware every day, has made them profoundly bitter. They have become sullen, mistrusting, skeptical. . . . They frequently foster deep hatred in their hearts toward the wealthy. We are very far removed from the times when the workers saw their bosses as family and frequently visited them, bringing gifts of chickens, eggs, and fruit. As modern communications bring communist texts to the countryside, and the agitators follow, the old-time affection is turned into skepticism and even inflamed into war. . . .

Today, the haves are much farther removed from the have-nots. And above all else, the people have lost the only thing that could give them spiritual peace and a profound happiness to live: religion. . . .

Father Alberto Hurtado (seated second row, facing camera) with Catholic activists in Valparaíso. Photographer unknown. Courtesy of El Centro de Estudios y Documentación "Padre Hurtado" of the Pontifica Universidad Católica de Chile.

The religion that has given so much happiness to our people has been completely lost. Religious practices are disappearing, and along with them, the Christian background will also disappear if we do not soon work with greater efficiency. . . .

Drifting from the Church

The falling away of the poor, whom Christ came to evangelize, is the greatest bitterness for the Church in our times. "The poor are evangelized," was what the teacher said to John's emissaries when they asked if he was the Messiah.

His Holiness Pius XI bitterly complained about the modern living conditions that force "most of humanity to be so absorbed in the task of getting its daily bread that it is almost impossible for them to think about the salvation of their souls." Modern civilization has multiplied its demands, and in order to satisfy them, we need money, a lot of money. Those who have money always want more in order to maintain a certain lifestyle that they deem necessary. . . Those who do not have any money want to have some, and they are envious of those who have it and whom they see as having everything. . . .

Added to all of this is the fact that we have a small number of priests to spiritually cultivate our nation in the necessary way for this modern life where faith needs to be better formed and more robust. The number of priests has not increased in proportion to either the increase in our population, or to the needs that new, specialized tasks require every day. These tasks take up many of our spiritual operations. At the same time, the Church in Chile does not have sufficient resources to carry out its educational tasks in a manner that is accessible to the people. Its schools can barely survive, and they barely stay open every year when the subsidies arrive late. The educational labors of the Church, such as they are, are carried out in the secondary schools, under the charge of priests and religious personnel, but the Church has had to charge money in order to maintain these very schools. In fact, the result has been that a Catholic education is only available to the wealthy. The Church, which is always lacking money for its charitable works to benefit the poor, has had to count on the benevolence of those who can donate money. It has had to approach these people asking for assistance, and many have therefore believed that it has aligned itself with the wealthy to defend the interests of the landowners. . . . The landowners have requested and organized the missions in the countryside. The missionaries have stayed in landowners' houses, where they have been kindly cared for. But now, this hospitality is frequently seen as an indication of the landowners' and priests' close conspiracy to keep the poor oppressed. . . .

All of this has persuaded the country that the Church works together with the wealthy and has taken a stance against the poor in the great social struggle which characterizes our century. An agitator recently wrote, "The Church is the assistant and instrument of the most impure forces of social oppression." Thanks to God, this concept has begun to fade, above all, due to the providential wisdom of our Prelates, who have been very careful to instill Christianity's social doctrine and the Church's complete separation from politics of parties several times. The Church, above and beyond the political parties, has been the slogan. The people have started to realize that this slogan is the way the ministers of the Church operate. . . .

It is a fact that the working masses in our cities have swollen the ranks of Marxism. This can only lead to more painful experiences than those which they have already suffered, that is, if Marxism were to become a reality. But if the people want to find a legitimate way to improve their lives, and turn to the Christian associations for a place where they can reach their goals without abandoning their faith, then unfortunately, we can not offer them anything in today's Chile. Where are the Catholic unions? Where are the multitudes? Where are the associations that defend workers' legitimate interests? Marxism offers them all of this; why don't the Catholics?

It is certainly not because the Roman Pontiffs have not spoken about this. It is not because our prelates have not repeated these teachings and have tried to apply them to Chile, but rather because they have not found any response among the Catholics. They have had no response because there are not enough priests dedicated to the task of social formation and organization, and because of how difficult this problem is in our country. The teachings of our Pontiffs, and our bishops who understand the Chilean reality, are still valid and constitute an urgent alarm, a grave obligation for all Chileans to obey and cooperate in this slow, difficult task, a task that has already failed in a thousand ways, the task of raising the social level of our working class.

Christian Life in Chile

What is the deepest root of all of these ills? We do not hesitate to affirm that it is the lack of religious education among the masses and the elites that leads to a weakening of the faith. Some believe that the faith endures among almost all Chileans. However, the results of surveys and statistics force us to think differently. It is true that most of our country still has a religious background that you can see from children being baptized, the icons that people have in their houses, and some practices, many of which are more superstitious than religious. Christian life, none the less, is weakening, almost to the point of disappearing in some regions.

If we simplify the results, we reach the conclusion that 9 PERCENT OF WOMEN AND 3 1/2 PERCENT OF MEN GO TO MASS ON SUNDAYS, AND 14 PERCENT OF THE FAITHFUL FOLLOW CHURCH INSTRUCTIONS. These statistics are even more pessimistic than that of the Chilean Episcopal's pastoral collective in November of 1939. The bishops estimated then that "an optimistic calculation of just 10 percent of the Chilean population goes to mass on Sundays and holidays."

Regarding marriage, we can say that 50 percent of the existing marital unions have been legitimized by the Church. Thus there are 50 percent of marriages that do not have God's blessing. In the Christian sense, *over half of the population is born illegitimately*. This percentage is terrifying.

On the other hand, a faithful background exists in our country. They have typically Christian virtues, and there is a desire not to drift from the Church. Even today, 98.2 percent baptize their children, which means that most of the population has a connection to Christianity. It is clear that they do not understand the deep meaning of baptism. Some baptize their children out of tradition, others do so because they have to name their children, so that they do not get the evil eye. . . .

If we consider the countryside, how much damage do some landowners, who say they are Catholic, frequently cause with their bad habits? An eager country priest writes, "Many times the scandalous behavior of a few Catholic *hacendados* offset the priest's efforts. I have verified this throughout my fifteen years as a country priest. Many times the children of the *hacendados* [landowners], who are educated in Catholic schools, are the perdition of the girls on the estates, and they set bad examples for the laborers. They take off with the servants' daughters in a car, and then turn up at the churches as if they were saints, displaying their apparent devotion to the sacraments. And woe unto the poor priest who criticizes these outrages!" . . .

The Gravest of Problems

In earlier chapters we have bitterly complained about the lack of education, the animal-like conditions in which many live, alcoholism, the degeneration of family, workers who embrace atheistic Marxism, the lack of a Christian lifestyle, the spread of Protestantism in our country, especially among the upper classes, but we have yet to discuss what we think is the gravest problem because it is the cause of many of the ills that we have discussed, at least in their acute forms that we see today. We are talking about the problem of priests.

And how many priests are there? How many faithful must each priest attend? The November 1939 Pastoral Collective affirms, "The Chilean population is greater than 4,600,000 inhabitants. *The number of priests is 780 in the secular clergy, and 835 religious personnel, for a total of 1,615* which leaves 1 priest for every 3,000 souls. Throughout the entire Republic, there are 451 parishes, so there is *an average of 10,000 faithful per parish.* If a parish priest can not attend to more than 1,000 faithful, then we can see how much is lacking, and we can say that the spiritual attention for the other 9,000 faithful is almost in vain. In more exact and impressive terms, we can say that *in Chile there are over 4 million faithful who are almost at the margins of the necessary pastoral action of their parishes.*

Could there be a more scandalous fact with greater consequences for the souls, the Church, and the Nation?

Translated by Ryan Judge

"I Told Myself I Must Find Work, I Cannot Continue Here": Interview with a Household Worker

While landlessness and rural poverty drove many men to seek work in distant min-
ing camps and factories, women increasingly traveled in search of service work in
Chile's capital and provincial cities. For most of the twentieth century, domestic
service remained the most common occupation for women in Chile, even as oppor-
tunities for office work and jobs in the textile industry expanded after 1930. The ar-
rival of young, rural women from southern Chile in Santiago attracted the attention
of Catholic clergy, who cultivated a following among domestic servants in the Na-
tional Association of Household Employees, a group of activists who worked with
the Church to provide legal support, vocational training, child care, and religious
services for female servants in the 1950s.

In this 2002 interview by Elizabeth Hutchison with Elba Bravo, one of the As-
sociation's founders tells her story of migrating from the rural town of Curicó to
Santiago to work as a domestic servant at age fourteen, recounting the hardship
of rural families that drove them to this difficult decision. Her account stresses the
isolation, onerous labor, and lack of basic rights suffered by many domestic workers
who began work as young girls. Bravo's account of her early activism also reflects the
Church's new emphasis on working with the poor and organizing Catholic associa-
tions in response to the decline in Catholic religious practice.

My name is Elba del Carmen Bravo Rojas and I was born in Illico and I was
baptized in Bichuquen, in Curicó. When I was very young I came to the
area around Licanten between Licanten and Iloca, on the seaside near Curicó . . . where I was raised until the age of twelve. And from there I went
with my family to a *fundo* [rural property/estate] called Maitenan, eight kilometers from Curicó, where my father was employed as a foreman. We were
eight children, and I studied until high school but we didn't have enough
resources and the school was very far away, and my mother didn't dare to
send me that far, so I never went beyond that (primary) education. . . .

When I arrived in Santiago my father continued working on that fundo. . . . I was fourteen. We didn't have enough food. My mother worked very hard, very hard, raising pigs and chickens and geese and turkeys, but we had very little clothing and we often went barefoot because there were no shoes and what we had we had to save for a particular celebration like the religious celebrations that *patrones* [estate owners] organized once a year, or when we went to the village. . . . One day the patrón of the fundo gave the order for me to go out to prune grape vines and my mother said "my daughter . . . is not going to go out [to work], my husband is paying to have a house [on the estate], but she is not going to go. And then they had an argument when I had gone, and I went to the banks of a river to look for firewood, and I sat down and I told myself I must find work, I cannot continue here. I worked, but I worked in whatever job there was to do on the plot of land they gave my father to cultivate, but he didn't have time, he had to pay for it, and I had to be counting sacks of potatoes, how many sacks of corn, how much they took to the market, but that was to buy food, that's all. So I said I'm going to speak with a lady who washed the clothes of the rich people on the estates, and I said to her "Is there any work in Santiago?" Santiago, I'm talking about the year 1948, was like going to another country, there was only the train. . . . She told me, "I'm going to speak with someone because they need a nanny." . . .

My father said, okay we will give you up, but if you are uncomfortable there come back, we tolerate poverty but not punishment, we heard that the patrones hit the girls when they didn't know how to do things correctly, punishment no said my father, no said my mother, you come back no matter what. They spoke with them and they [the patrones] said, "But she can't come back to see you before a year has passed." . . .

When my father was taking me to the train, we passed by a large fundo ten kilometers from Curicó where my fathers' cousins worked, and Uncle Juan Luis and Uncle Raimundo. The cousins told my father, "Look, Samuel, your daughter is going to return either pregnant or a prostitute."

The train came, and I was so sad, I held my father, we hugged, there were no words for it, my tears clouded my vision when I was on the train, my father cried, I cried, but, on the other hand, I said, I have to make something of my life, I can't sink into [the] poverty of my father and family, I can't, and I came to Santiago. But, my plans changed when I arrived at the house on Carrera Street and the lady told me, "Nanny? Not here, my daughter already has a nanny and the girl who cooks is the one who retired. . . . She was with us for many years so you will go to the kitchen." . . . I didn't know how to do anything, we were four servants, and I still was only fourteen, I burned the first rice I made, they got mad, and they told the woman who had retired to teach me to cook the food they liked, raviolis, the filling for empanadas, it was a lot to learn. . . . The family owned the estate next to the estate where my father worked so they spoke with my parents, but I couldn't go [home] until March. . . . They didn't give me permission to leave, and I didn't even have one day a week off, nothing, and my parents also warned me not to go out anywhere (in the city). . . .

There was a parish and they were Catholic, the family, and I asked permission to go to mass and they gave me permission, and I went to mass and spoke with the priest there, may he rest in peace, and then he told me that I could come to a meeting. I told him how I was suffering all alone, that the other maids were older, or not so old, but one was retired and the other was twenty-five, but all housewives. They did their work and took siestas while I wound up in the kitchen mopping, doing everything, and I had to keep ironing clothes that they themselves had washed, I had to keep ironing. I was the first to rise in the morning and the last one to go to bed. So I kept going, and the priest said to me, "Go ahead, ask for days off." They didn't give me days off. "Hmm, I'll speak with them," he told me, "so that you can come to Church on Wednesday or you can tell them if you dare," . . . "because here we have some literacy classes, learning to read and write, there's a class in fashion to learn how to knit clothing." And I was happy just being able to go out. . . . I kept going to the Church and I began to get to know other people who met there, and they said, "No, I get one day a week off, I go out late but I go out." So one day I said to the priest, "I am not going to go to the parish, today I have some things to do," because the lady of the house bought my clothing for me, she didn't allow me to go out to buy clothing, and I took a bus to the end of the line, and I returned on the same bus. It's that I wanted to get to know the city. There were people who put up with that, but I couldn't tolerate it. It's something that, no, no, no, made me suffer. The truth is that I suffered a great deal, my *compañeras* [comrades] were good, but each one just took care of herself, and they taught me some things, but it was slavery. Because at home we lived in a hut and there was a stream that passed right by, but we ate at the same table, we fought, we took things from one another, but it was my family, it was my family, and there I was sitting with some *señoras* who sometimes spoke and sometimes didn't speak, that's not right. That's what inspired me to give my all to the association.

First I began in the parish, I walked all the streets organizing people. We had 120 girls, maids, in the parish and we told each other our stories, we talked about how we got there, girls who didn't know how to read. I prepared letters for them to send to their parents. One Wednesday they brought responses that I read to them, and there we told each other our stories, and we cried together, sang together. When Christmas came we celebrated Christmas there and the priest gave us a lot of support, and then, I'm talking about 1948, 1949, Father Piñera arrived, there was a union, but I was terrified of the word "union," I didn't like it at all. . . . I went with a friend . . . because Father Piñera said, "These are workers' social organizations, it would be right for you to be there." So we went and Father Hurtado was there, but he was a priest like any other priest, and he got us involved in defending the rights that we should have, just as we had to get respect for our rights, do our jobs and fulfill our duties but also know how to defend our rights at the right moment, not be slaves, we were daughters of God, we had to know God, we had to struggle for the future. . . .

And that was how I met Father Piñera . . . who was for me The Priest. . . . And he spoke to us of this marvelous thing, of organizing an association, and that we had to respond to the needs of today's domestic worker, tomorrow's domestic worker, the domestic workers of the future, because they are born to poor families with few resources, that "today the young girls who will be born and who will migrate to Santiago, to the capital, who is going to meet them at the train station, there will be prostitutes waiting for them, there will be nobody, they fall sick and might die and nobody brings them a packet of tea, nobody brings them a tissue, nobody brings them medicine, nobody visits them or consoles them. What do they do when they are thrown out of the homes where they work? Where do they go the day they are thrown out? We are going to try to organize the thousands of domestic servants, there are thousands and thousands who are abandoned, and this cannot be. . . . You are going to solve many of your problems by yourselves, united, united with one common goal, with Christ, each one of you working and making your own contribution. I call on you in the name of God, in the name of all those who are suffering today, who [are] working when they are sick, who do not have the opportunity to take a day off to go see a doctor, all those who do not have work and are suffering injustice and who have to live locked inside the house, all those who cry with their families and cannot go to see their mothers, and if their families come to visit them there is no place to receive them, to all those who want to marry and have a family and cannot do so, have no place to celebrate a marriage, to court, to go out." . . . So I joined the movement, yes I did.

Translated by Elizabeth Q. Hutchison and Thomas Klubock

Fundamental Theoretical Principles of the Socialist Party

Julio César Jobet

The Chilean Socialist Party was founded following the brief establishment in 1932 of the Socialist Republic of Chile, led by the military officer Marmaduke Grove, which lasted only twelve days. The Socialist Party was a nationalist and leftist alternative to the Communist Party, with which it competed for a base among urban white-collar and blue-collar workers. The party distinguished itself among Chile's left parties through its independence from and critical stance toward the Soviet Union, its emphasis on nationalism and anti-imperialism, and its identification with Latin America (in comparison with the internationalism of the Soviet Comintern). The Socialist Party was also a major component of the Popular Front government elected in 1938, and of the Radical Party–headed governments that ruled between 1938 and 1952. Salvador Allende, one of the founders of the Chilean Socialist Party, began his "Chilean road to socialism" with the party's founding principles, described here by Julio César Jobet, outlining a distinctively Chilean and nationalist approach to revolutionary socialism.

1. Chilean Socialism is *anti-oligarchic* and *anti-aristocratic*. It combats the minority of large landowners, a small, compact nucleus of the dominant class with excessive influence on government leadership. The classic man of the right comes from this quintessentially reactionary sector. This man, by virtue of his interests, family traditions, lifestyle, education, way of being, doctrine and moral judgments, considers himself a superior being. He asserts the sacred right of his "elite" to run the country's affairs, thanks to their fortune, blood, and talent. He has elaborated an entire theory of natural law to justify these claims, while, in practice, a system of limited suffrage dominated by bribery assures him control over the government, ratifying this concept and giving him legal mandate.

2. Chilean Socialism is *anti-clerical*. It does not accept the intervention of the Church in politics and it denounces the Church's proselytiz-

ing activities, which are tightly linked to the aristocracy and defend its privileges and interests. It repudiates the clergy because they have placed their power at the service of the rich and powerful.

3. Chilean Socialism is *anti-capitalist*. It combats the economic exploitation of the capitalist system based on the privatization of the means of production, the pursuit of profit as an incentive for productive progress, and the exploitation of the worker as a means to become wealthy. On this front, Chilean Socialism attacks the clans of great industrialists, bankers and wholesale merchants, elements of the plutocracy, or rather the capitalist class as such. It combats political influence obtained by economic power, bribes, and corruption. It fights monopolies and speculation.

4. Chilean Socialism is *anti-imperialist*. It denounces the penetration of imperialist capital and the exploitation of the nation's natural resources, which transform the country into a colony of the great international monopolies. At the same time, Chilean Socialism's anti-imperialism exposes the support that the native oligarchy lends to the imperialists, facilitating their intervention and serving their interests.

5. Chilean Socialism is *anti-fascist*. It combats fascism because of its anti-worker terrorism, its support of big capital, and its militaristic and bellicose spirit. This fight is carried out ideologically, on a theoretical and political level, as much as it is in the streets, in direct, organized struggle.

6. Chilean Socialism is *anti-militaristic*. It combats the spirit of the barracks, national chauvinism, and the excessive development of the armed forces. It opposes any military intervention in politics.

7. Chilean Socialism is *anti-individualistic*. It distrusts the actions of solitary individuals, who are driven only by the egotism of greed, rooted in the exploitation of man by man. It repudiates the indifference of he who takes refuge in an ivory tower, removed from the social struggle for the emancipation of man and society. It opposes the rightist who, generally speaking, despises man and tries to subject the individual to the needs of public order and the cult of the State.

8. Chilean Socialism is *anti-statist*. It opposes the control of the police state, which operates at the service of the dominant, land-owning class and is used to repress the working classes. Chilean Socialism combats centralism and bureaucracy.

9. Chilean Socialism *criticizes the reformist Socialism of the Second International* because of its conformist position within the cogs of the democratic-bourgeois capitalist system. *It criticizes the Soviet Commu-*

nism of the Third International because of its dogmatic position regarding the exclusive defense of the USSR's interests; because of its pretentious theoretical formalist vanity which is sometimes extremist, often conciliatory, and always excessively rhetorical, as well as detrimental to the steadfast unity of the working classes.

In response to the *antis* listed above, Chilean Socialism announced the following positive declarations:

I.   Chilean Socialism is democratic: It has a profound confidence in human beings, and aims for total social equality; it strives to destroy all aristocratic privilege and to transform the current formal democracy, in which the artificial right to private property prevails over human rights, into an active, integral popular democracy. Its goal is to achieve the realization of a democratic workers' republic.

II. Chilean Socialism is secular, optimistic, and enemy to any who reject reason. It defends freethinking and freedom of conscience.

III. Chilean Socialism *advocates the replacement of the capitalist system with a socialist system* in which the collectivization of the means of production enables their organization in order to promote social services and the emancipation of the workers. It supports economic planning and, at the same time, defends the small producer's independence and personal autonomy.

IV. Chilean Socialism is *nationalist, a staunch defender of the country's economic and political independence.* It proposes a second national independence movement to rescue the country's natural wealth and means of production from the hands of international monopolies, and to eliminate imperialism. At the same time, it advocates the self-determination of peoples and a continental unity built upon the formation of an organic, anti-imperialist economy and a Latin American confederation of Socialist republics.

V.   Chilean Socialism *defends public liberties.* Socialism cannot exist without freedom, or it becomes vulnerable to all kinds of tyranny. It rejects the "cult of the State" as much as the "personality cults" of charismatic leaders, so characteristic of fascism and other systems of political terrorism.

VI. Chilean Socialism *struggles for peace and brotherhood among peoples.* It condemns war and favors arbitration in international disputes.

VII. Chilean Socialism is *economically collectivist, and profoundly respects human beings.* It strives to politically educate the working classes

so that they can fulfill their revolutionary duty: to destroy bourgeois society and build a classless society in which individuals can
achieve total material, social, and spiritual liberation.

VIII. Chilean Socialism *recognizes the indispensable role of a new State with
social, technical and planning services,* capable of prompting the suppression of all privileges and all antiquated institutions. It strives
to establish a direct democracy, one that effectively integrates all
workers within the economic, social, and political administration;
the workers' active participation supposes the real democratiza-
tion of the State and Society.

IX. Chilean Socialism is *revolutionary,* because it aims to change the relationship between work and property in order to bring about the
complete reconstruction of society. Socialist society will be based
on the public ownership of the means of production, the economic
planning of resources and the market, the democratic control and
management of the Economy and the State, the true validity of
the social and political rights of workers, and the propagation of
interest in the social as the people's motivation to action.

X. Chilean Socialism is *Latin-Americanist.* While it affirms the international scope of the Socialist doctrine and movement, it does not
dilute its ideas in remote global perspectives; rather, it roots them
in our continent, in a fraternal bond with the revolutionary movements of peoples united by race, language, customs and idiosyn-
crasies, by history, by similar problems, by their shared dreams
and their common enemies. It acts in solidarity with all of the oppressed peoples in the world and with their heroic struggles for
emancipation.

Translated by Jane Losaw and Ryan Judge

Public Health Crisis

Salvador Allende

This medical treatise on the socioeconomic causes of ill health in Chile by the young Popular Front minister of health and future Socialist president offers an expert analysis of the living conditions of the majority of Chileans in this era. It also offers insight into the reasons why Allende saw politics, rather than a medical practice, as the way to cure the conditions he observes and analyzes here. His concern about issues of public health echoed concerns enunciated by social reformers about Chile's extremely high rates of infant mortality and low levels of life expectancy. During the first decades of the twentieth century, reformers seeking answers to the "social question" had often employed eugenicist concepts to analyze the deterioration of the physical well-being of the Chilean "race," noting that national strength was eroded by alcoholism, lack of public hygiene in growing urban areas, and rates of infant mortality and illiteracy that ranked among the highest in the world. Allende's treatise, though marked by the revolutionary and anti-imperialist ideology of the Socialist Party, is consistent with decades of writing by social reformers who sought to establish the biological basis for national development by addressing the public health problems produced by economic modernization. While during the first decades of the century reformers had viewed problems like infant mortality and stagnant population levels as problems of hygiene to be treated as public health matters, Allende contended that without structural changes to the economy that would reduce poverty and inequality, medical measures would be ineffective.

Our country is passing through a historical era in which we struggle to escape from an old, autocratic, free-market economic system in order to organize society in terms of authentic social cooperation and well-being, for the benefit of both the popular and middle classes. For His Excellency, the President of the Republic, the Socialist Party and its Ministers, this is the real meaning of the Popular Front, which the people brought to power less than a year ago: we must revive the nation's social wealth and economic potential, managing, directing, and developing the nation for the benefit of all the country's citizens, without preference or exclusion. Moreover, because of this commitment, the government must return physical vitality to this race of people and the workers, returning to them the virility and health that were, until recently, their most striking characteristics; we must recuperate the physiological capacities of a strong people, and strengthen our immunity to epidemics, all of which would permit higher levels of national productivity and at the same time improve the people's ability to live and enjoy life. And, finally, the Popular Front must restore the right to culture, in all its forms and expressions, to the people of every class. An invigorated, healthy, and educated people: this is the slogan that we Chileans who wish to serve our country should uphold, and for which we struggle unceasingly, so that our people will overcome the exploitation and ignorance in which it has vegetated. . . .

Chile, just like most of the other South American countries, has lived at the mercy of the economic and cultural colonization that has blocked our social progress and development of natural wealth. Even worse, these factors have prevented the people from achieving a standard of living worthy of a civilized and relatively educated country. One hundred twenty years of independent political life have not been enough to incorporate the working classes into civic life within the normal scheme of development; this has barely been enough time to allow a small percentage of the poor to enjoy a little bit of the economic, technical, and cultural advances achieved by humanity.

The great majority of Chileans have been denied the great advances of industry, science, health and medicine, and the benefits of our cultural heritage, which are the definitive creators of public wealth. Our national economy has been, until very recently, exclusively dependent on two or three export products that constitute the principal source of the State's revenues, principally nitrates and copper; these are extractive industries that have not been exploited by Chilean investment, since they have always been in foreign hands and at the mercy of the interests of international economic imperialism. By contrast, agriculture and factory production have developed only in routine ways, thanks to the lack of foresight of previous regimes, the conservative sensibilities of almost all of the country's leaders, and the fact that technology has not spread to any significant degree into rural and industrial production. . . .

Our progress in levels of national production has not improved the well-being of the popular classes in any noticeable way because international capitalism—the economic and financial master of the great centers of production—is only interested in production to satisfy market demands, nothing more. Capitalist companies are not at all troubled by the existence

Salvador Allende, minister of health, 1941. Originally published with the caption "The Minister of Health inspects new medical equipment." Photograph by Miguel Rubio, Chile. Used by permission of Fernanda Rubio. Courtesy of Colección Museo Histórico Nacional de Chile.

of a population of workers who live in deplorable conditions, who risk being consumed by illness, and who vegetate in ignorance. . . .

Aware of the responsibility that he bears on his shoulders, the Minister of Health has tried to begin his work by completing a calm, well-documented, and realistic study of the health and hygiene conditions under which this government has taken power. A succinct and calculated analysis of our socio-medical situation is the best guarantee of being able to diagnose and consequently, apply the appropriate mechanisms that will reestablish the strength and vigor of our people. . . .

We must loyally declare that all of those medical steps that can be taken will only provide effective results if economic-financial policies are adopted that allow for the improvement in the standard of living of our fellow citizens. We can affirm that the fundamental elements that determine the well-being and progress of a people are precisely a good standard of living, adequate sanitary conditions and the wide diffusion of education among the popular classes. It also bears repeating that the volume and consistency of these elements relies heavily on economic growth, without which it is impossible to construct something serious from a hygienic or medical perspective, nor from an educational perspective, because it is not possible to provide health and knowledge to a people that is poorly fed, and that works at a level of miserable exploitation. . . .

Illness, malnutrition, alcoholism, disease, epidemics, and ignorance function and corrode from within any appearances and are inexorable in their effects. Our country has fallen victim to this process and this is why we are now facing an alarming medical-social reality.

Human capital, which is the fundamental basis for the economic prosperity of a country, has been underestimated and abandoned to its own devices. This is the principal cause of our population's failure to increase; this population must be improved and expanded via the number and quality of native inhabitants; population growth is the first condition for a country's prosperity, and the result of the health and educational conditions of its people. . . .

Anyone of progressive spirit must agree with the Minister of Health in that we must not lose any more time and that we must plan, organize, and set in motion the great task of restoring the nation in three fundamental respects: intensifying and expanding the mechanisms of profilaxis, national health, and intense literacy campaign among the unschooled sectors of the country. The Popular Front was created in order to achieve this immense task.

The Medical Convention of Chile, which was held in Valparaíso in 1936, had already declared that "our economic-social structure must be fundamentally changed in order to ensure that man will have the best welfare conditions by means of an equitable distribution of the products of his labor"; it also declared that the State must regulate "the production, distribution, and price of food and clothing"; it affirmed that "housing, as property, is essentially a social function and the State should intervene by regulating the quantity and quality of housing"; finally, it affirmed "that labor problems must be a medical concern because of the disastrous conditions under which work is performed, because of the high levels of mortality among the working classes, and because of the deficient regulation that governs relations between capital and labor." With which the Convention wished to indicate that the solution to the country's medical-social problem required precisely the resolution of economic problems that affect the proletarian classes.

With the directness typical of its political actions and in a manner completely consistent with its current responsibility, the Minister of Health therefore warns that the country should be considered in a state of emergency, and he indicates the pressing necessity of using all means necessary against this danger that threatens the very existence of the nation.

Translated by Elizabeth Q. Hutchison

"Progress for All Social Classes":
Campaigning for the Popular Front

Pedro Aguirre Cerda

As elsewhere in Latin America, the 1940s in Chile saw the rise of nationalist, populist governments that inaugurated a wave of new social and economic policies, including the expansion of public education and social welfare services, the incorporation of organized labor, and nationalist economic policies designed to produce economic diversification and industrialization. While in Brazil, Argentina, and elsewhere these populist and nationalist policies were implemented by figures like the Brazilian dictator Getulio Vargas and the Argentinian military man Juan Perón, in Chile, the election of the Popular Front reflected Chile's robust multiparty democracy and demonstrated the importance of political coalitions in electoral contests. This campaign speech by Pedro Aguirre Cerda, the head of the Radical Party, articulates the basic program and ideology of the Chilean Popular Front, an electoral coalition comprised of the Communist, Socialist, and Radical parties that later served as a blueprint for Salvador Allende's socialist Popular Unity government in 1970.

The march that occurred yesterday, which was the most extraordinary political demonstration that the Republic has seen, authorizes me to address the people of my Country in order to speak about the struggle in which we are involved.

This demonstration represented a call for political, social, and economic liberation issued by a people who have been underestimated, oppressed, and submerged in shameful misery—of both the lower and middle classes—in the face of the government's incomprehension. This government does not comprehend the nature of sovereignty, a sovereignty that is healthy, educated, and hard-won, and which should provide us with the feelings, ideas and actions that facilitate national cooperation and that, relying on this fraternity, should allow the fatherland to progress and grow. . . .

And women have participated in this [new] government, confirmed in their legitimate aspirations, and today they take their place in defense of new policies, which will protect her and her children, and which emerged not only from the political parties, but also from the MEMCH [Movement for the Emancipation of Chilean Women], and from university students and young athletes, who are the generous and visionary soul of social progress, and who, with the ideological enthusiasm that characterizes them, have allowed us to aspire to better days of justice and well-being.

Happily, the Popular Front has already begun to complete its promises, since, thanks to its unified efforts, progressive and industrious men and women have gathered in the United Leftist Front. They are joined in the conviction that immediate action is required in order that all the national forces, concentrated and mutually understood and respected, might mobilize the national wealth and make it serve the collective well-being of Chileans. The Popular Front wants the Country to be a caring mother that lends equal protection to all her children and not a stepmother that grants privileges that favor the least needy. Only in this way, united by bonds of affection and justice, will Chile be able to pose an insuperable obstacle to that other young nation [the United States], educated in principles of violence, that pushes to extend its threatening claw in order to snatch from us the few raw materials that we still have.

The Popular Front has formed a national political consciousness around this program, and it has found in me neither a political boss nor a Messiah, but rather the executor of those proposals that I have promised to complete, and which I will accomplish no matter what obstacles present themselves, because that program is the bare minimum of justice that we owe to our people.

And I will be the only one responsible for the realization of this program, because the Republic has plenty of laws to carry this out; if the laws have not been applied, it is not the fault of the parliamentarians, the political parties or the Opposition press, but rather of those in charge of executing them.

And that set of ideas concerning a program of collective well-being has been possible because the Radical Party—principally representing the middle class and in the face of the firm incomprehension of the Right— has taken a real step toward the Left in order to cordially ally itself with the working class, and because the Socialist and Communist Parties have moved closer to Radicalism in order to make use of its democratic strategies. With this alliance, the Republic has won, because it has exorcised all danger of violence that might have come from reactionary blindness, and we can now go on, democratically, using the constitutional tool of suffrage, to conquer civilization and make progress for all social classes.

The union of the Popular Front forces is not the rabble of 1920—disorderly, shapeless and with the secret hope of turning the existing order upside down—but rather it is composed of organized and responsible parties that do not seek demolition but rather an ordered social and economic reconstruction, one that will benefit all Chileans, whatever their religious or political creed.

With that goal in mind, the Socialist and Communist Parties have demanded neither Ministerial posts nor public jobs, but rather the fulfillment of an honorable and patriotic program for the general good, the details of which we are prepared to give to whomever should ask, a program that the country knows and that nobody will be able to censor.

Just as [the Socialist Party secretary general] Marmaduque Grove said, "The Socialist Party, which has found in the current situation no way other than direct action to solve the problems that affect the working classes, given that most of the middle classes remained undecided or indifferent, and having lost faith in democratic procedures, now pursues its goals through an alliance in the Popular Front; we have decided, loyally and bravely, to commit the mechanisms of the whole efficient national organization to the cause of assuring the democratic triumph of a single candidate, Don Pedro Aguirre Cerda. Our Party thus continues to struggle in this new era, facing a Chilean reality that assures victory and the conquest of Power, democratically, by the progressive forces that are united in the Popular Front, and with the efficient cooperation of the CTCH [Confederation of Chilean Workers], which has at its heart all the workers' organizations in our national territory."

The communist leaders have expressed similar ideas in a frank and public way during the several political excursions that we have carried out in the country.

The country is being pulled down by a lack of social justice.

A malnourished mother, who can not feed her children; a half-naked, shoeless, and rachitic student; an accumulation of sickly beings in a little room, united by common misery; 20,000 annual deaths due to tuberculosis; more than 40 percent excluded from military service because of physical disability; more that 3,000 lunatics secluded in Sanatoriums; a mortality rate higher than that of 37 countries; a life expectancy of 28 years, while in other nations it is more than 50 years; 500,000 people of marginal education because of a lack of schools and teachers; 730,000 illiterates older than 16 years of age; a youth unable to form a home because his lack of technical capacity prevents him from getting a job; 40 percent of cultivatable land unused; copper, nitrate, iron, electric power in the hands of international companies; industry, commerce, the agriculture, and mining, which still remain in Chilean hands, which have no guidance or instructors to update their progress and without access to low-interest capital that would allow them to raise their currently low production, which is not enough to serve even our small population; a minimal fiscal budget (without even taking into account the supplements that are apportioned daily) of 1,600,000,000 pesos; a municipal budget of 180,000,000 pesos; an annual deposit in Social Security of more than 400,000,000 pesos; the 240,000,000 peso payment of the external debt; which subtracts from a minimum group of producers and from a mass of salaried workers that pay them with hunger and misery without the proportional and proper investment in infrastructure that sends civilization out to the provinces; insufficient salaries and wages that have weakened commerce, industry and agriculture, since the middle and popular classes have no savings, investing all their wealth in their modest daily life; together with the freedom to speculate with necessary articles of life, the heavy restriction of freedom of speech, freedom of the press and of association, these are some of the many manifestations that demonstrate that our country is collapsing and that we must cooperate, and that all the forces of labor and production are prepared to fight with bravery and dignity to carry out a constitutional conquest of Power.

And we are in this fight, and we will know how to conquer, and nothing or nobody will be able to contain a nation thirsty for freedom, justice, and well-being.

Translated by Melissa Mann

Rural Workers, Landowners,

and the Politics of Compromise

The League of Poor Campesinos of Las Cabras

and the National Society of Agriculture

The petition here from a group of resident estate laborers (inquilinos), taken from a collection of peasant petitions edited by the historian Brian Loveman, reflects both the high level of organization among rural workers during the 1930s and 1940s and the hopes that the election of the Popular Front government of Pedro Aguirre Cerda (1938–1941) inspired among rural and urban laborers alike. The petition was written by inquilinos who had organized a union or "league" as part of the larger League of Poor Campesinos (Liga de Campesinos Pobres), which was led by the Trotskyist labor organizer and deputy Emilio Zapata. The call by the campesinos (peasants) for Aguirre Cerda and the Ministry of Labor to intervene to enforce the existing labor legislation in their conflicts with the patrón (estate owner) reflected the grow-ing demand to apply the labor rights enshrined in the 1931 labor code—including the right to legal unionization and strikes—to rural as well as urban workers. The public letter that follows, also addressed to Aguirre Cerda, is from the director of Chile's landowners' association, the Sociedad Nacional de Agricultura (National Agricultural Society; SNA), which grouped together members of some of Chile's most powerful families. The letter denounces the initiatives by members of the governing coalition, particularly in the Socialist and Communist parties, to extend the 1931 labor code to the countryside. The SNA opposed legal unionization of rural laborers, both inquilinos and peones (landless seasonal laborers), as well as the basic labor rights conferred on urban, industrial and white-collar workers, including the right to strike, a minimum wage, and the payment of family allowances. In this letter the SNA evokes the special nature of agricultural production and the traditional pa-ternalist relationship between inquilinos and patrones in which the estate laborer received a parcel of land to grow vegetables or pasture livestock and rudimentary housing as part of, or in some cases, most of his salary. While campesinos had or-ganized unions throughout Chile since the 1920s, few had acquired legal status, and the benefits of the 1931 labor code had yet to be extended to the countryside. As Love-man notes, the Popular Front and its successor left-center coalition governments led by the Radical Party basically acceded to the SNA's demands as a condition for the acceptance by the traditional political parties of social reforms that benefited urban blue- and white-collar workers. This political compromise meant that rural laborers continued to toil with few labor rights throughout the 1940s and 1950s.

The Peasants' Petition

> Your Excellency, Senor Pedro Aguirre Cerda
> La Moneda

Esteemed Senor,

The League of Poor Campesinos of Las Cabras, Santa Maria in the Department of San Felipe, appeals to your excellency for protection owing to the measures that the owner of said estate, Arturo Lyon, who lives in the Fundo de Jahuel, is taking against a number of *compañeros* [comrades].

Since May 1, for the sole crime of being unionized in this modest League, the above mentioned landowner proceeded to evict from the *fundo* [estate] the following *inquilinos* [estate laborers]: Julio Fernandez, Luis Henriquez, Manuel Gorigoitia, Felipe Lazcano and Abraham Henriquez.

Despite the fact that we have presented this *señor* on a number of occasions legal petitions [*pliego de peticiones*] he has never wanted to hear us, the reason for which we request that your excellency serve to arbitrate the measures of the case through the intermediary of the Ministry of Labor, with the goal of fulfilling the existing laws and bringing us that justice that corresponds to us.

Convinced of the spirit of equality and justice that must animate your excellency's good will, we petition for legal protection and we do not doubt that our just petition will be heard.

Translated by Thomas Klubock

Pedro Aguirre Cerda with domestic servants at his Conchalí estate, c. 1940. Photographer unknown. Courtesy of Colección Museo Histórico Nacional de Chile.

The Landowners' Public Letter

The institutions that we represent, constituting the greatest organized factor of production in the country, wish to stimulate the labor of their associates, which is, above and beyond any legal criteria, the only real source of the creation of wealth. The realization of this wish is obstructed by inconveniences derived from the present labor union legislation, which is unfeasible in the countryside. It is likewise obstructed by the coercive and arbitrary means with which said legislation is being put into practice, which will undoubtedly provoke, in the near future, the disruption of the agricultural economy, a social disturbance of pernicious consequences, and the deplorable failure of all aspiration to social harmony.

In these conditions production will inevitably tend to decline, provoking a natural regression to more primitive regimes of production, since the employment of the labor force will have to be avoided as the essential condition for maintaining the peace among the campesinos.

The traditional concept of the settlement of campesino families [on estates] will be disrupted as a result of the social agitation, thus causing mutual damage and a distancing [between workers and patrones] that for the present has not occurred but once produced will be irreparable.

The system of agricultural cultivation demands as a basis for success the opportunity for specific labors that, interrupted by any of the usual proceedings that collective conflicts originating in unions lead to, will result in the loss of an entire year of agricultural production. This situation does not occur in industry; a factory can compensate for the effects of a momentary strike with overproduction.

The same immunity from dismissal that the unionization law grants union leaders and even those workers who have presented a list of demands, constitutes a source of serious disruptions in the campesino lifestyle, in the harmonious coexistence of patrones and workers, that could lead to the establishment of a series of strikes. . . .

The establishment of the legal strike as a resource to force an understanding between patrones and industrial workers, because of the damages sustained by both parties with the cessation of production, does not have the same meaning in agricultural work. In the countryside, the majority of the salary is paid in housing, use of fences, pasture for livestock, and other benefits of partnership in working the soil, which cannot be suspended during strikes and that consequently place the patrón in a debilitated state and the inquilino in such a privileged position that it is difficult to imagine that he will not almost permanently maintain "legal" strikes.

A unionization law that takes the reality of agriculture into consideration and that cultivates harmony between capital and labor will never be resisted by the organizations of production that we represent since feelings of solidarity between patrones and workers are the best stimulus for production and collective well-being. . . .

These facts compel us to solicit the personal intervention of Your Excellency to put an end to the current situation so that the organs of the state suspend all activity regarding the unionization of campesinos until the dispositions that make the labor laws applicable to agricultural work are modified.

The profound conviction that the aforementioned reasons have produced in us and the imperative of our institution's honorable tradition of service in the public interest leads us to make known to Your Excellency the consequences that the unionization of the salaried workers in the countryside could have for the economy and the social organization of the country.

Translated by Jane Losaw

A Case of Frustrated Development

Aníbal Pinto

By the 1950s, Latin America's embrace of economic development through import-substituting industrialization (ISI) had produced disturbing trends toward stagnation, inflation, and trade imbalance. These changes preoccupied a generation of Latin American economists employed in the Latin American Economic Commission (CEPAL), a think tank created by the United Nations in 1948 that was housed in Santiago. A decade later, the CEPAL economist Aníbal Pinto contributed to widening debates on the limits of Chile's industrial development with his book Chile: A Case of Frustrated Development, *which provided a detailed critique of Chilean development strategies after 1939. Pinto explored the roots of the endemic inflation that characterized the protracted crisis of ISI in the 1950s, analyzing how state efforts to promote industrialization failed to promote the diversification of the export sector, in both agriculture and industry, which in turn provoked an endemic trade imbalance. Despite successful industrialization after 1930, he argued, Chile's economy continued to rely on the export of a single commodity, copper, to world markets, and was increasingly dependent on U.S. markets for its exports. On the other hand, Pinto noted, state-protected industrialization buffered the Chilean economy from fluctuations in the international economy, limiting the possible effects of any collapse as disastrous as the global depression of 1929–1933. The work of CEPAL economists like Pinto was widely disseminated throughout the region in this period and served as a precursor to theories of Latin American economic dependency (or "dependency theory") employed by Chilean leftists who promoted agrarian reform and the socialist transformation of the Chilean economy in the 1960s.*

A Critical Analysis of the Period

. . . In a general sense, we focus our critique on two aspects:

The first pertains to the insufficient clarity with respect to the chosen ends and means. The country, as we have seen, followed a general policy known as industrialization. Choosing this path had more to do with the immediate need to take action than through a conscious decision, which would involve mastery of its character, principles, and requirements. As such, incoherencies and contradictions have inevitably emerged. [The result has been] the pursuit of often incompatible goals and the selection of policies that are often as ineffective as they are at odds with other policies that were applied at the same time. . . .

The excessive specialization in the composition of their exports is one of the most injurious characteristics of the structure of underdeveloped countries. It is, without a doubt, the main cause of the vulnerability of their productive capacity. Therefore, one of the primordial objectives of their economic policy has been to improve that condition with the goal of diversifying exports.

This goal had especially important consequences for Chile because of the country's loss of position in world nitrate markets and the inauspicious conditions of the evolution of the demand and prices for its successor, copper, during the period. . . .

Unfortunately, the results have been disappointing as new and unexpected problems have joined the older, ugly ones that have constituted another aspect of Chile's dependence on exports.

It is worth pointing out that trade deficits have been common for the majority of underdeveloped countries that face the same challenge, which suggests that the task is particularly arduous and complex.

Let us think about some revealing statistics with regard to the Chilean case.

In the five-year period from 1925 to 1929, nitrate and copper represented 48.9 percent and 29.9 percent of total exports, respectively. Twenty years later, in the period from 1945 to 1949, copper's contribution rose to 52.6 percent and that of nitrate dropped to 16.8 percent. Altogether, mineral exports, which contributed 87 percent of the export revenues in 1928–29, averaged 78 percent between 1946 and 1953. Any slight progress in this regard seems offset by the sole importance of copper, which remained the supreme component of foreign trade.

Agricultural exports, which played an important role prior to the nitrate boom, contributed 10 percent of export revenues in 1928–29. Their value rose to between 16 percent and 18 percent between 1930 and 1939, mainly due to the decline of mining exports. Agriculture's contribution to total exports after 1940 returned to around 12 percent. . . .

The most encouraging aspect in the development of exports is the position that industrial exports have proceeded to fill, especially those proceeding from [the iron and steel company] Huachipato, which raised its relative importance from 3 percent in 1928–29 to 11 percent of total exports in 1952–1953.

Chuquicamata Copper Mine. Located north of Antofogasta, Chuquicamata is the world's largest open-pit copper mine. From its beginning Chuquicamata, like Chile's other major copper mines, was owned by North American companies, which fueled nationalist movements to expropriate the mines. Salvador Allende's socialist government nationalized the mines in 1970, and Chuquicamata still belongs to state-owned CODELCO, the largest copper mining enterprise in the world. Used by permission of CODELCO-CHILE. Photographer unknown. Courtesy of Colección Biblioteca Nacional de Chile.

The excessive specialization of the composition of exports has not changed. To make matters worse, a new element of distortion took shape: the lack of market diversity.

In the period from 1935 to 1939, around 65 percent of exports had the following destinations: 21 percent to the United States, 17 percent to Great Britain, and 27 percent to continental Europe. In the years 1950–1954, the situation reveals a profound change, one that has been developing since the war. The U.S. now absorbs more than 50 percent of Chile's exports, as a general rule, and Europe as a whole imports less than 30 percent. The only good news in this regard is the increase of the Latin American market and especially that of Argentina. Argentina imported less than 3 percent between 1935 and 1939, and increased its purchases to a little more than 15 percent in the years from 1950 to 1954.

Why has it been so hard to diversify and improve our exports?

We can list many reasons, but it suffices to emphasize the main one: It is very hard to promote new exports.

In this respect, it is again advisable to remember the result of the efforts to substitute imports. These efforts should have been complemented by the diversification (and the increase) of exports. The essence of a sensible policy would be to eliminate the trade deficit and speed up economic development.

In Chile, as in almost all the countries faced with the same problems and tasks, it has not been possible to advance in unison on those two fronts, because, again, the diversification of exports is much more difficult.

First of all, in terms of basic products, the adolescent countries encountered difficulties stemming from the limited variety of natural resources. Yet, even when they have them, the problem is not resolved. In order to place exports in a competitive position in international markets, it is necessary to produce them with a satisfactory degree of efficiency, that is, make production costs competitive with the costs of other exporting countries. Generally, this improvement requires considerable investments, and these countries often lack the necessary means as well as the institutional, political, and social will required to improve their exporting efficiency. Typically only foreign investors have been able to carry out this task. And, in this respect, we have already seen that the twenty-five-year period that we have studied has not been comparable to the previous century. Capital flows have been weak and, in addition, there has been a clear tendency toward developing industrial substitutes for many primary products. At the same time, many primary materials or basic goods have not been sufficiently attractive in the principal markets because of the slow growth of demand or other factors.

For their part, private investors in an adolescent country find themselves confronting foreign markets on a basis that frightens them. They know the markets are unstable and rigorously competitive. They understand the lure toward the monopolization of the productive and commercialization processes, and while their resources are relatively few, the strength of their organizations is even less.

If the difficulties seem great to the person studying the promotion of new exportable primary goods, they appear almost insurmountable when the goal is to sell finished or industrial products in foreign markets.

The companies linked to import substitution, however, face much more certain and promising outlooks. They know their demand, and because of official protection, they do not face constraints regarding productivity and costs. Finally, the habitual lack of foreign exchange restricts, if not eliminates, competition from other local businessmen.

Given these elements, it is not surprising that resources and energies are directed preferentially toward import substitution, with the consequent postponement of efforts to improve the structure of exports.

We have one example of this situation in the Chilean experience of export promotion. As was already indicated, the only new and significant contribution in this regard has been the iron and steel production of Huachipato. This company operates with the capitalization and scale of operations comparable to those of foreign factories, primarily because of the combination of foreign credit and determined, ample state support.

The case of the emerging paper and fiber industry is also illuminating. This has taken many years and its first stages of development are due to a combination of fortunate factors: a large private national company that purchases its products, the research and general backing of the Corporación de Fomento [State Development Agency], and credits from the Banco Internacional [International Development Bank].

One of the most interesting aspects related to that company, one that provides an idea of the very steep hill that this class of initiatives has to conquer, is the one that refers to the considerable investments of fixed social capital that they require. These investments include transportation infrastructure, housing for employees and workers, energy, etc. Generally, in a mature country, these obligations are satisfied by the State or other enterprises, and are the result of previous development, which is, precisely, one of the conditions that businessmen take into account when they begin a new activity. Our reality is different, especially when dealing with projects that are far away from sizable or available collective facilities. These difficulties imply larger investments, which reduce the likelihood of a satisfactory profit.

In this matter, a private or public national company faces a greater disadvantage than a foreign one. For example, the copper companies have had to make numerous complementary investments in their plants in the North or in Sewell, while their foreign counterparts have the backing of their mother companies as well as the certainty of being able to expand so as to satisfy a more or less certain demand. This has been the case for the subsidiary industries based in the North.

The Chilean economy remains vulnerable and dependent regarding trade because it has been unable to diversify the structure of its exports.

However, this circumstance should be analyzed in conjunction with another element that has a compensatory character, which is progress in the substitution of imports.

Let us recall what occurred in the past.

When trade contracted, a very considerable share of productive resources immediately became unemployed. Unemployment gave rise to misfortune and painful sacrifices that were exacerbated by local circumstances, such as the concentration of export activity in the Northern provinces. . . .

We need to consider one important fact when understanding the post-crisis, that is, the period after the economic readjustment that we have analyzed. There were no downturns that were comparable either in intensity or duration to those of the past in the five five-year periods. The ups and downs of international trade have been brief and relatively moderate, even though at times (for example, in 1949 and in 1953) they managed to cause concern and delicate problems, especially in the fiscal arena.

The new structure of the economy has not been subjected to a demanding test that allows us to draw an exact comparison.

However, it is possible and reasonable to discuss a few differences.

In the first place, especially during a brief downturn, employment income in the country would certainly be less affected because of the simple reason that the importance of the foreign sector has diminished. . . .

On the other hand, the decline in the capacity to import, which leads to a depression, will now affect the acquisition of primary materials, fuels, and capital goods more than that of consumer goods, as in the past. If an economic downturn is very acute and extended, it will end up restricting industrial activities and this . . . will lower income and demand, thereby setting off a depression-inducing "chain reaction." However, if the downturn does not radically affect the supply of primary goods and fuel, economic policy will be able to maintain and even increase business in those areas of the economy, especially industry, that produce for the internal market.

This change demonstrates the strengths of the current economic structure over the previous one. In the old economy, factors that were employed in the export sector did not easily transition to the domestic sector. In today's economy, however, because of our margin of installed capacity and basic supplies, industrial and other activities can, at the very least, temporarily compensate for the reduced demand for exports.

Translated by Ryan Judge and Melissa Mann

The Movement for the Emancipation of Chilean Women: Interview with Elena Caffarena

This selection provides an important look at the progressive feminist movement of the 1930s and 1940s. Closely aligned with the Popular Front, the Movement for the Emancipation of Chilean Women (MEMCH) organized both middle- and working-class women around feminist issues like the right to vote, access to birth control, and legalized divorce, as well as issues more typical of the leftist Popular Front like the cost of living, education, health care, and the unionization of women work-ers. Elena Caffarena, a lawyer and cofounder of the MEMCH, represented a new group of educated women who entered law, education, and social work, among other professions, and made new claims to legal and political equality for women. The MEMCH was not, however, limited to middle- and upper-class women. It was multiclass in character and included many working-class and working women as well. Thus, in addition to calls for universal suffrage, the MEMCH demanded legal protections for working mothers and a series of reforms to address the problems of working women. Chile finally passed universal suffrage for women in 1949, although women had begun voting in municipal elections in 1935. In this interview with the journalist Georgina Durand published in 1943, Caffarena describes the MEMCH's multiclass origins and diverse demands, insisting on the need for women's greater political and social rights.

What political or social phenomenon led to the formation of the MEMCH?

"The Movement for the Emancipation of Chilean Women was born in 1935. Then, as now, women were in an inferior situation to men legally, economically, and socially. Even though the Constitution emphatically declares that there are no privileged classes in Chile, and that we are all equal under the law, reality shows us something different. We see that women can not directly influence the republic's presidential and par-liamentary elections by voting. With some exceptions, those who have married are not able to administer their assets. Unless they are widowed, they have no rights over their children. They always have wages and salaries that are inferior to those of men. In many cases the rules governing public service prohibit them from being promoted above certain ranks. And when the rules do not explicitly state this, prejudice or a reactionary boss are enough to exclude women from important positions, etc. The feeling about this situation of women's limited ability to work for a living stimulated our energetic efforts to convince people that we need to unite all women's organizations in the fight for feminist demands, regardless of their class, religion, or political ideology. That is how the MEMCH was born, with a program that, in my opinion, constituted the most thought-out and serious planning about the needs and specific demands of our sex. That is where we thought about the situation of women as citizens and private persons: as youth, as mothers and heads of households, as single and married, as happily-married women, as well as unhappily-married women who need to fix their failed marriages. We considered their interests as workers, as maids, and as office workers. We thought about their spiritual needs, their educational demands, and also their material and economic problems."

Who were the leaders and founders of the movement?

"In its organization and internal structure, the MEMCH was a new kind of movement compared to existing Chilean women's organizations. I don't want what I am about to tell you about the other organizations to be taken in a negative way. I know that they emerged from a particular period, and they did work that we need to understand in relation to the environment and circumstances in which they operated. I think that until the MEMCH appeared, women's groups, more than mass organizations, were just groups of leaders, exclusive and elite groups, if we can call them that, and that is why individual leaders were extraordinarily important within them. In the MEMCH, individual personalities did not count much. In my opinion, what was interesting was the group. That is where something happened that had been unimaginable before then: women of all social classes worked together and in perfect harmony. There were maids working alongside doctors, lawyers next to peasants, high-class ladies alongside domestic workers, artists and writers next to women from the villages, who were often illiterate but understood the realities and problems of a hard life."

*Do you think that these women's groups are logical tools for winning the demands
that we seek?*

"Not only do I think that they are logical tools, but I consider them indispensable for achieving women's liberation. I think that if in Chile we
have not gone farther toward winning feminist demands, it is because
of a lack of unity and combativeness in women's organizations. I often
think that it was a mistake to skip the stage of the English and United
States style of militant, combative feminism. This is a statement I make
cautiously: I would gladly take it back if the women who participate in
the political parties could show me just one feminist demand that they
have secured, if they could show me just one campaign for women's
rights that they started and pursued. For example, think of the really
fantastic case, one worthy of being in *Ripley's Believe It or Not*, in which
women attending an assembly of the Radical Party themselves argued
that their party's convention should make a statement against granting
women the right to vote."

*Don't you think that it would make more sense to have women work with men
inside the political parties and other groups, rather than isolated from them as
they do now?*

"I think the one kind of work does not, and should not, preclude the
other. Women can and must work with the parties. But it is also necessary that there be a group of women who work independently, who
do not obey party interests, brandishing the flag of women's demands.
Without a doubt, this is one of the hottest problems that the Chilean
feminist movement has dealt with. At the same time, it is the one that
has been discussed the most around the world, especially in the vanguard movements. It is something that has been discussed in many con-
gresses and people have spilled a lot of ink over it. People argue that, if
women do not have fundamental problems that are different than those
faced by men, especially with respect to their economic needs, then
women should work alongside men [in the parties] because any type of
division will hinder the struggle for better living conditions. I think and
feel that I am a woman who works in the vanguard, but I respectfully
disagree with this way of thinking that, in my opinion, is the product
of simplistic theoretical logic. The truth is that women have to struggle
on two fronts: one is the struggle for basic demands, in which they
must accompany their children and work mates and life partners. The
other requires them to work for specific demands that stem from their

status as women, which can often put them in conflict with their own children and husbands. Six years of working for women's rights have convinced me that the political parties, even those that have beautiful feminist declarations in their programs, always have more pressing and important tasks to pursue rather than fulfilling these declarations. I am convinced that women's emancipation and achievement of all demands can only come about by a tenacious movement led by women and their organizations."

What are the most urgent victories for women to achieve today?

"The first one is the vote, not because this is the most important in and of itself, but because I consider it to be the tool, the key, to achieving other demands. The vote will allow women to be present in the laboratory of laws, to participate in order to modify the ones that reduce our rights and limit our possibilities. On the other hand, when women can vote, the political parties will suddenly have sympathy for, and interest in, us. I am looking forward to seeing the parties' concern for our culture, our education, our wages, our advances . . . for everything that they have never cared about or been interested in. Besides the female vote, as women we have important demands such as eliminating the married woman's lack of legal rights, in particular to replace the regime of communal property with one defined as an enterprise; obtain shared custody over children when husbands are present, and not only when there is no husband; eliminate all rules that exclude women from certain jobs, including the right to equal pay for equal work; the right to paid maternity leave, both before and after birth, etc."

Can women remain feminine if they dedicate so much time to social and political problems?

"In order to answer that, we would have to decide first what we mean by femininity because it connotes flirtation, and although femininity and flirting often go together, they are substantially different concepts. Flirting is objective, something that translates into material things, such as bracelets, curls, and silks; it is something that changes with time and fashion. Femininity, on the other hand, is subjective. It is a particular way of being a woman and remains fixed, constant across time. There is nothing to fear about the femininity of women who dedicate themselves to politics or social movements. If work influenced femininity, believe me there would no longer be any femininity left in the world. Remember women have been working the land for thousands of years and have labored as domestic servants, and that for more than one hundred years, women have been working with industrial machinery. Economic necessities have forced woman to earn her food in the factories and workshops. The census can document the thousands of women who work in the fields and mines, the hundreds of thousands who work as domestic servants. Has anyone ever worried about these women losing their femininity?"

Are you in favor of divorce?

"Look, Georgina, what would a doctor say if you asked him if he were in favor of amputations? He would tell you that he is not in favor of them, but in many cases they are necessary. I am not in favor of it, but I think that divorce is the solution, the remedy in some cases, for matrimonial gangrene. I don't understand why some people oppose divorce legislation, much less why some women view it as a threat to their homes. Those who are not guilty of something that would constitute grounds for divorce have nothing to fear. Nobody can be forced to seek a divorce. To be precise, divorce is the action that marital law gives an innocent spouse to punish the guilty partner. If, out of religious conviction or moral precepts a woman prefers to suffer her husband's offenses, that is her problem, but it would be selfish of her to apply this norm to people who do not have the same beliefs. We do not make laws to change or moralize about the customs of a particular era. On the other hand, for laws to be effective, we need to adapt them to the customs and needs of the times. The fact that the courts have had to accept arrangements that they know are fictional and artificial, such as the practice of nullifying marriages, tells us that divorce is considered to be a social fact and that we need a law to deal with it."

Translated by Ryan Judge

Poetry and Politics: *Memoirs* and

"The Heights of Macchu Picchu"

Pablo Neruda

In the selection from his autobiography here, Pablo Neruda reflects on the role of politics in his poetry. From his early days as a university student, Neruda was drawn to political and social activism. He later went on to become a leading figure in Chile's Communist Party, a senator for the northern mining province of Tarapacá, and the presidential candidate of the Communist Party in 1970, when he withdrew in favor of the nomination of Salvador Allende, the Socialist Party candidate, to lead the Popular Unity coalition. As a young man, Neruda worked in the foreign service, including a position as Chilean consul in Barcelona in 1936 at the outbreak of the Spanish Civil War. Neruda credited his experiences in Spain as fundamental to his growing politicization and eventual militancy in the Communist Party. His poetry reflected his political commitments, with poems on the Spanish Civil War, U.S. imperialism, and the working conditions of miners, and rural laborers. Neruda also makes clear that his poetry was rooted in the local specificities of Chilean life, Chile's natural landscapes, its history, and its people. At the same time, Neruda viewed himself as an American and an internationalist. His epic Canto General *provided a powerful and sweeping engagement with the history of the Americas from "the heights of Macchu Picchu" (excerpted here) and pre-Columbian civilizations and the Spanish conquest—including poems devoted to Pedro de Valdivia and the Mapuche leader Lautaro—to nineteenth- and twentieth-century history, including "José Martí," a poem about the Cuban revolutionary, and González Vidala's repression of workers and the Communist Party, in "The Traitor." Later sections of the epic concern the role of U.S. imperialism in the Americas, as in poems on the United Fruit Company in Guatemala and the Anaconda Copper Company in Chile. Neruda also wrote love poems and poems that evoked the experiences of southern Chile, where he was raised, the central coast near Isla Negra, where he lived during the latter years of his life, and the northern nitrate pampa, whose people he represented as a senator for the Communist Party. His poetry celebrated every aspect of daily life from southern Chile's forests, the fields and meadows of southern farms, the rocky Pacific coast, the arid northern deserts, and the many "common things," to which he wrote a book of odes.*

Memoirs

Life was changing in Chile.

The Chilean people's movement was starting up, clamoring, looking for stronger support among students and writers. On the one hand, the great leader of the petite bourgeoisie, Arturo Alessandri Palma, a dynamic and demagogic man, became President of the Republic, but not before he had rocked the country with his fiery and threatening speeches. In spite of his extraordinary personality, once in power he quickly turned into the classic ruler of our Americas; the dominant sector of the oligarchy, whom he had fought, opened its maw and swallowed him and his revolutionary speeches. The country continued to be torn apart by bitter strife.

At the same time, a working-class leader, Luis Emilio Recabarren, was extraordinarily active organizing the proletariat, setting up union centers, establishing nine or ten workers' newspapers throughout the country. An avalanche of unemployment sent the country's institutions staggering. I contributed weekly articles to *Claridad.* We students supported the rights of the people and were beaten up by the police in the streets of Santiago. Thousands of jobless nitrate and copper workers flocked to the capital. The demonstrations and the subsequent repression left a tragic stain on the life of the country.

From that time on, with interruptions now and then, politics became part of my poetry and my life. In my poems I could not shut the door to the street, just as I could not shut the door to love, life, joy, or sadness in my young poet's heart. . . .

MY COUNTRY IN DARKNESS

. . . I believe a man should live in his own country and I think the deracination of human beings leads to frustration, in one way or another obstructing the light of the soul. I can live only in my own country. I cannot live without having my feet and my hands on it and my ear against it, without feeling the movement of its waters and its shadows, without feeling my roots reach down into its soil for material nourishment.

But, before getting back to Chile, I made another discovery that was to add a new layer of growth to my poetry.

I stopped in Peru and made a trip to the ruins of Macchu Picchu. There was no highway then and we rode up on horseback. At the top I saw the ancient stone structures hedged in by the tall peaks of the verdant Andes. Torrents hurdled down from the citadel eaten away and weathered by the passage of the centuries. White fog drifted up in masses from the Wilkamayu River. I felt infinitely small in the center of that navel of rocks, the navel of a deserted world, proud, towering high, to which I somehow belonged. I felt that my own hands had labored there at some remote point in time, digging furrows, polishing the rocks.

I felt Chilean, Peruvian, American. On those difficult heights, among those glorious, scattered ruins, I had found the principles of faith I needed to continue my poetry. My poem *Alturas de Macchu Picchu* was born there.

The Nitrate Pampa   At the end of 1943 I arrived in Santiago once more. I settled down in a house I bought on the installment plan. I piled all my books into this house surrounded by huge trees, and took up the hard life again.

Once more I sought my country's beauty, the loveliness of its women, nature's overpowering splendor, the work of my fellows, the intelligence of my countrymen. The country had not changed. Fields and sleeping villages, heartbreaking poverty in the mining regions, elegant people crowding into the country clubs. I had to make a decision.

My decision brought me harassments as well as moments of glory.

What poet could have regretted that? . . .

These people without schooling or shoes elected me senator on March 4, 1945. I shall always cherish with pride the fact that thousands of people from Chile's most inhospitable region, the great mining region of copper and nitrate, gave me their vote.

Walking over the pampa was laborious and rough. It hasn't rained for half a century there, and the desert has done its work on the faces of the miners. They are men with scorched features; their solitude and the neglect they are consigned to has been fixed in the dark intensity of their eyes. Going from the desert up to the mountains, entering any needy home, getting to know the inhuman labor these people do, and feeling that the hopes of isolated and sunken men have been entrusted to you, is not a light responsibility. But my poetry opened the way for communication, making it possible for me to walk and move among them and be accepted as a lifelong brother by my countrymen, who led such a hard life. . . .

There are no elephants or camels in Chile. But I can see how puzzling a country can be that starts at the frozen South Pole and stretches upward to salt mines and deserts where it hasn't rained for eons. As senator-elect of the inhabitants of that wilderness, as representative of innumerable nitrate and copper workers who had never worn a shirt collar or a tie, I had to travel those deserts for many years.

Coming into those lowlands, facing those stretches of sand, is like visiting the moon. This region that looks like an empty planet holds my country's wealth, but the white fertilizer and the red mineral have to be extracted from the arid earth and the mountains of rock. There are few places in the world where life is so harsh and offers so little to live for. It takes untold sacrifices to transport water, to nurse a plant that yields the humblest flower, to raise a dog, a rabbit, a pig.

I come from the other end of the republic. I was born in a green country with huge, thickly wooded forests. I had a childhood filled with rain and snow. The mere act of facing that lunar desert was a turning point in my life. Representing those men in parliament—their isolation, their titanic land— was also a difficult task. The naked earth, without a single plant, without a drop of water, is an immense, elusive enigma. In the forests, alongside rivers, everything speaks to man. The desert, on the other hand, is uncommunicative. I couldn't understand its language: that is, its silence. . . . One afternoon I spoke to the laborers in a machine shop in the offices of the María Elena potassium-nitrate mine. The floor of the huge workshop was, as always, slushy with water, oil, and acids. The union leaders and I walked on a plank that kept us off that mire. "These planks," I was told, "cost us fifteen strikes in a row, eight years of petitioning, and seven dead." . . . My poetry and my life have advanced like an American river, a torrent of Chilean water born in the hidden heart or the southern mountains, endlessly steering the flow of its current toward the sea. My poetry rejected nothing it could carry along in its course; it accepted passion, unraveled mystery, and worked its way into the hearts of the people. . . .

POETRY IS AN OCCUPATION

The Power of Poetry   It has been the privilege of our time—with its wars, revolutions, and tremendous social upheavals—to cultivate more ground for poetry than anyone had ever imagined. The common man has had to confront it, attacking or attacked, in solitude or with an enormous mass of people at public rallies.

When I wrote my first lonely books, it never entered my mind that, with the passing years, I would find myself in squares, streets, factories, lecture halls, theaters, and gardens, reading my poems. I have gone into practically every corner of Chile, scattering my poetry like seed among the people of my country.

I am going to recount what happened to me in Vega Central, the largest and most popular market in Santiago, Chile. An endless line of pushcarts, horse wagons, oxcarts, and trucks come in at dawn, bringing vegetables, fruits, edibles from all the truck farms surrounding the voracious capital. The market men—a huge union whose members are badly paid and often go barefoot—swarm through the coffee shops, flophouses, and cheap eating places of the neighborhoods near the Vega.

One day someone came to fetch me in a car, which I climbed into without knowing exactly where or why I was going. I had a copy of my book *España en el corazón* (Spain in my heart) in my pocket. In the car they explained to me that I was going to give a lecture at the union hall of the Vega market loaders.

When I entered the ramshackle hall, a chill like that in José Asunción Silva's poem "Nocturno" ran through me, not only because winter was so far along but because the atmosphere in the place gave me quite a shock. About fifty men sat waiting for me on crates or improvised wooden benches. Some had a sack tied around their waist like an apron, others covered their bodies with old patched undershirts, and still others braved Chile's cold July bare from the waist up. I sat down behind a small table that separated me from the unusual audience. They all looked at me with the fixed, coal-black eyes of the people of my country. . . . How should I handle this audience? What could I speak to them about? What things in my life would hold their interest? I could not make up my mind, but disguising my desire to run out of there, I took the book I was carrying with me and said to them: "I was in Spain a short time back. A lot of fighting and a lot of shooting were going on there. Listen to what I've written about it."

I should explain that my book *España en el corazón* . . . has never seemed to me an easy book to understand. It tries to be clear, but it is steeped in the torrent of overwhelming and painful events.

Well, I thought I would just read a handful of poems, add a few words, and say goodbye. But it didn't work out that way. Reading poem after poem, hearing the deep well of silence into which my words were falling, watching those eyes and dark eyebrows following my verses so intently, I realized that my book was hitting its mark. I went on reading and reading, affected by the sound of my own poetry, shaken by the magnetic power that linked my poems and those forsaken souls.

The reading lasted more than an hour. As I was about to leave, one of the men rose to his feet. He was one of those who had a sack knotted around his waist. "I want to thank you for all of us," he spoke out. "I want to tell you, too, that nothing has ever moved us so much."

When he finished talking, he couldn't hold back a sob. Several others were also weeping. I walked out into the street between moist eyes and rough handclasps.

Can a poet still be the same after going through these trials of fire and ice?

Translated by Hardie St. Martin

The Heights of Macchu Picchu, VI

And so I scaled the ladder of the earth
amid the atrocious maze of lost jungles
up to you, Macchu Picchu
High citadel of terraced stones,
at long last the dwelling of him whom the earth
did not conceal in its slumbering vestments.
In you, as in two parallel lines,
the cradle of lightning and man
was rocked in a wind of thorns.

Mother of stone, sea spray of the condors.

Towering reef of human dawn.

Spade lost in the primal sand.

This was the dwelling, this is the site:
here the full kernels of corn rose
and fell again like red hailstones.

Here the golden fiber emerged from the vicuña
to clothe love, tombs, mothers,
the king, prayers, warriors.

Here man's feet rested at night
beside the eagle's feet, in the high gory
retreats, and at dawn
they trod the rarefied mist with feet of thunder
and touched lands and stones

until they recognized them in the night or in
    death.

I behold vestments and hands,
the vestige of water in the sonorous void,
the wall tempered by the touch of a face
that beheld with my eyes the earthen lamps,
that oiled with my hands the vanished
wood: because everything—clothing, skin, vessels,
words, wine, bread—
is gone, fallen to earth.

And the air flowed with orange-blossom
fingers over all the sleeping:
a thousand years of air, months, weeks of air,
of blue wind, of iron cordillera,
like gentle hurricanes of footsteps
polishing the solitary precinct of stone.

Translated by Jack Schmitt

Miners' Strikes and the Demise of the Popular Front: U.S. State Department Cables

Demanding salary increases and benefits, workers in Chile's coal and copper mines, where the Chilean Communist Party had a significant presence, threatened to paralyze the economy by engaging in massive strikes in 1946–1947. In response, the government of Gabriel González Videla imposed government arbitration on the copper company and the unions and later, as work stoppages continued, declared states of siege and sent in the military to take control of the mines and put an end to the strikes. The memos here, authored by Secretary of State Dean Acheson, Assistant Secretary of State Spruille Braden (son of the founder of Chile's El Teniente copper mine, later sold to Kennecott), and Claude Bowers, the U.S. ambassador to Chile, concerning strikes in El Teniente and the growing influence of the Communist Party among miners and workers, reflect the efforts of the United States to pressure the Chilean government to crack down on the Communist Party and the increasingly militant labor movement in Chile's coal and North American–owned copper mines. Copper mining company and U.S. government officials made it clear to the Chilean government that future investments, loans, and development assistance were contingent on putting an end to labor strife in the copper mines and removing the Communist Party from the governing coalition. After the military took control of the El Teniente mine, a number of miners identified as Communists were fired and detained; some were sent to the Pisagua concentration camp in the northern desert. Months later González Videla declared the Law for the Permanent Defense of Democracy banning the Communist Party.

The Acting Secretary of State [Dean Acheson] to Ambassador in Chile (Bowers)
Washington, November 9, 1946

[The State] Dept. has already informally pointed out to Chilean Chargé [in Chilean embassy in Washington] the embarrassing even untenable position in which this Govt. would be placed in considering Chile's request for further Eximbank loans and credits on Naval vessels at very time when proposed arbitrary settlement strike (described by Fon Min [Chilean foreign minister] himself as Communist plot, which would have grave consequences Chilean economy unless challenged) was jeopardizing highly important US investment copper industry. It was made clear to Chargé Rodríguez that with all good will in world for Chile this Govt. might be bitterly criticized by press and Congress if it were alleged that at time when interest of thousands of Kennecott stock holders were endangered American Govt. had made additional loans to Chile. . . .

MEMORANDUM OF CONVERSATION
by the Chief of the Division
of North and West Coast Affairs (Wells)
and Mr. Alexander Schnee of that Division

Participants:

Mr. E. T. Stannard, President, Kennecott Copper Corporation

Mr. Laylin, Washington lawyer for Kennecott

Mr. Spruille Braden, Assistant Secretary of State. . . .

Washington, November 12, 1946

President of Kennecott feels that cumulative concessions to Chilean Government's endeavoring to extricate itself from difficult political positions at the expense of the copper companies have placed Braden Copper Company in a tenuous economic position necessitating a clear-cut answer as to whether that Company will continue to be subject to such pressures; and inquires what further assistance can be expected from the Department, particularly in the event of intervention or expropriation by Chilean Government. . . .

The purpose of Stannard's visit was to review the strike situation up to the moment; and to inquire what further advice and assistance the Department could offer, particularly in the event of Chilean Government intervention or expropriation. . . . The whole history of the Company's relations with the Government in Chile has been one of continuous appeasement, one concession after another on taxes and special exchange rates, and of government pressure for political convenience on one issue after another. . . .

The present situation . . . is that President González Videla has given the Company until 12 noon, today, to accept arbitration on all points. . . .

Stannard is of the firm opinion that the Company should accept arbitration only on the wage demands, leaving the other demands, which the Company deems unconstitutional, for subsequent discussion, if necessary.

He feels the Company is faced with a crisis, and he would like to know (1) what further advice the State Department can offer, and (2) what the Department proposes to do if the Chilean Government intervenes or expropriates. . . . Mr. Stannard inquired whether, if the Company agreed to arbitrate on all points and if the arbitration award substantially met the demands of the Communist union, the Department would use its influence to prevent the Chilean Government from drawing on credits established by the Eximbank.

MEMORANDUM OF CONVERSATION,
by the Chief of the
Division of North and West Coast Affairs (Wells)

SECRET

Participants:
Señor Mario Rodríguez, Chilean Chargé d'Affaires
Mr. Spruille Braden, Assistant Secretary Of State

[Washington,] November 12, 1946

Mr. Braden reiterates this Government's grave concern over Chilean strike situation.

Mr. Braden took advantage of the Chargé's call . . . to reiterate the Department's very serious concern with the El Teniente (Braden Copper Company) strike situation. . . .

Mr. Braden impressed upon Señor Rodríguez the possible adverse effects on public opinion and Congress of precipitate action and subsequent settlement on terms that might prove tantamount to government intervention. In this connection, he mentioned that Kennecott's 90,000 stock holders not without influence. Should the situation develop to the point of irrevocably damaging this U.S. private investment in Chile, the Department, the Eximbank, and the Government as a whole would be in a most embarrassing position for having simultaneously extended large loans to Chile.

We had taken great pains to demonstrate good will toward President González Videla, this in spite of a feeling of uneasiness in certain quarters at the inclusion of Communists in the Chilean cabinet. Admittedly, the strike is Communist-directed, and is aimed at an American enterprise. . . . President González himself had expressed regret to the Company's manager that the Company was the victim of a squeeze between the Communists and Socialists.

The Ambassador in Chile (Bowers)
to Assistant Secretary of State (Braden)

CONFIDENTIAL

Santiago, November 18, 1946

In my conversation with the President [González Videla] I was left in no doubt as to his determination to do everything within the range of his possibilities to get some sort of agreement. He left me in no doubt whatever of his earnest desire to continue the very excellent relations between Chile and the United States. . . . He went over the conditions . . . that brought about the inclusion of Communists in the Ministry and, in this manner, more or less forced the mine issue upon him. He made it clear that he has no doubt that these Communists will not linger long in the Government.

States of Exception

Elena Caffarena

With the repression of miners' strikes in 1946 and 1947 and the outlawing of the Communist Party in 1948 in the infamous Law for the Permanent Protection of Democracy, President Gabriel González Videla became another in a long line of Chilean presidents to employ states of emergency and states of siege to crack down on strikes during moments of popular upheaval. The 1948 law sent the poet Pablo Neruda fleeing into exile across the Andes and numerous other militants of the Communist Party into concentration camps, including many who landed in a detention center in the northern desert town of Pisagua under the charge of a young officer named Augusto Pinochet. In her 1957 law thesis on the use of habeas corpus (a legal appeal for individual protection) and states of emergency, the prominent lawyer and feminist Elena Caffarena anticipated later legal defense of human rights in Chile by criticizing the executive's use of "states of exception," suspending basic political and civil rights, between 1930 and 1957 and arguing that these were unconstitutional acts of political repression that undermined democracy in Chile. In this document, Caffarena describes five states of siege imposed by the former military man President Carlos Ibáñez during the 1950s to quell an increasingly mobilized urban working-class population and enforce the unpopular Klein-Saks austerity measures designed to combat inflation. Caffarena insisted on the critical role of the courts in protecting a democratic society from executive and police powers, just one year before her own political rights were repressed under the anticommunist Law for the Permanent Defense of Democracy in 1958, which struck from Chile's electoral rolls the names of Caffarena and her husband, the Communist lawyer Jorge Jiles. The use of states of siege and political exclusion was the flip side of Chile's relatively stable multiparty democracy during the twentieth century, imposing important limitations on the exercise of individual liberties that moreover established legal precedents that would be invoked by Pinochet's military dictatorship after 1973.

Our courts have uniformly resolved that detentions and transfers ordered by the President of the Republic during periods of states of siege and extraordinary powers cannot be revised by them and have systematically rejected recourse to habeas corpus interposed in defense of the personal liberty of those affected.

In order for this doctrine to be exact, we would have to conclude that our Constitution and our laws contain iniquitous precepts, given that they surrender the liberty of the inhabitants of the country—although in periods of exception—to the arbitrary authority of the absolute sovereign. . . .

The problem becomes more serious if we consider that states of emergency are repeated each time with more frequency and, even worse, they are imposed to confront situations that are different from those foreseen by the Constitution.

Between the years 1900 and 1929, the first half of this century, only twice did the exceptional implementation of the state of siege come into play.

In contrast, in the years that follow, from 1930 to 1957, the country has suffered 16 laws or decree-laws involving extraordinary powers. They imposed upon us 44 months and 29 days of restricted liberties. The government of President Gabriel González Videla alone issued five laws of extraordinary powers that permitted him to govern for almost half of his term and, consecutively, two-and-a-half years with the suspension of constitutional guarantees of personal liberty.

In addition to these laws and decrees, laws of extraordinary powers, one must add at least a dozen decrees of states of siege imposed by various Presidents of the Republic during parliamentary recess.

The current President of the Republic, Mr. Carlos Ibáñez, has decreed states of siege on five occasions.

Has "internal disorder" really existed every time that a President of the Republic has decreed a state of siege? Has there been an urgent necessity for the defense of the State, for the conservation of the constitutional regime or for interior peace in the 16 times that, in the brief space of 27 years, the National Congress has granted the President of the Republic extraordinary powers?

Affirmatively answering these questions would mean accepting that our country has lived the last quarter of a century in constant internal anarchy, which nobody with a modicum of honesty could sustain. . . .

Why do our courts commit the grave error of sustaining that they do not have the power to revise the President's orders of detention during the state of siege, pretending not to understand their fundamental mission of being the bulwark of constitutional guarantees?

. . . It is fitting to point out one of the determinant reasons of this attitude of our judges: the conviction—which surely is sincere—that they are contributing to the maintenance of the social order.

But our magistrates forget that there can be no order where there is no justice, where arbitrariness reigns and is always found when an authority exercises his power without a counterweight and delegates that authority to subordinate functionaries.

Without intending to diminish the primordial responsibility of the President of the Republic and his ministers in the innumerable abuses that are committed during the periods of states of siege and extraordinary powers, it is important to emphasize that in these occasions the measures of restriction of personal liberty are generally resolved by police functionaries with little if any reliability; these functionaries act with irresponsibility and lack of honesty that nobody better than the judges have been able to verify over the course of their careers. It is just like the tranquility of many homes; liberty, health, and the life of citizens is surrendered to ineptitude, vengeance, denunciation, and the interplay of interests and the lowest passions.

We know of the dramatic case of the porter of Valaparaíso Oscar Rodriguez who was detained and transferred to Pisagua [concentration camp] because of a mistaken name during the state of siege declared in January of 1956. This humble citizen had to abandon his loved ones and suffer hard confinement for more than 20 days until the government removed the order; had recourse to legal appeal been put into effect, he would have obtained his freedom in 48 hours. . . .

The abuses and excesses of the Executive, the vacillations of the Judicial Power and the trampling of our rights that we now suffer were foreseen by the critics of the Organic Law of the Courts; the critics demanded the suppression of article 4 and the reenactment of the final clause of article 101 consigned in the original resolution. Jurists of the firm of Fabres, Letelier and Santa María pointed out the dangers. And what did the defenders of the resolution say? Simply that the fears were unfounded because nobody had ever thought of depriving the courts of their power of protecting individual liberty, a power that remained plainly contemplated in article 143 of the Constitution, which could not be eliminated or limited by any law.

This point will be studied with more detail in the body of this work. I have only wanted to put forward some ideas to point out the immense responsibility that corresponds to the courts upon leaving the citizens exposed to police arbitrariness, however laudable this purpose of defending the social order may be. When the citizens are convinced that they cannot expect justice, they look for the way of carrying it out for themselves, leading to the explosion of that "internal disorder" that no state of siege can detain.

Translated by Justin Delacour

The Birth of a Shantytown

Juan Lemuñir

The postwar decades were years of massive rural migration to Chile's cities by people too poor to pay slum rents and too many to be accommodated in inner-city con-ventillos (tenements). When the Chilean state failed to solve this growing housing deficit, the urban poor took the problem into their own hands and devised their own solution: squatting on vacant lands.

In this memoir, Juan Lemuñir describes the 1957 seizure of vacant suburban land in Santiago that led to the creation of the La Victoria shantytown. The memoir also traces the transformation of La Victoria into a combative shantytown and perma-nent población (settlement) in the 1960s, revealing as well the social organization and political links that were hallmarks of that era. La Victoria was the first of hun-dreds of such land seizures by homeless rural migrants and ill-housed urban workers that would reshape urban Chile during the next fifteen years. By 1972, one of every six inhabitants of the Santiago metropolitan region lived in such poblaciones, some of which were collections of tents, while others, like La Victoria, were composed of permanent houses built by the residents or the government. The history of La Victoria reflects a period of accelerated rural-urban migration that would remake both Chilean society and politics. By the 1960s, the urban poor residing in poblacio-nes would become targets for political organizing: the Christian Democratic Party attempted to build its electoral support by sending organizers into the mushroom-ing poblaciones throughout Santiago. The Left, however, had more success in both directing urban land occupations and organizing in poblaciones. La Victoria, for example, would become a bastion of the Chilean Communist Party and a major pil-lar of support for the socialist coalition headed by Salvador Allende during the 1970s.

It happened more than 30 years ago. Thousands of families . . . the majority from the banks of the Zanjón de la Aguada,[1] headed by the leaders Jorge Núñez and Navarrete among others, had organized themselves. They rep-resented the Frente de Pobladores [shantytown residents] which grouped families from several sectors.

The pobladores came demanding a solution to their problems. The marginalized presented many petitions and demands, but none of them produced results. It was during the second presidency of Carlos Ibáñez del Campo [1952–1958].

The drama of the marginalized was terrible and their living conditions were truly inhumane. The worst case was that of those who resided on the banks of the Zanjón, an arm of water that descended from the Colorado River filled with the city's waste. There their shacks were made of cardboard or in the more fortunate cases from lightweight building material. The rats, unfailing companions of misery and symbols of ruin, took charge of keeping the humble residents from their sleep.

But the pobladores were organized and had meetings constantly in order to put pressure on the authorities to search for solutions. One day in the third sector, a fire started and little by little consumed the weak dwellings. The affected families were transferred to the Municipal Stadium . . . while the other families remained in the same place because they had not been lucky enough to have their shacks burn down. There had already been two fires, one in the first sector where a disabled person perished. . . .

The second fire was in the fourth sector whose president was José Lobos; the last fire was in the third sector. This was the fire that moved the inhabitants of Zanjón to demand a solution. . . .

A commission was appointed composed of Jorge Moreno and Escudero. They held a meeting with the mayor, Julio Palestro. Later, a meeting in the Sala Chile took place; there an agreement was made to go talk with Councilwoman Iris Figueroa. That was how the Comisión Pro-Toma de Terrenos [Pro–Land Seizure Commission] was organized, composed of Mario Palestro, Julio Palestro and Iris Figueroa, who supported the land seizure. They sent two advisors: the well-known Communist Guatón Núñez and Navarrete, a member of the Socialist Party. . . .

Days passed and there was still no solution to the problem. The tension increased, and finally, motivated by the misfortune of the fire, a meeting was held that was definitive. From this point on, they had the kind of energy that springs from exhaustion; it was a moment in which mistreated human beings break into a cold sweat and begin to spit blood, exhausted by their impotence. The organization was already there, misery united them; the objective was one: land to live on. Thousands of eyes turned to the area south of the Zanjón, Las Chacras de la Feria, which was owned by the Corvi.[2]

In this way, the idea of seizing that which was denied them began to develop. They organized themselves into caravans of [horse-drawn] carts

Urban land occupation (*toma*) in Barrancas, Santiago, c. 1970. Originally captioned "Pobladores se toman terrenos en Barrancas." Photographer unknown. Used by permission of Empresa Zig-Zag. Courtesy of Colección Museo Histórico Nacional de Chile.

and started the trip toward the land that they had been promised. When they arrived at the place, the families lost themselves in the weeds, put up the tents, and at dawn on October 30, 1957, Chilean flags blossomed between the dust and the weeds.[3]

The first battle against misery had been won. Now it was necessary to resist, and with flags fluttering, jumping ditches, falling, and rising, but all with eyes shining with hope, tired of bureaucratic delays, of living abandoned in filth. Loud shouts were heard of "Viva Chile!"

The first thing was to investigate the police station. Jorge Moreno was in charge of this responsibility. He also cut the only telephone line that was installed in the Estadio Corvi [Corvi Stadium]. The transfer began at 1:30 A.M.; children, women, men, and the elderly. It didn't matter how they got there. All that mattered was to arrive! That was the thought of all the pobladores.

At six in the morning, a meeting was held where Jorge Núñez made it known that he would participate in a meeting that day, accompanied by Cardinal José María Caro, parliamentarians from FRAP,[4] the leaders of the land seizure, and Father Del Corro, the priest who had accompanied them. They would try to hold a meeting with the President of the Republic in order to avoid the eviction with which the police had threatened them. It was 9:00 A.M., and pobladores continued arriving, jumping ditches throughout the immense area abandoned by the Corvi.

The police cordoned off the entire area we had seized, trying to prevent people from entering or exiting the sector. For the first time in our country, thousands of flags could be seen fluttering in an area that would prophesy the future. The police force of that time felt a great respect for the flag, the national symbol, and for that reason they did not dare to wipe out all those families [gathered around their flags] who found themselves playing the lead part in their own history. Nobody thought that something unforgettable would happen for every one of them and for millions of other human beings that very night, that early morning, that day.

The first land occupation in Latin America, in the face of the threat of violent eviction, was a real feat. The intervention of Cardinal José María Caro was necessary and opportune.[5] It prevented the deaths of those valiant men and women who had tired of dreaming about having a home of their own and wanted to realize their dream. During those eventful days, they lived through more than a few moments of tension and fear. "To the line *compañeros* [comrades]" was the warning cry, and all of the pobladores armed themselves with wooden sticks and iron bars in order to defend those lands that by right belonged to them. And it seemed that even God was angry since the incessant rain at night and the burning sun of the day caused many to become sick. Around twelve babies died because of the epidemic that was unleashed as a consequence of the harshly alternating rain and sun.

The veiled threats of eviction continued. On October 31st, Cardinal José María Caro asked President Ibáñez personally not to use violence against the pobladores who had seized the La Feria land, because the press had been informed that Ibáñez had ordered the intendant of Santiago[6] to evict them forcibly. Later, the Subsecretary of the Interior, Fernándo Lagos, declared that for the time being there was no order of expulsion and that he would try to solve the problems of the land occupiers, respecting their human rights.

Yet, the pobladores did not stop. The leaders divided the lands and gave them out to the families. An *olla común*[7] was organized, and operated on the corner of the streets that today we know as Baldomero Lillo and 30 de Octubre, where there would later be the restaurant La Posada. The committee in charge was composed of Communist and Socialist leaders. . . .

"We want to make a better Chile," said the La Feria pobladores. Those were the newspaper headlines from that period. The pobladores, who from that moment began to call the area "Campamento[8] La Victoria," held a rally in order to celebrate their second triumph. Juan Acosta, the president of the Comando General [local government], gave a historical account of the movement from the beginning until the arrival at La Feria, stressing that unity and organization enabled the pobladores to realize their dreams. On the other hand, Núñez pointed out that this triumph did not belong to just one person but rather to the organization, and he added that these lands, a field of liberty where O'Higgins and San Martin had once camped, was now the camp of their own victory. In this way, La Victoria began between tears and shouts that were heard in what remained of the La Feria farms.

But time continued passing, and the La Victoria campamento could not stop itself. The inhabitants were already installed, and they had their first General Command, located on the streets that are today called Los Comandos and 30 de Octubre and where later the campamento's first school would be built through the pobladores' donations of 10 bricks each. Finally, a modest school was finished. It had curious characteristics not only because the pobladores had built it but also because it was round. Years later, at Raúl Fuica, 30 de Octubre, and Ramona Parra, the first police barracks was built. The Corporación de Vivienda donated the materials, and the pobladores built it.

Long lines grew in order to obtain water since there was only one faucet, which was at La Marina and La Feria. Obtaining this vital element was a true battle because the faucet could not supply the 3,000 families that needed water. At night, a cistern passed through distributing water. In this way the problem was partly solved. "The cask, comrades," they informed each other, and in that moment, the rattle of cans, shouts, laughter, and fights erupted in order to get a better place in line to obtain the liquid.

In November of 1957, they got the definitive answer: they would not be moved from the place that they were occupying. In that moment, the third triumph was won.

That is how the Población La Victoria was born and consolidated.

Translated by Melissa Mann

Notes

1. The Zanjón de la Aguada was a fetid canal on the southern border of Santiago, dividing it from the blue-collar bedroom suburb of San Miguel. It carried sewage and industrial wastes from the factories along its banks.
2. Corvi (Corporación de Vivienda) was the government agency in charge of public housing.
3. The pobladores believed that the police would not shoot a family gathered around a Chilean flag.
4. The Front for Popular Action, a political alliance composed mostly of Communists and Socialists. The Front's presidential candidate in 1958 would be Salvador Allende, then a Socialist senator.
5. Cardinal José María Caro was the archbishop of Santiago. His support for the pobladores would lead to one of the largest poblaciones being named after him. Ironically, in 1962, it would be a site of a notorious massacre of pobladores by police trying to evict them.
6. The top official appointed by the president to implement national government policies in the Santiago metropolitan region.
7. Literally "common pot"; a communal kitchen where poor people pooled their meager resources, solicited contributions of food, and cooked together a nutritious meal for the whole group. A long tradition among striking workers, the olla común was adopted by pobladores and would symbolize their organization and collective will to survive and win their demands.
8. A *campamento* (encampment) was the Chilean name for an informal community created by a land seizure, usually with temporary housing like tents. When the land seizure was recognized by the government and a more formal community was created, with permanent housing and urban services, it would become known as a población.

Klein-Saks: Chile's First Experiment
with Neoliberalism

Chile's turn to the right after 1948 continued with the election of Carlos Ibáñez in 1952 and González Videla's former finance minister Jorge Alessandri in 1958. Ibáñez implemented and Alessandri maintained a set of orthodox austerity measures designed by the 1955 North American Klein-Saks Mission. These policies put an end to the populist and redistributionist policies of the Popular Front era, slashing workers' real wages and benefits and cutting public spending. In addition, while the Popular Front governments had organized a government agency, the Development Corporation, to promote industrialization with significant state inputs and public-private ventures, the Ibáñez and Alessandri governments reduced the role of the Development Corporation and the state more generally in promoting development via industrialization and agricultural diversification. While urban workers suffered a reverse of the gains made during the 1940s, rural workers continued to labor under the same conditions that had characterized labor relations on large estates over the course of the century. In addition, large estates continued to monopolize arable land, and agricultural production stagnated during this period. By the early 1960s Chile's dependence on importing food from abroad would be a central cause of its chronic trade imbalance and would make the need for agrarian reform all the more pressing.

Klein-Saks political cartoon from *Topaze*, 15 November 1957. The caption reads: Don Tanprisco Carter: . . . and I recognize that the greatest weight of the economic measures fell on the workers. . . Verdejo: You're only waking up to this now? . . . Illustration by René Ríos Boettiger. Reprinted by permission of Sebastián Ríos O. Courtesy of Biblioteca Nacional de Chile.

VI

The Chilean Road to Socialism:
Reform and Revolution

If Che Guevara and Fidel Castro are the two most iconic figures in the pantheon of Cold War–era Latin American revolutionaries, Chile's Salvador Allende is not far behind them. When Allende led a coalition of leftist parties known as the Unidad Popular, or Popular Unity, to victory in 1970, he became the first democratically elected Marxist head of state in the western hemisphere. In Chile, Allende's election seemed to reflect the dramatic culmination of an exceptionally open, democratic political system. In a world riven by Cold War conflict, it was also an event of major international interest. Promising a "Chilean road to socialism," a revolution that worked within existing democratic institutions and respected the rule of law, the Popular Unity experiment was closely observed by critics and supporters alike. For an anxious United States, Allende's election posed a worrying new scenario: while Castro's guerrilla insurgency showed how the left could come to power through armed struggle, Allende showed how it might do so through a free, fair, and peaceful electoral process. For international observers sympathetic to its ideals, in contrast, Chile's democratic road to socialism became an inspiring model of a small, Third World country trying to produce development in the context of a socialist economy and democratic institutions—and in the shadow of a hostile superpower.

While it lasted just three years, Allende's revolutionary experiment wrought profound and sometimes chaotic changes, inspiring tremendous hopes as well as intense fears, and ending in a bloody military coup in 1973. The documents presented in this chapter seek to capture the heady political, cultural, and ideological climate that animated Chile in the 1960s and early 1970s, the period leading up to and culminating in Chile's revolutionary experiment under the Popular Unity government. The selections trace the revolution Allende sought to implement "from above," as well as the revolution "from below" of workers, peasants, and shantytown dwellers. These texts also project the voices of those who opposed the "Chilean road to socialism" and would eventually succeed in reversing its course.

Cold War Latin America was dominated by two divergent formulas for change: on the one hand Castro's Communist revolution and on the other the Alliance for Progress, a U.S. foreign policy initiative aimed at producing economic modernization and social reform from above as a means to avert future Cubas. This tension between reform and revolution was nowhere more evident than in Chile, where chronic problems of stagflation, economic dependence, and widespread poverty presented a deepening challenge to politics as usual. The story of Allende's truncated revolutionary project thus begins with the reformist period that preceded it.

The reformist option was embodied in the Christian Democratic government of Eduardo Frei (1964–1970), which sought solutions to Chile's perennial problems through land reform and industrial modernization. The Christian Democratic Party's roots went back to the 1930s, but it mushroomed rapidly after 1958 into Chile's largest and most "modern" party, the party of the expanding middle class. Drawing on the social Catholicism that animated Church leaders during the 1960s, as well as lay movements of students, workers, and women, the party positioned itself as a middle road between the heartless capitalism of the right and the godless communism of the left. In a speech made fifteen years before his election to the presidency, the party's standard-bearer, Eduardo Frei, articulated the Christian Democrats' proposed "Third Way."

Frei came to power in 1964 with a campaign pledging a "revolution in liberty," which highlighted his promise of meaningful social reform and economic modernization while presenting his government as a democratic alternative to Marxist totalitarianism. His development strategy was based on the purchase of a controlling share in the U.S.-owned copper mines, the promotion of consumer goods industries, and the transformation through agrarian reform of impoverished landless peasants into middle-class family farmers to buy those goods. In Chile as elsewhere in Latin America in the 1960s, the unequal distribution of land had become a major political issue. Frei proposed to expropriate large landed estates and promote the organization of rural workers. A government pamphlet reproduced here justifies agrarian reform in economic, social, and political terms, suggesting how land redistribution would lead to more efficient agricultural production, ameliorate social inequality, and give rights to rural workers. Agrarian reform was also a pointed political strategy. The Christian Democrats hoped that the beneficiaries of the reform would become party loyalists who would bar the way to either an Allende electoral victory or a Cuban-style rural guerrilla revolution.

Ultimately, Frei's revolution in liberty fell short on its promises. Purchase of half shares in the U.S.-owned copper mines was judged insufficient, and the industrial investment from abroad that Frei anticipated never materialized. The agrarian reform began late and reached too few. Chile remained mired in stagflation, high unemployment, and inequality. Meanwhile, growing political polarization and opposition from right and left, as well as the increasingly militant labor movement, weakened Frei's government, as did fractures within the Christian Democratic Party itself. A leftist faction influenced by liberation theology and disillusioned with the slow pace and limited scope of reform broke from the party and joined Allende's coalition. An essay here on "communitarian socialism" suggests how this Christian Left formulated a social critique that drew on both Catholic and Marxist ideas.

This divided and discredited Center, and the broader failure of the "revolution in liberty," opened the way for even more radical solutions to Chile's problems. The 1970 presidential election presented a three-way race between the Right, Center, and Left. The Left's candidate was Salvador Allende Gossens, a medical doctor and early standard-bearer of the Chilean Socialist Party who had served as minister of health and in both houses of Congress, including as president of the Senate. He was also a perennial presidential candidate, having run in the three preceding elections over the course of two decades. Representing a coalition of leftist parties under the Popular Unity banner, Allende promised followers a revolutionary program cast as a democratic road to socialism. As the electorate moved leftward, and the Right and Center failed to agree on a candidate who would unite the anti-Allende vote, the man who joked that his epitaph would read "here lies the next president of Chile" had a real shot at victory.

In response, the right-wing candidate and former president Jorge Alessandri led a well-financed campaign in the press and over the airwaves. Pursuing a strategy that had worked in 1964, his campaign sought to stoke the population's fears by presenting Allende's election as the victory of Stalinism in Chile, with images of Soviet tanks in the streets and children being ripped from their mothers' arms. Allende's Popular Unity coalition, meanwhile, countered this propaganda with a grassroots publicity campaign. "Brigades" of young political militants, many organized in the Communist Party's Ramona Parra Brigade, painted murals in the streets of Chile's towns and cities in support of Allende's candidacy. Meanwhile, the Center was represented by Radomiro Tomic, a founder and former president of the

Christian Democratic Party who led its left wing and who, like Allende, advocated deepening agrarian reform and the nationalization of copper. Although Allende's campaign had been written off as futile, even by members of his own coalition, the grassroots mobilization proved them wrong. In 1970 he triumphed by a small plurality to become Chile's first socialist president.

For the United States, Chile was an important country economically and strategically, one of South America's regional powers. In the context of the Cold War, politics in Chile were also of keen interest. As Henry Kissinger, the U.S. national security advisor, emphatically asserted to President Richard Nixon, "the election of Allende as President of Chile poses for us one of the most serious challenges [the U.S.] ever faced in this hemisphere." During the 1960s, the United States had banked on the Christian Democrats as the best hope for keeping the Left out of power, beginning with the 1964 Frei election campaign, which it masterminded and financed on a per capita scale that exceeded any U.S. election campaign. The United States then showered funds on Christian Democratic development programs, making Chile into a proving ground for the Alliance for Progress, which President John Kennedy launched in 1961.

In the 1970 election, the United States once again made secret contributions to and coordinated with Allende's opponents and, when he won at the polls, pursued other tactics to keep him out of power. Allende defeated Alessandri with only 36 percent of the popular vote but with a larger percentage and plurality of the votes than had elected Alessandri over Allende in 1958, triggering a constitutionally required congressional vote between the top two vote-getters—a routine procedure that always confirmed electoral victory for the first-place finisher. In 1958, Alessandri's 28 percent plurality had been enough to assure him the presidency, a victory that Allende had refused to contest. But in 1970 Alessandri led plots for a "congressional coup" in which he would be elected in the Congress with Christian Democratic votes and then resign and throw his support to Frei in a campaign for a new presidential term. Alessandri's plans were actively promoted by the United States, constituting "Track 1" of a secret strategy to prevent Allende from assuming the presidency. When President Frei refused to support the plot, the U.S. government turned to "Track 2," a plan to facilitate a dirty tricks military coup in Chile. Attempting to prevent Allende's inauguration, far-right Chilean operatives with links to the CIA planned to kidnap the commander-in-chief of the army, General René Schneider, who opposed military intervention in politics and pin the kidnapping on the Left. They botched the kidnapping and assassinated their target. This turn of events so shocked Chileans, as yet unaccustomed to such political violence, that it guaranteed the very congressional confirmation of Allende's election that it was intended to prevent. In two secret memoranda to President Nixon written just after Allende's inauguration, Kissinger laid out the argument for ending the Allende presidency, which he saw as an "insidious" model that would affect not only the U.S. position in Latin America but "even . . . our own conception of what our role in the world is." Recognizing the democratic legality of Allende's election, and in light of the fact that the Nixon administration was on record as supporting democratic self-determination, Kissinger argued for a "correct but cool" policy stance that would mask continued covert intervention to destabilize Allende's government and create the conditions for his ouster.

Allende did not have access to Kissinger's memos, but he was well aware of the U.S. hostility and the fragile situation he had inherited. During his first months in office, he was cautious in his actions, moderate in his discourse, and careful in his policies. Keynesian policies revived a recessed Chilean economy while large real wage gains enabled poor Chileans to purchase goods they had previously only dreamed about, creating "fiestas of consumption" that both helped the economy and increased political support for the Popular Unity coalition. Allende seemed to be fulfilling his campaign promise of a "revolution with red wine and *empanadas* [meat pies]"— a distinctly Chilean revolution without sacrifice, in which only the rich would lose and even they would retain much of their wealth, if not their banks, industries, and landed estates. As a result, in the April 1971 national municipal elections, widely viewed as a referendum on Allende's government, the Left received a majority of the vote for the first time in Chilean history. The Popular Unity hailed this election victory as a mandate to advance along the democratic road to socialism, embarking on the structural reforms that Allende had been reluctant to pursue during his first months as president. These more aggressive policies represented major revolutionary advances toward controlling "the commanding heights" of the economy but came at the cost of growing social tensions and increasing—and increasingly violent—political opposition.

In a speech in 1971, reproduced here, Allende describes this Chilean "revolutionary process" by summarizing the achievements and advances of his first year as president, including structural transformations that were far greater than those of any previous Chilean president in a corresponding time frame. Many of these advances—the nationalization of the foreign-owned copper mines by the unanimous vote of the Congress, for example, or the nationalization of banks by market purchase—were hallmarks of

Allende's carefully controlled "revolution from above," which employed old laws and institutions for new revolutionary purposes.

From the start of his presidency, Allende had to contend not only with the hostility of foreign and domestic opposition but also with the expectations of his social base. He owed his triumph at the polls in 1970 to profound changes in Chilean society. The preceding decades had witnessed a massive postwar migration of peasants and rural workers to Santiago and other cities, transforming Chile into an increasingly urban society. Migration exacerbated Chile's chronic urban housing deficit but also produced an urban lower class freed from the control of conservative rural landlords and available for political mobilization, which first Frei and then Allende sought to exploit. The 1960s were an era of burgeoning labor organization, when rural workers began to form unions and the number and percentage of unionized workers in Chile reached historic highs. It was also a period of grassroots organization and direct democracy, when peasants organized self-governing cooperatives on estates expropriated by the Frei agrarian reform and homeless *pobladores* (shantytown dwellers) seized vacant suburban lands and elected leaders to govern their new communities.

If the 1960s witnessed the growing radicalization of existing social movements and the mobilization of new ones, the triumph of the Popular Unity reinforced this trend. Chile under Allende was swept by a "revolution from below," in which pobladores, peasants, indigenous peoples, and urban workers took the revolution into their own hands, seizing farms, factories, and vacant lands, articulating their own vision of socialism by creating the revolution through direct local action, insisting that Allende explicitly support their vision by legalizing its advance. The revolution from below accelerated the revolutionary process, forcing the rapid advance of structural changes such as land reform and the nationalization of large industries, followed by peasant and worker control of production. Two texts provided here capture these dynamics. We hear the testimony of Mapuche peasants and the landowners involved in the first seizure of an estate by peasants seeking to expropriate it under the terms of the agrarian reform. We also hear an account of the workers who led the seizure of Yarur, Chile's largest textile mill, and succeeded in persuading Allende to nationalize their factory, against his better judgment. The tensions between the phased and controlled revolution from above and the more spontaneous and locally informed revolution from below were never resolved, constituting a fatal flaw in the Chilean revolutionary process.

In Chile as elsewhere in the world in the 1960s, politics were lived not only through elections but also through culture. The course of Chilean politics was shaped in part by this global cultural revolution, led by youth from Paris to Peking who challenged the cultural assumptions of their parents' generation. In Latin America, the young leaders of the Cuban revolution and the iconic Che Guevara lent this generational change a revolutionary political character, but for many Chileans, the Beatles were also revolutionaries. Chilean artists drew on diverse aspects of this international youth culture and added something of their own, producing a musical movement known as "New Song," which combined folk and indigenous music with political themes and spread throughout Latin America. Perhaps the most famous example of this movement's influence was Quilapayun's song "The People United Will Never Be Defeated," which emerged as the unofficial song of Allende's 1970 campaign and has remained an anthem of the Chilean and international Left ever since. The creation of this politicized popular culture is explored here through interviews with members of one of the signature music groups of the era, Inti-Illimani; and lyrics from Violeta Parra, the movement's founding mother; and Victor Jara, its most famous singer-songwriter.

If for some the Chilean road to socialism promised hope for a better Chile, for others it was a menace to the Chile they knew. The threat of the Left becoming the hegemonic force in Chilean politics pushed the Center into active opposition and into a deepening political alliance with the Right. In December 1971, in response to a visit by Fidel Castro to Chile, the first major opposition demonstration appeared on the streets of Santiago. The march was controversial, not only because traditionally the streets belonged to the Left but also because it was led by elite women, accompanied by armed men from the neo-fascist group Fatherland and Liberty as their bodyguards. The "March of the Empty Pots," as it came to be known, was led by middle- and upper-class housewives who banged on empty pots to protest government policies that they held responsible for food shortages that would only become serious during the following year. In an interview below, Carmen Saenz, one of the leaders of Feminine Power, the opposition movement that grew from the march, discusses how women mobilized against a government that was "destroying their homes, education, and the country's morality."

Opposition spread and deepened with growing economic dislocations in 1972 and 1973, characterized by accelerating inflation and multiplying consumer shortages. Ironically, these trends were in large part the result of a revolutionary "success." The combination of reforms from above and pressures from below raised average real wages by 30 percent during 1971, a dramatic jump in family incomes that led first to consumer spending sprees and a use of idle industrial capacity but then to growing shortages of food and other goods as demand outstripped supply. This situation was made worse by the understandable reluctance of Chilean entrepreneurs to invest in new machinery during a transition to socialism, and by the United States' "invisible blockade," which blocked international aid and reduced vital bank credit lines by 90 percent. The United States' aggressive economic interference made it hard for Chilean enterprises that depended on U.S. machinery to purchase spare parts and other imported inputs, let alone acquire new machinery to expand production.

Economic dislocations exacerbated social tensions, and both fed a growing political polarization, in which the opposition moved increasingly from the corridors of the Congress into the streets, where armed youth from both sides clashed in fights of growing violence. This increasingly counterrevolutionary opposition culminated in the October Strike, which combined a nationwide lockout by private sector businesses, most importantly the truck owners' association, with a work stoppage by professionals. The strike's goal was to halt the advances toward socialism by paralyzing the Chilean economy and creating the conditions for either legal impeachment or a military coup. In a manifesto from the October Strike, a group of *gremios* (professional and trade associations) articulated their opposition to Allende's policies. With the aid of the revolution from below, led by the *cordones industriales* (industrial belts), which represented a new form of territorial organizations of radicalized workers, the Allende government was able to stalemate the October Strike. Like the cordones industriales, the Movement of the Revolutionary Left, a leftist party outside Popular Unity that advocated militant revolutionary struggle, urged a deepening of the socialist revolutionary process as a response to the October Strike and the increasingly violent right-wing opposition to Popular Unity.

Instead, to end the strike, Allende negotiated an electoral truce in which the armed forces chiefs would serve as government ministers who would keep the peace until the midterm congressional elections in March 1973. The opposition won those elections but fell far short of its goal of a two-thirds majority that would have enabled them to impeach Allende; in fact, Popular Unity *gained* congressional seats, making it impossible to legally oust Allende before his scheduled term ended in 1976. In the face of this defeat, the opposition began to work for a military coup, pressing for the removal of the army's constitutionalist commander, General Carlos Prats, who, like his murdered predecessor General Schneider, espoused military nonintervention in politics. In Congress, Allende's opponents challenged his use of long-standing executive decree powers to nationalize enterprises, detonating a constitutional crisis that culminated in an August 1973 non-binding and partisan vote by the Chamber of Deputies (the lower house of Congress) that Allende's government was guilty of illegal acts. While the vote in one of Chile's two legislative branches had neither legal nor constitutional significance, it provided a fig leaf of legitimacy for a military coup.

The final weeks of the Allende presidency were characterized by acute tensions that played out in all areas of Chilean life, from worker-run factories and land occupations on rural estates to the streets, where demonstrators on both sides clashed with police and groups of counter-demonstrators. Meanwhile, controversies and conspiracies abounded within the military, as officers became increasingly politicized and joined coup plots in ever greater numbers. In addition to four unsuccessful coup attempts thwarted in 1973, the growth of military opposition to Allende was evident in a letter that several outraged military officers wrote in response to a revisionist history of Chile issued by a publishing house recently nationalized by the Allende government, a history they regarded as a slanderous, treasonous affront to national honor. Meanwhile, the vicissitudes of political conflict resonated far beyond Chile, as the U.S. government kept close tabs on the course of events. The motives and extent of U.S. involvement in plots to end Allende's presidency are sketched in painful detail in the Church Report, a 1976 study by the U.S. Senate committee charged with investigating U.S. involvement in Chile, which concluded that U.S. officials "may not always have succeeded in walking the thin line between monitoring indigenous coup plotting and actually stimulating it."

This collection of documents ends with two that, in hindsight, were prophetic. In a letter that compared Chileans to characters in a Greek tragedy, Radomiro Tomic, the Christian Democratic leader who had run against Allende in 1970, thanked the former army commander Carlos Prats for his stubborn commitment to democratic principles that had to that point stood as a bulwark against the "turbulent wave of bitter passion and violence" that "threatens to submerge the country, perhaps for many years to come." Two days earlier, as a result of his stalwart refusal to countenance military intervention, Prats had been pressured into resigning his post. The Greek tragedy Tomic prophesied culminated on September 11, 1973, when the Chilean armed forces initiated a concerted attack on the presidential palace, led by the supposedly apolitical general whom Prats had recommended as his replacement: Augusto Pinochet. Inside the besieged palace, Salvador Allende broadcast a farewell radio address in which he reminded his supporters, "History is ours and is made by the people." Within hours, he was dead, and a new chapter of Chilean history had begun.

Between Capitalism and Communism:
Social Christianity as a Third Way

Eduardo Frei

Although Eduardo Frei was not an original thinker, he was a good communicator and Chile's first "modern" politician, telegenic and Kennedyesque. Frei began his political career as a university student active in Catholic causes, a founding member in the 1930s of the Chilean Falange Nacional movement, an offshoot of the Conservative Party that advocated Catholic participation in social reform and electoral politics. In 1958, Frei became the first presidential candidate presented by the newly formed Christian Democratic Party. After losing that election he won a majority of the vote in 1964. His bid for the presidency benefited from support from both the United States and the Right, which feared a victory by his Socialist opponent, Salvador Allende, who had come very close to winning the presidency in 1958. In power, Frei followed the French model of dirigisme, in which the state oriented but did not replace the private sector in the economy, which became increasingly foreign-owned. This excerpt from a 1949 speech by the future president articulates the political philosophy that would orient the campaigns and policies of the Christian Democratic Party during the Cold War. Frei emphasizes his party's efforts to create a Social Christianity that would be a "Third Way" between capitalism and communism. The Christian Democratic promise to bring about a "revolution in liberty" was marked by both strident anticommunism and significant challenges to economic inequality.

Social Christianity must project itself beyond an obsolete capitalism. The task of this movement is to implement real solutions, in the here and now.
. . .

All peoples seek their future according to ideas that reflect their reality and search for justice through forms of social organization that grant them real liberty, as well as the dignity of participating in public life rather than being mere subjects of economic production, from which they receive nothing but humble crumbs.

This is why, just as in many other countries, we believe we have found in the ideas of Social Christianity the instruments that will allow us to realize our potential as a people. . . . One would have to be deaf to the noise of the world to be able to ignore the vast transformations that are taking place in the depths of human society. Communism, which has taken over huge areas, even whole continents, threatens Europe and we are called on to defend Western and Christian civilization.

And yet the big problem is how, why, and for whom we should provide this defense? . . .

And this is what Social Christianity is all about: the belief that Communism will never be stopped unless social and economic reform takes place, which in itself implies a revolutionary and creative change.

A Christian civilization like the Christian West is held together by Faith, Hope, and Charity, which does not consist in alms, but rather in loving our brothers and God. And yet they [the Right] want to maintain the West through capitalism, which is an egotistical pursuit; through rationalist skepticism, which negates faith; and through conserving their privileges, which is the way to kill all hope for the multitudes. . . .

Yet, in a world where a decisive fight between capitalism and communism has been unleashed, the Social Christian cannot just talk about principles in the abstract sense. This leads nowhere. Words often hide the truth better than they reveal it. Therefore, the people want to see actions that show what men are made of, they want to hear about concrete programs for the economy, trade-unions, and the laws that govern property and organize business. This is why the best people have worked for more than fifty years to define a set of policies that will put into action the ideas expressed in the papal encyclicals. This is the job facing those of us who are committed to political action. . . .

The Right affirms and supports the current system of rural land tenure, which Social Christianity wants to reform in order to give land ownership to thousands of families and to increase their participation in the economic life of the country. The Right consolidates, protects and sustains the organizations that represent capital, but it distrusts and tries to limit the organization of labor unions. . . . Throughout the world . . . Social Christians struggle to organize, strengthen, and expand these legitimate organizations, which represent the defense and instrument of social progress. . . .

At this moment in our South American continent, and consequently in Chile, a gigantic process of economic transformation and progressive industrialization is taking place. Massive amounts of capital will come from North America with increasing intensity.

The problem lies in discerning the sign of the times in this new era. Capital is essential in these lands, but it is necessary to question who will control this power and wealth.

Capital can come in the form of private or state capitalism, and instead of helping our peoples to be freer and live with greater dignity, can convert them into mere machines. Is that what we want? The State can do good, but if the State lacks morals and competence, it will merely replace the old entrepreneur with a high official or politician involved in shady business deals, and the moral values that defend a nation will sink and the people will not attain that new level of dignity, which is what should drive an economy that serves men, not greed.

That is the mission of Social Christianity: to orient this creative effort so that the capital that arrives not only leads to an economic change, but also to a human change. . . .

In the face of this reality, if Social Christianity wants to be heard and be influential, it should establish itself as a movement whose discipline, numbers, and clarity and firmness of purpose says to the entire nation, to men of all classes including the poorest, that through this movement they can imagine and achieve the yearnings of a great nation.

Translated by Melissa Mann

Property and Production:
A Pamphlet Promoting Christian
Democracy's Agrarian Reform

*That agrarian reform would figure so centrally in reformist and revolutionary agendas in Chile is not surprising, given the historic concentration of land ownership in the hands of a few. The large estates (*latifundios *or* fundos*) that dominated the Chilean countryside gave landowners, hence the political Right, control over rural constituencies that allowed them to stymie congressional attempts to alter the rural order. Chile, whose geography should have made it a major food exporter, had been a growing food importer since the 1930s, a failure that many critics ascribed to the concentration of landownership in the hands of a nonentrepreneurial "aristocracy" who were more interested in the social status and political power that accompanied landholding than in maximizing agricultural production.*

The agrarian reform, which proposed to expropriate the great landed estates and give them to the peasants who worked them, was a signature initiative of Frei's Christian Democratic government. Frei's administration encouraged peasant unionization and expropriated almost 20 percent of Chile's farmland over six years, programs that brought dramatic changes in rural labor relations, reduced the electoral power of the Right, and increased political polarization in the countryside. However, the slow process of land distribution and limited scope of the agrarian reform law also disillusioned peasants who did not receive the lands they expected and left-wing Christian Democrats who desired a more accelerated approach to the agrarian reform. By the end of the Frei government in 1970, only 20,000 peasants had received land. Both groups would desert the Christian Democrats in 1970 and support Salvador Allende's more radical program, which included a pledge to fully implement the Christian Democratic agrarian reform law.

In this 1966 government pamphlet, based on a speech President Frei gave at a meeting with peasant leaders at which he announced the reform, Frei makes the economic and social case for land reform, stressing its developmentalist and welfare goals. The pamphlet begins by identifying the problems with Chile's existing system of land tenure, including the grossly unequal distribution and speculative uses of land, the inefficient and unproductive agrarian economy, the poor living conditions of the rural population, as well as the exodus from the countryside that created social problems associated with rapid urbanization. Frei then proposes the remedy of land redistribution to promote agricultural modernization and social reform. Unstated in this speech are the political motives of the policy, which Christian Democrats hoped would win them the peasant vote, allowing them to become a hegemonic party by depriving both Left and Right of an important constituency.

How Land in Chile has been Cultivated

We are only cultivating two million of the 11 million hectares that could be cultivated. That is why it is absolutely necessary that we distribute this land among members of our national community in the broadest, most rational, and just way possible.

Sub-familial Farms,[1] of which there are 56,000, or 37 percent of the farms in Chile, have only 1 percent of the arable land in the country, and 2 percent of the entire irrigated land.

Family farms, of which there are more than 60,000, making up 40 percent of the total number of farms, control 12 percent of the total arable surface and 7 percent of irrigated land.

The more than 24,000 *medium sized farms* have 13 percent of irrigated land.

Large farms, of which there are 10,300, or 7 percent of all of the various types of farms, own 65 percent of the arable land and 78 percent of irrigated land.

Land is clearly concentrated in very few hands.

It is common that the small number of people who own the majority of irrigated land in the country are *not even farmers.* Sometimes they have obtained land as speculative investments to justify obtaining loans for other business ventures. In our country, land ownership does not obligate the owner to farm the land with maximum productivity or to share its harvests with the peasantry. It seems that it has always been more important for the large landowners to accumulate more land, acquire more estates, and extend their current fundos than to make productive investments and improve the conditions of the peasants.

The Farming Population

There are some 3 million Chilean peasants. Thirty percent of the economically active population works in the agricultural sector and currently only contributes between 7 and 10 percent of the nation's wealth each year.

The Ministry of Agriculture has determined that on large farms of more than 100 hectares in one county, 60 percent of the peasants' houses lacked sanitary services, 57 percent got their water from irrigation ditches, and people slept between two and six per room and in 90 percent of the surveyed houses, between one and four people used the same bed. How is it possible that in our day human beings, with dignity and equal rights, like our peasants, live in conditions that make us, as Chileans, ashamed?

The Peasant Flight to the Cities

All of this has produced an increasing exodus of peasants toward the cities, where they hope to improve their working and living conditions.

These peasants create serious problems when they arrive in Santiago or other cities, and seek shelter in the shantytowns. They generally do not have the technical capacity to work in industry or other activities, so they form a nucleus of sub-employed workers. *Because the country has not suitably dealt with the agrarian problem, it has transported misery from the countryside to the marginalized squatter settlements in the cities.* Peasants arriving in Santiago, Valparaíso, or Concepción take away opportunities from factory workers, while creating unused productive lands in the rural areas. All of this happens at the same time that we see an increasing need for agricultural products that satisfy the demand of our poorly fed population. However, because of the inadequate distribution of land and water, we can not utilize this enormous potential and respond to the historical needs of our times.

In response to this, President Frei has said, "It is undeniable, essential, and necessary that we carry out an authentic and effective agrarian reform."

Without it, the country will not be able to develop its industry, services, or other sectors, because, besides the peasants fleeing to the cities, where they join the marginalized population, they compete with the industrial worker and take away his opportunities to work. His lamentable poverty allows him to consume only a minimal amount of what industry produces. And they are 30 percent of the population of Chile!

At the same time, as ours is a democratic country, it is painful that the peasants, up until now, have not had the same opportunities as those who live in the city. By better incorporating the peasants into national life, we will improve our democratic system even more, and allow for equal conditions of development among all citizens.

Let us now turn to what this urgent Agrarian Reform will consist of.

Principal Objectives of the Agrarian Reform

(1) Giving land ownership to the thousands of peasants who are capable of working it. Making them owners of the land they work will fulfill an old and justified desire. They will have the opportunity to develop themselves individually as well as improve the lives of their families, which will in turn contribute to the development of the national community.

This law will attempt to extend and perfect property rights as well as to fulfill the social function of land.

(2) Improving agricultural production. Agrarian Reform will improve the general situation of our economy and will produce social development.

(3) Achieving the upward mobility of the authentic peasants and their families. *It can not be possible that 3 million people in our country in our time continue to be marginalized economically, socially, and culturally. They are fundamental for progress and democratic stability in Chile.*

*Guarantees for Current Landowners Who Work
the Land Well and Obey Social Laws*

In the meeting with the peasants, President Frei said that he was aware that some landowners are uncertain and feel uneasy [about the Agrarian Reform]. In many cases this was due to false information because *the Agrarian Reform will only take place within strictly legal channels.* . . .

Every landowner who works his lands in a normal manner will be able to keep a land reserve equivalent to 80 hectares of the best irrigated land. Along with this measure, every very efficient landowner who meets the following conditions will be allowed to maintain up to a total of 320 hectares of unexpropriable, irrigated land: if they work all of the land in an effective manner; obey social regulations and laws; pay wages that are higher than the prevailing wages in the zone; maintain a larger production than the regional average; conserve natural resources in an adequate manner.

How Many Landowners Will be Affected?

There are approximately 270,000 farms in Chile, which belong to approximately 250,000 owners. Of these, it is possible that only about 5,000 will be affected. Small and medium landowners, as well as large-scale owners who work the land in an optimal manner, will be automatically excluded from the reform.

Beneficiaries of the agrarian reform sign documents with a thumbprint, 1960s. Center for Agrarian Reform "Alcides Leal," Curicó. Photograph by Julio Troncoso. Courtesy of Colección Museo Histórico Nacional de Chile.

What is more, those 5,000 owners will keep an important part of their lands if these are not poorly worked. The Agrarian Reform Law gives the government the power to expropriate farms that contain more than 80 hectares of good irrigated land, or the equivalent in lower quality land.

Expropriated lands will be paid for in long-term bonds, through a just indemnification and in accordance with the official assessment of their value. Property improvements will also be paid for.

New Landowners and Settlements

It is said that Agrarian Reform could cause national production to fall in a sharp and dramatic fashion. *All of the necessary measures will be taken to ensure that this does not happen.*

To avoid disorganization of expropriated plots, these will be worked by the so-called "Peasant Settlements" [Asentamientos]. This will ensure that expropriated farms will not become paralyzed, as has happened in the past. The Settlement will be a partnership between the peasants who have freely elected a Committee to represent them, and the CORA (Agrarian Reform

Corporation). In this partnership the CORA will provide in a convenient manner the land, water, seeds, fertilizers, insecticides, and other inputs that are needed to work the land. The peasants will provide their labor, tools and equipment, as well as their experience in cultivating the land. This real partnership, which is what the Settlement is, will last for two years, and in exceptional cases three years. Upon the termination of this period, peasants who have proven themselves worthy of land ownership will receive lands and permanent land titles. . . .

Land Reform Is Not a Gift

Peasants will pay for their lands over thirty years. . . . *It is not a gift to anyone.* As the State will pay [the old owners] for the value of the expropriated lands, it will demand that peasant beneficiaries repay the value of the lands they receive.

This is essential to providing the necessary credits, technical assistance, and other requirements that must accompany land redistribution [for it to succeed].

The great majority of Chileans have their eyes on this great hope that the Agrarian Reform represents, especially the well-being that agricultural workers will receive from it. They have been our most neglected workers, and now their hour has come. It is time to give them the same rights as the rest of our citizens.

Translated by Ryan Judge

Note

1. Subfamilial farms (*minifundios*) were farms too small to support a family of five.

The Christian Left and

Communitarian Socialism

Jacques Chonchol and Julio Silva Solar

From its beginnings, the Christian Democratic Party was a multiclass, centrist political party with large right and left wings. Such internal divisions became increasingly acute in the late 1960s as the party was faced with questions about the pace, scope, and content of social reform. Conflicts over President Frei's agrarian reform policies proved especially divisive, ultimately leading the Christian Democrats' leftmost factions to splinter off and form new parties, the United Popular Action Movement (MAPU) and the Christian Left Party. With talented leaders, but far fewer followers than they had enjoyed as Christian Democrats, these parties would join Allende's Popular Unity coalition.

This essay, by two leading Christian Democrats is a key early statement of the philosophy of the Christian Democratic Left who, inspired by liberation theology in the 1960s, promoted "Communitarian Socialism," a political project inspired in Catholic principles of social justice that required the radical transformation of social and economic structures. The essay draws on both Church teachings and Marxist analysis to denounce private property and advocate the socialization of the economy. The political biography of Jacques Chonchol, one of the authors, illustrates the key role of the Marxist-Christian Left in the politics of this period: serving first under President Frei as head of the state agency that trained peasant leaders and promoted rural grassroots organization, Chonchol later served as Allende's minister of agriculture, directing the radicalization and expansion of the agrarian reform that he had helped design as a Christian Democrat.

Foundations of Communitarianism

How did the idea of the communitarian system arise?

It arose in the advanced Christian thought of our time, as a response to the capitalist system. Capitalist society is characterized by profound class inequalities that generate wealth and benefits for a privileged minority,

Women and children in a Santiago *población* (shantytown) in the early 1960s. Photographer unknown. Used by permission of Empresa Editora Zig-Zag. Courtesy of Colección Museo Histórico Nacional de Chile.

wealth created by the labor of the entire community, while the vast human masses of the poor only have what they need to survive on, and often not even that.

In the international community the same situation is produced. The developed industrial countries have increasingly concentrated in their hands large stocks of capital, exploit natural resources, human labor, commercial exchange and other important economic dimensions of less developed countries for their own benefit, so that the goods produced by the international community as a whole also have a tendency to accumulate in the main centers of the world economy, while the underdeveloped zones accumulate misery, illiteracy and backwardness or the many forms of the loss of human life. . . .

As the people become conscious of their exploitation and the fundamental injustice that this order of things represents for them, the struggle against it is born and grows. This struggle is given the generic name of social revolution. We live in an age of great social revolutions that have profoundly shaken the world. We must note, because of their repercussions, the Russian Revolution, the Chinese Revolution, the Cuban Revolution.

The formerly colonized world is also going through its national and social revolutions. The revolution of the peoples of the world against capitalist society, against the exploitation of global capital, is a historical process already under way that will not be contained. The revolutionary impulse is stronger in backward, underdeveloped societies, but the phenomenon is general. Capitalist society, including [in those countries] where it has led to greater prosperity, cannot expect much more from itself. Its historical cycle is exhausted. . . .

Therefore it is important to understand that the communitarian program goes much further than the simple reform of the capitalist enterprise or any other reform of capitalist structure.

What is the idea of communitarianism?

Communitarianism promotes a social structure founded on the principle that the land and productive goods (industrial, financial, commercial capital) belong to the workers. It proposes to transcend the fundamental conflict of the capitalist system—class conflict—where the antagonism between the small class of the owners of capital and the masses dispossessed of everything aside from their work, which must be at the service of capital in exchange for a salary, generates all types of obstacles to economic development and social justice.

This conflict can only be resolved in a social order with a communitarian character, where capital and work are no longer separated but united in the same people. . . .

The Step to the New Society

The communitarian idea describes this social change. But what is communitarianism? Is it a form of neocapitalism? Is it a form of socialism? Is it a third way? We believe that objectively it is a form of socialism, a communitarian socialism. Why? Because socialism is the system in which productive goods of a social character belong to the community. That is its base. That is also the base of the communitarian idea. In both cases it deals with a society of workers who possess in common the means of production. . . .

Private Property

. . . Private property is frequently presented almost as if it were a "dogma" of Christian doctrine. However, the so-called "Fathers of the Church," who were closest to Jesus and conserved his teachings best, and who belong to the first epochs of Christianity, frequently spoke against private property in favor of communal goods. To them property was not part of God's plan and was the cause of many evils. . . .

Not surprisingly, it was the principle of communal goods that Jesus himself put into practice in the Congregation he formed with his disciples, and his continued requests that people give up their properties or goods are well known, as are his harsh reproaches against the rich. This same principle was maintained among the first Christians according to the narrations in the Acts of the Apostles. . . .

An abyss exists between the aims of Jesus and those of the Christian bourgeoisie of our day, whose ideal of life, their best case scenario, exhausts itself in three main goals: become rich, form a family, and place their own privileges and individual liberties above all other values of the community. Whereas Jesus spent his entire life among the poor propagating the good news: the Kingdom of God, where private property cannot enter, where everything is for everyone, where man does not reach happiness through his individual or family egoism, nor through his wealth, nor through the power or superiority that he exercises over others, not even through the limited pleasure of a life consecrated to himself and his immediate family, but through the communion of all, through community based on love, where man becomes the true brother of mankind. . . .

In the encyclical *Mater et Magistra* [Pope John XXIII, 1961] it is made clear that socialization of the economy is a typical aspect of this age that should not be looked at as something negative, but rather something that unquestionably provides benefits for the people, specifically: the indispensable means of human sustenance, medical care, more advanced elementary education, complete professional formation, housing, work, convenient rest, recreation.

Translated by Carolyn Watson

The New Song Movement:
An Interview with Inti-Illimani

In Chile, as in much of the world, the 1960s was a decade of youth rebellion and cultural effervescence. One central aspect of the politicized popular culture was the Nueva Canción or New Song, a musical genre that combined folk and traditional music with political themes. Beginning in the 1960s and reaching its apex during the Allende years, the New Song movement in Chile reflected the cultural and political changes happening across Latin America. In this interview conducted by Luís Cifuentes Seves, members of Inti-Illimani, one of the leading groups of the New Song, talk about how their music emerged out of both international youth culture as well as the activist atmosphere that permeated Chilean universities in the 1960s.[1] Originally formed by several engineering students of the State Technical University (UTE) in Santiago, the ensemble adopted an Andean name that roughly translates as "sun of the Illimani mountains" in the Aymara language of the indigenous peoples of northern Chile, Peru, and Bolivia and refers to Bolivia's most famous peak. With its self-conscious mix of protest music, folk music, and indigenous Andean music and instruments, Inti-Illimani was emblematic of Chile's New Song movement. At the time of the 1973 coup they were touring in Europe, and they remained in exile there, not returning until 1988, when they were permitted to reenter Chile. Today Inti-Illimani continues to perform in Chile and around the world.

LUÍS CIFUENTES: The 1960s were one of those rare periods of history dominated by progressive cultural ideas. They were years of great hope, optimism, and mobilization. I believe that there were three fundamental factors that determined these characteristics. First, the 1960s saw the fruits of the postwar process of economic reconstruction and adjustment. This process produced an extraordinary growth of the world economy, which resulted in a considerable decline in unemployment levels, the massive production of consumer goods, and a significant rise in the standard of living in developed countries. Another result was the necessity of these countries to export goods and capital and to import pri

Inti-Illimani in concert, c. 1971. From Fernando Barraza, *La nueva canción chilena* (Santiago: Quimantú, 1972). Photographer unknown. Used by permission of Horacio Salinas of Inti-Illimani. Courtesy of Colección Archivo Fotográfico, Biblioteca Nacional de Chile.

mary materials, which also produced an activation of many Third World economies. Even when this process did not resolve the world's social or political problems and hardly touched the problem of extreme poverty, it did generate grand aspirations.

Furthermore, there was a progressive political climate with the liberation of many former colonies in Asia and Africa. The Cuban Revolution broke the geographic fatalism of Latin America and the Left grew to a world-class level. Marxist authors, like Marcuse and Althusser, were converted into bestsellers and a proletarian family background became a prestige factor in many intellectual circles.

Lastly, there was a significant technological advance with the emergence of the space race: *Sputnik* in 1957; Gagarin, the first man in space, in 1961; the first moon landing in 1969. The application of new electronic technology put communication within reach of hundreds of millions of people. Transistor radios really converted the planet into "a global village" and with them millenarian myths began to be shattered. All of this contributed to the climate of hope and optimism that some Chileans called "the revolution of aspirations." . . .

Another ingredient of the 1960s was rock and roll. I remember that the first time I became aware of the existence of rock was in January of 1957 when I listened to "Don't Be Cruel" by Elvis Presley. It really affected my sensibilities.

RENATO FREYGANG: Rock and roll was essentially a new language in the hands of the youth.

JOSÉ SEVES: Rock and roll was an alternative to the music "of the old people"—the tango, the Peruvian waltz, the bolero, the mambo. Holly Near[2] told me that Elvis Presley was her idol not only from a musical point of view but also as a revolutionary, with a popular connotation similar to that which Bruce Springsteen has today, but better. . . .

RENATO: Things generally arrive later in Latin America, but rock and roll arrived immediately. Its hits were number one in the entire world. I remember Bill Haley, Buddy Holly, Brenda Lee, and others. Rock and roll was intimately tied to black music, to jazz; it's blues with more tempo. . . .

JOSÉ: An ex-member of the rock group The Ramblers offered guitar classes to eight or ten kids in my neighborhood. Among other songs, he taught us "La Nochera," an Argentine samba. This was the most difficult song that I knew until the Beatles appeared. They broke with the four positions and attempted more complex harmonies. With time one realized that they corresponded to a new level of development in musical technology and in the organization of multinational recording labels. Better quality recordings, better publicity, etc. I was in a group that mimicked Beatles' songs.

If you examine their musical development, you will realize that they were always introducing something new, enriching the orchestrations and the timbre of their sound with an honest and spontaneous composition that was not conditioned by the "divine laws" of supply and demand.

LUÍS: There's no doubt that popular music was not the same after the Beatles.

MAX BERRÚ: Their more romantic themes reached me the most. The sweetness of the music and their vocal arrangements were a background for my own loves.

JORGE COULÓN: In my opinion, rock and roll's force lies in its primitive, tribal, and instinctual character. The Beatles were the first to give it a more sophisticated form. They were like a musical provocation. I had been an opponent of rock and roll, but later, I noticed that it had been converted into a universal language.

LUÍS: Another intense process of the 1960s was that which arose around the student movement. Jorge, could you tell us about your experiences?

JORGE: One of the activist groups in which I participated was the University Movement for All [MUPT]. It was driven by the FEUT [Federación Estudiantes de la Universidad Técnica][3] and had the main objective of publicizing the problems of secondary students, the large majority of whom were qualified for university studies but found their access to higher education severely limited. It was also a link between the university student movement and the secondary student movement. The MUPT was the result of a leadership training school [of the FEUT]. . . .

Simultaneously, Summer [Voluntary] Work was organized. Summer Work consisted of projects, such as the construction of schools, clinics, etc., in the rural and most underdeveloped regions of the country. These projects were financed by the Frei government and later by the Allende government. Summer [Voluntary] Work was an extraordinary source of social, political, and cultural experience.

I believe that the "secret" was the attractiveness of the ideas generated by the student movement. They mobilized a massive enthusiasm and seemed to have a master plan for change and the multifaceted advance of Chilean society that could include all these individual tasks. We wanted to position the University in resonance with the will of the great majority of Chileans. As a consequence of the tremendous support that these ideas had, it can never be said that they were proselytizing or narrow. . . .

One thing that has always caught my attention is the idea of some people that these great social processes were in some way managed by the political parties. The truth was that all of them, including the student movement, had their own dynamic; things happened spontaneously. Communists, socialists, etc., followed the lead of the student movement. Also, the velocity of people's incorporation into these activities was such that it was never possible to indoctrinate or manipulate.

One time, I was speaking to Esteban Tomíc[4] on a long trip to Bulgaria. He expressed an interest in this, and he said: "Don't think that this is a trick question. Did the Communist Party organize the New Song movement?" I told him that even if the CP had wanted to direct the movement, it would not have been able to do so . . .

Translated by Melissa Mann

Notes

1. The editors are grateful to Luís Cifuentes Seves for sharing his Inti-Illimani interviews (1987–1988) with our readers. They were first published by Cifuentes in *Fragmentos de un sueño: Inti-Illimani y la generación de los 60* (Santiago, 1989). A second revised online edition was published in 2000, available at www.cancioneros.com/co/3775/2/los-anos-de-la-

esperanza-por-luis-cifuentes-seves. This selection is excerpted from the chapter "Los años de la esperanza," in both editions.

2. U.S. folksinger and political activist who recorded many English-language versions of Chilean New Song and toured with Inti-Illimani in 1984.

3. Federación Estudiantes de la Universidad Técnica, the student government of the State Technical University (UTE), today the University of Santiago (USACH).

4. Esteban Tomíc: the son of Radomiro Tomíc, the leader of the left wing of the Christian Democratic Party and its presidential candidate in 1970.

Lyrics of the New Song Movement

Violeta Parra and Victor Jara

Violeta Parra and Victor Jara were the two most important singer-songwriters of the New Song movement. Together they illustrate both the cultural revolution that their movement helped define and the politicization of popular culture during the 1960s and early 1970s. Artists as well as activists, they personalized the political in their songs, while using their art to "raise consciousness" and mobilize politically. They also brought the music and folklore of the indigenous peoples of Chile into a Chilean musical repertoire that had long ignored the country's Andean location and indigenous culture. Violeta Parra was born into a talented rural family in the south of Chile that included Nicanor Parra, the country's leading "antipoet." A folklorist as well as an artist, she spent years collecting the folklore of southern Chile and championed the culture and cause of the Mapuche, work that is illustrated in her song "Arauco Has a Sadness." Considered the founding mother of the New Song movement, she popularized the peña, a gathering for the performance of live, politicized folk music. Many of the singer-songwriters of the New Song movement got their start in such gatherings, including Victor Jara. Her last testament in song, "Thanks to Life," became an international hit, made popular by singers such as Joan Baez and the Argentine Mercedes Sosa. Unlucky in love, Parra committed suicide in 1967.

The most famous singer-songwriter of the Popular Unity era, Victor Jara came from a working-class background and identified strongly with popular struggles for social justice. In 1972 he completed the concept album La Población, *an oral history of the founding by homeless squatters of a Santiago* población *(squatter settlement) in 1967. In the course of the* toma—*the squatters' takeover of the land—a young girl, Herminda, was killed by the police. The founders named the* población Herminda de la Victoria *in her honor. In* La Población, *Jara blended the voices of the* pobladores *(residents of poblaciones) and their oral testimonies with his own voice and songs. In 1973, a few months before the coup, Jara wrote and recorded an even darker song, "Winds of the People," alternately prophetic and defiant, in which he warns of the threat of new massacres of "the people" and promises to lend his words and voice to their struggle until "death takes me away." Tragically, Victor Jara himself became one of the first victims of the military coup, tortured and then publicly executed in the Santiago stadium that today bears his name.*

Violeta Parra

ARAUCO HAS A SADNESS

Arauco has a sadness that cannot be silenced
it is the injustice of centuries revealed for all to see
No one has put a stop to it though there is a remedy
Rise up Huenchullán![1]

One day from afar the demon conqueror arrives
searching for mountains of gold which the Indian never looked for
for the Indian, enough is the gold that sparkles forth from the sun
Rise up Curimon!

Then the blood runs, the Indian knows not what to do
his land will be taken, he must defend it
Dead falls the Indian at the feet of the invader
Rise up Manquilef!

Since the year fourteen hundred the Indian is oppressed
in the shadow of his *ruca* [hut] you can see him weep a torrent of five
   centuries
Never will it dry
Rise up Calful!

Arauco has a sadness even more black than his *chamal* [poncho]
no longer are the Spanish those who make him cry
The Chileans themselves take away his bread
Rise up Huenchullán!

Translated by Gloria Alvarez and Ericka Verba

THANKS TO LIFE

Thanks to life that has given me so much
It has given me two eyes, that when I open
I can distinguish the black from the white
and in the highest sky, its starry depths
and among the multitudes, the man I love

Thanks to life that has given me so much
It has given me my ears, that in all of their breadth
Capture night and day, crickets and canaries
Hammers, turbines, dogs barking, the rain falling
And the tender voice of the one I love

Thanks to life that has given me so much
It has given me sound and the alphabet
And with them the words that I think and declare
"Mother," "friend," "brother," and light that illuminates
The path to the soul of the one I love

Thanks to life that has given me so much
It has given me the footsteps of my tired feet
They have taken me to cities and swamps
Beaches and deserts, mountains and plains
And to your house, your street, and your patio

Thanks to life that has given me so much
It has given me a heart that beats steady
when I contemplate the fruit of human wisdom
when I contemplate goodness so far from evil
when I look into the depths of your clear eyes

Thanks to life that has given me so much
It has given me laughter and it has given me tears
I can thus distinguish joy from sorrow
the two elements that make up my song
and your song that is also my song
and everyone's song that is also my song

Translated by Gloria Alvarez and Ericka Verba

Victor Jara

HERMINDA DE LA VICTORIA

Herminda de la Victoria
died without having fought.
She went straight to heaven
with her chest pierced.
The bullets of the police
killed the innocent child.
Mothers and brothers wept
among the crowd of people.

All became brothers
brothers in misfortune
fighting against the wolves
fighting for a home.

Herminda de la Victoria
was born in the mud
grew like a butterfly
on waste land won over.

We built our community
and it has rained for three winters

Herminda, in our hearts
we will keep your memory.

Translated by Victor Jara Foundation

WINDS OF THE PEOPLE

Once more they want to stain
my country with workers' blood,
those who talk of liberty
and whose hands are soiled,
those who wish to separate
mothers from their sons
and want to reconstruct
the cross that Christ bore.

They try to hide the infamy,
their legacy of centuries
but the colour of murderers
cannot be wiped from their faces.
Already thousands of thousands
have sacrificed their blood
and its generous streams
have multiplied the loaves

Now I want to live
beside my son and brother
building the springtime
on which we all work every day.
You can't scare me with your threats
You masters of misery.

The star of hope
continues to be ours.

Winds of the people speak to me.
Winds of the people carry me.
They scatter my heart
And blow through my throat.
So the poet will go on singing
As long as my soul has the power
down the roads of the people
both now and forever.

Translated by Victor Jara Foundation

Note

1. Seventeenth-century Mapuche leader who fought the Spanish.

The Election of 1970

In the hotly contested presidential election of 1970, three candidates, representing the right, center, and left, faced off in what was billed by all sides as a referendum on Chile's future. In part because of increased literacy and popular political participation in the 1960s, but also because of the sharply distinct ideological positions at stake, the campaign leading up to the 1970 election was among the most vigorous and contentious in the nation's history. The center and left campaigns organized large street rallies, promoted popular art, and held mass music and theater events. Colorful murals appeared on walls and buildings, the work of a Communist Youth organization known as the Ramona Parra Brigades. Meanwhile, the newly invigorated Right, eschewing an electoral alliance with the Christian Democrats, sought to convince voters through sympathetic newspapers and poster- and letter-writing campaigns that Allende's election would mean the imposition of a Soviet-style regime in Chile.

When the votes were counted, Allende had eked out a victory, receiving 36 percent of the vote—compared to 35 percent for the right's candidate and 28 percent for the centrist Christian Democrat. Because no candidate had received an absolute majority, according to Chilean law it fell to Congress to ratify the result. Despite an active and ultimately violent campaign to deny Allende victory—a campaign in which the CIA was secretly involved—the Chilean congress confirmed Allende as president six weeks later, making him the first democratically elected Marxist head of state in the hemisphere.

A youth brigade paints a political mural, 1970. The political and aesthetic ferment embodied in the New Song movement had its counterpoint in the realm of visual arts in the public mural. With the streets of Chile's towns and cities as their canvas, artists such as those associated with the Communist Youth painted political murals that drew on Andean and indigenous aesthetic forms and portrayed peasants, workers, and *pobladores* (shantytown residents). Chilean muralists also drew from the Mexican muralist movement embodied by artists such as Diego Rivera earlier in the twentieth century, as well as from the imagery and style of Picasso's later work. Photograph by Ximena Castillo. Courtesy of Colección Archivo Fotográfico Biblioteca Nacional de Chile.

Protesting Allende, 1970. This Alessandri supporter holds a sign declaring "I would rather die than live with the Russians." Photograph by Ximena Castillo. Courtesy of Colección Archivo Fotográfico Biblioteca Nacional de Chile.

Election day, 1970. A newspaper kiosk advertises Chile's choice on the eve of the 1970 election in headlines that blare competing predictions of the outcome. During the campaign—and to an even greater extent during the Popular Unity period—newspapers displayed polarizing and increasingly violent rhetoric in defense of their competing political agendas. Photograph by Ximena Castillo. Courtesy of Colección Archivo Fotográfico Biblioteca Nacional de Chile.

The Election of Salvador Allende:
Declassified U.S. Government Documents

As the date of Chile's 1970 presidential election approached, the U.S. government grew increasingly interventive. Its covert action to prevent the election of the Socialist candidate Salvador Allende had actually begun in 1964, when the United States secretly financed more than half of the winning presidential campaign of the Christian Democrat Eduardo Frei and masterminded a propaganda "terror campaign" in the media against Allende's candidacy that alleged that if Allende was elected Chile would become a Communist country, fathers would disappear, and Chilean children would be sent to Cuba. It continued through the Frei presidency and, when U.S. covert action failed to prevent Allende from winning a plurality at the polls in 1970, President Richard Nixon directed the CIA to prevent Allende's inauguration, instructing his aides to "make the Chilean economy scream." The national security advisor, Henry Kissinger, advised the CIA that "it is firm and continuing policy that Allende be overthrown by a coup."

Having failed to block Allende's inauguration as the hemisphere's first democratically elected Marxist president, Washington faced the dilemma of what policy to adopt toward his administration. Only two days after Allende's inauguration, and at the secret urging of Kissinger, Nixon opted for a hostile policy of covert action—including an invisible economic blockade that pressured public and private lenders and investors, as well as domestic and international aid agencies, to deny Chile credit, investments, and assistance—masked by a "correct but cool" public stance. Its goal was to "destabilize" the Allende government and prepare the way for its ouster. Recently declassified memos detailing this policy, two of which are reproduced here, reveal both the real U.S. policy toward Allende's Chile and that the reasoning behind it was Kissinger's concern that a successful democratic socialism in Chile would prove attractive to Western Europe as well. The memos also underscore the immense importance U.S. government officials ascribed to Allende's Chile in the context of global Cold War struggles and the lengths to which they would go in order to end his government.

Salvador Allende receives the presidential sash from the president of the Senate as
outgoing president Eduardo Frei looks on. Photograph by Sonia Aravena Derpich.
Used by permission of the photographer. Courtesy of Colección Archivo Fotográfico,
Biblioteca Nacional de Chile.

November 5, 1970

MEMORANDUM FOR THE PRESIDENT

FROM: Henry A. Kissinger
SUBJECT: NSC Meeting, November 6—Chile

This meeting will consider the questions of what strategy we should adopt
to deal with an Allende Government in Chile.

A. DIMENSIONS OF THE PROBLEM

The election of Allende as President of Chile poses for us one of the most
serious challenges ever faced in this hemisphere. Your decision as to what
to do about it may be the most historic and difficult foreign affairs decision
you will have to make this year, for what happens in Chile over the next six
to twelve months will have ramifications that will go far beyond just US-
Chilean relations. They will have an effect on what happens in the rest of
Latin America and the developing world; on what our future position will
be in the hemisphere; and on the larger world picture, including our relations with USSR. They will even affect our own conception of what our role
in the world is.

Allende is a tough, dedicated Marxist. He comes to power with a profound anti-US bias. The Communist and Socialist parties form the core of

the political coalition that is his power base. *Everyone agrees that Allende will purposefully seek:*

- –to establish a socialist, Marxist state in Chile;
- –to eliminate US influence from Chile and the hemisphere;
- –to establish close relations and linkages with the USSR, Cuba and other Socialist countries.

The consolidation of Allende in power in Chile, therefore, *would pose some very serious threats to our interests and positions in the hemisphere,* and would affect developments and our relations to them elsewhere in the world:

- –US investments (totaling some one billion dollars) may be lost, at least in part; Chile may default on debts (about $1.5 billion) owed to the US Government and private US banks.
- –Chile would probably become a leader of opposition to us in the inter-American system, a source of disruption in the hemisphere, and a focal point for subversion in the rest of Latin America.
- –It would become part of the Soviet/Socialist world, not only philosophically but in terms of power dynamics; it might constitute a support base and entry point for expansion of Soviet and Cuban presence and activity in the region.
- –The example of a successful elected Marxist government in Chile would surely have an impact on—and even the precedent value for— other parts of the world, especially in Italy; the imitative spread of similar phenomena elsewhere would in turn significantly affect the world balance and our own position in it.

While events in Chile pose these potentially very adverse consequences for us, *they are taking a form which makes them extremely difficult for us to deal with or offset,* and which in fact poses *some very painful dilemmas for us:*

a. Allende was elected legally, the first Marxist government ever to come to power by free elections. He *has* legitimacy in the eyes of Chileans and most of the world; there is nothing we can do to deny him that legitimacy or claim he does not have it.

b. We are strongly on record in support of self-determination and respect for free elections; you are firmly on record for non-intervention in the internal affairs of this hemisphere and of accepting nations "as they are." It would therefore be very costly for us to act in ways that appear to violate those principles, and Latin Americans and others in the world will view our policy as a test of the credibility of our rhetoric. On the other hand, our failure to react to this situation risks being perceived in Latin America and in Europe as indifference or impotence in the face of clearly adverse developments in a region long considered our sphere of influence.

c. Allende's government is likely to move along lines that will make it very difficult to marshal international or hemispheric censure of him—he is most likely to appear as an "independent" socialist country rather than a Soviet satellite or "Communist government." Yet a Titoist government in Latin America would be far more dangerous to us than it is in Europe, precisely because it can move against our policies and interests more easily and ambiguously and because its "model" effect can be insidious.

National Security Council
Washington, D.C. 20506
November 9, 1970

TOP SECRET. SENSITIVE/EYES ONLY
National Security Decision Memorandum 93

To: Secretary of State
        Secretary of Defense
        Director of Emergency Preparedness
        Director of Central Intelligence

SUBJECT: Policy Towards Chile

Following the discussion at the meeting of the National Security Council on November 6, 1970, the President has decided that the basis for our policy towards Chile will be the concept underlying Option C of the Inter-agency paper submitted November 3, 1970 by the Department of State for the consideration of the National Security Council as outlined in the guidelines set forth below.

The President has decided that (1) the public posture of the United States will be correct but cool, to avoid giving the Allende government a basis on which to rally domestic and international support for consolidation of the regime; but that (2) the United States will seek to maximize pressures on the Allende government to prevent its consolidation and limit its ability to implement policies contrary to U.S. and hemisphere interests.

Specifically, the President has directed that within the context of a publicly cool and correct posture toward Chile:

– vigorous efforts be undertaken to assure that other governments in Latin America understand fully that the U.S. opposes consolidation of a communist state in Chile hostile to the interests of the United States and other hemisphere nations, and to the extent possible encourage them to adopt a similar posture.

– close consultation be established with key governments in Latin America, particularly Brazil and Argentina, to coordinate efforts to oppose Chilean moves which may be contrary to our mutual interests; in pursuit of this objective, efforts should be increased to establish and maintain close relations with friendly military leaders in the hemisphere.

– necessary actions be taken to:

    a. exclude, to the extent possible, further financing assistance or guarantees for U.S. private investment in Chile, including those related to the Investment Guarantee Program or the operations of the Export-Import Bank;

    b. determine the extent to which existing guarantees and financing arrangements can be terminated or reduced;

    c. bring maximum feasible influence to bear in international financial institutions to limit credit or other financing assistance to Chile (in this connection, efforts should be made to coordinate with and gain maximum support for this policy from other nations, particularly those in Latin America, with the objective of lessening unilateral U.S. exposure); and

    d. assure that U.S. private business interests having investments or operations in Chile are made aware of the concern with which the U.S. Government views the Government of Chile and the restrictive nature of the policies which the U.S. Government intends to follow.

– no new bilateral economic aid commitments be undertaken with the Government of Chile (programs of a humanitarian or private social agency character will be considered on a case by case basis); existing commitments will be fulfilled but ways in which, if the U.S. desires to do so, they could be reduced, delayed or terminated should be examined.

The President has directed that the Director of the Office of Emergency Preparedness prepare a study which sets forth the implications of possible developments in world copper markets, stockpile disposal actions and other factors as they may affect the marketing of Chilean copper and our relationship with Chile.

The President also has directed that the Senior Review Group meet monthly or more frequently as necessary to consider specific policy issues within the framework of this general posture, to report actions which have been taken, and to present to him further specific policy questions which may require his decision. To facilitate this process the President has directed the establishment of an Ad Hoc Interagency Working Group, comprising representatives of the Secretaries of State and Defense, the Director of Central Intelligence, and the President's Assistant for National Security Affairs, and chaired by the representative of the Secretary of State, to prepare options for specific courses of action and related action plans for the consideration of the Senior Review Group and to coordinate implementation of approved courses of action.

[Signed] Henry A. Kissinger

Cc: Secretary of the Treasury
    Administrator, A.I.D.
    Director, Office of Management and Budget
    Chairman, Joint Chiefs of Staff

The Mapuche Land Takeover at Rucalán:
Interviews with Peasants and Landowners

Allende's inauguration and promise not to use Chile's security forces against "the people" was a license for newly empowered Chileans to take the revolution into their own hands in order to realize their historic dreams. The result was a revolution from below that began with the Mapuches, Chile's largest indigenous group. Almost as soon as Allende was inaugurated, Mapuche communities in the southern province of Cautín began to move the fences back to where they had been before non-Mapuche settlers, aided by the Chilean state and a corrupt judiciary, had taken the lands from them during the late nineteenth and early twentieth centuries. This "running of the fences" was also accompanied by the seizure of landed estates (tomas de fundo) on which Mapuche laborers, along with other rural workers, had been hired hands. In the early hours of the morning of December 20, 1970, an alliance of peasants from several Mapuche communities and day laborers from a nearby estate invaded the fundo Rucalán. Four days later, on Christmas Eve, the owner of the farm, Juan Bautista Landarretche, returned with a band of family members and fellow landowners and retook the property, wounding several peasants in the resulting melee. Government officials then arrested Landarretche and some of his conspirators, put them on trial, and turned Rucalán over to the peasants to establish an asentamiento, or agrarian reform cooperative.

As the first rural land occupation carried out under the Allende government, as well as the first case of an attempted reoccupation by landowners, Rucalán became a cause célèbre for both the Popular Unity government and the landowner-led opposition. In January 1971, Allende instructed Jacques Chonchol to move his Agriculture Ministry to Cautín and accelerate the agrarian reform there in order to solve the problem the tomas had created and restore social peace. But soon the wave of rural tomas spread north through the Central Valley. The lesson that Chile's peasants and rural workers had drawn from Rucalán and other early occupations was that the way to get the government to prioritize expropriating a given fundo was to seize it, creating a "social problem" that the government had to resolve without delay. As a result of this rural revolution from below, the agrarian reform projected to take six years to fully implement was completed in eighteen months. After 1973, the military regime quickly returned many expropriated properties—including Rucalán—to their former owners.

The oral history interviews with key actors in the toma of Rucalán were collected by the historian Florencia Mallon in 1997, seven years after the transition to democracy. Don Heriberto Ailío, leader of the community of Ailío and founding member of the Revolutionary Peasant Movement (MCR), the peasant front organization of the far-left Movement of the Revolutionary Left (MIR), together with his wife, Doña Marta Antinao, represent the occupying peasants. At the end of his testimony, don Heriberto makes clear how, for the Mapuche in particular, the question of the land had a longer and deeper history connected to the autonomy of indigenous territory, still of recent memory, and going back centuries. Violeta Maffei de Landarretche, the widow of Juan Landarretche, and her son Luciano represent the landowners' point of view, explaining how the tomas, which they attributed to outside agitators from the MIR, disrupted their family's security and livelihood. As these interviews demonstrate, the conflicts that animated the peasant tomas and landowners' responses continue to echo in today's divided views of Chile's past.[1]

The Toma de Fundo at Rucalán

DOÑA MARTA ANTINAO: We divided ourselves up, the women went in a boat, the men went first. When we got there we entered the farm and made a group, there was a large barn and that's where we arrived. There were only a few women, me, my husband's aunt, my mother. We cooked for the men, we made a fire and cooked in a common pot for everyone. Every day we were more united, fighting for the land.

DON HERIBERTO AILÍO: Here in the community people always fought for their land. Later a politics of class, of political parties, became a part of it. So we agreed with that, we said, that's ours, too. If the *peñi* (brothers) there are fighting for their labor, for their ideas, we must also struggle, since we don't have work, we don't have land. So that's when we said, all right, we should invade the land.

I didn't participate immediately with the leaders, but I always loved to express my opinions and to collaborate with them. Well, then they began to trust me, and I became a trusted member of the movement [MCR]. They . . . put me in a position with responsibility, and it was serious. The first fence running was when we took over the fundo Rucalán, at the end of 1970. We went by night, about forty men heads of household. We men went on foot and the women went in a boat on the Imperial River. My aunt, may she rest in peace, was there. We loved her because she was very brave, she really inspired people, she had a voice; if she yelled, she could reach people on the other side of the river.

We arrived on a Monday, and we put the women in a place where they'd be safe, and then the men, we went ahead to talk to the rich guy. We had two, maybe three people who were prepared, so those three approached him. They said "Excuse us, but we've taken over the farm, at this point it's taken," so we said we needed to search the house, and they went inside and did the search, and they found revolvers, shotguns, too, old carbines, and we took them. And then we told them to stay calm, to go back to sleep peacefully, but in the morning they'd have to leave because the property was ours.

DOÑA VIOLETA MAFFEI DE LANDARRETCHE: When they knocked on our door at three-thirty in the morning, for us it was, well, maybe a logical thing given the government we had, but for us it was a total surprise. Of course, when they knocked we didn't wake up, but the maid did and she came to our bedroom and told my husband, "Boss, the farm has been taken over, you must get up, because there's a person out there who is demanding that you come to the door." Juan got up and went to the door and talked with one of the people from the MIR who put a revolver to his head. Then he came back and said, "What do you think?" Well, yeah, I said, we can't do anything, look at all the people who are out there in the yard.

The house was surrounded, completely surrounded. At first I thought someone could take a message to the other farm, but we couldn't get out, not even through the window. So I said, I think the best thing is to turn it over, and I began packing up a few things just to see if they'd let me take them, my jewelry, some clothes, things like that. Look, I said, I think that right now we can't do anything. Later, when I was getting in the car, the guy from the MIR told me to open my suitcase, but I said I wouldn't. So finally he let me go.

When we arrived at the neighboring farm that belonged to my husband's cousins, he said to my son here, who was sixteen at the time, "Go and herd the animals that are there behind the property, you can ask for help here, and go herd as many animals as you can." So Luciano got help from one of the men who worked for us, and between the two of them they took the animals to the neighboring farm, and that was what we lived on.

LUCIANO LANDARRETCHE: My older brother and I got up and went out to the yard to see what was going on and try to talk to these people. There was a big fight because the whole yard was occupied, it was still night but there were probably sixty people, more or less, maybe seventy. . . . But there were a lot, because they had the house surrounded, and at that moment Father tried to talk with the one who was in charge who was from the MIR and with one other person we later found out was Ricardo Mora Carrillo. This guy worked on the farm of a friend of ours . . . but he was the leader of the movement in the community of Ailío.

So Father and Ricardo Mora had an altercation, and Father even threw a punch and at that moment I thought, they're going to shoot him, but instead they forced him to hand over the keys. The guy from the MIR, who calmed everyone down, told my father that he would authorize us to leave in two cars for [the nearby town of] Carahue, but that we could only take our personal effects.

Retaking the Farm

LUCIANO LANDARRETCHE: We decided to retake the farm because my father realized he was about to lose everything, and besides, there was a lot of talk about land takeovers, usurpations, and this was a way to stop this thing, and somebody had to do it. Added to this was that, on December 23, Salvador Allende was in Temuco and in his speech he kept warning the landowners not to arm themselves against the peasant movement. So in this political climate it seemed necessary to try and get the farm back.

Now this was a very complicated situation, because it was the first takeover in our municipality, and there were fifteen, twenty, forty, who knows how many guys from the MIR in there, so it was pretty risky. And we thought that surely we'd confront machine guns, submachine guns, things like that. But we had a good plan. We organized ourselves in three groups, one advancing in each of three small ravines that go north to south, to surround them. At that moment we yelled to them that they should evacuate, because we were retaking the property, and we didn't want anybody to get wounded, we didn't want any dead. Because after all, our family is not a family of delinquents. But they immediately answered us with shots and several charges of dynamite, one of which exploded not more than twenty meters from me. That's when the shootout began, and it didn't last more than fifteen minutes, because after all, it was December 24, early in the afternoon, and they were preparing a big party. They'd killed a steer and were getting ready for a big party.

The only way out they had was downhill, across a stream. Mora Carrillo and the others who later claimed they had bullet wounds got caught up in the barbed wire or the brambles, because at no point did we shoot to kill. We could have done so if we wanted, since we were shooting from at most ten meters away, but Father had asked us not to, because he didn't want problems with the law. The next day, on Christmas, the police arrived and arrested my father and older brother.

DOÑA MARTA ANTINAO: When I left the farm's orchard up there, running straight down we had to cross a canal. Some of the older ladies, they ended up serving as a human bridge, because the young folks just got there and crossed first right over them. I had a brother with me, he was pretty young too, and he caught my little boy. I got to the edge there, and in my hurry I just threw the little boy across the canal. The canal was really wide, and I just threw my little boy across to my brother. I had a basket with me, the kind we use for potatoes, I'd thrown what I could into it, I thought to myself, well, if they're throwing us out, then we won't be back, so I took what I could in my basket and took off running. And I told my brother to go ahead with the basket and I'd follow with the kid. I'd put him here in front of me so that they wouldn't . . . I was afraid they'd kill him . . . better that I put my little boy in front of me.

My husband was in Temuco, it seems he was coming back and was going to get off the bus and another gentleman went up to him and said, "Don't get off, because they're throwing the people off [the fundo] over there, do you want to be killed?" So that's how they stopped him and he just stayed on the bus until further along, where we were hiding, and that's where he got off.

DON HERIBERTO AILÍO: Four days after the toma they retook the farm and chased us out, guns blazing. Bullets and water rained down on us that day. No one escaped, everybody running, soaked, people buried in mud, passing through a tremendous stream. It was the capitalists who were armed in those days. Sure, they were all civilians who arrived, but there had to be some policemen mixed up in it. They had a good plan for how to kick us out, but it took a long time for people to get out. They didn't dare come close, they just kept shooting from far away.

When the case was decided in our favor, the court appointed an administrator who confirmed the situation on the farm, then put out an order to start work once again. And the government official came to get us here in the community, and the same ones who had been in the takeover, all of them, and from the communities of Pichingual, Rucahue, they all supported us, helped us.

Since we took nothing with us, the State sent us people from INDAP [National Institute for Agricultural and Livestock Development], and they were our ambassadors. At that time it was CORA [the Agrarian Reform Corporation], and CORA gave everything—tractors to replace the oxen, cows, seeds, fertilizers—everything the farm needed for the peasants to work it. So we said, let's each take two hectares of land, for each member of the asentamiento, but since the members didn't have time to work those two hectares, they'd find a partner from outside, from nearby. We'd provide the seed, fertilizers, and the land, and they'd provide the work, two crops, weeding, all those things. And at the end, we split the harvest fifty-fifty.

CORA did a good job back then, because they gave us the right to distribute some of what we planted to people. So we'd give out, say, wheat or potatoes by the load. Each family would get, for example, six sacks of wheat per load. And that's how we maintained ourselves and bought the other things we needed. Because we also had a cooperative. We were able to keep the cooperative stocked, in fact we watched it grow, we were able to do things right in those years, no one was left owing money, we all came out well. Things were well organized back then.

People worked well there. We kept that farm clean as a whistle, we grew many crops, potatoes, wheat, everything we planted grew well. The bad part was that then, later, the soldiers arrived, and everything was given back to them again.

Taking the farm at the time we did was totally illegal, but we said it wasn't illegal. Why? Whose permission had they asked earlier when they'd taken over our lands in the first place? Nobody's. They just arrived and they said, OK, move over that way, this land is ours now. So afterward we also said to them, clear as day: this land is ours. You get out, tomorrow you grab your things because the farm is ours now. That's the conclusion we reached, clear as day.

A long time ago, according to history, the "peacemakers" arrived, but they were soldiers who came to find out if there were people here in Chile, because who knew if there really were Mapuche people? Those were the years when the *winkas* [non-Mapuches], as we call them now, arrived. That's when this whole thing got started.

My father, may he rest in peace, told me how my grandfather climbed the hill here, there was a large ulmo tree and they had fixed it so you could climb it. So the old man would climb up there and looking out he'd yell to people, "Look, you see out there, all those lands, they're ours. And so are these others, this part over here." With his hand he drew the lines for them, they had their way of marking what belonged to them.

Translated by Florencia Mallon

Note

1. This case and the broader context for the Mapuche movement for land restitution are explored in Florencia E. Mallon, *Courage Tastes of Blood: The Mapuche Community of Nicolás Ailío and the Chilean State, 1906–2001* (Durham, N.C.: Duke University Press, 2005). The editors are grateful to the author for sharing these materials.

Revolution in the Factory: Interviews with Workers at the Yarur Cotton Mill

One of the central tenets of "the Chilean road to socialism," dating back to Allende's earliest presidential campaigns, was his personal promise to make workers' welfare and participation central to the revolutionary process. Following Popular Unity's intervention in mining, agriculture, and banking and municipal elections majority in early 1971, workers' demands to initiate the nationalization of Chile's largest manufacturing firms became uncontainable. Beginning with the Yarur cotton mill in April of that year, workers in these enterprises took the revolution into their own hands by seizing control of their workplaces, demanding that the government nationalize them and affirm worker participation in management decisions. As this "revolution from below" spread from factory to factory and sector to sector, it accelerated the road to socialism but threatened Allende's carefully phased "revolution from above," raising the question of who in fact was leading the Chilean revolution, the government or the workers?

Santiago's Yarur mill was Chile's largest and most emblematic textile factory, with a near monopoly of important product lines and financial dealings that put the Yarurs, a family of Palestinian Arab descent (called "Turks" in Chile because they emigrated when Palestine was still under Turkish rule and so arrived in Chile with Turkish passports) with business interests in banking as well as textiles, at the center of the Chilean economy. The Yarurs were also notorious for their political influence and their repression of labor rights. In 1970, during the Allende presidential campaign, a group of young workers organized in secret to win an independent union and were further encouraged by Allende's promise during a campaign speech at the factory that if elected he would take it over and turn its management over to the workers. When the Yarurs rejected the new union's demand for improved working conditions, workers went on strike and demanded the factory's expropriation by the government. But Allende resisted, worried—with good reason—that the seizure and socialization of the factory threatened to inspire similar acts across the industrial sector, jeopardizing the success of the revolutionary process as a whole. In the end, the Allende government was persuaded to legalize the Yarur toma (seizure). As the vice-minister of economy declared: "The Popular Unity program is very clear: we must put an end to monopolies. And in the textile industry, Yarur is an example of the concentration of power."

The interviews with Yarur workers here were conducted by the historian Peter Winn shortly after the creation of "Ex-Yarur," the worker-controlled factory. They convey the character and spontaneity of the revolution from below and its conflict with Allende's revolution from above. The interviews begin with the workers' account of a boisterous union meeting in which they respond to the management's refusal to meet with the union delegation.[1]

The Yarur Union Meeting

SILVIO CASTILLO: For the first time, I was a little surprised at a union meeting. Normally in meetings most *compañeros* [fellow workers][2] never ask for the floor; and when they do, it is with a certain prudence—trying not to attack the company . . . But in the meeting where the strike was declared, I was amazed at the courage of many compañeros shouting out to demand the floor. They told the union president, Compañero Rojas, that we *had* to go on strike, that once and for all "we had to fix the wagon of these Turkish thieves." And many compañeros who normally never speak valiantly asked for the floor to say these things.

RAMÓN FERNÁNDEZ [OFFICER OF THE CENTRAL UNICA DE TRABA-JADORES (CUT), CHILE'S NATIONAL LABOR CONFEDERATION]: I have never in my life seen anything like this . . . When the union officers told them that the company didn't want to receive them and had denied all their demands, the people stopped them and began to cry: "Socialization! Socialization!" It was incredible. It was *revolution!* Two thousand workers standing and shouting: "We want socialization!" And the women calling out: "No more exploitation!" They were in a state of euphoria. . . .

Then they asked me to take the floor . . . because they wanted to hear the opinion of the CUT . . . and I didn't know what to say because I had to get up and speak before two thousand workers all demanding "socialization" . . . and Allende had told me *"no,* not yet." He said: "First, [we will socialize] Radio Balmaceda, which is going to be given to the CUT, then deal with the mortgage question, and third, after that [we will socialize] the textile enterprise." That is what Compañero Allende told me only a week before the Yarur meeting.

But at that point the only thing that I could do was to go and instruct the compañeros on how they should proceed. So I said: "Compañeros! You have decided that this enterprise should pass to the social property area. My duty is to demand this of the government." Then an old-timer

Workers of the "Ex-Yarur" factory march in downtown Santiago. In this photograph from May Day 1972, the workers of the nationalized "Ex-Yarur" cotton mill marched down Santiago's main thoroughfare in a demonstration of their new protagonism and their support for the Allende government. Photograph by Peter Winn.

banged his fist on the table and shouted out: "And right now, compañeros! We are going on strike and we won't go back to work so long as those sharks are inside!" And all the old-timers shouted their approval. It was overwhelming.

Meetings with President Allende

RAMÓN FERNÁNDEZ: The president received me . . . He dressed me down for half an hour, saying, "I told you this could *not* be!" I asked him, "What would *you* say to two thousand workers who are all on their feet demanding socialization . . . demanding that the president fulfill his promises? . . . What would you say? 'No, you can't'? They would throw me out of there feet first!" At that point, Allende touched the bell and [four of his key advisors including the heads of the Communist and Socialist parties] entered. And he began to spout pure nonsense: "I am the one who gives orders here, and I do not agree that Yarur should be incorporated into the social property area right now. . . ."

There was a big argument that lasted more than an hour . . . and I had to tell the story of Yarur all over again. . . . [The Communist Party president] Luís Corvalán argued: "We have to make the workers understand that this is going to be a legal action, which will mean a delay of four or five days, but that the enterprise is going to pass into the socialized sector." Allende responded, "If I give a green light to this one, there is going to be another and another and another, just because one was already gotten out of me . . ."

Finally, Allende said he would order a study of the economic and legal situation of the enterprise, because there were various questions that were in bad shape: arrears of taxes, unpaid welfare benefits, a thousand and one legal questions, saying "We will do this study and then we will see."

Then I had to go to the factory to tell the union officers that they had to go and talk with *el compañero presidente* [that evening],[3] and all of them were scared to death at the prospect. [When we got there,] Allende asked me, "Who are these people that you have brought here? Are you the union officers? You are? Well, you had better tell me what happened there."

ANTONIO LARA: So we began to tell the whole story all over again. We explained the pressures that we were submitted to daily and the drop in production and the repression in the industry . . . and how we had drawn up a ten point petition . . . and how Yarur had rejected all of them and that we had left it up to the Assembly to decide . . . and that the compañeros had demanded that we go out on strike.

RAMÓN FERNÁNDEZ: And Allende said, "You are not going to convince *me* that the whole thing was spontaneous. There was work behind the scenes . . . an effort to motivate people to react in this way, because they wouldn't react that way by themselves."

ORLANDO ROJAS: After scolding us a bit more, Allende began to lecture us in serious tones: "Successful revolutionary processes are directed by a firm guiding hand, consciously, deliberately—not by chance . . . The masses can not go beyond their leaders, because the leaders have an obligation to direct the process and not to leave it to be directed by the masses . . . I am the president and it is I who give the orders here!"

RAMÓN FERNÁNDEZ: And Allende said "And this thing we are going to have to study. You have created a difficult situation by bringing all the people out on strike. Come back here on Wednesday and see if I have an answer for you."

DAVID SEPULVEDA: [The next day] Allende summoned us [the Socialist union leaders Sepulveda and Abudaye] to give us a warning . . . and in very harsh terms. We went to his house on Tómas Moro Street . . . the day after the toma . . . and well, he warned us that we had gotten out of control and that either we marched in step with the government, or we didn't march at all . . . It was practically the same as the other day . . . except that we had already heard the conversation. We didn't come to any resolution, and in the end he threw us out of his house . . . Allende seemed like a changed guy . . . because he saw that he was dancing on a tightrope in those moments.

EDUARDO CÁDIZ: [The following day,] we had a duel with el compañero president [in the presidential palace]. Straight out Compañero Allende said that there would be no requisition. Then he really blasted our ear drums. He said that the workers by themselves could not make decisions. That if he had been elected president, it was to plan in conjunction with them, but not to leave him on the sidelines of the decisions that the government should take. That if what they wanted was to have a government that would play the role of a figurehead, then he would resign his post, and they could elect another president . . . We responded that he knew how they did things here [at Yarur], that he had been to the factory and . . . knew how much exploitation there was at Yarur and that he had said so himself in some of his speeches. That at one time he was a friend of the Yarurs . . . and therefore Amador Yarur was taking advantage of this and had even said: "I am a friend of the president, and he is not going to abandon me" . . . that he was flaunting it in front of us. But Allende approached it by saying that we had many good arguments, but that he had the authority . . .

Then Compañero Toha [the interior minister] told us, "So! The president has made a decision that you will have an *interventor* [government manager] this afternoon with orders to start up the production lines." This would have thrown the whole process overboard, because to bring in an interventor was to deny the authority of the union leaders.

ORLANDO ROJAS: It was at that point that I intervened and told Compañero Toha that our movement was not a movement that was made for economic gain. If we asked for the requisition of the industry, it wasn't as if we were doing it thinking that we were going to gain a better salary and that we were going to line our pockets with silver, but rather that we were asking because the situation here had become unbearable, that we couldn't take it anymore, and that we were asking because we were conscious that we were doing it in the interest of the people and the government itself. The only thing that we had asked as representatives of the workers was that they [the government] should grant us this demand that was, after all, within the plans of the government, and that the Yarur workers would demonstrate thereafter with actions that they [the government] had not committed an error in granting us this right and taking this opportunity to requisition the industry.

Compañero Toha listened intently, took notes, and even got a journalist who was there to record part of it . . . Toha told us that he would stand up to the President during lunch. . . .

We returned to the factory a little demoralized and a little worried, because we really thought that they weren't going to requisition the industry just when our desire for it was greatest. We mixed with the people but didn't tell them anything. We didn't want them to know what had happened at the meeting. So we just went on with the strike. That's all.

The union officers didn't sleep that night . . . We remained with the compañeros making the rounds with them of the factory walls. Here it was really a fiesta; it didn't even seem like a strike. The workers were all happy, everybody content with what they were doing. We were receiving mutual aid from other workers. Congressmen visited us, the Mexican press came, and also the French television, all of them expecting the industry to be requisitioned and interviewing the compañeros. . . .

The Factory Is Liberated

EDUARDO CÁDIZ: [The following day,] at about 4:30 in the afternoon, [Oscar Guillermo] Garreton [the vice-minister of economy] phoned us once again and said, "Come immediately to the Ministry" . . . One last time we went over there. We arrived at about five and they told us that the government and the Popular Unity had agreed to intervene in the industry . . . Garreton showed us the requisition decree with the names of the compañeros who would be coming as government managers.

ARMANDO CARRERA: It was about seven in the evening that the news reached [the Yarur mill] that [the government] had requisitioned the factory, that they had named Interventors, and that they were all en route back to the factory. With that people began to sing and dance in the streets surrounding the factory . . . and we began to call all the people together in the Plaza Yarur alongside the factory gates . . . and at about eight at night they all arrived . . . the three interventors arrived . . . along with Compañero Garreton, and they called an assembly.

RAMÓN FERNÁNDEZ: I also went to that assembly . . . When they announced that the enterprise was requisitioned, there were women crying with joy, Old-timers embracing each other. They embraced each other crying: "The Yoke is lifted!" It was really moving.

ORLANDO ROJAS: The joy was really indescribable . . . something very difficult to translate into words successfully . . . It was a very special moment . . . all joy and happiness, as at last we had achieved something that had cost so much, for which moreover we had struggled so hard and so long, something for which so many had been fired and remained without work . . . there were Old-timers there who remembered all this, and when I entered with the Compañero Ministro [Pedro Vuskovic, minister of the economy] and some of these compañeros approached us to embrace me and greet me, it was with tears in their eyes. They also embraced the Compañero Ministro. Many of the women workers kissed him and . . . it was very special, you understand. It was the kind of thing that remains in your mind forever . . . At bottom, there was a sense of . . . *liberation*.

OSCAR GUILLERMO GARRETON [VICE MINISTER OF ECONOMY]: The requisition of Yarur was very special. For someone like myself . . . from the middle class and the university, it was thrilling . . . In the square between those two huge factory buildings, there were workers singing, dancing, crying . . . I have talked thousands of times about "the Chilean Revolution," but this was the first time that I really understood what it was.

Translated by Peter Winn

Notes

1. The history of the Yarur cotton mill and its workers is explored in Peter Winn, *Weavers of Revolution: The Yarur Workers and Chile's Road to Socialism* (Oxford: Oxford University Press, 1986), in which parts of these testimonies also appear.
2. In Chilean working-class communities, the term *compañero* could refer to anything from a close friend or partner to a political ally. But within the context of a socialized factory like Ex-Yarur, *compañero* was a common form of address that became to the Chilean Revolution what *citoyen* (citizen) was to the French Revolution, a leveling term of address that replaced hierarchical terms like *Don* or *caballero*.
3. Allende referred to himself as the *compañero presidente* in order to show that he remained a man of the people even after his election. Unlike his predecessors, he would not be known as the "honorable" president but by this familiar phrase that reduced the social distance between himself and his supporters.

The Chilean Revolution One Year In

Salvador Allende Gossens

Allende's first year in office, particularly in the first five months, was spectacularly successful. His government's Keynesian policies restored prosperity to Chile's recessed economy, despite the U.S. covert economic hostility. The expansion of employment and consumption that resulted from Popular Unity policies benefited many poor Chileans, while the coalition's moderate policies and the promotion of participatory democracy at the grassroots relieved middle-class fears that an Allende government would be a Communist dictatorship. The Left then went on to win a majority for the first time in the municipal elections of April 1971, which the Allende government considered a popular mandate to accelerate its policies and proceeded to completely nationalize the U.S.-owned copper mines, hasten the implementation of the Christian Democratic land reform, and advance the nationalization of the banking sector by means of stock purchases. But as 1971 drew to a close, these early successes were beginning to be undermined by economic dislocations, social tensions, and political polarization.

In this November 1971 speech marking the first anniversary of his presidency, Allende gives an account of what his government has accomplished during its first year in office and warns against the growing autonomy of popular sectors and fractious politics within his own coalition, which in Allende's view threatened the advances of his administration.

I have come to render account to the People. In accordance with the Constitution, I have the duty to inaugurate the ordinary sessions of Congress every May 21st, and to render on that occasion an administrative, political, and economic account to the Congress and to the country. But we are breaking with the old molds, and year after year we will give an account of our government in this same stadium, or even larger spaces, in dialogue with the People—the key element in the Chilean revolutionary process.

I stated [a year ago] that taking power was different from conquering the government. On November 3rd [1970] we assumed the responsibility to govern this country by virtue of the popular will expressed by ballots and ratified by Congress.

Juntas de Abastecimiento y Precios (Supply and Price Committees). The JAPs in each neighborhood made sure that local merchants (pictured here) sold consumer goods at official, not black market prices. They also distributed a basket of necessary goods at subsidized prices to every family that joined the JAP, protecting Allende's social base from the worst effects of inflation and shortages. Photograph by Pedro González. Courtesy of Colección Museo Histórico Nacional de Chile.

Today I come to declare that slowly but surely we have been conquering power and producing the revolutionary changes set forth in the Popular Unity program.

The people of Chile have recovered what belongs to them. They have recovered their basic wealth from the hands of foreign capital. They have defeated the monopolies that belong to the oligarchy. This is the only way to break the chains of underdevelopment; the only way to put an end to the institutionalized violence that punished and still punishes the immense majority of the country.

Fulfilling the Program

That is why we are here: to signal that we have advanced in the construction of the Social Property Area, which is the base of the economic program, the foundation of power for the People.

We control 90 percent of what were the private banks. Sixteen among the most powerful banks . . . are today the property of Chile and its people.

More than 70 monopolistic and strategic companies have been expropriated, intervened, requisitioned, or nationalized. We are owners!

Today we can say: *Our* copper! *Our* coal! *Our* iron! *Our* nitrates! *Our* steel! The key bases of heavy industry today belong to Chile and the Chileans.

We have extended and deepened the agrarian reform process; 1,300 big estates, totaling 2.4 million hectares, have been expropriated. Sixteen thousand families are living in them today, and there is space for another 10,000 families. . . .

But . . . it is even more important to have made peasants feel that they are citizens and understand the great task of joining with the People, with the workers, in order to make it possible for our people to eat more. The peasants sow their crops the entire length of the fatherland and that represents better health and welfare for all Chileans.

For that reason we have created the Peasant Councils and we have begun to change labor relations. Today, the workers are conscious that *they* are the government, and that their attitudes have to be different. . . . For that reason, we have also sent to Congress a proposed law that will assure worker participation in the management of state enterprises and mixed ownership enterprises, and the participation of private sector workers in Production Committees. . . .

I want to signal that the Government has been concerned, through the Ministry of Agriculture, for a sector of Chileans who have been discriminated against: the Mapuches . . . the root of our race, who have always been left behind. . . .

We want the Mapuches to have equal rights . . . and we want to raise their cultural, material and political levels so that they can join with us in the great battle to liberate the Fatherland.

Income Redistribution

. . . we have come to power: to incorporate neglected groups and sectors. Our concern has been to strengthen democracy and broaden liberty through a redistribution of income, an economic liberation. This Government wants an authentic democracy and a concrete liberty for all Chileans. Democracy and liberty are incompatible with unemployment, with a lack of housing, a lack of culture, with illiteracy, with illness. How do you enhance democracy? Giving more work. Redistributing better. Constructing more housing. Giving more education, culture, and health to the People. As you can see, workers, that is what we have done.

For more than a century, this country has been punished with a brutal unemployment. In September 1970 we had an 8.3 percent unemployment rate; by September 1971 we had lowered it to 4.8 percent. . . . Another important factor to enhance democracy is to level incomes in order to diminish the tremendous inequality in remunerations of the capitalist system. . . . In 1970, wage earners received 50 percent of the national income; in 1971 they are receiving 59 percent of the national income. . . .

Economic Policy

We have sent to Congress our proposal for a law creating the different areas of the economy. . . . We want to nationalize 120 to 150 companies of Chile's more than 35,000 companies. Monopolies and the big entrepreneurs know that, after proper payment, their companies will be incorporated into the social area [public sector]. But the 35,000 or more small and middle-size entrepreneurs, industrialists, tradesmen have nothing, absolutely nothing, to fear from the People's Government. . . .

But if it is important to strengthen democracy by all these means, it is also necessary to understand that a revolution cannot be defended only through political measures. For this reason I talked frankly to the People on May 1st, calling for a great campaign to raise production. Today, I come to tell you the following: for the first time in the last ten years, industrial production is going to grow [in 1971] 12 percent more than in prior years. . . . All the nationalized industries have put to work their idle capacity, raising production enormously . . .

Revolutionary Character

I want to point out that what we have achieved is mainly due to the workers' response, to the workers' identification with the government. We mobilized the masses in order to defend our copper, we needed and got the People's support for the expropriations and nationalizations; we also got the workers' understanding in the battle of production; and the People have been present and mobilized, showing their political consciousness in order to dissuade the counterrevolution. A vigilant people is the supreme guarantee of the stability of the revolutionary government, which the People have created.

But I want to reiterate. Nobody who really knows the Marxist doctrine can doubt the revolutionary character of the Chilean Popular Government and the road it chose and is following. There is no revolution without a transformation of social structure. Every Revolutionary Government has the obligation to keep public order. Both premises are united in our own Government.

The public order of a Revolutionary Government is not the public order of a bourgeois democracy. Our public order is based on social equality; persuasion is its tool. That is the order we need in order to make structural changes. It is the order of the People made Government, it is the public order of a revolutionary country. . . .

That is why we need the workers to be present in every act of life with their class consciousness and their revolutionary will. That is why we do not accept pressure. We have said it with the honesty of revolutionaries: we are against the indiscriminate seizures of rural estates, which create anarchy in production and which will end up pitting peasants against peasants or peasants against small farmers. (Applause.)

We are against the seizure of housing that harms the workers who saved the payments to buy them. We are against the take-over of small and middle-size factories by their workers; the nationalization and requisition of enterprises have to obey a government plan and not the anarchy of the voluntaristic impulses of a few factory workers. . . .

The Authentic Chilean Road to Socialism

. . . and here we are, traveling the Chilean Road to Socialism in order to make our revolution without mentors or tutors, according to Chile's history: a pluralistic, democratic, revolution in liberty, comrades. . . .

We Chileans have done more during this year than was done during the first year of the Cuban revolution—and I say this without diminishing the Cubans. I am going to ask Fidel Castro about this when he comes here; but I know what his answer will be. Also keep in mind that we have made our revolution without social costs. I can assure you that there is no other country in the world that has taken the revolutionary road with the [low] social costs of your People's Government. We have done this together, and this has a great value in terms of human lives and for the economy of the country.

That's why I want to point out that the solid base of the revolutionary process is a conscious, organized, and disciplined people with political parties that loyally understand unity, the workers organized in their unions, in their federations, in their Central Unica [labor union confederation]. And because this is a road within the legal order, the Armed Forces and the Carabineros [Chile's militarized national police]—I say it and I underline it—are part of that base. To them, to the people in uniform, I render homage for their loyalty to the Constitution and the popular will expressed through the ballots by the citizens. . . .

Political Pluralism

In order to win [state] power, the [class] conscious workers first have to win a majority [of the votes]. This cannot be achieved by creating a climate of insecurity, and eventually of chaos and violence . . . We cannot avoid the fact that, objectively, the middle and petit bourgeoisie are, and have to be, on our side. Similarly, we need the support of the middle and small producers, artisans, shopkeepers, technicians and professionals.

That is why, now more than ever, we have to be conscious of what is the Chilean road, a road that is authentically ours, a road of pluralism, democracy, and freedom. This is the road that opens the door to Socialism. . . .

A revolution is a process with stages that we have to observe. The singularity of Chile's revolution is maintaining public order and adjusting the legal and institutional order to the new social reality, and not the other way around. . . .

Self-Criticism

Today we have fulfilled one stage [of the revolutionary process]. We have advanced, we have realized goals, we have made conquests. The People are with us. But it is necessary to make a self-criticism.

We have to end sectarian politics and political exclusion. . . .

We have to end centralization and bureaucracy. . . .

We have to make it understood that the political quota system for public offices cannot be the base of the Popular Unity. . . .

We have to end dogmatism. . . .

We must end absenteeism in the workplace. . . .

Compañeros[1] workers: . . . I thank you for your attention and stress what our revolution means: it is authentically Chilean. But millions of people beyond our borders look with passion and interest on what we are doing. The Chilean revolution is also the revolution of the dependent countries struggling for their liberation.

Translated by Enrique Garguin

Note

1. Here, a common form of address that became to the Chilean revolution what *citoyen* (citizen) was to the French Revolution, a leveling term of address that replaced hierarchical terms like *Don* and *caballero*. See notes 2 and 3 in the preceding chapter.

Women Lead the Opposition to Allende: Interview with Carmen Saenz

*Even as electoral support for Popular Unity grew over time, Allende's political op-
ponents became increasingly visible and vocal. They included significant numbers
of women, who came to play an important role in creating the conditions for a successful military coup. Led by female members of opposition parties, middle- and
upper-class women first took to the streets in December 1971 in the "March of the
Empty Pots," a dramatic anti-Allende protest in which participants beat noisily on
pots in order to draw attention to alleged consumer shortages and the accelerating
inflation affecting their families.[1] The unprecedented presence of upper- and middle-
class women in these street demonstrations had a major impact, as did the participation of "Fatherland and Liberty," a right-wing paramilitary group that showed
up to "protect" the female protestors. Encouraged by their success, the anti-Allende
women's movement coalesced in Poder Femenino (Feminine Power), a group that
became the visible face of an increasingly strident opposition. As electoral and legislative strategies repeatedly failed to hold the Allende government in check, Poder Femenino's protests against Popular Unity became more explicitly political and their
demands more extreme, culminating in 1973 in public calls for Allende's overthrow.*

*In this interview conducted by the scholars Lisa Baldez and Margaret Power in
the early 1990s, Carmen Saenz, vice-president of the rightist National Party and a
Poder Femenino leader, explains the reasons for her outspoken opposition to Popular Unity.[2] Her account reflects the dominant ideological critiques and anti–Popular Unity propaganda launched by the Right and the Christian Democratic Party
during 1972–1973, which argued that the Popular Unity was responsible for food
shortages and that a privileged minority with ties to the Popular Unity enjoyed
access to basic goods at low prices unavailable to the rest of the population, and
accused Allende supporters of instigating street violence (ignoring the leading role
of the armed, neo-fascist Fatherland and Liberty in the street violence). The interview also reflects the opposition's central claim that in supporting a military
coup to replace a democratically elected government, they were acting in defense
of democracy.*

Women took to the streets to march with pots and pans during the Allende years. They confronted something that was destroying their homes, education, and the country's morality. And you could see how they took to the streets and confronted the resistance forces of the Allende government, and defended what was theirs. . . .

The discontent was so great—there were long lines to buy a kilo of bread—that was what it was like. In the *poblaciones* [shantytowns] people had to depend on the JAPs [Supply and Price Committees], which were the Popular Distribution Boards that the government used to give food to its supporters. For example, there would be only so much chicken, and they would divide it and sell it within a certain circle to get enough money to buy a piece of meat. In order to buy bread, meat, or anything else you had to wait in line and take a number. But the black market was immense—to the extent that if you had money you could go and buy some flour and bake your bread at home. There was no fuel. It was worse than a country in the middle of a revolution or a country after a war, where a very small sector of the population had everything and the rest of the people didn't have anything. So there were radio stations that began to carry on a campaign that we should speak out in order to discredit the government, a government that was discrediting itself, one that had even been declared unconstitutional by the Chamber of Deputies on August 23rd in the year of the military coup. . . .

This march of the pots and pans was not my idea. I always had meetings with people from the shantytowns, from the Mothers' Centers,[3] people who had worked with me on the 1958 presidential campaign of Don Jorge Alessandri . . . and we began to get together. There was a short, stocky girl, a woman who was really lower class, and she said, "Why don't we take to the streets with empty pots and pans and bang on them?" I think this had been done in a small town in Brazil. And so through Radio Agricultura and Radio Cooperativa[4] we began to work with an extraordinary journalist, Carmen Puelma . . . she began to work with the radio stations to invite people with whom we were going to unite. One day I met with her. I was the vice-president of the National Party. . . . We met with the different political parties, the Christian Democrats, the Radical Party . . . and the leaders of the National Party, and we agreed not to use party banners, only Chilean flags and an empty pot. We agreed to meet at Baquedano Plaza.[5] When I arrived there was nobody . . . But at five in the afternoon, women, women, and more women began to arrive in buses and then all at once there were huge numbers of women and we began to march toward downtown in an orderly fashion . . . Of course when they saw how many of us there were they

"March of the Empty Pots," early 1970s. This photograph expresses the moment in December 1971 when middle- and upper-class women first marched banging empty pots to protest consumer shortages that would become serious in 1972–1973. During those years, protesting women would become the visible face of the opposition to Allende and his road to socialism. Photographer unknown. Courtesy of the Photographic Archives of *El Mercurio*.

began to send people to scare us away. They began scaring us off by throwing pellets and rocks . . . they took up positions in what is now the Diego Portales [Gabriela Mistral] building, which was being built at the time, and from there they began to throw rocks. That was like lighting a fire . . . That's what woke the men up, it was like, "Hey, where are you guys?" After that people began to understand. We had to push the military men to take this burden off of us. And we threw chicken feed at any military man who passed by, as a way of telling him that he was a coward, a chicken. . . .

Factories were taken over and production stopped. To buy a diaper you had to go to Buenos Aires and buy cloth because at that time there were no disposable diapers. When a woman got married, she couldn't find cloth for her sheets because all the factories had been taken over. Nobody was working. For me, this was like the end of a party, like when the whole cake has been eaten and only crumbs are left, when you wanted to taste the cake for yourself. There was nothing left to destroy in Chile, this is really what happened. Unfortunately young people today didn't live through it, but if you talk to anyone who is a little older, they'll tell you the same thing. You were afraid then to send your kids to school because the Ministry of Education and the Ministry of Foreign Affairs were running the educational system in much the same way as the Russians ran theirs. The Chamber of Deputies and the Catholic Church both rejected this system.[6]

There were so many things that happened in those three years. It was a very short period in the country's history, and many people have forgotten all that happened, such as the number of deaths caused by the violence, how people killed others just for the sake of killing . . .[7] In sum, I don't regret anything that happened. First and foremost, I have always supported democracy, and I always supported the September 11th military coup because Chile had no other alternative.

Translated by Ryan Judge

Notes

1. In December 1971, there were few consumer shortages, and inflation, which had been low by Chilean standards in 1971, was only beginning to accelerate. During 1972–1973, both would become serious economic problems.

2. The editors would like to thank Margaret Power and Lisa Baldez for their permission to use this interview. The movement of rightist women and their role in the opposition to and overthrow of the Allende government is explored in Margaret Power, *Right-Wing Women in Chile: Feminine Power and the Struggle Against Allende, 1964–1973* (Philadelphia: Penn State University Press, 1998), and women's political mobilization on the right and the left, under Allende and Pinochet, is examined in Lisa Baldez, *Why Women Protest: Women's Movements in Chile* (Cambridge: Cambridge University Press, 2001).

3. Mothers' Centers: community organizations, first formed under President Frei, that offered state assistance to women in poor districts and also served as instruments of political mobilization for both the Left and the Right.

4. Key opposition radio stations that received aid and advice from the CIA in its "covert action" to destabilize the Allende government.

5. Plaza Baquedano, better known as the Plaza Italia, is the midpoint of Santiago and a common start and end point of political demonstrations.

6. The Unified National School (ENU) reform of 1973 was a plan to secularize public and parochial school curricula and replace them with a combination of socialist and "traditional Chilean values." This reform proposal, which was never approved by Congress, prompted widespread opposition from the Church and among the middle and upper classes and became a potent rallying cry for the opposition.

7. Approximately 100 Chileans died in political conflicts during the Allende regime: three-quarters of them were killed by opposition groups such as Fatherland and Liberty.

"So That Chile Can Renew
Its March Forward"

Chilean Business and Professional Associations

Chile's road to socialism was beset not only by the intransigence of Allende's po-
litical opponents in Congress but also by the increasing mobilization of upper- and
middle-class business owners and professionals against the regime. By September
1972, Christian Democratic and leftist congressional leaders had failed to reach a
compromise deal on Allende's proposed socialist reforms, further polarizing politi-
cal debate and fueling an opposition movement that spilled out from the corridors
of Congress into the streets, which were filled with ever more frequent and violent
protests. In October of that year, truck owners in the distant southern province of
Aysén launched a strike to protest a plan to create a public sector trucking enterprise
in that province, a movement that mushroomed rapidly into a nationwide trucking
and bus service boycott, widespread lockouts of workers by their employers, and
strikes led by the gremios, *powerful trade associations of business owners and pro-*
fessionals that were closely connected to opposition parties and movements financed
covertly by the CIA.

The goals of the so-called October Strike were revealed in "The Demands of
Chile," a statement published in the national press and signed by fifteen student,
professional, and business gremios. This manifesto openly called for the rever-
sal of Allende's policies, including the reprivatization of key industries, an end to
agrarian reform, and prohibition of Allende's use of executive decree powers. It also
revealed how Allende's opponents sought to paralyze the economy and create the
conditions for congressional impeachment or a military coup. Their list of demands
made it clear that the Popular Unity government faced active opposition not only
from an increasingly militant and radicalized political Right, which controlled the
judiciary and the Congress, but also from ever more hostile upper- and middle-class
business and professional associations.

Due to the country's current situation, the National Command for Trade Association Defense presents "the Demands of Chile," which contains immediate and definitive measures to be taken for the good of the country.

Respect for Trade Association Freedom and Rights: Within the country's democratic system, every trade association has the right to present its demands and points of view in the same form as every other worker's organization and has the right not to have its legal status attacked. In this regard we demand the following:

(a) The immediate cancellation of all the court cases and government actions against trade association leaders and members, as well as the immediate freeing of them throughout the country.
(b) The immediate rehiring of any worker—including professionals, functionaries, technicians, employees and workers—who has been fired because of their trade association actions. The immediate cancellation of any repressive measures that have been taken, or will be taken, against these workers. These measures include transfers, working conditions, etc.
(c) The immediate return to their legitimate owners of properties requisitioned or confiscated since August 21st, along with any corresponding compensation payments, including payments for damages that said properties may have suffered. . . .

The Complete Restitution of the Right to Information and Expression, so that trade associations can exercise their freedom effectively—by any means of communication, freely and without a prior censorship—our right to transmit opinions and information. In this regard, we demand the following:

(a) The immediate end to the obligatory national network of radio stations and respect for the Republic's General Accounting Office ruling on the Supreme Decree that forms the base of such a measure.[1]
(b) The cancellation of orders to suspend broadcasts of Radio Agricultura of Los Angeles and of any other radio station whose operations have been suspended, without restrictions of any kind.[2]
(c) The end of the slow asphyxiation of La Papelera paper company and the immediate establishment of fixed, fair paper prices as determined by law, in accordance with the real costs and the findings of technical studies, which have the support of the workers of that company.[3] Keep this industry in private hands, thus guaranteeing the existence of free enterprise.

(d) The immediate publication in the *Diario Oficial*[4] of the law that finances radio stations and establishes the extension of university television channels in the times that congress approves.

(e) The immediate cancellation of charges against journalists that have been filed because of the trade associations' strike.

Changes That Are within the Law

The process to change laws must conform to the Constitution and be legal. It must also respect the will of the people, as expressed in the National Congress. In order to have a functional rule of law, the State must respect the Judiciary's ability and authority to issue rulings.

(a) The immediate passage of the constitutional reform regarding the economy as Congress has expressed it, or submit this reform to a PLEBISCITE within 48 hours.

(b) The sending of the proposed Bank Reform law that rejects the concept of a sole banking system to Congress within 48 hours. We also demand the immediate end of the administrative measures adopted by the Central Bank to nationalize and centralize credit and foreign trade.

(c) The strict implementation of the current Agrarian Reform law as well as sanctions for those functionaries who do not enforce it.

(d) The inclusion with an "Urgent" designation of the proposed Law of Guarantees for Small and Medium-sized Enterprises in the agenda of the Extraordinary Legislative Session [of the Congress], accepting the trade associations' proposals for it.

(e) The complete respect for the competency and integrity of the judiciary, an end to the smear campaign against it, and the implementation of judicial rulings. . . .

Workplace Safety and an End to the Violence

In order for the country to work and produce in a useful manner, it is absolutely imperative that we have peace, a sense of calm, and freedom in the workplace. In this regard, we demand the following:

(a) The immediate publication in the *Diario Oficial* of the law on arms control that Congress has already approved.[5]

(b) The disarming of violent groups within 24 hours.

(c) The expulsion, within 48 hours, of those foreign extremists who are in the country illegally and whom the corresponding official services have detected. They are intervening in politics by forming and training armed groups.

(d) The application of the Law of Internal State Security without distinction among the violent groups.

The Freedom for Chileans to Leave or Enter the Republic

We demand the following:

(a) The immediate cancellation of the currency controls that the Central Bank imposed illegally as well as the Internal Taxes that have created a bureaucratic wall that prevents Chileans from freely leaving the country, or traveling freely within it.

Political Control

We demand the immediate end to political and economic controls. We demand the immediate termination of the controlling actions of the JAPs, CUPs, and the Self-defense Committees of the Revolution because they are totalitarian organizations.[6] . . .

We are adopting a position of solidarity among trade associations because of the deep and inalterable principles of democracy and freedom that drive us. We will only consider these NATIONAL DEMANDS satisfied once the petitions contained herein are met.

Signed,

National Confederation of Chilean Truck Owners
Confederation of Retail Commerce and Small Industry in Chile
Central Chamber of Commerce of Chile
The National Confederation of Small Industry and Artisans
National Confederation of Agrarian Reform Cooperatives and
    Settlements
National Confederation of Small Farmers of Chile
National Confederation of Agricultural Workers of the United Agricul-
    tural Provinces
National Manufacturers Society (Sofofa)
Provincial Bank Council of Santiago
Chilean Chamber of Construction Enterprises

United Command of Professional Associations in Conflict
National Front of Professionals
Student Federation of the Catholic University of Chile
National Confederation of Taxi Drivers of Chile
Federation of Private Education Employees

Translated by Ryan Judge

Notes

1. Allende used his executive powers occasionally to form a national radio network that ensured that all stations would broadcast presidential speeches and other public announcements. His opponents argued that this deprived opposition radio stations of their ability to criticize the government.

2. Radio Agricultura was a right-wing radio station in southern Chile whose operations were suspended by the government when it was accused of inciting violence on the air.

3. La Papelera, Chile's largest paper company, had close ties to right-wing parties and successfully resisted the Allende government's attempt to take it over. The government then used other measures, such as price controls, to weaken La Papelera and its domination of Chile's paper supply, prompting opposition claims that government measures threatened freedom of the press.

4. The *Diario Oficial* was a government "newspaper" that published government decrees and other official communications.

5. The Arms Control Law authorized the armed forces and police to raid any place where illegal arms were suspected to be, on the basis of evidence as limited as anonymous tips.

6. Popular Unity organizations with diverse functions that all mobilized in support of Popular Unity during the October Strike.

The Demands of the People

Movement of the Revolutionary Left

Chile's Movement of the Revolutionary Left (MIR) dated back to 1965, when it was founded in Concepción by university students with strong Socialist Party ties and a diverse older generation of Trotskyists, Maoists, and anarchists. It evolved into a guerrilla group influenced by Che Guevara and the Cuban revolution and spent the late 1960s preparing for "armed struggle" against the Chilean "bourgeois state." But when Allende was elected president, the MIR (which was not part of the Popular Unity coalition) shelved those plans, put down its arms, and began organizing at the grassroots, focusing in particular on groups that had not already been organized by the rival Communist and Socialist parties. The MIR's goal was to radicalize Allende's road to socialism, making its "reformism" revolutionary. It had a strong impact on the rural revolution, promoting land occupations that accelerated agrarian reform in indigenous areas of southern Chile as well as in the Central Valley, the country's rural heartland. It also played a key role in the movement of urban pobladores (shantytown residents), transforming recently seized empty lots into planned squatter communities that were impressive for their organization, internal democracy, and political activism. The MIR was less successful in winning acceptance among the urban working class, which tended to support the leftist parties of the Popular Unity coalition, the Communist and Socialist parties. The MIR became the conscience of the Chilean revolutionary left, offering critical support to the Allende government while pushing for more sweeping revolutionary measures.

In this selection, the MIR analyzes the lessons of the October Strike and juxtaposes against the "Demands of Chile," published by the "bourgeois" strikers, a revolutionary vision of the "Demands of the People." The MIR opposed the incorporation of military officers into Allende's cabinet, promoted a strategy of class conflict (as opposed to Allende's much-vaunted cross-class alliance), and advocated direct democracy and poder popular, a people's power constructed through "revolutionary" popular organizations, including municipal councils of workers, peasants, and pobladores and a national "people's assembly." Taken together, the "bosses' manifesto" and the MIR's rejoinder reflect the increasingly irreconcilable perspectives that characterized Chile's polarized political climate.

In response to the demands of the bosses, we present the demands of the working class, the rural and urban poor, and all Chilean workers.

I. The Bosses' Strike

1. The Bosses' Strike and Civil Resistance were designed to paralyze the country so that they could overthrow the government and oppress the people. Those have been the goals of the wealthy owners who control transportation, trade, industry and agriculture. Their economic and political power is still immense. They use it to capitalize on the permanent campaign of sabotage that they have carried out since September 4, 1970.

2. The bosses displayed all of their force with the trade and transportation strike. The petit bourgeoisie used its privileges within Congress, the Office of the Comptroller and the Courts. They displayed the power of their wealth. But they could not paralyze the country because the workers and the People kept it going. At the same time, they have been unable to drag officials and soldiers into their dirty and criminal acts. . . .

II. We Do Not Need The Bosses

1. These events have taught us that the workers do not need the bosses in order to make the economy work. Through their desperate attempts to paralyze the country, they have revealed their parasitic nature to the nation. They have isolated themselves along with a small constituency of those who control the privileged sectors. THE CONCLUSION IS CLEAR: WE DO NOT NEED THE BOSSES. The bosses have attacked the People, and they will continue to do so. But they did not achieve their goals. . . .

2. They want to return to the "normalcy" of before, which means that we would go backward and become weak like we were before. THEY WANT TO KEEP THE TOOLS THAT HAVE ALLOWED THEM TO CONTINUE SABOTAGING PRODUCTION, WITHHOLDING INVESTMENT, SPECULATING, WASTING RESOURCES, AND BECOMING EVEN RICHER THROUGH THE BLACK MARKET. That would enable the bosses to create the conditions to overthrow the government and savagely oppress the workers by making them pay in blood for the fear that we have made them feel. That is why we, as workers, cannot ease up in this struggle. To do so would allow the capitalists to return to the "normalcy" of twenty days ago. It would allow them to take back the control that they held over industry, agriculture, transportation, trade, the press, and the institutions of the State.

"Soldiers, don't fire on the people!" In this poster, photographed just days before the coup, the MIR appealed to the conscience of the conscript army as a way to forestall military intervention. Photo by Peter Winn.

III. The Tasks of the Workers

1. Our recent efforts have left us extraordinarily strong. We have strengthened our organization, and people are more politically conscious than before. The working classes in the country and city have reinforced their leadership roles among the poor and all of society. As the workers and the People, we are the primary strength that will allow us to advance, confront, and defeat the bosses and their politicians.

2. Throughout this movement we have created new organizations, THE MUNICIPAL COUNCILS OF THE WORKERS, which will greatly increase our

strength. From these councils we workers, poor farmers, and students will make our enemies feel the power of our movement with THE PEOPLE'S DEMANDS.

3. Part of the people, the soldiers, have confronted as never before the social and political activities of a class that is fighting fiercely and unscrupulously to preserve its privileges. They [the soldiers] have seen the actions of the People that they are a part of, that have proven themselves capable of maintaining production, feeding and transporting the People, and defending Chile's wealth from the sabotage of the bosses.

IV. Let's Build The Road Toward Popular Power

1. Given recent political conditions, including the isolation and exposure of the bosses, as well as the strength of the working class and the People, these DEMANDS will unite us and provide us with a clear sense of direction for each of our attacks.

The Immediate Tasks of the Working Class, Workers, and the People

The working class and the People currently face the fundamental political task of moving from an essentially defensive position against the bosses' attacks toward one of openly attacking the exploiters. The actions of the working class during the bosses' strike have created a new relation of power between the proletariat and the bourgeoisie within factories. This new relation not only allows the working class and the People to "normalize" the productive apparatus and distribution systems, but demands that they go one step farther. The working class must take greater control. It must take greater control of the economic system by nationalizing the large companies that were taken over or occupied during the capitalist strike. The workers must now take control of every sector in which the working class has advanced sufficiently to do so. . . .

On the political front, the crisis cannot be solved by negotiating concessions and alliances with a few high-ranking military officers, but rather with every soldier and officer, regardless of rank, who supports the People's Demands. The military cabinet is a political alliance, and the People only make political alliances with those who support and take part in our movement. We need to carry out a permanent offensive that will be communicated through the People's Demands, and have support from the working class and popular masses.

By mobilizing workers, this movement will be able to develop, strengthen, extend and multiply the early efforts to create an alternative form of popular power that has already begun to appear in the form of dozens of coordinating committees across the country. These coordinating committees are the birthplace of the Workers' Municipal Councils. They are tools for organizing and mobilizing the working class and popular masses in the struggle for power. . . .

ONLY SOCIALISM CAN SOLVE THE PROBLEMS OF THE WORKING CLASS, WORKERS AND THE PEOPLE BECAUSE SOCIALISM IS POWER FOR THE PEOPLE, THE EMPOWERMENT OF THE PEOPLE.

Translated by Ryan Judge

"A Treasonous History"

A Group of Retired Generals and Admirals

*The Popular Unity also tried to promote a cultural revolution, in which the govern-
ment sought to extend the benefits of literary culture and education to the majority of
Chileans and to raise political consciousness in the process. To this end, the Allende
government nationalized Zig-Zag, the country's largest publisher, and transformed
it into a "revolutionary" press. Editorial Quimantú—a Mapuche word meaning
"know the sun"—was a commercial and political success, publishing books at low
cost for Chileans with limited reading skills. In August 1973, the press published*
Chapters in the History of Chile, *a highly revisionist popular history of Chile that
challenged such nationalist conventional wisdoms as the heroism of Chile's founding
father, Bernardo O'Higgins, and triumphalist accounts of Chile's role in the War of
the Pacific. The author's provocative pseudonym, "Ranquil," alluded to a notorious
1934 rebellion and then massacre of rural workers by the Chilean army. This unconventional history unleashed a controversy that illustrated the culture wars of the era
and cast a prophetic pall over Chilean political life. A group of retired military officers
published a letter of protest in* El Mercurio, *the leading opposition newspaper, denouncing Editorial Quimantú for its "high treason" and "slander" and summoning
all patriotic Chileans to a public event commemorating Bernardo O'Higgins.*

*The generals' letter illustrates the strong sense of nationalism and honor that
informed military identity and the way in which the past, not just the present or
future, became a subject of heated contention in the polarized climate of the Popular
Unity's final days in government. The letter also demonstrated military intolerance
for ideas it opposed, presaging the censorship and lack of freedom of thought that
would characterize the dictatorship to come. Shortly after the military coup that
followed a few weeks later, Editorial Quimantú was closed and reprivatized.*

With astonishment, the public has become aware of the publication of the
work *Chapters in the History of Chile*, which is dedicated to our workers in
the city and the country. A considerable number of these books have been
distributed to these workers, which is why it is difficult to find this book in
the market.

This work, which it would be impossible to analyze completely here—

countering this pile of malicious stories, adorned with the most false and obscene interpretations of our national achievements and the actions of our most illustrious men—uses a well-known pseudo-scientific approach to analyze our History. It is enough to cite only two cases to see that it constitutes a true sacrilege against the entire Fatherland. First, the book systematically denigrates the memory of the Father of the Fatherland, Captain General Don Bernardo O'Higgins Riquelme. Second, the work simply represents a betrayal that could seriously jeopardize the nation's international prestige and its national patrimony.

O'Higgins is presented as a persecutor of the patriots who were more audacious than himself in the struggle for independence; as a servant of the Creole oligarchy; as a traitor who plotted with the Royalists; as an instrument of [Argentina's] General San Martín; as a supporter of the monarchical system; and finally as an exploiter of slaves at his hacienda in Peru during his exile. We all know that this is the vilest plot of whimsical interpretations, the product of a sectarian and deviant mind.

And now the treason. The war of 1879–1884,[1] that great enterprise that fills us with legitimate pride, is interpreted as an imperialist act of plunder that benefited the Chilean capitalist bourgeoisie and harmed their Peruvian and Bolivian counterparts. And about the military glory that we won: nothing. Such a dogmatic and sectarian interpretation is treason, because it fuels the revenge of our past adversaries, one of whom makes no mystery about it and points to 1979 as the "Year of Revenge." . . . These examples are clear enough to demonstrate the general framework of the book that has been published with the clear objective of changing consciousness.

So much slander, such pointed treason must not go unpunished. This is why we are calling a meeting to make amends to the memory of the Father of the Fatherland, Captain General Don Bernardo O'Higgins, and to our history, which has been so deeply offended.

We do not doubt that your patriotism will make you answer our call and that whatever the sacrifices may be, we will be able to count on the massive expression of true Chilean spirit on August 22nd, according to the instructions that we will make available beforehand in the Santiago press.

Translated by Ryan Judge

Note

1. A reference to the War of the Pacific, a conflict in which Chile defeated an alliance of Peru and Bolivia, seized the nitrate-rich deserts of what is today Chile's Norte Grande, and deprived Bolivia of its access to the sea. The conflict has served as a focal point for Chilean nationalism.

United States Policy and Covert Action against Allende

The Church Committee

Despite the U.S. government's official position of tolerance toward the Allende administration, covert activities by the CIA, State Department, and diplomatic corps, as well as economic policy, suggest a different story. As President Allende declared before the United Nations General Assembly in 1972: "We are the victims of almost invisible actions, usually concealed with remarks and statements that pay lip service to respect for the sovereignty and dignity of our country."[1] Such "invisible actions" included the Nixon administration's unofficial economic blockade, which denied Chile loans, investments, credit lines, and aid, as well as the interference of U.S. companies such as International Telephone and Telegraph and Kennecott in Chilean affairs. They included a U.S. government outlay of some $7 million on covert activities and the cultivation of ties with military officers and civilian elites. Overall, these actions were aimed at creating the political, social, and economic conditions propitious for a military coup to overthrow Allende.

After that coup came to pass, the U.S. Senate Intelligence Committee convened to investigate rumors of U.S. involvement in the sequence of events. Chaired by Senator Frank Church, the committee produced a staff report in 1975, "Covert Action in Chile, 1963–1973," that for a generation became the official story of U.S. interference in Chile's internal politics during a crucial decade of Chilean history.[2] The excerpt here provides an overview of the committee's findings with regard to the political rationale for and basic contours of U.S. involvement in Chile from 1970 to 1973. Documents declassified much later revealed that both the CIA and Nixon's national security advisor, Henry Kissinger, covered up the full extent of U.S. involvement in their testimony to the Church committee. Although the Church report's deliberate omission of the activities of the U.S. Defense Intelligence Agency (DIA) makes it a less than complete account of the covert war against Allende, it remains the most important official version of U.S. secret efforts first to prevent him from becoming president and later to remove him from power. Authorized at the highest levels of the U.S. government, these efforts included bribery, kidnapping, and murder.

In his 1971 State of the World Message, released February 25, 1971, President Nixon announced: "We are prepared to have the kind of relationship with the Chilean government that it is prepared to have with us." This public articulation of American policy followed internal discussions during the [National Security Council meeting of November 6, 1970]. Charles Meyer, Assistant Secretary of State for Inter-American Affairs, elaborated that "correct but minimal" line in his 1973 testimony before the Senate Foreign Relations Subcommittee on Multinational Corporations: "The policy of the Government, Mr. Chairman, was that there would be no intervention in the political affairs of Chile. We were consistent in that we financed no candidates, no political parties before or September 8, or September 4. . . . The policy of the United States was that Chile's problem was a Chilean problem, to be settled by Chile. As the President stated in October of 1969, 'we will deal with governments as they are.'"

Yet public pronouncements notwithstanding, after Allende's inauguration the 40 Committee[3] approved a total of over seven million dollars in covert support to opposition groups in Chile. That money also funded an extensive anti-Allende propaganda campaign. Of the total authorized by the 40 Committee, over six million dollars was spent during the Allende presidency and $84,000 was expended shortly thereafter for commitments made before the coup. The total amount spent on covert action in Chile during 1970–73 was approximately $7 million, including project funds not requiring 40 Committee approval.

Broadly speaking, U.S. policy sought to maximize pressures on the Allende government to prevent its consolidation and limit its ability to implement policies contrary to U.S. and hemispheric interests. That objective was stated clearly in National Security Decision Memorandum (NSDM) 93, issued in early November 1970. Other governments were encouraged to adopt similar policies, and the U.S. increased efforts to maintain close relations with friendly military leaders in the hemisphere. The "cool but correct" overt posture denied the Allende government a handy foreign enemy to use as a domestic and international rallying point. At the same time, covert action was one reflection of the concerns felt in Washington: the desire to frustrate Allende's experiment in the Western Hemisphere and thus limit its attractiveness as a model; the fear that a Chile under Allende might harbor subversives from other Latin American countries; and the determination to sustain the principles of compensation for U.S. firms nationalized by the Allende government.

Henry Kissinger outlined several of these concerns in a background briefing to the press on September 16, 1970, in the wake of Allende's election plurality: "Now it is fairly easy for one to predict that if Allende wins, there is a good chance that he will establish over a period of years some sort of communist government. In that case you would have one not on an island off the coast which has not a traditional relationship and impact on Latin America, but in a major Latin American country you would have a Communist government, joining, for example, Argentina, which is already deeply divided, along a long frontier; joining Peru, which has already been heading in directions that have been difficult to deal with, and joining Bolivia, which has also gone in a more leftist, anti-U.S. direction, even without any of these developments.

So I don't think we should delude ourselves that an Allende takeover in Chile would not present massive problems for us, and for democratic forces and for pro-U.S. forces in Latin America, and indeed to the whole Western Hemisphere. What would happen to the Western Hemisphere Defense Board, or to the Organization of America States, and so forth, in [*sic*] extremely problematical. . . . It is one of those situations which is not too happy for American interests."

As the discussion of National Intelligence Estimate in Section IV of this paper makes clear the more extreme fears about the effects of Allende's election were ill-founded; there never was a significant threat of a Soviet military presence; the "export" of Allende's revolution was limited, and its value as a model more restricted still; and Allende was little more hospitable to activist exiles from other Latin American countries than his predecessor has been. Nevertheless, those fears, often exaggerated, appear to have activated officials in Washington.

The "cool but correct" public posture and extensive clandestine activities formed two-thirds of a triad of official actions. The third was economic pressure, both overt and covert, intended to exacerbate the difficulties felt by Chile's economy. The United States cut off economic aid, denied credits, and made efforts—partially successful—to enlist the cooperation of international financial institutions and private firms in tightening the economic "squeeze" on Chile. That international "squeeze" intensified the effect of the economic measures taken by opposition groups within Chile, particularly the crippling strikes in the mining and transportation sectors. For instance the combined effect of foreign credit squeeze and domestic copper strikes on Chile's foreign exchange position was devastating. Throughout the Allende years, the U.S. maintained close contact with the Chilean armed forces, both through the CIA and through U.S. military attachés. The basic purpose of these contacts was the gathering of intelligence, to detect any inclination within the Chilean armed forces to intervene. But U.S. officials also were instructed to seek influence within the Chilean military and to be generally supportive of its activities without appearing to promise U.S. support for military efforts which might be premature. For instance, in November 1971, the Station was instructed to put the U.S. government in a position to take future advantage of either a political or a military solution to the Chilean dilemma, depending on developments within the country and the latter's impact on the military themselves.

There is no hard evidence of direct U.S. assistance to the coup, despite frequent allegations of such aid. Rather the United States—by its previous actions during Track II, its existing general posture of opposition to Allende, and the nature of its contacts with the Chilean military—probably gave the impression that it would not look with disfavor on a military coup. And U.S. officials in the years before 1973 may not always have succeeded in walking the thin line between monitoring indigenous coup plotting and actually stimulating it.

Notes

1 Salvador Allende Gossens, "Address to the United Nations General Assembly, December 4, 1972," in James D. Cockroft and Jane Canning, eds., *Salvador Allende Reader: Chile's Voice of Democracy* (Melbourne, Australia: Ocean Press, 2000), 200–221.

2. See U.S. Senate, Select Committee to Study Governmental Operations with Respect to Intelligence Activities, Staff Report, "Covert Action in Chile, 1963–1973," Washington, D.C., 1975. See also U.S. Department of State, Freedom of Information Act website, http://foia .state.gov/Reports/ChurchReport.asp, accessed 14 May 2013.

3. The 40 Committee was an interagency group of officials convened by the U.S. Executive to oversee covert activities.

"Everyone Knows What Is Going to Happen"

Radomiro Tomíc to General Carlos Prats

By August 1973, President Allende's only hope for averting a military coup was to reach an agreement with Christian Democratic leaders, including his proposal to convene a national plebiscite on his presidency. Allende's planned announcement of the plebiscite the night before the coup was fatally delayed as he waited for a sign of Christian Democratic support, a sign that never came. Radomiro Tomíc, Allende's Christian Democratic opponent in the 1970 presidential election and the leader of his party's left wing, favored the plan for a plebiscite but was unable to convince his party. In its absence, only the constitutionalist stance of the army commander General Carlos Prats stood in the way of the coup plotters, who by this time had already made four attempts to bring down the Allende government. Prats had personally led loyal troops to crush a coup attempt in June and then rejoined Allende's cabinet, after which opposition leaders focused on ways to embarrass Prats into resigning his position; they finally succeeded in mid-August, when the wives of his army officers protested outside his house, calling him a coward for not supporting military intervention. When his generals refused to provide him with a vote of confidence, Prats resigned.

In the letter here Radomiro Tomíc, celebrated by the government newspaper as "a distinguished politician who is not afraid of telling the truth" and who inspires "faith in the Nation's destiny," paid tribute to Prats's constitutionalist loyalty and warned prophetically of an imminent military coup whose inevitability made the actions of the protagonists appear as in a "Greek tragedy." On Prats's advice, Allende named General Augusto Pinochet, the army's second in command and reputedly an apolitical "soldier's soldier," to succeed him as head of the army. Less than a month later, Pinochet would join an existing group of conspirators in the violent coup that overthrew the Allende government.

Esteemed General Prats,

We have met only occasionally through the years, and I cannot consider myself your friend in the usual sense of the word.

Maybe it is best that way because this letter does not contain personal feelings of affection, but rather objective thoughts about your actions in critical moments to promote public peace and the national interest.

I do not write you as a friend, but rather as a Chilean who expresses his solidarity and in advance, modestly associates himself with the homage that history's judgment will pay you because of your patriotic integrity and clear perception of the demands that the delicate moment in which Chile lives has placed upon you in your role as a soldier and as Commander in Chief of the Army.

That is how you acted in October of 1972, along with other distinguished representatives of the Armed Forces when you allowed for the degree of consensus necessary for the country to overcome the general strike at that time. That is how you acted in March of 1973 when you guaranteed that the parliamentary elections take place under an impartial framework on behalf of the Government. That is how it is now, in August of 1973, up to the point when you were able to do something.

A turbulent wave of bitter passion and violence—of moral blindness and irresponsibility, of weakness and abandonment that shakes every sector of the nation, and one way or another is the work of all of us— threatens to submerge the country, perhaps for many years to come.

It would be unjust to deny that some are more responsible for this than others, but while some are more and others less, all of us are pushing Chilean democracy towards the slaughterhouse.

As in the tragedies of classical Greek theater, everyone knows what is going to happen, everyone hopes that it does not happen, but each person does exactly what is needed for the tragedy to occur, even as he tries to prevent it.

And in relation to you sir, this is the responsibility that history will not place upon your shoulders if confrontation, dictatorship, systematic repression, each time deeper and bloodier, mutilate the essential unity of Chileans.

You did everything you could, as a soldier and a Chilean, to prevent it. I would not say this if I were not in a position to do so. Because of this, allow me to send you my congratulations and solidarity.

Translated by Ryan Judge

"These Are My Final Words"

Salvador Allende Gossens

The military coup that some feared and others sought, but which surprised few, finally came to pass on a gray winter morning, on Tuesday, September 11, 1973. The coup began at dawn in the naval base of Valparaíso and spread rapidly to the army and the air force. President Allende was awakened and rushed to La Moneda to take charge. At first, the Carabineros, the powerful militarized national police, remained loyal, providing Allende with his presidential guard and the hope that this coup, like the other attempts, might be thwarted. But in the end the Carabineros succumbed to the pressure of the military branches and joined the coup despite the refusal of the seven most senior Carabinero generals to betray their oath of loyalty to the civilian government. With the armed forces united, the outcome of the coup was no longer in doubt. But Allende refused to surrender, even though his presidential palace was ringed by attacking troops and tanks, denying the military junta the legitimacy it sought. It was in this context that Allende broadcast his final words to his supporters, using the one leftist radio station whose tower had not yet been destroyed by the military.

It was a spontaneous address, delivered without notes, yet it was the most eloquent, most quoted, and most remembered speech of his long political career. In it, he thanked his supporters—women, men, and youth; workers, peasants, and intellectuals—for their loyalty. Significantly, he did not call on them to risk their lives to defend him in such unequal combat: instead, the "Compañero Presidente" offered himself as a sacrifice for their loyalty and expressed his Marxist faith that the workers would win in the end, that history "is made by the people." But Allende also issued a searing indictment of those responsible for the coup, from the military commanders who led it to the foreign capitalists and Chilean elites who supported it. Chileans everywhere—from his supporters to those who promoted his ouster—clustered around their radios to listen to the president's last words.

A few hours later Salvador Allende was dead in the smoldering ruins of the presidential palace, set aflame in bombing runs conducted by Chile's own air force. Within days, armed resistance to the coup was overcome, bringing Chile's "democratic road to socialism" to a sudden, violent end. The military's devastating as-

In one of the most iconic images of the 1973 coup, army snipers lay siege to La Moneda, Chile's presidential palace and the seat of Allende's government, as army tanks and air force planes attack the smoking building on the morning of September 11, eventually setting it aflame. When Pinochet repaired the devastated eighteenth-century building after the coup, he covered and sealed shut the executive entrance on Morandé Street used by elected civilian presidents, transforming the "disappeared door" into a symbol of the military's "disappearance" of Chilean democracy and thousands of citizens. One of the first acts of the new civilian democratic government in 1990 was to repair and recondition La Moneda, and in 2003, on the thirtieth anniversary of the coup, President Ricardo Lagos, the first Socialist president since Allende, reopened the executive side entrance that the military had kept sealed since the day that it was used to remove Allende's body. Photograph by AP/Enrique Aracena, image no. 730911037. © 1973 The Associated Press. Used with permission.

sault on the presidential palace, and Allende's resistance and martyrdom, were instantly transformed in both domestic and international arenas into symbols of the military's attack on Chilean democracy and on the welfare of its people. They would serve as rallying points for civilian opposition to military rule over the next seventeen years.

Compatriots:

This will certainly be the last opportunity I have to address you. The Air Force has bombed the towers of Radio Portales and Radio Corporación.

My words do not spring from bitterness, but rather from disappointment, and these words will be the moral punishment for the men who have betrayed their oath: Chilean soldiers, the appointed commanders-in-chief as well as Admiral Merino (who appointed himself), plus the despicable

General Mendoza, who only yesterday declared his fidelity and loyalty to the government and who has also named himself Director General of the Carabineros.

In light of these events, I have only one thing to say to the workers: *I will not resign!*

In this historic juncture, I will pay with my life for the loyalty of the People. I tell you that I am certain that the seedlings that we have planted in the dignified consciousness of thousands and thousands of Chileans will not be cut short forever. They [the military] have the force. They can subdue us. But social change will not be held back by crime or by force. History is ours, and it is made by the people.

Workers of my fatherland: I want to thank you for the loyalty that you've always demonstrated, for the trust you invested in one man who merely interpreted the great longing for justice, a man who gave his word to respect the Constitution and the law, and kept that promise. In this decisive moment, the last time I will be able to speak to you, I want you to learn this lesson: foreign capital, and imperialism allied with the reactionary forces, created this climate so that the armed forces would break with their tradition [of nonintervention in politics], a tradition taught by General Schneider and reaffirmed by Commander Araya, victims of the same social class that today will be waiting in their houses to recapture power with alien hands, so that they can go on defending their properties and their privileges.[1]

Above all, I speak here to the modest women of our land; to the peasant women who believed in us; to the grandmothers who worked harder; to the mothers who understood our concern for children. I address the professionals of the nation, the patriotic professionals who for many days have continued working against the sedition sponsored by the professional associations, classist associations that also defend the benefits that capitalist society gave to just a few. I also speak to the youth, to those who sang and contributed their joy and spirit to the struggle. I address the men of Chile—the workers, the peasants, the intellectuals—those who will be persecuted because fascism reemerged in our nation some time ago, as evidenced by the terrorist acts of blowing up bridges, cutting railway lines, and destroying oil and gas pipelines, acts which were met with silence by those whose duty it was to respond to what was happening. They were committed [to this coup]. History will judge them.

Surely Radio Magallanes will be silenced, and the calm sound of my voice will no longer reach you. But it doesn't matter, for you will continue to hear it. I will always be at your side. At least I will be remembered as a dignified man who was loyal to the Fatherland.

The People should defend themselves, but not sacrifice themselves. The People should not let themselves be destroyed or shot to pieces, but they also can not let themselves be humiliated.

Workers of my Fatherland: I have faith in Chile and in its destiny. Other men will transcend this gray and bitter moment in which treason seeks to impose its will. Carry on in the knowledge that, sooner rather than later, the great avenues along which free men will pass to build a better society will open wide again.

Long live Chile!

Long live the People!

Long live the Workers!

These are my final words and I am sure that my sacrifice will not be in vain. I am certain that my sacrifice will at least serve as a moral lesson that will punish crime, cowardice, and treason.

Translated by Trevor Martenson

Note

1. General René Schneider, the constitutionalist commander-in-chief of the Chilean army, was assassinated in 1970 in a neo-fascist and CIA plot to prevent Allende's inauguration. Commander Arturo Araya Peeters, Allende's naval attaché and bridge to constitutionalist officers in the navy, was assassinated several months before the coup.

VII

The Pinochet Dictatorship:
Military Rule and Neoliberal Economics

On September 11, 1973, Chile witnessed the overthrow by a military coup of Salvador Allende's Popular Unity government, one of many democracies to fall victim to the wave of military interventions that swept Latin America during the Cold War. But it was among the most infamous, as much for the Chilean military's brutality and human rights abuses as for its evisceration of democratic norms. Yet its leader, General Augusto Pinochet, would use legal mechanisms to try to legitimize and prolong his dictatorship. When Pinochet finally relinquished power in a peaceful transition to elected civilian leadership in 1990, his seventeen-year regime had outlasted all other dictatorships in the Southern Cone, leaving behind a society deeply transformed by the military's authoritarian political and neoliberal economic projects, through which its leaders sought to permanently inoculate Chile against future revolutionary experiments and statist policies. Although Pinochet himself was eventually driven from power by a combination of resurgent social protest and Chileans' return to the ballot box, the long and difficult path to redemocratization after 1990 demonstrates just how profoundly Chile was changed by the military dictatorship.

The reasons for the military intervention of 1973 were many, both long- and short-term in their origins, the result of both domestic and international pressures. Moreover, the military coup that ousted Allende was as brutal as it was decisive, representing one of the most dramatic ruptures in Chile's modern history. For many years after the coup, the causes of the violent fall of the Allende government were fervently debated by participants and observers, with most explanations reflecting Chile's deep political divisions in 1973: while Popular Unity sympathizers pointed to the collusion of Chilean military and civilian actors with the U.S. government and private corporations, Popular Unity detractors held the Allende government and its supporters accountable for pursuing rapid, unsound economic and political strategies in their quest for revolutionary change. Now, at some decades' distance from Chile's September 11 coup, a more balanced interpretation that combines many of these factors is possible. Among them is the important role of U.S. actors in creating conditions for the successful coup: the ongoing declassification of U.S. government documents, due to the tireless work of Chilean solidarity activists and the National Security Archive (an NGO housed at George Washington University), has provided ample evidence of U.S. executive, State Department, and CIA actions to destabilize the Chilean economy and promote political and military opposition to Allende. Nor is there as much controversy about the nature of the political tensions and conflicts—both within the governing coalition and between the government and both its grassroots supporters and its opponents—that helped create the conditions for a successful military intervention. The selections in the previous part of this book offer insight into the many factors—internal and external—that combined to produce the 1973 coup.

What constitutes the focus of the selections here, then, is not the question *why* the coup occurred but what its consequences were for life in Chile during the ensuing seventeen years of military rule. This group of selections presents some of the most compelling documents and images from the period so as to show the systematic brutality of the military regime, explain its longevity, and examine its policies, which imposed profound changes at all levels of Chilean economy, society, and politics. The story of Chile's military period is also one of constant struggle, as Chilean civilians, as well as some men in uniform, denounced the authoritarian regime, defended human rights, and called for the return to democracy. What best characterizes this important period in Chilean history is the profound tension between the shifting strategies of the military leadership, which began as a collective leadership of armed forces commanders but rather quickly devolved into a highly personalistic dictatorship led by Pinochet, and Chileans' adaptation and resistance (as well as international solidarity and protest). In 1988, a combination of opposition to Pinochet and political mechanisms installed by the regime in its 1980 Constitution led to a historic national plebiscite that brought an end to the dictatorship. But the transition to democracy that followed has only partially addressed the profound changes the military regime introduced, leaving subsequent civilian governments to deal with the combined legacies of military abuse of human rights, free-market economic policies, and the legal marginalization of the Left. The demise of the military regime and the transition to civilian democracy in 1990 initiated a process of gradual change that many judge still incomplete more than two decades later.

On the fateful morning of September 11, 1973, Chileans awoke to radio reports of a military coup. Residents of Santiago watched as tanks shelled and fighter jets bombed La Moneda, Chile's presidential place, setting it aflame. Meanwhile, troops fanned out across the country detaining Popular Unity loyalists. The tenor of that day is captured in the diary of Peter Winn, a U.S. researcher living in Santiago. As a state of siege was imposed in the capital and throughout the country, military forces clamped down on leftist industrial belts, shantytowns, universities, and land reform centers, and Chile was engulfed in an unprecedented wave of systematic state violence. Among the early victims was the famed singer-songwriter Victor Jara, who was detained with students at the State Technical University on the day of the coup and executed at the nearby indoor stadium that now bears his name.

In the ensuing days and months, the ruling junta—made up of the commanders of the four branches of the Chilean armed forces, including the national police (Carabineros)—sought to destroy popular support for the Popular Unity project and publicize the "reasons for the junta." They justified the coup with the claim that Allende had brought Chile to a state of civil war in which Popular Unity supporters planned to defend their government through armed force. During the first three months of military rule, security forces subjected thousands of leftists to illegal detention, torture, and execution, with frequent recourse to "disappearance," the kidnapping and prolonged detention of civilians without the filing of criminal charges against them or acknowledging that they were being held prisoner. From the very moment the coup began, military officials disseminated throughout the country lists of hundreds of individuals wanted by the regime because of their support for the Allende government and its coalition parties or other leftist movements. As the journalist Patricia Verdugo's account of events in the northern city of Antofagasta illustrates, on learning of these orders, many Chileans turned themselves in to local officials, expecting to be rewarded for their cooperation (and innocence) with quick release. Others were taken from their homes, classrooms, offices, factories or farms, even from the streets in full daylight, and were summarily detained with no notice to friends or family of where they were being held or on what charges. This practice of forced disappearance was usually only the first step in the systematic application of state terror, in which "the disappeared" were taken to sports stadiums and secret detention centers and subjected to relentless physical and psychological torture for weeks or months or longer before their eventual execution or release. Although later official investigations put the minimum number of those disappeared and killed at 3,216—most of those occurring in the first four years after the coup—higher estimates include those whose detention or death has never been officially verified. Further, a focus on those who were "disappeared" and then executed has at times obscured the much greater numbers of civilians subjected to the regime's elaborate torture and imprisonment apparatus. A later investigation by the Valech Commission would determine that more than 38,000 civilians were imprisoned and tortured by agents of the military regime, with more than 100,000 who were tortured during military searches of *poblaciones* (shantytowns) not entering into these official calculations. The best-known cases of military repression at the time of the coup were those of prominent Popular Unity political leaders, many of whom suffered detention and severe torture at secret detention centers before negotiating their release into foreign exile. An estimated 200,000 Chileans went into exile during the military period, or 2 percent of the total population. Most of those who were swept up in the expanding network of repression in Chile were workers, peasants, and *pobladores* (the residents of shantytowns) whose participation in local political, union, community, or land reform organizations made them principal—and vulnerable—targets. By 1974, these ad hoc repressive practices were institutionalized in the Office of National Intelligence (the DINA), a permanent apparatus that was coordinated by army officials close to Pinochet and charged with the continuing surveillance, disappearance, detention, and torture of the regime's opponents. Significantly, many of those who were disappeared and executed were "punished" for actions that were not crimes when they performed them—such as working with or supporting the democratically elected government.

The overwhelming international response to the military intervention was swift and negative, but several key international actors supported it, including the U.S. government, which defended the coup with its diplomacy and quietly offered support to the military commanders and the parties of the Right. Meanwhile, the centrist Christian Democrats, long acrimonious rivals of the Popular Unity, supported the coup that ended the Allende government but expected a speedy restoration of democracy that would permit former President Eduardo Frei's return to the presidency. The military's very public and systematic violation of human rights, as well as increasingly explicit intention to remain in power indefinitely, however, led to sustained Christian Democratic opposition by 1975, although the regime enjoyed steadfast support among the Right.

Prominent in the opposition—evidenced at first through quiet actions and only later through prophetic denunciation—was the Catholic Church, which assisted victims and their families. When military leaders pressed religious leaders to cease their activities, Cardinal Raúl Silva Henríquez intervened to establish an organization wholly protected by the Catholic Church, the Vicarate of Solidarity. From its founding in 1976, the Vicarate functioned in offices adjacent to the Cathedral of Santiago (and in similar offices throughout Chile), allowing teams of lawyers, social workers, psychologists, and educators to offer support and services to those directly affected by military repression. Along with a number of other human rights groups established as the regime wore on, the Vicarate gave aid to thousands of the persecuted and documented the systematic violation of human rights.

The pattern of sustained military violence unleashed by the coup was neither novel—in terms of military dictatorships already established elsewhere in Cold War Latin America—nor contained within Chilean borders. Chilean military and security forces borrowed techniques such as disappearance and torture from other regional authoritarian regimes such as Brazil, a process facilitated by officers' shared experiences at U.S. training centers for foreign officers in Panama and the United States and the exchange of experts in interrogation techniques. These transnational linkages also multiplied Chile's impact on regional security forces, particularly after November 1976, when Manuel Contreras, a colonel in the Chilean army and director of the DINA, convened the First Interamerican Meeting on National Intelligence in Santiago. With representatives of the Argentine, Uruguayan, Paraguayan, and Bolivian security forces in attendance, the initiative known as "Operation Condor" was born. A transnational network of South American national security forces, Operation Condor established a central database of political opponents of each regime, created a communication system, and set up regular meetings for participating countries (which later included Brazil), with the goal of identifying, detaining, interrogating and often disappearing and executing "enemies" of the region's dictatorships who had escaped into exile in other participating countries. In addition, Operation Condor carried out a series of high-profile assassinations—most infamously the 1976 car-bombing of the former Allende minister and ambassador Orlando Letelier in Washington, D.C.—and regularly repatriated exiled activists to an almost certain death. As the declassified cable included here demonstrates, news of Condor's activities reached the highest level of CIA, FBI, and diplomatic communications, but the U.S. government response under presidents Nixon and Ford to these illegal activities was ambiguous and contradictory, essentially giving the green light to the operation of a South American terror network until it began to operate in Europe and the United States.

The leaders of the military regime understood the destruction of the

Popular Unity regime in global, Cold War terms as merely one step in a larger campaign to extirpate the "cancer" of Marxism and end Soviet and Cuban influence in Chile and the western hemisphere. More important, the broadening scope of repression banned not only the parties of the Left but, by 1977, the centrist Christian Democrats as well. This reflected military leaders' fundamental distrust not just of the Left but of democratic politics generally, which they portrayed as the playground of self-interested, incompetent, and irresponsible civilian leaders. Military leaders defined "real democracy" as social peace and the protection of private property, a human "right" enshrined in the military's new Constitution, which was ratified in 1980 by a fraud-ridden plebiscite. According to this fundamentally antipolitical vision of society, in a proper democracy the popular will—previously expressed in Chile through elections and popular mobilization and long venerated by the country's center and left parties—would be restrained by a controlled political system that outlawed not only Marxist ideology but all ideas or principles supposedly threatening to the nation. The military leaders' hostility to liberal democratic freedoms was also repeatedly expressed through its police apparatus (which severely punished political dissent through censorship and repression) and in a series of decree-laws through which it sought to reorder labor relations, economic development, and political activity.

By 1976, the Pinochet regime had decided to marry its authoritarian politics to a long-term project of economic transformation based on the dictates of neoclassical or neoliberal free-market economics. Pinochet's growing reliance on a group of Chilean economists influenced by the Austrian Nobel laureate Friedrich Hayek and trained by University of Chicago economists, including Milton Friedman and Arnold Harberger, set Chile on the path to aggressive neoliberal restructuring. Under the guidance of these so-called Chicago Boys, Chile became an early proving ground for economic policies that were later associated with U.S. Reaganomics and Britain's Margaret Thatcher and that as the Washington Consensus would pervade Latin America in the 1990s. Because the incoming military leaders had no experience with economic policy, they turned at first to Christian Democratic and other technocratic and business advisors in an attempt to stabilize Chile's economy and reverse the expansion of the state sector, which had accelerated under both Frei and Allende. In the first two years of military rule, virtually all the enterprises nationalized under Allende were reprivatized, with the notable exception of the copper mines, the foundation of the Chilean state's budget and military appropriations; trade barriers and tariffs were reduced or eliminated; Chilean currency was devalued and exchange rates fixed; and a series of counterinflationary measures were implemented, such as freezing wage levels, restricting the money supply, and cutting state social welfare budgets. By 1975 the still sluggish economic recovery influenced Pinochet's increasing reliance on the Chicago Boys, who inaugurated a so-called shock treatment of neoliberal economic restructuring. The combination of monetary policies, speculative investment in the deregulated financial sector, and nontraditional export promotion led to a gradual but noticeable recovery after 1975, as evidenced by the rapid growth of exports in new sectors (fruit, fish, and forest products), high annual growth rates hovering around 8 percent, low (for Chile) inflation rates of about 9.5 percent by 1979, and increased national reserves. These policies also resulted in a flood of inexpensive imports from abroad, which undermined Chile's once dynamic domestic manufacturing sector, driving many factories, notably in the textile sector, out of business. While the economic indicators appeared to reflect a Chilean economic "miracle," the period of growth between 1976 and 1981 was underwritten by a flood of inexpensive petrodollars—inexpensive loans on the global market that poured into Chile's deregulated financial sector.

Chile's widely touted "economic miracle" under the guidance of the Chicago Boy technocrats dovetailed nicely with the military regime's broader agenda of social demobilization and shrinking the state. New labor laws decreed in 1978–1981, for example, placed strict controls on labor contracts, organization, and strikes, thereby codifying employers' greater control over labor (which they had enjoyed since the coup) and further curtailing leftist influence over organized labor. As the "silent revolution" described by Joaquín Lavín here also makes clear, the military regime's social policies also "modernized" health care, pensions, and education in Chile by spurring their rapid privatization. Indeed, Chile's social security and school voucher systems are today invoked as models by those who advocate privatization elsewhere in the world—and as cautionaries by those who oppose it. They were part of the regime's so-called Seven Modernizations, through which it sought to justify its extended rule and to transform Chile.

Other more negative effects of economic restructuring were painfully evident as the regime's neoliberal reforms took effect. Despite its positive macroeconomic indicators, Chile's "economic miracle" was also associated with increased unemployment (reaching 25–30 percent by 1983), widespread poverty (affecting 45 percent of Chileans by 1988), and an increasingly unequal distribution of income (among the worst in Latin America, the world's most unequal region). Negative as well were worsening health indicators, amid declining earnings prospects for vulnerable population sectors and the privatization of Chile's historic public health care system, leaving the poor without adequate medical care at a time of growing need. Moreover, Chile's neoliberal "miracle" was fueled by speculative foreign capital attracted by the high short-term returns in Chile's unregulated financial sector and was vulnerable to external shocks. When recession hit the United States and the world economy in 1980–1981, with a general hike in interest rates to adjust to the jump in oil prices, the speculative bubble inflated by the Chicago Boys' policies burst, and Chile's major financial conglomerates went belly up, forcing the military government to renationalize a significant part of the economy, from banks and insurance companies to major industries in mining, textiles, fisheries, and forestry. It was Chile's worst economic crisis in half a century, in which the economy shrank by 14 percent during 1982–1983 and unemployment rose to 31 percent, with another 15 percent barely surviving on $1 a day public make-work programs.

The crisis also fueled a rising tide of opposition that exploded in widespread popular protest from 1983 to 1986. Despite the relative stability that marked the regime's institutionalization (most clearly reflected in the passage of the 1980 Constitution), the economic crisis of 1982–1983 sparked a new phase of protest by organized labor, the women's movement, and student and shantytown organizations, but their expectations that Pinochet would be forced by the crisis to resign proved illusory. However, the profound and lengthy crisis revealed growing dissent within the military regime and the shaky basis of an economic miracle funded largely by cheap credit and inexpensive imports during the late 1970s. A few years later, when Pinochet sought an additional eight years in power through the 1988 plebiscite, regime opponents such as Ernesto Tironi and Alejandro Foxley would use the negative effects of the regime's economic policies to discredit the narrative of "economic miracle" in Chile. Moreover, younger officers, who had risen through the ranks in Pinochet's Chile in the period after the cessation of the most egregious and public abuses of human rights, began to chafe under the regime's unyielding adherence to neoliberal economic models, its status as international human rights pariah, and the growing personalization of the regime around the figure of the aging Pinochet, who refused to let go of the reins of power. When a 1986 attempt by Communist guerrillas to assassinate him failed, Pinochet's opponents were left with only one alternative: the 1988 plebiscite on his continued rule established in his 1980 Constitution.

As Chile's political opposition gradually reemerged from the tumult of the social movements of the 1980s, the 1980 Constitution—first conceived as a mechanism to perpetuate and legitimate Pinochet's hold on power—

was reluctantly transformed into a roadmap for the return of civilian rule. When Chile's political parties of the Center-Left (except for the excluded Communist Party) merged into a unified coalition—the Concertación for the NO (i.e., the "No" vote on Pinochet's continued rule)—in February 1988, they set their sights on winning the October 1988 plebiscite, running aggressive grassroots and media campaigns to drive Pinochet from power. This strategy was not without its detractors, of course, many of whom continued to view the 1980 Constitution as fraudulent and expected the plebiscite to be as well. The Communist Party, which for decades before the coup had adhered to democratic methods of revolutionary struggle, during the 1980s responded to the Sandinista rebellion in Nicaragua and a wave of street protests and widespread repression and discontent in Chile by sanctioning armed struggle against the dictatorship. The failed assassination attempt against Pinochet undertaken by the Communist Frente Patriótico Manuel Rodríguez in September 1986, however, further marginalized the Communists from the political opposition, who now were convinced that they had no option but to contest Pinochet's 1988 plebiscite as the instrument of a transition to democracy.

In a climate of considerable fear and uncertainty—but with a liberalization of censorship and media access negotiated by the U.S. Embassy and unprecedented political participation throughout Chile—the historic plebiscite held on October 5, 1988, resulted in Pinochet's defeat by a decisive vote of 54 percent to 42 percent of the electorate. As a report by international observers illustrates, on the day of the plebiscite and in the weeks and months that followed, Chileans both celebrated the victory of the "No" and watched anxiously to see how military leaders would respond. The acquiescence of military leaders to this result, including, reluctantly, Pinochet himself, marked an extraordinary turn in an evolving political transition. The formal transition concluded with the 1990 inauguration of Patricio Aylwin Azócar, who in 1973 had led the procoup Christian Democratic opposition to Allende, as Chile's first civilian president since the coup. The country's recent history had come full circle, as Chileans used the ballot box to reassert civilian control over the government and bring Pinochet's seventeen-year dictatorial rule to an end.

Diary of a Coup

Peter Winn

In this essay, the historian Peter Winn quotes from his own diary to provide an eyewitness account of the 1973 military coup as it developed in downtown Santiago. During the September 11 military intervention, the fifth coup attempted that year, civilians gathered to observe and wonder at the spectacle, even as troops were dispatched to universities, workplaces, and private homes throughout the country, arresting, torturing, and sometimes executing former government officials and Allende supporters. Winn's testimony reflects the jarring realization—common among many Chileans—of the radical change portended by the events unfolding before them. Like other foreigners who had come to live in Chile to witness Popular Unity's experiment in democratic revolution, Winn shared in the culture of fear created by the military's unrelenting and systematic attack on the civilian population, although unlike the U.S. citizen Charles Horman, a journalist whose murder was the basis for the Costa-Gavras film Missing, *he lived to tell about it. The arrest and disappearance of foreigners in the days following the coup sparked some of the earliest criticisms of the military regime by foreign governments, although the U.S. Embassy in Chile refused to investigate or protest the disappearance of their own citizens as a result of military violence.*

I awoke at dawn on that gray and chilly late winter day, after a night of too little sleep, filled with dreams of foreboding, and left my house early in the morning to get to the downtown offices of Identificaciones before they opened in order to get my Chilean resident ID Card. I had been there the Friday before, but there were so many people on line to get their safe conducts to leave the country that I had waited in vain to be seen.

One of them was Andre Gunder Frank, the leftist intellectual and adviser to the MIR, the Revolutionary Left Movement, who gave me the incredulous look reserved for fools and madmen when I told him what I was there for. "Don't you know that there is going to be a rightist military coup?" he said pointedly. I had just been told by the head of Allende's Foreign Press Office that it would be on September 12th.

"Yes," I said, trying to sound brave and principled, "but I'm staying." So, I scoped out where the staircase was closest to the office where I needed to go and which outside door to enter to get there fast. When the doors opened on September 11, I was first on line outside the ID card office. The young woman who had not been able to assist me the day before smiled at me and said she would call me in five minutes. But when she returned a few minutes later it was with a worried look on her face and a hurried statement that she would not be able to process my request—or anyone else's—that day, that her office—which had scarcely opened, was about to close for the day. Something in her voice stopped me. "Why?" I asked. "Is something wrong?" Her response was so classically Chilean that I have to use her words: "Me parece que hay un problemita en La Moneda"—"It seems as if there is a little problem at the presidential palace."

This was it. I raced down the stairs and out the door heading for the Plaza de la Constitución. Next door to the offices of Identificaciones were the offices of Investigaciones, the Chilean FBI, the one security service that Allende had been able to staff with his loyalists. As I passed its doorway two detectives sprinted out carrying submachine guns and heading for a squad car. I asked them if anything had happened. One shouted over his shoulder—"No . . . todavía"—"No . . . not yet." I walked rapidly to the Foreign Press Office—which overlooked the presidential palace and Constitution Plaza. The head of the office was not there, but my friend his assistant was. I asked what was happening. "It seems that there is an uprising of the armed forces," he replied. "All of them?" I asked. "No," he said. "Just the Army, the Navy and the Air Force." That was not as crazy a statement as it sounds. It meant that the Carabineros, the militarized national police, the second largest force in Chile, with bases in every city, town, and village in Chile, was still loyal to the Allende government. If that remained true, a resistance to the coup could be mounted. I went to the window and saw the Carabinero buses disgorging dozens of uniformed police with heavy machine guns to take up defensive positions around La Moneda, joined by *tanquetas*, the light tanks of the Carabineros.

The telephone rang and my friend picked it up: "Sí, sí, sí . . ." I heard him say disconsolately. He put down the phone and turned to me. "And now the Carabineros," he said sadly. I looked out the window and saw the tanquetas begin to leave the square and the Carabineros pick up their machine guns and get back on the bus leaving the presidential palace all but unguarded. "Where is Allende?" I asked. "He is inside La Moneda. He has said that he will only leave feet first."

It was just after 9 A.M., and they had orders to lock the doors and the building. I was welcome to stay if I wanted to, I was told. I debated for a minute. The office had a great view of the presidential palace and the square in front of it. I would be able to see perfectly whatever happened. But I remembered the Swedish photographer who was shot and killed in a similar window during the *tancazo* armored regiment mutiny.[1] Moreover, if the coup succeeded, I would be in effect a prisoner in what its leaders would consider enemy territory. Most of all, I did not like the idea of being shut up, unable to leave no matter what happened.

So, I thanked him and wished him luck and dashed out of the building just as its front gates were being locked. I decided to watch what happened from the far corner of the square, so that I would not have to cross it to retreat towards my building roughly a mile away. It was 9:30 and there was a small crowd of people, most of them workers from suddenly closed government offices milling around in the street. Most of them were Allende supporters who were hoping for loyal troops who would rescue the government, as had happened in the tancazo two months before.

Suddenly Carabineros arrived and began to push the crowd back from the square. I took out my journalist credentials and tried to talk with them, but the look of rage with which they regarded me—and the civilians around me—stopped me. "This is going to be a very different coup than people expected," I thought.

Close to 10 A.M. army tanks suddenly arrived in front of La Moneda and one took up position at the corner of the square near us, its gun turret facing away from the presidential palace. The crowd cheered, thinking that it was there to defend Allende. Then, slowly, its gun turret wheeled and aimed at the presidential palace. There was first stunned silence and then an audible gasp. We were standing near a shopping arcade. The Carabineros told everyone to go into the arcade, whose gates would be pulled shut and locked.

There they would be safe from the fighting. I considered it but rejected the image. It looked too much like being shut up in a jail. I decided to take my chances out on the street. Weeks later I learned that after the coup, people inside the arcade were taken to the National Stadium for interrogation and some of them disappeared forever.

A few minutes after ten, however, it looked like a bad decision. The tanks started firing on La Moneda and suddenly there were bullets everywhere, raining down from the government office buildings where the Socialist Youth were posted as snipers to defend the presidential palace. The corner was untenable. There were people lying wounded around me. I made my way back down Morandé Street hugging the walls to the next doorway, where I took refuge behind its neo-classical columns.

In back of me, the tanks and machine guns were firing away, but in front

Prisoners held at Chile's National Stadium, 1973. From September 11 to November 7, over 12,000 of those detained by the military in Santiago were held for weeks without criminal charges at Chile's premier sports arena. Allowed outside on the stands during the day, detainees spent their nights crowded into the arena's locker rooms without beds or blankets, dreading their next trip to the makeshift torture chamber at the bike track adjacent to the stadium. Photograph by Marcelo Montecino Slaughter. Used by permission of the photographer.

of us the street was alive with sniper bullets. There seemed no escape. Opposite were the offices of *El Mercurio*, the leading rightist newspaper. From its second floor window a telescopic sight suddenly appeared pointing at me. There was nowhere for me to hide. If it was a gun, I was dead. I watched transfixed as the sight slowly swiveled and faced the presidential palace, revealing a camera with a long telephoto lens. I breathed a sigh of relief.

Then the firing stopped, as suddenly as it had begun. People came out from their hiding places, at first gingerly and then with greater confidence, as if it was all over. It was a symbolic corner, with the Congress building and the court building. They gathered in between these two symbols of Chile's constitutional democracy and being Allende's Chile, they began to argue: who was responsible? Was it the Left? Was it the Right? Was it the Center? Was it the United States? I listened with a sense of prophetic nostalgia, thinking to myself: "This may be the last public political debate that you will hear in Chile for a very long time." But I also noticed that the debate in front of me was getting more and more acrimonious. Then, just when I thought it would come to blows—itself emblematic of the political polarization in

Chile by September 11, 1973—the firing started again, and the antagonists all took refuge under the newspapers and magazines representing Left, Center, and Right hanging down from the newspaper kiosk at the corner, itself a symbol of the political pluralism and free press that was about to disappear.

The bullets were all around me now. A man standing next to me got hit and I decided it was time to leave. I began to run down Morandé Street, along the side of the Congress, when suddenly I was stopped by what seemed to be a red puddle in the middle of the street—it was a pool of blood. . . . I began to run again, faster this time. As I passed the street where the headquarters of the Communist Party and the CUT (Central Unica de Trabajadores) labor confederation were located, I saw the Carabinero tanquetas firing away. Shots rang out near me and the tanqueta wheeled and began to fire in my direction. I ducked around the corner and kept running until I reached the old market close to the river. As I emerged from behind an overturned fruit cart, I saw them: there all along the broad boulevard of the Parque Forestal along the River Mapocho was the army, two regiments' worth . . . with tanks and machine guns. The soldiers seemed very young, conscripts of 17 or 18—and they were very nervous. If I had been afraid that the Carabineros near the Plaza would kill us civilians out of rage, here I was concerned that they could kill me out of nervousness and inexperience.

They were herding civilians across the river, outside of their battle station perimeter. I crossed the bridge near the Mapocho railway station and turned east toward my apartment and the Plaza Italia. More and more people were crowding Costanera Avenue as buses were stopped and their riders were forced into the street at gunpoint, many of them with their hands over their heads out of fear, like refugees from some war movie. Manicured men in business suits, together with down and out beggars and street peddlers.

But for the first time, the firing seemed distant. I stopped to rest and looked back across the river toward the downtown battle zone that I had just escaped. Someone had a transistor radio tuned to the military warning that they would bomb the presidential palace if Allende would not surrender. The young woman next to me began to cry. I assumed that she was an Allende supporter, but I was mistaken. She was mostly apolitical, she explained, but leaning toward the Right. She had voted for the rightist candidate Jorge Alessandri in 1970 and said to me: "Two days before I would have been happy to see Allende hanging from a lamppost, but this—the Chilean military attacking the presidential palace, the symbol of Chilean democracy, this should not happen. This is not the Chilean way." The sky was getting darker, with a hint of rain. "El cielo no querrá ver lo que pasará,"— "Heaven doesn't want to see what is going to happen," she said.

I decided that I had to try and return to my apartment while I still could. I asked a young soldier where I could cross. He motioned to a bridge upriver near Estados Unidos Street. It took me past the old U.S. Consulate. . . . I headed down a little side street toward the Alameda, the main thoroughfare that I had to cross to reach my apartment in the Torres San Borja complex, opposite what would become the headquarters of the military regime. I passed a group of worried but determined men coming out of a doorway with a Socialist Party banner. Two of them had pistols tucked into their belts. I overheard them making plans for what they would do when the troops arrived. I stole a last glance at their tense, sad faces, at a determination born more out of desperation than optimism. . . .

I turned the corner toward the Alameda passing by the headquarters of the neo-fascist Patria y Libertad and the Communist "Comité de Pobladores Sin Casa"—opposite poles of a Chilean pluralism. . . . I expected sniper fire, but there was none. The Alameda, normally a raucous river of traffic, was empty and silent. I crossed with surprising ease and made my way to my building opposite the Marcoleta market. Near its entrance was a crowd of people downing liter bottles of milk from an abandoned stand, as if they were chugging beers, looking at each other and laughing as if they had shared an illicit pleasure, but their laughs bordered on hysteria.

I made it to my building and took the elevator to my apartment on the 19th floor, finally safe, feeling myself a privileged foreigner in that security. I turned on the radio in time to hear the final threat to bomb the presidential palace. I got my camera out in time to track the Hawker Hunter jets streaking toward La Moneda with my telephoto lens, wishing it was a telescopic sight instead, squeezing the trigger over and over again, but to no avail. In the near distance I heard the sound of the impact of their rockets. From my window I could see black smoke billowing from the presidential palace. . . .

I took out my tape recorder and began to record the military announcements. There would be an indefinite curfew. . . . Then came the shock: a list of leftist leaders who would turn themselves in to the nearest military post or police station. It was a strange list, including many people I knew who were moderates in the Allende government, people who posed no threat to the military coup. . . . This list was followed by another, a list of foreigners who were also to turn themselves in at once. . . . Andre Gunder Frank's name was on the list. I breathed a silent prayer that he had left the country in time. Then, in a moment of terror, I suddenly realized that if other innocuous people were on the wanted list, mine might be there too. . . . I might not be safe after all. . . . It was a terrifying realization which brought home to me the new Chile that was about to be born. . . .

Phone calls began to come in, from friends and Chileans who saw me as a foreign journalist who could get the word out. Not to despair [they said] . . . loyal troops were on the way . . . recently retired General Prats was leading them. . . . loyal provincial commanders in the north were still holding out—all of them false rumors or wishful thinking. . . .

By nightfall, phone calls brought truer but grimmer tidings—Allende's death in the ruins of La Moneda, the triumph of the coup throughout the country. Outside my window, fighting continued. The city was blacked out, and from my window high over Santiago, I could see the helicopter gunships home in on leftist factories and shantytowns, a horrific lightshow of headlights and tracer bullets lighting up the darkened city sky. I slept fitfully, awakened at 4 A.M. by a loud bomb explosion. In the distance something large was on fire. I couldn't sleep.

The firing went on all the following day, along with reports of the targets attacked—the Pedagógico, the leftist education school of the University of Chile; the Sumar textile factory, the working-class districts of San Miguel, the "Red County," the shantytowns near the Cordillera. That night the Armed Forces commanders, the new Junta de Gobierno, appeared on television for the first time. Each one addressed the nation in turn. Pinochet was the most enigmatic, terse and anti-Marxist, but vague, as if he hadn't thought about what he would say or wanted to do. The most scarily rightist was the Air Force commander Gustavo Leigh, who talked of "the struggle to excise the Marxist cancer from the Chilean body politick and of the need to reverse the preceding 50 years of Chilean history"—i.e., not just the three years of Allende's road to socialism, but also the Alliance for Progress reforms of the Christian Democratic government of the 1960s, the welfare state and labor reforms of the Popular Front of the 1930s, even Arturo Alessandri's introduction of mass democratic politics of the 1920s. Clearly this was not going to be a "soft coup," a brief period of military rule to calm things down and then return power to the civilian political leaders as in the past.

Later that night I was awakened by the sound of animals roaring in agony. It was the lions in the zoo across the river, who had not been fed for two days. It seemed to me that they were expressing what too many Chileans felt that night, that they were symbolic of a nation in agony.

Note

1. On June 29, 1973, a tank regiment of the Chilean army surrounded La Moneda but was repelled by forces loyal to Commander Carlos Prats.

"In the Eyes of God and History"

Government Junta of the Armed Forces
and Carabineros of Chile

In this public declaration issued on the day of the coup, the four-officer military junta detailed in fourteen points the allegedly illegal actions of the Popular Unity government that, in the view of the junta, legitimized the military intervention of September 11, 1973. Citing the will of the people, the junta explained that it would "hold power only for the length of time demanded by circumstances," thereby laying the foundation for an indefinite period of military rule, first by the junta, and by 1975 by its principal leader, General Augusto Pinochet. The junta's declaration has all of the key attributes of the "antipolitics" rhetoric typical of military regimes in Cold War Latin America, excoriating civilian leaders for supposedly uncontrolled corruption and political conflict, denouncing purported Soviet and Cuban intervention in Chilean affairs, and invoking moral and even divine authority for military actions against the democratic regime. The unity of purpose exhibited by these military officers on the heels of the coup would quickly devolve into conflicts over economic and security policies, as well as tensions among the officers over Pinochet's ascendancy within the junta.

Taking into account:

1. That the Allende Government has become deeply illegitimate, demonstrated by its violation of fundamental rights such as liberty of expression, freedom of education, the right of association, the right to strike, the right to petition, the right to property, and the general right to a dignified and secure existence;

2. That this same government has destroyed national unity, artificially fomenting a sterile and, in many cases, bloody class struggle, thereby squandering the valuable contribution that every Chilean could make to the well-being of the Fatherland and resulting in a fratricidal and blind struggle, following ideas that are foreign to our national character, as well as false and demonstrably unsuccessful;

3. That this same Government has shown itself incapable of keeping the peace among Chileans because it did not comply with or enforce the rule of law, which has been seriously damaged on repeated occasions;

4. That, in addition, the Government has acted outside of the Constitution on multiple occasions, using questionable judgments and twisted or manipulative constitutional interpretations—some of them flagrantly so—interpretations that have, for a variety of reasons, gone unsanctioned;

5. That, likewise, relying on a subterfuge that they themselves have called "legal loopholes," this government failed to implement some laws while trampling on others, creating situations that were illegitimate from the beginning;

6. That this government has repeatedly ruptured the mutual respect that should exist between the branches of government, rendering impotent the decisions issued by the National Congress, the Judiciary, and the Comptroller General, using unacceptable excuses or no explanation at all;

7. That the executive branch has visibly and deliberately over-reached its power, seeking to amass huge amounts of political and economic power, to the detriment of vital national activities and placing all of the rights and liberties of the country's inhabitants in grave danger;

8. That the President of the Republic has openly shown that his personal authority is constrained by the decisions coming from committees and directorates made up of the political parties and groups allied with him, and has lost the role that the Constitution assigns him as the country's highest authority, and therefore the presidential nature of the Government;

9. That the agricultural, commercial, and industrial economy of the country is now stagnant or in recession while inflation is increasing quickly, and the Government has given no indication that it is concerned with these problems, but rather has completely ignored them and acted as if it were merely a spectator;

10. That in the country there is anarchy, liberties have been crushed, there is moral and economic crisis, and, within the Government, an absolute irresponsibility and incompetence, which has worsened Chile's situation and prevented the country from achieving the position it deserves as one of the greatest nations of the continent;

11. That all of the above-mentioned facts are sufficient to conclude that the internal and external security of the country is in danger, that the very survival of our Independent State is at risk and that the con-

General Augusto Pinochet (second from left) flanked by members of the junta. Pinochet exploited his position as the junta's most prominent spokesman to expand control over security operations and secure the junta's support for his policy directives. By 1978, struggles over the fundamental objectives of the military regime forced the resignation of the air force general Gustavo Leigh (far left), the only member with sufficient institutional weight and charisma to threaten Pinochet's dominance. Photograph by AP, image no. 061210042349. © 2006. The Associated Press. Used with permission.

tinuation of this Government undermines the highest interests of the Republic and its sovereign people;

12. From the perspective of the classical doctrine that characterizes our historical thinking, the facts mentioned above are enough to justify our intervention to remove this illegitimate and immoral Government, one that does not represent the national spirit, thereby preventing an even worse outcome that could be produced in the present power vacuum; there are no other reasonably successful ways to achieve this, if our goal is to reestablish normal social and economic relations in the country, as well as the peace, tranquility and safety it has lost;

13. For all of the reasons already expressed, the Armed Forces has assumed the moral duty imposed upon it by the Fatherland, that of destroying a Government that—although legitimate at first—has become flagrantly illegitimate; the Armed Forces will assume power only for the period of time demanded by these circumstances, supported by the evident feelings of the great majority of Chileans which, in the eyes of God and History, justify the Armed Forces' actions and, at the same time, the resolutions, rules and instructions that we issue

to attain the common good and fulfill the highest possible patriotic interests;

14. Therefore, since the military's instructions are legitimate, they are also obligatory for all citizens, and everyone, especially public officials, should obey and carry them out.

Translated by Justin Delacour

Pinochet's Caravan of Death

Patricia Verdugo

The "Caravan of Death" was a military operation that swept Chile during the weeks following the coup, terrorizing conscripts and imposing internal order within the military. Orchestrated by General Sergio Arellano Stark from his Puma helicopter, the campaign increased the sentences dictated by military courts and clandestinely executed and buried seventy-five political prisoners. Published in 1985, banned by the government, and then circulated clandestinely, the investigative journalist Patricia Verdugo's Los Zarapazos del Puma *("The Claws of the Puma," a reference to the type of military helicopter in which General Arellano traveled) told the story of this, one of the most infamous of the dictatorship's repressive campaigns. Verdugo drew on extensive interviews with military personnel and residents of Antofagasta to provide a detailed account of events there following the arrival of General Arellano and his entourage on October 17, one month after the coup. As Verdugo notes, according to General Joaquín Lagos Osorio, commander of the region's military forces and Arellano's immediate superior, Arellano "brought an order from the Commander in Chief of the Army, General Augusto Pinochet Ugarte, to regularize the standards applied in the administration of justice." Pinochet also visited the Antofagasta regiment as General Arellano carried out his orders. Verdugo's bold report, which provided some of the first incontrovertible evidence of Pinochet's direct involvement in political executions, contributed to the erosion of Pinochet's legacy in the 1980s and became a critical source for human rights cases brought against Pinochet and other military commanders after 1990. The excerpt begins with General Lagos's account of his own discovery of what his subordinate's forces had been up to since their arrival in Antofagasta.*

Major Manuel Matta Sotomayor, chief of public relations, asked to speak to him (Lagos). Matta came into the office with a contorted face, General Lagos recalled:

"'What are we going to do now, General?' asked Major Matta.

"'Do about what?' I said, intrigued.

"'But what? Don't you know, General, what happened last night?' Matta asked with a mixture of amazement and consternation.

"'What are you talking about?' I asked.

"'But . . . you really don't know, General?' Major Matta stammered.

"'No, I do not know what you are talking about. Say it immediately, Major!' I demanded, irritated.

"Then he told me that during that night, the General's entourage took fourteen detainees, whose cases were in process, from the place where they were being held to a ravine called Quebrada del Way and killed all of them with submachine gunfire and repeater rifles. After that, they took the bodies to the Antofagasta Hospital morgue, and since it was very small and all the bodies didn't fit, most were left outside. All of the bodies were mutilated, with approximately 40 bullet wounds each. At that time, they were lying out in the sun so that everyone passing by could see them.

"When I heard about this horrible massacre, I was stupefied, and I felt enormous indignation for these crimes perpetrated behind my back in my area of jurisdiction. I gave orders to the military and civilian doctors to reassemble the mangled bodies and to notify the relatives so that the bodies could be returned to them in the most respectable and expeditious manner. While I was doing that, I received a telephone call from my wife at home, who demanded an explanation of what had happened because there were more than 20 women standing in front of our house, crying loudly. They were asking for the reason why their husbands, sons, or brothers had been killed, and they begged her to intercede so that the bodies would be returned to them. . . .

"That day was very hard for me: arranging for and organizing the transfer of the bodies to the relatives. I recall that I even asked Father José Donoso, whom I had appointed chaplain of the jail, to tell some of the relatives about the execution of their loved ones. I tried to telephone General Pinochet, which turned out to be impossible because he was traveling between Iquique and Arica. I urgently wanted to tell him what General Arellano and his entourage had done.". . .

"Imagine my state of mind! A general of the Republic had been my guest for a few hours and, behind my back, had ordered the murder of 14 detainees, prisoners who for the most part had given themselves up voluntarily, trusting in me. I was responsible for those prisoners, according to the Geneva Convention! In military school and in war games, we were taught to respect the Geneva Convention regarding the treatment of prisoners. We had to protect them from every violent act, and we had to make every effort to be good 'lawyers' if we were assigned to serve in their defense in the court-martial. It was outrageous—they had massacred 14 defenseless prisoners behind my back!" . . .

To try to understand what happened in Antofagasta, it is important to look more closely at the actual story of some of these individuals, for example, Tocopilla's Mayor, Marcos de la Vega, age 46, a building contractor, who was married with three children. The story told by his sister is heartrending:

"After the coup, the people told him to leave Tocopilla, to go somewhere safe. But Marcos would answer, 'Why should I leave if I haven't stolen a peso, if I haven't taken anyone's job away, if all the books in the mayor's office are up-to-date, if I haven't done anything bad?' Thus, he worked until September 16th in his office. That day the newspaper published that all the authorities of Tocopilla would be arrested. So he came home in the afternoon, asked for thick clothing, ate, asked for a hot cup of *mate*, and he sat down to wait for them. The police surrounded the house, entered with submachine guns, and took him away. They treated him very badly. One day the wife of Governor Mario Arqueros went to speak with a military prosecutor, and she saw him (Marcos) in the Tocopilla jail. He embraced us firmly, and he asked us for a field bed because he was being taken to Antofagasta the next day. From then on, we took clean clothes to him every day in Antofagasta. But on Saturday the 20th, they rejected my clothes at the jail. And then on Sunday the 21st, one of the guards told us that the chaplain wanted to talk to us. He told me he was dead. We couldn't believe him because Marcos was not ill. On Monday the 22nd, we went to the morgue, telling ourselves that they were wrong and that there must have been some mistake."

But there was no mistake. Marcos de la Vega, mayor of Tocopilla, was there. "They gave us his blood-soaked clothes in a plastic bag. We could only see his face and one hand that had a wound as if a nail had been driven through it. The truth is that several bodies had the same mark on their hands. It was a deep wound. . . ."

The family of Eugenio Ruiz-Tagle Orrego, manager of INACESA (Industria Nacional de Cemento) until the military coup, also had to endure the same kinds of repeated lies. Eugenio's mother, Alicia Orrego, remembered, "Eugenio gave himself up on September 12 to the new authorities after his name appeared in a military proclamation. From that day on, he suffered physical abuse and was never allowed to speak with his lawyer. In fact, lawyers Cruzat and Fernandois spoke with General Lagos, and he promised to rescind Eugenio's incommunicado status. I reached Antofagasta on Octo-

Members of the Agrupación de Familiares de Detenidos-Desaparecidos
(Association of Family Members of the Detained-Disappeared) protest
in Santiago's Plaza de Armas. Formed shortly after the coup by family
members searching for loved ones kidnapped by security forces, the
Agrupación became a focal point of protest against the military regime.
Members of the Agrupación worked tirelessly to document the fate of the
desaparecidos and raise public awareness about the regime's systematic
use of illegal detention, torture, and assassination against its opponents.
Used by permission of the Fundación de Documentación y Archivo de la
Vicaría de la Solidaridad.

ber 18 at night. The next morning, I was told at the jail that I could see him on the following day. When I arrived (on the 20th), I was told that he was incommunicado."

The authorities did not dare tell Alicia Orrego that her son was already dead. She found out through one of the official communiqués that appeared in the press on October 21. "They didn't let me go into the morgue. I was only able to see my son's body already in a casket, with the window part sealed. I cannot give first-hand information about the physical torture that he endured. I didn't see his body, but the attorney and the employee of the funeral home both told me about it. I can speak about his neck, his face, and his head. What they described is etched with fire in my memory forever. He was missing his left eye. The lids were swollen, but he had no wounds or cuts. They took out his eye with something in cold blood. His nose was broken, pierced, swollen on the inside, and detached as far as one of the nostrils. His lower jaw was broken in several places. The mouth was a swollen bloody mass, and you could not see his teeth. On his neck, he had a long, wide cut that was not very deep. The right ear was swollen, cut, and torn from the lobe upward. He had signs of burns or, perhaps, a superficial bullet wound in the right cheek that was very deep. His forehead had small cuts and bruises. His head was turned at a strange angle, which made me think that he had a broken neck. I know he had two bullets in his body, one in his shoulder and the other in his stomach." . . .

General Joaquín Lagos Osorio decided to end his military career. It was clear that he could not be relied upon for the "work" that the military power demanded. In February 1974, General Lagos was transferred to Santiago, and eight months later he was retired. Thirteen years after the murders, in 1986, General Lagos raised some questions about certain points contained in his previous testimony and said, in a sworn statement, "There are still the following questions in my mind: Why did General Arellano do everything behind my back? Why wasn't a court-martial convened, an institution in which all the people charged have the right to a lawyer?"

Translated by Marcelo Montecino

Women and Torture

National Commission on Political Detention

and Torture

In a report commissioned by the democratic administration of President Ricardo Lagos in 2003, the "Valech Commission" documented the military regime's widespread and systematic use of torture against Chileans through its network of approximately 1,200 torture centers. The National Intelligence Directorate coordinated the work of army, police, and civilian paramilitary operatives in the surveillance, detention, torture, and execution of the regime's suspected opponents. In contrast to neighboring Argentina, which executed and disappeared over 8,960 civilians, the Chilean regime murdered fewer civilians but relied just as heavily on the systematic application of severe physical and psychological torture, administered in military barracks, urban jails, sports stadiums, and secret detention centers throughout the country. Although more than 3,000 civilians arrested and tortured by the National Intelligence Directorate were subsequently disappeared, tens of thousands more were released after enduring weeks, sometimes months, of the tortures described in the testimony here.

Among the more horrifying realities revealed by the Valech Commission was the torture of women, who made up roughly 14 percent of the 27,255 ex-prisoners who gave confirmed testimony to the Commission. Although the majority of human rights victims were men—owing in part to the regime's strategy of decapitating existing political leadership, as well as the persistence of gender roles that encouraged male political activism—women were also regularly detained and were typically subjected to a variety of sexual tortures, from systematic harassment to gang rape. The section of the government report excerpted here presents the Commission's summary comments and evidence culled from thousands of women's testimonies, identified only by the region and year in which the victim was tortured.

Situations That the Commission Knows About

This Commission received testimony from 3,399 women, which corresponds to 12.5 percent of those who offered testimony. More than half of these women were detained in 1973. Almost all of these women reported being victims of sexual violence, regardless of their age, and 316 testified that they were raped. However, we believe that the number of raped women is greater [because it is so difficult to talk about] and because many who were arrested have testified that they witnessed rapes at a large number of detention facilities. The torture that under-aged or pregnant women suffered highlights the brutality of these acts and the grave consequences that they live with. It is worth mentioning that 229 of the women who testified before this Commission said they were detained while pregnant, and 11 of those said that they had been raped. Due to the torture they suffered, 20 women miscarried and 15 gave birth in detention facilities.

The testimonies speak for themselves.

Prison and Sexual Violence

"They beat and shocked me in the police station [name omitted].[1] The most severe torture happened in [a Navy facility], where I suffered the submarine,[2] lack of food, simulated executions every night, burns from cigarettes. . . . In the [omitted] station, they raped me with bottles, and damage to my genitalia, blows to the head that put me in the Fuerte medical clinic for a week, but I never received any medication." VIII Region, 1973.

"When they detained me I was held incommunicado in a cell where a soldier raped me while they interrogated me. They said horrible things to me. They put a sword to my neck and told me that the whole squad was going to rape me if I did not talk." VII Region, 1973.

"I became pregnant when the torturers raped me. I miscarried in jail. I suffered electrical shocks, hangings, "pau-arara," "submarines," simulated executions, and cigarette burns.[3] They forced me to consume drugs and raped and sexually harassed me with dogs, put live rats in my vagina and all of my body. They forced me to have sexual relations with my father and brother who were also detained. I also had to watch and listen to them torturing my brother and father. They did the "telephone" to me.[4] They put me on a grid, and cut my abdomen with a yataghan sword. I was twenty-five. I was detained until 1976. I was never tried." Metropolitan region, 1974. . . .

Prison and Sexual Violence against Pregnant Women
Who Were Raped in Captivity

"Thirty years have passed and I still cry. I was three months pregnant when they arrested me. I was in the police station [name omitted]. The carabinero in charge threatened to rape me. In a tent in the yard they forced a union leader to rape me and grope me in front of two carabineros who were in charge. They threatened to pull out my toenails (they did not do that to me, but they did do it to others). There I suffered a simulated execution. . . . I was held incommunicado on the bleachers day and night. I was blindfolded the whole time. They forced me to watch as they tortured others and they threatened to rape me again. They would take off my clothes and grope me in the interrogations and sat me in a dentist chair and shocked my breasts, throat, abdomen, legs . . . I went to the hospital in December 1973." X Region, 1973.

"I was three months pregnant when they arrested me and took me to the National Stadium. They beat me there, and I suffered a simulated execution. I was forced into difficult positions in which I could not move. . . . They forced me to watch them torture and rape other women. Even though I was pregnant, a group of soldiers tortured, raped, and groped me." Metropolitan Region, 1973.

"They took me to an unknown location. They beat me. I was a month and a half pregnant. They punched and kicked me, and hit me with their guns. They shocked me. Two men violently, brutally raped me . . . they asked me about my dad who was also detained. In the torture house in [place omitted] they beat and kicked me. I told them that I was pregnant and they offered me an abortion." X Region, 1973.

"I was detained in 1973 in [place omitted], and they tortured me. I was two months pregnant. Soldiers of the Army raped me, which led to my miscarriage. I was under house arrest for two months. I was released." IV Region, 1973.

"I suffered beatings and electrical shocks to my entire body. They hung me by my feet and hands and covered my mouth with a towel. I was pregnant at the time (one month). Several men raped me while my hands and feet were tied. They put me in water, and later applied electrical shocks to me, especially to my genitalia, fingers, and abdomen. I also suffered psychological torture, when they threatened to kill my nine month old daughter, who was under their control." Metropolitan Region, 1975.

"They blindfolded me when they detained me . . . and took me to [a facility of the National Intelligence Directorate]. One of the men requested a special treatment for me because they were going to send me to another place. That treatment consisted of beating my ears and giving me electrical shocks. They took me to Tejas Verdes:[5] all the while I was blindfolded and held incommunicado in a barracks. . . . They tied us up, placed hoods over our heads, and took us in a refrigerated truck to our interrogation session. They took off our clothes and placed us in cells to wait. The torture sessions would last about twelve hours. They did this to us every day. I was three months pregnant. They beat me on the abdomen. They beat my legs with wet bags. They tied me to a post and threw buckets of water on me. They tied me up for hours with ropes under my legs. I suffered simulated executions and rape. They pulled out my toenails from my little toes and burned my body. I heard other prisoners being tortured and they made me listen to a recording of children whimpering and told me they were my children. They made me eat excrement. In the [place omitted] I miscarried because they tortured me. I never received medical attention." V Region, 1974. . . .

Women Who Were Raped and Became Pregnant in Prison

Many women were raped and became pregnant. Many of them miscarried or had abortions. Others gave birth.

"I was held incommunicado, blindfolded with a hood over my head. They beat me and shocked me with electricity. They hung me and raped me. I had a broken rib and toes. They pulled out my fingernails. I was in several locations. I think I was in [a National Intelligence Directorate office] and in another place. They repeated the torture everywhere I went. I could hear the cries. I had an ectopic pregnancy from being raped." Metropolitan Region, 1973.

"The soldiers came to my office and detained me . . . they tied me up and took me to the regiment, where they interrogated me about my political militancy and my leftist family. . . . They took me to [place omitted] and then to a jail in [place omitted] in October of 1973, and in January 1974, they returned me to jail at [place omitted]. While I was transported from one place to another, the soldiers beat and raped me. In 1974, I became pregnant while in I was being held, and miscarried in the fifth month in the [name omitted] hospital." VIII Region, 1974.

"They tortured me, tied me up, and blindfolded me at a secret location. They kicked and punched me. They applied electrical shocks to various parts of my body. They knocked out my front teeth with a rifle butt. I suffered sexual abuse and was repeatedly raped, which led to my becoming pregnant." Metropolitan Region, 1975.

A twenty-nine-year old woman testified to the Commission. Her mother became pregnant while detained and was 15 years old. When she was released, she gave birth to the woman who testified to the Commission. In her testimony she declared:

"I represent living proof; I represent the greatest pain and the worst experience of my mother's life . . . There was a lot of rage inside of her; I felt it. This has shaped my life and is eternal: I cannot be born into another family, nor can I change what happened. I have had to deal with this rage, with my mom's frustrations, but I was also bitter. I had no place to go. My mom would go to the Vicariate,[6] but what about me? I could barely talk to my best friend about it! I have had to carry this eternal weight. . . . I began to drink after they told me, I would hide and drink all weekend. . . .

I am someone who was really affected by the coup. I believe that we, the children who were born just like me, were just as much prisoners and torture victims as those who were detained. . . . You can be a victim, but nobody recognizes it. We are never taken into account. How many mothers see the features of their rapists in their children (and therefore reject them)? Some people bear the burden of their disappeared loved ones, while others were themselves tortured, but I also have a burden: that I was detained without my knowledge. I cannot even explain the emptiness it has created inside of me. . . . All of the damage that they caused me is internal: I have no physical marks. A woman who has been tortured sees things very differently than I do. It is the same problem but we see it from different perspectives. This Commission does not include this vision. We cannot bury it; we must expose it." VII Region, 1974.

Translated by Ryan Judge

Notes

1. As indicated in the law establishing the Commission on Torture, the names of perpetrators and the specific military institutions where torture was conducted were omitted from the Commission's final report. Likewise, the transcripts of the extensive testimony received by the Commission are closed to public scrutiny (and the possibility of their use in criminal cases) for fifty years.

2. See the following note.

3. The *pau de arara* or "parrot's perch" was a form of torture invented by the Brazilian dictatorship in which the victim was hung from a horizontal pole with hands and feet tied, often subjected to additional tortures. In the "submarine," torturers submerged the victim's covered head in water or excrement.

4. In the "telephone," torturers clapped their hands repeatedly over a victim's ears.

5. Tejas Verdes, a former beach resort near the port of San Antonio, housed the Army School of Engineers, which served after the coup as one of the regime's most infamous torture centers, under the command of the army general Manuel Contreras.

6. The Vicariate of Solidarity, a human rights organization created by Cardinal Raúl Silva Henríquez in 1976, offered legal defense and other support to victims of the regime (and their families) and served over time as an important site of resistance to military rule.

Operation Condor and the Transnationalization of Terror

U.S. Federal Bureau of Investigation

*Within months of the military coup, Chilean military and intelligence officials be-
gan to coordinate efforts with their counterparts in Argentina—and later in Uruguay, Bolivia, Paraguay, Brazil, Ecuador, and Peru—creating a covert transnational security network known by late 1975 as "Operation Condor." Officials from
these countries created a shared database of political dissidents, sponsored counter-
insurgency training courses, and coordinated military and paramilitary efforts to
kidnap, torture, interrogate, disappear, and force repatriation of hundreds of victims between 1975 and 1977. Most notoriously, Operation Condor was responsible for
the public assassination of former Chilean diplomat Orlando Letelier and his U.S.
colleague Ronni Moffitt in a Washington, D.C., car-bombing on September 21, 1976.
This document—a secret cable sent to Washington by the FBI legal attaché Robert
Scherrer in Buenos Aires just one week after Letelier's murder—is one of several
that demonstrate U.S. government knowledge of Operation Condor, although in this
case the author was trying to blow the whistle on it. Despite the Carter administration's public position protesting Chile's human rights record and U.S. concern when
Condor operations reached into North America and Europe, Operation Condor continued to operate in Latin America until at least 1980. This declassified document,
which remains incomplete because parts of the text have been blacked out, is one of
thousands that have been released by various U.S. government agencies in response
to Freedom of Information Act requests and by the Clinton administration at the
request of the Spanish magistrate Baltasar Garzón for cooperation in his 1998–1999
case against Pinochet for human rights crimes.*

*An important catalog of declassified U.S. documents on Chile under Pinochet is
available through the online National Security Archive (www.gwu.edu/~nsarchiv/),
a nongovernmental research institute housed at George Washington University. The*

more than 24,000 documents declassified by the Clinton administration are available at www.foia.state.gov in the "Chile Collection."

"Operation Condor" is the code name for the collection, exchange, and storage of intelligence data concerning so-called "Leftists," Communists, and Marxists, which was recently established between cooperating intelligence services in South America in order to eliminate Marxist terrorist activities in the area. In addition, "Operation Condor" provides for joint operations against terrorist targets in member countries of "Operation Condor." Chile is the center for "Operation Condor" and in addition to Chile its members include Argentina, Bolivia, Paraguay, and Uruguay. Brazil also is tentatively agreed to supply intelligence input for "Operation Condor." Members of "Operation Condor" showing the most enthusiasm to date have been Argentina, Uruguay, and Chile. The latter three countries have engaged in joint operations, primarily in Argentina, against the terrorist target. During the week of September 20, 1976, the [two lines deleted] with respect to "Operation Condor."

A third and most secret phase of "Operation Condor" involves the formation of special teams from member countries who are to travel anywhere in the world to non-member countries to carry out sanctions up to assassination against terrorists or supporters of terrorist organizations from "Operation Condor" member countries. For example, should a terrorist or a supporter of terrorist organizations from a member country of "Operation Condor" be located in a European country, a special team from "Operation Condor" would be dispatched to locate and surveil the target. When the location and surveillance operation has terminated, a second team from "Operation Condor" would be dispatched to carry out the actual sanction against the target. Special teams would be issued false documentation from member countries of "Operation Condor" and may be composed exclusively of individuals from one member nation of "Operation Condor" or may be composed of a mixed group from various "Operation Condor" member nations. European countries, specifically mentioned for possible sanctions under the third phase of "Operation Condor" were France and Portugal.

The special team has been organized [words blacked out] which are being prepared for possible future action under the third phase of "Operation Condor."

It should be noted that no information has been developed indicating that sanctions under the third phase of "Operation Condor" have been planned to be carried out in the United States. However, it is not beyond the realm of possibility that the recent assassination of Orlando Letelier in Washing-

Operation Condor planned the assassination of dozens of Pinochet's Chilean opponents living in foreign countries, including a failed attempt against the Christian Democrat Bernardo Leighton and his wife in Rome, the murder of General Carlos Prats and his wife in Buenos Aires, and, pictured here, the 1976 car-bombing of Orlando Letelier, in which the former Allende minister and his assistant, Ronni Moffit, were killed on Embassy Row in Washington, D.C. Photograph by AP, image no. 7607201410. © 1976 The Associated Press. Used with permission.

ton, D.C. may have been carried out as a third phase of action of "Operation Condor." As noted above, information available to the [confidential source of information in this cable] indicates that particular emphasis was placed on the third phase actions of "Operation Condor" in Europe, specifically France and Portugal. This office will remain alert for any information indicating that the assassination of Letelier may be part of "Operation Condor" action.

Protected Democracy and

the 1980 Constitution

Jaime Guzmán

In this text, the principal ideologue of the military regime outlines the objectives and strategies of the Constitution it promulgated in 1980. A lawyer trained at Chile's Catholic University, Jaime Guzmán was a leader of the gremialistas (from trade association or guild), a conservative university student movement that opposed the Allende regime and actively supported the military regime after 1973. The 1980 Constitution that he helped to write is considered the foundational document of Chile's "protected democracy," the euphemism by which the military and its supporters referred to the political regime. The Constitution reaffirmed states of constitutional exception, created the National Security Council, a body of military and legal officials appointed by Pinochet, and stipulated the selection of "Designated Senators," thereby establishing the permanent tutelage of the armed forces over the institutions of civilian government and limiting the power of elected representatives in Congress. Left-wing political parties were further marginalized through the Constitution's criminalization of "doctrines that attack the family, propose violence, or that maintain a view of society, the State, or the judiciary that is totalitarian or founded on class struggle." Furthermore, the constitutional plan advocated by Guzmán defined not only a political system but also an economic one, enshrining in constitutional principle "a free economic system, founded on the private ownership of the means of production and on individual initiative as the fundamental motors of the economy." The Constitution also served as a mechanism for returning Chile to civilian democratic rule, stipulating that a plebiscite be held in 1988 to determine whether Pinochet would serve as "President" for another eight years—or not. In 1991, shortly after the return to democracy, Guzmán was assassinated on a Santiago street corner, an act that heightened fears of renewed military intervention and delayed the advance of criminal cases against military officials. In this essay, published just prior to the fraudulent constitutional plebiscite of 1980, Guzmán explains the authoritarian notions of democracy distinctive to the Chilean military regime, principles that through the Constitution still constrain democracy in Chile today.

We connect the best traditions of the Chilean Republic with our creative resolve in order to meet the challenges we face in terms of global realities and the Chilean experience, which allows us to speak of this as a new Constitution for a new democracy. This does not mean we have the absurd pretension of inventing a wholly new political system, but rather the desire to efficiently imbue our future democracy with the values of freedom, security, progress, and justice, thus abandoning the basic neutrality toward these values that characterized the Chilean institutional regime until September of 1973. It was precisely this neutrality that allowed our democracy to serve its enemies as a useful instrument, which they used to advance their opposing "values": totalitarianism and statism, which infringe and curtail freedom; terrorism and subversive violence, which threaten security; and demagogy, which undermines economic progress and social justice. The whole effort to produce a new founding document has been shaped by this emphasis. . . .

(2) The Promise of the New Constitution

. . . It might seem odd that it has been necessary, in debates on the Chilean constitution, to waste so much time on the non-democratic regimes of Chile's past, which some have suggested are normal systems, supposedly valid for our future.

Those efforts stem, however, from the understandable distrust produced by Chileans' experience of how democracy was used not to serve but rather to destroy and undermine freedom, security, progress, and justice.

The new constitutional model diverges completely from the position of those who, because of recent events in Chile, or because of the threats of today's world reality, defend the values mentioned above by denying that democracy has any validity. We believe, on the contrary, that a well-conceived democracy, adequately and opportunely implemented, is the ideal system to serve these values.

Nevertheless, we must not forget that no form of government is an end in and of itself. Democracy is just a means, which retains its legitimacy and validity only insofar as it promotes the desired objectives and way of life. Only in this way will we avoid repeating recent experiences, which produced a democracy that opposed freedom, given its weakness in the face of totalitarian and statist threats; an uncertain democracy, because of its inability to take a stand against violence and all other forms of subversion; in sum, a demagogic democracy, because of its failure to provide support for the kind of political, economic, and social leadership that permits progress and effective justice.

Just as the new constitutional scheme offers a new kind of democracy, it is very different from corporatism and from the elitist, closed illusions of the past, insofar as it makes a clear commitment to values. It is also quite distant from the mere "reestablishment" of democracy proposed by the current political opposition. Their goal is to return to the institutional regime that existed before 1973, as if what happened in Chile under the Marxist government was the result of an unfortunate gamble, rather than the complete breakdown of a system whose gradual and inexorable collapse had been evident for a long time. . . .

(3) The Limits of Ideological Pluralism

We have already shown how ideological pluralism is inherent in the very differences that exist within a free society such as our own. But just as without difference, there is no liberty, without a minimal level of consensus that is respected by everyone, community disappears. It is no accident that the word community is derived from "common unity." Once this is broken, coexistence devolves into anarchy, and differences into civil war. At the same time, when community disappears, obviously the possibility of having civil disagreements comes to an end.

The unrestricted nature of pluralism therefore also becomes, paradoxically, the greatest threat to pluralism itself. Even if the aforementioned minimal consensus should flow spontaneously within every community, we cannot deny the reality that this does not always happen. It is necessary then to prevent a minority from attacking pluralism. If this minority grows to the point of driving the division to civil war, it becomes a necessity that in this case is imposed on a broken society. It is certain that the thought of prohibiting the advocacy of certain ideas, which many people might support in good faith, runs counter to the tolerant Chilean character. But the much greater pains experienced by our country in the recent past, when it reached a clear situation of civil war, leave no doubt about the necessity of excluding certain doctrines from civic life, at least whenever—as in the Chilean case—these doctrines represent a potentially significant threat to the survival of this minimal consensus that holds the nation together.

If we recognized the right of every community to defend its existence as such, that is, to defend its very identity, we can then agree on the legitimacy of the above-mentioned civic prohibition [on certain doctrines].

The proposed constitutional framework suggests that we exclude from civic life those doctrines that attack the family, that promote violence, and

Lucia Hiriart de Pinochet on a school visit, c. 1976. As director of the state-run Mothers' Centers, Pinochet's wife, Lucia Hiriart, proved a key figure in the public face of the regime, promoting its populist programs in housing and unemployment as well as traditional norms for Chilean women. Speaking on behalf of the government plan to rename International Women's Day the "National Year of the Woman," Hiriart explained that "we want to add to our year the concept of GENEROSITY, which is what Chilean women have heaped upon this country, with even greater intensity since the eleventh of September 1973." Photographer unknown. Courtesy of Colección Museo Histórico Nacional de Chile.

that support a totalitarian vision of society, the State, and the legal system, or based on class struggle. Significantly, this stipulation does not refer to just any kind of action that attacks the family or promotes class struggle, since that could lead to excesses that everyone rejects. The law applies only to doctrines, that is to say, to global conceptions that, for example, attack the family or promote a whole social perspective founded in class struggle. In terms of which doctrines fall in this category, as well as which ones are totalitarian and violent, there is and will always be easy agreement within an organism like the Constitutional Tribunal, which is convened to examine and define jurisprudence, since without the influence that inevitably occurs in the application of legal values to specific cases, we are dealing with concepts about which all Chileans who are not Marxists clearly agree.

It is therefore useful to refute the falsehood that some repeat, which is that this law would lead to "punishing ideas and not acts," or that it would apply the same totalitarian criterion as the Marxists, except from the opposite ideological position.

From the start, it is not correct to say that this law would punish ideas, because in a person's heart of hearts, conscience is inviolate and sacred. It is not about the State getting involved in people's private lives, either, which would lead to an unacceptable "witch hunt." It would certainly not stop intellectual or academic work within any doctrine. What the proposed law specifically sanctions is the "propagation" of the specified doctrines, that is, their dissemination with intent to proselytize. In this manner, the law punishes not the idea, but the act of proselytizing a doctrine, and of the serious social repercussions that result from its dissemination.

Those who apply this kind of criteria must then admit that someone who promotes a terrorist ideology or armed struggle, even if he doesn't personally engage in these practices, would remain immune from punishment. In this manner, criminal sanctions would only apply to people who—out of imbalance or immaturity—follow the ideologue of violence, but never to the ideologue himself. The uneven injustice of that criterion makes it difficult to take the objection seriously. And if, on the contrary, we accept that someone who promotes violence deserves to be punished, we already agree on the fundamental thesis that motivates the new constitutional scheme, leaving us only to debate which doctrines should be sanctioned if they are propagated. At this point, the text of the constitutional proposal becomes difficult to oppose in its precise, moderate content.

In reference to those who try to compare in this way the new Chilean constitutional regime with a totalitarian regime such as the Marxist one, it is enough to point out the following key differences: while totalitarian regimes establish a single official and acceptable doctrine, and sanction those declared "dissident" from that doctrine by the Government or its courts, thereby depriving people of their most fundamental human rights, including their personal liberty, the new Chilean institutions by contrast leave open many options within the range of acceptable ideological pluralism, with the exception only of certain extreme doctrines. The Constitutional Tribunal—a completely independent body—then punishes only those responsible for propagating those doctrines, by temporarily suspending the principal civic rights that are most essential to human beings. . . .

The final defeat of all totalitarianism, and in particular of Marxism, requires without a doubt that we engage in a permanent anti-subversive struggle, in economic and social development that eliminates extreme poverty as the easy terrain for the cultivation of subversion, and in an ideological struggle that wins over the very consciousness of the people. . . .

(4) Adoption of a Free Economic System

Some have argued that the constitutional project would link the Constitution to a determined political-economic project. Since the Constitution is always subject to multiple and changing conditions, it should be obvious that a Constitution should never be tied to a specific political economic model. In reality, there is nothing in this constitutional project that justifies such an unfounded fear.

What the project achieves is something very different. It is not linked to any political economy, but it does define the basic system of economic organization that is necessary to keep the country stable. A constitution, as its name indicates, should deal with "substance," with what is essential. And it would be very difficult to argue today that the foundations of a Nation's economic structure are not part of its social existence. It strikes us as a capricious and erroneous thesis to argue that a contemporary Constitution should define the nature of a political regime—to choose, for example, between presidentialism and parliamentarianism—and also to argue that it should abstain from making pronouncements about the virtues of a collective versus a free economy. The very same Constitution cannot serve both collectivism and liberty, because it would then lack the qualities of the so-called "fundamental law" of the country. Something very fundamental would remain undefined. The fact that we went as a country from what we had in 1970, to another economy that was openly collectivist and Marxist, without any constitutional reforms whatsoever, eloquently demonstrates how easy it was to convert our old democracy into an anti-libertarian regime.

The new constitutional framework is resolutely defined by a free economic system, founded on the private ownership of the means of production and on individual initiative as the fundamental motors of the economy.

Translated by Ryan Judge

Shantytown Protest:
Interviews with Pobladores

On taking power, the ruling military junta moved quickly to eliminate working-class political and social organizations. Despite—and in response to—repression and the economic crash of 1975, residents of poblaciones *(shantytowns) were among the first to organize against the dictatorship. Shantytown residents, or* pobladores, *constituted a heterogeneous social sector, including party militants, labor activists, the unemployed, Catholics, atheists, students, housewives, and more. A single individual usually held multiple identities and affiliations. The first organizations to emerge in opposition to the dictatorship capitalized on these interlocking networks and identities. They included clandestine left-wing political parties and subsistence organizations, such as unemployed people's groups and soup kitchens, which operated under the shelter of the Catholic Church. The organizations spread throughout Santiago's* poblaciones, *as* pobladores *quietly reconstructed social and political networks. By 1981, when the economy crashed a second time,* pobladores *were in a position to work with other disaffected social sectors, especially organized labor, to lead the first national protests against the dictatorship.*

In 1978, the military regime imposed a new labor code that reintroduced limited collective bargaining, while severely curtailing workers' labor rights. In response, workers who were organized in unions, especially the powerful copper miners' unions, turned to protest, calling for a national movement to overthrow the dictatorship. The copper workers' call for a day of national protest in 1983 sparked the first mass mobilizations against the Pinochet regime, including not just workers, but members of the poblaciones *and the urban poor, especially women, who had suffered under the economic shock of the 1970s and again during the deep recession of 1982–1983 that pushed unemployment rates close to thirty percent. The national protests began in May 1983 and continued through 1986, at least in the* poblaciones. *The protests forced the regime into negotiations, which would lead to the plebiscite that eventually ended the dictatorship. Post-1990 civilian governments have disinherited the working-class organization and protests that made the transition possible, but the* pobladores *have not forgotten. In the interviews here, conducted in 2004–2005 by the historian Alison Bruey,* pobladores *reflect on working-class resistance to the dictatorship in the 1970s.*[1]

LUISA: "The desperation of doing nothing was so great that you had to participate in something. The dictatorship eliminated all of the neighborhood associations, mothers' centers, all forms of organization. It eliminated everything, swept it away, so that nothing was left standing, no organization. And under these circumstances the priest shows up and organized the Christian community, known as Christ the Liberator, which was the only thing there was, the only space that was created. He was a revolutionary priest, one who pulled everyone together, the activist Christians and the people from political parties who had nowhere to organize."

JUAN: "When we arrived in the Christian community, the rest of the people from the Christian community knew that we were Communists. For us it was very clear that we supported a principle, the principle of social justice. Our goal was to find out what happened to the detained-disappeared and the Catholic Church took on that challenge. The detained-disappeared weren't Christians: the majority were Communists and some were MIRistas. . . . We met, at that time, in a kind of worship that was a Catholic meeting, a spiritual gathering, but that was combined with social activism."

MARIO: "Sunday was the day of worship, which was different from Mass. Mass was celebrated only once a month. And Sunday worship was a small assembly, perhaps as the Church originally wanted it to be, of the people of God. And what this assembly did was to share a relevant event or experience from that week: something concrete that was happening in the country like the change to the pension system, the latest unemployment rates, or news from other countries like the repression in Nicaragua as the Sandinista Revolution advanced. Because of these discussions, the community was a great place for political, cultural, and religious learning. There was no place where those things could be discussed, well not in the press, even less on television, and spaces for people to gather just didn't exist. And the worship meeting was structured: it began with a hymn and general prayer, but immediately the weekly theme for discussion was introduced, then those assembled could speak, so that everyone could express opinions and ask questions. Obviously, promoting the community was not only the work of Christians, but also of the persecuted Left. And therefore the Communist Party, that is Communist militants, had a strong presence in the community, many of whom had before then been very distant from the Church. And so these meetings produced a re-encounter at the very base of the community between Christians and Communists. So it was difficult: it was a space for political reflection, but at the same time it was the space of a faith community."

JUAN: "In those days, we met and spoke about these prohibited things in an old, dilapidated house. And it became a gloomy environment because the repression by the DINA [National Intelligence Directorate], which was the armed branch of the dictatorship, was terrible, it was feared. And we were a group that was there talking about what was prohibited at that time, I mean, about advancing people's rights, how to reorganize, how to fight, how to make them feel that we should be respected."

LUISA: "Communion was very special, for example. Not just anyone received communion. It wasn't given to just anyone, to someone who just opened her mouth to receive the host, no. The priest would say, "I don't want people to come to swallow wafers, I want people who have a commitment to our suffering people." And one took Communion to gather the strength one needed to continue working, and so it was very striking, very strong, very wonderful. It proved really attractive even to political people. Everything revolved around each person's commitment. And we evaluated this on work days: you had to talk about what you were doing. I mean, people who weren't doing anything weren't accepted. In confession, for example, the priest would say, 'I don't want you to come here to tell me you stole candy or that you swore at your neighbor. Here the most serious sin is not participating in the liberation of the Chilean people. That is what I want to hear. If there is anyone who wants to tell me that, I will listen. The rest of you can just go home.'"

IRENE: "After the coup, people got much closer to the Christian community because it was there that we found a way to speak, to express ourselves. People began losing their jobs and unemployment began. At the end of '74, the unemployment began. Right away the priest created the committee of unemployed, bringing together all of the workers [who had been] expelled from the unionized industries and [who] had been organized. Later, in December of '74, we created the children's soup kitchen because we already had three families of detained-disappeared and there were other people who no longer had enough to eat; they had malnourished children. Later, after 1975 when unemployment increased, this project expanded; it was no longer only the children who went but entire families."

GINA: "All of these organizations were informal, rather than official. They began to form networks. In these networks health teams from this población organized with the team from the next población and became very attached to the church, especially the Catholic Church. . . . And this social network began to build, as quietly as possible. In fact, we would go to the street market and take bags full of pamphlets that we would scatter. The social networking was mobilized mainly by women and young people. So there was a lot of complicity between children and their mothers, whether they were housewives, women, or grandmothers. Fathers often didn't know that their families were involved. So later, by 1978, we already had a well-organized network, camouflaged if you like, but well organized, because in '79 the biggest meetings began to take place."

LUISA: "We all began to get inspired, to go out into the streets to protest. For example on May 1, while we were still under dictatorship, we took everything into the streets. The priest said that we had to go out as families, taking the entire family with us, to the street, to make demands, to shout. It was a big deal because they could kill you in the street and I remember having gone out with the Christian community, taking my husband Manuel and all of the children with me, one May Day. There were more than 100 people, which was a lot of people at that time. This event paved the way for what would come later, for those national protests."

MARÍA TERESA: "The Christian community began to represent a type of social work, a commitment to address these big structural issues. But then people began to say, 'So who is really committed to changing society? It's not the Church.' So where was that commitment? In a political party. Then, many people got involved in the parties and many young people left their studies because of this. In addition, in the years '78, '79, and '80 we had the sense that the revolution was about to begin."

LUISA: "It was due to participating in this Christian community space that many people—especially young people—made a serious commitment to fighting the criminal dictatorship. The youth committed themselves very seriously, and at a political level. They began to work clandestinely, and the political parties began to function again. But at that point, the Christian community worked like a trampoline for that commitment. Many people left the community and began to open new spaces for protest: and the national protests were born."

JUAN: "The breeding ground for the national protests was the appalling levels of injustice, that's how they got started."

SILVIA: "Many people went to the street spontaneously, many people did, but there was also plenty of preparation beforehand. It's not that the protests just broke out one day: it took years to organize them bit by bit, because the political parties had to reorganize and get stronger. All of this took a lot of effort, and took years. We had been preparing for the protests. Making use of the spaces offered by the Church, political and social organizations met and reached an agreement on how to carry out together what became known as the first national protest and the ones that followed."

Street protest in the Plaza de Armas, 1983. The photographer Juan Carlos Cácares captured a tense moment during one of the many protests that marked Santiago in that period. Photograph by Juan Carlos Cácares. Used by permission of the photographer.

JUAN: "It was a broad call and everyone did his own thing in terms of preparing for it, for example turning off the lights at night, cutting electricity to prevent the repression from reaching the neighborhoods involved in the protest."

SILVIA: "People thought up actions on their own. I took care of that. I wanted to see what happened with the woman who had never done anything, to see what that kind of person would do. That's why the protests of the empty pots and pans[2] were so successful, because they weren't scared, because they could protest from their bedrooms, with the kids kept at home or hidden under the bed. Or they could put them in the bathroom, because they knew it was solid, that the bullets wouldn't get through."

GINA: "When the protests happened the kids went out into the night and we opened the doors for them. We women opened the doors, turned off the lights, and when the cops came the kids came inside. We organized them, we began to whistle. For example, if the cop was coming to one house, the neighbor turned on a light. Then we told them, 'it's up to you: if you're brave, shout, blow the whistle, or turn on the radio.' But the least one could do was turn the light off and on, that was the minimum.

In 1986, Alvaro Hoppe captured this image of a march in downtown Santiago that commemorated the assassination of André Jarlan, a Catholic priest whose death at the hands of police in the La Victoria shantytown two years earlier helped galvanize popular opposition to the military regime. Photograph by Alvaro Hoppe. Used by permission of the photographer.

So we never insisted that they commit 100 percent, only that each person do what they could for the protests. And in fact, all the kids in the población, even the policemen's children, everyone's children, all of them were involved."

JUANITA: "During the day you could be like a social group, working at different activities. But that same group was also participating politically. In general the older women from the neighborhood worked with us and helped us. They were the ones who bought us the gasoline for the barricades.[3] Often, at the gas station, if a young person went to buy a lot of liters of gas, they wouldn't sell it to you and you could be arrested. But they brought things for us, found houses for us to stay in if there was repression, and they also participated directly in all of the protests."

ALEJANDRA: "That was really critical. Of course the doors were open. So when the cops came you could go into a house. If those people hadn't opened the doors, it would have been really complicated. And the barricades, that was also a big job because you had to look very late at night for tires and you had to take them to a house and then take them out for the day of the protest. It was very risky. There were a lot of young people doing that job. They organized into teams so that some kept watch and others broke into the tire dump to remove them. Sometimes there were 20, 30, or 40 youth getting the tires."

SILVIA: "Bread and milk began to arrive, which fed the fighters. That's how we talked, 'we have to feed the combatants' in the street, because they went around all day breathing the smoke from the barricades. So we would make bread in the morning and deliver it at 12 and then at 5 in the afternoon. . . . Later the Patriotic Front appeared.[4] The pobladores hoped the Front would appear. When the cops were crushing us, everyone looked around hoping the Front would appear so the Front could take on the police and the pobladores could go home. The Front fulfilled a major role in the poblaciones, I mean, without the Front the massacre would have been much greater because they took charge and told us to fall back. They also told us how to do things and they also said, 'now, now!' and people followed them with confidence . . . One comrade from the Front saw everyone running away because armored tanks were arriving and he stopped us and said to us, 'don't run away, don't run away, I'm going to show you.' . . . And he got up on the tank and it began to back up, and people went on like that advancing, and the dumb ass in the tank didn't know what to do because people were not afraid. . . . The comrade showed us that the tanks were used to intimidate, but that now they couldn't fire on a crowd because all the international organizations were here. The people didn't know that and so it was the comrades from the Front who taught everyone not to be afraid."

CARMEN: "We survived all of this. And the most important point was when the plebiscite happened. I think that without the plebiscite, this gentleman Pinochet, or his military guys, would still be in charge. We were afraid of what could happen, what with all the horrific things that had occurred."

ALEJANDRA: "In the debate about power, about how the transition from Pinochet to democracy will happen, our dead are the ones who have no voice. And I believe it's true: without the protests, without any resistance, I think we would have continued with Pinocho.[5] These are things that, for better or for worse, paved the way."

Translated by Carolyn Watson

Notes

1. In *Bread, Justice, and Liberty: Organizing Grassroots Opposition in Pinochet's Chile* (forthcoming), Alison Bruey uses these oral histories to document the impact of shantytown organizing on urban communities during the 1970s and 1980s. The editors are grateful to the author for sharing these materials and their contextualization. All the notes that follow are hers.
2. Here Silvia refers to protests that included activists banging on empty pots, a technique earlier made famous by women protesting the Allende regime in the early 1970s.
3. Protestors in this period often erected barricades of burning tires, which demarcated urban areas held by protestors and slowed police incursions into certain poblaciones.
4. The Frente Patriótico Manuel Rodríguez (FPMR) was an urban guerrilla group made up of Communist Party youth.
5. "Pinocho," or Pinocchio, is the name derisively used to refer to Pinochet.

"There Is No Feminism without Democracy"

Julieta Kirkwood

In the 1980s, many Latin American countries witnessed not only a wave of transitions from military rule but also an upsurge of feminist political activism, which was inseparable from the democratic ferment in which they occurred. In that period, economic dislocation and recession provoked a wave of popular protests against the dictatorship in poor urban neighborhoods and poblaciones (shantytowns). "Las protestas" were often led by working-class women, who organized together with middle-class feminists and women human rights activists to link their demands for democracy and social justice to demands for women's rights. Like other feminist intellectuals, the Chilean sociologist Julieta Kirkwood combined scholarship with activism to define the reemergent Chilean women's movement in the period of dictatorship. In 1986 Kirkwood wrote the foundational text of the women's movement, "Women's Politics in Chile" (Ser política en Chile), in which she examined the history of women's twentieth-century participation in Chilean politics and provided a searing critique of the subordination of women and feminism in Chilean political parties. Calling for "democracy in the country and in the home," women's movements throughout Latin America were notable for their antiauthoritarian discourse and their challenges to the sexism of Left parties. In this excerpt, Kirkwood set out to write "a simple and personal essay about two ways that women behave politically. I am referring here to the feminists and the 'políticas,'" a term that referred to women who participated in or identified with a political party.

In the last decade, we have seen the emergence and growing visibility of a new socio-political actor in Chile's democratic opposition: the women's groups. These groups have varied histories, timing, significance, and constituencies, and they may have different origins in the superstructure or the base, and interclass or intraclass characteristics, but they have in common the novelty of being constituted and generated fundamentally by women and/or for women, and these organizations embrace the widest possible range of activities and objectives.

All different kinds of groups have emerged, including those dedicated

Women mobilize against Pinochet. Overcoming the partisan divisions and strategic disagreements that had weakened opposition to the military regime, the women's movement was among the first to constitute a broad coalition across parties and groups. In December 1983, Mujeres por la Vida (Women for Life) convened thousands of women for the "Caupolicanazo," a meeting in the Caupolicán Theater of Santiago. Featuring topics from women's rights to strategies for advancing the transition to democracy, this massive event set the stage for the creation of similarly broad coalitions among other political and social actors. Photograph by Juan Pablo Cárdenas, from "Caupolicanazo, 29 de Diciembre 1983" *Análisis* 7, no. 73 (January 1984), 17. Used by permission of the photographer.

to urban and rural action and protest, personal reflection and growth, the study of women's condition, solidarity work and/or self-help activities, and political training and action. Grassroots activist groups have formed among the homeless and *arpilleristas*, for unemployment relief and soup kitchens.[1] Women's groups have been active at critical moments in national affairs, including their constant defense of human rights, support for the denunciations levied by the relatives of political prisoners and for the disappeared, and for those in foreign and internal exile, by lobbying for their return. Women's organizations have defended health care, fought the impact of drugs, protected defenseless children and youth, and much more. . . .

Both feminists and *políticas* seem to agree on one goal: that of gaining recognition for this historic and civilizing possibility of achieving woman's emancipation. Where there seems to be less agreement altogether, is about what goals, objectives, methods, theories, practices, and priorities will be addressed in the process of society's full liberation. It is worth noting that feminists and políticas do not agree about how this social liberation will run its course.

Both approaches stem from a distinct set of value judgments.

The first—in broad strokes—refers to the need for a politics elaborated *by women themselves*, a politics that arises from the limitations and marginality specific to women's position. The other, more traditional, approach sees women as mere *additions*, and with their mass incorporation into existing political projects, the assumption is that women's demands will be included in the future.

This division in two camps can be explained by looking at our recent history. From the very first women's political assemblies, which brought together the whole gamut of groups and political currents associated with women, two positions constantly emerged in every topic and situation.

One of these is summed up in the phrase "There is no feminism without democracy," which means, in other words, that the only form of women's organization possible NOW is one of support, that is of joining the struggle against the authoritarian government; the specific problems stemming from women's discrimination are secondary to this struggle against dictatorship and can be treated after or *only if* they do not hamper that struggle. This position is maintained by political women *(las políticas)*.

The second position, diametrically opposed to the first, inverts these terms and affirms that "There is no democracy without feminism." Setting aside the question of priorities and any hierarchy of social contradictions, this perspective affirms the constitutive nature of all forms of oppression that contribute to the private and public forms of women's domination, discrimination, and subordination. At the same time, it shows that movements for change that do not consider the private realm have sanctified and predetermined women's roles within a conservative ideology and political practice; these arguments cite data on women's participation and the history of women's support for the most conservative and passive ways of thinking.

This argument stresses the possibility of speaking and showing *together* all forms of oppression, not stratified from without, but in a new synthesis.

If we delve deeper into the discourse developed from this second proposal we might say that, feminist analysis has, since its inception, derived from its audacious critique of democracy, and of the re-evaluation and re-covery of its meaning.

Very quickly, this reflection allows us to perceive that there is a large and profound distance between, on the one hand, democratic values and proposals such as equality, anti-discrimination, liberty, and solidarity, and on the other what we experience and assume to be our reality.

Based on the difference between proposals and experience, we women recognize and can testify to the fact that our concrete, daily reality is one of *authoritarianism*. We know that women experience—and have always experienced—authoritarianism within the family, women's recognized arena for work and experience. We know that what the family structures and institutionalizes is precisely the undisputed Authority of the head of the family, of the father; it structures gender discrimination and subordination, as well as the hierarchy and disciplining of a vertical order, which is imposed as natural, and which subsequently is projected outward to all social events.

This leads us to argue that there are *two areas* or realms of action in relation to politics, which are completely separate and mutually exclusive, and which correspond to sexual divisions, a "natural" division which was not invented by the authoritarian regime that cut down democracy. On the contrary, this division preceded the regime, deriving instead from civilization itself.

Those realms, as we have said, are the *public*—where politics dominate along with the possibility of participating in the promise and search for liberty—and the *private*, solidly rooted in that which is domestic and necessary.[2] What women do, as a cultural group or category, is pushed into this private space. In this sense women have been deprived and politically marginalized.

From the vantage point of the political parties, whether they are more or less progressive, or promoting incipient or fully realized plans for social change, women's political action is always understood as a problem of barriers and incorporation, and how to get women's support for tactical and strategic models. For feminists, this position is problematic because it posits that the sense and meaning of women's political action, as we mentioned earlier, derives from the denial of women's identity, not an actual political identity.

When we argue that *it is possible to see the private as public*—at least in terms of social action—two things happen at once. In the first place, we see that today's notions of politics/public are very narrow, and in the second place, that ideas about who are the political subjects and actors are also limited, if we think about these things from the perspective of restoring democracy.

Translated by Melissa Mann

Notes

1. Among the local groups that proliferated under the dictatorship, women stood out for their leadership in sewing circles that produced and sold small tapestries (*arpilleras*) that reflected themes of social and political protest, as well as the *ollas communes* or "common pots" through which *pobladoras* (shantytown residents [feminine]) procured, prepared, and distributed meals in their neighborhoods.

2. The following note is provided here by the author:

See Hannah Arendt, "La condición humana," Seix Barral, Barcelona, 1974.

The Kids of Barrio Alto

Alberto Fuguet

Alberto Fuguet's best-selling 1991 novel of alienation among upper-class Chilean youth during the 1980s presents a searing portrait of the culture of a new wealthy class created under the dictatorship. Raised in California, Alberto Fuguet returned to Chile in 1977 at the age of fourteen and went on to study journalism, later contributing to a new wave of literature on the dictatorship known as "the new Chilean narrative." Fuguet's novel captures the idioms of youth culture, the spread of consumerism, and the identification with the United States in Chile's upper class during the 1980s. The isolation of this upper class is juxtaposed with the political changes occurring in the background of the novel, marked by the 1980 plebiscite on the Constitution. The novel follows the teenage protagonist Matías Vicuña—often compared to Holden Caulfield of J. D. Salinger's Catcher in the Rye—*during a week's time, recounting his travels in Rio de Janeiro and Santiago, regular drug and alcohol use, and idle conversations. In the excerpts here, Matías starts the day with a drink and aggressive chatter with the family maid and ends it with cocaine and conversation with bartender-student Alejandro Paz. It reflects Fuguet's skillful use of narrative detail, such as references to U.S. and British rock bands, popular consumer brands, and Santiago landmarks, to sketch the political apathy and global consumerism characteristic of his fictional subjects, as well as the stark class differences that continued to mark daily life in Chile in the 1980s.*

Friday September 5, 1980. Santiago, Chile.
I go into our kitchen. Carmen, our housekeeper, with those smudgy Coke-bottle glasses, wearing that blue apron I can't stand, is older and uglier than I remember. She doesn't even look at me. She's washing a pan, and I can tell she's about to leave. It's her day off. No one's going to be home tonight anyway, so it's a good day for her to take it. I notice that Rommy isn't here. She's a redhead, Irish, or so she says: "Just like O'Higgins, the founding father of our country." That's what she said to my mother anyway. So maybe it's true.—[like O'Higgins] she's from Chillán, so it's possible.
    "Rommy's not here, Carmen?"

"No, and that little cunt isn't coming back either. Your mother fired her while you were away. She was stealing. What a whore—I never saw a hornier bitch in my life . . . what a nerve she had. So a friend of mine is going to help out for a little while. I can't do all this work by myself. You people in this house are trying to kill me."

"Oh, shut up. Just give me a glass of tomato juice, will you?"

Rommy sure didn't last very long. I never even got a chance to make a move on her, much less get her in bed, and she was pretty hot. Not even twenty years old. One time she went out with [Vicuña's friend] Lerner and they ended up in bed together in some sleazy hotel near the train station. He told me all about it—said it was amazing, that she was insatiable, etc. She overheard the conversation, though, when we were on the phone and afterward told me that he was all talk and that the whole thing wasn't so hot and heavy. Not at all.

"Here's your juice. Hurry up and drink it because I want to get out of here. I've got to take two buses."

"Well then, go if you want to."

I go over to the bar and pour a little Stoli into the juice and bring it to my room. Nobody's around. I close the door and turn on the stereo: Earth, Wind and Fire, "September." The pits. I put on "Tangerine Dream" instead. Familiar, predictable, nothing great, but lets me think for a little while. I take a sip of my Bloody Mary, lean back, and feel the effect. I try to sleep a little, since I'm still wiped out. . . .

I try to read the paper. No way, though, too depressing. Gustavo Leigh, the guy who bombed La Moneda, switched parties and now he's voting for the "NO." And Jaime Guzmán, that fucking nerd, talks all day about justifying the "SI." Pinochet himself is pathetic, but he's smart, because he surrounds himself with good advisors, like Guzmán. This month's slogan is: "Good today, better tomorrow."

My sister Francisca, who is now old enough, is going to vote for the "SI." She and all her poser friends are for Pinochet's Constitución de la Libertad. They talk nonstop about how Chile is now the most important country in Latin America for advertising. All the other countries come here to film their commercials. I could care less about politics. The truth is, I just don't know very much, outside of those documentaries on TV that are against the Allende administration. They're the ones they show on Channel 7. They're actually kind of entertaining, because Chile seems like such a different place on them. It's as if it were another country: men with long beards, girls in miniskirts, and posters and demonstrations and sit-ins and riots. My mother says it was the worst time ever in Chile, but I don't see that at all—it looks great to me. She's always exaggerating, my mother. Some of what she says is true, I guess. At the very least, though, it's a hell of a lot more interesting than what's going on these days. . . .

All right, Matías, *the night is young.* I imagine that I'm in Rio or Los Angeles, speeding down a street lined with palm trees. If only Santiago had freeways and highways to roar down: I could get up to 100, maybe even 110, on my parents' Accord. But Santiago is in Chile and the only things we have are those four-way intersections and endless, useless traffic circles packed with cars going round and round and round. I'm in the traffic circle at the Portada de Vitacura, going around and around, as usual. I've already gone around four times; I suppose I should try to exit already. First, I look at the digital clock on the dashboard: 22:18. Early. The curfew tonight is 3:00 A.M. Nacho said "late" so I have some time to kill. I decide to go for a ride, to get lost for a little while. . . .

I finally get to El Bosque: I park in front of Juancho's. . . . Juancho's is the place where all the "chosen ones" go; the hangout of the "golden children," as Luisa calls us. Luisa, who never even comes here. She's right, though. Not just anyone can come here. There's a bouncer at the door who checks that everyone coming in is "people like us." Before, I thought it was just lucky getting into Juancho's considering my age, and being a student and all. But El Toro, the owner, believes in cultivating his future clientele, if you will, and has no problem letting me and my friends in. He also knows that underage shits like us will pay whatever it costs. And it's true. Everyone under eighteen—pre–driver's license—that comes here, everyone I know, spoiled little fuckers that come from the country club or Reñaca or from school, all have the good fortune of not looking their age. They all dress well, get the "look" just right, and spend shitloads of money. That's why everyone gets in.

One of the major selling points of Juancho's is that El Toro (whose real name is Juan) trusts us. What that means is that he has various "open" accounts where he keeps tabs on what people spend. If, at the end of the month, you don't have enough money to pay it off, he and his little gang bill your parents directly. The great thing about this arrangement is that the parents always pay, because El Toro is somehow associated with the local Godfather as well as with Pinochet's nephew. That's what connects this whole network of bars, pubs, cabarets, drug dealers, hookers, massage parlors, saunas, and who knows what else. That's how Nacho's account works. They just add his expenses to his father's bill. And every time his father leaves Krazy Kat or Private VIPs, he's so nervous that Nacho's mother is going to find out that he just whips out his Mont Blanc and signs. And Nacho, of course, drinks and drinks. I guess everyone gets their revenge in their own way. In my case, though, it's harder to charge me. My parents only go to Regine's, where they're members, or else they go to the Red Pub. So what ends up happening is that when I'm broke, it's Nacho's father who ends up subsidizing my vices. That's why I come; it works out great for me. No loss on my part.

When I go inside Juancho's, the latest, horrendous Queen album over-takes me, penetrates my ears. I almost lose my balance. The place seems smaller somehow, slightly more Chilean than I remembered it. The big movie screen is still there with its bad picture and bad tracking. Jim Mor-rison is puking all over some flowers. The sound never quite matches the video. El Chalo, the disc jockey, is more into changing the music than the music itself. He then plays "Another One Bites the Dust," full blast. As I look at him, he just lifts those bushy eyebrows of his that just about meet in the middle, smiles a shit-eating grin, and then puts on "Bohemian Rhapsody" to piss me off. Fuck him. . . .

The Great Alejandro Paz of Chile does a lot more than just serve drinks. He hangs out, talks to everybody, fulfills all the standard, stereotyped re-quirements of the bartender. Just like you see in the movies. He's a good guy, and I get along pretty well with him, better than most around here, and I kind of think I know why. He's sort of a working-class type, so his favorite thing is to piss off all of us who come into Juancho's. He criticizes and criti-cizes. So I tell them he's a spy, a secret agent from Frei's regime, or maybe even of the "NO." Yeah, sure. He dies laughing whenever I tell him that.

"To undermine this society, Matías, you have to get at it from the inside," is what he once said to me. "You'll understand when you get to university. Mark my words. . . ."

At the university, everyone thinks he's really arrogant and "imperial-ized" (the poor guy suffers from an unmistakable, almost unforgivable "Yankee-mania"); here, on the other hand, at Juancho's, he takes on the role of proletarian-exploited-by-society-who-feeds-alcoholic-drinks-to-the-children-of-the-ruling-class.

Alejandro Paz, of course, is a member of the bourgeoisie. Four years older than me, he tells this (far too familiar) story of his life, that's just a little bit beyond my understanding. But I do get it. He lives alone, he's told me, and spends all the money he earns at Juancho's (plus the extra he makes off trafficking his joints and other "medicinal substances") on music, books in English, and subscriptions to magazines like *Rolling Stone* (which I also get) or *Interview* (which I hate). His dream is to go to the United States, a country that he has turned into his total obsession, almost like a sickness with him.

He idealizes it to the extent that he probably knows more about America than practically any normal American does.

I've only been to Miami, with my parents and my sisters, a few years ago. We also went to Orlando: Disney World, Cape Kennedy, the usual. I liked it, sure, but it wasn't an obsession or anything. It all seemed incredible to me, though, like the ideal place to go, to be whoever you want to be, in a country where everything happens, where nobody notices you, nobody judges you, zero opinions, and full of things you never dreamed of. It seemed like a place where it would be impossible to get bored. For Paz, it's all that and more: it's heaven, the only perfect place. That's exactly why I think he's never gone there, though, and he probably won't, ever. Because if he gets there, and the United States disappoints him somehow, and treats him badly, the poor guy will just crack up. It'll destroy him.

In any event, it's this strange communion with the United States that continues to bond me and the Great Alejandro Paz of Chile. We always talk in English. Me with my good little accent and everything. According to him, I speak it well because, just like him, my background has been "nontraditional." Meaning, more than in school and those classes at the North American Institute, you learn "American" from the radio, the movies, music, magazines, or screwing some American girl over here on one of those "Youth for Understanding" programs. In fact, Paz once introduced me to a girl from Texas, Joyce something, who was here on an exchange program. Paz is the kind of guy who loves making exotic drinks. He invents these concoctions with names like "A Drink on the Wild Side" or "Atlantic City Blues," which no one ever dares to order. It's inevitable with him—when we get to talking, he always starts dolling out advice. Before I went to Rio, he said to me:

"You should go on a real trip, one that'll hurt you, get it? So you can see how things really are. Not with your teacher or with those spoiled little brats in your school. You should go alone. Go cross-country on Greyhound, for example. Get stranded in Wichita, eat a taco in front of the Alamo, sleep in a cheap motel full of bums in Tulsa, Oklahoma. Or go to New York, man; go to CBGBs, go see Patti Smith in concert. That's life, man, not this! One day in Manhattan is like six months in Santiago. To come back to Chile is insanity, it sucks, with all the fucking military all over the place, add all its phobias, and the total backwardness, it's so *heavy*. It's more than heavy, it's *hard-core*, man. All you have to do is turn on the radio to see how bad off we are, Matías. When are they going to start playing the Ramones or the Sex Pistols here? Listen to me, man, and take a trip: go west, my son, go west." . . .

"This fucking place is boring," I say to Paz, who is washing some glasses.

"It's as if nothing ever changes, all the images just repeat themselves over and over again."

"That's what I always said to you, and that's exactly what I've always thought."

"Everything's so small, so familiar. I feel like I know everyone in this little world of Chile, and I know exactly what's going to happen here."

"You've got to get out. Escape before it gets too late. Nothing happens, and nothing's ever going to happen here. Much less now. This whole thing with the referendum and the constitution and that mess, these motherfuckers are going to stay in office at least another eight years, and maybe more. Eight years, and then another sixteen. That's twenty-four years, buddy. That's serious, *hot stuff*, you know, no bullshit. Just imagine what that'll be like. The worst part of it all is that it's the little assholes like you who are going to vote for the 'sí.'"

"I don't vote. I'm not even eighteen yet . . ."

"But if you did, you'd vote for the 'sí.' You know you would."

"I'd have to think about it."

"Think because what! It's because of people like you that we're in the situation we're in. Thanks to you, I'm stuck here, only dreaming about escaping. What do you think, Matías, that it's fun to feel like you have no country, that you have no future, and basically no way out? Do you?"

"Stop it, okay? Get off my back. I'm wired and annoyed enough as it is, and the last thing I need is to listen to your bullshit little speech, that I don't believe and neither do you anyway. What's this 'no future' crap you're talking about? How much money do you make here on a good night? God only knows you make enough to buy all the music you could ever want. On top of that, you're a student, you study the most indulgent, useless subject that you'll never be able to use to make any money, but that's your problem, man. If you wanted, you could switch to business. In this country, that's where there's opportunities for everyone."

"Who are you trying to kid, motherfucker?"

"Eat shit, Paz. You're a communist who dreams about the United States. You'd sell your mother to write an article for *Rolling Stone* or serve drinks at the famous Palladium you're always talking about. Give me a tequila, straight up, will you? With limes and salt and everything. And put it on Nacho's tab. That motherfucker should've been here a long time ago."

Translated by Kristina Cordero

Sexuality and Soccer

Pedro Lemebel

Gay activists became prominent in struggles against the military dictatorship in the 1980s, both through Chile's first gay rights organization, El Móvil (The Movement), and less openly through other political and social movements (feminist, party, neighborhood, etc.). A founder and participant in the art collective Las Yeguas del Apocalipsis (Mares of the Apocalypse), Pedro Lemebel performed the politics of protest, transvestism, and sexuality in the waning years of dictatorship and transition to democracy. Through his fiction, Lemebel made homosexuals and transvestites visible, challenging the traditionalism and apparent homogeneity of official culture. Lemebel's short story "How Could I Not Love You (or the Micropolitics of Soccer Fans' Gangs)" takes its title from one of the anthems sung by fans of the soccer team Colo-Colo and describes a Chilean soccer game in explicitly sexualized terms. In Chile as elsewhere, professional soccer is considered a staunchly heterosexual male venue, one where open expressions of gender difference and sexuality are not tolerated. In this story, Los de Abajo (literally, Those from Below, or The Riffraff) is the name of the University of Chile team's fans, while La Garra Blanca (The White Claw) refers to itself as La Hinchada Popular (The Popular Fan Club). Playing on the ritualized opposition enacted by fans both inside and outside the stadium, Lemebel explores the linkages between the fans' sexual excitement—even as they antagonize a gay fan—and the challenge to authoritarian control manifest in the political destape (opening or liberalization) of the 1980s.

Having come loose from the branch of civic control, the gangs of soccer fans overfill stadiums, wobbling or knocking down the fences that authorities place to delimit the youthful fever, the adolescent mass weaving ties of complicity under the soccer teams' heraldry. This is how each confrontation between the "Garra Blanca" and "Los de Abajo" leaves in its wake a trail of sticks, stones, and broken glass, as the two opposing attitudes of the fans' gangs shatter the calm of well-bred homes with the periphery's mongoloid echoes.

Both fanaticisms are let loose in the mass's very center, the same romantic vandalism disrupting the regulatory apparatus that systematizes and silences the kids' euphoria.

The supposed resentments between the two gangs are played out between neighbors who soften financial hardships by drooling on a shared box of wine or in the acidic vapors of the joints that are passed around amid the sparkling embers that the fight revives. But beyond the rivalry for goals or last-minute penalty kicks, they know that they come from the same place, they remind one another of time spent buddying up behind the anti-dictatorship barricade and they're sure that the policeman's boots will not differentiate between them when striking their butts. They know that they really get together to fake a heinous opposition that in turn summons the true rival; the policeman, securing democratic order, who now strikes back in power's rump.

They could even be called juvenile eruptions that parade their bastard triumph screaming out "Blue, I love you, you're always in my heart," always under their skin, in the youthful hubbub of those who untiringly sing "Como no te voy a querer" ("How Could I Not Love You"). Despite the heat that tickles in the trickling drop of sweat that makes its way down the burning crotch, despite the stickiness of the nude torsos wet with excitement, the guys hug and squeeze, atremble from the blast of a forward who scores, slashing through the hymen of the goal's anal door. So the goal is an excuse for fans to cop a feel, raised and bundled together in the feverish wave that climbs the protective fences.

These juvenile shows mute out the democratic pastoral; they are uprisings of teens who, in the delirious tide that wets the stadiums, display the erection visible through the jean, cut off at the knee or at half of the buttock, the fashionable cut showing a dark cheek, part of a hairy thigh. A state of confidence in which no one is safe because the bottle spins in the air and can blow up in any distracted fan's face. No one is protected, least of all the flamer with the indigenous-looking belt who, acting like a male, managed to blend in amid the heartless waving flags. That very same flamer who hates soccer, who as a little girl was never able to kick a ball, elevated as she was in the fragile imagination of her high-heels. But she was overtaken by the desire to be there, amid all these jumping bodies rubbing up against one another, and her, adrift from the soaked bodies who discharge their soccer-ballistic might in the fit of a "Te quiero adicto."[1]

It was a struggle for her to be admitted in the center of the group of fans, the evil heart rocking her in the midst of the slogans. She slipped through, bending her legs, pushing some and dirtying her tongue with soccer's slang's "I knew they would, man," "Would you believe that" and so many others. But she finally made it and, while she pretends to be watching the game, following the ball rolling on the field, and bouncing, as are all the balls that are jumping right next to her, juicy in the hairy nest that cradles the dance. While she pretends to stumble, lightly running into someone and losing her balance, having to hang on to whatever is within reach, to the steamy pack of the kid who had been onto her for a while. And who was just waiting for the flamer to cop a feel to scream out: There's a fag here. It would then seem that upon hearing the word fag the entire stadium suddenly froze into silence, the ball suspended in the air, right about to pass the crossbar and the scream of goal also suspended in the "oa" without reaching the triumph of the "l." The perplexed players point toward the gallery, toward the gang of fans' very center, where the terrified flamer has been left speechless. Like a sacred heart awaiting martyrdom. A cramp in her throat makes her vomit the *goal* and the awaited word shakes up the coliseum, as the wicked stew once again bubbles.

And so, spun in the confusion, the flamer slips away in the moistness of the hugs, fleeing and sliding froth-like toward the corridors where the washrooms are seething with men in the urinal's ammonia.

There, this familiar smell revives her sucking ball-hogging mouth's crimson thirst. Protected by the profane scriptures, she calms down in the dialogue of moldy grafittis that preach "Here I gave it to Bluey" or "The Claw sucks it so good." Each tremulous sentence soaked through with the desire to bumfuck the rival, to sit him with such virility on the hanging post. As if pleasure and punishment were a shared ritual, a metaphor of injection that punishes and rewards with semen the opposite flag.

This is how the eye-cum-guiding-ring glances the wall, gleaning notes and phallic sketches from each hurried drawing, like roses on wallpaper turned sepia by the traces of urine. Iodine flowers slice the flamer's iris, teaching her to read the signs faded by the public toilet's solitude. A voyeuristic chronicle that learns its ABCs by expectantly peeping at the contiguous stall from that hole in the wall. Looking at the golden trickle of ejected beer. Ejected from a teen who has also spotted the flamer's lens transfixed on his member with her ruby eye desperately drilling through the wall. And then, at the first sign, the flamer changes teams, introducing herself in the neighboring stall where the guy awaits her shaking his red card in his hands. The closed door then shuts them off from the loud horde that follows the ball. The stadium outside erupts when a center forward zigzags the ball between his legs, barely brushing it, kicks it, rocking it by the pelvis all the way to the chest, enjoying it as he heads it and zoom gets both body and ball through the gate's opening.

At the game's end, fans sing "Como no te voy a querer" at the top of their lungs and both gangs then disperse throughout the city, knocking down the authorities' signposts, peeing in every street-corner where they find a camera installed by these authorities to watch over them with their punitive gaze.

Human tidal waves in shorts and torn sneakers challenge the repression as it whistles its tear gases and dents the rocks with water-throwing trucks. Then the racket scatters throughout the streets, amid the honking, drumming and whistling that liven up the rocker kids' partying. The home-grown *cumbia* [Latin dance music with Afro-Caribbean roots] that moves the trasher [a punk, someone who drinks and does drugs] along to the rhythm of the by now beloved "Como no te voy a querer," scribbled everywhere, shouted out on the walls in the subversive lyricism of its spelling. A nomad writing, sprayed-by-hand, whose traces are found in the strokes' gothic style. The graffiti's runaway grammar that practices its writing striking at the happy city's walls, at the continent's neoliberal face, stained by the black lipstick that the street kids pour on it.

We'll see if they find them, if the team's directors assume responsibility for the disasters caused by its members, declared a public menace by the mayor, a bad example for other youngsters who don't get drunk or sink into drug use. Our lads, sound of spirit, with their shirts white and their jeans freshly ironed, involved in social services, taking elderly people for walks and cleaning up the mud after floods. So different from the swarm of offenders that derailed a train for the fun of it because they did not want to continue to ride along the same path outlined by the traffic lights. It was enough for one *loco* [crazy guy] to unhook the car in which they were returning after a match, for everyone to go along with it, smoked up as they were, without rhyme or reason, as they watched the locomotive roll away on its own along the railroad line, laughing their heads off, thinking that the driver was sure of taking them along the monotony of the right track. They once dreamed of the electric train of the rich kids' childhoods and this time they had a real train that they would take to Woodstock far away from the 'hood's dried earth, from the law that's on their heels, and always running away, always in school, jail and hospital problems.

That's why they think that they're rebels in a mutiny, surpassing the metropolis's harmonic tone. They think that they're drunks drowning their sorrows, or else, drunks celebrating their team's triumph. Like a small victory of faded angels who continue chanting and ringing in the cheer beyond the limits of what's permitted, rupturing the official eardrum with the sullen song that returns to the margins, fading away, drowned out by the police cars' sirens that direct juvenile circulation in the bullet-proof spikes of order.

Translated by Beatriz E. Rodríguez-Balanta

Note

1. "Te quiero adicto" can be translated as "I love you like an addiction." It refers to a common theme in the chants of the Colo-Colo soccer club's fans, who refer to their love for the club as an addiction.

Competing Perspectives on Dictatorship as Revolution

Joaquín Lavín and Ernesto Tironi

On the eve of the 1988 plebiscite on Pinochet's rule, contentious debates on the na-
ture and accomplishments of the military regime raged throughout Chilean society.
Part of these debates concerned the economic effects of the military regime, and the
very definition of Chilean "progress," an issue explored in two widely read works:
Joaquín Lavín's Chile, A Quiet Revolution *and Ernesto Tironi's response,* The
Silences of the Revolution. *Lavín, a key advisor to Pinochet and a leader of the*
Chilean Right today, hailed the modernizing trends evident in the commercial ar-
chitecture, increased consumption, and cosmopolitan entertainments enjoyed by
many Chileans in the 1980s. Citing the privatization of health care and education as
keys to this modernization, Lavín celebrated Chile as a "society of choice," in which
Chileans choose from the many options proffered by the market rather than the two
or three alternatives offered by state-run programs. The sociologist Ernesto Tironi,
a major figure in the opposition to the Pinochet regime, answered Lavín by describ-
ing the failures and limits of Chile's free-market revolution. Tironi highlighted those
left behind by the expansion of the market system, focusing his attention on the
increasing impoverishment of the urban poor, who faced deindustrialization, high
prices, unemployment, and urban resettlement, as well as the temporeros (seasonal
agricultural workers), whose ranks swelled dramatically after the reversal of agrar-
ian reform and the growth of the protected fruit industry. Taken together, Lavín
and Tironi represent the polarized views of the dictatorship's economic legacy that
circulated during the plebiscite campaigns in 1988 as well as after the transition to
democracy.

Chile: A Quiet Revolution, *by Joaquín Lavín*

During the last decade, Chile has experienced profound changes, transformations that are modifying the way in which new generations of Chileans
live, think, study, work, and rest. The way in which they dress, the food

they acquire, the way in which they use their free time, the cities in which they prefer to live, the professions they want to pursue. . . . Everything is changing.

These changes are the consequence of three principal factors: the dramatic shift in the world economy, which, because of amazing technological developments, has moved in just a few years from the "industrial era" to the "information era"; a deliberate politics of global integration, initiated in 1975, that not only eliminated commercial barriers, but also expanded Chilean horizons, giving them access to information, technology, and consumer goods that were previously available only through infrequent foreign travel; and all of this happened in an environment that has favored individual initiative, creativity, innovation, boldness, and entrepreneurial capacity.

This experiment with three ingredients has produced an explosive mixture: millions of Chileans making free decisions with all the available information in a country connected to a world that is advancing at supersonic speed. They are making a true revolution. . . .

Between 1970 and 1986, more than one million people joined the workforce, the majority of whom will retire as members of the [privatized pension funds] Provida, Santa María or Habitat Pension Fund Associations, and not the Social Security Service or the Public or Private Employees Fund of their parents' generation. This new generation has a much higher educational level than their parents, and their greater years of study mean that they enter the labor market later, as well. In 1960, only 8 percent of the population of Santiago had finished high school. Today that percentage is 31 percent. Whereas in 1970 a total of 302,000 young Chileans went on to secondary education, in 1985 this number surpassed 670,000. Likewise, in the last six years the number of students who entered higher education grew by 74 percent, and four of every ten no longer graduate from the University of Chile, the Catholic University, or other traditional universities, but rather from [newly created private universities].

Advances in the health standards of the population mean that every Chilean born today will enjoy 35,000 more hours in his lifetime than those who were born in 1970.

Progress brings with it profound changes that modify how families live. Because people have more choices, time becomes ever more scarce, and life always moves more quickly. Women, who enjoy ever better access to more advanced education, can aspire to higher salaries, which makes it more difficult—"more expensive," in economists' language—if they choose to stay home. In fact, in the last decade the growth rate of female employment was twice as great as that of men, which means that more than four

Pope John Paul II visits Chile, April 1987. The papal visit erupted in controversy, as both Pinochet and his opponents sought to use the visit to shine the light of international attention on Chile. Here, Pinochet greets the pope on his arrival; later, his public mass in O'Higgins Park dissolved in conflict between police and opposition protestors. The papal visit was an attempt to smooth the long-standing tensions between the Chilean Church and the regime but the reality of Catholic leadership in human rights and political movements that opposed the dictator could not be escaped. Photograph by AP/Pete Leabo, image no. 8704010159 © 1987 The Associated Press. Used with permission.

of every ten Chileans incorporated into the labor market today are women. As in other parts of the world, this phenomenon has given rise to the development of technologies destined to save women's time in household tasks, leading to an increase in consumer acquisition of washing machines, vacuums, dishwashers, microwave ovens, disposable diapers, "fast food" industries, microwavable dinners, restaurants, and large commercial centers and supermarkets, where it is possible to find, in a single location, a wide variety of articles without wasting time in several trips or in search of parking. . . .

THE TENDENCIES OF THE SILENT REVOLUTION: GLOBAL INTEGRATION

Chile has become integrated with the world. While we sell our products to the world, we also acquire its fashions, its technology, and its language. Until a few years ago, a film that won the "Oscar" was delayed many months, and even years, before it was exhibited in the theaters of our capital. In contrast, people in Santiago could see "Platoon," the film that won the "Oscar" in 1987, almost simultaneously with the American audience, and could also watch the live ceremony in which the film was awarded. Our connection with the world has caused a boom in courses and institutes for English instruction, as well as a shift in high school and college language programs.

Greater commercial possibilities have meant that the number of cars on the streets grew by 445,000 in the last fifteen years, while boasting a total of two million homes with a television, Chile has one of the highest rates of televisions per family in South America.

The so-called cartoon and Atari generation—children and young people who spend several hours a day in front of the television or computer—is much better informed than their parents were at the same age, a situation whose effects are still unknown. At the same time, those children sitting in front of the television constitute a new market for Chile, one that is exploding and revolutionizing the world of advertising and consumer habits. In the last five years, the consumption of yogurt has increased significantly, and young people also drink more sodas and less wine. . . .

MADE IN CHILE

The world's population has reached five billion, just as Chilean exports are also reaching the five billion mark. This means that today we sell a dollar's worth of merchandise to every inhabitant of the planet, a record that hundreds of Chileans are contributing to by exporting everything from popsicles to spiders, as well as kiwis, toys, weapons, books, and software programs.

Contrary to what the technocrats tried to create fifteen years ago [under the Popular Unity], the market redrew the maps and went beyond geography so that today, rather than producing parts and pieces that integrate us into the Peruvian, Bolivian, or Ecuadorian economies, we are associating with New Zealand and confronting together the world market for wood, sea products, and fruit. In the last twelve months, the "New Zealand connection," [which stems from increased investment by New Zealand companies in Chilean ones], has been extended to other areas of economic activity. . . .

A "CUSTOMER-FRIENDLY" ECONOMY

Orientation toward the client, which is so characteristic of competitive market economies, has encouraged businesses to yield much better service, because they consider consumers' different tastes, ease in financial transactions, and need to save time.

A few years ago it was not possible for a Chilean to cash a check in any branch of his bank, much less withdraw money or make deposits on the weekend. Now 800,000 transactions per month are carried out at the 160 automatic tellers installed in different locations throughout the country.

Supermarkets have expanded noticeably, everywhere displacing the "corner grocery store." Every day, there are more conveniences: 5,000 Santiago families, especially those in which husbands and wives both work, do their weekly shopping by telephone and have their groceries delivered to their homes by the Telemercados Europa trucking fleet. Client services are more and more sophisticated: on the receipt of Almac supermarkets, a housewife can read in complete detail how much of each product she bought with its corresponding price. The big malls such as Parque Arauco and Apumanque welcome more than one million people each month and compete to attract clients; they have transformed shopping into a true weekend outing for the family. At the same time Visa, Diners, Mastercard, and American Express credit cards help thousands of families with their purchases, a system that big department stores like Falabella, Almacenes París, Ripley, and others have begun to utilize by issuing their own credit cards.

It is possible to travel to Concepción at night, in sleeper buses, with televisions and VCRs, for a lower price than the same travel by train, and it is possible to telephone from Panguipulli—a southern city of 30,000 inhabitants—to any place in the world by dialing direct. A revolution in services? This is a reality that the Chilean consumer already enjoys.

NEW PRIVATE SECTOR BUSINESSES

Work that was before only reserved for the public sector has begun to be successfully carried out by private enterprises. The health insurance agencies, better known as Isapres, that serve one million beneficiaries, have generated a demand for health coverage in the private sector. The blocks of Salvador Street in Santiago today constitute a true "medical neighborhood," a half kilometer on which laboratories, dental clinics, and health centers compete for clients.

Private insurance is a reality for more than two million affiliates of the Pension Fund Associations (known as AFPs), and for hundreds of retirees and pensioners who belong to the new system.

As in many other activities, the private sector has also penetrated deeply into the field of education, where it has created numerous private colleges and 2,700 private schools subsidized by the State. Centers of technical training, professional institutes, and even universities today constitute new private alternatives for those who finish their primary education. . . .

CHILE'S GLOBAL INTEGRATION: EMERGING VERSUS DYING INDUSTRIES

The global economic market, integrated with the world, represents a complete re-adaptation of the productive apparatus. Certain activities have been expanded, while others have become less important. Today's growth industries are those that have been able to modernize when they compete in international markets, industries for which the country has special advantages, and those which offer services that support the export sector.

According to what John Naisbitt explains in his best-seller *Megatrends* (Warner Books, New York, 1984), there are currently two economies in the United States: one that is emerging and one that is slowly retreating. The same thing is happening in Chile: we have a situation that is generating a dual economy, which confuses those who try to analyze it according to old indicators, indicators that are dying along with the economic scheme they represent. We used to measure agricultural growth with an index of fourteen products, but this index did not include grapes, which today is the principal agricultural product and Chile's second-most important export; it also excluded wood, apples, asparagus, and kiwis.

At the same time, part of the country is growing, and the other is in recession. Even as unemployment rises above 12 percent in the Fifth Region, particularly because of the problems faced in Valparaíso, work can be found now in other places. Unemployment has fallen below 6 percent in Copiapó, in the Sixth Region, in the Tenth, and in Aysén. In the zones where export-agriculture and fishing are expanding, there is labor scarcity.

The industries that are expanding can be found, in general, far from Santiago, and are not visible to those living in the capital, since those regions trade directly with the world. Iquique provides fishmeal, Concepción sends wood, Copiapó sells grapes from its vineyards, and Puerto Montt and Aysén export salmon. The total catch from fishing grew from 1.2 million tons in 1977 to 5.4 million in 1986. Production levels in cellulose grew from 350,000 tons in 1973 to 846,000 tons in 1986, at the same time that agricultural production grew by more than ten times.

THE MODERNIZATION OF AGRICULTURE

Among those sectors of the economy that have modernized, agriculture— without a doubt—holds a very special place. Fruit exports grew 25 times between 1973 and 1986. That sector today relies on the most modern infrastructure in terms of refrigeration, controlled atmosphere, and drip systems. While the United States still produces grapes with seeds, the Chilean varieties—which are more modern—do not have seeds. The land devoted to industrial fruit production in the main export districts grew from 49,000 to 105,000 hectares; Chile led the world market in table grapes, peaches, and nectarines. In 1986 Chile imported 2,875 tractors, a statistic that represents a 149 percent increase over the previous year, as well as the second highest number ever imported in the history of Chile. . . .

Confronted with tough external competition, national industry must become efficient to compete. Capital goods imports, which in 1984 represented 16 percent of Chilean purchases in the international market, now constitute 25 percent, and consist mainly of industrial machinery that has permitted the improvement of production techniques. . . .

THE MALLS

Born in the 1940s in the United States, shopping centers or malls have developed very rapidly in the last few years. In Santiago today, malls account for more than fifty important commercial centers, but none of them can compete with the two market giants: Parque Arauco and Apumanque. Both situated in the Las Condes district, they welcome more than one million visitors a month, with record-breaking sales that improve year after year.

Parque Arauco opened its doors in 1982, through the fruitful initiative of a group of Chilean construction entrepreneurs. . . . They invested more than $40 million in a gigantic building of 40,000 square meters, which houses more than 140 commercial sites. . . . This mall, which recently underwent an important expansion, has parking, a movie theater, service stations, special bus transportation to the subway, Ñuñoa, and La Reina districts, and a closed circuit television system that provides permanent surveillance of all entrances. The Apumanque, for its part, with 42,000 square meters and 335 stores, boasts the equivalent of nineteen blocks of shop windows.

Paralleling the development of malls is the expansion of the great department stores, such as Falabella, Almacenes París, Ripley and others, which have expanded their coverage and modernized their system of attending to the public. All of them offer their clients the benefit of credit cards. Also, thanks to the help of a centralized computer, Falabella credit card holders can use their cards in any of the four cities in the country where that store does business.

Translated by Carolyn Watson

The Silences of the Revolution, *by Ernesto Tironi*

THE OTHER SANTIAGO

"They descend in the hundreds from [the working-class district of] Peñalolén, they go together, advancing along Américo Vespucio Avenue from the southern sector toward the upper-class neighborhood, they ascend San Cristóbal Hill via Conchalí on the way to Las Condes, or they walk through the streets of the periphery in the direction of their places of work in the center of city." This is how the magazine *Qué Pasa* described part of the movement of human beings taking place in Santiago each morning. However, from their automobiles, descending along new highways, or crossing recently inaugurated bridges toward schools or offices located more often "above," many inhabitants of the same valley hardly realize the existence of this other city that is also part of Santiago, nor of their momentary convergence with it. Only after eight, ten, or twelve hours, do they rub elbows, as each inhabitant returns to his territory: while some go speedily toward their homes in the upper neighborhood, the others descend to their shantytowns in crowded microbuses, or simply on foot.

TWO CITIES

The inhabitants of the other Santiago, those who live poorly in the "marginal belt" of the city, are commonly called *pobladores*. They account for around 2.3 million people, which is equal to half of the total population of the Metropolitan Region. Harshly assaulted by unemployment, declining income, and the deterioration of public services, and forced to concentrate in poorer and less equipped urban areas, the pobladores have clearly remained on the other side of the border that divides Santiago into two cities; not in the city in "expansion" that is now being "born" but in that which "decays" and "dies."

Each inhabitant of a city has in his memory an imaginary map of it, where, with almost exact precision, its "good" and "bad" neighborhoods are situated. In Santiago, the segregation between these two worlds is social, and it is also spatial, and the latter has not only been accentuated in the last decade, but has been planned by public policies.

Among the explicit purposes of the recent municipal reform, for example, was "the identification of certain more homogenous areas," which resulted in a redefinition of the districts of the Metropolitan Region. To create "homogenous areas," all those zones with a greater density of poor people were separated from the rich and intermediary districts, and new districts were created where they could concentrate. One illustration of this policy is Ñuñoa, where two groups with a high concentration of pobladores were relocated, to comprise two new districts: Peñalolén and Macul. As a result, Ñuñoa was in one sweep converted into a homogenous intermediate level district, through which its socio-economic status increased spectacularly.

The constitution of two cities in Santiago—one "cultured" and another "barbaric" . . . the latter located in the periphery of the city center—has allowed more comfortable families to avoid seeing poverty. It no longer forms part of their daily environment nor their personal responsibility, and they only perceive it as a diffuse threat to public order and tranquility.

The delimitation of an urban border and the constitution of ecologically and administratively homogenous zones responds precisely to this last vision, because it facilitates the control of the State over the coming "threat" of the other city, that of the pobladores. This was the same intention of the celebrated Baron Haussman, who after the Commune Rebellion in 1848 remodeled Paris with the intention of protecting it from the "dangerous classes."

RELOCATION

In housing policy, the military regime decided at the beginning to give priority to families without the capacity to save and who inhabit camps devoid of urban infrastructure and property titles. In some cases, this emergency situation was the result of the installation of the pobladores in the site in which they were; in others they were relocated to different areas of the city, where they were given land, ownership titles, and small, urbanized houses.

This last procedure was employed in the case of the settlements located in zones that were economically and socially more valuable in Santiago, which were emptied out, their residents relocated in the extreme periphery of the city. The procedure received the official name of "eradications," and between 1979 and 1984 it affected 28,703 families, or 4 percent of the Regional Metropolitan population.

The principal justification of the policy of eradications was economic: the relocation to zones with lower land values would permit a housing solution for a greater number of pobladores. However, diverse studies have proven that, if all the additional costs are taken into account that installing a family in the urban limits implies (transportation, widening of roads, basic services, etc), the investment surpasses that necessary for their establishment in central areas of the city 17 times over.

An additional problem, which tends to aggravate the situation, is that the receiving districts of those eradicated are precisely those that in the Metropolitan Region have fewer resources in education, health, transportation, and other basic services. The inequality that threatens these districts has not yet been reversed, and therefore the investment per capita of the public sector in the districts that eliminated the settlers surpassed the investment destined for receiving districts five times in the period 1980–1984.

"FAR WEST"

With their eradication from the rich districts, the pobladores were also exiled from a social medium where they had access to integrating and social mobility mechanisms, where they could turn to certain basic social services, and where they could access a job market composed of service occupations, such as gardening, laundry, domestic service, repairs. They became alienated, without means—neither they nor their children—to leave marginality. What did they receive in exchange? A "housing solution" that consisted of houses smaller than 500 square feet, with sites no bigger than 1,614 square feet. And these were the fortunate ones because others had to live together in units of three or four floors with densities of more than 800 people per hectare.

THE OUTER DISTRICTS

. . . The aspiration to have a city with "homogenous areas" has given rise to districts reminiscent of South African townships. In Santiago, certainly, there are no barriers between those districts and the rest of the city; however, other factors serve to limit that communication and create a situation of severe alienation in the poorest districts.

At the end of 1985 in the La Pintana district, there were only seven telephones, one for every 22,000 inhabitants; in the sectors where the eradicated are concentrated, they could not count on even one nearby telephone. Suffice it to say that, to that date, there was neither a post office nor a telegraph agency. Collective transportation is not sufficient either, considering that 63 percent of the residential urban streets are not paved, which makes transit in buses impossible; for the rest, the buses are routinely assaulted by common delinquents, which leads to the interruption of the routes.

But alienation does not only affect La Pintana; it is shared by lower Santiago in its totality. Take as an example what happens with collective transportation. The inhabitants of the peripheral districts actually travel less toward the rest of the city than they did a decade ago, and when they travel, they must frequently do so on foot. This is because in 1980 to make fifty trips per month on public transportation meant spending 4 percent of the minimum salary, and today it means spending 26 percent. As a consequence, while in 1977, 18 percent of trips were made on foot, in 1986 these reached 25 percent.

It is known that the number of automobiles in the country went from 262,000 in 1976 to more than 600,000 in 1985. But this boom obviously has not benefited the other Santiago. In 1984, for example, the [wealthy] district of Providencia had 697 automobiles for every thousand inhabitants, whereas [poor] La Granja had 15. . . .

SURVIVING

Poor women have an obsession that makes them uneasy during all hours of the day: how to eat today—first the children, then the husband, and finally themselves—and, then, what to do so that there is no shortage of food tomorrow. There is no better indicator of poverty than hunger, and in fact this is a phantom that prowls through the other Santiago without resting.

In 1986, eight of every ten families living in the *poblaciones* [shantytowns] of Santiago consumed fewer calories than the minimum recommended by the Food and Agricultural Organization/World Health Organization. Despite this, food accounts for up to 70 percent of family expenses: "We do not eat anything at night. We have a late cup of tea and almost nothing remains by night. The children drink a cup of tea, or see if anything is left in the pot, which is very difficult," points out a woman interviewed for the cited study. The poor family, therefore, orients all of its forces toward survival: other expenses are eliminated with the goal of leaving something for food; [the poor family] tries to have all of its members conducting some activity that generates earnings; it turns to the support of friends and relatives; it looks for help from the government. If this is not enough, it proceeds to selling goods or articles bought during when times were good. At last, it resorts to an extreme solution: feeding itself in soup kitchens, supported by the Church and sometimes by the municipalities. . . .

NECESSITY CREATES THE MEANS

For the inhabitants of the other Santiago, the hidden face of poverty is unemployment. According to all the polls, this is the problem that they consider a priority. In the last fourteen years it has affected one-fifth of the work force (on average), which triples the historical levels (between 1960 and 1970, the rate of unemployment reached 6.4 percent). Among the pobladores however, it has reached, on average, one-third of the work force; and among the youth, unemployment and labor marginality are more intense still. . . . Unemployment has begun to form part of the daily experience of the poorest groups. Without employment there certainly are no incomes, but neither is there personal dignity nor family stability. . . .

TO MARKET

. . . In order to "flexibilize" the job market, the new labor legislation gives the boss the possibility of firing his personnel simply because of "the needs of the company," which generates a climate of instability among workers. At the same time, it permits the expansion of the work day to 12 hours, which has become a very extensive practice, especially in sectors such as the railway, collective transportation, fishing, services and commerce (think, for example, about the vendors in the malls like Apumanque or Parque Arauco, in Santiago, which remain open until nine o'clock at night, including Sundays and holidays).

The "flexibilization" that the new Labor Code introduces also induces the substitution of daily work for salaried work, through contract or by piecework: by piece, in the shoe and clothing industries; by catch bonus in industrial fishing; by fare commissions in urban transportation. This also facilitates temporary contracts, and induces the replacement of permanent personnel with contracted workers, who take on lateral functions at a much lower cost. In copper mining and the railways, for example, the increase of contract workers has become a growing concern for stable workers, who fear becoming displaced by them.

In terms of union organization and collective bargaining, the new labor institutionalism favors multiple unions [per enterprise], reduces the range of issues that can be negotiated, and the participation of sectoral [labor] federations in negotiations, excludes numerous sectors from collective bargaining, meticulously restricts the right to strike, and promotes non-union agreements between employers and workers. The purpose, obviously, is the creation of a type of union movement that is focused on micro-economic issues (at the level of the business), and has no interest in or influence on national level politics. In addition, there are special dispositions that prohibit union leaders from serving in a political party, a standard that is not applied, however, to the managers.

What has the new labor institutionalism meant? Essentially, organized labor—always considered weaker than employers—has lost the protection it traditionally found in the State; workers and unions are now at the mercy of the market. Today workers can be fired at the same moment when their employer finds cheaper alternatives in the market (that is to say: another worker). Workers are obliged to improve their earnings; and the unions themselves compete for workers' preference and affiliation. For the unions, then, the possibility of making up for their structural weakness [in the economy and labor relations system] by offering institutional protection disappears, and the possibilities of presenting a united front against their employers are reduced. . . .

BEHIND THE FRUIT

The Chilean countryside, after almost two decades of different types of experiments, entered into a process of sustained development at the beginning of the eighties. The agricultural boom, as it has been baptized, has been based in the security and high protection that the price lists fixed by the State provide to its products and in the extraordinary expansion of the fruit and forestry export sectors. Another component of this boom, however, is often forgotten: the availability of abundant, cheap labor lacking any kind of union organization.

After 1973, 45,000 small landholders created by the Agrarian Reform received their property titles. In the following years, totally abandoned by the State, whose support organizations were literally dismantled, without credit or technical consultation, the majority of them had to sell their land. . . .

At the same time, the new business logic that took hold in the countryside meant the expulsion of thousands of tenants who lived dispersed on the old estates. Gradually, they were installed along the edges of roads or railways, the banks of rivers, or on the slopes of hills. Today they are also found on the periphery of rural towns close to fruit plantations and sites of forest exploitation. They do not migrate to the city, like their ancestors: they know that there they will not find work; they are still waiting—even the young people—for employment that agriculture might some day offer them.

In the Chilean countryside a figure who seemed to have vanished reappeared: the "migrant worker" (*afuerino*), the peon without land (man or woman), the same one who in the nineteenth century went from one hacienda to the other taking any job, adjusting to occasional work, poorly remunerated. They are the current "seasonal workers" [temporeros], who lack stable employment and move through the countryside working according to the demands of different types of production. Between 1964–65 and 1986–87, stable agricultural workers were reduced by half . . . ; the number of seasonal workers, in turn, doubled. . . .

The salaries of the seasonal workers are substantially above the minimum wage. Nevertheless, the Ministry of Agriculture declared a short time ago: "We cannot talk about the boom of the Chilean economy and have balance sheets showing great profits without distributing part of those earnings to the workers." . . . For example, the kiwi has generated profits of $25,000 per hectare, but while in New Zealand (the principal worldwide exporter) the worker is paid $64 daily, in Chile his salary fluctuates between two and four dollars.

Translated by Carolyn Watson

The Whole World Was Watching:

The 1988 Plebiscite

The Observer Group of the Latin American

Studies Association

In a historic plebiscite held October 5, 1988, Chileans were asked to vote "Yes" or "No" on an eight-year extension of Pinochet's rule. In a climate of increasing anxiety as the date of the plebiscite approached, a coalition of opposition parties mounted an extraordinary campaign in favor of the "No" vote—including television advertising, grassroots organizing to get out the vote, and street parades. The day of the election was remarkably free of violence but yielded a stunning result: after the votes were counted, the opposition "No" had won with 54.71 percent of the vote. In this report, observers from the Latin American Studies Association (LASA), an international organization of scholars who study the region, describe the day of the referendum, noting the population's palpable fear of military reprisal, popular enthusiasm for the "No," and the common decency that pervaded the day's events. The presence of powerful international observers and discontent among younger military officers and the more moderate right-wing Renovación Nacional (National Renovation) Party, along with clear signals from the U.S. and foreign governments in favor of a free and fair election, together created considerable pressure on the regime to validate the majority vote against Pinochet.[1]

October 5, 1988, the day of the plebiscite, was an extraordinary event in the life of the Chilean nation.[2] Ninety-seven percent of the registered voters, or 90 percent of the eligible population, turned out to vote, the highest percentage in the nation's history. Members of the LASA delegation fanned out across Santiago; one member went to the port city of Valparaíso, and two members went to provincial capitals and rural towns to observe the vote. From the Instituto Nacional, where Pinochet arrived to vote at 11 o'clock, receiving a subdued reception by the long lines of male voters awaiting their turn to vote, to the working-class neighborhood of San Miguel, to the shantytowns of San Ramón, thousands of Chileans queued up peacefully to vote. Because most voters chose to arrive early, lines were often long and many people stood for three hours or more in the hot sun. Voters waited cheerfully without incident, occasionally debating in a good humored way the political alternatives Chileans faced. Among the many moving scenes was the arrival at polling places of invalids and bed-ridden persons with the aid of relatives or nurses and of senior citizens dressed in their Sunday best.

By mid-afternoon, opposition leaders became concerned that the voting was proceeding too slowly. They feared that many voters would get tired and go home or find that the voting place had closed by the time they reached the front of the line. For the most part, the slowness with which the *mesas* [voting stations] began operation and undertook their work was due to the inexperience of many of the polling officials after fifteen years without fair elections and the complicated instructions they were supposed to follow. Even so, Juan Ignacio García, the head of the electoral service, gave assurances to opposition leaders that his office would see to it that the voting process was speeded up.

There was no evidence, however, that the military authorities were trying to slow down the voting process in working-class neighborhoods or otherwise hinder the voting process. In fact military commanders from the different services were very polite to the voters and were anxious to ensure a fair and impartial procedure. At one voting place in San Joaquín, for example, the young paratrooper in charge had looked into every conceivable contingency, from having ambulances stationed outside in case someone had a heart attack to an elaborate evacuation plan in case of an earthquake. Finally, both foreign and domestic observers were allowed to watch the proceedings without hindrance.

Less accommodating than most of the military authorities were some officials and private parties in scattered rural areas. For example, some Yes partisans hired all of the buses and denied transportation to people from communities that were identified with the No. In a few instances individuals were denied the right to vote since their names had been removed from the electoral registries because they were subject to prosecution for political offenses against the state. In some localities individuals who were openly supporting the No campaign had had their identity cards requisitioned by the police, making it impossible for them to vote. These incidents, however, pale by comparison with the fact that the overwhelming majority of Chileans voted without impediment. The authorities were committed to a clean and fair electoral process. In many polling places, voters embraced soldiers and officers, thanking them for guaranteeing a peaceful election.

(above, left) Vote for Pinochet. In this mimeographed leaflet from the "Sí" campaign, Pinochet's supporters touted Pinochet's role in returning Chile to democratic rule. Other leaflets, distributed at rallies and marches in the months leading up to the vote, boasted of the regime's economic success, while still others showed vintage photographs of masked, marching workers wielding clubs in the early 1970s. Pamphlet reproduced in *El Panfleto: Plebiscito 1988 a través de panfletos y volantes,* by Crístián Cottet Villalobos (Santiago: n.p., 1989), n.p.

(above, right) The vote for the "No." As the date of the 1988 plebiscite approached, Pinochet's opponents intensified their public campaign by focusing squarely on the regime's systematic abuse of human rights. The text of prominent artist Nemesio Antúnez's poster reads: "No more internal exile, burnings, exile, throat-slittings, executions, torture, rape, intimidation, censorship, persecution. We want democracy! Social justice = peace." "Throat-slitting" is an explicit reference to the "caso degollados" ("case of the throat-slitting") in which three Communist human rights activists were executed by security forces in 1985. The horrible and public nature of the crime and its commission after the 1978 Amnesty Law was passed provoked a judicial investigation that sparked the resignation of General César Mendoza, head of the Carabineros and founding member of the military junta, and led to life sentences for six members of the security forces. Illustration by Nemesio Antúnez. Pamphlet reproduced in *Por Que No: El NO de los escritores y los artistas plásticos chilenos,* edited by Arturo Navarro (Santiago: Comando Nacional por el NO.© 2012 Artists Rights Society (ARS), New York / CREAIMAGEN, Santiago.

As early as 5:00 P.M. some mesas closed and the vote count began. Interested voters and observers alike were allowed in to watch the count. It took close to two hours at each mesa, as polling officials counted all of the signatures, ballot stubs and ballots to see that there was an equal number of each. The president and secretary of each mesa also signed each ballot before they were opened. The results of the vote were read aloud by the president after the secretary opened each ballot. The poll watchers for the candidate and the opposition parties closely scrutinized each vote. Sometimes the crowd around the mesa spoke up to argue against questioning the validity of a vote, for example in the case of a voter having marked an X over his preference rather than a single vertical line.

Throughout the country, however, the counting went on without serious incident, and citizens and officials alike treated each other with respect and civility. When the count was finished, the No, Yes, blank, and contested ballots were placed in envelopes and sealed with lacquer, as were the ballot stubs. Each poll watcher received an official form signed by the president and secretary of the mesa certifying the results. Opposition poll watchers quickly sent their information to Santiago to be tabulated in the computers of the Command for the No. Many Yes and No partisans exuded civic pride in the peaceful electoral process, concluding that "Chile was the winner." When the LASA delegation asked a representative of the Yes how he felt about losing his mesa to the No he replied, "I feel that it is a great day for Chile." That shared sense of reclaiming the country's democratic heritage helped hold the nation together in the tense hours ahead.

Soon after the polls closed, it became apparent to opposition leaders that the No was winning. The Committee for Free Elections (CEL),[3] concerned that false information not be broadcast, had agreed that it would not give a preliminary count until it had information for at least 600 mesas, and only after it had informed the Yes campaign of its results. The No campaign was equally concerned about not raising false hopes so it agreed not to issue results until later in the evening. Radio stations supporting both the government and the opposition, however, began to broadcast partial results from polling places across the country, underscoring the fact that those tallies did not represent any particular trend. Television, almost totally controlled by the authorities, gave a decidedly different impression, conveying to viewers the certainty of a victory for the Yes.

The opposition strategy—to wait until substantial results had come in—was altered when the Undersecretary of Interior, Alberto Cardemil, appeared at 7:30 P.M., an hour and half after he was supposed to give preliminary returns. He reported the results of only 79 mesas or 0.36 percent of the total with a vote favorable to the Yes. By that time the opposition already had counted over half a million votes, which were showing a clear trend for the No. Cardemil said he would have further results in an hour, but an hour went by and he gave none. In view of the refusal of the authorities to issue results, the opposition decided to broadcast its own figures at 9:00 P.M. Sergio Molina of the CEL also released his count with 735 mesas tabulated, after unsuccessfully trying to reach the Yes campaign on the telephone. That count favored the No and, in retrospect, turned out to be surprisingly close to the final tally. Television, however, refused to broadcast opposition figures. In fact, Secretary General of the Government Hernán Poblete later called the stations warning them that to broadcast any opposition news would have the "gravest" consequences.

When Cardemil appeared on television at 10:00 P.M. to announce that with 677 mesas the Yes was still winning, and national television began showing reruns of U.S. sitcoms, the level of tension increased in opposition headquarters. Leaders of the pro-Yes National Renovation Party also became upset with what they perceived to be an effort in governmental circles to provoke some kind of incident. Some of them believed that the government had been stunned by the results and was looking for some way out, short of openly recognizing the No victory. Renovation leaders contacted the Ministry of the Interior directly, warning them not to do anything "stupid."

Some government officials, led by the Minister of the Interior Sergio Fernández, actually were considering a plan to issue a statement around midnight declaring the Yes was winning on the basis of more than a million votes counted. Since they knew that the No was really ahead, such a plan required the careful selection of actual polling places to provide the desired totals—a very difficult task, particularly since there was an overwhelming tendency in favor of the No. The plan also envisioned calling on partisans of the Yes to converge on the center of Santiago to celebrate their "victory." What made such a scenario especially sinister was that some government officials simultaneously considered asking for the withdrawal of police and troops who had cordoned off the center of Santiago. Removal of the armed forces would not only permit the Yes partisans to congregate downtown, but also would heighten the risk of a dangerous clash between partisans of both sides if No supporters rushed there to protect their "victory." The authorities might then impose a state of siege and put into place military contingency plans to cope with disorder and violence. This could give the Pinochet government the upper hand and an excuse to blame elements of the opposition for provoking the incidents and not recognizing the fairness of the count. It also could permit a suspension of the vote count or, if the unrest was widespread, a cancellation of the plebiscite. At the very least, the policy of not reporting returns was only adding to the tension in the country and the potential for confrontation.[4]

Despite the bitterness of the election campaign, political leaders of the Right and other junta members were more willing to accept the count of the opposition than the results given out by the government authorities and showed their determination to guarantee a fair electoral process. National Renovation maintained contact with the opposition as well as with the government and had access to the count from the Committee for Free Elections. Data from opposition computers were also taken directly to Generals Fernando Matthei, Commander-in-Chief of the Air Force, and Rodolfo Stange, Director General of the Police. Both junta members also obtained information from their own institutions confirming opposition results. Sergio Onofre Jarpa, the President of Renovation, went on television at midnight with Patricio Aylwin, president of the Christian Democratic party, to participate in a program that had been scheduled much earlier. The leader of Chile's Right was prepared to accept the defeat of the Yes and said that his impression was that there was a "majority tendency in favor of the No." His statement had an extraordinary impact. It immediately defused the tension in the No headquarters and calmed listeners all over the country who could not understand why opposition radio stations were broadcasting figures continuously while the authorities remained silent.

Even more important in providing reassurance to a nervous nation was the declaration along the same lines by General Matthei at 1:00 A.M. He was on the way to the presidential palace to meet with General Pinochet and the other junta members for a meeting that had been scheduled originally at 9:30. Like some leaders of the Right, Generals Matthei and Stange had not been able to reach the Ministry of the Interior nor the Moneda palace to find out what was going on. Their annoyance was clear when they arrived at the palace, there to be greeted by an enraged Pinochet; but they refused to sign a decree that interior Minister Fernández had prepared, giving General Pinochet broad emergency powers. According to some accounts they also had harsh words with the minister when he tried to argue that the Yes had actually won because Pinochet obtained an extraordinary vote for someone who had been in office for fifteen years. In a testy exchange with the minister and with Pinochet, all three junta members (including Admiral José Toribio Merino) made it very clear that there was no alternative but to recognize the defeat and to adhere strictly to the constitution.

It was not only Renovation leaders and the other junta members who helped defuse tension and dissuade government officials from any desperate last minute attempt to salvage a catastrophic loss. General Jorge Zincke, commander of the Santiago garrison, had refused to go along with the request that security forces be removed from the center of Santiago. At two o'clock Cardemil recognized that the No had won. Opposition leaders in the crowded press room of the No campaign openly embraced and wept before the cameras of the world.

In the final analysis the most important reasons for the absence of confrontations or incidents the night of the plebiscite were the maturity and good sense of ordinary citizens who followed the instructions of the No command and stayed home. The Communist Party's willingness to follow the directions of the Command for the No and to forego celebrating victory was crucial. The vast majority of Chileans waited patiently until the next day or until the mass rally at the Parque O'Higgins on Friday October 7, to celebrate what most had thought impossible only weeks earlier—the defeat at his own game of the 72-year-old dictator, who had prided himself on having won every previous test.

Notes

1. The LASA commission was chaired by Paul Drake (University of California, San Diego) and Arturo Valenzuela (Georgetown University). Commission members included: Adolfo Aguilar Zinser (Carnegie Endowment), Alan Angell (Oxford University), Marcelo Cavarozzi (CEDES, Argentina), Federico Gil (University of North Carolina), Larissa Lomnitz (UNAM, Mexico), Brian Loveman (San Diego State University), Amparo Menéndez-Carrión (FLACSO-Ecuador), Frederick Nunn (Portland State University), Luis Pásara (CEDYS, Peru), Paul Sigmund (Princeton University), Barbara Stallings (University of Wisconsin), and Peter Winn (Tufts University). The report was written by Paul Drake and Arturo Valenzuela, incorporating suggestions from each of the commission members. The full report was published in *LASA Forum* 19:4 (Winter 1989).

2. The following note is placed in an earlier section of the complete report but is relevant to the section of the report selected here:

This section and the longer section below dealing with the night of the plebiscite is based on conversations by a Commission member with key sources in the government, the opposition, and the diplomatic service. At first the events described here were denied by government supporters. Eventually, most of the events were confirmed in subsequent published reports. The first published revelations of the events of the night of October 5th appeared in veiled form in Acanio Cavallo's column "La hora de los audaces" in *La Epoca*, October 9, 1988, p. 8, and Pamela Constable, "Chile Factions United to Safeguard Voting," the *Boston Globe*, October 13, 1988, p. 1. Because of its close ties to the government, the most politically significant account appeared in the rightist *Qué pasa*, no. 914 (November 13–19, 1988), "La noche más larga . . . ," pp. 6–7, under

Patricia O'Shea's byline. Another good report, which draws on the *Qué Pasa* account, is Nibaldo Mosciatti's "La historia de un golpe frustrado," *APSI* (24–30 October 1988), pp. 4–7. The most complete description of what happened published to date is Ascanio Cavallo, Manuel Salazar, and Oscar Sepulveda, "La historia oculta del régimen militar: 5 de octubre," Special Supplement 53 of *La Epoca*.

3. This was one of the groups organized to carry out a parallel count of the vote, in an effort to reduce the likelihood of a fraudulent count. Because of a bombing attack at the CEL's headquarters in the week prior to the plebiscite, organizers coordinated the delivery of voting data to a network of computers hidden in private homes. The Yes campaign carried out its own parallel count, relying not on selected exit polls but on data received from government sources.

4. The following note is provided at this point in the report:

Renato Gazmuri, a leader of Renovación Nacional, caused a sensation when he agreed with these accounts and noted in a public forum that "hot heads surrounding the President" had tried to "provoke a grave confrontation that would have resulted in military intervention . . . [and] maintain the government beyond the results of the plebiscite." See also *Las Ultimas Noticias*, November 10, 1988, p. 7. See also *La Epoca*, November 10, 1988, p. 10.

VIII

Returning to Democracy: Transition and Continuity

The remarkable victory of the democratic opposition in the 1988 plebiscite marked the beginning of the end for the Pinochet dictatorship. Its defeat was sealed the following year, when democratic presidential elections were held in Chile for the first time since 1970. Christian Democrat Patricio Aylwin soundly defeated Pinochet's handpicked candidate with 55 percent of the vote, successfully campaigning at the head of the Coalition of Parties for Democracy (the Concertación), a coalition that included Aylwin's own Christian Democratic Party and the Socialist Party of former President Allende, as well as the new center-left Party for Democracy. The Concertación strategy brought together old political rivals from the center and left (with the exception of the Communist Party) in a coalition remarkable for its longevity and success: it would govern uninterrupted from 1990 to 2010, shaping the course of the transition to democracy and the rules of political engagement, but within inherited constraints. Unlike neighboring Argentina, whose rapid democratic transition of 1983 was precipitated by the military's disastrous invasion of the Malvinas and followed by the trial and conviction of the military government's leadership, Chileans pursued a gradual and negotiated transition that prioritized political stability, a route beset during the 1990s by Pinochet's open challenges to civilian leadership in defense of himself, his family members, and military colleagues. Hindered by the 1978 Amnesty Law, an antidemocratic electoral law that overrepresented the Right, a Constitution that constrained congressional majorities for the governing coalition, and the Concertación's own reluctance to encourage participatory democracy, the coalition's first decade in power illustrated the limits of the negotiated transition and the persistence of authoritarian enclaves in Chilean political life. Despite some significant advances, such as the Rettig truth commission (1990), which established officially that thousands of executed and disappeared Chileans had been victims of state terror under Pinochet, as well as the proliferation of civil and criminal cases against members of the regime's security forces and the gradual erosion of the legislative veto enjoyed by sympathizers of the military regime, the first decade of democratic rule promised to end, as it started, with impunity for military leaders and insecurity for civilian ones.

Pinochet's 1998 detention in London at the request of Spanish authorities seeking to try him for human rights violations dramatically shifted the balance of military and civilian power in Chile. Pinochet's detention also transformed the viability of international law in such cases: thereafter, dictators and others accused of human rights and other crimes could no longer assume effective diplomatic immunity while traveling in foreign countries. Held under house arrest and in a humiliating legal limbo for nineteen months while British authorities debated a Spanish request for his extradition, Pinochet was ultimately judged too senile to stand trial and was returned to Chile in 2000. But as several documents in this group of selections illustrate, Pinochet's arrest renewed debates over his legacy between his supporters and opponents, while further emboldening the Chilean judiciary to take action against him and other military officers. Although he was never successfully brought to trial, he would be dogged by legal travails in Chile, his reputation further tarnished by revelations of corruption, including millions of dollars held in secret U.S. accounts, until his death in 2006. The first years of the twenty-first century were also marked by open and unprecedented debate on the question of military impunity. These developments both contributed to and were catalyzed by the creation in 2003 of the Valech Commission, a historic presidential truth commission charged with investigating cases of political prison and torture under the military dictatorship and recommending reparations for the victims. The Commission's report revealed the military regime's systematic torture of all political prisoners, including the sexualized torture of women prisoners. Under President Michelle Bachelet (2006–2010), who had herself been a political prisoner in the 1970s, a wave of memorial-building underscored the Concertación's commitment to a political culture of "Never Again!" Yet, while the transition governments reversed many of the key anti-democratic pieces of the 1980 Constitution (including the appointment of "designated" senators), Pinochet's 1978 Self-Amnesty remained law.

The Concertación also achieved significant economic success during its two decades of rule. During the 1990s, in particular, seven straight years of high economic growth combined with low inflation and unemployment and a halving of the high poverty rate inherited from Pinochet was hailed as "the Chilean Miracle" and made Chile's neoliberal democracy look like a model to be emulated. However, the Concertación was much less successful in addressing inequality. Indeed, according to a 2011 study by the Organization for Economic Co-operation and Development—the international economic development organization for developed countries, which Chile joined in 2010—Chile ranks as the country with the most unequal distribution of income in the developed world, more unequal than Mexico or Turkey. In addition, the Concertación failed to reform significantly the dictatorship's regressive Labor Code, which imposed severe restrictions on workers' rights and unionization, or to roll back the regime's privatizations of social security, health care, and education—although by 2010 it had softened them somewhat, creating a "neoliberalism with a human face." But neoliberal policies that privatized the economy, favored loan repayment over social welfare, and discouraged popular mobilization were a glaring continuity with the dictatorship, and a key point of controversy, during the years of the Concertación governments.

The 2000 presidential election in many ways represented a watershed in Chilean politics, signaling the renewed vitality of the Right and some of the early signs of a weakened and fractious governing Center-Left coalition, while also ushering in a shift to the Left within the Concertación, from Christian Democratic domination to the ascendancy of the "progressive pole" of Socialists and the Party for Democracy (Partido por la Democracia), which would elect two Socialist presidents during the first decade of the new century. But, while Ricardo Lagos, the first Socialist presidential candidate to win the Concertación nomination, defined his campaign in terms of the unfinished business of the transition, his right-wing opponent Joaquín Lavín (whose celebration of a "society of choice" was presented earlier) touted the posttransition period as one in which the history of the Pinochet dictatorship was a closed book. The transformation in the presidential campaign of Lavín's public image from an extreme-right member of Opus Dei who worked for the Pinochet dictatorship into a popular "modern" politician "who gets things done" heralded significant changes in the Chilean Right, even as Lagos ultimately won the election in a second round of balloting by linking Lavín to Pinochet, who was about to return from his period of house arrest in London. The continuing transformation of the Chilean Right, and popular frustration with successive Concertación governments, culminated in the election in 2010 of Sebastián Piñera, a successful businessman from the more moderate right-wing National Renovation Party, in the first post-Pinochet election. The Concertación's loss to Piñera, particularly galling because it followed the enormously popular presidency of Chile's first woman president, the Socialist Michelle Bachelet, ushered in the first democratically elected conservative government since 1958 and represented a significant realignment of political forces in Chile.

What the Concertación may ultimately be remembered for, however, is the modernization of Chile, from public institutions and family law (including Chile's first divorce law) to mass media. Under the Concertación censorship ended, and Chileans embraced international popular culture and consumerism. Other key transformations in Chilean society after military rule include the country's dramatic opening to a variety of social and cultural changes, from relative improvements in women's and gay rights to successive challenges to the primacy of the Catholic Church in family and political life. In Chile as elsewhere, in a period following authoritarian rule, the turn to democracy opened up spaces, both public and private, for the expression and pursuit of rights and participation by women, homosexuals, and indigenous populations. While these movements have been treated very differently by political parties and gained vastly different footholds in government policy, they nevertheless signal both the activist legacy of the "hijos de Pinochet"—Chileans who grew up under Pinochet—and the politics of the younger, post-Pinochet generation, tied less to party politics than to international movements. In fact, the increasing frequency and scale of new social movements in recent years—including a wave of Mapuche land invasions or "recuperations" of forestry estates in southern Chile from the 1990s to the 2011 "Chilean winter" of student-led protest—have generated ongoing criticism not only of the military period and of elite complicity with the dictatorship's neoliberal policies and authoritarian practice but also of Chilean politics and society during and after the democratic transition, stressing the continuities in authoritarian politics, neoliberal economic development, and social conservatism before and after 1990.

This final part of *The Chile Reader* also addresses the "earthquakes," both seismic and political, that have shaken Chilean society since early 2010. In February 2010 a massive earthquake rocked southern Chile, sparking tsunamis that devastated coastal and island communities and caused $30 billion in damages. Chileans subsequently criticized both the outgoing President Michelle Bachelet and the incoming President Sebastián Piñera (inaugurated in March) for the state's failure to address crises in housing and employment afflicting poor communities hit by the disaster. As the Chilean author Ariel Dorfman noted in the *Los Angeles Times*, "the earthquake did not only split Chile's ground and swamp entire towns with a deadly tsunami. It also revealed fractures in Chile's social and moral fabric—the slow tsunami of persistent poverty and the cosmetic quality of the vaunted modernization that the country has undergone over the last decades." The first months of

Piñera's presidency, the first right-wing civilian administration to assume power since the end of military rule, were further troubled in July by the start of a lengthy hunger strike by thirty-four Mapuche activists in protest of their imprisonment and poor treatment under antiterrorist laws. Boosted temporarily in popular opinion by media attention surrounding the dramatic rescue of thirty-three copper miners trapped underground for three months, thereafter President Piñera battled spiraling controversy and popular opposition stemming from the "Great Educational Reform" his government proposed in November. Criticizing the Reform's recommendation to reduce the curriculum in history, geography and social science by 25 percent, the historian Fernando Purcell wrote: "one should say that we cannot advance into the future if we do not do so with full knowledge about who we are and how we have gotten here." By July of the following year, discontent with unequal, for-profit, and low-quality education, together with rejection of the Piñera educational reform, boiled over into three months of student-led street protests and strikes, including the largest demonstrations since the end of the dictatorship, sparking controversy over the role of popular mobilization, neoliberal development, and the value of state-led versus private initiatives in education, health care, and the economy. Opinion polls showed overwhelming public support for the protestors and disillusionment with parties and politicians of all stripes. The protestors' largest demand—a new democratic constitution—suggested that a new era of Chilean history might be about to begin.

Justice "To the Degree Possible": The Rettig Report

Patricio Aylwin Azócar

On March 4, 1991, roughly a year after taking office, President Patricio Aylwin went on television to announce the findings of the government's Commission on Truth and Reconciliation, a committee charged with investigating and substantiating deaths and disappearances under military rule, discovering the whereabouts of their remains, recommending state reparation to victims' families, and recommending measures to prevent the recurrence of such human rights violations in Chile. The Commission was not empowered to subpoena witnesses or prosecute those charged with committing crimes. The Rettig Commission—so named after its chair, Raúl Rettig, a respected Radical Party politician and former ambassador—worked for nine months with scores of lawyers, human rights groups, and victims to document extralegal deaths in Chile and collected evidence of over 3,400 cases. In its final report, the Commission certified the names of 2,115 victims killed in political violence between 1973 and 1990. Although the Rettig Report was roundly criticized by both the armed forces (as a politically motivated campaign by its opponents) and the human rights movement (for its failure to name perpetrators or investigate torture), the work of the Commission gave official recognition to victims of human rights abuses, promoting public debate about Chile's past and legitimizing civil cases against torturers and military commanders.

In his televised presentation of the Commission's final report, President Aylwin offered a somewhat unexpected apology to the victims of human rights abuses and their family members, on behalf of the Chilean state. Laying out the nature and extent of the military repression, Aylwin emphasized the significance of clarifying the truth of Chile's recent past, while arguing for "justice . . . to the degree possible," alluding to the political constraints that prevented more aggressive action. However limited by the military's legal impunity and the Right's legislative opposition, the Rettig Report and President Aylwin's public defense of its findings served as a shocking repudiation of the military regime in the tense early years of restored civilian rule and helped consolidate a historical memory of the dictatorship as a period of state terrorism.

I would now like to take this opportunity to share some reflections that weigh on my conscience as a human being, as a Chilean, and as President of the Republic. These reflections emerge from my reading of the Report and from the many discussions about it that I have shared with individuals from diverse parts of our country.

The Subject of Truth

All co-existence is based on the reign of truth. This principle holds true at multiple levels of social relations, from the home up through the universal community; it applies equally to relations in the family and in the heart of nations, and even to relations between countries.

Where truth is not respected, trust between people is broken; this leads to the expression of doubt, dismissive insults and, consequently, hatred and violent tendencies. Lies are the predecessors of violence and are incompatible with peace.

In terms of the human rights violations that took place in this country, the truth has been hidden for a long time. While some people denounced them, others—who knew about them—denied it, and those who should have investigated failed to do so. This explains why many people, perhaps even a majority, did not believe that the violations occurred. And this discrepancy became a new source of division and hatred among Chileans.

The Report that I make public today brings the truth to light. Because of the nature of the Report, and the qualifications of its authors—many of whom were participants in or supporters of the previous regime—everyone should accept its findings. Nobody could, in good faith deny this truth.

I am not saying that this is an "official" truth. The State does not have the right to "impose" a single truth. However, because I am convinced that the Report is true, I call upon all my compatriots to accept it and to act accordingly. When shared by all, this truth—however cruel and painful it may be—will eradicate a cause of argument and division among Chileans.

The act of affirming this truth is independent from the different opinions that people may hold about the politics of the time period, especially the legitimacy of September 11, 1973. All this will be judged by history; but no specific criterion could erase the fact that the human rights violations described in the Report were indeed committed. As the Report asserts, "the situation of 11 September 1973 and its consequences objectively placed human rights

Monument to the Detained-Disappeared, Santiago General Cemetery. Photograph by Marcos González Valdéz. Used by permission of the photographer.

at risk and made their transgression more likely, but in no case did it justify their violation" (pp. 24).

No one can point to the existence of an "internal war," or the need to defend the country from terrorism, to deny or excuse this truth. We all know—and the Report confirms—that the Armed Forces took control of the country very quickly, within a few days at most. On the other hand, war also has its own rules. Nothing justifies the torture and execution of prisoners, or the disappearance of their remains.

The Subject of Forgiveness and Reconciliation

Many compatriots feel that this is the time to put a "full stop" to this issue.[1] For the good of Chile we need to look toward a future that unites us more than the past can separate us. We have too much to do—building a truly democratic society, advancing development, and achieving social justice— to waste our energy mulling over wounds that are beyond repair. This reminds us of the words of the Holy Father John Paul II during his visit: "Chile is called to understanding, not to confrontation. Progress cannot be made by making divisions deeper. It is the time of forgiveness and reconciliation." Who does not share these desires? In order to realize them, however, we need to distinguish those who have been offended and are asked to forgive,

Coordinadora Nacional de Organizaciones por los Derechos Humanos

Several months before Aylwin's inauguration, the remains of nineteen bodies were un-earthed in the northern desert of Pisagua, near a military camp where prisoners were held, tortured, and executed after the 1973 coup, refuting military claims that they had been shot while trying to escape. Grisly photos of the victims' tortured bodies dominated front pages of Chile's major newspapers for weeks after the discovery, and this image of a blindfolded prisoner became ubiquitous in campaigns against military impunity. This poster by the artist Ricardo Morales reads: "Truth/Justice/Liberty. It was not a war, it was slaughter." Poster by Ricardo Morales. Used by permission of the artist.

from those offenders who need to be forgiven. I cannot forgive in place of another. Forgiveness cannot be imposed by decree. Forgiveness requires re-pentance of one party, and generosity of the other.

In circumstances such as this, when those who caused such suffering were agents of the State, and the appropriate State agencies, could not—or did not know how to—avoid or sanction the ghastly situation; when the social response that could have ended the situation simply did not exist; the State and the entire society are responsible for what happens, through their actions or their failure to act. It is Chilean society that is indebted to the victims of human rights violations.

For this reason, the suggestions for moral and material reparation for-mulated by the Report fall upon all sectors of society.

This is why I dare, in my position as President of the Republic, to represent the entire country to ask forgiveness, in the name of the nation, from the families of the victims.

For this same reason, I solemnly ask the Armed Forces, and to all those who participated in the excesses committed, to make gestures of recognition for the suffering they have caused and to cooperate in efforts to diminish this pain.

The people of Chile have always loved and admired their Armed Forces. We identify them with the glory of the Fatherland, with the manly spirit of Chileans, and with the selfless actions they undertake in our daily lives and in the face of grave emergencies. The desire for reconciliation, in a truly united Chile, requires that we remove the obstacles that still hinder these feelings. We all must contribute to this process.

I have stated on more than one occasion that my greatest aspiration as leader is to achieve national unity in democracy. Such a task demands that each and every person make a great effort to place himself in another's shoes and try to understand different perspectives. It also demands the humility to recognize one's own faults and limitations and the generosity to forgive the faults and limitations of others.

The Subject of Justice

Justice is the greatest of all social virtues, the irreplaceable foundation of peace.

We know that, because of the very limitations of the human condition, perfect justice is an unattainable good in this world, but we still constantly long to achieve the greatest possible justice.

Justice is not revenge: on the contrary, justice excludes revenge. One wrong is not sanctioned or made right by the commission of another. No one has the right to cause damage to his or her neighbor, much less to attempt to take the life of another under the pretext of justice. Those who commit such actions are likewise guilty of human rights violations and deserve the greatest social condemnation. To permit private vengeance is to supplant the law with violence, in which the law of force prevails over reason and justice.

In the topic of human rights violations, the clarification and acceptance of the truth, as established by the Report, is already an important step in obtaining justice for the victims. It is also justice that the Report proposes the moral vindication of the victims' dignity and reparations for their families.

But this is not enough. Justice also demands that we know the resting places of the disappeared, and that we determine who is personally responsible for the violations.

In regard to the first point, the truth established in the Report is incomplete, given that, in most cases of the detained-disappeared and executed, because the victims' remains were not returned to their families, the Commission had no way to determine their final resting places.

In terms of determining criminal responsibility, in a Society of Laws this task corresponds to the Legal Courts, consistent with judicial regulations and the guarantees of due process. The Commission of Truth and Reconciliation could not enter into this terrain because its founding mandate denied the Commission this ability in recognition of clear constitutional principles.

In any case, the Commission has turned all the pertinent information over to the appropriate courts. I hope that these agencies will perform their duties properly and carry out exhaustive investigations which, in my opinion, should not be blocked by the existing amnesty law.[2]

Terrorism and Violence

These criteria I discuss here can by no means be interpreted as signs of weakness or tolerance in our struggle against terrorism and the violence of extremist sectors.

My government is resolved to energetically combat terrorism and all forms of violence, regardless of who propagates it. What matters is that we find efficient methods to defeat and bring to an end terrorism and violence. The experiences of other countries demonstrate that the law provides the most effective path to this goal rather than simple armed confrontation. We refuse to accept the idea that to combat terrorism—a contemptible crime in part because it violates human rights—one must employ methods that result in similar violations, because those methods, which are morally unacceptable, serve as a catalyst for the spiral of violence. . . .

I Implore All Chileans

To conclude this speech, I implore my fellow Chileans to have the strength to accept these truths with integrity and responsibility. We must be able to learn from this experience so that NEVER AGAIN will something similar happen in Chile. This is a task for all of us, a task from which no one is exempt.

If the pain, the terror and the righteous indignation were to move us to act with hatred and violence, we would soon repeat the past. It would mean a return to fratricidal struggle, the destruction of our newly-revived democracy, and renouncing the desire for peace that we all cherish.

All Chileans can have the certainty that the Government will fulfill its duties in accordance with the moral principles that guide it and only in pursuit of justice, reconciliation, and the common good of our nation.

But this is not the task of the government alone. It is just as much the task of the other branches of the State, or the Armed Forces, of the religious authorities, the social organizations, and the entire national community. I ask that everyone cooperate so that together, with mutual respect and mutual support, with understanding and with generosity, we can do what is necessary to heal the wounds of the past and construct a future of justice, progress, and peace for all of Chile.

Translated by Trevor Martenson

Notes

1. Aylwin uses the phrase "punto final," referencing the practice in other postauthoritarian regimes such as Argentina, where in 1986 President Alfonsín placed a time limit on new criminal prosecutions of human rights violations.
2. Aylwin here refers to the 1978 Decree-Law 2191 issued by the military government, which granted amnesty for crimes committed during the State of Siege between September 1973 and March 1978. The idea that the courts should investigate and document human rights crimes before applying the Amnesty Decree-law is known as the Aylwin Doctrine.

Surveillance Within and Without:

The Custody of the Eyes

Diamela Eltit

During the 1980s and 1990s Diamela Eltit emerged as one of Chile's most prominent writers. This excerpt from her prize-winning 1994 novel The Custody of the Eyes *reflects some of the major preoccupations of women's writing during this period. Eltit is well known for her avant-garde experimental style, and this novel is orga-nized around the stream-of-consciousness narrative of a young boy and letters from his mother to his father, an anonymous patriarchal presence who remains silent. When the mother and son leave the custody of their home to venture out into an un-named city, they confront an alienating and chilly landscape where they are under constant surveillance by neighbors. Eltit links a general atmosphere of political and social repression (represented by the neighbor's "eyes" and the cold covering the city) to the mother's internalization of surveillance in her apparently coerced responses in the letters to the father's accusations. Both the home and the family, like the wider society, have become prisons. The novel meditates on the ways in which authori-tarianism is related to patriarchy within families and explores how the Pinochet dictatorship, represented by the father, produced fractured and distorted personal relations defined by self-policing, surveillance, and suspicion. Written during the transition to democracy, the novel suggests that authoritarianism in Chile cannot be reduced to the dictatorship but is insinuated in the fibers of all spheres of social life.*

The whole night long my heart has harassed me without letup. During all these hours I have felt crippled, assailed by a truly disturbing weariness. A prisoner of diverse anxieties, even the most trifling, I could wish only for a quick death. But I couldn't guess that more punishments awaited me, punishments revealed in certain fleeting dreams about mutilations. In my brief dreams, a mangled body lies across my hands. Just imagine, I was the cause of that death and yet I didn't know where the final resting place of those remains ought to be. I don't know how I survive that dream in which

I saw myself astounded, holding some corpse's mutilated viscera for which I was responsible. My heart has humiliated me all night long. Hearts beat, beat, beat, but mine, during this night, was irregular. It beat in frightening arrhythmia. My heart has behaved in such a hurtful way that I'm in no condition to reply to the question you ask me.

I know I owe this bad night to my neighbor. My neighbor keeps her eye on me and keeps her eye on your son. She has put aside her own family and now devotes herself solely to spying on my every move. She's an absurd woman whose rancor has vanquished her and left her prey to the power of her envy. My neighbor seems to perk up only when she sees me walking down the street, looking for some food. Then I come face to face with her eyes shamelessly following me from her window, with a malicious cast to them in which I can read her worst thoughts. Then she goes out and it would even be possible to swear that sometimes she has followed me. You know I have a keen sense when I feel observed.

I could swear that she has shadowed my footsteps on my only trip across town. Now I know my neighbor, in spite of the cold, is going from house to house and I'm sure that I'm the motive for her rounds and the reason for her conversations. Her look is definitely tendentious and I can sense how evil is creeping up behind my back, jumping me from behind, leaving me clawed by cruel defamations. I just don't understand from which of her innumerable hatreds she's chosen to make me her opponent.

You know that my own neighbor spies on me. The questions you ask me only reproduce the spying within me. Your son's not attending school isn't a sign of our living together indecorously. I warned you this moment would come. If you haven't put a stop to it, why then must I follow your order? We remain, we stay according to your will in a city that is progressively going mad. My neighbor keeps her eye on me and keeps her eye on your son and when it grows dark, I can hear her desperate weeping. She cries because her Western life has turned upside down, because the cold has taken another turn and, from its contagion, tonight even my heart has revolted.

Your son and I spend this time committed to a rhythm that doesn't merit the slightest reproach and I don't see why I should have to give you a detailed account of how we spend the day. But, in short, you must know that our hours go by mocking the cold that is reaching truly monstrous proportions. Your son wards it off by playing his games and sidesteps it with the clamor of his deafening horselaughs. I keep vigil by day and I'm vigilant during the night. But how can I make you understand that my neighbor lashes out at me shamefully? So quite wearing me down with totally unfounded arguments. Your son was expelled from school on account of his behavior and we are confined to the house. What is it you really fear? What harm could threaten people who lived locked up between four walls?

Oh, my neighbor is looking to vilify us. Her pupils, always crouching and ready to pounce, never fail to show an incomprehensible fury toward us. Your son, who has understood, now also plays by crouching down. We are kept under surveillance by a woman who's been reduced to gesticulating flesh, a woman terrified of herself, who with the power of her gaze snatches a few moments of enthusiasm to ease her monotonous life. From her window she executes disconnected and to a large degree apathetic actions, a series of actions in which she scarcely conceals a stuttering stream of offensive words. My neighbor is the best representative of a city-person's procedure that strikes me as increasingly scabrous. A procedure by which she stirs up the badly aligned chromosomes deep within her miserable anatomy.

The surveillance is extended now and encloses the city. This surveillance supports the neighbors' instituting laws, which, they assert, could curb the decadence they observe. They have taken up activities lacking any basis whatsoever, expect to grant them some exercise that lets them get the stiffness out of their numbed limbs. Your son and I now move amid glances and an inconceivable chill. Nevertheless, you dare to doubt my words and thereby seek to excuse my neighbor. You accuse me of being the one responsible for a thought that, according to you, alludes to an astonishingly ambiguous position, or you claim that my assertions, as you have stated, result from the anesthetic effect of a dangerous dream.

Through your judgments you are trying to turn me into the image of a lying woman. A lying woman, driven by a mounting delirium. I tell you—and this you know full well—that your words represent the best-known and most treacherous way of discrediting me. In this way you refuse to accept that my neighbor spies on me and spied on your son, and at this moment it seems to me that you yourself have taken advantage of her sick staring to further your own ends.

I ask myself, what is it that prejudices you against our behavior? If I rightly understood your recent letter, you are disturbed that I want to foster in your son's thinking what seems opposed to your beliefs. You also say that I'm the one trying to lead your son away from a proper education, and you even go so far as to assert that it's my own conduct that arouses your distrust, since more than one neighbor has described my curious movements to you.

Could it be the delirium in which you implicate me that really informs your writing? Could you be forgetting perhaps that I myself was the one who foresaw the school problems your son faced? And aren't you forgetting, as well, that my words were granted no attention at all by you? Your son was expelled from school and now I ought to concern myself with his education. I ought to do it in spite of the violent cold that grips the city in near paralysis. Oh, the cold continues and continues slicing through the house, freezing even the tiniest corners. Your son moves amid this unacceptable temperature so actively that I'm always surprised. He runs through the house at full speed and, on occasion, he bumps into the walls. His bumps, however, don't alarm me. I have bumped myself too often in sudden falls, in unavoidable accidents, from legitimate distractions. His bumps, then, don't frighten me. What upsets me are his horselaughs which seem to multiply in the midst of this cold, as if he were trying with his laughter to defeat this unbearable freezing. Your son laughs with a noise as harsh to me as the cold that falls upon us and he pays no attention to the malaise these noises provoke in me. I spend my days between putting up with his laugh and dodging the custody of my insistent neighbor's eyes.

Translated by Helen Lane and Ronald Christ

Legislating Gender Equality?
Voices from Congress and Civil Society

Among the many issues that roiled the politics of transition in the 1990s was the question of women's role in Chilean society. Whereas the military government had publicly celebrated women's domestic role—a campaign championed by First Lady Lucía Hiriart de Pinochet—the Aylwin government followed through on a campaign promise to feminist supporters by creating the National Service for Women (SERNAM), a state agency with cabinet rank, but more influence than power to address gender inequalities in Chilean society, such as women's economic inequality and violence against women. From the start, debates over SERNAM's creation exposed disagreements on women's issues, both within the governing Concertación and with its political opponents. The women's movement, itself divided since the fall of Pinochet over issues of organization and strategy, was also divided in its assessment of SERNAM: while many activists participated in SERNAM's operations, others criticized the marginalization of feminist and activist perspectives within the agency.

These tensions came to a head in 1995, when SERNAM presented its Plan for Equality of Opportunity for Women, a position paper on the status of women in Chile prepared for the official Chilean delegation to the United Nations' Fourth World Congress on the Status of Women in Beijing. In keeping with existing international agreements, the Chilean Plan proposed sweeping changes to address women's subordination, such as the reform of constitutional and legal barriers to gender equality, as well as measures to provide women with better economic opportunity, improved reproductive health, and equal education. These interviews, conducted by the Chilean journalist Pilar Molina, illustrate the debate about the Plan that ensued among legislators, women's rights advocates, clergy, doctors, and other public figures. The controversy led President Frei to demand changes in the Plan, including the elimination of feminist language and affirmation of Chilean support of family and opposition to abortion. The dispute also brought new problems for the struggling SERNAM, which saw its public influence and budget severely curtailed in subsequent years.[1]

Work and Domestic Labor

In the chapter that aims to facilitate women's access to and improve their position in the job market, the Plan reports that the population of women active in the job market increased by 83 percent from 1970 to 1990, and that women today make up 34 percent of the Chilean labor force. But it adds that "even though they understand the benefits of paid work, more than two-thirds of working-age women remain inactive," principally because they are occupied with child care and domestic duties. The report therefore argues for the need "to increase women's availability to work through a more equitable division of household responsibilities." And it proposes a series of measures to train and help women so that they find work: promoting of child-care programs, researching flexible work schedules for men and women, studying optional post-natal leave for fathers, along with making maternity leave more accessible to household workers, a bill that is almost ready.

The Christian Democratic Senator Nicolás Díaz is not convinced that men and women can have interchangeable roles, in which the man works half time so that he can do housework or use paternity leave. From his perspective as a doctor, the senator argues that "Men cannot replace women in the work of breastfeeding, which is not just about the provision of carbohydrates, protein, and resistance to illness, but also creates the intimate mother-child emotional relationship."

According to journalist Fernanda Otero, as in other areas the Plan also takes a feminist and materialist approach to women's employment. "All these measures indicate that women should work outside the home, to advance the country's economic development as well as their domestic standard of living, and fail to consider that, according to a study from the University of Chile, women's greatest contribution to the Gross Domestic Product is that which they make through domestic labor. In the 71 pages that make up this document, nowhere is there a single motion to support or give recognition to women for the role they play in the family by educating children and transmitting values and social stability; it is as if power resided only in the political sphere, and it were just a matter of giving women access to those institutions. The Plan says that 'the isolation that most women suffer is related to the sexual division of labor, which keeps them shut up in domestic spaces with the exclusive responsibility for child-rearing . . . under male authority,' thereby applying the dialectic of the class war to male-female relations."

The subdirector of SERNAM, the socialist feminist lawyer Paulina Veloso, responds "yes, this shows that women are discriminated against." She recognizes that in the Plan, "there is a strong tendency to propose the incorporation of women into the labor market. But that is because today a large percentage of women don't have that option, and women who enjoy higher incomes must work more [than men]. It's not that we want all women to have a job or that we don't value domestic labor; rather it is about creating the right conditions for women who want to work, who cannot do so now because of the inequalities that exist in the labor market."

And this is happening, adds Veloso, because the State offers assistance with child care—a project under study—as another way to make sure the care of children is not the sole responsibility of women. "Children have to be the responsibility of society, of men, not just of women. It can't be that women earn less because of children, and also have smaller pensions because of children, so that in effect they are punished because they perpetuate the species."

Mariana Aylwin also defends these changing roles, "because it is also an opportunity for men to participate in family life, an activity that society doesn't value today because women take care of it." Representative Antonieta Saa explains that in Sweden—where a group of parliament members just traveled to learn about policies for gender equality there—80 percent of women work and the birth rate has started to rise, "because maternity no longer implies that women can't work, and raising children is the responsibility of the whole society. There is total coverage for child care, more time for the family, and methods for incorporating fathers into the childrearing process."

Fernanda Otero also thinks that fathers must be better incorporated into family life, but this decision must be made in private by each family, and under no circumstances should it mean men and women should just switch roles. "The basic problem of The Plan is that it doesn't recognize that many of the problems that we have as women stem from the fact that we are different from men; because we are different, these problems cannot be solved with greater equality, but rather by accepting those differences."

Changing Sexist Education

The aspiration of SERNAM to create equal opportunities for women relies in large part on producing cultural changes through a "non-sexist" education. The Plan indicates that today "there is a very pronounced division by sex in the selection of fields of study and specializations." And although women are not discriminated against in their pursuit of education (they attend school as much as men), they continue to be the object of discrimination because of the stereotypes that education transmits and the "sexist practices of teaching staff."

"Research has concluded that school texts still show women as involved in the private domestic sphere and men engaged as providers, and that teachers stress the development of skills for public life for men, and skills for domestic life for women," adds Rosalba Todaro, the author of the Plan for Equality and Opportunities for Women.

But the majority of the remedies the Plan proposes to eliminate sexism in education have provoked bitterness. Representative Angélica Crísti is concerned about the ambiguous outcomes that will result from, for example, the creation of workshops to identify "sexist practices" in classrooms or to ensure that sexual education is developed from a "non-sexist" perspective.

The Christian Democratic Senator Nicolás Días also disagrees with another part of the Plan, the "attempt to eliminate the division between boys and girls in manual, non-academic subjects as well as the sexist slant in physical education." "The attempt to create equality in all areas is absurd. We have anatomically and biologically distinct constitutions, to the point where we even endure different illnesses. I don't know of a single great female musical composer or philosopher. We have different intellects, which are neither superior nor inferior to one another, but are just different. Our two Nobel Prize poets are equally brilliant in their poetry, although [Pablo] Neruda is cosmic and Gabriela [Mistral] is intimate, and reflects on the internal world."

Fernando Otero, on the other hand, fails to see what The Plan is referring to when it points out "sexist slants," and when it proposes that school texts and didactic materials should be revised to eliminate those biases. "Aren't men and women significantly different? Is it that nobody should excel, or do we all have to all succeed at the same pace, even though women's fine motor skills are better developed? They are going to revise school texts based on the vision of bureaucrats rather than parents: they ask for 'non-sexist' sexual education as if the sexes were not different from one another, and they consider women's choice of careers a form of 'sex segregation.' Certainly there are cultural elements at work in these choices, but it also reflects the fact that men and women are different, a fact that The Plan never recognizes, and because of this it contains a variety of proposals for how to push women to study 'non-traditional' careers."

Paulina Veloso (married with two children) defends her position: "we don't care if women study education, but we want them to have the same chance to study engineering, which does not happen today because we are conditioned to it. Ninety percent of the images in textbooks show men as athletes and heroes, and women cleaning up or caring for men. The idea is not that nobody can do well, but rather that this should be valued, that women aren't seen in just one role and that men can also succeed."

"Reproductive Rights"

Various themes treated in the chapter on improving women's health have proven to be controversial.

Objective 6.7 proposes "to secure [women's] ability to exercise their reproductive rights and get what they need to freely choose the number and timing of children." To do this the Plan would establish large campaigns to provide "exhaustive information about birth control methods for all women of childbearing age."

And to prevent teen pregnancy and provide total treatment when it happens, the Plan would provide "scientific information about preventing pregnancy" in the "final years of elementary and middle school," creating special programs for adolescent education that would focus on reproductive health, sexually transmitted diseases, the prevention of unwanted pregnancies, and promote increased access to contraception.

Although Senator Andrés Zaldívar subscribes to the SERNAM Plan in general terms, he adds that on this point "there is a great deal of vagueness, because 'scientific information' could also include things such as abortion."

For Doctor Fernando Orrego, the above points are the worst part of the document. "They show that feminism has a merely zoological approach to women's condition. The only thing that the Plan proposes is that contraceptive use be increased, as if preventing pregnancy were not also connected to the vulgarization and banalization of sex between adolescents. It seems incredible to me that under the pretense of modernity they are trying to apply Planned Parenthood's strategies, which failed in high schools in the United States. This is how they avoid speaking about the effects of divorce—which SERNAM promotes—well-documented in Chile and in the rest of the world, on sexual promiscuity, drug addiction, and criminal behavior among adolescents."

In addition to those who oppose state involvement in the education and sexual lives of children and society, others such as Representative Christi also observe that the SERNAM document incorporates ambiguous and erroneous terms, such as "reproductive rights" or "a full and complete sexual life," in areas which the Plan proposes new programs.

Translated by David Schreiner

Note

1. The authors would like to thank Pilar Molina for her permission to use interview materials from the article "SERNAM's Plan for Women: Equality or Feminist Totalitarianism?," *El Mercurio*, 29 May 1995.

Gender and Sexuality in Transition

Even as Chile inaugurated its first civilian president in 1990, the impact of dictatorship was still everywhere in evidence, from the new government's embrace of neoliberal economic policies to the glaring persistence of authoritarian enclaves. One of the most immediate cultural effects of the end of dictatorship, however, was evident in the transformation of existing social movements and the emergence of new mobilizations, including many pressing for change in public discourses and policies on gender and sexuality. Activists drew on experience garnered during years of struggle against the dictatorship in order to articulate demands for radical change to persistent norms regarding gender, sexual identity, and family in Chile.

Throughout the early 1990s, activists seized on the destape *(loosening, opening) of the postdictatorship era to make their demands visible through public marches, electoral campaigns, and grassroots organization. In so doing, they contributed to what critics dubbed the "moral crisis" of the period. A number of issues, from reforms of family law to sex discrimination, inspired public discussion and debate, but among the most controversial were abortion and gay rights. Feminists led political and public health campaigns to address Chile's high abortion rates, while gay rights activists set about building a substantial, visible gay rights movement for the first time in Chile's history. These social movements have not always achieved the transformations they sought, but they have opened up public debate and have changed the calculus of political campaigns as well as the public positions of many political leaders and organizations with respect to gender and sexuality.*

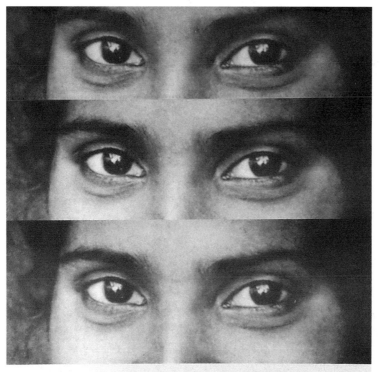

EN CHILE CADA AÑO 190 000 ABORTOS
CADA MES 4 MUJERES MUEREN POR ABORTO

¡ES PROBLEMA NUESTRO!

GICAMS • INSTITUTO DE LA MUJER • CODEM • CATOLICAS POR EL DERECHO A DECIDIR • REVISTA PAGINA ABIERTA • FORO ABIERTO DE SALUD Y DERECHOS REPRODUCTIVOS
CORSAPS • CASA DE LA MUJER LA MORADA • TIERRA NUESTRA • CIASPO • RED DE SALUD/ISIS INTERNACIONAL • COLECTIVO EL TELAR • OFICINA PARLAMENTARIA LAURA
RODRIGUEZ • MEMCH • EPES • COORDINADORA METROPOLITANA DE SALUD POBLACIONAL • CASA DE LA MUJER/VALPARAISO • COLEGIO DE ENFERMERAS DE CHILE

Abortion is "our problem." Abortion has been a recognized public health issue in Chile for most of the twentieth century, not least because of extremely high maternal mortality rates. As his final act before stepping down, Pinochet signed a law criminalizing abortions in all circumstances, with no exceptions for rape, incest, fetal viability, or the mother's life, making it one of Latin America's most restrictive abortion laws. Chile has nevertheless continued to have among the highest abortion rates in the hemisphere, with an estimated 5.5 abortions for every 10 live births in the early 1990s. Poster by Foro Abierto de Salud y Derechos Reproductivos. "'It's our problem' abortion rights poster" courtesy of The Sam Slick Collection of Latin American and Iberian Posters (Pict 000–674–3755), Center for Southwest Research and Special Collections, University Libraries, University of New Mexico.

One example of how activists emerged from and worked across social movements in the transition period is that of the journalist and human rights activist Victor Hugo Robles, who became a prominent figure in public protests against the military regime in the 1990s. Robles is known for his public performances of "El Che de los Gays," a role depicting Che Guevara in drag that expresses Robles's simultaneous protest of political authoritarianism and sexual repression in Chile. In this image, "El Che de los Gays" holds a sign reading "Try Pinochet," a demand for criminal prosecution of the ex-dictator. Photographer unknown. Used by permision of Victor Hugo Robles.

The Credit-Card Citizen

Tomás Moulián

In the context of the fundamental continuity of neoliberal economic policies that characterized Chile's transition to democracy (see the later selection by Alejandro Foxley), trends in labor relations and financial dealings also continued unchecked. Such continuities were evident, for example, in the ongoing deindustrialization and "flexibilization" of Chile's workforce, as well as the rapid expansion of personal credit, an industry first established in Chile in the late 1970s by the business mogul and future president Sebastián Piñera. Critical both of the neoliberal development model and the officialist discourse celebrating the "society of choice," in 1997 the Marxist sociologist Tomás Moulián published Chile Today: Anatomy of a Myth, *a surprise best seller that captured the critical mood of Chilean society in the mid-1990s, when Pinochet remained commander of the army, criminal charges for human rights violations under the previous regime were scarce and largely fruitless, and the Concertación pressed forward Chile's neoliberal economic project inherited from the dictatorship. Moulián's sweeping reflection on the Chilean malaise began not with an indictment of the Pinochet regime but with the transformation of citizens into consumers in this selection about "the credit-card citizen," an extended description and critical diagnosis of Chilean consumerism in the 1990s. Pointing to the continuities between the neoliberal economic planning of the dictatorship and the first two governments of the Concertación, Moulián analyzed the relationship between consumption, debt, citizenship, and modernity in postdictatorial Chile, where consumption and markets had eroded past practices and spaces for the expression of community and citizenship.*

By building up credit, one exercises a kind of citizenship—the "credit-card citizen"—which is part of a massive chain of consumption with deferred payment. This chain expands the power of money-wages. Besides being a way to pay "today," it also signifies an individual's ability to make financial commitments in the future.

This credit-card citizen is normalized, "put in order," and regulated by consumption with deferred payment. He has to subordinate his conflict strategies to his survival strategies as a salaried worker. He has learned that his future lies in continuing to be a credible worker. It is this credibility, linked to his submission, that opens the door to increased future consumption: the color television, the car, his own house. Credit is a remarkable factor of discipline, and more efficient because it is completely commodified: it works because it is driven by economics.

If that salaried worker stops paying, his citizenship disappears. Once he exhausts his ability to consume material goods, the only thing left is the illusion of suffrage. He stops being a credit-card citizen and returns to being only a political citizen. He is someone who has lost the possibility of access to the almost magical extension of his possibilities and powers, to a bigger salary, and becomes once again a nobody—he is no longer a consumer client.

He becomes once again another kind of "client," one who depends completely on the ups and downs of politics. He cannot plan for a "better life" on his own; the doors of credit (such as they are) are closed. Alienated by the individualist illusion of consumption, it is unlikely that he can rediscover the path he lost to community participation.

There is a close connection between the idea of weekend-citizen and the credit-card citizen. Both center their lives on the family and the home, on what is theirs, although the local citizen (at least) also pays attention to the public space around him. They have the same goals: a comfortable home, education for their children, and green spaces—that is to say, "portable" objectives. It is only through the thick veil of delinquency that both attend to social problems, when they are able for example to see in the pickpocket or assailant a deviant form of integration into the market, a compulsive realization of their own consumerist purposes. They see in these cases a perverted form of the passion of consumerism, people who seek the shortest path to economic success, regardless of the means.

Weekend citizenship and credit citizenship are forms of depoliticizing citizenship, to the extent that citizens no longer see politics as offering the possibility of deliberation, much less critical questioning. Both "forms" represent conservative models of citizenship, ones that are functional in the world as it is. Citizenship understood as local administration means not questioning a global social order that is determined a priori. Credit citizenship assumes that the power to which one should aspire is only that of exercising the rights of the consumer. The two forms entail, therefore, the conscious or unconscious acceptance of goals framed in this way.

Here I should provide a definition of "consumerism," which I use in a measurable and instrumental way. In this essay "consumerism" refers to acts of consumption that surpass the wage possibilities of the individual and turn into indebtedness, betting on time so to speak. The individual restricts his leeway for future maneuvers, and he operates as if he could be certain about things that the logic of production has made uncertain. To calm his consumerist anxiety, he mortgages the future and must pay the cost of this boldness, which he does by increasing his discipline, his merits as a worker, and his respect for orders. This type of consumption has multiple impacts in terms of comfort, prestige and self-esteem, but those effects are not considered because what matters most is this gamble with a future salary, played by those who are practically incapable of controlling their consumption.

"Consumerism" usually elicits open rejection and all kinds of moral preaching, not only by ecclesiastics. The critical literature of a certain period, from Fromm to Marcuse, saw in "consumerism" a sign of the banality of mass society and a loss of consciousness and energy in superficial things. Does it make sense to consider "consumerism" a form of alienation, as the enclosure of the human spirit in the desert of nonsense, or as a way of being that is marked by the futility of objects and the banality of entertainment?

In reality it is much more interesting to recognize the double face of consumerism. One side: as a mechanism of domestication, as a prominent and subtle device of domination. The other: its connection with pleasure. That is to say, it is important to analyze consumerism in its positive and negative aspects.

Chile Today combines a flexible labor market with the extremely restrained power of unions cloistered within the company and an extension of credit that operates as the most efficient form of achieving the dream of comfort. Credit, much more than the union, appears as the instrument of progress. The individual strategy of financial purity is considered much more profitable than a strategy of association. In Chile Today the individual is more important than the group.

Credit is both a resource and a marker of identity. The credit card (Visa or Falabella [a Chilean department store], they're the same) makes us individual "paymasters" to realize our desires without the ascetic Puritanism of waiting. If we possess these resources it shows that we are honorable; it reflects the stability of our earnings and the solvency of our economic behavior. The "untouchable," the metaphorical equivalent of the "pariah," is he whose "purity" has been denied by all the verifying mechanisms. He's the one whose past behavior and present salary do not make him worthy of financial confidence. He is no one, nothing, and all roads to progress have been closed to him. He is the one who will slosh around in the swamp of mediocrity, far from the things he wants. On the contrary, financial solvency allows for hedonism, that form of imitating happiness.

The credit-card citizen is not someone who feels chained to the discipline of making monthly payments, but rather pays them to conserve his power and his credentials as a "real" citizen. By preserving those credentials, he stays in the world of instant gratification, in the universe of pleasure, compensated by consumption for the ascetic discipline of wage labor.

As a mechanism of domination, this discipline is tied to satisfaction, to the expectation of realizing one's desire. That is its great force, so different from the "normal" discipline of work. I call "normal discipline" the individual's subjugation to norms for no other reason than to satisfy material reproduction, that is, the discipline that does not address the "self-realization" of the individual or some other strategy of empowerment.

The everyday culture of Chile Today is penetrated by the symbolism of consumption. At a subjective level this means that in great measure the identity of Me is constructed through objects, and that the distinction between "image" and being has been lost. The trappings of Me, the objects that indicate status or comfort level, are confused with the attributes of Me. . . . This Me has become a mirror image, trapped in the culture of outward appearances. I am the car I have in the driveway or the improvements to the house that make it different from others in the same shantytown. I am the school where the children study.

Here I must insist: this exacerbation of consumption through the extension of credit is discipline and pleasure at the same time. It is never purely negative. Consumption is at once the purgatory of increased exploitation and the heaven of an increasing capacity to consume. The most important fact is that the good and bad aspects of this always happen together. If they were produced separately, the charm would be gone and the mechanics of domination would not function.

The emphasis on consumption as human fulfillment contradicts traditional approaches. Saint Simon and especially Marx emphasize work as the space for fulfilling human potential. From this perspective, even if work becomes alienated, the way to overcome the problem is to change production relations. Consumption can never be the solution: it is just considered a variable of material reproduction or non-fulfillment because it is the use, or rather the mere use-digestion-contemplation of things created by others.

Nevertheless, certain contemporary perspectives in the analysis of consumption allow us to understand two dimensions hidden by the traditional perspective: consumption as desire-pleasure and as a construction in itself.

In truth, if we ignore these dimensions of consumption, we deny important aspects of it. Imprisoned by certain ideologies of traditional criticism we are tempted to deny the importance that certain forms of consumption have acquired, or read them as pure alienation. . . .

In Chile Today, where the economy creates false and simulated ways to protect the individual from economic inequality—providing him with credit that gives him a concrete, feasible hope that the great, abstract ideologies cannot provide—it is easy to fall into the temptation of a life lived between the pressure of work and the relaxation offered by the mall or the television. In this context, what end would politics, participation or public action serve? These activities cannot compete with credit as a source for hedonistic pleasure, and they are not able to do what consumption does: provide good, faithful clients with the hope of ever-increasing comfort, the constant renewal of the passive pleasures of entertainment, and a future filled with more and more objects.

People no longer find pleasure in those community festivals of days gone by, in the mass demonstrations where feelings of communion and comradeship flourished and produced lively and unforgettable feelings. Those were, obviously, exceptional moments. But today people don't even find pleasure in the Sunday stroll through the park or the San Cristóbal or Santa Lucía Hills. Today, pleasure consists of a stroll through the mall, where many families have the experience of fulfilling their commercial desires voyeuristically, without consuming anything: they consume a microwave, or a better heater, just by looking. But for many other families happiness consists in affirming that it is not necessary to postpone their desires. In spite of poor wages, the festival of objects is within reach of the hand . . . That is the incorporative power of the credit card.

Then, moreover, there are the consumers from the tenth quartile, the slightly more than one million people who earn 40.8 percent of Chilean income.[1] Before 1973, conspicuous consumption was almost impossible because imports were regulated, but also because of the moral condemnation it invited. In a time when waste and splendor were rejected, the rich often led an austere life in public: their houses were not very ostentatious, and their cars were discreet. . . . Flaunting wealth was considered dangerous, because it provoked envy. The rich felt they were being watched. Therefore, they showed themselves as such only in their enclaves, the great mansions of their haciendas, the beach resort of Zapallar, and the polo and golf clubs.

The crux of the matter resided in that feeling of being watched, which revealed their guilty feelings. It is not that Chile's dominant classes were naturally ascetic. We can see how the period of the nitrate boom revealed this as another myth. What was really happening was the fear of showing one's wealth in the face of social criticism, against the pressure of an egalitarian culture, which was fed by the Church's social Christianity and the existence of class parties.

Today, on the contrary, living luxuriously is a sign of prestige. The fifty thousand dollar car is shown as a medal of commercial heroism and shrewd struggle in a competitive market. It is necessary to have a huge house if you want to be someone on the road to success. It's a good idea to cover your walls with famous painters so that culture is associated with wealth. It is indispensable to dress in the latest fashion. To be rich it is necessary to get together with other rich people, and you must do it in the right places. Wealth is not private, it is there to be flaunted. It is in bad taste to hide it. It is like remembering that, in another time, it was necessary to disguise oneself as middle class.

Translated by Carolyn Watson

Note

1. The following note is provided at this point by the author:

The exact number is 1,080,180, which is the result of multiplying the 353,000 people of the top 100 percent of income-earners by the average household size, which is 3.06 for this sector.

"Chile's Greatest Addition to the Spanish Language": *Huevón*

John Brennan and Alvaro Taboada

The Spanish language that is spoken in Chile, like variants spoken throughout Latin America and Iberia, can be a critical signifier of nationality, regional origin, generation, class, and even ideology. In Chile, the malleability of the language has made it particularly important for expressing changing class and political identities, while the penchant for wordplay—the use of double entendre, for example— has marked Chilean literary and political discourse. For non-Chileans, the most striking aspects of Chileans' spoken Spanish is its rapid pace and frequent use of slang expressions that draw on both native and foreign words, which make Chileans abroad easy to identify but can make communication more difficult for non-native Spanish speakers for a time. Among the key slang terms frequently employed by Chileans in informal contexts is the word huevón *(a variant of huevo, or egg), which has taken on so many variations in usage that it earned a separate entry in the reference book for English-speakers* How to Survive in the Chilean Jungle. *The term and its variations are as vulgar as they are ubiquitous, but without it, the English-speaking traveler in modern Chile will be at a considerable disadvantage in everyday conversation.*

huevón-ona: Pronounced *gueón*.
(1) *n. & adj.* Once described as Chile's greatest addition to the Spanish language, a whole book could be written about this all too common word, whose closest American English equivalent is "Dude." There are essentially two meanings: friend or not friend and even a friend who is not acting like a friend is a *huevón*, as well as a person you would not want to be friends with. Is that everybody? Ex. "Oye gueón, el asado fue una güeá increíble, que manera de huevear." "¿No gueí?" "Si po, soy un güeá por no haber ido." (2) *n.* "Asshole," "Fuck head"; A very disagreeable or bad person.

hacerse el huevón: *exp-vr.* "To play dumb"; To act like one doesn't know what another is talking about.

ahuevonado-a: *n. & adj.* "Bonehead"; Stupid, idiotic.

huevada (güeá): *n.* (1) "Thing" as in anything. Ex. Watching a football game and speaking of the ball, a Chilean might say, "¡Patea la güeá!" (2) A stupid thing, as in an action, a comment, etc.

puta la huevada (güeá): *exp.* "Shit"; An expression used after a frustrating and/or annoying experience.

qué huevada (qué güeá): *exp.* (1) As a question: "What's that?" Said when one does not understand what has been said, or what is going on. (2) Exclamation of minor distress.

huevas: *n. pl.* "Balls," "Nuts"; Testicles.

saco de huevas (güeás): *exp.* "Dick head"; Big idiot and Fool.

mata de huevas (güeá): Same as *saco de huevas*.

como las huevas (güeás): *exp-v. estar*: To be really bad. *sentir:* To feel "shitty"—really bad.

huevear: *v.* (1) To bother, to annoy. (2) "To goof off"; To have fun esp. to not act seriously.

hueveo: *n.* Fooling around, not serious behavior, unfocused attitude.

agarrar para el hueveo: *exp-v.* "To pick on someone"; To tease someone.

hueveta: *n.* Superficial person, person given to the simple pleasures of life.

huevonaje: *n.* Everyone, the whole group, esp. a specific group.

huevonazo: *n.* Super *huevón*.

huevoncito: *n.* For referring to a *huevón* in a derogatory sense.

huevonear: *v.* To refer to someone as *huevón*, instead of referring to someone by his name.

"I Never Looked for Power"

Augusto Pinochet Ugarte

After the transfer of formal power to President Aylwin in March 1990, General Pinochet remained active in military and political affairs, regularly participating in public life and continuing to defend his legacy as the man who had rescued Chile from communism and steered the country back to democracy. After the return to democracy, Pinochet continued as commander-in-chief of the army until 1998 under the provisions of the transition agreement. He then served as an unelected "senator for life," a position he enjoyed thanks to a clause in his 1980 Constitution designating former heads of state as lifetime senators. Pinochet remained a truculent, unapologetic, and outspoken defender of his legacy; in an interview shortly before his arrest he quipped, "I was only an aspiring dictator."

His arrest in October 1998 in London for human rights violations put Pinochet on the defensive, but it did not shake his arrogant confidence in his story of heroism and sacrifice for the nation. In this "Letter to the Chileans," published in the British and Chilean press, Pinochet publicly defends both his honor and his legacy. In an appeal designed to galvanize public support for his release, Pinochet thanked his supporters, reminded Chileans of his historic role as their savior who had rescued Chile from civil war, and lamented his continuing victimization at the hands of an international leftist conspiracy. His letter is a rigid defense of his dictatorship almost a decade after the plebiscite that brought it to an end, and illustrates the degree to which the regime's legacy was tied to Pinochet's reputation as a reluctant but passionate anticommunist crusader, motivated only by love of country.

Impeded from returning to my country, and living through the hardest and most unjust experience of my life, I would like to thank my compatriots for all their noble gestures of affection and support, without which these hours of trial and loneliness would be incomparably sadder for both me and my family. I would like to express my gratitude with some reflections that have come to my mind during these painful days, which might help us discover the truth and justice of the history that is now being judged.

The country knows that I never looked for power. That is why I never

EL PACIENTE INGLES   2ᵃ parte

The English patient. Pinochet's detention in London dominated the Chilean media, reigniting old arguments for and against the military regime. The Chilean satirist Guillo ridicules Pinochet's arrest in this cartoon, which borrows its title from the 1996 Hollywood film. Cartoon by Guillo Bastías. Used by permission of the artist.

clung to the power that I exercised, and when the time came for me to leave office, I did so in accordance with the laws of our Constitution. No historian, not even the most biased and least objective, could ever sincerely argue in good faith that my public conduct resulted from personal ambition, or any other motive aside from the good of Chile. On the contrary, I always thought that I should answer the call to serve my country—which beat in my heart since I was a child—through a career in the military. I always knew that I would fulfill the oath that I made as a young man before God and our flag. Precisely because of our sound moral education, early on we soldiers learn how much pain and irreparable loss is caused by war. That is why as the nation's leader I demonstrated an indefatigable and unconquerable will to avoid armed conflict, to seek peace for Chile at all times, even though threats of all kinds have loomed over us.

Even when faced with the dramatic crossroads that the Popular Unity government brought to our nation, I hesitated to act until the very end, despite the clamor of citizens who pounded on the doors of our barracks, begging us to intervene. I waited not out of fear, but rather out of a secret

Pinochet's supporters rally for his release in London.
Photograph by AP/Roberto Candia, image no. 99021901446.
© 1999 The Associated Press. Used with permission.

hope that we would overcome peacefully the extreme institutional crisis, which had already been denounced by the Most Excellent Supreme Court, the Honorable Chamber of Deputies and other members of our polity. A soldier knows better than anyone just how uncontrollable armed confrontations can be when they are not directed against a regular army. The conflict became unavoidable, however, and we finally had to seize control of the nation on that historic eleventh of September, but not before entrusting our success to God and the Holy Virgin of Carmen, the patron saint of the Air Force and the Queen of Chile. In my heart I will always cherish this memory and savor the deepest feelings of gratitude and admiration for that generation of soldiers, sailors, aviators and police officers who participated in that patriotic journey and made so many heroic sacrifices.

About such an important gesture, I offer just one reflection. The Armed Forces did not destroy an exemplary democracy, nor interrupt a process of development and well-being, nor was Chile in those days a model of liberty and justice. Everything had been destroyed, and we men of arms served as a moral reserve for a disintegrating country, a country controlled by people who wanted to submit us to Soviet control. . . .

Today, I feel that destiny has again placed on my shoulders the enormous responsibility of helping to sow the seeds of peace that will make the greatness and unity of my Fatherland possible. Beyond my own suffering and a soul wounded by the unjust humiliation to which I have been subjected, and beyond the indignation that I feel seeing the sovereignty and independence of my country attacked, denied the respect it deserves, I want to declare that I accept this new cross, with the humility of a Christian and the composure of a soldier, if by doing so I can serve Chile and its people. I desire nothing more than to see us overcome the divisions and the sterile rancor among us.

Although I am already nearing the end of my life, and despite the injustice and misunderstanding that has brought me fatigue and suffering, I assure you that even if the adversities had been greater, my spirit would never be defeated. Nothing will bend my convictions or my firm will to serve my Fatherland, just as I promised on the day that I joined the Chilean Army. My deepest desire right now is to ensure that there are no more victims in our beloved land, no more pain than that which foreign ideologies have already created within the Chilean family. I hope that mine will be the last sacrifice. May my suffering and the attacks to which I have fallen victim satisfy the ever-insatiable appetite for revenge, and mean that those who remain steeped in rancor might make peace with themselves. God willing, those people will be able to stop living in such a perturbed state, and never again in our Fatherland will we hear the revolutionary sermons that sowed such violence and division among Chileans.

Those of us who believe in forgiveness and true reconciliation need to continue working hard for the future. Soon will come the day when a new generation of compatriots will study the history of our nation and discover the truth of our actions, which allowed us to build a society of free and dignified Chileans, to build a better Fatherland that would be for all, not just for one group or party, which was the reality we were about to experience in 1973.

I have been the victim of political-legal machinations, sly and cowardly scheming, that have no moral value whatsoever. While the European continent, especially the countries that condemn me with spurious judges, has witnessed how communism has murdered millions of human beings in this century, they persecute *me* for having defeated this evil doctrine in Chile, thereby saving the country from virtual civil war. Our actions resulted in three thousand deaths, one third of whom were soldiers and civilians who fell victim to extremist terrorism.

I have been falsely judged in numerous European countries, in an operation directed by those who declare themselves my enemies, without even the remotest possibility that those who prejudge and condemn me will ever comprehend our history or understand the spirit in which we acted. I am absolutely innocent of all the crimes and actions of which they irrationally accuse me. However, it seems to me that those who condemn me have never been—nor will they ever be—able to listen to reason or accept the truth. . . .

My faith in God and the principles that have guided me throughout my life remain unshaken. I firmly believe that the Lord, in his infinite mercy, is making me suffer deeply on behalf of those who died so unfairly in those years of conflict. Those who believe or argue that one group has a monopoly on mourning the bloodshed in our Fatherland are mistaken. We have all suffered for the victims. It seems to me that those who did not provoke this confrontation have suffered the most, those who never sought or desired the conflict, but who ended up being its innocent victims. A soldier always looks to protect his compatriots. I have never wanted anyone to die, and I am sincerely pained by all the Chileans who lost their lives in those years.

With great humility I have asked God to give me the acceptance and clarity needed to understand and accept this cross, and to ensure that this pain I bear deep in my spirit turn into a fruitful seed planted in the soul of the Chilean nation. If my sufferings can put an end to the hatred that has been planted in our country, I tell you that I am ready to accept whatever fate holds, with the utmost confidence that God, in his infinite love, will know how to make the sacrifice that I offer fruitful so that peace may triumph, and in the dawn of the new century that is already upon us, see to it that all Chileans join together as the unified and reconciled nation that I have always dreamed I would live to see.

I love Chile above all else, and not even the most painful circumstances could stop me from repeating "Long live Chile" with all the force of my spirit—even at this distance—a thousand and one times.

Translated by Trevor Martenson

Historians Critique Pinochet's "Anti-History"

Eleven Chilean Historians

In response to Pinochet's "Letter to the Chilean People," a group of Chile's leading historians issued "The Historians' Manifesto," which appeared in several of Chile's major newspapers.[1] The manifesto offers an analysis of the history leading up to the 1973 coup that directly refutes the historical account offered by Pinochet and his supporters. Through these public exchanges, debate about the nature of the military regime—and the political crisis that preceded it—reached an unprecedented peak in Chile, reflecting the degree to which Pinochet's arrest broadened the legitimate arena of criticizing the regime and its legacy. Although Pinochet was released from house arrest in March 2000, the discussion about his criminal responsibility continued within Chile. These discussions had concrete repercussions when, shortly after his return from England, the Chilean Congress stripped the ex-dictator of his senatorial immunity. A series of criminal and civil suits would dog Pinochet until his death in 2006.

Recently we have noted a notorious intensification in the tendency to manipulate and accommodate the truth on public matters pertaining to the last fifty years of Chile's history. The purpose of this manipulation has been to exaggerate some actions and to silence others in order to justify certain deeds. Nearly always, there is a tendency among some groups to lend legitimacy to the impermissible, and to present as true and objective what cannot be so, in an effort to give substance to their desired self-image. This tendency is facilitated by the almost exclusive access to the mass media that these sectors and groups possess. By means of extensive and all-powerful media control, they have managed to give an appearance of public truth to what is in reality only the historically distorted expression of private partisan interests. . . .

The manipulation is manifest, to a large extent, in the historical appraisal of:

EXCLUSIVO... FOTO INÉDITA DE LA LLEGADA DE PINOCHET

"Exclusive: Unedited Photo of Pinochet's Arrival." During Pinochet's house arrest in London, Chilean humorists founded a satirical weekly publication, the *Clinic*—so named for the London hospital where Pinochet was placed under arrest—that offered a scathing repudiation of the arguments made by the general's supporters and of the Concertación government for advocating his release and return to Chile. According to one of the publication's founders, "I suppose we realized that together with everyone else, the dictatorship—which was over, and yet continued—had tried to deprive us of our sense of humor, and this is why so much was left over from it. Through humor, we could destroy the heart of the regime's ideology and even its memory." In this fashion, this photo and its caption mocks Pinochet's actual arrival after his London imprisonment, when he stood from his wheelchair to offer a triumphant greeting to the throngs of supporters who greeted him at the airport. From *The Clinic . . . firme junto al pueblo . . .* © Ediciones y Publicaciones Bobby S.A. (Santiago, 2002), p. 1.

Memorializing Allende. From the moment a statue to Allende was proposed in Congress in 1991, the Chilean public debated the merits of Allende's legacy, the placement of the statue, and how he would be represented. In 2000, after nearly ten years of heated discussion in Congress and the media, and following the Socialists' concession to approve a similar statue for the Pinochet advisor Jaime Guzmán, Allende's statue was unveiled in front of the presidential palace. Photo by Bruce Nelson. Used by permission of the photographer.

(a) the democratic process prior to the 1973 military coup;
(b) the subsequent political process under dictatorial rule;
(c) the issues of human rights and sovereignty arising during and after the dictatorship.

We consider that that manipulation is present on its more extreme and simple form in the "Letter to the Chileans" by the former general Augusto Pinochet. . . .

Therefore, we feel compelled to state the following:

II

In his "Letter to the Chileans" ex-general Pinochet proclaims, among others, three 'historical truths'.

(a) That the dictatorial intervention of the military between 1973 and 1990 was a "heroic deed, a Homeric feat, an epic achievement" of national character;

(b) That the political crisis of the former democratic system was the exclusive making of the Popular Unity, whose manifesto sought to impose—with "the preaching of hatred, vengeance and division" and the "sinister ideology of Marxist socialism"—an "atheistic and materialistic vision . . . an implacably oppressive system against freedom and rights . . . the rule of lies and hatred";

(c) That the "men of arms" acted as the "moral reserves of the nation" to reintroduce "unity for the country . . . not for a sector or a party," "respect for human dignity" and the "freedom of the Chileans," and to give "true opportunities to the poor and the neglected."

In relation to the first assertion, we wish to point out that in History we only employ expressions such as "heroic deed . . . Homeric feat . . . epic achievement" when a whole nation, or country, or national community have joined forces, taken decisions and carried out actions, as a whole, in the exercise of their sovereignty. This was the case when, for centuries, the Mapuche people fought against the Spanish invaders, or when the Chilean people mobilized themselves after 1879 in the Pacific War. To use these terms to characterize the armed action undertaken by one sector of Chileans against another, implies a peculiar, abusive and opportunistic use of concepts which have a more edifying meaning than this. In truth, that kind of action is not a national epic deed but a seditious action (independently of whether it is successful or not). If those Chileans who performed and supported the 1973 military coup consider that their action was an "epic deed," then it follows that the attempt to attain national economic development carried out by legal means by the defeated faction between 1932 and 1973 against another faction opposed to and obstructive toward their plans during all that time, should also be considered an "epic deed." It is necessary to differentiate between the "opposition" that operated within the rule of law (the case of the defeated ones in 1973) and the opposition that operated with the use of force (the case of the victors of 1973). The actions of a democratic and legal movement seem closer to being "epic" than those of an armed one.

In relation to the second assertion, we have to state that the 1973 crisis was not due exclusively to the conduct of the Government of the Popular Unity. Truthfully, no serious historian would caricature that conduct by reducing it to the "preaching of hatred," to the implementation of "sinister" ideologies, to the "oppression" that its reforms inflicted on certain interests and rights, or the "rule of lies" that would have formed the basis of its reforms. That conduct was also due, and in no small measure, to historic processes of long duration, whose origins can be traced back to the XIX Century, or even before.

In fact, the Popular Unity administered (and precipitated) a crisis that was not only political but mainly economical and social. This crisis had been slowly growing for at least a century, a period in which historic responsibility cannot be attributed to the Marxist ideology or to the center-left parties, but to the chronic and inept governmental rotation of power between the oligarchic elites of Chile. It must be pointed out here . . . that the "pre-populist" crises of 1851, 1859, 1890–91, 1907–8, 1924, 1930–32, and the "developmental" crises of 1943, 1947, 1955, 1962 and 1967–69, taken as a whole, reveal that the structural damage caused by a century of oligarchic and neo-oligarchic governments was difficult to be resolved through democratic means. For this reason, the attempts to reduce the *structural* crisis of Chilean society to the *political* crisis of the 1970–73 period, and to attribute strategic historical responsibility to the reformist program of the Popular Unity government, have no place within the logic of scientific analysis, even if they have a role within the logic of factional arguments. This approach should not feature in the vision of true statesmen, who should examine the situation of all Chileans and consider the country's history in its entirety.

It is deplorable that in Pinochet's "Letter to the Chileans" neither the logic of historical science nor that of a true statesman can be found. The derogatory expressions used by the former general to refer to the sovereign options and actions of a faction of Chileans who in March 1973 attained 43.3 percent of the national electorate (not including those who voted for the centrist Christian Democrats) exposes the logic of a factional chieftain rather than the discernment of a national statesman. Why condemn in a derogatory manner the sovereign actions of nearly half of the Chilean citizens? Is that discredit necessary to displace the blame onto nearly half the national electorate for not only the responsibility for their own mistakes but also the responsibility for all the mistakes of the oligarchy from the past and to all the excesses of the triumphalist faction of the present? And, if one should blame others for one's own deeds—is it necessary to revile?

With reference to the third assertion (that "the men of arms" acting as the "moral reserves" fought for the unity of the country and the human dignity of the Chileans, etc.) we have to say that nobody is fighting for the unity of the nation when the "arms of the nation" are used against nearly half of their fellow countrymen. Nobody is fighting for the dignity of the Chileans when the human rights of thousands of disappeared prisoners, hundreds of thousands of tortured people, or prisoners, or dismissed workers, etc. are violated. Nobody guarantees "true opportunities for the poor and under-privileged" when the labor market, imposed by despotic means, is based on the widespread instability of employment and on a hyper-commercialized higher education system. We cannot describe as the "moral reserves of the nation" those who in a partisan way declare a "dirty war" against half the nation, and who violate the human dignity of their fellow countrymen or carry out assassinations of political opponents inside and outside the country. Nor can we apply that description to those who invoke the superior principle of *sovereignty* in an attempt to justify and give immunity to attacks perpetrated against this very sovereignty. The arms of the nation must not be used by one faction against another, nor to the exclusive benefit of a minority, nor to usurp the sovereignty of all. When they are used in that way, the offense committed is against sovereignty. And that offense cannot be covered under a puerile mantle of devotion and public protestations, claiming the personal assistance of God and the Holy Virgin Mary. . . .

IV

These days we have seen on TV government authorities and high military officers defending, with rare enthusiasm, the thesis that the indictment against ex-general Pinochet initiated in Great Britain and Spain is an affront to national sovereignty, and that to defend him with all the resources of the State is a patriotic duty. Furthermore, if he has to be judged, it must be under Chilean laws. It has been proclaimed and maintained, to this effect, the thesis that the "principle" of national sovereignty (following in this case the 1980 constitutional text) is above not only the "criminal acts" of any fellow national, but also above the international consensus on human rights. The government has given this principle, within and outside the country, supreme validity, postponing and subordinating any other principle, even the demand for justice that comes from the thousands of Chilean victims of those violations and from the citizens of the world who support them. On this, the following questions are pertinent: Considering the crimes against humanity, what is worthier? The "principle" of national sovereignty—as defined by the Constitution, laws and decrees promulgated by the same dictatorial government that "commanded" those crimes—Or the "principle" of justice that both victims and humankind demand to be brought to bear? What is the Chilean State defending today?

It seems to us that the ultimate, essential subject of History is the question of sovereignty and human rights. Sovereignty emanates from individual and collective freedom, and human rights represent the universal legal establishing of that sovereign dignity. History is no more than the exercise of that sovereignty and the continuous validation of those rights. The Constitution and the Laws are legitimate as long as they express the sovereign will of the national community. If—and only if—they express it, can it be stated that they represent sovereignty. When the legislative will of the community is respected, the most fundamental of human rights is also respected, i.e. the possibility that that community may by itself build the reality that it sees fit to build. When people's sovereignty is usurped by a few, when those few pass laws for a minority, and they try to impose them on all, when those laws are imposed by the force of arms and not by the free and informed will of all the people, then it is not the people's sovereignty what prevails—we are witnessing the usurpation of that sovereignty. Laws that are passed under a state of sovereign misappropriation are illegitimate. The tribunals, judges, and police that act upholding them are not expressing sovereign justice but the interests of the minority that misappropriated it and benefited from it. This is not true justice. The legal mechanisms imposed by the usurpers, to protect themselves from sovereign justice or from international justice, is not an expression of sovereignty. This is, simply, a mockery of it.

We regret that in today's Chile the ruling classes have "deduced" sovereignty from the Constitution of 1980, disregarding whether this was the sovereign product of an informed popular decision, or a partisan imposition of autocratic powers. It does not matter to them whether "that" sovereignty is used to defend the rights of the people, or to defend the interests of the dictators who usurped and violated the rights of the people; likewise, this notion of sovereignty can be used either to pursue justice on behalf of the assassinated and tortured, or to protect those who were complicit in those crimes.

In this way, it is not history that is written, but anti-history. For this reason, to put those "principles" before factual truth and sovereign rights reveals not a vocation of public service but a slanted mockery against public interest from the part of a minority.

V

History is not only the past, but also, and principally, the present and the future. History is projection. It is the social construction of future reality. The most important of human rights consists of the respect to the ability of the people themselves to forge the future reality that they need. Not to recognise that right, to usurp or to falsify that right, is to impose, above all, not the truth, but a historic lie. It is to negate the very moral reserves of humankind.

Translated by: Enrique Zapata

Note

1. The manifesto was signed by eleven Chilean historians and seventy-three other scholars.

The Mapuche Nation and
the Chilean Nation

Elicura Chihuailaf

The Mapuche movement began during the late 1970s as indigenous communities rejected a Pinochet law designed to break up and privatize communally held lands. By the 1990s, Mapuche communities had begun to invade and "recuperate" land usurped by large estates and now often held by large forestry conglomerates. They were led by organizations like Ad-Mapu and the Consejo de Todas las Tierras. By the late 1990s, a large number of militant communities, often affiliated with the Coordinadora de Comunidades en Conflicto Arauco-Malleco, had taken over land on forestry estates often covered with pine plantations, recovering land that had been usurped from their communities over generations. Mapuche organizations like the Coordinadora also made more sweeping demands for national and territorial ethnic autonomy in southern Chile. In response, the governments of Eduardo Frei (1994–2000) and Ricardo Lagos (2000–2006) employed antiterrorism laws dating back to the 1950s, as well as newer laws created by the Pinochet regime, to prosecute and jail Mapuche activists. The crimes they were charged with included setting fire to forestry trucks and tree plantations and issuing threats against forestry companies. As the text here by the Mapuche poet Elicura Chihuailaf makes clear, Mapuche organizations and communities increasingly linked their demands for land and territorial autonomy to an ecological critique of the impact of forestry and tree plantations on the biodiversity of southern Chile's native temperate rainforest.

In a colloquium with high school students, I was speaking about the old Mapuche Nation, whose territory covers parts of what is now Argentina and Chile. I discussed the fact that the mountain range that is currently known as the Andes was never the "creator" of what the states would later, in an almost simultaneous manner, designate the Chilean Mapuches on one side and the Argentine Mapuches on the other. But, I told them, in spite of that, we are still part of a Nation of Peoples.

I later tried to answer some questions.

One student asked me, "But why do you insist so much on talking about Chileans and Mapuches? Are you not Chilean? Do you not feel Chilean?" I told him, "I was born and raised in a Mapuche community where we see the everyday and spiritual worlds in our own way. We view the world through Mapudungun and in the later imposed Spanish, in our brownness, and in the memory of the arrival of the Chilean state that "gave us" our nationality. It was "also" certainly the arrival of large landholdings from which we were excluded. . . .

[Our group] continues toward the communities of Temulemu, Didaico and El Pantano. You can see the pine forests of the Mininco Timber Company. We arrive at a bridge that takes you into the zone. Police have set up a checkpoint to watch over the area. It resembles a border crossing point or a large police station. The police ask for the truck's registration and identification from all of us. Are the police "writing down our information? Are they checking our IDs against lists? . . ." They make us wait. They then "allow us to enter."

We go in silence. It appears to be another country. We think that this country is different. The road is soft, and covered with a wet residue because of the watering truck that constantly wets it. One after another, the owners of the road, the logging trucks, come down with their golden trunks of Chile's "successful development." Farther up, the "hysterical" machines are destroying the land. The wind does not move one leaf, plant, or drop of rain that is not pine.

There is nobody walking around in the tense darkness of the day. Police vehicles drive past. They come and go from one of the two mobile barracks along the edges of the pine forests. All the while, our memories talk about the years of the "Pacification."[1]

We go on for a long time. But suddenly a peaceful circle of soft hills opens up. We have reached the Temulemu community (Forest of the Temu Tree). The sign on the gate reads "Do not enter. Mapuche Territory." We enter. We also belong here. The Lonko (chief) Pascual Pichun is not at home. His *kure* [wife] tells us, "He is in the El Pantano community with the Machi [healer] in a Geykurewen or Ñeikurwen ceremony for renewing wisdom and power. . . . Later on, some detectives walk into the area bringing with them a summons for the Lonko who has been accused of "violent actions." He is to appear before the Traiguén Magistrate. The pine forests that surround the community feel like ropes around a neck that conspiring hands slowly begin to tighten.

We begin our journey again. Along the way we observe the Mininco Timber Company's "operations center" off to the side of the road and below. There is a police barracks immediately next to it on top of the hill. . . .

We arrive at the El Pantano community. The blue and white flags tell us where to go. The Machi are carrying out their ritual there. The Lonko is also there. A police vehicle also drives by a short distance away. "The *peñi* [brothers] are taking care of me. They won't let me out" the Lonko says with a sense of humor.

The Machi Maria Ancamilla tells us, "The Winka [non-Mapuche] have broken the harmony here. They have destroyed the balance between our Land Above and the Land Where We Walk. They work with negative energies, those from the Land Below, that is why the water has dried up here and the medicinal plants and herbs have disappeared. They have taken away our remedies. We have to go far way to collect them. The Winka's pine trees have dried up the water and have killed off the medicinal plants and herbs. That is why we have gotten sick, and our animals have too. The Winka are making our Mother Earth sick."

The breeze is freezing while the mist begins to moisten our silence. The Lonko has asked us to take him home. It rains while we go along our communities' roads and look at ourselves and the extensive pine forests through the fogged up windows without talking. The road is uneven. The vehicle's constant bumps make us occasionally hear the vibration of the *Kultrun* [ceremonial drum] that one of the Lonko's children is holding firmly, while we also hear the accordion that I am holding decide to play some notes from time to time.

We arrive. It is cold, and the Lonko invites us in to his home. His wife offers us a bowl of soup and some fresh baked bread. We drink mate. The Lonko says, "There are five hundred of us in this community; more than two hundred live as visitors in others' homes. Most of our families occupy lands that range from one-half to three hectares in size. The timber companies have taken over our lands. The Chilean state, the government, has not met our demands. We are tired, our patience is running out, but we are not the ones who are interested in creating violence. We have been asking for a sincere dialogue, one that respects our community, for a long time. Our communities are very poor, but our movement focuses on the Mapuche's survival. That is why we need our land."

They say that life has changed around these parts. Families wait for their daughters and their young sons outside of the school. The harassment is constant. Nobody walks alone at night. It is a police state. The state protects the "timber neighbors" who occupy our lands to ensure the success of the market. They say that land, nature, the Mapuche community, and Chilean sovereignty are goods on the "free market. . . ."

The State talks about assimilation and integration, but our people say that we are fighting to coexist.

That's why Alfonso Reiman (Flor del Cóndor) says "A community that doesn't fight will never be free." And he says that we have been meeting to find common strategies and find solutions to the largest problems that affect us as Mapuches. In Lumaco (Water from the Luma Tree), we have always had a spirit of conversation and commitment. There have always been organizations, but many of them were manipulated by different ideologies, political parties, or religions. Of course, these outside organizations have always had different goals than ours. That is why we have had this process of dialogue and analysis with leaders so that we could clarify our objectives as well as the role that our Ñankucheo Association would play. We organized our ideas and different projects.

One of the most important tasks that we have taken on has dealt with making our rights as a community respected. We have worked on recovering these rights. As everyone in society knows, land is the most important thing for us, the Mapuche. And in that regard, there are communities here in Lumaco that have serious land-related problems because each community has an average of 250 hectares and 50 families. And because we were pushed into the mountains, most of our lands are very steep and have serious erosion problems. For example, using intensive farming practices implies quickly eroding our soils because of the natural erosion process that exists when farming mixes with water and wind on steep slopes.

That is why one of our most important demands has been the demand for land. We restarted our movement for our ancestral rights in the region in 1930. Some communities were able to increase the size of the territories by using land subsidies from the Conadi (National Indigenous Development Corporation), but that institution is no longer able to meet the many demands for land. It certainly does not have enough resources, but that is the State's, or government's fault. So the communities and their organizations believe that it is an institution that simply will not satisfy their demands. The Conadi is an inadequate institution for our communities.

The communities have decided to carry out mobilizations and create social pressure, as the only way to increase our land holdings. I am talking about taking back our lands. Around here, 80 percent of the communities are proposing or implementing this option.

It is clear that the land invasions that the timber companies carry out have caused immense problems regarding the environment and the quality of life for people living here. This understanding has led to rejection and hatred of the timber companies. As a community we have simply proposed to begin expelling them from our lands. Because even though they try to make us believe that they provide jobs for us, even though they try to make us believe that they will employ us, we have seen that this is not the case. It is a big lie. Up until now we have only seen the damage that they cause to our environment. I should also say that this environmental damage has led to the drying up of water and disappearance of medicinal plants. As our Machi say, without these plants we can not practice Mapuche medicine.

We now need to discuss migration. Why do so many of us, our brothers and sisters, our descendants of this people which had so much land, have to beg, and live as we presently do? Why do 50 percent of our people live in marginalized conditions in the large cities, living in the lowest social levels of Chilean society?

This migration also means the loss of culture, language, our knowledge, history, and all of the cultural values that we have as Mapuches. This is why we are proposing the reconstruction of our Mapuche territory, and along with it, validation, the rebuilding of our Mapuche organizations and authorities: our Lonko, our Machi. We need them to be valued and respected as leaders of any society would be. We are holding conversations with other Territorial Identities about this proposal. For example, we can say that our [indigenous] structure was of the dual sort, and not vertical like the Winka organizations.

That is a topic that we are going to continue to work on regarding the abilities of each Territorial Identity to consolidate itself as well as generate discussion and analysis to rebuild our organization as Mapuches and recover our validity vis-à-vis the state. . . .

This time the State has become more violent toward us. This is where the demand for our territory has been the longest. Beginning on October 13, 1997, our communities in Pichiloncoyan and Pilimapu began to see that the Conadi had run out of resources as an institution, and they decided to take back their lands. That is when the mobilizations began in many communities while others began to prepare themselves for similar actions.

And this conflict has brought about the persecution and incarceration of many of our leaders. It seems like that is how the government wants to respond to our legitimate demands. It has even dedicated many resources and secret agents to infiltrate the Mapuche movement and find a way to persuade and bribe our leaders. The State, the government, has not wanted to deal with this problem in a serious manner. It has not wanted to realize that our demands are just and legitimate, that we are doing all of this out of necessity.

So far we have not seen any signs that they want to work with us. We have only seen militarization and the deployment of undercover and uniformed police in our territories. There are even some places where the police stop and document everyone who is going from one community to another. We are supposed to be in a "democratic" and "free" country. They are harassing us. We believe that the State is betting on us disappearing as a culture and people. . . .

As Mapuches, we will not be able to change the development policies in this country by ourselves. We have seen examples in which Indigenous and Chilean society have worked together. We can work together.

That is why we are clarifying our situation, among ourselves, so that we can put forth proposals for the rest of society. We want to work with those who are marginalized and excluded from the system. We want to speak and work with groups and organizations that have transformed this country, with groups that have played important roles such as student groups, university groups, labor unions, farmers groups and even the Church if its views are similar to what we are proposing.

And regarding the accusations of the logging companies and government that the Mapuches have decided to burn the forests that they have not been able to obtain through mobilizations; we believe that it is possible that the logging companies started most of the fires. We think that because the export demand for wood has decreased due to the Asian crisis, they are setting fires and earning money from their insurance policies. But it is possible; it is possible, that the communities begin to use that type of action in the future.

We are saying here that we will undertake any type of action to expel the timber companies from our lands because they have always had an inflexible attitude. They do not want to admit that planting pines and eucalyptus destroys the native forests. They do not want to admit that their actions have dried up streams, lakes, and marshes. They do not want to admit the damage that their aerial fumigations cause. They do not want to admit the soil deterioration that pine and eucalyptus plantations cause. If we were to calculate the price of each of these damages, we would have to be talking about reimbursements of 50 percent of their profits for the Mapuche communities.

However, we are proposing expelling the timber companies. Who can foresee what will happen if the destruction of our lands continues? We explained these concerns to the government. Today the projects of CORMA, the National Timber Trade Association, have the objective of tripling the currently planted area. This will happen in Mapuche territory. And this means that this entire problem, falling living standards, deterioration and loss of territory, will continue to worsen.

The farmers of Colliupulli (Red Lands) say that they have organized themselves into "self-defense committees," as they are called, to defend their lands. Our elders tell us that the wealthy landowners in this area have always held anti-Mapuche views, so these actions do not surprise us. But if the government has been capable of designating visiting ministers to "solve" our conflicts, we will see if it is capable of designating a visiting minister to investigate the formation of the landowners' paramilitary groups. They would have to begin by investigating how many and what type of arms they have. Maybe if they would have heard that the Mapuche were responsible for these events they would not have taken so long to designate a visiting minister. The attitudes of the wealthy landowners and the rich can lead to very unfortunate consequences.

We tell Chileans that they must accept that this is a multi-cultural country. Our culture is different from Chilean culture, and we believe that we have legitimacy in being who we are. We want to continue existing as a people. We want to maintain our language, and keep using Lonko and Machi. We want to regain our rights as Mapuches. We want to be the ones who design and control our lives.

And we want Chilean society to understand that the conditions in which the Mapuche live today have transformed us into the poorest of the poor. We want them to know that we also know that a large part of Chilean society lives in the same conditions as the Mapuche. That is why we understand them and want to establish an alliance with those whom the system marginalizes and excludes. No single group, not the workers' organizations or any other, nor the Mapuche will be able to create a transformation when facing such a powerful enemy alone. So we must all have the spirit, will, and clarity to talk to one another with respect in order to create an alliance that will allow us to aspire to a better and more just society for this country.

Translated by Ryan Judge

Note

1. The "pacification" refers to Chilean military campaigns to defeat the Mapuche south of the Bío Bío River in the late nineteenth century.

Growth with Equity

Alejandro Foxley

Following on a leading campaign promise of the forces that defeated Pinochet, the governments of the Concertación devoted considerable energy to the so-called growth with equity strategy, a plan that sought to combine successful macroeconomic performance with increases in public spending on housing, education, health care, and other antipoverty measures, all of which had contracted under the military government. The strategy succeeded. The Aylwin government obtained congressional approval for a series of major tax increases in 1991–1993, $500 million of which was earmarked for social spending and aggressive antipoverty measures. During 1990–1997, Chile experienced an impressive 7.7 percent average annual rate of growth, lower inflation rates, increased foreign investment, and low unemployment rates. In combination with the targeted social spending, this "Chilean economic miracle" enabled the Concertación to boast that in a single decade they had reduced Chile's rate of poverty from the staggering 45 percent of the final years of the dictatorship to 22 percent in 1998.

The principal architect and defender of this plan was Alejandro Foxley, a Christian Democratic economist trained in the United States, who had repeatedly criticized the negative economic and social effects of the military regime's radical neoliberalism. In 1990 Foxley took the helm of economic planning as minister of finance, an appointment that carried with it high expectations of social equalization and a reversal of neoliberal policies from the Concertación's supporters, as well as fears of radical change from the pro-Pinochet business community. Expectations and fears alike proved exaggerated, however, when the center-left regime steadfastly opted for continuity in the economic policy arena. Concerned both with courting business support and staving off populist demands, Foxley produced a plan for democratic Chile that left most of the inherited economic model intact, despite the high social costs it had inflicted under the military regime. When asked about this seeming contradiction, Foxley argued memorably that "we have already paid the social costs of these neoliberal policies, so we might as well enjoy their economic benefits." In this 2004 study prepared for a World Bank conference on poverty, Foxley explains the eco-

nomic objectives of the government, describes its antipoverty policies, and defends the Concertación economic policy—including its record of income distribution—in the 1990s.[1]

The Social Impact of a Pro-growth Strategy

Poverty eradication has been at the core of development strategies in Chile during the 1990s. The Aylwin, Frei and Lagos administrations have persisted in the fight against poverty as a high priority policy goal. We will explore in this paper the nature of the policies undertaken to reduce poverty, evaluate the results, and draw lessons from what worked or did not work in the antipoverty policy approach pursued for more than a decade now.

The social policies of the 1990s were heavily influenced by a particularly adverse starting point. The Chilean economy had gone through a deep financial crisis in 1982. When looking at the relevant figures, what comes to mind is the Argentina crisis of 2001, as a similar type of economic shock. Chile's GDP fell by 16 percent in 1982 and 1983. The collapse of the financial sector cost Chilean taxpayers between 30 and 40 percent of GDP.[2] Unemployment shot up to 30 percent. Around 50 percent of the population went below the poverty line, a figure not unlike Argentina's in the early 2000s. Extreme poverty affected 30 percent of the population.[3]

Starting in 1985, a new Minister of Finance shifted the focus of economic policies towards recuperating financial solvency and economic growth. The effort was successful. Exports grew rapidly and unemployment went down. However, on the poverty front, results were less successful. People living below a poverty line still represented 45 percent of the population in 1987. Additionally, a key decision, that of reducing taxes and government expenditures in 1988, had a further negative impact in social policies. . . .

A tax reduction of 4 percent of GDP, undertaken by the Pinochet government in the late 1980s, forced a decrease in social expenditures equivalent to 3 percent of GDP. This meant a severe deterioration in the coverage and quality of public health services, lower wages for teachers and lower pensions for the elderly.

It is against this background that the newly elected democratic government of Patricio Aylwin came into office in 1990. The new government immediately put the fight against poverty at the top of the agenda, as part of a "growth with equity" development strategy.

In thus defining the government programme, growth with equity, the new administration was making a strong statement: a successful poverty eradication would not be possible unless it was based on an unambiguous pro-growth strategy but one that would be accompanied by active social policies. . . .

The pro-growth policies included a commitment to a permanent budget surplus, to retiring government debt as an insurance against future financial shocks, as that experienced in 1982; to a further unilateral reduction of external tariffs that would be followed by free trade agreements to be negotiated with Chile's main trading partners, including Latin American countries, the European Union, the United States and Canada.

The pro-growth policies also considered a deepening of the capital market, by allowing for a gradual diversification of financial instruments, where privatized pension funds and other financial intermediaries could invest in. All these policies were pursued with vigour and continuity by the three Center-left governments of Aylwin, Frei and Lagos.

The pro-growth agenda produced generally good results. . . . In fact, the Chilean economy grew by more than 6 percent a year for the decade, in spite of a slowdown caused by the Asian crisis in 1998 and 1999. Productivity grew at a respectable 4.4 percent annually. Real wages increased by 3.3 percent a year. The rate of investment reached an all time high. The same is true of domestic savings. The budget surplus objective was achieved. It reached 1.3 percent of GDP as an average for the decade.

The robust growth performance provided a solid foundation for the anti-poverty objective. Both real wages and employment increased significantly. New job opportunities for the unemployed and higher disposable incomes had an immediate impact on poverty reduction.

But such a positive result had to be reinforced by aggressive social policies designed to further improve the lot of the poor. The financing of such an effort could only be achieved by redressing the drastic tax reduction undertaken in the later years of the Pinochet regime.

A tax reform was proposed in 1990 increasing taxes across the board, including corporate and personal income taxes, the value added tax and reducing tax evasion in sectors like the farm sector. The tax reform passed the Congress by a large majority in less than two months.[4]

As a consequence, tax collection increased by 3 percent of GDP in subsequent years. The government committed itself to spend 100 percent of the additional revenues in the social sectors. The commitment was fulfilled, with a dramatic reduction in the number of families living below the poverty level. Indigence also decreased sharply.

These results are the most successful when compared with other Latin

American countries in a similar period of time. . . . The results also compare favourably with similar efforts undertaken by countries such as Indonesia, Malaysia, Pakistan and others.[5]

Antipoverty Strategies

Having inherited deep social imbalances and massive poverty, the Aylwin government took strong initial action to provide a minimum income to poorer families. The minimum wage was increased by 17 percent in real terms between 1989 and 1991.[6] Family allowances and various subsidies for disadvantaged families, for disabilities and for the unemployed were also increased, as well as pensions.

The next step was to expand social expenditures in public health, housing for the poor and education. The public health system had been seriously neglected by the military regime in the hope of forcing a complete privatization. Hospitals had to be provided with basic equipment, including bed sheets, heating and standard drugs required by patients.

Investment in public hospitals and primary care units increased from US$10 million a year to US$100 million annually during the Aylwin administration. Sharp increases in primary health care subsidies administered by municipalities were implemented, as well as a significant improvement in salaries paid to hospital personnel. However, no changes were made to highly centralized institutional arrangements and deficient management practices in public hospitals, something that would be regretted at a later stage.

The initial effort to increase the coverage and quality of public health was continued under Presidents Frei and Lagos. In a ten-year period, public expenditures in health had increased by 250 percent. . . . Housing subsidies were also expanded by 160 percent in the decade, with an emphasis in the lower income quintile, in rural communities and in urban renewal programs.

But where the main effort was concentrated, was in improving the quality and equity in education. Public resources increased almost threefold in the decade. The notion was to improve on the coverage of education by including pre-school children, and to upgrade the quality of primary and secondary education.[7]

The first stage in educational reform involved concentrating resources on the 10 percent of primary schools with poorest learning outcomes. Funds were used to repair schools, improve teaching methods, provide access to books and, later, to computers, as well as reinforcing the school lunches program. After a few years, the two thousand schools in the program had an improvement of 12 percent in the reading and math skills scores, vis-à-vis 9 percent in the rest of the municipal schools, a modest but positive result.

This was followed by a systemic intervention at the primary and secondary school levels. The effort included all schools public and private, oriented towards low income families. Upgrading teaching materials, libraries and networking schools through the Internet in the Enlaces program was part of the effort. The rest consisted in providing funds for school or teacher generated innovative projects. The idea was to induce changes in teaching methods from below.

A third phase in education reform extended the school day to 8 pedagogical hours, 1200 hours a year, in order to allow for a more sustained effort at improving the quality of education in poor schools. The whole process was accompanied by huge wage increases for teachers, more than doubling their salaries in real terms in ten years.

However, teachers and particularly the National Teachers Union were reluctant partners in the effort. The Teachers Union forced the government to accept a Teachers Statute in 1991, that essentially gave tenure to teachers and school administrators, irrespective of their performance, and established a highly centralized national collective bargaining process for teachers' salaries. Teachers could not be fired even if school enrollment fell. And they would be paid identical salaries irrespective of local conditions. . . .

Social expenditures more than doubled in the decade. As many incidence studies have demonstrated, the impact of these programs in reducing income disparities was very significant. The World Bank concludes that by 1996, a monetary income differential of 1 to 20 between the poorer 20 percent of the population and the 20 percent richer had been reduced to 1 to 11 because of the redistributive effects of social expenditures.[8]

In fact, income distribution when considering only monetary income improved between 1990 and 1994 but had deteriorated by 1998. However, when income distribution is adjusted for cash and in-kind transfers, the situation drastically improves. Anti-poverty programs had a clear redistributive impact.

A key to understanding the rapid reduction in poverty ratios in Chile lies in the balanced nature of the equation: an active pro-growth agenda and aggressive social policies focused on poverty reduction. Studies by Meller[9] and by Cowan and de Gregorio ask the following question: did active social policies make a difference in the case of Chile or is good growth performance the sole driving force behind poverty reduction? These authors compare the effectiveness of each additional point in growth rates on the percentage of poverty reduction achieved with two different growth strategies: the trickle-down strategy of the 1980s as compared to the growth-with-equity strategy of the 1990s. The conclusion is that active social policies do matter. In fact they explain 40 percent of poverty reduction. Economic growth maintained at the level of the late 1980s, and identical growth rates as experienced in the 1990s, poverty in 1996 would have been 28 percent of the population, instead of the 23 percent actually achieved. Social policies did make a difference.

Notes

1. *Editors' note:* The citations in this chapter are from the original publication.
2. Gunther Held and Luis Felipe Jiménez, "Liberalización, crisis y reforma del sistema bancario: 1974–1999," in Ricardo Ffrench-Davis and Barbara Stallings, eds., *Reformas, crecimiento y políticas sociales en Chile desde 1973* (Santiago: CEPAL, 2001).
3. Dagmar Raczynski and Claudia Serrano, "Eventos de Quiebre de Ingreso y Mecanismos de Protección Social," paper prepared for the World Bank (2001).
4. Alejandro Foxley, "Development Lessons of the 1990s: Chile," paper prepared for the Practitioners of Development Conferences by the World Bank (2003).
5. Kevin Cowan and José de Gregorio, "Distribución y Pobreza en Chile," *Estudios Públicos* 64 (Spring 1996).
6. Alejandra Mizala and Pilar Romaguera, "La legislación laboral y el mercado del trabajo: 1975–2000," in Ffrench-Davis and Stallings, *Reformas, crecimiento y políticas sociales.*
7. Cristián Cox and María José Lemaitre, "Market and State Principles of Reform in Chilean Education," in Guillermo Perry and Danny M. Leipziger, eds., *Chile: Recent Policy Lessons and Emerging Challenges* (Washington, D.C.: World Bank, 1999).
8. World Bank, *Chile's High Growth Economy, Poverty, and Income Distribution, 1987–1998* (Washington, D.C.: World Bank, 2002).
9. Patricio Meller, "Pobreza y Distribución del Ingreso en Chile en la Década del 90," paper presented to "Conference on Chile, 1990–1999," University of California, San Diego, December 1998, and Cowan and de Gregorio, "Distribución y Pobreza en Chile."

So Conservative and Yet So Modern?

The Politics of Concertación

Alfredo Jocelyn-Holt

In this short piece published for a U.S. audience, Alfredo Jocelyn-Holt, a leading Rightist public intellectual, assesses the progress and limitations of Chilean society during the first decade of Concertación rule. His analysis of two divergent political viewpoints and the political apathy that lies between them provides a concise sketch of how stalling economic growth, political scandals, limited redress for human rights violations, and uneven development undermined public confidence in political parties and democratic process at the turn of the millennium. Asking "How is it that a country can be so conservative and yet so apparently modern?" Jocelyn-Holt shows some of the complexity and ambivalence of Chilean politics three decades after the military coup and just one decade after the end of the dictatorship.

Two divergent views seek to define Chile today, one tends to be self-complacent, optimistic and officialist. The other is more marginal, skeptical and sour.

The first of these visions builds on the premise that Chileans have suffered too much and too long. A different country is what they deserve; one no longer torn by dissension nor economically destitute, ruled by civilians, but as unlike as possible from the radical Allende regime which brought us to the brink of civil war. In short, a consumer market economy, open to new international opportunities, bound to economic growth and orthodox fiscal policies, respected by international financial agencies and foreign investors, without forgetting the poor and the less competitive. In other words, it is a line of thinking that envisions a government not willing to waive its right to raise taxes when it finds it convenient nor wanting to relinquish the control of copper and other strategic industries in order to maintain macroeconomic balances.

This position more or less coincides with what the military tried to accomplish. Paradoxically, though, this time former opponents—watched over firmly by the armed forces as constitutional "guarantors"—are in charge of the implementation of these goals. As if this were not enough oversight, a number of additional institutional mechanisms require the consensual agreement of the powerful right-wing opposition. This is a scheme hard to swallow—but not without its benefits. After all, it has given an electoral advantage to three centre-left Concertación governments, in power since 1990 when Pinochet lost the 1988 plebiscite that sought to perpetuate his regime yet another eight years. Former socialist-minded politicians have been able to leave behind their past reputation as poor administrators and radical subversives to the point that no member of the establishment would at present care to disdain them. And, whatever their past ideology, the fact that they can control a still-potent state—if not wealthier now, at least more businesslike—has given them the chance to carry out what they have always aimed to achieve, to engineer revolutionary change from above, nowadays via the market. That they may be the envy of Latin America, not unlike when they were being proclaimed revolutionary models, has given them a further cause to be boastful—enough to pass over the bad years, and any remorse for what they are now defending. History, for them today as well as 30 years ago, is not so much dead as surmountable.

The other position holds that the Concertación governments have compromised too much. They were elected to reform the Constitution and the neoliberal system, put an end to dictatorship and bring about some justice in compensation for the atrocious human rights violations. Since none of these objectives has been fully met, the Concertación appears to be a mere machination to perpetuate the military legacy, while the Right awaits its comeback, gaining more at this stage by being in the opposition than in La Moneda. Consequently, this critique questions the moral motives of those who are [in 2004] in power, seeing them as a self-serving coterie bound to ideological betrayal, accommodation and personal ambition. Needless to say, people holding this view are seldom admitted to political circles. They are labeled nostalgic, bitter, unrealistic, premodern, elitist, and too quarrelsome. Without any effective organization behind them, nor any concrete alternative proposal, these Chileans are often viewed as a chorus of lamentation that should be left alone, marginalized and generally unheeded.

Fortunately or not, this group cannot be dismissed so easily. What they have to say periodically generates debate. In 1997 and 1998, a number of best-selling publications diagnosed a growing climate of frustration. They could not have been more timely: in 1997, the Concertación lost popular support in the parliamentary elections. Almost four million Chileans (40 percent) either did not register, abstained, annulled their votes or left the ballot blank.

The economy also accounts for this increasing malaise. Annual economic growth from 1998 to 2002 was 2.4 percent, compared to 7.7 percent between 1990 and 1997. If in the earlier period employment rose 2.4 percent annually, in these last years, the average increase in new jobs has been a poor 0.4 percent. If the number of Chileans below poverty level descended abruptly from 5 million in 1990, the number has remained around 3.1 million since 1998 (21 percent). Other variables point to a more complex picture. According to the 2002 census, 87 percent of households own a color television; one out of five families owns a computer; one out of ten is connected to Internet; 51 percent has at least one cell-phone, and three out of four families are homeowners. However, the 2002 United Nation Development Programme (UNDP) report still posed anguished questions such as: "We Chileans: Who are we? What is happening to us? Where are we going? Answers were even more sulky; at least 52 percent felt they were "losers," 54 percent expressed doubts with respect to the economy, and 43 percent said that their incomes barely allowed them to live decently.

A number of recent events have damaged public confidence in institutions. Pinochet's London detention and his subsequent acquittal by Chilean courts, as well as a streak of scandals involving the illegal appropriation of public monies by high government officials to finance their political parties, may explain why only 50 percent of people polled in 2002 answer that democracy is the best political system; 30 percent think "it does not matter"; only 23 percent have confidence on the judiciary; and a mere 12 percent trust political parties. . . .

In addition to this panorama of mistrust and corruption, disturbing statistics show that 61 percent of crimes go unreported; 40 percent of Chileans show some form of mental disorder; half of Chilean women suffer family violence; and 19,000 children are mistreated each year. Data on education is contradictory. University attendance may have increased from 120,000 twenty years ago, to approximately 500,000 at present. However, one of the 70 new private universities can invest $8 million in a brand new library—and have only 40,000 volumes in its shelves; tax breaks explain high expenditures in infrastructure, while effective research commitment is still to be seen. Chile systematically ranks well below average in almost all international tests, and reading levels could not be poorer; nevertheless the Minister of Education insists on making Chile a bilingual English-speaking country. Supposedly, this ought to make us more "globalized." Let us hope so; the main daily devotes 14 pages to "social life" against 4 dealing with international news. In the last years of dictatorship we had a more progressive and critical press than today. According to Human Rights Watch, Chile ranks immediately above Cuba as having the worst record in freedom of speech in all of Latin America. In terms of personal freedom, it is not doing that well either; there is still no divorce law.

How is it that a country can be so conservative and yet so apparently modern? The obvious explanation is that it is meant to work that way and has been doing so ever since the Pinochet years. Whoever rules Chile has to be acrobatic. . . .

What are we to make of all this? My guess is that Chile is an unstable society undergoing rapid change. It obliquely deals with its past traumas, all of which center on violence, in the absence of a strong consensual agreement that would permit us to deal with them frankly on an institutional level. Consensus politics is built into the Constitution. However, in many cases, it simply serves to maintain fragile equilibria amongst powerful sectors. Chile is not an open society and has a long way to go before it can meet the standards of a demanding modern world. It may be progressive economically, but only to a point. Poverty and unequal distribution of wealth are pressing dilemmas that neither the military nor the Concertación have solved adequately. . . .

Finally, if we have learned anything during these past years, it is that Chilean society resists any clear-cut definitions. This situation is not unlike what happened, back in the early 1970s, when it turned out that we were not the Latin American exception that confirmed the rule, nor as institutionally bound as everyone wanted to think. If so, in the near future, Chile will be a far more surprising place than anyone in or out of power, self-assured or not, might be guessing at this present time.

The Catholic Church Today

Antonio Delfau, S.J.

After the return to democratic rule, the Catholic Church was the most prestigious institution in Chile, largely because of its courageous defense of human rights during the dictatorship. But the Church leadership of the 1990s was no longer the progressive Church influenced by liberation theology but a more conservative hierarchy appointed by Pope John Paul II, which used the Church's hard-won legitimacy for conservative purposes, such as resisting the legalization of divorce and abortion. In this article Father Antonio Delfau, editor of the respected Jesuit monthly Mensaje, *examines the decline of the progressive Church and the challenges facing the Chilean Church in the new millennium. For Delfau, this decline is evident not only in Chile's "changing culture and traditions" but also in the clergy's failure to communicate effectively in a secular world. Echoing Father Alberto Hurtado's 1941 "Is Chile a Catholic Country?" Delfau questions Chilean values in an era of materialism and social conservatism.*

Cultural and ethical traditions are changing rapidly in Chile. Chileans' greater appreciation for individual freedom has challenged the Church's ability to offer a compelling religious discourse. Although the Church's priorities do not always have to coincide with those of larger society, it does seem that the priests are no longer able to effectively communicate their principal concerns.

Many people think that, as Catholics, we are not responding to the concerns, questions, and problems of the world today. They do not see us proposing new answers, answers derived from our faith, to the challenges raised by cultural changes. Instead, they see us as being ill equipped, reacting without proper preparation to the issues raised by others. This, along with accusations of sexual abuse, has resulted in a slow but steady deterioration of our credibility, capacity for conversion, and presence as a Community of God in Chile.

The Trust Wanes

In our country the separation of Church and State occurred in 1925. Nevertheless, since then political authorities have shown a special deference toward the Catholic hierarchy. The vast majority of our democratic governments have tried to respect the Church and have maintained good relations with its hierarchy. For their part, the priests have been wise enough to use this space for the advancement of noble causes and, through focusing on Chile's best interest, have made the President, legislators and the public see their point of view.

Lately, however, this respect and deference toward Church authorities has been weakening. Parliamentarians, public authorities, academics and the media are criticizing some bishops and their proposals. Complaints have gradually arisen—some, in addition to being unjust, are outright offensive—against certain priests and their ideas.

The difficulties the Church faces in being heard are not simply the result of real or supposed anti-Catholic campaigns. Nor should the discrepancy of some of these claims be seen as easy evidence that we are walking along the path of persecution the Lord promised to his disciples. These denunciations do not always prove that we are doing the right thing. We need to discern whether or not this discredit and loss of trust in both the Church and its authorities, especially among the youth, can be attributed to the defense of sacred values, to cultural changes, or to inappropriate strategies and formulations.

Various surveys indeed show a "divorce" between the feeling of the believers and the discourse of some of their pastors. There are Catholics who, while not abandoning the Church, remain in it without abiding by all of its customs. For their part, lately some prelates give the impression of having made loyalty and fidelity to the Church equivalent with consenting to some forthcoming pronouncements and approaches that are indeed questionable. They have also assumed disloyalty or ethical relativism among those who try to find areas of agreement and dialog with the diverse sectors of Chilean society, the media, the academic and scientific world, and politicians.

Listen Attentively and Compassionately

The Catholic hierarchy in Chile has the right and the obligation to guide social life, teaching the doctrine that best relates to current trends and situations. Those who wish to hide such doctrine in the vestries or who think that only loyal Catholics should hear its interpretations are mistaken. Nevertheless, we must admit that today the Catholic Church does not command the prestige, trust, and privileges that it enjoyed in the not so distant past. We are facing serious difficulties in communicating our message to a society that values its autonomy more and more every day.

We must learn the lessons of history, recognize its mistakes, open a process of reflection about our situation in Chilean society and hopefully thus improve the way that we offer our points of view. More and more devout Catholics are beginning to understand this. We believe that the search for ways to inculcate Christian values in Chile is solved by seriously considering the context, feeling, possibilities and real life problems of the people.

We will be able to overcome the difficulties faced in the Church's dialogue with society if, moved by an immense love for the world in which we are living and taking into account the cultural changes that are now occurring in Chile, we look for a more appropriate language for these new feelings. That is how it was done by the apostles, the evangelicals, and Saint Paul himself when they adapted their preaching and emphasis for new cultural contexts. By always being ready to give reason to our faith, the clarity of our convictions and approaches will not prevent us from listening attentively to those of others. The difficulties and defeats that we are dealing with should not make us more rigid. Rather, they should inspire us to be more creative and more willing to find the necessary language, tones, and ways to evangelize considering the cultural changes happening in Chile today.

Translated by Carson Morris

"To Never Again Live It, To Never Again Deny It": The Valech Report on Torture

Ricardo Lagos

Of all the repressive measures instituted by the Pinochet regime, none was more widespread—or more sinister and hidden—than the systematic application of torture. Despite this pervasive practice, torture in Chile remained largely a private crime whose victims found it difficult to disclose for psychological and political reasons. Torture was, consequently, one of the more difficult crimes around which to mobilize public protest and remained outside of official discussions of human rights violations and reparations well into the transition to democracy. In September 2003, however, after apologizing to the victims of torture and declaring that "there is no tomorrow without yesterday," President Ricardo Lagos convened a presidential truth commission charged with documenting politically motivated imprisonment and torture carried out by the military regime. It was on the basis of the report of this commission, named the Valech Commission after its chair, Bishop Sergio Valech, that the systematic practice of torture in Chile became part of the country's official history. The Commission concluded that all political prisoners were tortured, and documented some 27,255 cases in 1,132 political prisons, military barracks, and clandestine detention centers. In the wake of the report, the government established pensions as well as free education, health care, and housing for torture victims. Moreover, while a fifty-year moratorium on testimonies collected by the Commission prevented their use in criminal trials against specific perpetrators, the report's release dramatically eroded lingering positive public opinion about the Pinochet regime in both civilian and military circles. In his prologue to the Valech Report, excerpted here, Lagos also amplified the remarks of the army commander Juan Emilio Cheyre, published just days earlier, in which Cheyre broke with earlier positions taken by military leaders and rejected any justification for the commission of human rights violations.

The Reading of the Report

I have carefully read and analyzed this Report. The victims' stories have touched me. They relate disturbing experiences, to the point that one's emotions make them difficult to read. I have intimately felt the magnitude of the suffering, the injustice of extreme cruelty, and the immensity of the pain.

I express here, as President of all Chilean people, my solidarity with and my affection for all the victims and their families.

No one who reads this report can remain indifferent. I am sure that the overwhelming majority of my compatriots will empathize with those who have suffered and will reaffirm their support for freedom and human rights.

Upon Reading the Report, Various Questions Continue to Bother Us

How do we explain such horror? What could provoke such human behaviors? I do not have an answer to these questions. As with other places and historical moments, there is no rationale that can explain those human behaviors that are epitomized by extreme cruelty. How can we explain that 94 percent of the detained demonstrated that they had suffered torture? How can we explain that, of the 3,400 women who offered testimony, almost all declared that they had been subjected to sexual violence?

And there are other questions. How were we able to live in 30 years of silence? We know that silence was a consequence of fear during the dictatorship, but that does not explain everything. From the victims' perspective silence is the result of a desire to preserve their basic dignity. The report states that: "removing the veil of torture, of humiliation, of physical and psychological abuse, is a very difficult task, even with [victims'] own spouses. And this understandable silence intensified the pain of those unshared sufferings, which we prefer to put on the shelf of nightmares and remove from the files of history."

Behind the Report are the broken lives, destroyed families, maimed personal perspectives, and inability to give one's children a better life. All of this was covered up for a very long time by a thick, unhealthy silence. That had to end, and it has ended.

The will of the victims and of their relatives, combined with that of the people and institutions that were always by their side, prevented this silence from turning into forgetting. And that is where we find the moral strength of the victims.

Some will ask if it makes sense to compose a report so many years after the fact. The report itself answers this question by pointing out that "the experience of political imprisonment and torture represented a fundamental break that traversed every dimension of the victims' existence and that of their families, and it accompanies them through the present."

We are not only dealing with the horrors of the past, but also with the pain that still remains. Furthermore, it is only appropriate that we face this traumatic part of the truth and complete the process of justice and healing that the victims rightfully deserve.

In those dark days of yesterday, imprisonment and torture served as an attempt to forever strip the victims and their families of their dignity. Vindicating them thirty years later is a means of exalting their enduring dignity. Indeed, it was this very dignity that had served as moral support in the battle to return to democracy. . . .

The Basic Lessons

I have said on various occasions that the break in democracy and in the foundations of our coexistence was produced in the midst of political and ideological storms that we were incapable of controlling. The institutional rupture and the subsequent establishment of arbitrariness and terror were the consequences of these collective and individual errors.

The context of political intransigence before the military coup, with the erroneous transformation of adversary into enemy and the international impact of the Cold War, can be understood as antecedents to the institutional rupture. But there is no justification for the harshness that then followed. I clearly share, then, what the Commander in Chief of the Army affirmed: "Does the setting of global conflict described above excuse the human rights violations that occurred in Chile? My answer is one and the same: no. Human rights violations never and for no one can have an ethical justification."

No! One thousand times, No! There will never be ethical justification for the atrocities that were committed and that are detailed in the report. Never Again!

The acknowledgment of this sad chapter of our history allows all Chileans today to feel part of one community and of one destiny. This recognition allows us to feel that our armed institutions belong to all Chilean people.

Recognizing the delirium and the loss of direction that in a single moment of the past allowed the armed institutions and the State to stray from their historical tradition, from the very doctrines that defined their foundation and development, is a necessary condition to retaking the path always taken by the founders of the Republic.

The report recounts the places where torture was practiced, indicates the State agents who carried it out, establishes the practices employed by diverse public entities, identifies the laws that protected acts of repression, and describes the proceedings of the tribunals. The long list of military bases, police stations, units, ships, regional government offices, prison camps and clandestine spaces covers the national territory. The conclusion is clear and undeniable: political imprisonment and torture were institutional practices of the State, at once absolutely unacceptable and completely outside of Chilean historical tradition.

Today we can peacefully look at our past. We are constructing a democracy that is every day more solid, and we are fighting for progress and social justice, the essential bases of a united nation. We have regained the necessary harmony between a society and its armed institutions. We have the strength needed to transform the pain into memory and the memory into national unity, in a shared future. . . .

Final Words

The road to taking responsibility for our past has been long, difficult, and complex. Accepting the brutal truth of what happened and the responsibility for these acts has not been easy for any Chilean.

As a society we have been opening our eyes to the reality of those compatriots who were disappeared, executed, exiled, and blacklisted, and now, to those who suffered political imprisonment and torture.

As a nation, to the degree that it is possible, we have been proposing and defining methods of moral, symbolic and economic reparations for all those people who were victims of crimes against their most basic rights. By recognizing those victims of political imprisonment and torture we complete a chapter through which we needed to pass.

Translated by Carson Morris

The Chilean Army after Pinochet

Juan Emilio Cheyre Espinosa

Even before Chile's transition to democratic rule, Pinochet's authority over the armed forces was not absolute, and tensions were part of the ambivalence toward the Pinochetista project felt by a younger generation of army commanders such as Juan Emilio Cheyre, who rose through the ranks to become commander-in-chief from 2002 to 2006. Cheyre actively distanced the army from Pinochet and worked to change it into an institution for a new era of civilian democracy, making public his efforts to cooperate with civilian leaders. In 2003, he stunned observers by releasing a statement on civil-military relations, "The Chilean Army: The End of a Vision," in which he announced that the Chilean army had abandoned a Cold War vision of its role in society, a role that had reached its maximum expression in the Pinochet regime. It was in this context that General Cheyre emphatically denounced the military's involvement in human rights abuses, inaugurating a new period of relative cooperation between civilian and military authorities under Ricardo Lagos and subsequently President Michelle Bachelet. In this letter to the editor of El Mercurio, *published February 8, 2005, General Cheyre responds to recent articles that, in Cheyre's view, portrayed the army in a negative light. He is at pains to illustrate the role that the army under his command will not play in Chilean politics.*

Esteemed Editor,

I am writing in regard to *El Mercurio*'s "Week in Politics" from last Sunday, which described—among other things—the Army's reaction to recent events as "a tepid response," and also made the following assertion in the general context of the editorial: "in short, the Armed Forces have ended up watching how history is written by their adversaries and by those who, either out of convenience or cowardice, changed sides." It is my duty to state that these arguments are of grave concern.

In my opinion, it is a serious matter because this type of characterization reflects a particular line of argument, a line that a newspaper of the importance and journalistic tradition such as *El Mercurio* has been showing in its coverage of current political and judicial topics, in news articles, opinion pieces, headlines, and—this past Sunday—in this editorial.

We might ask, in effect: how does *El Mercurio* expect the Chilean Army to act? If the author of this editorial, who contributes nothing constructive to the debate (something typical of this type of background piece) describes the Army's response as a "tepid response," it means that the author expects or implies a different kind of reaction. Or might another, less "tepid," response from the Army include the following:

- Approving military insubordination regarding judicial decisions.
- Accepting improper pressures from someone who has been affected by court rulings and thinks these rulings are wrong and lack due process.
- Exerting pressure on the State and other public officials.
- Using the Army's capabilities, which society has given it to defend Chile, to employ different levels and kinds of force.
- Assisting, promoting, or accepting internal acts of military rebellion within a hierarchical and disciplined institution.
- Using threats, either directly or indirectly, to guarantee that the Army's own view of the problem at hand (which the author does not wish to address) is the one that prevails.

This is a problem that I, as Commander in Chief, have thoroughly addressed on repeated occasions throughout the country, via the appropriate channels, and in all of its dimensions since the beginning of my term.

No, esteemed editor, it is my responsibility—regardless of the characterization that this member of the media uses to describe the institution—to ensure that every Chilean knows that the Army remains loyal to the current constitutional order, in which our fellow citizens can see that we all belong to the same society (I must remind you, by the way, that the Army does not see any Chilean as its "adversary") and that the institution maintains a level of professionalism and efficiency that provides Chile with security, defense, and peace.

Additionally—and this is the heart of the matter!—with respect to the past, its dramatic denouement and the unresolved issues that affect all of us—victims and comrades in arms alike—it behooves us to remember that it is not the Army, but rather society, along with its public authorities and State powers, that must ensure a definitive solution to the ongoing impact of a political crisis that began more than three decades ago.

In spite of this fact, the Army has never been indifferent to the fate of its members (in active service or retired), especially when we have lately witnessed the kind of public redress affecting those who have been condemned for Human Rights violations, who must now add to their sentences the kinds of taunts that are reprehensible under a democratic regime.

Among the most unjust assertions about this are the views expressed in the editorial "end of an era," as well as others that this newspaper publishes in line with this view, which it has maintained as a consistent point of view. As far as I understand, this runs counter to the essence of what the Chilean Army should be, which a research article (in Section B of the same paper) containing the opinion and analysis of experts from a variety of tendencies documents so well.

I sincerely believe that *El Mercurio* has made, and makes, a significant contribution—on every topic—to the process of building the Army that we all hope for, except for when it publishes articles to which I feel compelled to object. I express this with all due respect for freedom of opinion and the independence of the press, as well as my personal respect for what this newspaper represents for the development of the country.

I conclude by restating my hope that Chileans will find the way to solve the still unresolved and painful issues of the past. The Army has thoroughly and broadly dealt with the topic of Human Rights, and will continue to contribute, because of its moral and legal mandate, to those legal cases wherever they may arise. I am confident that on this topic *El Mercurio,* along with the rest of the media, will collaborate in solving such a pressing topic in a rational fashion.

Translated by Ryan Judge

La Señora Presidenta

Michelle Bachelet

In 2006, Michelle Bachelet won a runoff election to become Chile's first female president and the fourth woman elected to this office in the Americas since President Isabel Perón assumed office in Argentina in 1974. As the fourth Concertación president and the second Socialist chief executive since the end of the dictatorship, Bachelet's presidency signified both the ruling coalition's continuity with the past and a new informal style of politics that stemmed in no small part from her personal biography. A Socialist Party activist since her youth, like many of her contemporaries Bachelet was personally affected by the dictatorship. Her father, an air force general who had served in the Allende government, died while in military custody, and she and her mother experienced detention, torture, and exile. After four years of exile in East Germany, Bachelet returned to Chile to finish her medical studies, emerging in the 1990s as a popular Socialist politician who served as minister of health and then of national defense. The national and international press never tired of pointing out other distinguishing characteristics of her profile, such as her status as a divorcee, a single mother, and an atheist, characteristics that made Bachelet come across as a real person, not just another politician, and a style that apparently resonated with much of the Chilean electorate.

Bachelet's presidency advanced gender equality in Chilean politics beyond the mere fact of placing a woman in power, however. Her government made advances toward gender parity and more open government, implementing gender quotas and antipoverty measures while remaining responsive to popular pressure. President Bachelet navigated carefully but publicly the challenges posed by her status as a woman in a male-dominated political world, expressing her empathy for the circumstances faced by other single mothers even as she avoided close association with Chile's outspoken feminist movements. In this 2007 speech, delivered at a women's conference in Quito, Ecuador, President Bachelet discusses the implications of Chile's choice of a "Presidenta" and describes the creation and implementation of public policies with a "gender perspective." Ultimately Bachelet was remarkably successful at overcoming the initial unease her presidency provoked among some *sectors of the electorate: she ended her term in office with approval ratings at 84–96 percent, higher than those of any Chilean president in living memory. Barred from a consecutive term in office, beginning in 2010 Bachelet served as executive director of the United Nations Entity for Gender Equality and the Empowerment of Women, until the presidential elections of 2013, in which she was the leading candidate.*

When we speak here about the situation of women what we are talking about is equity in our societies. We are talking about all the peoples of Latin America working together for societies that are more just, have more humane relations, where there is no longer room for inequality, arbitrariness, abuse, abuse of power, where all people, men and women, have equal opportunity. . . .

Because many forms of exclusion persist in Latin America, and there are many forms of exclusion in my own country, Chile. But my election as president is precisely that: a defeat of exclusion, a defeat for those who believe there is an imminent and untouchable order in our societies that sanctions exclusion.

My presence here today as the first woman president of Chile symbolizes our having won a victory for inclusion. "We are all Chile" was my campaign slogan.

That is why I say, dear *amigas* and *amigos* [friends]: Let us never lose that ethical horizon before us: a more inclusive, and therefore more just, society is possible if we work for it. . . .

Let me also share with you something that is a bit more personal, some general reflections on women, politics and public policy that are also based on practice. And let me do so based on my own experience as the first woman president of Chile.

Every day, and I insist every day, I see even in the smallest details how my country faces a new and different experience—from etiquette and protocol, where people don't know whether to call me Presidente or Presidenta, to the notorious discomfort of some people who don't know whether to shake my hand or give me a peck on the cheek.

From the sexist criticisms of some to the differential treatment that the press gives us. The press worries about the color of my dress, shoes or purse. I never heard them making any comments about my predecessors at all. At most you might hear something like this about the men presidents: "The blue suit looks better on him than the gray." But the press is concerned even about my haircut.

But, well, I knew it would be like that, and if I bring it up it's not to complain, but because it's in our power to work to change those prejudices and to create a more open and more democratic culture, more accepting of difference.

But there is much more. There is a whole symbolic and semiotic load behind all this. A woman holding the reins of a country, with her style, signs and forms, is serving I think as a catalyst to the cultural changes that move us toward greater equality and toward the more horizontal relations which we are already seeing in our countries. . . .

And I notice this every day in Chile, when I visit schools and girls say with all naturalness that they want to be like me when they grow up. Before they used to say that they wanted to be doctor like me; now they say "Presidenta" of course.

I don't mean this as an anecdote, because when I was eight years old, at a time when power was essentially masculine in its form, gestures and style, I probably would not have even thought about that.

The symbolism of being able to reach the highest rung is very powerful, and it's changing Chilean society. When I celebrated International Women's Day for the first time as president, I said, "Equality is no longer a dream."

But there's more. How does being a woman translate into the public arena? Is it the same as being a man but with a skirt? No. I have always believed that being a woman also adds something.

How do you translate a woman's rich interior world—full of ways of seeing and reflecting that allow her to understand the worth of human beings and of life—into public?

To be a woman is to love life and to express it as we vibrate, laugh, cry, love, with all the richness those emotions bring. To be a woman is to relate to others with the tremendous ability of putting yourself in the place of others. And those feelings express themselves naturally and in all their intensity in private.

To break through that boundary and deploy them in public is a new adventure I am fully committed to, at times hard and difficult but tremendously gratifying.

Without doubt there are different ways of seeing, and for modern societies where women are in all walks of life for good, I insist that the challenge is to be able to integrate masculine and feminine ways of seeing into a harmonious whole.

That more properly masculine *ethics of results*, in which what you achieve is what matters most and not how you get there, can be virtuously combined with women's *ethics of process*, where it also matters what path you take, the costs, how much involuntary damage you inflict, how many disturbances you occasion.

Now, it is hard to break those barriers and sometimes you are forced to play with what we might call the masculine within each woman. I have had to do it many times, to be sure. It's tempting, easier, just to stay in the same place, relate to others using codes that have been the tonic of the patriarchal world. That is clearly not the choice I want to make.

Still, I am convinced that our people want a greater integration of those worlds. I believe that men as well as women want to leave behind a daily existence that endlessly repeats meaningless routines that seem necessary for reasons we can't figure out, and that we don't know how to change. . . .

When a woman enters politics alone, she changes. When many women enter politics, politics changes. And, clearly, improving the quality of political life is one of the greatest challenges of our democracy, one of the most urgent necessities.

That is why I celebrate the fact that this Conference is discussing and recommending affirmative action measures that can ensure the full participation of women in public office and in elected positions. . . .

If we think, and we do think, that we want equity, that minorities should be respected and properly represented, then it is even more evident that majorities, and in this case women, are under-represented in politics.

And this is not just a question of numbers. It's a question of democratic principles, of noting shortcomings in representative government and therefore justifiably putting in place measures, even if they are temporary, to overcome those shortcomings. . . .

And, in this regard, I want to . . . announce that in September I will send to Congress a law that modifies the Electoral Law and the Law of Political Parties, so that we can establish a minimum number of women candidates that political groups must put forward as candidates in congressional and municipal elections.

We know that women candidates encounter a series of difficulties. That's why I will propose that women candidates get additional public financing. . . . And we'll also propose less state financing for groups that put fewer women on the ballot.

And I will propose that we provide incentives for political parties that provide equal opportunity for men and women in the exercise of internal democracy and in the selection of party authorities, and that secure gender balance in party members' access to, and exercise of, positions of authority within the party and in public service.

And this will be, without doubt, an important step forward for Chilean democracy.

The incorporation of women into politics is valuable in and of itself because it helps make our institutions more representative.

But that's not all. It also contributes to a better "delivery" of our policies, better results. It allows us to incorporate a gender perspective in our public policies . . .

We want to incorporate that perspective in every public policy. Let me give some examples:

In Chile, one of the great reforms we are initiating is a reform of the pension system. . . . Among the many measures we are putting in place, we are putting in place several measures to give women a subsidy equivalent to one year of pension contributions for each child they give birth to, so as to compensate them for the time they are out of the workforce because they are caring for their children.

Another measure we are proposing is a basic solidarity pension for the poorest 60 percent of citizens who have not contributed enough to their pensions to fund their retirement.

What does this mean? Often women work at home without pay and because of that women are going to receive this pension in greater proportion than men. That will mean growing old with fewer fears, but also greater dignity for women.

And I want to tell you that when I was a candidate, I did not propose this because I looked at all the countries in the world and none of them gave housewives a pension. The cost was very high. . . .

But having said that I couldn't guarantee this, I formed a multidisciplinary commission made up of politicians, experts, representatives of unions and trade associations [gremios] and asked them, although I had not seen this problem solved anywhere else, "Find a solution so we can give housewives a pension."

And today I am satisfied because I didn't promise it, since I wasn't sure we could achieve it, but now we are going to achieve it, and we expect that next year we'll be paying out pensions to a large number of people.

Or take what we are doing in the worlds of work and education. We have the most ambitious plan ever to build daycare centers in Chile. In the first year of my presidency, we built more nurseries than in all our country's history. I am talking about free, public nurseries.

Why this concern? Because we know that inequality starts at birth, and from that very moment we need to provide girls and boys with more opportunities. Because we also know that only 20 percent of women who have small children work for wages, because they don't have a place to leave their children.

And so this is how we are setting in place public politics by incorporating women's perspectives.

In education, we promote programs of study that avoid prejudices and stereotypes regarding the domestic roles of boys and girls; as a way of preventing violence and abuse, we promote respect between the sexes in our educational programs starting in preschool. And we've launched a strong offensive against violence against women.

And I am not going to ignore this sad reality. In what goes of this year, already 32 women have been killed by their partners. Some say *sexism kills*.

And I cannot accept this. So in Congress we are proposing stiffer penalties for those who attack or kill women.

In addition, with the Minister of Women, we are creating a network of shelters throughout the country, to help and house victims of severe cases of violence or threats. . . .

But wait: all this concern for women is not just the feminist outburst of a president. It's not just that, to be sure. It's not just an ethical imperative. It's not just a political imperative. It's also crucial to the development of our countries.

How is it possible for our countries not to take advantage of the talents of more than half of their population? If we are serious about developing, developing integrally, we have to take advantage of all our potential. . . .

We are not yet a society of free men and women with equal rights and opportunities. To reach that goal, we have to deepen the cultural changes already under way. . . .

Because equality cannot be only a dream: we have to rebuild it with women's stubbornness and perseverance.

The writer Isabel Allende used to say that the masculine ethic is pessimistic. I am not. If I weren't optimistic—historically optimistic, I should add—I would certainly not be president of Chile.

So: more women, more democracy, more justice, more humanity, more progress, more equality. Equality is not a dream.

Translated by Karin Alejandra Rosemblatt

The Bicentennial Generation

In 2010, Chile commemorated the bicentennial of its independence in a year that proved unusually eventful. In January, Chile received international recognition as a model democracy and economic success when it became the second country in Latin America to join the OECD, the club of developed nations. In February the country was rocked by a magnitude 8.8 earthquake that devastated the country's south-central region. A month later, Sebastian Piñera took the oath of office, becoming the first rightist president elected in half a century. In July, Mapuche prisoners jailed under dictatorship-era antiterrorist legislation declared a hunger strike, and in August a catastrophic collapse trapped thirty-three miners underground. Their fate commanded the world's attention when they were successfully rescued three months later. President Piñera closed the year with an article in the Economist *radiating optimism about Chile's steady march into development without poverty—an idea that resonated powerfully with the long history of Chilean exceptionalism. He celebrated Chile's "bicentennial generation" as one destined to overcome the challenges of the modern era: underdevelopment, poverty, and inequality.[1]*

The dramatic events of 2010 also demonstrated the continuing resonance of other themes explored in The Chile Reader, *including the tension between optimistic and more critical assessments of Chile's progress. On the one hand, OECD membership and the electoral milestone seemed to speak to the political and economic modernity of neoliberal Chile; on the other, Chile was revealed to be the most unequal of OECD nations. The powerful earthquake that wrought extensive damage and loss of life reminded Chileans that geography and nature will continue to impact even a developed Chile. The dramatic rescue of the miners—an event swathed in Chilean flags and broadcast around the world—underscored a nation projecting itself as modern, successful, and capable; but critical observers pointed to the mining accident's roots in weakened unions and inadequate environmental and labor regulation. The Mapuche hunger strike underscored that Chile's conflictual relations with its indigenous peoples, rooted in persistent landed inequality, ecological degradation, and their historic exclusion from the nation, remain unresolved.*

The buoyant optimism of Piñera's bicentennial assessment was challenged by other voices. In retrospect, 2010 marked a commemoration of the past, but also a new chapter of the future, one animated by a cycle of social mobilization that by

2011 included ongoing Mapuche protests, environmental mobilizations, and a student movement whose street demonstrations drew more than half a million and recalled the heyday of protest against the dictatorship. If Piñera imagined a bicentennial generation destined to secure Chilean progress, these movements were considerably less sanguine about the prospects for equality and citizenship for all. Indeed, the real bicentennial generation, those who came of age around 2010, is the first of the post-Pinochet era and thus the first generation since 1973 without fear of political violence. They take for granted the transition to democracy and focus instead on the limits of that democracy and the high social and environmental costs of Chile's economic "miracle." Piñera is correct that they will write the next chapter of Chile's history, but whether they will write the history he envisioned remains to be seen.

Note

1. Sebastián Piñera, "We, the Bicentennials," *Economist*, 27 November 2010, p. 60.

"We are well in the shelter, all 33 of us." After an August 5, 2010, cave-in at the San José copper mine in northern Chile left thirty-three miners trapped underground, Chilean and foreign rescue teams worked to keep them alive until they could be brought to the surface sixty-nine days later. In an incident subjected to 24/7 coverage in the international news media, President Piñera—here shown embracing one of the first miners to emerge—celebrated the tenacity and bravery of the trapped miners, along with the technological finesse and dedication of the Chileans who rescued them. Photograph by Hugo Infante/Government of Chile.

Protest over Mapuche political prisoners. News of the trapped miners completely eclipsed media coverage of the simultaneous eighty-two-day hunger strike of thirty-four Mapuche prisoners who protested, along with their families and a widening tide of social mobilization, the state's use of a Pinochet-era antiterrorist law to justify their continued detention. Photograph by Guido Vargas. Used by permission of the photographer.

Selected Readings

General Works on Chile

The Chilean website "Memoria Chilena" (www.memoriachilena.cl/) has an extraordinary wealth of primary documents and images covering the entirety of Chilean history. Documents include classic works in literature, history, and social analysis, accompanied by first-rate explanatory essays by leading Chilean scholars.

Aylwin, Mariana, Bascuñan, Carlos, Correa, Sofía, Gazmuri Cristián, Serrano, Sol, and Tagle, Matías. *Chile en el siglo XX.* Santiago: Editorial Emisión, 1990.

Bengoa, José. *Historia del pueblo mapuche (siglo XIX y XX).* Santiago: Ediciones SUR, 1996.

Bethell, Leslie, ed. *Chile since Independence.* Cambridge: Cambridge University Press, 1993.

Collier, Simon, and Sater, William. *A History of Chile: 1808–2002.* Cambridge: Cambridge University Press, 2004.

Correa, Sofía, Figueroa, Consuelo, Jocelyn-Holt, Alfredo, Rolle, Claudio, and Vicuña, Manuel. *Documentos del siglo XX chileno.* Santiago: Editorial Sudamericana, 2001.

———. *Historia del siglo XX chileno.* Santiago: Editorial Sudamericana, 2001.

Godoy, Lorena, Hutchison, Elizabeth, Rosemblatt, Karin, and Zárate, M. Soledad. *Disciplina y desacato: La construcción de identidad en Chile, siglos XIX y XX.* Santiago: SUR-CEDEM, 1995).

Grez Toso, Sergio, ed. *La cuestión social en Chile: Ideas y debates precursores, 1804–1902.* Collected, edited, and with a critical introduction by Sergio Grez Toso. Santiago: DIBAM, 1995.

Lira, Elizabeth, and Loveman, Brian. *Las acusaciones constitucionales en Chile. Una perspectiva histórica.* Santiago: FLACSO-LOM, 2000.

———. *Las ardientes cenizas del olvido: Vía chilena de reconciliación política, 1932–1994.* Santiago: DIBAM-LOM, 2000.

———. *Las suaves cenizas del olvido: Vía Chilena de reconciliación política 1814–1932.* Santiago: DIBAM/LOM, 1999. 2nd ed., corrected and expanded (July 2000).

———. *Leyes de reconciliación en Chile: Amnistías, indultos y reparaciones 1819–1999.* Santiago: DIBAM/Centro de Investigaciones Diego Barros Arana, 2001.

Loveman, Brian. *Chile: The Legacy of Hispanic Capitalism.* Oxford: Oxford University Press, 2000.

Pinto Vallejos, Julio, and Salazar, Gabriel. *Historia contemporánea de Chile.* 5 vols. Santiago: LOM, 1999–2002.

Ramón, Armando de. *Santiago de Chile: (1541–1991): historia de una sociedad urbana.* Santiago: Editorial Sudamericana, 2000.

Vitale, Luis. *Interpretación Marxista de la Historia de Chile.* 7 vols. Santiago: LOM, 2011 and 2012.

Part II. Chile before Chile: Indigenous Peoples, Conquest, and Colonial Society

Aldunate, Carlos, Hidalgo, Jorge, Niemeyer, Hans, Schiapacasse, Virgilio, and Solimano, Iván, eds. *Culturas de Chile Prehistórica: Desde sus origenes hasta los albores de la conquista.* Editorial Andrés Bello, 1989.

Dillehay, Tom D. *Monte Verde: A Pleistocene Settlement in Chile.* Washington, D.C.: Smithsonian Institution Press, 1997.

———. *Monuments, Empires and Resistance: The Araucanian Polity and Ritual Narratives.* Cambridge University Press, 2007.

Góngora, Mario. *Encomenderos y estancieros: Estudios acerca de la constitución social aristocrática de Chile después de la conquista, 1580–1660.* Santiago: Universidad de Chile, 1970.

———. *Origen de los inquilinos de Chile central.* Santiago: Universidad de Chile, 1960.

Jara, Alvaro. *Guerra y sociedad en Chile: La transformación de la Guerra de Arauco y la esclavitud de los indios.* Santiago: Editorial Universitaria, 1971.

Korth, Eugene. *Spanish Policy in Colonial Chile: The Struggle for Social Justice, 1535–1700.* Palo Alto: Stanford University Press, 1968.

León, Leonardo. *Maloqueros y conchavadores: En araucanía y las pampas, 1700–1800.* Temuco, Chile: Eds. Universidad de la Frontera, 1991.

Mellafe, Rolando. *La introducción de la esclavitud negra en Chile: Tráfico y rutas.* Santiago: Universidad de Chile, 1959.

Padden, Robert Charles. "Cultural Change and Military Resistance in Araucanian Chile, 1550–1730," *Southwestern Journal of Anthropology* 13:1 (spring 1957), 103–121.

Schiaffino, Santiago Lorenzo, and Urbina, Rodolfo B. *La política de poblaciones en Chile durante el siglo XVIII.* Quillota: Editorial El Observador, 1978.

Part III. The Honorable Exception: The New Chilean Nation in the Nineteenth Century

Bauer, Arnold. *Chilean Rural Society: From the Spanish Conquest to 1930.* Cambridge: Cambridge University Press, 2008.

Bello, Andrés. *Selected Writings of Andrés Bello.* Oxford: Oxford University Press, 1997.

Collier, Simon. *Ideas and Politics of Chilean Independence, 1808–1833.* Cambridge University Press, 1967.

Gazmuri R., Cristián. *El "48" chileno: Igualitarios, reformistas radicales, masones y bomberos.* Santiago: Editorial Universitaria, 1999.

Graham, Maria. *Journal of a Residence in Chile in the Year 1822; and, A Voyage from Chile to Brazil.* Edited by Jennifer Hayward. Charlottesville: University of Virginia Press, 2003.

Jaksic, Ivan. *Andrés Bello: Scholarship and Nation-Building in Nineteenth-Century Latin America.* Cambridge: Cambridge University Press, 2006.

Jocelyn-Holt, Alfredo. *La Independencia de Chile: Tradición, modernización y mito.* Santiago: Planeta/Ariel, 1999.

Milanich, Nara. *Children of Fate: Childhood, Class, and the State in Chile, 1850–1930.* Durham, N.C.: Duke University Press, 2009.

Pérez Rosales, Vicente. *Times Gone By: Memoirs of a Man of Action.* Oxford: Oxford University Press, 2003.

Romero, Luis Alberto. *¿Qué hacer con los pobres? Elite y sectores populares en Santiago de Chile 1840–1895.* Buenos Aires: Editorial Sudamericana, 1997.

Salazar Vergara, Gabriel. *Labradores, peones y proletarios: Formación y crisis de la sociedad popular chilena del siglo XIX.* Santiago: Sur Editores, 1985.

Serrano, Sol. *Universidad y nación: Chile en el siglo XIX.* Santiago: Editorial Universitaria, 1994.

Sommer, Doris. *Foundational Fictions: The National Romances of Latin America.* Berkeley: University of California Press, 1991.

Vicuña Mackenna, Benjamín. *The Girondins of Chile: Reminiscences of an Eyewitness.* Oxford: Oxford University Press, 2003.

Part IV. Building a Modern Nation: Politics and the Social Question in the Nitrate Era

Agosín, Marjorie. *Gabriela Mistral: The Audacious Traveler.* Athens: Ohio University Press, 2003.

Barr-Melej, Patrick. *Reforming Chile: Cultural Politics, Nationalism, and the Rise of the Middle Class.* Chapel Hill: University of North Carolina Press, 2000.

Bengoa, José. *Historia del pueblo mapuche (siglos XIX y XX).* Santiago: Ediciones SUR, 1996.

———. *Historia de u conflicto: El estado y los mapuches en el siglo XX.* Santiago: Planeta, 1999.

Blakemore, Harold. *British Nitrates and Chilean Politics, 1886–1896: Balmaceda and North.* London: Institute of Latin American Studies, 1974.

Coña, Pascual, and de Moesbach, Ernesto Wilheim. *Lonko Pascual Coña: Testimonio de un cacique mapuche.* Santiago: Pehuen, 1992.

DeShazo, Peter. *Urban Workers and Labor Unions in Chile, 1902–1927.* Madison: University of Wisconsin Press, 1983.

Donoso, Ricardo. *Alessandri, agitador, demoledor: Cincuenta años de historia política de Chile.* Mexico: Fondo de Cultura Económia, 1952–1954.

Gazmuri, Cristián. "Alberto Edwards y La Fronda Aristocrática." *Historia* 1:37 (January–June 2004).

González Miranda, Sergio. *A los 90 años de los sucesos de la Escuela Santa María de Iquique.* Santiago: LOM, 1998.

————. *Hombres y mujeres de la pampa: Tarapacá en el ciclo de la expansión del salitre.* Santiago: DIBAM-LOM, 2002.

Harambour Ross, Alberto. "Ya No con las Manos Vacias: Huelga y Sangre Obrera en el Alto San Antonio. Los 'sucesos' de La Coruña, Junio de 1925." In Sergio González Miranda, *A los 90 años de los sucesos de la Escuela Santa María de Iquique.* Santiago: LOM, 1998.

Huidobro, Vicente. *The Selected Poetry of Vicente Huidobro.* Edited and with an introduction by David M. Guss. New York: New Directions, 1981.

Hutchison, Elizabeth Quay. *Labors Appropriate to Their Sex: Gender, Labor, and Politics in Urban Chile, 1900–1930.* Durham, N.C.: Duke University Press, 2001.

Lafertte, Elías. *Vida de un comunista.* Santiago, 1961.

Lavrin, Asunción. *Women, Feminism, and Social Change in Argentina, Chile, and Uruguay, 1890–1940.* Lincoln: University of Nebraska Press, 1995.

Miller, Nicola. "Recasting the Role of the Intellectual: Chilean Poet Gabriela Mistral." *Feminist Review* 79 (2005).

Monteon, Michael. *Chile in the Nitrate Era: The Evolution of Economic Dependence, 1880–1930.* Madison: University of Wisconsin Press, 1982.

Navarrete Araya, Micaela. *Balmaceda en la poesía popular, 1886–1896.* Santiago: DIBAM, 1993.

Obrien, Thomas F. *The Nitrate Industry and Chile's Crucial Transition: 1870–1891.* New York: New York University Press, 1982.

Ortega, Luis. *La guerra civil de 1891: 100 años hoy.* Santiago: Universidad de Santiago de Chile, 1993.

————. "Nitrates, Chilean Entrepreneurs and the Origins of the War of the Pacific." *Journal of Latin American Studies* 16:2 (November 1984).

Ortega, Luis, and Pinto Vallejos, Julio. *Expansión minera y desarrollo industrial: Un caso de crecimiento asociado: Chile, 1850–1914.* Santiago: Universidad de Santiago de Chile, 1990.

Pernet, Corinne A., "Chilean Feminists, the International Women's Movement, and Suffrage, 1915–1950." *Pacific Historical Review,* Vol. 64, No. 4 (November 2000).

Pinto Vallejos, Julio. *Trabajos y rebeldias en la pampa salitrera: El ciclo del salitre y la reconfiguracion de las identidades populares (1850–1900).* Santiago: Editorial Universidad de Santiago, 1998.

Pinto Vallejos, Juilo, and Valdivia O., Verónica. *Revolución proletaria o querida chusma: Socialismo y Alessandrismo en la pugna por la politización pampina (1911–1932).* Santiago: LOM Ediciones, 2001.

Rojas, Claudia, Lopestri, Lorella, Jiles, Ximena, and Gaviola, Edda. *Queremos votar en las próximas elecciones: Historia del movimiento sufragista chileno, 1913–1952* Santiago: LOM Ediciones, 2007.

Rojas Flores, Jorge. *La dictadura de Ibáñez y los sindicatos, 1927–1931.* Santiago: DIBAM, 1993.

Sater, William. *Chile and the War of the Pacific.* Lincoln: University of Nebraska Press, 1985.

Solberg, Carl. *Immigration and Nationalism: Argentina and Chile, 1890–1914.* Austin: University of Texas Press, 1970.

Vitale, Luis. *Interpretación marxista de la historia de Chile: De la república parlamentaria a la república socialista (1891–1932)*. Santiago: LOM, 2011.

Part V. Depression, Development, and the Politics of Compromise

Bengoa, José. *Haciendas y campesinos: Historia social de la agricultura*. Vol. 2. Santiago: Ediciones SUR, 1990.

Bowers, Claude. *Chile through Embassy Windows, 1939–1953*. New York: Simon and Schuster, 1958.

Drake, Paul W. *Socialism and Populism in Chile, 1932–1952*. Urbana-Champagne: University of Illinois Press, 1978.

Garcés, Mario. *Tomando su sitio: El movimiento de pobladores de Santiago, 1957–1970*. Santiago: LOM Ediciones, 2002.

Klubock, Thomas Miller. *Contested Communities: Class, Gender, and Politics in Chile's El Teniente Copper Mine, 1904–1951*. Durham, N.C.: Duke University Press, 1998.

Loveman, Brian. *El campesino chileno le escribe a su excelencia*. Santiago: ICIRA, 1971.

Mamalakis, Markos, and Reynolds, Clark. *Essays on the Chilean Economy*. Homewood, Ill.: R. D. Irwin, 1965.

Moran, Theodore. *Multinational Corporations and the Politics of Dependence: Copper in Chile*. Princeton: Princeton University Press, 1977.

Neruda, Pablo. *The Poetry of Pablo Neruda*. Edited and with an introduction by Ilan Stavans. New York: Farrar, Straus and Giroux, 2005.

———. *Canto General*. Translated by Jack Schmitt. With an introduction by Roberto González Echevarría. Berkeley: University of California Press, 1991.

Pavilack, Jody. *Mining for the Nation: The Politics of Chile's Coal Communities from the Popular Front to the Cold War*. College Park: Pennsylvania State University Press, 2011.

Pinto, Aníbal. *Chile: Un caso de desarrollo frustrado*. Santiago: Editorial Universitaria, 1962.

Rosemblatt, Karen Alejandra. *Gendered Compromises: Political Cultures and the State in Chile, 1920–1950*. Chapel Hill: University of North Carolina Press, 2000.

Valdivia Ortiz de Zárate, Verónica. *Las milicianas republicanas: Los civiles en armas, 1932–1936*. Santiago: DIBAM, 1992.

Part VI. The Chilean Road to Socialism: Reform and Revolution

Arriagada, Genaro. *De la vía chilena a la vía insurreccional*. Santiago: Editorial del Pacifico, 1974.

Baldez, Lisa. *Why Women Protest: Women's Movements in Chile*. Cambridge: Cambridge University Press, 2002.

Bitar, Sergio. *Chile: Experiment in Democracy*. Institute for the Study of Human Issues, 1986.

Cockcroft, James, ed. *Salvador Allende Reader*. New York: Ocean Press, 2000.

Debray, Regis. *The Chilean Revolution: Conversations with Allende*. New York: Pantheon Books, 1972.

De Vylder, Stefan. *Allende's Chile: The Political Economy of the Rise and Fall of the Unidad Popular*. Cambridge: Cambridge University Press, 2009.

Fleet, Michael. *The Rise and Fall of Chilean Christian Democracy*. Princeton: Princeton University Press, 1985.

Garcés, Mario. *Tomando su sitio: El movimiento de pobladores de Santiago, 1957–1970*. Santiago: LOM Ediciones, 2002.

Gaudichaud, Frank. *Poder popular y cordones industriales: Testimonios Sobre El Movimiento Popular Urbano, 1970–1973*. Santiago: LOM Ediciones, 2004.

Gustafson, Kristian. *Hostile Intent: U.S. Covert Operations in Chile, 1964–1974*. Dulles, Va.: Potomac Books, 2007.

Kornbluh, Peter. *The Pinochet File: A Declassified Dossier on Atrocity and Accountability*. New York: New Press, 2004.

Loveman, Brian. *Struggle in the Countryside: Politics and Rural Labor in Chile, 1919–1973*. Bloomington: Indiana University Press, 1976.

Mallon, Florencia. *Courage Tastes of Blood: The Mapuche Community of Nicolas Ailio and the Chilean State, 1906–2001*. Durham, N.C.: Duke University Press, 2005.

Naranjo, Pedro, Ahumada, Mauricio, et al., eds. *Miguel Enriquez: El proyecto revolucionario en Chile: Discursos y Documentos del Movimiento de Izquierda Revolucionaria*. Santiago: LOM Ediciones, 2004.

Petras, James. *Politics and Social Forces in Chilean Development*. Berkeley: University of California Press, 1972.

Pinto, Julio, and Garces, Mario. *Cuando hicimos la historia: La experiencia de la Unidad Popular*. Santiago: LOM Ediciones, 2005.

Power, Margaret. *Right Wing Women in Chile: Feminine Power and the Struggle against Allende, 1964–73*. College Park: Pennsylvania State University Press, 1998.

Sigmund, Paul. *The Overthrow of Allende and the Politics of Chile, 1964–1973*. Pittsburgh: University of Pittsburgh Press, 1977.

Stallings, Barbara. *Class Conflict and Economic Development in Chile, 1958–1973*. Stanford: Stanford Univesity Press, 1978.

Tinsman, Heidi. *Partners in Conflict: The Politics of Gender, Sexuality, and Labor in the Chilean Agrarian Reform, 1950–1973*. Durham, N.C.: Duke University Press, 2002.

United States Senate. Select Committee to Study Governmental Operations with Respect to Intelligence Activities. Staff Report. "Covert Action in Chile, 1963 1973." Washington, D.C., 1975. See also U.S. Department of State, Freedom of Information Act website, http://foia.state.gov/Reports/ChurchReport.asp, accessed 14 May 2013.

Valenzuela, Arturo. *Breakdown of Democratic Regimes: Chile*. Baltimore: Johns Hopkins University Press, 1978.

Winn, Peter. *Weavers of Revolution: The Yarur Workers and Chile's Road to Socialism*. Oxford: Oxford University Press, 1989.

Part VII. The Pinochet Dictatorship: Military Rule and Neoliberal Economics

Agosín, Marjorie. *Tapestries of Hope, Threads of Love: The Arpillera Movement in Chile*. Lanhham, Md.: Rowman and Littlefield, 2007.

Arriagada, Genaro. *Por la razón o la fuerza: Chile bajo Pinochet*. Santiago: Editorial Sudamericana, 1998.

Collins, Joseph, and Lear, John. *Chile's Free-Market Miracle: A Second Look.* Oakland, Calif.: Institute for Food and Development Policy, 1995.

Constable, Pamela, and Valenzuela, Arturo. *A Nation of Enemies: Chile under Pinochet.* New York: Norton, 1993.

Díaz, Alvaro, and Martínez, Javier. *Chile: The Great Transformation.* Washington, D.C.: Brookings Institution Press, 1996.

Garretón, Manuel Antonio. *The Chilean Political Process.* New York: HarperCollins, 1989.

Kornbluh, Peter. *The Pinochet File: A Declassified Dossier on Atrocity and Accountability.* New York: New Press, 2004.

Mallon, Florenica E. *Courage Tastes of Blood: The Mapuche Community of Nicolás Ailio and the Chilean State, 1906–2001.* Durham, N.C.: Duke University Press, 2005.

Politzer, Patricia. *Fear in Chile: Lives under Pinochet.* New York: New Press, 2001.

Schneider, Cathy Lisa. *Shantytown Protest in Pinochet's Chile.* Philadelphia: Temple University Press, 1995.

Stern, Steve J. *Battling for Hearts and Minds: Memory Struggles in Pinochet's Chile, 1973–1988.* Durham, N.C.: Duke University Press, 2006.

Tironi, Eugenio. *Los silencios de la revolución: Chile, la otra cara de la modernización.* Santiago: La Puerta Abierta, 1988.

Valdés, Teresa. *Las mujeres y la dictadura militar en Chile.* Santiago: FLACSO, 1987.

Verdugo, Patricia. *Chile, Pinochet, and the Caravan of Death.* Miami: University of Miami North South Center Press, 2001.

Winn, Peter. *Victims of the Miracle: Workers and Neoliberalism in the Pinochet Era, 1973–2002.* Durham, N.C.: Duke University Press, 2004.

Part VIII. Returning to Democracy: Transition and Continuity

Chihuailaf, Elicura. *Recado confidencial a los chilenos.* Santiago: LOM, 1999.

Defensores del Bosque Chileno. *La tragedia del bosque chileno.* Santiago: Ocho Libros Editores, 1999.

De la Parra, Marco. *La mala memoria: Historia personal de Chile contemporáneo.* Santiago: Editorial Planeta, 1997.

Drake, Paul, and Jaksic, Iván, eds. *El modelo chileno: Democracia y desarrollo en los noventa.* Santiago: LOM, 1999.

———. *The Struggle for Democracy in Chile.* Lincoln: University of Nebraska Press, 1995.

Haughney, Diane. *Neoliberal Economics, Democratic Transition, and Mapuche Demands for Rights in Chile.* Gainesville: University Press of Florida, 2006.

Lira, Elizabeth, and Loveman, Brian. *El espejismo de la reconciliación política: Chile 1990–2002.* Santiago: DIBAM-LOM, 2002.

———. *Políticas de reparación: Chile 1990–2004.* Santiago: LOM Ediciones, 2005.

Marimán, Pablo, Caniuqueo, Sergio, Millalén, José, and Levil, Rodrigo. *¡ . . . Escucha winka . . . ! Cuatro ensayos de historia nacional mapuche y un epílogo sobre el futuro.* Santiago: LOM, 2006.

Moulian, Tomás. *Chile actual: Anatomia de un mito.* Santiago: LOM, 1997.

Namancura, Domingo. *Ralco: ¿Represa o pobreza?* Santiago: LOM, 1999.

Paley, Julia. *Marketing Democracy: Power and Social Movements in Post-dictatorship Chile.* Berkeley: University of California Press, 2001.

Petras, James, and Leiva, Fernando Ignacio. *Democracy and Poverty in Chile: The Limits to Electoral Politics.* Boulder, Colo.: Westview Press, 1994.

Quiroga Martínez, Rayén. *El tigre sin selva: Consecuencias ambientales de la transformación económica de Chile: 1974–1993.* Santiago: Instituto de Ecología Política, 1994.

Report of the Chilean National Commission on Truth and Reconciliation. Notre Dame, Ind.: University of Notre Dame Press, 1993. www.usip.org/files/resources/collections/truth_commissions/Chile90-Report/Chile90-Report.pdf, accessed 20 May 2013.

Richards, Patricia. *Pobladoras, Indigenas, and the State: Conflicts over Women's Rights in Chile.* New Brunswick: Rutgers University Press, 2004.

Rueque Paillalef, Rosa Isolde, and Mallon, Florencia E., eds. *When a Flower Is Reborn: The Life and Times of a Mapuche Feminist.* Durham, N.C.: Duke University Press, 2002.

Stern, Steve J. *Reckoning with Pinochet: The Memory Question in Democratic Chile, 1989–2006.* Durham, N.C.: Duke University Press, 2010.

———. *Remembering Pinochet's Chile: On the Eve of London 1998.* Durham, N.C.: Duke University Press, 2006.

Acknowledgment of Copyrights and Sources

Part I. Environment and History

"'No Better Land,'" by Pedro de Valdivia, previously published as "Carta al Emperador Carlos V, escrita en La Serena en 1545," from *Cartas de Relación de la Conquista
de Chile,* by Pedro de Valdivia (Santiago: Editorial Universitaria), 26–34, 39–48
(abridged).

"The Poetry of Place," by Gabriela Mistral, previously published as "My Country,"
U.N. World (May 1950), 51. Reprinted by permission of La Orden Franciscana de
Chile.

"Crazy Geography," by Benjamín Subercaseaux, from *Chile: A Geographic Extravaganza,*
translated by Ángel Flores (New York: Macmillan, 1943), 17–21 (abridged). Used by
permission of Juan Flores and Barbara Flores Dederick.

"Catastrophe and National Character," by Rolando Mellafe, from "Collective Percep-
tions and Representations of Catastrophes in Chile, 1556–1956," in *La memoria de
américa colonial: Inconciente colectivo y vida cotidiana,* edited by Rolando Mellafe
Rojas and Lorena Loyola (Santiago: Editorial Universitaria, 1994), 102–103, 112–115
(abridged). Used by permission of Editorial Universitaria.

"Deforestation in Chile: An Early Report," by Claudio Gay, previously published as
"Sobre la disminución de los montes de la provincial de Coquimbo," *El Araucano*
399 (April 1838) (abridged).

"'Catastrophe in Sewell,'" by Pablo Neruda, in *Canto General,* translated by Jack
Schmitt (University of California Press, 1991), 252 (abridged). © 1991 by the Fun-
dación Pablo Neruda. Reprinted by permission of the University of California
Press. In the original Spanish by Pablo Neruda, "Catástrofe en Sewell," *Canto
General* © Fundación Pablo Neruda, 2011. Reprinted electronically by permission of
the Fundación Pablo Neruda.

"A Call to Conservation," by Rafael Elizalde Mac-Clure, from *La sobrevivencia de
Chile: La conservación de sus recursos naturales renovables* (Santiago: Ministerio de
Agricultura-Servicio Agrícola Ganadero, 1970), 2nd ed., 33–36 (abridged).

"In Defense of the Forests," by Ricardo Carrere, from "Efectos de la sustitución de
bosque nativos por plantaciones exóticas en Chile," in *La tragedia del bosque chileno,*
edited by Los Defensores del Bosque (Santiago: Ocho Libros Editores, 1998),
285–293 (abridged). Used by permission of María Isabel Cárcamo.

"Pollution and Politics in Greater Santiago," by Saar Van Hauwermeiren, from "Con
secuencias del crecimiento económico sobre el medio ambiente: casos ilustrativos,"

in *El tigre sin selva: Consecuencias ambientales de la transformación económica de Chile, 1974–1993,* edited by Rayén Quiroga (Santiago: Instituto de Ecología Política, 1994), 207–220 (abridged). Used by permission of the author.

Part II. Chile before Chile: Indigenous Peoples, Conquest, and Colonial Society

"The Inca Meet the Mapuche," by Garcilaso de la Vega el Inca, from *Comentarios Reales de los Incas. Primera Parte* (Lisbon: Crasbeeck, 1609) (abridged).

"A Conquistador Pleads His Case to the King," by Pedro de Valdivia, previously published as "Carta al Emperador Carlos V, escrita en La Serena en 1545," in *Cartas de relación de la conquista de Chile* (Santiago: Editorial Universitaria, 1970) (abridged).

"Exalting the Noble Savage," by Alonso de Ercilla y Zúñiga, from *The Araucaniad, a Version in English Poetry of Alonso de Ercilla y Zúñiga's "La Araucana,"* translated by Charles Maywell Lancaster and Paul Thomas Manchett (Nashville: Vanderbilt University Press, 1945) (abridged). Used by permission of Vanderbilt University Press.

"Debating Indian Slavery," (1) by Melchor Calderón, from "Treatise on the Importance and Utility of Slavery," in *Biblioteca Hispano-Chilena (1523–1817),* compiled by José Toribio Medina (Chile, 1899) (abridged). (2) By Father Diego de Rosales, from "Treatise Acknowledging the Damage Caused by Slavery in the Kingdom of Chile," in *Las encomiendas de indígenas en Chile,* edited by Domingo Amunátegui y Solar (Santiago: Imprenta Cervantes, 1909–10) (abridged).

"'To Sell, Give, Donate, Trade, or Exchange,'" 1657 certification of Indian enslavement, *Fuentes para la historia del trabajo en el Reino de Chile: Legislación 1546–1810,* edited by Alvaro Jara and Sonia Pinto, vol. 2 (Santiago: Editorial Andres Bello, 1983) (abridged).

"Portrait of Late Colonial Santiago," by Vicente Carvallo y Goyeneche, previously published as "Descripción histórica-geográfica del Reino de Chile," in *Colección de historiadores de Chile y de documentos relativos a la historia nacional,* vol. 9 (Santiago: Impresa del Ferrocarril, 1875) (abridged).

"From War to Diplomacy: The Summit of Tapihue," from *El Parlamento de Tapihue, 1774.* Original archival document located and transcribed by Leonardo León (abridged). Currently housed in El Archivo de Indias, Seville, and El Archivo Nacional de Chile.

"'The Insolence of Peons,'" by the mine owners of Copiapó, from *Fuentes para la historia del trabajo en el Reino de Chile: Legislación 1546–1810,* edited by Alvaro Jara and Sonia Pinto, vol. 2 (Santiago: Editorial Andres Bello, 1983) (abridged).

Part III. The Honorable Exception: The New Chilean Nation in the Nineteenth Century

"A Revolutionary Journalist: 'Fundamental Notions of the Rights of Peoples,'" by Camilo Henríquez, from "Nociones fundamentales sobre los derechos de los pueblos," *Aurora de Chile* 1 (13 February 1812), 1–3 (abridged).

"An Englishwoman Observes the New Nation," by Maria Graham, from *Journal of a Residence in Chile during the Year 1822* (London: Longman, Hurst, Rees, Orne, Brown, and Green, and J. Murray, 1824), 69–74 (abridged).

"The Authoritarian Republic," by Diego Portales, from *El peso de la noche*, edited by Guillermo Feliú Cruz (Santiago: Imprenta de la Dirección General de Prisiones 1938) vol. 2, letter 247, 226–230, and vol. 3, letter 572, 486–487.

"A Political Catechism," by Francisco Bilbao, from "El Soberano," in *El evangelio americano* (Buenos Aires: Impr. de la Soc. Tip. Bonaerense, 1864), 11–19 (abridged).

"A Literature of Its Own," by Alberto Blest Gana, from *Martín Rivas: A Novel of Politico-Social Customs*, translated by Tess O'Dwyer (Oxford: Oxford University Press, 2000), 5–91 (abridged). Used by permission of Oxford University Press, USA.

"The University and the Nation," by Andrés Bello, from "Address Delivered at the Inauguration of the University of Chile, 17 September 1843," in *Selected Writings of Andrés Bello,* edited by Iván Jaksi, translated by Frances M. López-Morillas (New York: Oxford University Press, 1997), 124–137 (abridged). © 1997 by Oxford University Press, Inc. Used by permission of Oxford University Press, USA.

"A Polish Scientist among the Mapuche," by Ignacio Domeyko, from *Araucanía y sus habitantes* (Buenos Aires: Editorial Francisco de Aguirre, 1971 [1845]) (abridged).

"German Immigrants in the South," by Vicente Pérez Rosales, from *Times Gone By: Memoirs of a Man of Action*, translated by John H. R. Polt (Oxford: Oxford University Press, 2003), 303–358 (abridged). © 2003 by Oxford University Press, Inc. Used by permission of Oxford University Press, USA.

"*The Beagle Diary*: 'A Peculiar Race of Men,'" by Charles Darwin, from *The Voyage of the Beagle* (New York: P. F. Collier, c. 1909), 265, 269–71, 343–45 (abridged).

"How to Run an Hacienda," by Manuel José Balmaceda, from *Manual del hacendado chileno: Instrucciones para la dirección i gobierno de los fundos que en Chile se llaman haciendas.* (Santiago: Imprenta Franklin, 1875) (abridged).

"A Franco-Chilean in the California Gold Rush," by Pedro Isidoro Combet, from *We Were 49ers: Chilean Accounts of the California Gold Rush,* edited and translated by Edwin Beilharz and Carlos U. López (Ward Ritchie Press, Los Angeles, 1976), 151–185 (abridged). Reprinted by permission of Alan Beilharz and Evelyn López.

"'The Worst Misery'": Letters to the Santiago Orphanage, from Libros de Entradas [Entry Registries] of the Casa de Huérfanos of Santiago, vols. 1873–1882; 1883–1889; 1896–1898, currently held at the Casa Nacional del Niño, Santiago (abridged).

"'A Race of Vagabonds,'" by Augusto Orrego Luco, from *La cuestión social* (Santiago: Imprenta Barcelona, 1897) (abridged).

Part IV. Building a Modern Nation: Politics and the Social Question in the Nitrate Era

"'Audacious and Cruel Spoilations': The War of the Pacific," by Alejandro Fierro, from *Manifiesto que el gobierno de Chile dirije a las potencias amigas con motive del estado de Guerra con el gobierno del Perú* (Santiago: Imprenta Nacional, 1879) (abridged).

"A Mapuche Chieftain Remembers 'Pacification,'" by Pascual Coña, from *Testimonio de un cacique mapuche,* edited by Ernesto Wilhelm De Moesbach (Santiago: Pehuén, 1995) (abridged). Used by permission of Pehuén Editores.

"Race, Nation, and the 'Roto Chileno,'" by Nicolás Palacios, from *La raza chilena: Libro escrito por un chileno para los chilenos* (Valparaíso: Imprente y Litografía Alemana, 1904), 1–12 (abridged).

"Nitrates, Nationalism, and the End of the Autocratic Republic," (1) by José Manuel Balmaceda, from "Discurso del Presidente de la Republica Pronunciado en el Banquete con que fue Festado a su llegada a Iquique," *La Industria*, Iquique, 7 March 1889, reprinted in *Documentos del siglo* xx *chileno*, edited by Sofía Correa et al. (Santiago: Editorial Sudamericana, 2001), 185–187 (abridged). (2) By Arturo Alessandri, from *Revolución de 1891: Mi actuación* (Santiago: Editorial Nascimiento, 1950), 161–177, quoted in *1891 visto por sus protagonistas*, by Patricia Arancibia Clavel (Santiago: Editorial Fundación, Santiago, 1991), 632–637 (abridged). (3) By a popular poet, from "La balmacedista," in *Parnaso balmacedista: recopilación completa de todas las poesías que se han escrito en homenaje a la memoria de Balmaceda desde el día de su sacrificio, 19 de Septiembre de 1891*, edited by Virgilio Figueroa and José Manuel Balmaceda (Santiago: La Nueva República, 1897), 89–90.

"A Manifesto to the Chilean People," by the Democratic Party, from "Manifiesto del Partido Democrático al pueblo de Chile," *El Ferrocarril*, 23 November 1888 (abridged).

"'God Distributes His Gifts Unequally,'" by Archbishop Mariano Casanova, "Pastoral que el Illmo. y Rmo. Sr. D. Mariano Casanova, arzobispo de Santiago de Chile, dirige al clero y pueblo sobre la propaganda de doctrinas irreligiosas y anti-sociales," reprinted in *La "cuestión social" en Chile: Ideas y debates precursors: (1804–1902)*, edited by Sergio Grez Toso (Santiago: DIBAM, 1995), 401–413 (abridged).

"Workers' Movements and the Birth of the Chilean Left," by Luis Emilio Recabarren, from "Carta a Abdón Diaz," in *La "Cuestion Social" en Chile: Ideas y debates precursores (1804–1902)*, edited by Sergio Grez Toso (Santiago: DIBAM, 1995), 551–54.

"Nitrate Workers and State Violence: The Massacre at Escuela Santa María de Iquique," by Elías Gaviño Lafertte, from *Vida de un comunista: Páginas autobiográficas* (Santiago: Talleres Graficos Lautaro, 1957), 52–68 and 28–51 (abridged).

"Women, Work and Labor Politics," by Esther Valdés de Díaz, from "La celebración del segundo aniversario de la Asociación de Costurcras," *La Palanca* 1, no. 4 (August 1908), 44–47.

"The Lion of Tarapacá," by Arturo Alessandri, from "Discurso por Arturo Alessandri Agradeciendo su designación como candidato a la Presidencia de la República, pronunciado en la Convención Presidencial el 25 de Abril de 1920," in Arturo Alessandri Palma, *Recuerdos de Gobierno* (Santiago: Editorial Nascimiento, 1967), 395–404 (abridged).

"Autocrats versus Aristocrats," by Alberto Edwards Vives, from *La fronda aristocrática en Chile* (Santiago: Imprenta Nacional, 1928).

"Rescuing the Body Politic: Manifesto of a Military Coup," the military coup pronouncement of 1924, *El Mercurio*, 13 September 1924 (abridged).

"The Poet as Creator of Worlds," by Vicente Huidobro, from "Preface," in *Altazor or the Parachute Voyage* (Middletown, Conn.: Wesleyan University Press, 2003). Translation © 2003 Eliot Weinberger. Reprinted by permission of Wesleyan University Press.

"Mother of Chile"? by Gabriela Mistral, from (1) "Sufragio Femenino," in *Pensando a Chile: Una tentativa contra lo imposible,* compiled by Jaime Quezada (Santiago: Comisión Bicentenario, Presidencia de la Republica 2004), 238–239. Used by permission of La Orden Franciscana de Chile. (2) "Valle de Elqui," by Gabriela Mistral, in *Selected Poems of Gabriela Mistral,* translated by Ursula K. LeGuin (Albuquerque: University of New Mexico Press), 337–339. © 2012 University of New Mexico Press.

Part V. Depression, Development, and the Politics of Compromise

"'Their Work Has Laid the Foundation for Greatness,'" (1) interview with Juan Yarur, *Mundo Arabe* 1, no. 16 (February 20, 1936), 13 (abridged). (2) By La Asociación Comercial Sirio-Palestina, from *Las industrias de las colectividades de habla árabe en Chile* (Santiago: Imprenta y Litografía Universo, 1937) (abridged).

"*Is Chile a Catholic Country?,*" by Alberto Hurtado, from *¿Es Chile un país Católico?* (Santiago: Ediciones "Splendor," 1941), 68–132 (abridged). Used by permission of the Fundación Padre Hurtado.

"'I Told Myself I Must Find Work, I Cannot Continue Here,'" interview with Elba Bravo by Elizabeth Hutchison, 5 July 2002.

"Fundamental Theoretical Principles of the Socialist Party," by Julio César Jobet, from *El Partido Socialista de Chile* (Santiago: Ediciones Documentas, 1987 [1971]) 2nd ed., 114–117 (abridged).

"Public Health Crisis," by Salvador Allende, from *La realidad médico-social chilena* (Santiago: Ministro de Salubridad, 1939) (abridged).

"'Progress for All Social Classes,'" by Pedro Aguirre Cerda, "Nada ni nadie podrá contener a un pueblo sediento de libertad," *La Hora,* 18 July 1938, 5.

"Rural Workers, Landowners, and the Politics of Compromise," (1) by The League of Poor Campesinos of Las Cabras, from *Antecedentes para el estudio del movimiento campesino chileno: Pliegos de peticiones, huelgas y sindicatos agrícolas, 1932–1966,* edited by Brian Loveman (Santiago: ICIRA, 1971). Used by permission of Brian Loveman. (2) "La actual legislación sindical es impracticable en los campos," letter from The National Agriculture Society to President Pedro Aguirre Cerda, *El Campesino,* 17 March 1939.

"*A Case of Frustrated Development,*" by Aníbal Pinto, from *Chile: Un caso de desarrollo frustrado* (Santiago: Editorial Universitaria, 1962), 122–176 (abridged). Used by permission of the author.

"The Movement for the Emancipation of Chilean Women," interview with Elena Caffarena by Georgina Durand, from *Mis entrevistas* (Santiago: Nascimiento, 1943) (abridged).

"Poetry and Politics," by Pablo Neruda (1) excerpts from "The Roads of the World," "Lost in the City," "My Country in Darkness," and "Poetry Is an Occupation," from *Memoirs,* by Pablo Neruda, translated by Hardie St. Martin. Translation copyright © 1977 by Farrar, Straus and Giroux, Inc. Reprinted by permission of Farrar, Straus and Giroux, LLC. Excerpts from the original Spanish by Pablo Neruda, *Confieso que he vivido* © Fundación Pablo Neruda, 2012. Reprinted electronically by permission of the Fundación Pablo Neruda. (2) "The Heights of Macchu Picchu," in *Canto General,* translated by Jack Schmitt (University of California Press, 1991), 29–41 (abridged). © 1991 by the Fundación Pablo Neruda. Reprinted by permission of the

University of California Press. Excerpt from the original Spanish by Pablo Neruda, "Alturas de Macchu Picchu," *Canto General* © Fundación Pablo Neruda, 2012. Reprinted electronically by permission of the Fundación Pablo Neruda.

"Miners' Strikes and the Demise of the Popular Front," by U.S. Department of State, from "1946 Memoranda from US Diplomatic Officials," in *Foreign Relations of the United States, 1946*, vol. 11, *The American Republics* (Washington, D.C.: Government Printing Office, 1960) (abridged).

"States of Exception," by Elena Caffarena, from "Palabras preliminares," in *El Recurso de Amparo Frente a los Regímenes de Emergencia* (Santiago: Editorial Jurídica, 1957), 21–30 (abridged).

"The Birth of a Shantytown," by Juan Lemuñir, in *Crónicas de la Victoria: Testimonio de un poblador* (Santiago: CENPROS, 1990), 10–18 (abridged). Used by permission of the author.

"Klein-Saks," political cartoon from *Topaze*, November 15, 1957. Illustration by René Ríos Boettiger. Reprinted by permission of Sebastián Ríos O. Courtesy of Colección Biblioteca Nacional de Chile.

Part VI. The Chilean Road to Socialism: Reform and Revolution

"Between Capitalism and Communism," by Eduardo Frei Montalva, from "La misión del socialcristianismo en Chile," in *Obras Escogidas*, edited by Oscar Pinochet de la Barra (Santiago: Editores del Centro de Estudios Políticos Latinoamericanos Simon Bolívar, 1993), 152, 155–160 (abridged). Used by permission of the Fundación Eduardo Frei.

"Property and Production," pamphlet promoting Christian Democracy's agrarian reform, from "Chile Avanza: Reforma Agraria," Biblioteca del Congreso Nacional del Chile (Santiago, Imprenta Servicio de Prisiones, 1966) (abridged). Available at http://www.memoriachilena.cl/archivos2/pdfs/MC0023352.pdf. Accessed on February 14, 2006.

"The Christian Left and Communitarian Socialism," by Jacques Chonchol and Julio Silva Solar, from *El desarrollo de la nueva sociedad en América Latina* (Santiago: LOM Ediciones, 2009), 22–49 (abridged). Used by permission of LOM ediciones.

"The New Song Movement," by Luis Cifuentes, from *Fragmentos de un sueño: Inti-Illimani y la generación de los 60* (Santiago: Logos, 1989), 38–50 (abridged). Used by permission of the author.

"Lyrics of the New Song Movement," (1) by Violeta Parra, "Arauco tiene una Pena." Used by courtesy of NFC editions musicales, Paris-France. Translation © Ericka Verba. (2) "Gracias a la vida," words and music by Violeta Parra © (Renewed) Warner/Chappell de Artgentina S.A. All rights administered by Rightsong Music, Inc. All rights reserved. Used by Permission. Translation © Gloria Alvarez. (3) By Victor Jara, "Herminda de la Victoria," from *Población* (Odeon/Alerce/Warner, 1972). (4) By Victor Jara, "Vientos del Pueblo," from *Vientos del Pueblo* (Monitor, 1976). Used by permission of the Fundación Victor Jara.

"The Election of Salvador Allende," declassified government documents, (1) by Henry Kissinger, from "Secret/Sensitive Memorandum to President Nixon," November 5,

1970. Declassified document from the National Security Archive. Available at http://www.gwu.edu/~nsarchiv/NSAEBB/NSAEBB110/chile02.pdf. Accessed July 12, 2010. (2) By Henry Kissinger, from "National Security Decision Memorandum 93: Policy Towards Chile," November 9, 1970. Declassified document from the National Security Archive. Available at http://www.gwu.edu/~nsarchiv/NSAEBB/NSAEBB8/docs/doc09.pdf. Accessed on May 25, 2009.

"The Mapuche Land Takeover at Rucalán," interviews with peasants and landowners by Florencia Mallon, 1997. Used by permission of Florencia Mallon.

"Revolution in the Factory," interviews with workers at the Yarur cotton mill by Peter Winn, conducted between 1972 and 1974.

"The Chilean Revolution One Year In," by Salvador Allende, from "Speech at the National Stadium in Santiago on November 4, 1971," *La Nación*, 5 November 1971 (abridged).

"Women Lead the Opposition to Allende," interview with Señora Carmen Saenz by Margaret Power and Lisa Baldez, December, 27 1993. Used by permission of the interviewers.

"'So That Chile Can Renew Its March Forward,'" by Chilean Business and Professional Associations, "El pliego de Chile," *El Mercurio*, 21 October 1972 (abridged). Used by permission of the Central Unitaria de Trabajadores, Chile.

"The Demands of the People," by the Movement of the Revolutionary Left (MIR), from "El Pliego del Pueblo," in *Miguel Enríquez y el proyecto revolucionario en Chile*, edited by Pedro Naranjo, Mauricio Ahumada, Mario Garcés, and Julio Pinto (Santiago: LOM, 2004), 185–188 (abridged).

"'A Treasonous History,'" by a group of retired generals and admirals, from "Desagravio a la memoria de O'Higgins," *El Mercurio*, 17 August 1973, 20.

"United States Policy and Covert Action against Allende," by The Church Committee, from *Church Report: Covert Action in Chile 1963–1973*, *94th Congress*. S. Rep. No. 63–372 (December 18, 1975) (abridged). Available at http://foia.state.gov/Reports/ChurchReport.asp. Accessed on November 3, 2010.

"'Everyone Knows What Is Going to Happen,'" by Radomiro Tomíc, in "Usted hizo todo lo que pudo como soldado y chileno," *La Nación*, 29 August 1973, 7. Used by permission of Esteban Tomíc on behalf of the Tomíc Family.

"'These Are My Final Words,'" by Salvador Allende, from "Último Discurso," presidential address, La Moneda Palace, Radio Magallanes, 11 September 1973, radio broadcast.

Part VII. The Pinochet Dictatorship: Military Rule and Neoliberal Economics

"Diary of a Coup," by Peter Winn, from "The Other 9/11: Coup Diary," keynote address at The Bildner Center for Western Hemisphere Studies, CUNY, September 10, 2003. Used by permission of Peter Winn.

"'In the Eyes of God and History,'" by Government Junta of the Armed Forces and Carabineros of Chile, in *Razones de la junta: Tres años de destrucción* (Santiago: Associación Impresores de Chile, c. 1973).

"Pinochet's Caravan of Death," by Patricia Verdugo, in *Chile, Pinochet, and the Caravan of Death*, translated by Marcelo Montecino (Miami: North-South Center Press, University of Miami, 2001), 105–168 (abridged). Used by Permission of Susan Davis, The Center for Hemispheric Policy, University of Miami.

"Women and Torture," by National Commission on Political Detention and Torture, from "Capítulo V: Métodos de tortura: Definiciones y testimonios," in *Informe de la Comisión Nacional sobre Prisión Política y Tortura* (Santiago: Comisión Nacional sobre Prisión Política y Tortura, 2005), 252–256 (abridged).

"Operation Condor and the Transnationalization of Terror," by U.S. Federal Bureau of Investigation, from "The Operation Condor Cable," September 28, 1976. Declassified document from the National Security Archive. Available at http://www.gwu.edu/~nsarchiv/NSAEBB/NSAEBB8/docs/doc23.pdf. Accessed on December 1, 2009.

"Protected Democracy and the 1980 Constitution," by Jaime Guzmán, "La definición constitucional," *Revista Realidad* 2, no. 3 (August 1980), 17–39 (abridged). Used by permission of the Fundación Jaime Guzmán.

"Shantytown Protest," interviews with *pobladores* by Alison Bruey and Ricardo Balladares, 2004. Used by permission of Alison Bruey and Ricardo Balladares.

"'There Is No Feminism without Democracy,'" by Julieta Kirkwood, *Ser política en Chile: Las feministas y los partidos* (Santiago: FLACSO, 1986), 218–233 (abridged). Used by permission of Pablo Sabat Kirkwood.

"The Kids of Barrio Alto," by Alberto Fuguet, from *Bad Vibes*, translated by Kristina Cordero (New York: St. Martin's Press, 1997) (abridged). Used by permission of Guillermo Schavelzon Literary Agency on behalf of the author and by permission of Kristina Cordero.

"Sexuality and Soccer," by Pedro Lemebel, from "Como no te voy a querer," in *La esquina es mi corazón: Crónica Urbana* (Santiago: Cuarto Propio, 1995). Used by permission of the author and Grupo Planeta.

"Competing Perspectives on Dictatorship as Revolution," (1) by Joaquín Lavín, from *Chile, una revolución silenciosa* (Santiago: Zig-Zag, 1988). 11–34, 79–80, 120–121 and 151–152 (abridged). Used by permission of the author and Editora Zig-Zag. (2) By Ernesto Tironi, from *Los silencios de la revolución: Chile, la otra cara de la modernización* (Santiago de Chile: Ediciones SUR, 1988), 21–32, 70–81. Used by permission of the author.

"The Whole World Was Watching," by the Observer Group of the Latin American Studies Association, from "The Chilean Plebiscite: A First Step toward Redemocratization," by Paul Drake and Arturo Valenzuela et al., *LASA Forum*, 19, no. 4 (Winter 1989) (abridged). Used by permission of the authors.

Part VIII. Returning to Democracy: Transition and Continuity

"Justice 'To the Degree Possible,'" by Patricio Aylwin Azócar, from "Discurso al dar a conocer a la ciudadanía el Informe de la Comisión Verdad y Reconciliación," *El Mercurio*, 5 March 1991 (abridged).

"Surveillance Within and Without," by Diamela Eltit, from *Custody of the Eyes*, translated by Helen Lane and Ronald Christ (Santa Fe, N.M.: Lumen Inc./Sites Books, 2005), 23–26 (abridged). © 2004 Lumen Books. Translation © 2005 Ronald Christ. Used by permission of Ronald Christ.

"Legislating Gender Equality?" by Pilar Molina Armas, from "Plan del SERNAM para la mujer: ¿Igualdad o Totalitarismo Feminista?," *El Mercurio*, 29 May 1995 (abridged). Used by permission of the author.

"The Credit-Card Citizen," by Tomás Moulián, from *Chile Actual: Anatomia de un Mito* (Santiago: ARCIS/LOM, 1997), 102–110 (abridged). Used by permission of the author and LOM ediciones.

"'Chile's Greatest Addition to the Spanish Language,'" by John Brennan and Alvaro Taboada, from *How to Survive in the Chilean Jungle* (Santiago: Dolmen Editorial, 1996), 102. Used by permission of JC Sáez Editor.

"'I Never Looked for Power,'" by Augusto Pinochet Ugarte, from "Carta a los chilenos," *El Mercurio*, 28 December 1998.

"Historians Critique Pinochet's 'Anti-History,'" by eleven Chilean historians, from *The Historians' Manifesto*, edited by Sergio Grez Toso and Gabriel Salazar, translated by Enrique Zapata. Remember Chile. (Abridged). Available at http://www.remember-chile.org.uk/declarations/manhist.htm . Accessed on 15 March 2012. Used by permission of Gabriel Salazar and Enrique Zapata.

"The Mapuche Nation and the Chilean Nation," by Elicura Chihuailaf, from *Message to Chileans*, translated by Celso Cambiazo (Victoria, B.C.: Trafford Publishing, 2009) (abridged). Used by permission of the author.

"Growth with Equity," by Alejandro Foxley, "Successes and Failures in Poverty Eradication: Chile," World Bank (August 2004) (abridged). Used by permission of the author and The World Bank.

"So Conservative and Yet So Modern?," by Alfredo Jocelyn-Holt, from "Chile Today," *ReVista: Harvard Review of Latin America* III, no. 3 (spring 2004), 10–13 (abridged). Used by permission of the author and the David Rockefeller Center for Latin American Studies, Harvard University.

"The Catholic Church Today," by Antonio Delfau, S.J., from "La Iglesia Católica en el Chile de hoy," *Mensaje* 228 (July 2004), 4–5 (abridged). Used by permission of *Revista Mensaje*.

"'To Never Again Live It, To Never Again Deny It,'" by Ricardo Lagos, "Para nunca mas vivirlo, nunca mas negarlo," from the prologue to *Informe de la Comisión Nacional Sobre Prisión Política y Tortura* (Santiago: Ministerio del Interior, 2005) (abridged).

"The Chilean Army after Pinochet," by Juan Emilio Cheyre Espinosa, a letter to the editor, *El Mercurio*, 8 February 2005. Used by permission of the author.

"*La Señora Presidenta*," by Michelle Bachelet, from "Her Excellency, President of the Republic Michelle Bachelet, Speech before the Tenth Regional Conference on Women in Latin America and the Caribbean (CEPAL), Quito, Ecuador, 6 August 2007," translated by Karin Alejandra Rosemblatt, in *Documenting Latin America: Gender, Race, and Nation,* edited by Eric O'Connor and Leo Garofalo, vol. 2, 1st ed. (abridged) © 2011. Printed and Electronically reproduced by permission of Pearson Education Inc., Upper Saddle River, New Jersey.

Every reasonable effort has been made to obtain permission. We invite copyright holders to inform us of any oversights.

Index

agrarian reform: Agrarian Reform Corporation (CORA) and, 360–61, 391; *asentamientos*, 360–61, 386; Christian Democracy and, 356–61; Eduardo Frei and, 344–45, 348, 356–61, 362; Salvador Allende and, 402. *See also* Mapuche

Aguirre Cerda, Pedro, 301–7

Alessandri, Arturo, 220–22, 251–56, 259, 321

Alessandri, Jorge, 276, 340, 407, 447

Allende, Salvador: death of 428–29; election of, 345–47, 376–79; final words, 428–31; inauguration of, 380; military coup and, 426–31; plots against, 346–47, 426–27; public health and, 297–300; "revolution from above" and "revolution from below," 348, 393–99, 400–405. *See also* Popular Unity; U.S. intervention; military coup of 1973

Amnesty Law of 1978, 514, 521–22, 532

anarchism, 197, 245, 259, 415

antipolitics, 438, 450

Antofagasta, 11, 199, 435, 454–56

Araucania, 11. *See also* Mapuche

archaeology, 60, 67–71

Armed Forces. *See* military

arpilleristas, 484, 486, pl. 5

Association of Families of the Detained-Disappeared (AFDD): 457; pl. 5

Atacama Desert, 7, 9, 12, 17, 21, 23, 64, 68, 75–77, 80, 169, 193, 199

Aurora de Chile, 122, 129, 132

authoritarianism: feminism and, 485; patriarchy and, 482–86, 534–37; psychological effects of, 534–37. *See also* Autocratic Republic; Pinochet dictatorship; states of siege

Autocratic Republic, 139–42, 151, 217, 256

Aylwin Azócar, Patricio, 441, 521; Rettig Commission and, 521–22, 527–33

Bachelet, Michelle, 522–24, 592, 595–600

Balmaceda, José Manuel, 172–77, 196, 199, 217–24. *See also* Civil War of 1891

Balmes, José, pl. 4

Bello, Andrés, 124, 153–56, 180

bicentennial, 1, 4–5, 601–3

Bilbao, Francisco, 123–24, 143–46

Bío Bío River, 11, 23, 51, 92, 115n3, 124, 157, 205, 574n1

Blest Gana, Alberto, 124, 147–52

borders, 11, 210; Argentina and, 11; Bolivia and, 7, 11, 142n1, 193–95, 199–205, 210; Peru and, 7, 11, 21, 142n1, 193–95, 199, 203–5, 210. *See also* War of the Pacific

bourgeoisie: rise of, 147

British merchants, 7, 125, 133, 217

Caffarena, Elena, 274, 315–19, 331–33

Calderón, Melchor, 92–97

California gold rush, 126, 178–82

Carrere, Ricardo, 48–51

Carvallo y Goyeneche, Vicente, 102–8

Casanova, Mariano, 227–32

Castro, Fidel, 343; Allende and, 349, 404

Catholic Action, 274, 284

Catholic Church: changing influence of, 227–32, 284–88, 585–87; Pinochet dictatorship and, 436–37, 500; Social Catholicism, 274; socialism and, 227–32; university education and, 155

censorship, 7, 411, 420, 438, 441, 514

Chicago Boys, 438–39

Chihuailaf, Elicura, 568–74

623